Peter Norton's User's Guide to

Windows™ 3.1

Peter Norton's User's Guide to Windows™ 3.1

Peter Norton
and
Peter Kent

BANTAM BOOKS
NEW YORK • TORONTO • LONDON • SYDNEY • AUCKLAND

Peter Norton's User's Guide to Windows 3.1
A Bantam Book / January 1993

All rights reserved.
Copyright © 1993 by Peter Norton
Cover design © 1993 by Bantam Books
Interior design by Nancy Sugihara
Produced by Micro Text Productions, Inc.
Composed by Context Publishing Services

No part of this book may be reproduced or transmitted in any form or by any means, electronic or mechanical, including photocopying, recording, or by any information storage and retrieval system, without permission in writing from the publisher. For information address: Bantam Books

Throughout the book, tradenames and trademarks of some companies and products have been used, and no such uses are intended to convey endorsement of or other affiliations with the book.

ISBN 0-553-37148-7

Published simultaneously in the United States and Canada

Bantam Books are published by Bantam Books, a division of Bantam Doubleday Dell Publishing Group, Inc. Its trademark, consisting of the words "Bantam Books" and the portrayal of a rooster, is Registered in U.S. Patent and Trademark Office and in other countries. Marca Registrada, Bantam Books, 666 Fifth Avenue, New York, New York 10103.

PRINTED IN THE UNITED STATES OF AMERICA

0 9 8 7 6 5 4 3 2 1

Contents

Part 3 Windows' Major Accessories

Part 4 Windows' "Desktop" Accessories

Part 5 Windows' Multimedia

Part 6 Sharing Data

Introduction

This book is about working with Microsoft Windows 3.1, the most recent version of the Windows "graphical user interface." Windows 3.1 is a great improvement over earlier versions. It's faster, easier to use, and it does more. It prints documents faster, carries out file operations faster, and runs your applications faster. And although at first glance it looks the same as Windows 3.0, there are hundreds of improvements, some minor, some major.

Many people use Windows to run one or two applications. Their word processor or spreadsheet requires Windows, so they use Windows. But Windows is much more than simply an "operating system" in which you run applications. It has its own applications that are quite capable and can save you a lot of money. If your word processing needs extend only to writing a few letters and memos, don't buy a word processor, use Windows Write. It lets you use different typefaces and even add graphics. If your database needs stretch no farther than to storing a few addresses, use Cardfile. If you use your computer telecommunications "now and again," use Terminal. Want to create a few simple illustrations for a document? Use Paintbrush.

There's much more to Windows than people realize. Explore a little and you will find a macro builder, Recorder, that lets you automate tasks in any Windows application. Use Sound Recorder to add voice messages to your documents. Use Character Map to help you insert special characters into almost any Windows document—in word processing or desktop publishing applications, for example. Use Notepad to build DOS batch files, or Calculator to figure out averages or standard deviations. Use Microsoft Diagnostics to view hardware configuration data such as IRQs and the status of the communication ports.

If you had heard about the data sharing capabilities of Windows 3.0, but never had the time to fight your way through the confusing commands and procedures, take another look. The major new feature of Windows 3.1 is OLE, Object Linking and Embedding, and this book describes it in detail. Now you can place information from one application—pictures, text, numbers, or even sounds—into another, and keep the information up to date automatically. You can even place "packages" containing executable commands into an application—double-click on the package and another application starts, or a DOS command is carried out.

There's much to discover in Windows, and we've tried to make it easy for you to understand it all. This book provides detailed information about all aspects of Windows, from how to create pictures in Windows Paintbrush, to how to use Windows' troubleshooting tools; from how to record your voice and place a sound "package" into a letter, to the strategies that will help you win at Minesweeper.

One of Windows' great strengths is the consistency of commands between applications. It's not perfect—you will sometimes find software that seems to use unusual commands for carrying out common procedures. But in general, common procedures use common, consistent commands. For instance, the **File | Open**, **File | Save**, and **File | Save As** commands are used by almost all Windows applications, and they work in a similar way in each. This conformity makes learning a new program easy, because once you've worked with Windows for a little while you will know how to carry out many procedures—you don't have to start from the beginning each time you use a new application. You will understand how to work with files; cut, copy, and paste data; undo mistakes; work with the application's Help system; select a printer and print a document; and close the application when you've finished working with it.

Common procedures also make it easier to describe new applications. We are not going to explain the same commands over and over again. We will explain basic commands and procedures early in the book and assume that by the time you get to the later chapters you will understand them. For instance, we don't repeat the explanation of **File | Open** every time it appears in an application: in Cardfile, Calendar, Notepad, Windows Write, Windows Paintbrush, and so on.

For this reason, if you are new to Windows it is a good idea to make sure you read the early chapters before leaping into later subjects. Learn the basics first, and the more advanced topics will be easier to understand. In later chapters we won't explain every click of the mouse, every key pressed. Rather, we assume that by the time you have read the first few chapters you understand the basics. Later in the book, when we tell you to select an option from a drop-down list box, we will assume you understand what to do. When we tell you to click on a button, we assume you know how or, if you don't have a mouse, you know how to duplicate the mouse click using the keyboard. So if you are not already familiar with Windows, make sure you read the early chapters.

One more thing before we start. We are going to use a shortcut that we feel is easier to read, especially if you are scanning quickly through a chapter looking for information. When we tell you to select a command from a menu, we are going to describe the command in this manner: *menuname* | *commandname*. We are not going to say "open the File menu and select the Save As option." Rather, we will say "select File | Save As."

Part 1

Getting Started

1

Installing Windows

The Windows installation procedure makes setting up Windows a relatively simple task. It lets you choose between the Express Setup (which quickly installs as much as it can, with little interaction from you) and the Custom Setup (which lets you decide exactly what you want installed and how). There are also special options for installing on a network server, a network workstation, and for automating installation on a large number of workstations.

System Requirements

Windows runs in two modes, *Standard* and *386 Enhanced*. These modes are explained in detail in Chapter 2. Suffice it to say that 386 Enhanced mode is the most capable, although there may be some occasions when you would run in Standard mode. The hardware on which you install Windows determines the mode in which you can run.

Standard Mode

Absolute Minimum: 80286 processor, 1 MB (megabyte) RAM, 6.5 MB hard-disk space, EGA (Enhanced Graphics Adapter) graphics

Recommended Minimum: 80286 processor, 2 MB RAM, 9 MB hard-disk space, VGA (Video Graphics Array) graphics

386 Enhanced Mode

Absolute Minimum: 80386SX processor, 2 MB RAM, 8 MB hard-disk space, EGA graphics

Recommended Minimum: 80386SX processor, 4 MB RAM, 10.5 MB hard-disk space, VGA graphics

By absolute minimum we mean the level below which you simply cannot run this mode. For instance, Windows won't run on anything less than a 286 with EGA graphics. The recommended minimums are Microsoft's suggestions. Although you can run 386 Enhanced mode with 2 MB of RAM (1.6 actually, but computers these days won't accept fractions of a megabyte), Microsoft says that you would actually be better off using 4 MB of RAM.

The recommended configurations are, to some degree, arbitrary. You would be better off with 8 or 16 MB of RAM, for instance, and you'll need a lot more than 10.5 MB of hard-disk space once you start working with Windows applications.

As a general rule of thumb, "more is better." Windows is slower than DOS. If you are a newcomer to Windows you may be shocked as to how much slower a Windows word processor or database is, for instance. So fast processors and fast disk drives make working with Windows easier. You may find that some Windows applications are simply too slow to run on a 286, or even a 386SX. They'll run, but you seem to spend most of your time waiting. If you are using your machine for business—and time on your computer is money—the amount you save by purchasing a 286 is quickly lost while you sit twiddling your thumbs. In particular, graphics programs are often very slow, as are desktop-publishing packages—the sort of software that Windows was designed for.

Hard disks always seem to be too small, but Windows application files are often larger than DOS files, so drives fill even more quickly. (Why are they larger? Because Windows applications take advantage of Windows graphics and sound abilities, and that takes space.) And while EGA may be okay in DOS, it doesn't do Windows justice. The ideal video configuration is a large monitor (17 inches or more), running Super VGA or higher.

You also need a mouse. It's not absolutely essential, but Windows is a graphical user interface, and "GUIs" are designed for use with a mouse. Most operations can be carried out without a mouse—most, though not all, commands can be selected using either mouse or keyboard—but you will find that a mouse makes working with Windows much easier.

You also require MS-DOS 3.1 or later, which you almost certainly have if you have a 286 or higher processor. Ideally, you should have the latest MS-DOS (currently 5.0). DOS's memory management has improved dramatically since 3.1, freeing more memory for Windows to work in.

Preparing to Install Windows

The first thing you should do before running the installation program is to remove TSRs (memory-resident programs) from your AUTOEXEC.BAT file. Some of them may prevent Windows from installing. Also disable any network messaging systems; if your system receives a message while you are running Setup it may cause problems.

You should also back up your hard disk before beginning. Loading Windows is a major change, so a complete backup will allow a complete recovery if something goes wrong.

Beginning Installation

Start the installation procedure by placing the Windows disk #1 in your floppy disk drive. At the DOS prompt, type **A:** (or type **B:** if the disk is in the B: drive) and press **Enter**. Then type **setup** and press **Enter**. Windows loads the Setup program.

Setup begins by scanning the computer's memory, checking for programs that may interfere with it. (If it finds one it will display a message, informing you that you must remove the program and start again.) Next you see a "Welcome to Setup" screen. Just press **Enter** to continue. You are then given two options: **Express Setup** or **Custom Setup**. We recommend that you use the Custom Setup. It is not particularly complicated, and it has a few important advantages. First, the Express Setup examines your hardware's configuration and loads drivers according to what it finds—even if what it finds is not correct. For instance, there's a chance that it won't recognize your mouse, so it won't install a mouse driver. It also won't update some of your drivers: It will update any drivers installed with Windows 3.0, but not drivers that were provided by manufacturers and added to your Windows 3.0 installation later, even though the Windows 3.1 disks may have more recent drivers.

▼ ***Note*** If you use Express and Windows gets your hardware configuration wrong, you may be able to use the Windows Setup from within Windows to correct the settings—see later in this chapter. If Windows won't start because the configuration is wrong—perhaps it picked the wrong display adapter—change to the WINDOWS directory in DOS, type **setup** and press **Enter**, and you will be able to modify the settings.

The Custom Setup, however, lets you modify Setup's hardware choices, so if it makes a wrong choice, you can correct it before continuing. It also gives you far more flexibility in choosing what files should be installed; you can even see the amount of disk space the files will take up, to compare with the amount of disk space you have available. Press **Enter** to use Express, **C** to use Custom.

Custom Installation

After you select Custom Installation you see a screen that asks in which directory you want to place Windows. It suggests using a directory called C:\WINDOWS (or the directory in which you currently have a copy of Windows), although you can change the name. If you already have Windows 3.0, you have the choice to create a new Windows installation or to copy the files over the old installation. (Windows will maintain your program groups and icons if you upgrade.)

When you press **Enter**, Setup checks your computer's configuration and then displays a screen similar to Figure 1.1. This shows the hardware that Setup *thinks* you are using. Read it carefully, because it may not be correct.

If one of the hardware options doesn't match your system, use the **arrow keys** to move to the option and press **Enter**. You will be shown a list of options. Again, use the **arrow keys** to move to the option and press **Enter**. When you finally press **Enter** in the Hardware Configuration screen, Setup begins to load files. It will prompt you to change disks if necessary.

After a minute or two Setup will have loaded enough of Windows to actually run a different interface. If you have used Windows before you will understand how to use these dialog boxes. If you are new to Windows, here are a few pointers:

- If you have a mouse, "click" on buttons to activate them.
- If you have a mouse, select items from lists, check boxes, or option buttons by clicking on them.

```
Windows Setup

    Setup has determined that your system includes the following hardware
    and software components. If your computer or network appears on the
    Hardware Compatibility List with an asterisk, press F1 for Help.

        Computer:         MS-DOS System
        Display:          VGA
        Mouse:            No mouse or other pointing device
        Keyboard:         Enhanced 101 or 102 key US and Non US keyboards
        Keyboard Layout:  US
        Language:         English (American)
        Network:          No Network Installed

        No Changes:       The above list matches my computer.

    If all the items in the list are correct, press ENTER to indicate
    "No Changes." If you want to change any item in the list, press the
    UP or DOWN ARROW key to move the highlight to the item you want to
    change. Then press ENTER to see alternatives for that item.

  ENTER=Continue  F1=Help  F3=Exit
```

Figure 1.1 The Hardware Configuration screen

- If you don't have a mouse, operate a button by holding down **Alt** while you press the letter underlined in the button's name.
- If the button doesn't have an underlined letter, press **Tab** until the button is highlighted, then press **Enter**.
- Select from a list box by holding **Alt** while you press the letter underlined in the list box's name, use the arrow keys to move to the item you want to select, then press **Spacebar** to select the item.

The first dialog box you see asks for your name and company name. Enter the information and then use the Continue button. Verify that the information is correct in the next box, then use the Continue button again.

Now you will see three check boxes. You can choose to select the Windows components you want to set up. (For instance, you will be able to tell Setup you don't want to install the wallpaper files or the games.) If you want to install *all* the components, click on the first check box to remove the X (or press **Alt-W**).

The SetUp Printers check box has an X in it. That means Windows will help you install a printer driver. You can always install a driver later using the Control Panel. To skip this procedure, click on this check box also (or press **Alt-P**).

The last option makes Windows search your hard drive for applications. If you are upgrading from 3.0 you probably don't need to do this, and you can always add icons later in Program Manager. To skip this procedure, click on the check box or press **Alt-A**.

When you click on Continue (or press **Alt-o**), the Windows Setup dialog box appears. This is very similar to the Windows Setup dialog box we describe later in this chapter (used from within Windows to modify your Windows installation—see Figure 1.5). This box lets you decide which of the *optional files* you are going to install. The files have been grouped into various categories—Readme files, Accessories (such as Paintbrush, Notepad, and Write), Games, Screen Savers, and Wallpaper & Misc. (sample sounds and desktop wallpaper).

The dialog box also shows you how much hard-disk space each category takes up, the total of all the selected files, and how much space you have available. If you want to install all the files in a category, make sure there's an X in its check box. If you don't want *any* of the category files loaded, click on the check box to remove the X (or press **Alt** and the underlined letter). If you want to select specific files, click on the appropriate Files button to see another dialog box with a list of file types (or press **Tab** to move to the Files button you want, and press **Enter**). To select files that you don't want to load, click on them in the right-side list box, or press **Alt-I**, use the arrow keys, and press **Spacebar** to select a file. Then use the Remove button to move the files to the right list box, and click on OK to continue.

When you click on Continue in the Windows Setup dialog box, Setup closes the dialog box and creates a *swapfile* (if you are installing Windows on a system that can run 386 Enhanced mode). If you don't understand what's going on, don't worry about it now; you can modify the swapfile later (see Chapter 8 for information). In the next step Setup loads more files. It will tell you when to insert each disk. Then it asks you if it can modify the CONFIG.SYS and AUTOEXEC.BAT. You have the option of letting Setup do so, making Setup show you the changes before it makes them, or not allowing it to make any changes. (If it makes the changes it will rename and save the current files, so you have a backup.) By the way, if you don't have a mouse you can select another option by pressing the **Down Arrow** key and then pressing **Enter**. If you don't understand these files, you should let Windows make the changes for you.

The next step is to select a *printer* (if you chose that option earlier). When the list of printers appears, use the Down Arrow key to select the printer you have, and use the Install button to install that driver. If you understand how this dialog box works, you can then attach the printer to a port and set up the printer. If you aren't sure how to do this, don't worry about it now; you can do it later from the Control Panel's Printers dialog box (see Chapter 8). Use the Continue button to proceed (press **Tab** several times to get to the button, and press **Enter**).

Next Setup builds *Program Manager* and then prepares to search for applications (if you chose that option earlier). Use the Down Arrow key and Spacebar to select the drives you want to search, then press **Enter**. Setup searches for executable program files it recognizes. It can set up all the Windows applications it finds, but it can only set up DOS applications that it recognizes (ones for which it has a *PIF*, a Program Information File). When it finds a DOS application it *thinks* it recognizes, it shows you the path and filename and a list of application names. Select the correct application name, and press **Enter** to continue. If you select the "None of the above" option, Setup will not install an icon for the file.

Setup then displays a list of all the applications it found. Click on the Add All button if you want Setup to create program icons for every application, or select certain applications and click on the Add button. Then click on OK. You should probably use the second method, because some of the applications will be ones you do not wish to run in Windows, and others will be applications that are not run directly—.EXE and .COM files that are run from other applications.

Setup then gives you the choice of using the *Tutorial* or skipping it. Finally, you have the choice to Reboot the computer (so you can immediately start Windows) or return to DOS. Press **Alt-R** to reboot, or **Alt-D** to return to DOS. If you decide to return to DOS, you must reboot before opening Windows, so the AUTOEXEC.BAT and CONFIG.SYS changes take effect.

Express Setup

If you decide to use Express Setup, you will have fewer choices. The Express Setup begins by checking your hardware configuration, but it won't give you a chance to change what it finds. (If it is wrong, you can use the Windows Setup program later to fix the problem—to install a mouse driver, for instance. See Future Changes, later in this chapter.)

Express Setup also won't let you select the files you want to load; instead, it loads as much as your disk space allows. Nor will you be able to modify the swapfile, although that's not really a problem. As we mentioned earlier, you can use the Control Panel to change it later. It changes your AUTOEXEC.BAT and CONFIG.SYS files, but you won't have a chance to view the changes first. Express Setup does make selecting a printer just a little bit easier than Custom Setup by using two simple dialog boxes—one to select the printer and one to select the port to which it should be connected.

You also won't have a choice about the application search. Express Setup automatically searches your hard drive for applications and automatically creates icons for each one. The final dialog box in Express Setup has *three* options. As with Custom Setup, you can Reboot and Return to DOS. But you can also use the Restart Windows to reboot your computer and automatically start Windows.

Using FastDisk

You may have heard about a new Windows feature called *FastDisk*, or *32-bit Disk Access*. With certain disk drives Windows can directly access the hard-disk controller, bypassing the ROM BIOS. This means that disk reads and writes are much quicker. It also means that you can run more DOS applications in Windows, because it can create more *virtual* DOS machines, by swapping applications to hard disk quicker.

When you load Windows, however, FastDisk is *turned off* by default. If you want to use this feature you must turn it on yourself, using Control Panel's 386 Enhanced dialog box. That's because Microsoft doesn't want to turn on a feature that can harm your hard-disk data in some circumstances. If you want to use FastDisk, read Chapter 8. Make sure you read the warnings about FastDisk before using it.

Two Versions of Windows

If you have Windows 3.0 on your computer, you can either update or install a completely separate version of Windows 3.1. Why would you want *both* versions? If you use your computer for business, then time working with Windows is money. You may want to make sure that Windows 3.1 will run all your applications without problems before you do away with Windows 3.0. Most applications will have no problems—or, at least, no important ones. Still, better safe than sorry (especially when a few hours of lost time can cost so much). For information about application compatibility, see Chapter 5.

You can install a new version by simply entering a new name when Setup prompts you for the directory. But remember that Setup is going to update your AUTOEXEC.BAT and CONFIG.SYS files. When you want to run the Windows 3.0 version, you must move or rename the new ones, copy the old ones back to the root directory of your C: drive, and reboot your computer. When you want to go back to Windows 3.1, copy the new ones back to C: and reboot again. You may want to create a batch file that will help you swap the files quickly.

Troubleshooting Setup

If you have trouble running Windows Setup, make sure you have removed all the TSRs from your AUTOEXEC.BAT file. Read the SETUP.TXT file (it's on Windows Disk # 1). Then start Setup by typing **setup /l**. Setup will create a log as it works, and the last line will indicate at which point it hangs up. This log file (BOOTLOG.TXT) can then be used to help technical support figure out your problem.

A few other options may be of help. Typing **setup /i** tells Setup not to run through the hardware detection. Instead it will display a typical configuration, and you will have to select the correct settings, if necessary. You can also try **setup /t**, which makes Setup search the drive for programs that shouldn't run at the same time as Setup or Windows 3.1. **Setup /c** turns off the search for memory resident programs, and **setup /b** sets up Windows with monochrome display attributes.

Setting Up on a Network

You can, of course, run Windows on a network. Why would you want to? To save disk space on your workstation, perhaps, or to run Windows on a *diskless* workstation—a computer with no disk drive. You can run Windows with as little as 300 K of "personal" files, which may be on your workstation's hard disk, or even in a private network directory. There are drawbacks to running Windows from the network, as there are with any application. It will run slower, and it will not be available when the network is not functioning. If all your applications are Windows applications, when the network is down you have an expensive paperweight on your desk.

If you want to install Windows on a workstation as a stand-alone version, use the normal installation procedure. If you want to run Windows from the network server, you must use one of the special network installations.

Before carrying out any of these network procedures, remove TSRs and turn off the messaging system.

Creating an Administrative Copy: Setup /a

You can copy Windows files to a network server so they may be accessed by workstations. The Administrative Setup doesn't create a usable version of Windows, it simply copies files into a directory so that workstations can run Setup from the server.

At a workstation, connect to the network drive on which you are going to load the files; you must have write access to this drive. With the Windows disk #1 in the floppy drive, at the DOS prompt change to that drive, type **setup /a**, and press **Enter**. Windows will prompt you for the directory in which you want the files, a group name, and a company name. It then expands all the files and installs them. They will be marked as read-only. The files will use about 16 MB of disk space.

Installing on a Workstation: Setup

To load a copy of Windows from the server, go to a workstation, connect to the network and the directory on which you installed the Administrative copy of Windows, type **setup /n**, and press **Enter**. You can then install Windows in the same way you would from the disks; you can even select Express or Custom setup. You will be prompted for a Windows directory. This will normally be on the workstation's hard disk. If you have a diskless workstation, you should select the workstation's private network directory.

Setup will then install a few files into this directory—the .INI initialization files and the .GRP files (which create Program Manager). This lets each workstation have a unique Windows configuration while using very little disk space.

Creating Custom Installations

If you administer many PCs, you may want to consider creating your own custom installation. Windows uses setup installation files to control how the installation procedure works.

SETUP.SHH	Instructs Automated Setup (**setup /h**) which type of automated setup you want to use (you can create several).
SETUP.INF	Stores information about Windows' system and application files and creates program groups in Program Manager.

CONTROL.INF Stores information about printers and international settings.

APPS.INF Stores information about applications. You can modify this file to customize the way in which Windows will run certain applications.

You use this Setup by typing **setup /h:** [***drive:\path\system_settings_filename***]. The system settings filename determines the type of automated setup that will be carried out. The installation proceeds with little input from the user. Thus you can create several different types of setup for several different types of systems on your network.

You can modify these files to install Windows in a very specific way. If you only have a few PCs there's not much point spending the time creating a custom installation. But if you have many PCs that must be configured in the same way, a custom installation can save time and help maintain system uniformity. The Microsoft Windows Resource Kit explains how to create your own installation files. Contact Microsoft for details on how to obtain this kit.

Future Changes: Using Windows Setup

If your computer's configuration changes after you have installed Windows, you can modify the setup using the Windows Setup program. For instance, you add a new monitor and display adapter and want to operate at a higher resolution; you install a new mouse; you are connected to a new network, or need to install a new network driver; you install a different type of keyboard; you install a new hard drive, so now you have the room to install programs that you originally told Windows not to install.

▼ ***Note*** You can also make these changes from DOS. Change to the WINDOWS directory, type **setup**, and press **Enter**.

There are changes for which you will *not* need Setup. If you install a new printer, you will load the new printer driver using the Control Panel's Printers dialog box (see Chapter 8). If you install MIDI (Musical Instrument Digital Interface) equipment, a sound board, or other unusual equipment (such as a digitizing tablet), you will install the drivers using the Control Panel's Drivers dialog box.

Double-click on the Windows Setup icon in the Program Manager's Main program group. Or select **File | Run** and run **SETUP**. The Windows Setup dialog box appears (see Figure 1.2). As you can see, this dialog box shows you some

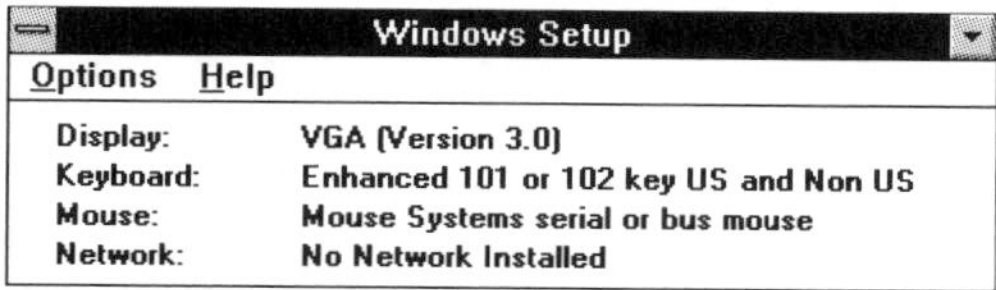

Figure 1.2 The Windows Setup dialog box

important system configuration information: the display, keyboard, mouse, and network you are using.

▼ *Note* Windows Setup will not open if the SYSTEM.INI file is loaded in a text editor.

Changing System Settings

To change any of the four items listed in the Windows Setup window, select **Options | Change System Settings**. The dialog box shown in Figure 1.3 appears. You may now select a new option from any of the four drop-down list boxes. Each option has an "Other" option at the bottom of the list ("Other mouse," "Other network," and so on). Select one of these if you have a disk provided by the manufacturer.

If you select the Other option, a dialog box pops up immediately, asking you to insert the disk into drive A:\ (change this to B:\ if appropriate). Click on OK to load the driver.

If you selected one of the other options from the list, you must click on OK and Windows searches the SYSTEM directory to see if the driver file is already there (if it is, Windows asks if you want to use it or load a new one). Then it looks at the A: drive to see if there's a disk containing the driver. Finally, it asks you to insert the appropriate disk into drive A:\ (again, change this to B:\ if necessary). Windows tells you which disk from the installation set contains the driver, but if you

Change System Settings
Display: VGA (Version 3.0)
Keyboard: Enhanced 101 or 102 key US and Non US keyboards
Mouse: Mouse Systems serial or bus mouse
Network: No Network Installed
OK Cancel Help

Figure 1.3 The Change System Settings dialog box

have an updated driver you can use that disk instead, or name the directory on your hard drive containing the new driver.

Finally, Windows shows a dialog box telling you that you must Restart Windows. You don't have to do so immediately, unless you want to use the new driver right away.

▼ ***Note*** You can get updated device drivers from Microsoft Customer Support (1-800-426-9400), or from various bulletin boards. See Chapter 14 for information.

Setting Up Applications

You can use Windows Setup to create program icons for applications, although you probably won't do so—it's usually simpler to create them in Program Manager (see Chapter 4). You may want to do so, however, if you told Windows not to search for applications during the installation procedure; you can now come back and have Windows create icons for all your applications.

To create new program icons, select **Options | Set Up Applications**. Windows asks if you want to "Search for applications" or "Specify an application." The first option is the same as the one available during the installation procedure. You will be able to specify a drive and tell Windows to search for .EXE and .COM files. If Windows finds DOS applications that it thinks it recognizes—those for which it has Program Information Files (PIFs)—it displays a list of possibilities from which you can select. It cannot set up a DOS application for which it doesn't have a PIF.

When it has searched the entire drive, it displays the dialog box shown in Figure 1.4. You can move through the list on the left and decide which applications you want to add. The easiest way to do this is to use the Down Arrow key to move through the list and look at the path and filename below the list box. When you find an application for which you want to create an icon, press **Spacebar**. When you have selected all you need, click on the Add button to copy them over to the other list box, and then click on OK to continue.

Windows will either create a new program group, called Applications, or add the new icons to the existing Applications group. If it finds that you have selected a DOS application that is already set up, it lets you decide whether you want to replace the existing one; create a new one, so the application may operate differently depending on the one you use; or not create an icon for that application.

If you want to set up just one application, you will select the "Ask you to specify an application" option. Setup displays a dialog box in which you can name the application and select a program group in which you want to place the icon. When you click on OK, Setup creates the icon. If it's a DOS program, Setup can only

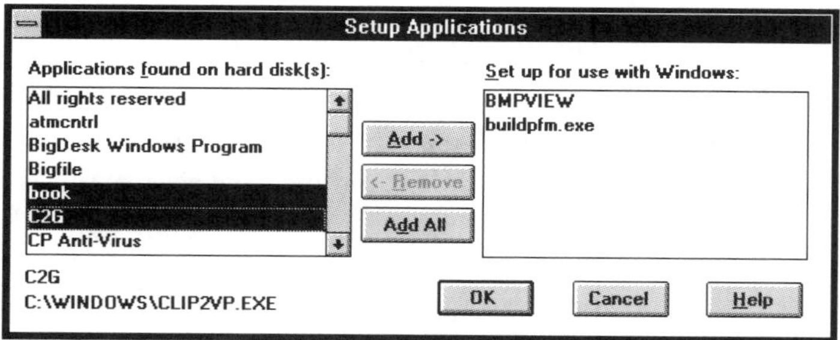

Figure 1.4 The Setup Applications dialog box

create an icon if it has a matching PIF. If it doesn't, you will have to use the methods described in Chapter 4 to create the icon.

Adding and Removing Software

You can use the Windows Setup to modify the Windows software. Perhaps you didn't load everything and now want to add certain components. Or perhaps you are running out of space and want to remove certain Windows accessories. Select **Options|Add/Remove Windows Components**. You will see the dialog box shown in Figure 1.5.

This dialog box indicates what you already have installed on your system. Each check box shows if any files of the associated type are on your hard drive; if there is

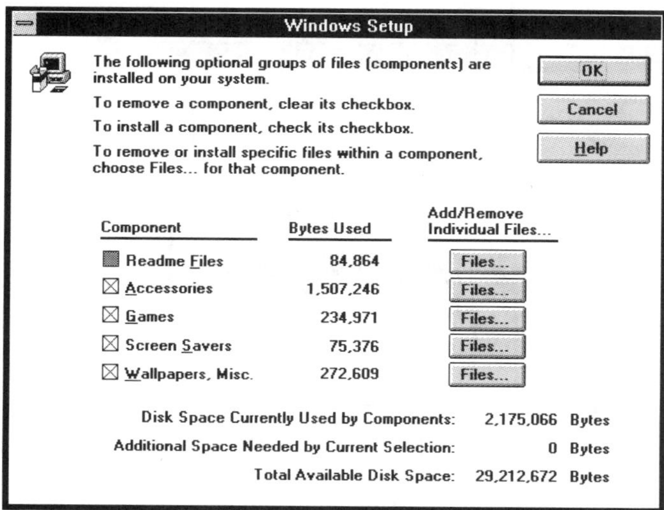

Figure 1.5 The Windows Setup dialog box

a check mark in a box, it means all of the files are on the system. If there is no check mark, it means that none of those files are on the system. If the check box is shaded (as is the Readme Files check box in Figure 1.5), it means *some* of the files are on the system. So, if you want to make sure that *all* the associated files are loaded, click on the button until the check mark appears. If you want to *remove* all the associated files, click until the box is clear.

If you want to see exactly what files are on your system, or if you want to add and remove selected files, click on the **Files** button. For instance, the Readme Files dialog box, shown in Figure 1.6, indicates that you have two Readme files installed. These dialog boxes may be a little confusing, because the labels above the list boxes are not correct. If you didn't click on the check box in the Windows Setup dialog box, then the list boxes show the current situation. The label on the left should read "These files are *not* installed," and the one on the right should read "These files *are* installed." If you *did* click on the check box, these list boxes show what Windows Setup plans to do—install those files when you have completed the operation.

You can now add or remove specific files. To add files, select the ones you want from the left list box (click on each one by one, or select each with the arrow keys and press **Spacebar**), then click on **Add**. Or click on **Add All** if you want to install all the files that are not yet loaded. If you want to remove files from your hard drive, select them from the right list box and click on **Remove**.

Now the list boxes show what the configuration *will be* once you have completed the operation (the right list box should read "These files will be on your hard disk"). Click on the OK button, and Windows closes the dialog box. You can now click on another Files button to select more files to load or remove.

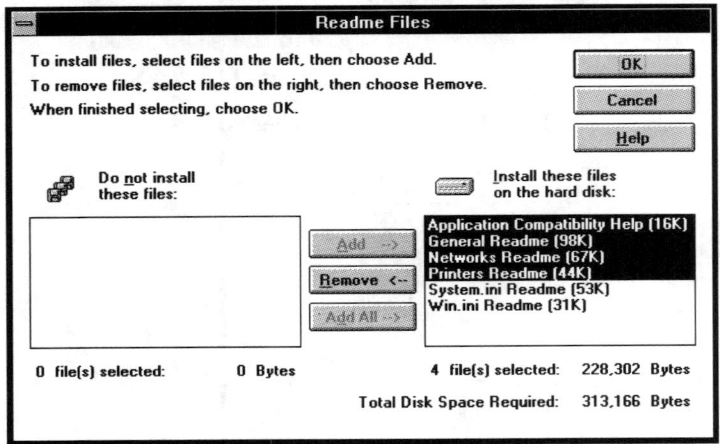

Figure 1.6 The Readme Files dialog box

When you have finished all your selections, click on the OK button in the Windows Setup dialog box. Windows begins by deleting the files you asked it to remove. Setup will prompt you to confirm that you want to delete the first file; you can click on Yes to delete that one file, or Yes to All, to delete all the files you selected without being prompted for each one.

Then Windows tells you to insert a disk, so it can begin loading the files you want to install. It will tell you to place the disk in drive A:, so change it to B: if necessary.

The information under *Expanding Windows Files*, later in this chapter, provides a simple example of how this all works—loading the file expansion utility.

Recovering from Setup Problems

It's possible, if you install the wrong driver, to set up Windows so it won't run. This is most likely to happen if you specify a display driver that your display adapter can't use. You can correct the problem by running Setup in DOS.

At the DOS prompt change to the Windows directory, type **setup**, and press **Enter**. When the System Information Screen appears, select the option you need to change, select the appropriate driver, and press **Enter**. (Don't try to run Setup at a DOS prompt inside Windows; you must be outside Windows to run Setup this way.)

Changing the Code Page

You can also run Setup in DOS if you need to change the code page, the character set you want to use for DOS applications running in Windows (determined by the language in which you are working). When you install Windows, it automatically selects the same code page used by DOS. You only need to change the setting if you modify DOS's code page.

Change to the WINDOWS directory, type **setup**, and press **Enter**. The hardware configuration screen appears. Select the Code Page from the System Information screen. Setup will display instructions and prompt you to install the correct disk.

Expanding Windows Files

You can selectively extract files from the Windows installation set to replace damaged or missing files. During installation Windows may have installed the EXPAND.EXE file in the Windows directory. If it didn't, or if the file has been removed, you can use Windows Setup to load it. Select **Options|Add/Remove**

Windows Components, and then click on the **Files** button on the **Accessories** line. If EXPAND.EXE is not on your hard drive, you will see **File Expansion Utility** in the left list box. Select it and click on the **Add** button. Then Click on **OK**.

Click on **OK** in the Windows Setup dialog box, and Windows will tell you which disk you must place in the floppy-disk drive. (Remember to change A:\ to B:\ if necessary.) Place the disk in the drive and click on **OK**. Windows loads the file.

Compressed files on the disks have underscores as the last character of the file's extension. For instance, DRWATSON.EXE is named DRWATSON.EX_ on the disks.

Copy the compressed file into your Windows directory, then follow this procedure to extract the file from the compressed file.

1. Open a DOS window.
2. Type **cd C:\WINDOWS** and press **Enter** to change to the Windows directory.
3. Type **EXPAND A:*FILENAME* C:*DIRECTORY* *FILENAME*** and press **Enter**. This extracts the file and copies it into the specified directory with the specified name.
4. Delete the compressed file.

2

Opening and Closing Windows

In this chapter you are going to learn how to start and run Windows, from the very beginning—the DOS prompt. Windows can operate in two modes—*Standard* and *386 Enhanced*. If you have a 286 computer you have no choice—you must use Standard mode. If you have a 386 or 486 with 2 MB of RAM or more, you can select either mode. We are going to learn about the two modes and their advantages and disadvantages. We will also look at a few ways to start Windows and open applications at the same time.

Windows' Modes

In some cases you will be forced to run in Standard mode. There may be times that you *want* to run in that mode, even though your machine can run in 386 Enhanced mode.

The main difference between the two modes is how they *multitask*. Multitasking is the ability to run two or more applications at the same time. For instance, you might be typing in one application, while another is printing a document, and while yet another carries out some lengthy calculations or sorts a database. Although PC-compatibles cannot really do two things at a time—processes are carried out one at a time, one after another—Windows lets applications multitask by jumping between applications very quickly. It spends a few milliseconds here, a few there, then the next application, and so on. Sometimes it works so well that it's hard to tell if anything is going on in other applications. In some cases, though, the application in which you are working may slow down considerably.

We say that the application in which you are currently working is the *active*, *current*, or *foreground* application. Applications running operations that are not active are known as *inactive* or *background* applications.

Although Windows 3.0 had another mode—*real mode*—which could not multitask, both modes of Windows 3.1 can multitask Windows-specific applications, those applications that were written for the Windows environment. However, only 386 Enhanced mode can multitask DOS applications—those applications not written for Windows but intended to run on the MS-DOS or PC-DOS operating systems.

▼ ***Note*** To find out how to improve multitasking performance, read Chapter 11 on printing. Printing is the most common process that you will want to multitask. Also see the 386 Enhanced information in Chapter 8, information about creating a DOS application's PIF file in Chapter 7, and information about optimizing Windows in Appendix A.

Let's take a look at the differences between the modes.

Standard Mode

Windows will automatically run in Standard mode if you are using a 286 machine, or if your 386 or 486 has less than 2 MB of RAM. Standard mode runs Windows applications well—often quicker than 386 Enhanced mode—but it doesn't work with DOS applications very well. While Standard mode can multitask many Windows applications at the same time, it has to stop everything to run one DOS application. The advantages of Standard mode are as follows:

- If you are running only Windows applications, Standard mode may be quicker than 386 Enhanced mode.
- This mode can let DOS applications use expanded memory installed on your machine, if the applications require it. (386 Enhanced mode cannot use expanded memory, although it can use extended memory to simulate it.)
- Standard mode may be able to run on some machines that are not fully hardware compatible with Windows, and on which 386 Enhanced mode will not run.

The disadvantages of Standard mode are as follows:

- It can't run DOS applications in the background—a DOS application will freeze while you are running another application.
- While you are using a DOS application, the Windows applications freeze.
- If your application needs expanded memory and you have a 286, you must have an expanded memory board installed—Windows cannot simulate expanded memory in Standard mode.

- Some DOS programs that use DOS *extenders* cannot run in Standard mode, because they conflict with Windows' use of extended memory. If the application uses DPMI (DOS Protected Mode Interface), it should be able to run.
- You can only run DOS applications "full screen"; that is, you cannot run them in a window, nor can you modify the font used.
- This mode won't use a permanent *swapfile* on your hard disk to simulate more memory. It will use a temporary swapfile for DOS applications, though.

386 Enhanced Mode

You can use 386 Enhanced mode on any 386SX, 386, or 486 machine that has at least 2 MB of RAM. 386 Enhanced mode can do everything Standard mode can—though it may run Windows applications slightly slower—but it can do a lot that Standard mode *cannot* do. If you plan to use DOS applications at the same time you run Windows applications, you will probably want to use this mode.

386 Enhanced mode sets up *virtual machines*. The 386 and 486 processors can block off areas of extended memory—the memory above 1 MB—to look like conventional memory. Thus, each DOS application can run in its own block of memory, like a separate DOS machine. When you swap between applications, Windows simply swaps between blocks of memory. Standard mode, on the other hand, has to move information in and out of memory (onto the hard disk) when you swap to and from DOS applications. The advantages of 386 Enhanced mode are as follows:

- You can multitask DOS applications, so they don't freeze when you swap to another application; a DOS application can continue printing, for example.
- When you are running DOS applications, Windows applications can continue running in the background.
- This mode switches between DOS and Windows applications much more quickly than Standard mode.
- If your DOS application needs expanded memory, Windows can simulate it—your machine doesn't need an expanded-memory board.
- Although Standard mode may be quicker than 386 Enhanced when running only Windows applications, it may not be noticeably quicker.
- DOS applications can run in windows, which can be sized and moved.
- You can change the font used in DOS-application windows, which will improve clarity and modify the window's size and the amount of information held.
- You can copy graphics or selected text from a DOS application into the Windows Clipboard. (Standard mode can only copy an entire "text image" of the application.)

- You can paste data from the Clipboard to DOS applications more easily.
- This mode can use your hard-disk drive to simulate memory, letting you run more applications than your actual RAM would allow. See Chapter 8 for more information on *swapfiles*.
- This mode can monitor COM-port use, and sort out problems when a DOS application tries to use the COM port at the same time as another DOS or Windows application.

Although 386-Enhanced mode may be slightly slower than Standard mode, it is the default mode for 386 machines and higher. The speed difference is not always significant, but the mode does have some important advantages over Standard mode. It runs DOS programs more effectively than Standard mode.

▼ ***Note*** Although 386 Enhanced mode *can* multitask DOS applications, by default it *doesn't*. If you want a DOS application to continue running while another application is active, you must turn on the **Execution: Background** option in its PIF (see Chapter 7 for more information).

Starting from DOS

When you installed Windows, the installation program probably modified the AUTOEXEC.BAT file, adding your WINDOWS directory to the PATH statement. (The only case in which it *didn't* change AUTOEXEC.BAT was if you used the Custom Setup and told it not to change the file.) This allows you to start Windows from anywhere: You don't need to change to the Windows directory first. Simply type **WIN** and press **Enter**. This will start Windows in 386-Enhanced mode (if you have an 80386 or higher computer, with at least 2 MB of memory), or Standard mode (if you have an 80286 with at least 1 MB of memory, or an 80386 with less than 2 MB).

Tip Will you *always* be working in Windows? You can add the WIN command to the end of your AUTOEXEC.BAT command to run Windows automatically whenever you start your computer. If you need to run DOS programs, you can still run them from Windows itself. And if you ever need to return to DOS, you can close Windows.

You can check in which mode your computer is working by selecting the About command from any of Windows' Help menus. At the bottom of the About dialog box Windows shows the mode and the amount of memory and system resources available.

The WIN Command

The simplest way to start windows is to type **win** and press **Enter** at the DOS prompt. But you can do more. You can start Windows in a number of ways by typing information after WIN. You may tell Windows

- to run in a particular mode
- to automatically open an application
- to automatically open an application and load a file
- to automatically open Recorder, load a macro file, and run a macro
- to use several special troubleshooting tools

Selecting a Mode

Although you can run your 386SX, 386, or 486 in 386 Enhanced mode, you may want to start it in Standard mode, perhaps because you are having hardware problems in 386 Enhanced mode, or because you want to see if it will run faster.

You can also *force* Windows to run in 386 Enhanced mode, although you will probably never do this. If your computer has the equipment to run in 386 Enhanced mode it will do so automatically. You may want to try forcing Windows into 386 Enhanced mode as a troubleshooting exercise, if it is going into Standard mode when it should go into 386 Enhanced mode.

To start in Standard mode, type **win /s** or **win /2**. To start in 386 Enhanced mode, type **win /3**.

Note The space between win and / is not essential.

Running an Application

You can tell Windows to begin running and automatically load an application. For instance, you might type **win calendar.exe** to start Windows and automatically load the Windows Calendar (CALENDAR.EXE). Because CALENDAR.EXE is in the Windows directory, you don't need to use the pathname. Nor do you need the path if the application is in a directory named in your DOS PATH (the PATH is usually created in your AUTOEXEC.BAT file). If you want to load a file that is in another directory, you should name the full directory. For instance, you might type **win c:\windows\draw\draw.exe** to run DRAW.EXE in the DRAW subdirectory.

▼ *Note* You can normally omit the file extension if you wish. For instance, type **win calendar**.

You can even open a DOS program automatically in this way. You will learn in Chapter 7 how to create PIFs (Program Information Files). These control the way in which DOS applications operate. You can call a PIF in the same way you would call a Windows application. For instance, **win dosprmpt.pif** will open Windows and start DOSPRMPT.PIF, the PIF that creates a DOS prompt. Or **win c:\tax91\pte.pif** would start a PIF called PTE.PIF. Or you may open the DOS application directly by typing its path and filename.

Running an Application and Loading a File

You can also automatically open a Windows application and load a file (you can't do this with a DOS application). There are two ways to do this. The first is to name a Windows application and then include the filename. For instance, **win c:\windows\draw\draw.exe animal.drw** will open the DRAW.EXE application and load the ANIMAL.DRW file into the application.

The other way to do it is to simply name the file itself. The file must be *associated* with an application. For instance, .CAL files are associated with CALENDAR.EXE, .TXT files are associated with NOTEPAD.EXE, and so on. So, if you type **win c:\data\data.txt**, Windows will automatically load NOTEPAD.EXE and load the document named DATA.TXT into it.

Many Windows applications automatically associate their file types with their executable files. For instance, Windows Draw (a Micrografx product) associates .DRW files with DRAW.EXE. So typing **win c:\mgxlibs\clipart\animal.drw** would automatically start DRAW.EXE and load the ANIMAL.DRW file.

You can also associate file types with applications yourself. Read Chapter 9 for more information on which files are associated with which applications, and how to create your own associations.

Loading a Program with a Switch

Some programs have special *switches* that make the program run in a particular way. Many DOS programs use such switches—you can include the switches after the filename in the same way you would if you were starting the program in DOS. Some Windows applications also use switches. For instance, **win c:\winword.exe**

/mfile1 tells Windows to open Word for Windows and load the last file that was saved (not the last file opened, or the last file closed, but the last one actually *saved*).

Using Windows Recorder

Windows Recorder is a special application, included with Windows, that lets you create simple macros. It's quite easy to use, and you could create startup macros, macros that you want to run when you start Windows. A macro could open a group of applications for you, or select a specific printer, or even open Terminal and automatically begin a communications session. You could create a number of macros, one for each way in which you use Windows, and then use a special command to open Windows and automatically run the macro.

We explain in detail how to run macros in Chapter 15, but here's an example. Typing **win recorder -h ^+f16 startup** will start Recorder, load the .REC file named STARTUP, and then use the Ctrl-Shift-F16 keyboard shortcut to run a macro. (You can use this shortcut, in this manner, even if you don't have an F16 on your keyboard.)

Combining Commands

Some of these commands can be combined. You can combine the mode switch with any of the other commands. For instance, **win /s c:\windows\draw** will start Windows in Standard mode and automatically start DRAW.EXE. If you know you are not going to open any DOS applications you may want to start a Windows application in Standard mode, to make it run just a little quicker. You can also open two applications at the same time. Typing **win calendar calc** will open both CALENDAR.EXE and CALC.EXE, the calculator. (However, in some cases—if you are combining another method of opening an application, as we discuss in a moment—only one of these named files will open.)

Using Batch Files

You may want to create several batch files, so you can open Windows differently according to your needs at the time. For instance, you might create a simple batch file with this line: **win winword /mfile1**. Name the file LWORD.BAT, and each time you want to open Word for Windows and work on the last file you saved, all you have to do is type **/word** and press **Enter**. You could place **win winword** in a file called WORD.BAT, so you could open Word with a blank document by simply typing **word** and pressing **Enter**.

If you create Recorder macros to open various applications, you could also create a batch file for each macro: COMPSRV.BAT to make Recorder open Windows Terminal and begin a communications session with CompuServe; CALC.BAT to get Recorder to load Microsoft Money and the Calculator, so you can do your accounts; DRAW.BAT to load Windows Draw, Paintbrush, and a screen snapshot program. The combinations are endless. Creating Recorder macros is quite simple, and they let you begin a Windows session in any way you want.

Summary

Here's a quick summary of the different ways to open Windows:

WIN /S Opens Windows in Standard mode

WIN /2 Opens Windows in Standard mode (exactly the same as WIN /S)

WIN /3 Opens Windows in 386 Enhanced mode

WIN *application*
Opens Windows and starts the named application

WIN *application filename*
Opens Windows, starts the application, and loads the file

WIN *filename* Opens Windows and loads the file into its associated application

WIN *application switch*
Opens Windows and starts the application, using the command "switch"

WIN recorder -h *macroshortcut filename*
Opens Windows, starts Recorder, loads the named file, and uses the keyboard shortcut to run a macro

The following commands are for troubleshooting, when you are having trouble starting Windows:

WIN /b Use if Windows won't start. Windows will create a BOOTLOG.TXT file that keeps a log of each file loaded as it boots. You can read this log to find the *last* file, the one with which Windows hung up. Replace that file and try again. (Use the EXPAND command. See Chapter 1.)

WIN /d:x Also try this if Windows can't start. It stops Windows from scanning the upper memory block for unused space, so you can start if a memory block is causing problems. If the system works with this switch, add the line

```
EMMExclude=A000-FFFF
```

to the SYSTEM.INI file.

WIN /d:f Turns off 32-bit disk access. If this helps, turn 32-bit disk access off from the Control Panel's 386 Enhanced dialog box. See Chapter 8 for a discussion of this feature.

WIN /d:s Stops Windows from using a ROM address space between F000:0000 and 1 MB for a break point. Some memory managers require that this area be off limits to Windows. If the system works with this switch, add the line

```
SystemROMBreakPoint=Off
```

in the SYSTEM.INI file.

WIN /d:v Specifies that the ROM routine will handle interrupts from the hard disk controller. If the system works with this switch, add the line

```
VirtualHDIRQ=Off
```

in the SYSTEM.INI file.

WIN /? Displays this list of optional switches.

Starting Applications Automatically

You have just seen several ways in which you can start applications automatically when you start Windows. You can include the application after WIN in the command line; you can name a document file that has been "associated" with the application file; and you can use Windows Recorder to run a macro that could open applications for you.

There are some other ways. The easiest way is to use Program Manager's **StartUp** program group. If you place an application icon in this group, Windows will automatically open the application each time you open Windows. See Chapter 4 for more information.

You can also use the **Load=** and **Run=** lines in the **WIN.INI** initialization file. An application named on the Load= line is started and then *minimized* (converted to an icon at the bottom of your screen). An application named on the Run= line is started and remains at its normal (*restored*) size. See Appendix B for more information. Notice that the StartUp program group and the Load= and Run= lines are independent of each other. Placing an icon in the StartUp group does *not* add it to the WIN.INI file.

Which startup methods have priority? Windows will open applications in this order:

1st	The applications named in the Load= line of WIN.INI
2nd	The applications named in the Run= line of WIN.INI

3rd	The application you name at the DOS prompt
4th	The application in the top left corner of the StartUp window
5th, and so on	The applications in the StartUp window, in sequence (from left to right along the top row, then the next row, and so on)

▼ ***Note*** If one of the applications is a DOS application, it will be pulled out of sequence and loaded *last*.

There's one last way to start applications automatically. You can add **startup=*group name*** to the [Settings] section of the PROGMAN.INI file. This turns the named group into the StartUp group. In other words, the applications in the named group will open, but the applications in the actual StartUp group will not. See Chapter 4 for more information on the StartUp group and Appendix B for more information on modifying the PROGMAN.INI file.

Closing Windows

In Chapter 3 you will find out how to work in Windows. However, if you have been playing with the different ways to open Windows and want to know how to close it, simply press **Alt-F4**. If the Program Manager is displayed (on top of all the other windows, if you started some applications), this will close Windows. If another application is displayed instead, it will close that application. Continue pressing **Alt-F4** to close all the applications and Windows itself.

3

Windows Basics

If you are completely new to Windows it's easy to get lost the first time you run it. And if you have never used any type of GUI (Graphical User Interface), you won't understand any of the conventions that have become standards in the GUI world—the purpose of icons, how to open menus, what windows and dialog boxes are, and so on.

So we are going to take it slowly, beginning with what you will see when you open Windows using the basic WIN command at the DOS prompt.

The Windows Environment

The first thing you will see when you open Windows is a *window* called Program Manager (see Figure 3.1). This is similar to a Windows menu and equivalent to a command line, the place from which all other applications are run. Remember, Windows is no longer simply a "shell" so much as an operating system. Although you do need DOS to run Windows, Windows 3.1 actually bypasses DOS for most operations. Although it needs DOS for file-management procedures, it can bypass DOS to print, for example. In the same way that DOS is an operating system that lets you run DOS programs, Windows is an operating system that lets you run Windows programs *and* DOS programs.

In DOS you start a program by typing a command and pressing **Enter**. In Windows you have a number of ways to start programs. Most of those little pictures, or *program icons*, you see in Program Manager represent applications. You can start an application by selecting an icon and pressing **Enter**, or by double-clicking on the icon with the mouse. There are several other ways to start an application, which we will discuss in Chapter 4. (The icons you may see outside the Program Manager windows—such as those shown in Figure 3.3—represent appli-

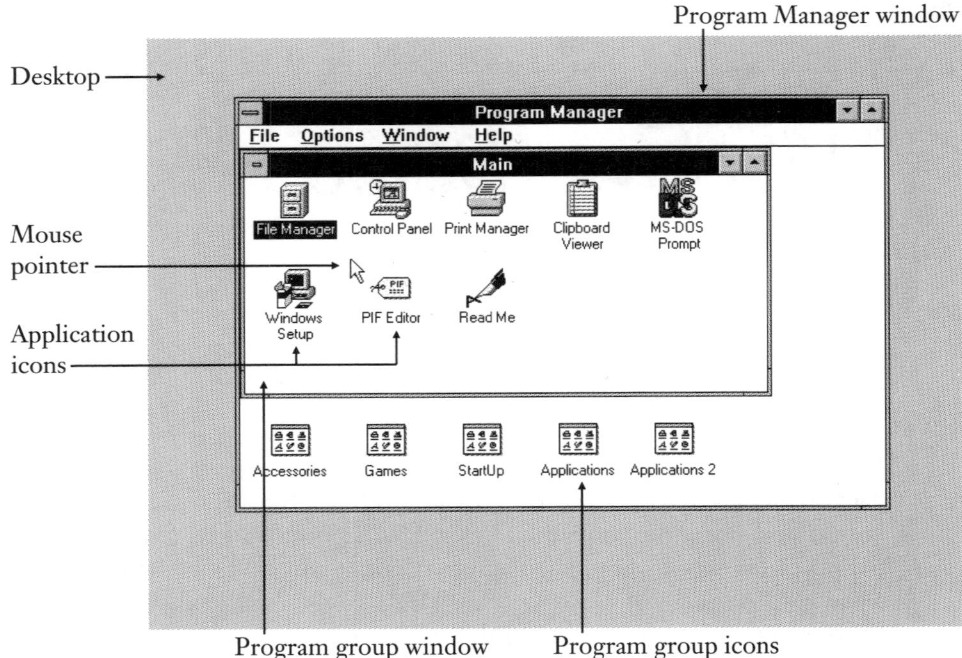

Figure 3.1 Windows Program Manager

cations that are running. The applications have been minimized, and the icons are known as *application icons*.)

▼ *Note* Are you using a copy of Windows that someone else has been using? Did another program appear on your screen instead of Program Manager? The other user may have configured Windows to start the other program—or several programs—automatically whenever Windows starts, as we discussed in Chapter 2. Press **Alt-Esc** to see the Task List dialog box. This dialog box lists all the open applications. Select one (anything but Program Manager) by pressing the **Down Arrow** key to highlight it. Then press **Alt-E** to close the application. Repeat the operation for each application except Program Manager.

A *window* is a special box in which an application runs. Program Manager is an application that lets you run other applications, so it has its own window. If you use a Windows word processor, spreadsheet, or database, each will run in its own window. You can change a window's size or move it around the screen. You will learn about the different parts of the window later in this chapter. Let's begin by learning how to move around in Program Manager, using the keyboard or the mouse.

Using a Mouse

You need a mouse. Yes, you *can* use Windows without one, and even if you have one you will still use the keyboard for many operations. But Windows was designed for use with a mouse, and many operations are much more efficient and much quicker when carried out with a mouse.

▼ ***Note*** We are going to use the term *mouse* throughout this book. You may, however, use any Windows-compatible pointing device—trackballs, digitizing tablets, mouse "pens," and so on—that can move the mouse pointer across your computer screen.

Many Windows programmers seem to have forgotten that some users don't have a mouse. Some programs intentionally require a mouse. For instance, you cannot use the Micrografx Windows Draw without a mouse, because many of the most basic commands can only be selected by pointing and clicking. Other programs accidentally forget keyboard equivalents for some commands. While a program may be planned as a mouse or keyboard application, programmers sometimes forget to add certain keyboard commands. You will be able to use most of the program without a mouse, but you will occasionally find commands that can be selected only with a mouse.

These problems may occur with applications you buy for Windows. Windows itself supports both mouse and keyboard for almost all commands. (There are just a few instances in which you need a mouse—while playing the Minesweeper game, for example.) We are going to explain both methods, but suggest that you buy a mouse if you don't already have one.

Tip Some mice are falsely advertised as "high-resolution" mice. The resolution controls how far you must move your hand to move the on-screen mouse pointer a certain distance. The higher the resolution, the shorter the distance you have to move. Windows lets you control the resolution to some degree, but still, a low resolution mouse may be irritatingly sluggish. Maximum resolutions measured in hundreds of dpi (dots per inch) are too low. Look for thousands or tens of thousands of dpi. When buying a mouse ask about the *maximum* resolution, not the default.

The mouse—or any other pointing device you are using—provides a way to move a pointer across the computer screen and to carry out certain operations by clicking the device's buttons. (The arrow pointing at the File Manager icon in Figure 3.1 is the mouse pointer.)

Two basic types of mice are available—mechanical and optical mice. A mechanical mouse has a small ball on the underside. As you move the mouse across a flat surface, the ball rolls and moves special roller-switches inside the body of the mouse. These switches control the pointer. An optical mouse reflects light off its mouse pad. The pad has a special grid, and the reflections from the grid lines are used by the mouse to determine in which direction and how far it is moving.

By moving the mouse you can move the pointer into any position on the screen. Then, using the mouse's keys, you can carry out certain operations. These are the terms we will be using in this book to describe mouse procedures:

Point to	Move the pointer on top of an object on the screen.
Click	Press the mouse button.
Double-click	Press the mouse button twice, quickly.
Press	Press the mouse button and hold it down.
Click on the	Point at the object and click the mouse button.
Double-click on the	Point at the object and double-click the mouse button.
Drag the	Point at the object, press the mouse button, and move the mouse: The object will move across the screen.

We've used the term *mouse button* several times, but your mouse has at least two, or maybe three, buttons. Which one do we mean? Generally, we mean the *dominant* mouse button, usually the left mouse button. If you are right-handed you will move the mouse with your right hand, resting your index finger on the left button—the dominant button. If you are left-handed and bought a special "left-handed" mouse, the mouse is wired back-to-front. You will move the mouse with your left hand, with your index finger resting on the *right* button—which, for you, is the dominant button.

If you are left-handed and use mainly Windows programs, you don't need a special left-handed mouse, because Windows lets you swap the mouse button (we'll explain how in a moment). If you swap the buttons, then the dominant button is the *right* button (on a normal mouse).

The other buttons are used less frequently. The right button is used by many Windows applications for special procedures. The middle button—if you have a three-button mouse—is used by only a few special applications.

▼ ***Note*** If we say "click" a mouse button, but don't say *which* button, we mean the dominant button. If we want you to click the other button we will specify it. We will not refer to the middle button.

Incidentally, double-clicking is difficult for some new mouse users. The speed has to be just right, or the operation you are trying to carry out will not work. As a test, point at the title bar in Program Manager (the colored bar at the top of the window). Double-clicking this title bar *maximizes* the window—that is, the window goes to maximum size, covering your computer's screen. Double-clicking again returns it to the original size (*restores* it, in Windows-speak). Experiment until you get just the right speed. (The double-click speed can be adjusted in the Control Panel. See Chapter 8.)

If you are new to using a mouse—or if you want to swap the mouse buttons—try Windows' mouse tutorial. Move the mouse until the pointer rests on the word Help in the menu bar. Click the dominant button once. A menu "drops down." Click on the line that says **Windows Tutorial**. The tutorial begins. Type **M** and press **Enter** to begin the mouse tutorial. The tutorial will lead you through various screens and exercises: Just follow the instructions. It will also give you a chance to swap the mouse buttons.

At the end of the mouse tutorial you will have the option to "Go on to the Windows Basics tutorial." Select that option to learn about Windows components and procedures.

Using the Keyboard

Almost everything you can do using the mouse, you can do using the keyboard, at least in Windows itself (as we mentioned earlier, this may not be true in some Windows applications you buy). As we describe the various components of Windows we will explain both mouse and keyboard operations. Later in this book we will assume that you understand how to duplicate mouse operations using the keyboard and will explain only the mouse procedures. For now, if you want to use the Windows tutorial, press **Alt-H** and type **W**. Then follow the tutorial's instructions.

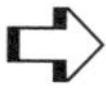 **Tip** As a general rule, if you see a label with one letter underlined, you can hold Alt and press the underlined letter to operate the labeled component. For instance, menus have one underlined letter, as do most buttons, list boxes, option buttons, and so on.

There's one very important thing to remember about the keyboard. If you are using the cursor-movement keys on your keyboard's numeric keypad, *turn off the Num Lock!* These keys won't work while you have the Num Lock turned on.

Windows' Components

We are now going to take a look at the Windows "environment," using Program Manager as an example. Most of what you are about to learn applies to Windows in general: how to move and size windows, how to select menu options, working with dialog boxes, and so on. When we've covered these basic components and procedures, we will move on to Chapter 4 and examine Program Manager in detail.

A Windows Components

As you saw in Figure 3.1, Program Manager is contained in what is known as a *window*. A window is a box containing various objects. A window can be moved or changed in size. When the window is not maximized—that is, when it isn't covering your entire screen—you can see a border around it.

The window is the basic Microsoft Windows component. Each application runs in an *application window* and may contain a variety of objects. A word processor contains a document, a spreadsheet contains spreadsheet cells. Program Manager is a special application that lets you manage and run your other applications. The Program Manager contains several other small windows. These windows within the window usually are known as *document windows*. For instance, a word processor or spreadsheet might contain several open document windows, each holding a different document or spreadsheet.

In Program Manager the document windows are called *program-group windows*, or just *group windows*. Each icon in Program Manager's group windows represents a program. You only really need one group window—you could put all your programs in that window. But it's easier to build several groups for different types of programs. This might seem similar to the way you create different directories in DOS to group different applications. Windows' group windows are more flexible. While Windows still uses the DOS file and directory structure to store information on your hard disk, you can place any kind of program icon in a group window from many different DOS directories.

▼ ***Note*** We are going to describe Program Manager in more detail in Chapter 4. In general, you can press **Ctrl-Tab** or **Ctrl-F6** to move to the next document window in an application window. Some applications also have a Next command in the Control menu.

Group windows can be *minimized*. A minimized window is one that has been shrunk down to an icon. In Figure 3.2 you can see several group-window icons at the bottom of the Program Manager window. It consists of a small picture of a window with a title underneath. Windows of all sorts can be minimized to simply get them out of the way. Once icon-size you can use them when you need them; but they are not taking up precious room on your screen.

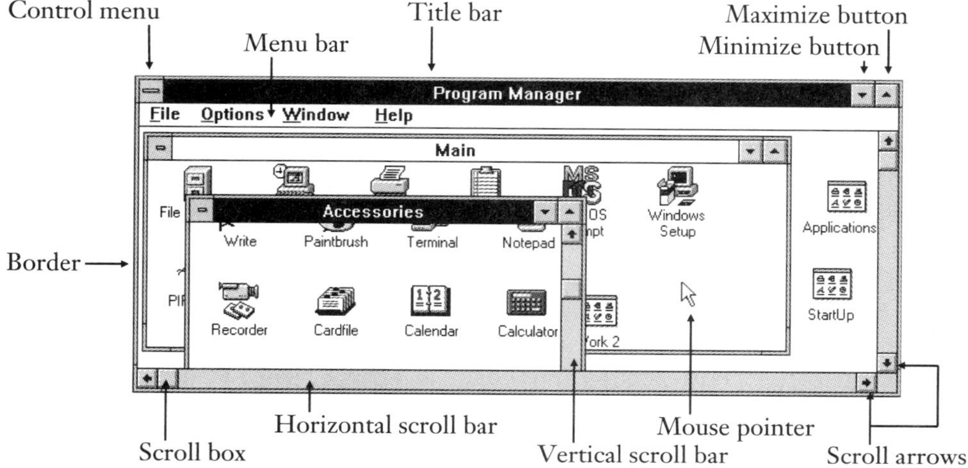

Figure 3.2 Windows components

Let's look at the other components that most windows contain. Take a look at Figure 3.2, and you should see the following:

Title bar The name of the application (in some applications the title bar includes the name of the open file). In Program Manager the group windows' title bars show the group names. (When you maximize a group or document window, the title is added to the main window's title bar.)

Control-menu box A special menu drops down from here when you click on the box or when you press **Alt-Spacebar**.

Minimize button Click this button to change a window into an icon.

Maximize button Click this button to maximize the window—to make an application window cover the entire screen, or make a document window fill the application window. If the window is already maximized, this button will display two triangles, one pointing up and one down. Clicking on the button *restores* the window, changing it to its previous size.

Menu bar Menu bars contain several words. Clicking on a word makes a list of options "drop down." These are often called *drop-down menus*, or simply *menus*.

Mouse pointer The pointer controlled by the mouse movement and used to select objects.

Scroll bar A bar used to move through a document vertically or horizontally. For instance, Windows adds a scroll bar to a group window if it contains more icons than will fit in the window. You can use the scroll bar to view the other icons.

Scroll arrow Click on a scroll arrow to scroll through the window slowly.

Scroll box Drag the scroll box to scroll quickly through the window.

Border Displayed only when the window is not maximized nor minimized. You can use the border to change the window's size.

The menu bar is usually found only in an application window—although some applications also have menu bars in document windows (none of Windows' own applications do). Most of the components we have just looked at may be found in both the application and document windows.

Some of these components—scroll bars, borders, minimize and maximize buttons—can be used only with a mouse. There are keyboard equivalents, however, ways in which you can carry out the same operation using the keyboard. Other components—the Control menu and menu bar—may be used by both mouse and keyboard.

Using the Menus

You can select most Windows application commands from the menus. A number of menus are common to most applications, including Program Manager. Three are described here:

Control The Control menu contains commands that let you move and size the window, switch to other applications, and close the application. Some windows have one or two extra commands. Program Manager's group windows, for instance, contain a Next command, which makes the next group window the active one.

File The File menu is commonly used to open, save, and close the file. It also has a command that lets you close the application itself. When a document window has a Close command, it may close the file or simply minimize the window (the command minimizes Program Manager's group windows).

Help The Help menu contains commands that let you access the application's Help system, as well as an About command that provides the application version number and related information. Windows' Help system is described in Chapter 10.

The easiest way to use a menu is to point and click. Point at the name of the menu you want to open, then click the mouse button. (If you want to open the Control menu, click on the box in the top-left corner.) A menu "drops down" below the name. Click on one of the menu options to select that command.

If you prefer to use the keyboard, you have several options:

- Press **F10** to activate the menu bar, then press the **Left** and **Right Arrows** to move to a menu, and the **Up** and **Down Arrows** to open the menu. (F10 won't work in some Windows applications.)

- Press and hold **Alt**, then press the letter underlined in the menu name. To open the Control menu, press **Alt-Spacebar**. To open a document window's Control menu, press **Alt-Hyphen** (-). If the document window is maximized you may be able to open its Control menu by pressing and releasing **Alt**, then pressing **Enter**.
- When a menu is open, press the letter *underlined* in the menu-option name to select the option.
- When a menu is open, use the **Up** and **Down Arrows** to highlight a menu option, and press **Enter** to select it.
- When a menu is open, press the **Left** and **Right Arrows** to open another menu.

Many menu options also have keyboard shortcuts, which are shown in the menu next to the option name. The File menu in Program Manager has several keyboard shortcuts. These shortcuts let you select a command without even opening a menu. Pressing **Alt-Enter**, for instance, automatically selects the Properties command.

Important Throughout this book you are going to see menu names and options in the following format: *menuname* | *optionname*. This means, "select the *optionname* option from the *menuname* menu." For instance, "select File | Properties" means "select the Properties option from the File menu."

What happens when you select a menu option? That depends. It may

- carry out a command immediately.
- display a dialog box into which you can enter information before the command is carried out.
- select a default setting or *preference*.
- display yet another menu (a *cascading menu*), which will drop down to one side of the option name.
- do nothing.

Menus often indicate what an option will do. If the option is dimmed (also called *disabled* or *ghosted*), the option is not available, so it won't do anything. You may have to select something or use another command before the option becomes available. If there's an ellipsis (. . .) after the option name, that option will lead to a dialog box (some Windows programmers forget to include the ellipsis, although all the appropriate menu options in Windows itself include it). Several of the options in Program Manager's File menu have ellipses.

If there's a small triangle (next to the option name, pointing to the right), selecting the option will display yet another menu, a cascading menu, which drops down to one side. Some menu options set application *preferences*. You will see this term used by many Windows applications: It simply means "the way you want the program to run." For instance, if you select the Options | Minimize on Use option in Program Manager, you are telling the application that you want Program Manager to be minimized—to be changed into an icon—each time you start an application. To show you that the preference has been selected, an application will display a check mark (✓) next to the option name. Many programs also use Preferences dialog boxes when there are too many options to place in the menus themselves.

Sizing Windows

You can adjust a window's size to move it out of the way of other windows or so that you may see more of the application document. Let's take a quick look at how you can change the size of a window.

- Place the pointer over the **window's border**. It changes to a two-headed arrow. Drag the border to change the size.
- Place the arrow on the **border's corner**. Dragging the two-headed arrow adjusts both horizontal and vertical size.
- Click on the **maximize button**. An application window maximizes, filling your screen and covering the desktop and any icons or other windows. The window's border disappears. Clicking on a document window's maximize button makes it fill the application window. In some applications maximizing one document window maximizes all of them (not so in Program Manager).
- Click on the **minimize button.** The application is minimized, changed into an icon at the bottom of the screen. (Figure 3.3 shows examples of application icons.) If that area is covered by another window, you will not be able to see the icon. Clicking on a document window's minimize button usually reduces it to an icon at the bottom of the application window (in some applications, such as Word for Windows, it simply reduces it in size until you can see borders around it).
- Click on the **restore button** (the two-triangle button that appears in place of the maximize button when the window is maximized). The window is restored to its last open size (not to an icon).
- Double-click on the **title bar**. If the window is maximized, it is restored. If it is *not* maximized, double-clicking maximizes it. Double-clicking a document window's title bar maximizes it only—once maximized the title bar disappears, so you can't use it to restore the window.

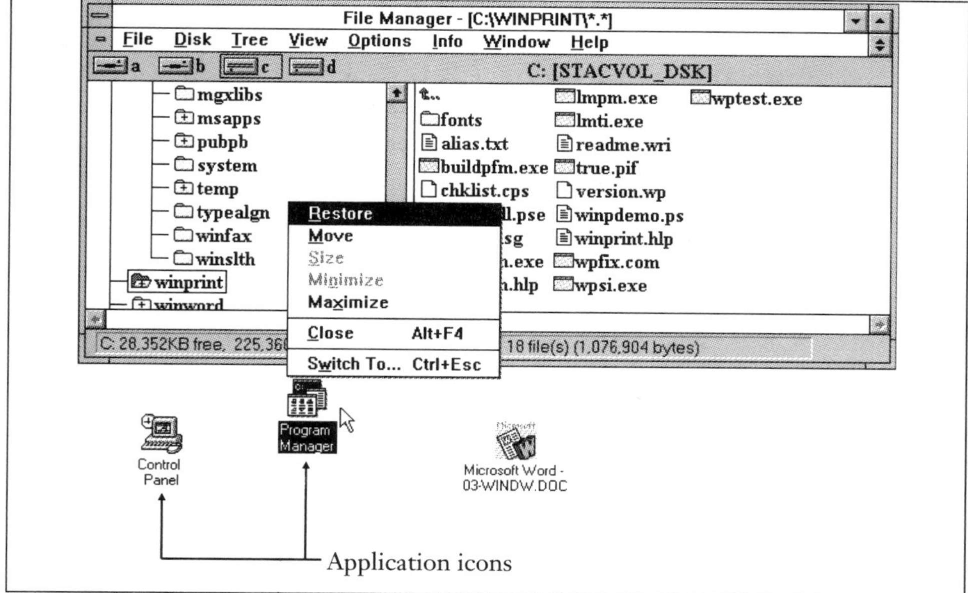

Figure 3.3 Application icons on the desktop

Incidentally, some applications may have slightly different methods. Word for Windows, for instance, lets you use the keyboard to operate the restore button; press **F10** and then the **Right Arrow** several times. You can then press **Enter** to restore the document window.

You can also use the **Control menu** to change a window's size. Open the Control menu and use the following commands:

- **Restore** restores the window (the same as clicking the restore button). This option is only available if the window is maximized or minimized.
- **Size** lets you modify the window's size using the arrow keys. This option is only available if the window is restored.
- **Minimize** reduces the window to an icon. This option is only available if the window is maximized or restored.
- **Maximize** makes the window fill your screen, covering all the other windows and icons. This option is only available if the window is restored or minimized.

The **Size** option is not quite as simple as using the mouse, of course, but easy to use nonetheless. When you select the option a four-headed pointer appears. When you press an arrow key Windows selects the border you can move. For instance, press the **Up Arrow** to move the top border or the **Left Arrow** to move the left border. Then use the arrow keys to move that border in or out. If you press a vertical arrow followed by a horizontal arrow—or vice versa—Windows selects a corner. For instance, press **Up Arrow** followed by **Left Arrow** to select the top-left corner. Then you can move the corner up, down, left, or right using the arrow keys. When you have the window the size you want, press **Enter**. You can also press **Esc** to abandon the operation.

▼ *Note* Remember that you can also size document windows within an application window. If you want to use the Control menu to do so, select the document window (by clicking on it or pressing **Ctrl-Tab** or **Ctrl-F6**), then press **Alt-Hyphen** (-) to open the menu.

Moving Windows

You can also move windows around on your screen. You may want to do this—in combination with sizing—to place two applications on your window so you can see them both, for instance. The quickest way to move a window is to simply **drag** the **title bar**. You can also drag an icon to any position on the screen. Of course you can't move a maximized window, because it is using the entire screen (if it's maximized, there's nowhere to move the window to).

If you don't have a mouse, use the Move option on the Control menu. This option is only available if the window is not maximized, or if it is an icon. When you select the option the same four-headed pointer appears that you use for sizing a window. Press the arrow keys to move the window around, and then press **Enter** when you have it in the position you want it. Again, you can press **Esc** to abandon the operation if you wish.

▼ *Note* If you can't seem to move or size the window into the position you want—if it seems to jump past the position—you probably have a large Granularity setting in the Control Panel's Desktop dialog box. See Chapter 8 for information.

Using Icons

Once minimized, an application window becomes an icon at the bottom of the *desktop*, the area of your screen on which all Windows components are based. (You might imagine your screen as a desk, and the windows as open books. An icon is like a closed book.) You can move icons in the same way you move a window. You can simply drag the icon into the position in which you want it. As long as the icon is selected, it is the active application. If you place this icon on top of an open window, you will still be able to see it. However, once you click on the open window, it becomes the active application and the icon disappears below the window.

You can also open an icon's Control menu. Simply click once on the icon or, if the icon is already selected, press **Alt-Spacebar**. (If you are in another application, you can select the icon by pressing **Alt-Esc** one or more times. In Chapter 5 you will learn more ways to move between applications.) Figure 3.3 shows the File Manager window open, with several icons on the desktop. The Program Manager icon has its Control menu open.

You can then use the Move command to move the icon to another position, or the Maximize or Restore commands to open the window.

Many applications, such as Program Manager, also let you minimize document windows. You can see examples of these icons in Figure 3.1. These can be moved around inside the window the same way you move application icons around the desktop.

Using Scroll Bars

Windows uses scroll bars as an easy way to move around in a window. When you are working in a word processor, spreadsheet, or desktop publishing program, for instance, you will find that you need to move around in the document. Of course you can use the keyboard's PgUp, PgDn, and arrow keys to move around, and applications often have menu commands to help you find a specific page. But the scroll bars let you use the mouse to scroll through a page, a screen, or an entire document.

As you can see in Figure 3.2, the Program Manager application window and group windows sometimes contain scroll bars. If a window contains more icons than can be seen, Windows adds scroll bars so you can move through the window. So changing a window's size often adds or removes scroll bars. Try changing the size of the Main window, for example. If you reduce this window by dragging one corner into the center, Windows will have to add scroll bars so you can get to some of the icons.

A scroll bar contains several elements. The bar itself runs the length or width of the workspace inside the window. At each end of the bar is a *scroll arrow*. And inside the bar is a *scroll box*. The scroll box indicates the relative position of the information currently displayed in the window. For instance, if the scroll box is in the middle of the bar, the information displayed is in the middle of the document.

This is how you can use the scroll bars:

- Drag the scroll box along the scroll bar and release it. The window scrolls to the relative position in which you released the box. In some applications the information in the window scrolls as you move the box. In others the information remains still until you release it.

- Point at the scroll bar above or below the box (or to the left or right of the box in a horizontal scroll bar) and click the mouse button. The information in the screen jumps in the appropriate direction, generally one screenful. Hold the mouse button down to move quickly, screen by screen.
- Point at one of the arrows and click the mouse button. The information in the screen jumps in the appropriate direction, generally one line. Hold the mouse button down to move quickly, line by line.

You will also see scroll bars elsewhere, not just in windows. Many list boxes have them so you can use the mouse to move through a list of options. Program Manager also uses scroll bars in its Change Icon dialog box so that you can view a series of icons. And while scroll bars are permanently affixed to some windows and components, in other cases they only appear as needed. Like Program Manager (which, as you've just seen, only adds scroll bars if there are icons that are not visible), many list boxes only add the bars when there are more options in the list than will fit in the box. Even some applications only add scroll bars when the amount of information in the window, or the manner in which the information is being viewed, necessitates the use of scroll bars.

Most applications use the following keyboard equivalents for scroll bar actions:

One line up or down	Up Arrow or Down Arrow
One screen up or down	PgUp or PgDn
One screen left or right	Ctrl-PgUp and Ctrl-PgDn
To the beginning of a line	Home
To the end of a line	End
To the beginning of a document	Ctrl-Home
To the end of a document	Ctrl-End

Not all applications will use all of these and there may be some slight variations, so check the application's documentation. You can use the arrow keys to move around in Program Manager's group windows.

Working with Dialog Boxes

Windows uses *dialog boxes* as a sort of interface between you and Windows applications. You enter text or numbers, or select options, to provide an application with information about what you want the program to do: what words to search for, what colors to use, what calculations to make, and so on. Figure 3.4 shows an example of a dialog box that you can open from Program Manager; select an icon and then select **File | Properties**.

Windows also uses special dialog boxes simply to provide you with information. Such boxes are more commonly known as *message boxes*. A message box might

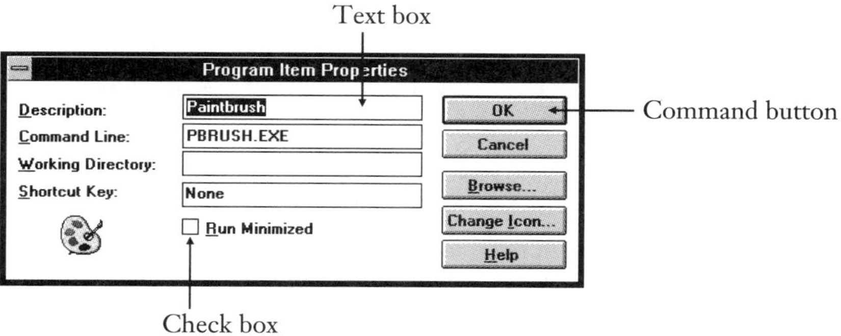

Figure 3.4 The Program Item Properties dialog box

inform you that your printer is not working, that you entered invalid information into a spreadsheet cell, or tell you that you don't have enough information to complete an operation. These messages sometimes contain suggested solutions to the problem. Figure 3.5 shows a typical message box.

There are several ways to close dialog boxes. You can click on the OK button to close the box and carry out the command; click on the Cancel button or press **Esc** to close the box without carrying out the command; press **Alt-F4**; or select Close from the box's Control menu or double-click on the menu, if it has one.

These are the dialog box components:

Command buttons Clicking on a button carries out an operation.

Text boxes Text boxes display information. You may be able to modify the text.

List boxes List boxes display a list of options from which you may choose.

Drop-down list boxes A drop-down list box looks like a text box with a down arrow on the right side. When you click on the down arrow (or, in some cases, press **F4**), a list of options "drops down."

Option buttons Option buttons generally appear in groups: you can select only one of the option buttons in the group.

Check boxes Check boxes turn on certain settings.

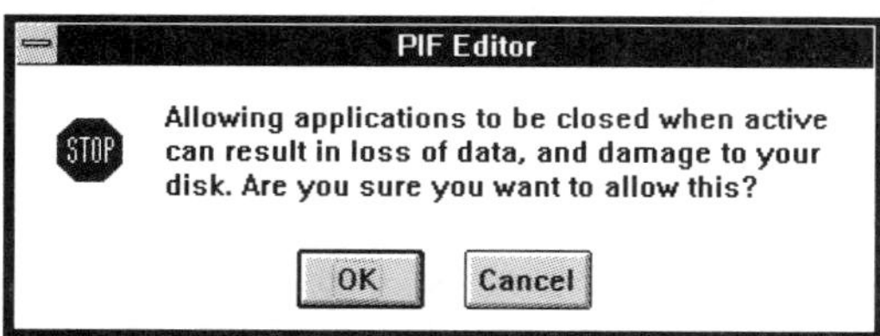

Figure 3.5 A typical message box

Incrementer boxes Incrementer boxes let you enter a number by typing it or clicking on small arrows to increase or decrease the existing number.

Scroll bars Some dialog boxes let you make adjustments by moving the scroll box along a scroll bar.

Figures 3.4 and 3.6 through 3.9 show these components. Program Manager's dialog boxes don't contain all of these components, so one of our example illustrations comes from a different application.

You can use dialog box components in a variety of ways. To select or activate a component you can click on it, but you may also press **Tab** to move a highlight between components. (Pressing **Shift-Tab** moves the highlight in the opposite direction.)

Most components also have an underlined letter in their name. This allows you to select the component by pressing and holding **Alt** and then pressing the underlined letter. In the case of a button, using this method will actually activate the button, the equivalent of clicking on it. The currently selected component is highlighted in some way. For instance, in Figure 3.4 the Description text box is selected; you can tell because the word Paintbrush is highlighted. In Figure 3.5 the OK button is selected; you can tell by the dotted line around the button's label. When an option button or check box is selected the label is also surrounded by a dotted line. When a scroll bar is selected the scroll box flashes each second.

COMMAND BUTTONS

Command buttons are the components that tell the application to carry out the operation indicated by the title on the button. Most dialog boxes have at least an OK button and a Cancel button. Clicking on the OK button carries out the operation, using the information in the dialog box. For instance, in Figure 3.4 clicking on OK would create the program icon using the information provided.

Sometimes the dialog box uses a Yes button instead of OK, or another title that indicates the action that is about to be carried out: Print, Copy, Delete, and so on. In many dialog boxes you can press **Enter** to duplicate the action of clicking on the OK (or Yes, or Print, or whatever) button. (If the button is highlighted, you can press **Enter** to operate it.)

The **Cancel** button makes the application close the dialog box and abandon the operation. In many dialog boxes you can press **Esc** to duplicate the action of clicking on the Cancel button.

Another button often found in dialog boxes is the **Help** button. Clicking on Help displays context-sensitive help, that is, information about the dialog box in which you are working. And many other buttons may be used in dialog boxes. For instance, Figure 3.4 has a Browse button (which lets you "browse" through the directories looking for the executable file you want to add to the Command Line text box), and a Change Icon button, which lets you select another icon. Notice the ellipsis after the button names (Browse. . . and Change Icon. . .). Like ellipses in menus, this indicates that clicking on the button will display another dialog box. (Ellipses on buttons are common, but by no means universal. Many Windows applications do *not* have ellipses on the buttons that display dialog boxes.) Some command buttons have "greater than" signs (>>) on them. This type of button presents more options and information by expanding the dialog box.

Activate a button by clicking on it, by pressing **Alt** and the **underlined letter**, or by pressing **Tab** until the button is highlighted and then pressing **Enter**. (When a button is highlighted its outline is thicker than the other buttons.)

TEXT BOXES

Figure 3.4 shows several text boxes. A text box is a rectangular box that displays a line of text (some text boxes have space for more than one line, but most are single-line boxes). When the dialog box first appears it may already show text in the text box or it may be blank. Either way, you can normally enter your own information.

To get to the text box, you can simply click on the box. A text cursor is placed inside. Or press **Tab** to move to the box, or press **Alt** and the letter underlined in the text box's title. If you use one of these two methods, the text in the box is highlighted; if you begin typing the text is immediately replaced by the new text.

You may type text into the text box or paste it in. If you have text in the Windows Clipboard, you can press **Ctrl-V** or **Shift-Ins** to copy it into the text box. (The Clipboard is a special application used to transfer text and graphics from one application to another or within applications. You will learn more about it in a later chapter.) You can edit text also. Use the following keys:

arrow keys to move the cursor within the text box

Ctrl-arrow keys to move the cursor a word at a time

Home to place the cursor before the first character

End to place the cursor after the last character

Shift- combined with cursor-movement keys to select characters. For instance, Shift-Ctrl-Left Arrow selects the word immediately to the left.

Del to delete the character immediately to the right

Backspace to delete a character immediately to the left

LIST BOXES

A list box looks like a multiline text box but contains a list of options. You can generally select one of the options, although in some special cases you may be able

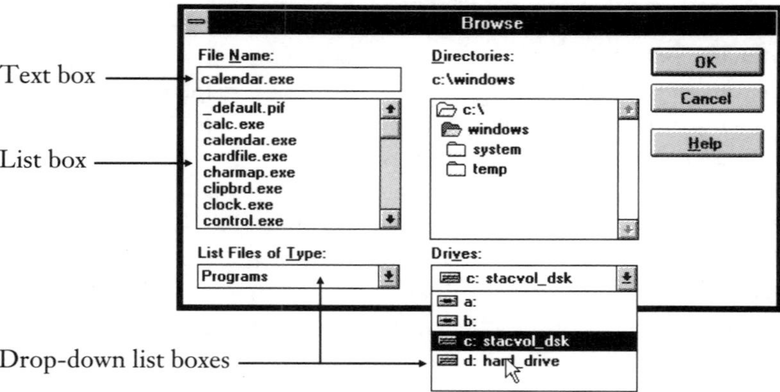

Figure 3.6 The Browse dialog box, showing list boxes and drop-down list boxes.

to select several or all of the entries. Figure 3.6 shows the Browse dialog box displayed when you click on the Browse button in the Program Item Properties dialog box (you can display this dialog box by selecting a program icon and pressing **Alt-Enter**). The Browse dialog box contains two list boxes; the one on the right shows a list of directories, and the one on the left shows the files in the selected directory.

Notice that the list box on the left has a scroll bar, allowing you to scroll down through the list. The box on the right has a scroll bar, but it is disabled because there are not enough directories in the list to require scrolling. Some applications actually remove scroll bars entirely when they are not required.

You can reach a list box in the usual ways; press **Tab** until a highlight appears in the list or click in the list. In some cases you may be able to press **Alt** and the underlined letter. For instance, in the illustration you can press **Alt-D** to place the highlight in the list of directories. But to reach the list of files you must press **Alt-F**—which places the highlight in the text box above the list—and then press **Tab** to move into the list itself. (Some similar dialog boxes may require that you press **Down Arrow** to move into the list itself, especially if there is no gap between the text box and the list box.)

Once in the list, you can use a variety of ways to move around and select an option. You can use the scroll bars to move around or use the **arrow keys** to move up and down. You can also press **PgUp** and **PgDn** to move through the list one boxful at a time, **End** to select the last item in the list, and **Home** to select the first item in the list. Dragging the **scroll box** lets you quickly see all the list entries as you move down the list.

You can select an item by **clicking** on it and carry out an action by **double-clicking** on it. In the list of directories, for instance, you can click on a directory and then click on OK, or **double-click** on it to select it and display its contents in

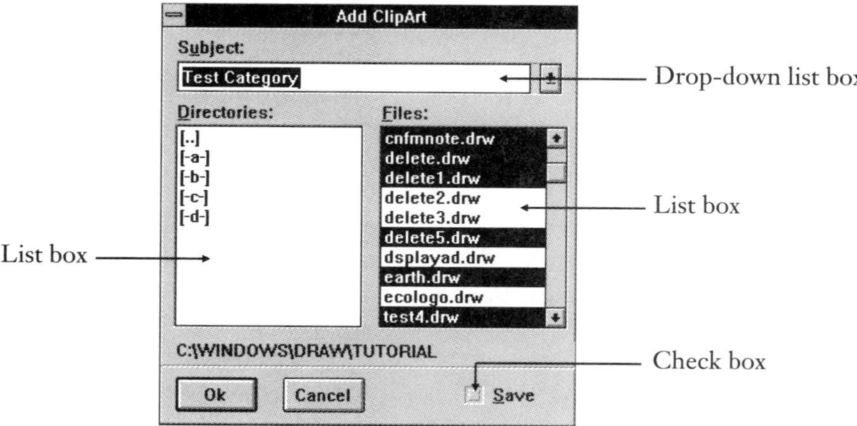

Figure 3.7 Windows Draw's Add ClipArt dialog box, showing several selected filenames

the Files list box. (You can also highlight the directory and then press **Enter**.) In the list of files you can select an option by simply clicking on it once. If you **double-click**, you not only select the option but close the dialog box. Why the difference between the actions of a double-click?

Tip Many list boxes let you type a letter to move to the first item that starts with that letter. Press the letter again to go to the next one. When you get to the last one, press again to go back to the first in the list. This is very useful when you are selecting from long lists, such as choosing a file in a directory.

It makes perfect sense, if you consider the purpose of the dialog box. The purpose of the dialog box in Figure 3.6 is to let you select the name of an executable file. If you double-click on a filename you are telling the dialog box that you've found the file you want. On the other hand, double-clicking on a directory name simply opens the directory. There's no point closing the dialog box, because you haven't finished yet—you still need to find the filename.

Some list boxes let you select several options from the list. For instance, Figure 3.7 shows a list box from the Micrografx Windows Draw. In this box you may select as many of the files in the right-side list box as you wish (they are being added to a clip-art library). You can select multiple files in several ways:

- Click on each one.
- Some list boxes require that you hold **Ctrl** while you click on each option.

- Click on the first in a group, move to the last in the group, hold **Shift**, and click again.
- Press the mouse button and drag the pointer across the files.
- Press **Shift** and press the **Up** or **Down Arrow** to select a group.

When you select an option from a list, Windows often displays that option somewhere. For instance, when you select a directory in the Browse dialog box, the pathname appears immediately above the directory list. When you click on a filename, the name appears in the text box above the list.

DROP-DOWN LIST BOXES

Some dialog boxes use a special sort of list box that at first glance looks like a text box. If you look again you notice that there's a small down-arrow on the right end of the text box. Examples of drop-down list boxes are shown in Figures 3.6 and 3.7.

In general there are three ways to open a drop-down list box: click the arrow; click on the **text** itself; or press **Tab** to move to the text box and then press **Down Arrow.** This won't always open the list box; it may simply move the next option in the list box into the text box. In such a drop-down list box pressing **F4** will usually open it.

Drop-down list boxes are used to save space in cramped dialog boxes, or in situations in which a user probably won't need to select from the list. For instance, in Figure 3.6 the user will always need to select from the list of files, and often from the list of directories. But the need to select from the file types or disk drives is rare, so those lists can be tucked away, to appear only when needed. It's all up to the judgment of the programmer: List boxes and drop-down list boxes are in many ways interchangeable.

You may also be able to type an entry into a drop-down list box, which you cannot do in a list box. If the programmer has used a list box but wants to let you type an entry, a text box will be included with the list box (as in the File Name text and list boxes in Figure 3.6). Drop-down list boxes often let you type an entry, because they are a combination of a text box and a list box.

OPTION BUTTONS

Sometimes known as *radio buttons*, option buttons let you select one option from a group. For example, if you click on the Program Group button in the dialog box shown in Figure 3.8, the other option button is automatically *deselected.* (This dialog box is displayed by selecting File|New in Program Manager.)

You can see why the term radio button—more common for Macintosh applications—has been used to describe this feature. It's an analogy with the sort of

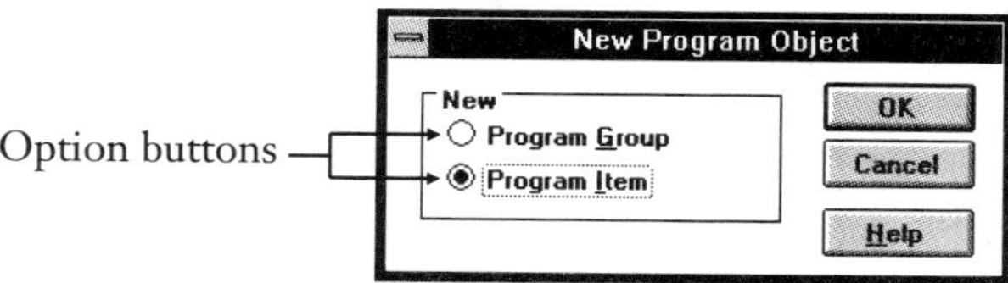

Figure 3.8 The New Program Object dialog box

channel-selection buttons often found on old car radios: Press one button in and another button pops out.

You can also select an option button by pressing **Alt** and the underlined letter, or by pressing **Tab** until you reach the option-button group, and then using the **arrow keys** to move to the option you want to select.

Some Windows applications let you double-click on option buttons to both select the option and close the dialog box. Windows itself won't work like this, but some other programs (such as Word for Windows) will, on occasion, let you do so, as long as the dialog box has all the information it needs to carry out the requested operation.

You can quickly tell if an option button has been selected: If it is filled with a circle, it's selected; if it is empty, it is not.

CHECK BOXES

Figure 3.4 shows a check box at the bottom of a dialog box. Check boxes select nonexclusive options. In this case selecting the check box tells Windows that you want the application to run minimized—as an icon—when you use the program icon to start it. Unlike option buttons, selecting a check box does not normally deselect another check box. You may be able to select several from a group.

You can select or deselect a check box by clicking on it or by pressing **Alt** and the underlined letter. Or press **Tab** to move to the check box, and press **Spacebar**. When you select a check box it fills with a diagonal cross, as you can see in Figure 3.9. (Some applications, such as the Micrografx Windows Draw, have a slightly different type of check box; when it's selected, it's filled with a colored square. See Figure 3.7.)

▼ ***Note*** You will sometimes see a check box that is "shaded," or gray. This usually happens when you have selected several items and opened a dialog box that shows you information about those items. For instance, if you select several words in a word processor and open a dialog box that shows you character formats, the Bold check box may be shaded. This would mean that some of the selected characters are bold and some are not.

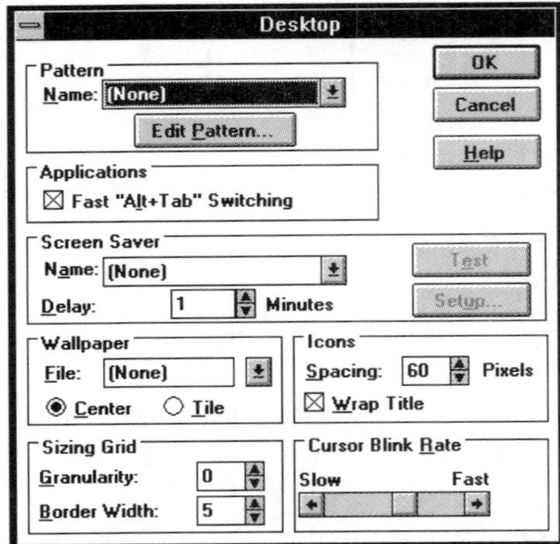

Figure 3.9 Control Panel's Desktop dialog box

INCREMENTER BOXES

An *incrementer box* contains a number and has two arrows on one side of the box. Clicking on the up arrow increases the number in the box, while clicking on the down arrow reduces the number. Figure 3.9 shows the Control Panel's Desktop dialog box, in which you can use several incrementer boxes to modify various settings: increase the Screen Saver time and modify the Icon Spacing, Granularity, and Border Width.

As usual, you can get to an incrementer box by holding **Alt** and pressing the letter that is underlined in the incrementer's label. For instance, pressing **Alt-D** would take you to the Delay incrementer in the Desktop dialog box. The number in the incrementer is highlighted and is replaced by the number you type. You may also place the cursor in the incrementer by clicking inside it.

SCROLL BARS

As you can see in Figure 3.9, in some dialog boxes you may adjust a setting using a scroll bar. The Cursor Blink Rate can be adjusted by dragging the scroll box along the bar, by clicking on one of the arrows, or by pointing at the bar between the scroll box and one of the arrows and clicking. If you don't have a mouse you can select the scroll bar (press **Alt-R**), and use the arrow keys to move the scroll box along the bar.

ESC KEY

The Esc key is a general purpose "cancel" key. Pressing **Esc** while a dialog box is open will close it. Pressing it after selecting the menu bar deselects the bar, after opening a menu closes the menu. Pressing **Esc** also cancels many other operations, such as moving or sizing windows. And different applications will use Esc to cancel their own specific operations. For instance, you can press **Esc** while File Manager is reading a disk to stop it and display what it has found so far.

Closing Windows

Let's take a quick look at how to close Windows. You can close Windows by closing Program Manager itself. Use one of these methods:

- Select **Close** from Program Manager's Control menu.
- **Double-click** on the Control menu.
- Select **File | Exit**.
- Press **Alt-F4**.

You can use the same methods to close an application.

This may all seem a little confusing—there are so many ways to do things, and Windows is not as consistent in the way it uses components as perhaps it should be. But once you get rolling you will find that the different components soon make sense and are easy to understand, even when they vary slightly from the norm.

There is probably no such thing as a truly "intuitive" computer program, industry-hype to the contrary. But you will find that when you have used Windows for awhile, you start to understand new programs the first time you work with them. Components look familiar, menu and command names immediately make sense. In many cases you will find that you can learn a program's basics without opening the documentation, because you already understand "the language" the software's programmer is "speaking."

That's Windows' greatest strength, a consistent user interface that really does make learning new programs much easier. As soon as you have a feel for how these various components work, you will be able to start working with a variety of different programs with relatively little time spent learning.

Spend a little time playing with the different components and seeing what they do. As we describe the various features and commands of Windows we are going to assume that you understand the basic components and how to use them. If you get stuck with a particular component later in the book, just return to this chapter and review how it functions.

4

Program Manager

When you install Windows, it automatically creates several program groups in Program Manager:

Main Contains important Windows applications: File Manager, Control Panel, Print Manager, Clipboard Viewer, MS-DOS Prompt, Windows Setup, PIF Editor, and Read Me (a Windows Write file). If you upgraded from Windows 3.0, the PIF Editor remains in the Accessories group.

Accessories Contains the Windows accessories applications: Write, Terminal, Clock, Calendar, Calculator, Notepad, Cardfile, Character Map, Object Packager, Media Player, Sound Recorder, Recorder.

Games Contains Windows' games, Minesweeper and Solitaire.

StartUp This window is empty at first, but if you place a program icon inside it that program will open automatically each time you open Windows.

Applications Contains applications that it has found on your hard drive. If you have a lot of applications, Windows may actually open more than one Application program group, calling them Application, Application 2, and so on.

You can adjust these groups. You can move icons to whichever group you want; add, rename, or remove group windows; and place the same icon in two or more groups. You can also size and move the group windows. See Figure 4.1 for an example of Program Manager and these program groups.

Moving Around in Program Manager

Let's find out how you move around in Program Manager. The quickest and easiest way to select another group window is to click on it. For instance, if you

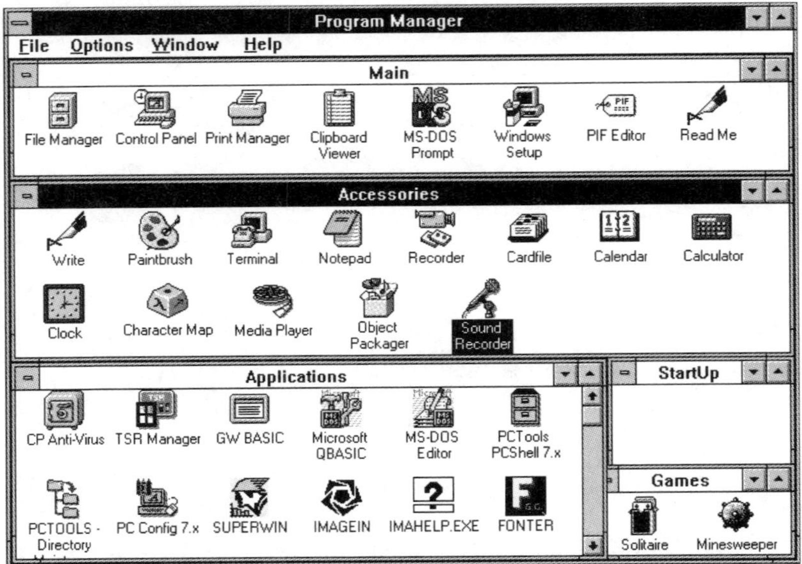

Figure 4.1 Program Manager and the initial program groups

want to start an application whose icon is in a window that is partly underneath another, clicking on the window brings it to the front. That makes it the *active* group, the one that Windows assumes you want to work with next.

If the group window you want is minimized, you may be able to see its icon. If so, just double-click on it and it will open. Another way to find the group window you want is by pressing **Ctrl-Tab** or **Ctrl-F6**. Ctrl-Tab displays each group-window's title bar or icon title. Holding Ctrl and pressing Tab repeatedly moves through the windows one by one. Release Ctrl when you reach the one you want. If it is minimized—an icon—press **Enter** to open it.

If you have a lot of group windows, you may want to use the Window menu to select the one you want. This menu displays a list of the group names. If there are more than nine, an extra option More Windows, is added. Select this option to see the Select Window dialog box (as in Figure 4.2). Use the scroll bar to move through the list of groups, or press the **Down Arrow** until you reach the window you are looking for. Then click on **OK** or press **Enter**, or **double-click** on the window name, and Program Manager makes the selected group window the active one. (As with most list boxes you can also use Home, End, PgDn, and PgUp to move around in the list.)

Within a program group you can use the mouse to select icons—just click on them—or use the arrow keys to move from icon to icon. If a group window has scroll bars, you can use the mouse to bring other icons into view. If you use the

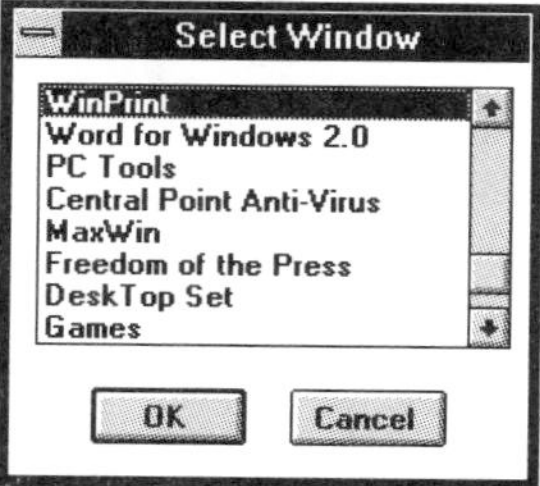

Figure 4.2 The Select Window dialog box

arrow keys, though, the window will scroll automatically as you jump between icons.

Creating and Editing Icons

What exactly is a program icon? Each icon represents information that you can modify: the picture itself; the application that it represents; a working directory; a keyboard shortcut that you can use to open the application or to jump to the open application; and an optional instruction telling Program Manager to minimize itself each time the icon's application is run. You may add up to 40 icons to each Program Group. There are three ways to create these icons: using Windows Setup, using Program Manager's File|New command, and dragging files from File Manager into a Program Manager group.

Using File|New and File|Properties

All the information about a program icon is stored in the Program Item Properties dialog box (see Figure 4.3), which you can see by selecting an icon and pressing **Alt-Enter**, or by selecting the icon and choosing **File|Properties**. (If you want to create a new icon, select the group window in which you want to place it, select **File|New**, then when the New Program Object dialog box appears click on OK. You will learn more about this box in a little while.)

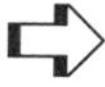 **Tip** Here's a quick way to open the Program Item Properties dialog box. Hold **Alt** and **double-click** on the icon you want to modify. If you want to create a new icon, point at a blank area in the group window in which you want to place the icon, hold Alt, and double-click.

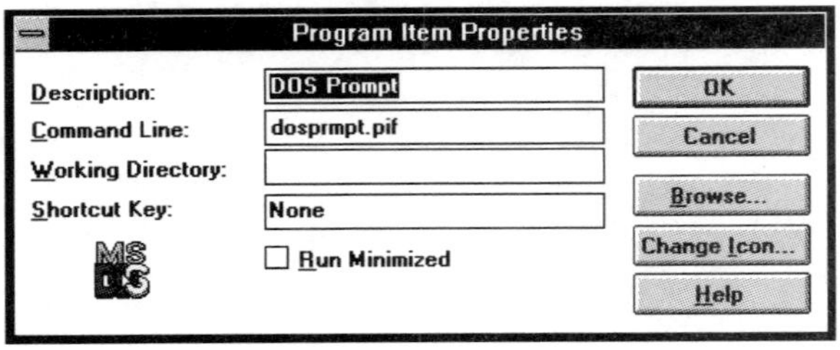

Figure 4.3 The Program Item Properties dialog box

The first piece of information in the dialog box is the **Description**. This is the title that appears below the icon, and it may be up to 36 characters long. Long titles are generally wrapped onto two lines, though if you prefer not to wrap the icon titles you can modify this feature using the Control Panel (see Customizing Program Manager later in this chapter). The title may be the application name, or a filename if the icon loads a file into an application. An icon *must* have a title. If you don't add one, Windows will use the name of the application file represented by the icon.

If you are creating an icon for a DOS application—rather than an application written specifically for Microsoft Windows—the text you enter into this text box also appears in the application window's title bar. (If you run the application in a window, that is. You can also run DOS applications "full screen." See Chapter 7 for more information.) Windows applications determine their own title-bar text, so the Description only changes the icon label.

Tip You can make an icon appear to have no title. Simply type a single space into the Description text box.

The next piece of information is the **Command Line**. This is the file that Windows must run when you want to start the icon. If the file is in the Windows directory, you can just enter the filename; otherwise you should enter the path and filename. (You don't have to include the file extension.) You can put an .EXE, .COM, .BAT, or .PIF file in here. (A PIF—Program Information File—is used to determine how Windows will run a DOS application. You'll learn more about them in Chapter 7.) If you are not sure about the path or filename, click on the **Browse** button. The dialog box shown in Figure 4.4 appears.

This dialog box lets you search through any disk drive. If necessary, begin by selecting the drive from the **Drives** drop-down list box (the drive on which the WINDOWS directory is installed will be displayed automatically). Then use the

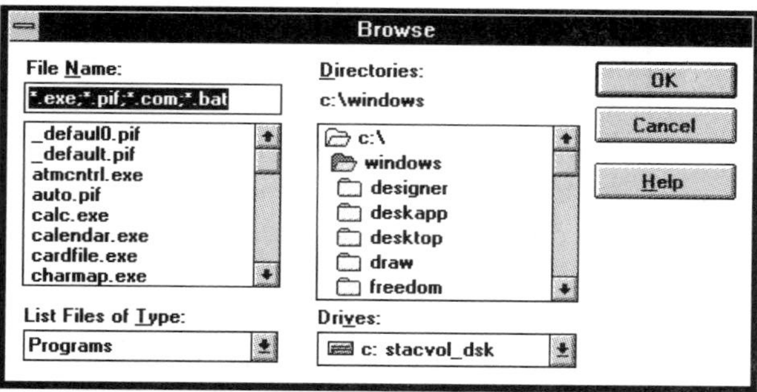

Figure 4.4 The Browse dialog box

Directories drop-down list box to find the directory that contains the file you want; double-click on a "closed folder" icon to open that directory, or double-click on an "open folder" icon to close that directory, moving you up the "directory tree." For instance, if you want to see all the directories in the root directory, double-click on the c:\ line. (Instead of double-clicking, you can select the line you want and press **Enter**.)

When you find the directory you want, select the file from the **File Name** list box. Double-click on the filename, or select it and press **Enter**. Windows closes the Browse dialog box and automatically adds the path and filename to the Command Line text box.

▼ ***Note*** We describe the file-selection dialog boxes in more detail in Chapter 6.

Three optional pieces of information may be included. The icon may tell Windows what **Working Directory** to use, the directory in which the application should look for data files. The application may not need this information—it may not use data files, or it may have another method of storing the path to the data-file directory. If you don't enter a working directory, Windows will automatically assume that the working directory should be the one in which the application file is stored.

The icon may also contain a **keyboard shortcut**. This shortcut lets you do two things: You can use it to start the application, if Program Manager is the active window; or you can use it to swap to the application from another, if it is already open. The shortcut must be in one of these formats:

- Ctrl-Alt-*character*
- Ctrl-Shift-*character*
- Ctrl-Alt-Shift-*character*

The character can be just about any key on your keyboard. You cannot use Esc, Enter, Tab, Spacebar, Print Screen, or Backspace, but you can use the function keys, number keys, or numeric keypad keys.

Place the cursor in the box and then press the combination (don't type it). For instance, press **Ctrl-Shift-1**, don't actually type C t r l - S h i f t - 1. Or simply type a character into the box and Windows automatically adds Ctrl-Alt in front.

▼ ***Note*** Make sure you don't choose a shortcut used by one of the applications you are likely to be using when you want to use this new shortcut. The icon's shortcut will override the application shortcuts.

The next option is the **Run Minimized** check box. If you select this check box, each time you use the icon to open the application it is automatically minimized—changed into an icon at the bottom of your desktop. You may want to do this when you are opening several applications that you plan to use together—if, for instance, you add icons to the StartUp program group.

Finally, in the bottom left corner of the Program Item Properties dialog box, there's the application's actual icon—the picture that will represent the application in Program Manager. All Windows applications have at least one picture that may be used as the icon—some applications even let you select from several. And if you don't like the ones provided by the application, Windows lets you select from two libraries of about 150 icons.

If you would like to select another icon, click on the **Change Icon** button. If you are installing a DOS application, you will see a message saying that there are no icons available for the file. Just click on OK to see the Change Icon dialog box (shown in Figure 4.5). This box shows the name of the file that contains the icon. In most cases that will be the same as the program file itself, because each Windows application has one or more icons "attached" to its executable file.

In some cases the File Name will show the name of a different file, one that contains one or more icons that may be used. When you are creating a DOS application icon, Windows automatically shows the icons in the **PROGMAN.EXE** file. This file contains 46 icons. Another file, **MORICONS.DLL**, contains over 100. Some applications load more libraries for you. For instance, PC Tools 7.x loads a file called **CPSICONS.DLL** which contains 14 icons.

You can use this dialog box to attach any icon to any application. You don't have to use one of these "library" files; you can attach one application's icon to another. For instance, you could use the Windows Paintbrush icon for a DOS paint program. Select the file that contains the icon by typing the name into the File Name text box and clicking OK or by clicking on the Browse button and selecting

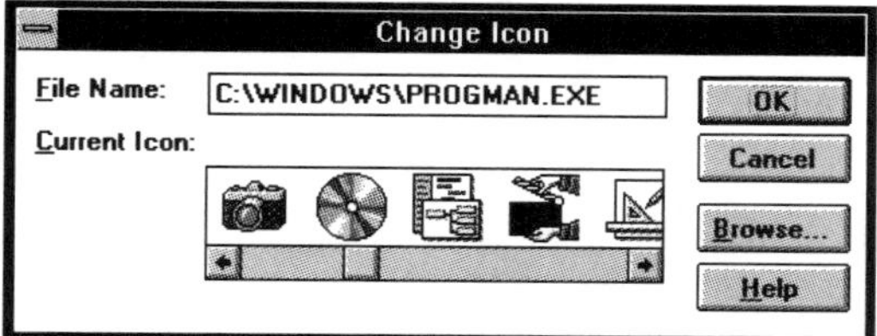

Figure 4.5 The Change Icon dialog box

from the Browse dialog box. Then select the icon from the list—scroll through the list and double-click on the one you want, or use the arrow keys and press **Enter**. (You can also move through the list using Home, End, PgUp, and PgDn.)

Now that you have entered all the Program Item Properties information, click on OK to shut the dialog box and create or modify the icon.

Loading Application Files and Using Switches

There are a few ways to make an icon automatically load application files. Suppose you want to be able to open a Cardfile file automatically (Windows Cardfile is a simple database; you can find more information in Chapter 18). Instead of opening the application and using the File | Open command to open the file, you can make Windows do both at the same time. In the **Command Line** text box simply enter the name of the application, followed by the name of the file. For instance,

```
cardfile c:\windows\data\address.crd
```

tells Windows to open Cardfile and load the file called ADDRESS.CRD. Of course you don't need the path if the file is in the same directory as the executable file.

▼ ***Note*** You cannot use this method with DOS applications.

The second method depends on the file type being *associated* with a particular application. Windows automatically associates certain files with certain applications. Files with the .CRD extension are associated with CARDFILE.EXE, those with .TXT are associated with NOTEPAD.EXE, and so on. Many applications associate their own files when you install them. For instance, if you install the Micrografx Windows Draw, it automatically associates .DRW files with DRAW.EXE.

If a file has been associated with an application you can simply enter the name of the file into the Command Line text box. For instance, simply type

```
address.crd
```

and Windows will know which application you want to open. You can change or add file associations using File Manager. See Chapter 9 for more information.

You may also add "switches" to the Command line. For example, if you use Microsoft's Word for Windows, you tell Windows to open the last file in which you were working. Type this in the Command Line text box:

```
winword.exe /mfile1.
```

Or you might want to start Windows Recorder, open a file, and run a macro, all at the same time. Type

```
recorder -h ^+n filename
```

to open Recorder, open the file, and carry out the macro that uses the Ctrl-Shift-*n* keyboard shortcut.

You may even want to create several icons for an application, each one opening the application in a different way, or each one loading a different file.

Using Windows Setup

You can use Windows Setup to create icons in the same way it did when you installed Windows. Double-click on the Windows Setup icon in the Main program group. Or select **File|Run** and run **SETUP**. When the Setup window appears, select **Options|Set Up Applications**. A dialog box appears, offering you two options: You can make Windows search for applications (in which case you will be able to specify which disk drive), and you can tell Windows to ask you to specify an application. This is the option you will use when you want to create just one or two icons. In the dialog box that appears you will enter a filename (or use the Browse button to search for one) and select the program group into which you want to place it.

When you click on OK Windows creates the icon for you. If you are creating an icon for a DOS application it may ask you for more information: It may present a list of DOS applications and ask you to choose the correct one.

This is not always the best way to create an icon. If Windows can't identify a DOS application—if it doesn't have a PIF for that application—it won't be able to add the icon. And if you want to select the other options for the icon (another picture, the keyboard shortcut, run minimized, and the working directory), you have to open the Program Item Properties dialog box anyway.

Using File Manager

There's one more way to create icons. You can open the File Manager window, size and position Program Manager and File Manager so you can see them both, and drag a file—.EXE, .COM, .PIF, or .BAT file—from File Manager to a program group. Windows will automatically create an icon for you, using the default settings. For more information about File Manager, see Chapter 9.

Creating and Editing Program Groups

You are not stuck with the program-group windows that Windows gives you. You can combine them, delete them, or create your own. Also, many Windows applications create new program groups when you install them, to hold their program icons.

To create a new program group, select **File | New**. Windows displays the New Program Object dialog box. Make sure the Program Group option button is selected (if you selected an open program-group window first, the Program Item option button is selected). Then click on OK to see the Program Group Properties dialog box (as in Figure 4.6).

First you must enter the name of the program group in the Description text box. This is the name that appears in the window's title bar. Enter something useful, like Account Files or Calendars, whatever describes the purpose of your new group.

You may now press **Tab** and enter the Group File name if you wish. You probably won't want or need to do so, however. Each program group has a file with the extension .GRP. This file is stored in the WINDOWS directory and contains information about all the groups' icons. The Program Manager initialization file (PROGMAN.INI) contains a reference to each .GRP file, so when Windows starts the Program Manager knows where to find the necessary information for each group.

If you don't enter a group-file name, Windows will provide one for you. It takes the first eight characters of the name you gave the group and adds the .GRP

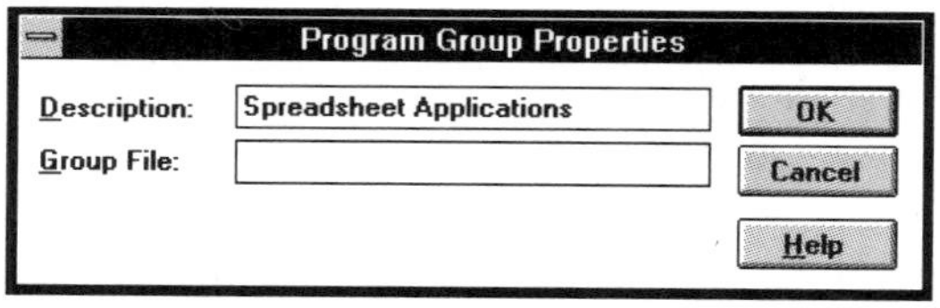

Figure 4.6 The Program Group Properties dialog box

extension. If you already have a group whose name matches the first eight characters of the new group, Windows replaces the eighth character with a number. So if you have groups named Applications, Applications 1, and Applications 2, the files will be called APPLICAT.GRP, APPLICA0.GRP, and APPLICA1.GRP. There is almost never a reason for you to enter a group-file name, so simply click on OK and Windows creates the new group window.

Now that you have a new program group you can add icons to it by creating new ones or by moving and copying icons from other groups—as we will see in a moment. But before we move on, let's look at how you can rename a program group. If you want to change a program group's name, you must first minimize the window. Then select the icon and choose **File | Properties**. (You can also open the Program Group Properties dialog box by holding **Alt** and double-clicking on the program-group icon.) The Program Group Properties dialog box appears again, but this time there is a filename in the Group File text box. You don't need to change it. Simply type a new name into the Description text box and click on OK.

Tip The Program Group Properties dialog box lets you add existing program groups. If you want to copy a program group from another computer, or from a Windows 3.0 installation, copy the .GRP file into the WINDOWS directory, then open the Program Group Properties dialog box. Type the name of the .GRP file into the Group File text box, then click on OK. Remember that copying .GRP files will overwrite existing .GRP files with the same names, so you probably don't want to copy the MAIN.GRP or ACCESSOR.GRP files.

Managing Program Groups

You can organize your program groups in several ways. If you have only the ones Windows provided you and you are not going to add many applications, you could arrange them as shown in Figure 4.1, so they are all visible. Use the program groups' Control menus, minimize buttons, and maximize buttons to size and position them appropriately. Remember that you can size the Program Manager window itself to make more room.

Another method is to place just one or two groups—the ones containing the icons you use most of the time—so that they fill the Program Manager window. You can leave the other program-group windows as open windows—below the ones you want to use most of the time—or as icons. Then, when you need to use one of them, simply swap to it using the methods we learned at the beginning of this chapter.

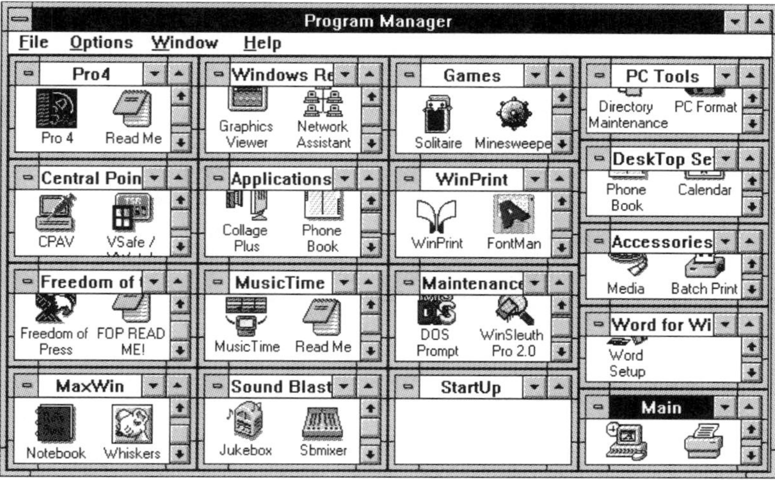

Figure 4.7 Program groups after using the Window | Tile command

Another method you might use is to open all the windows, then select the **Window | Tile** command. The windows will be placed next to each other, each with the same amount of space, as shown in Figure 4.7. If you have a lot of windows things may look cluttered. But when you want to use a window you can simply click on its maximize button to make it fill the Program Manager window. When you have finished, click on the button again to restore it to its original size and position—it will drop back into its original tiled position.

A similar method is to minimize all the groups, and then select the **Window | Arrange Icons** command. Windows straightens out the icons and places them at the bottom of the Program Manager window. Double-click on an icon when you need to use it, and click on its minimize button when you want to put it back in place.

You can also use the **Window | Cascade** command to sort the open windows. The windows will be placed so that each title bar is visible, and each window is offset to the right slightly, like a deck of cards (see Figure 4.8). If more windows are open than can fit into the Program Manager window in this manner, Windows starts over and begins another cascaded series, on top of the first one. This method is awkward if you have a lot of program groups, because they keep disappearing below the others.

Both the Tile and Cascade commands also straighten out any group-window icons you may have in the Program Manager window, lining them up at the bottom of the window. So you can combine methods: Leave some groups minimized, tile or cascade the others, and make sure the Program Manager is large enough so you can see the icons at the bottom.

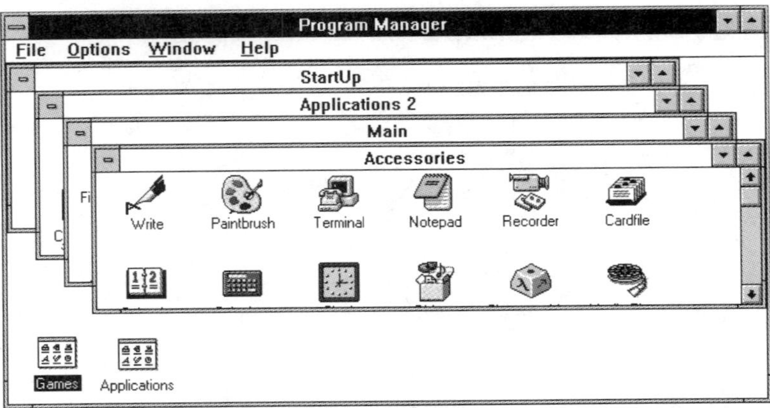

Figure 4.8 Four cascaded group windows

The **File | Arrange Icons** command also works on the selected, open group window. The icons are lined up in the active group window, spaced equally. The other, nonactive windows, are not affected. There's also an **Options | Auto Arrange** command, which makes sure that the icons in each group window are *always* neatly spaced: If you drag one out of line Windows will pop it back into position. This command has no effect on the group icons.

SAVING SETTINGS

When you create new program groups and icons Windows automatically saves them. However, when you shuffle groups and icons around, Windows does not save their positions. Let's say you have all your frequently used icons in one group. You place the icons in the order and positions in which you want them, and position and size the group window. This information is not saved automatically. Nor are the other settings in the Options menu saved.

To make sure the groups and icons always appear in the same positions when you open Windows, select **Options | Save Settings on Exit** (if there is already a check mark next to the name, don't select the option—it is already enabled). Now, when you close Windows it will automatically save the positions and Options settings.

There's a good reason *not* to use this method, though; if you do, each time you modify Program Manager—open another group window, for example—and then close Windows, the new positions will be saved. In fact you never need to use this option. Instead, try this: Make your adjustments, press and hold **Shift**, and select **File | Exit Windows**. Windows will save the settings—regardless of Save Settings on Exit—without closing.

Moving and Copying Icons

Eventually you will want to move or copy icons. The simplest way to do both operations is to use the mouse. To move an icon, simply drag it to where you want it. If you want to place it in another group window, simply drag it from one to the other.

If you want the icon to make a copy of the icon, press Ctrl while you drag it. You may want copies for a couple of reasons. First, you may want to be able to open the application from two or more group windows. You also may want to open an application using various different methods. If several people have Calendar files on the same computer, you could produce several icons—one for each user—and set up each icon so that it opens a specific file. Or open an application using different command-line switches; you can create an icon for each individual startup command, if the application has such switches. Figure 4.9 shows several examples of multiple-icon uses.

You can also use the menu commands to copy and move icons. Select the icon and then choose **File | Copy** or **File | Move**. You will see the Copy Program Item or Move Program Item dialog box (both look and work the same; see Figure 4.10). Simply select the name of the group to which you want to copy or move the icon from the To Group drop-down list box and click on OK.

You can delete both icons and program groups. Remember that these items only *represent* applications. Deleting an icon, for example, does *not* affect the application

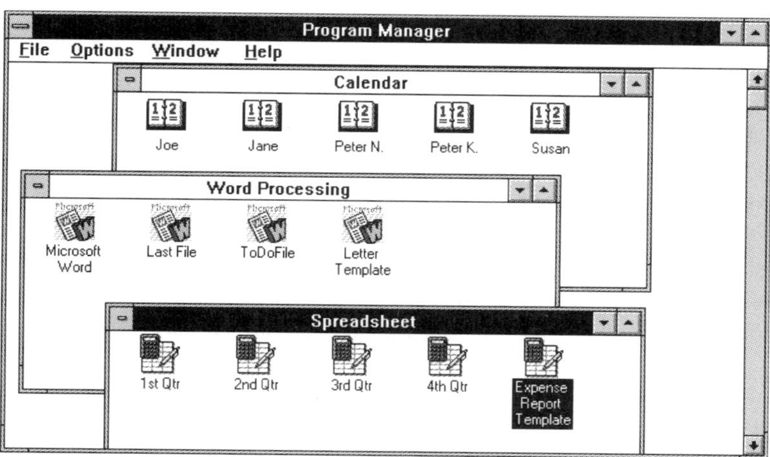

Figure 4.9 Multiple icons let you start the same application using different methods.

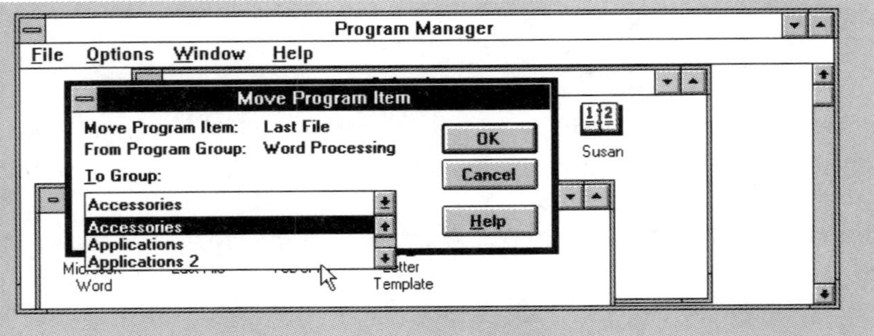

Figure 4.10 The Move Program Item dialog box

file. Also, removing a program from your disk does not remove the corresponding icon.

To delete an icon, select it and press **Del** or choose **File | Delete**. Windows will display a message box asking if you are sure you want to delete the icon. (The message names the icon, so read the message just to confirm that you selected the correct icon.) Click on the Yes button and Windows removes the icon.

If a group window is empty when you press Del, Windows asks if you want to remove the group itself. If you wish to delete a group and all its icons with one operation, however, minimize the group, select the icon, and *then* press Del. The entire group, icons and all, is removed. (The icon's Control menu must not be displayed when you press Del. Clicking on the icon displays the Control menu, so you will have to click again to close it.)

Tip If you accidentally remove an entire group or a large number of icons, you may be able to recover the group. You must recover the .GRP file associated with the group, which you can do in two ways. First, if you make regular backups you can copy the .GRP file from your backup tapes or disks into the WINDOWS directory. Then open the Program Group Properties dialog box and enter the name of the .GRP file into the Group File text box and click on OK (this adds the group to the PROGMAN.INI file).

The other method is to use a file undelete utility to immediately recover the .GRP file. DOS 5.0 has an UNDELETE command, as do many file-utility programs. You will also have to use the Program Group Properties dialog box to add the group to the PROGMAN.INI file. Once you have made the changes, you will have to restart Windows to make the group window reappear.

Customizing Program Manager

There are a few more ways in which you can customize Program Manager. In Chapter 8 you will learn about the Control Panel, a special application that lets you customize all sorts of Windows features, from the color of the title bar to the screen saver that is displayed when you leave your computer unattended. You can modify the Desktop features to adjust the horizontal spacing between the icons in the group windows, and make the icon's titles display in a straight line (by default the icons are wrapped onto the next line if they are very long).

You may also modify WIN.INI, a system initialization file that tells Windows how to work each time you start it. You can use the MenuDropAlignment= and MenuShowDelay= commands to modify the way the menus are displayed (these commands will affect *all* Windows applications, not just Program Manager); the IconTitleFaceName= and IconTitleSize= lines to change the font and font size used by the icon titles; and IconVerticalSpacing= to change the vertical spacing between icons. If you find your hand moves slightly when you double-click on an icon, you can adjust the tolerances by changing the DoubleClickHeight= and DoubleclickWidth= lines to modify how far the mouse pointer can move while you are double-clicking. (Again, this is a systemwide option.) For more information about WIN.INI, see Appendix B.

Replacing Program Manager

Some people don't like Program Manager. That's okay; they don't have to use it. You can make another application open in Program Manager's place. For instance, you could make File Manager open instead, or buy one of the many Program Manager replacements that are available. You can even make Windows open an application directly, so that your word processor or spreadsheet appears instead of Program Manager.

Replace Program Manager by changing the shell= command in the SYSTEM.INI initialization file, described in Appendix B. Remember that whatever application you put in its place, closing the application will also close Windows.

Closing Program Manager

Closing Program Manager actually closes Windows itself. You can close Program Manager in a variety of ways, as we saw in Chapter 3: You may select **Close** from the Control menu, **double-click** on the Control menu, select **File | Exit**, or press **Alt-F4**.

There's another way we haven't explained yet. Open the Task List dialog box (press **Ctrl-Esc** or select **Switch To** from the Control menu). Select Program Manager from the list of applications, then click on **End Task**. This lets you close Program Manager without displaying its window first.

Program Manager's Menu Options

Here's a quick summary of Program Manager's menu options:

File | New Lets you create a new group window or icon.

File | Open (Enter) Starts the application represented by the selected icon.

File | Move (F7) Lets you move an icon from one group to another.

File | Copy (F8) Lets you copy an icon from one group to another.

File | Delete (Del) Deletes an icon or program group.

File | Properties (Alt-Enter) Displays the selected icon's properties.

File | Run Lets you enter the name of an application you want to run.

File | Exit Windows Closes Windows.

Options | Auto Arrange Makes Program Manager keep the program icons lined up tidily.

Options | Minimize on Use Makes Program Manager minimize itself whenever you run an application.

Options | Save Settings on Exit Makes Program Manager automatically save its settings each time you close Windows.

Window | Cascade (Shift-F5) Places the open group windows on top of each other with each title bar visible.

Window | Tile (Shift-F4) Places the open group windows so that all are visible and all have the same amount of space.

Window | Arrange Icons Tidies up the icons, placing them in lines and equally spaced.

Window | *group names* Opens the selected group window.

Window | More Windows Lets you select and open a group window. This option appears only if you have more than nine group windows.

Help | *command name* The help commands, explained in Chapter 10.

▼ ***Note*** Virtually every Windows application has a Help menu. We are not going to describe Help menu options in each chapter. Rather, we have covered the Help system in detail in Chapter 10.

5

Running and Switching Applications

You have installed Windows and configured Program Manager; now you are ready to run a Windows application. This chapter explains how to start applications, and how to switch from one to another. Chapter 6 explains some background information about the way in which Windows applications operate, and Chapter 7 describes some important things you must know about running DOS applications in Windows.

The Windows Applications

Before we look at how to run an application, let's look at the icons Windows created when you loaded it. Windows opens the Main program group for you and minimizes the other groups at the bottom of the Program Manager. Let's start with the **Main** program group (see Figure 5.1).

File Manager Helps you manage your files. Carries out operations such as copy, delete, move, rename, and search.

Control Panel Lets you customize Windows by changing colors, the way the mouse and keyboard work, network setups, and so on.

Print Manager Manages the print queue. Print Manager lets you pause printing and move print jobs to different positions in the queue.

Clipboard Viewer Displays the data stored in the Clipboard. The Clipboard is Windows' main system for swapping data between applications.

MS-DOS Prompt Displays a DOS "window," letting you work with standard DOS commands.

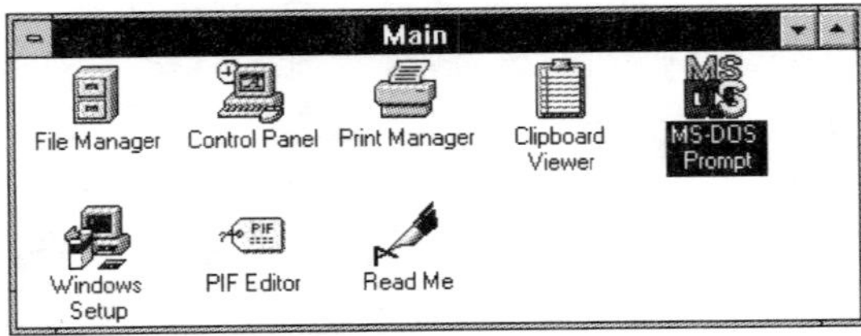

Figure 5.1 The Main program-group window

Windows Setup Lets you modify Windows' configuration. You can load new drivers, for instance, or remove items you no longer need.

PIF Editor Creates PIF files, which are used to configure windows in which DOS applications may be run.

Read Me Runs Windows Write, with the installation Read Me document displayed.

Figure 5.2 shows the **Accessories** program-group window. This window contains applications that you can use to get your work done: a word processor, a communications program, a database, a calculator, and so on.

Write A word processor.

Paintbrush A paint program, similar to PC Paintbrush.

Terminal A data communications program you can use if you have a modem.

Notepad An ASCII text editor, useful for editing DOS batch files and Windows initialization files.

Recorder A program that lets you build macros to automate any Windows application.

Calendar A simple calendar to keep track of important dates and appointments.

Cardfile A simple database, based on "cards" of information.

Calculator A calculator with two modes, Standard and Scientific.

Figure 5.2 The Accessories program-group window

Clock A clock that you can make stay above other Windows applications, so it is always visible.

Object Packager An application that moves "package" information from one application and places it in another. The package may then be "opened" to view or edit the information.

Character Map A utility that helps you use special characters in any Windows application.

Media Player A multimedia application that lets you play sound, MIDI sequencer files, and animations, and control CD-ROM and videodisk players.

Sound Recorder A sound-recording and editing application.

The **Games** program-group window contains two games (Figure 5.3).

Solitaire The popular card game you can play against yourself. You use the mouse to turn and move cards.

Minesweeper A game in which mines are hidden below squares in a grid. You must uncover the safe squares and mark the mined squares.

The **StartUp** group window is empty when you first open Windows. As you learned earlier, you can use StartUp to define which applications you want opened automatically when Windows starts. Simply drag an icon from another group window into StartUp (hold down **Ctrl** while dragging if you want to place a *copy* of the icon in StartUp, rather than moving it).

The **Applications** window (or windows, if you have a lot of applications) is only created if you let Windows search your hard-disk drive for applications during installation. The number of applications (and, consequently, the number of Applications windows) depends on how many applications Windows found (see Figure 5.4). Many of these applications may be of no use to you. A number, for example, are applications that cannot be run by themselves, they may be called only by an associated application. For instance, a graphics program may load another executable file when you want it to "vectorize" a bitmap. That other file will run only when called by the graphics application, but it will still appear in the Applications group window—Windows creates icons for all the WINDOWS .EXE and .PIF files it finds (it creates icons only for DOS applications that it recognizes).

Eventually you will want to weed out the icons that are of no use to you and perhaps rename some of the ones that remain.

Figure 5.3 The Games program-group window

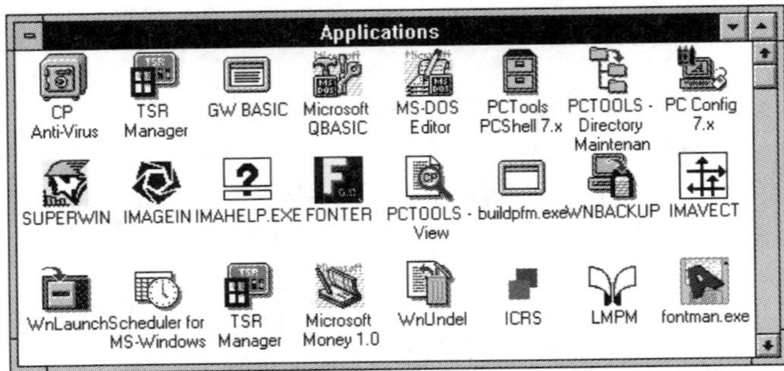

Figure 5.4 An example of the Applications program-group window

Starting Applications

Windows has a number of ways in which you can start applications, some of which we have seen already:

- **Double-click** on the icon.
- Select the icon and press **Enter**.
- Select the icon and select **File | Open**.
- Press the icon's **keyboard-shortcut** combination.
- Put the icon in the **StartUp** program group.
- Use the **File | Run** command, in Program Manager or File Manager.
- **Double-click** on the program file in File Manager.
- Select the icon in File Manager and press **Enter**.
- Select the icon in File Manager and select **File | Open**.
- In File Manager, **drag** a document file onto the program file.
- In File Manager, **drag** a document file onto the program's icon or title bar.
- Use Load= and File= in the **WIN.INI** file (as described in Chapter 2 and Appendix B).
- Use a **DOS command line** to open Windows and start applications (as described in Chapter 2).

Using Program Manager

The most common way to open applications is to use Program Manager. Simply double-click on an icon and Windows opens the application according to the information you provided in the Program Item Properties dialog box. If you don't have a mouse, select the icon and press **Enter**, or select it and then choose the **File | Open** command.

You can also use the **File | Run** command to start an application. You might use this to start an application for which you haven't created an icon, or if you simply don't want to search through group windows for the correct icon. When you select the command, the dialog box shown in Figure 5.5 appears. Type the filename into the Command Line text box—include the path if necessary and any command-line switches—and click on OK.

You can enter the name of any file that has been *associated* with an application. As you learned in the last chapter, Windows associates files with applications—.BMP files with Paintbrush, for instance. If you enter an associated file in the Run box and click on OK, that file's associated application is started and the file is loaded.

You may also enter the name of an application followed by the name of the document you want to load. For instance, typing

```
c:\winword\winword letter.txt
```

would load and open Word for Windows and load LETTER.TXT, even though .TXT files are normally associated with Notepad. (You can't use these methods for DOS applications, only for applications written specifically for Windows.)

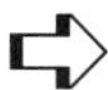 **Tip** If you use this method to load a document with *no* association into an application, Windows automatically creates the association for you. See Chapter 9 for more information about associating files.

Notice the **Run Minimized** check box in the Run dialog box. Select this if you want Windows to start the application and place it at the bottom of the desktop, as an application icon.

You can also use an icon's keyboard shortcut to start the application (we explained how to give an icon a shortcut in Chapter 4). Remember that Program Manager must be the active application when you use the shortcut.

Figure 5.5 The Run dialog box

Finally, there's the **StartUp** program group. Any icon in this program group will be opened automatically when you start Windows. First the icon in the top left of the group window is opened, then the one immediately to the right. Windows opens each one in the window, working along the row and then down to the first one on the next row, and so on. You can move or copy an icon into the StartUp group from another group.

Program Manager has a **Options | Minimize on Use** command. This tells Windows to minimize Program Manager—to get it out of the way—each time you use it to start an application. If you want this turned on permanently, make sure there is a check mark next to the option and then save your settings: Hold **Shift** and select **File | Exit**.

Using File Manager

You can also use File Manager to open applications. Double-click on the filename, select the file and press **Enter**, or select the file and then choose the **File | Open** command. File Manager also has a **File | Run** command that works in the same way as File | Run in Program Manager.

File Manager has a special way to open certain applications. Drag a document file onto the program file with which it is associated. If the application supports that type of operation—not all do—Windows opens the application and loads the file. You can even drag the file from File Manager onto the program's icon or title bar.

Moving Between Windows

The whole purpose of Windows is to let you run more than one application at once. In fact, you almost always run at least two applications: Program Manager itself is an application. (It is possible to run an application without Program Manager by using the shell= line in the SYSTEM.INI file. See Appendix B for more information.)

Only one window or icon is *active* at any time. The active window or icon is the one on which the next operation will be carried out. Windows indicates the active window in several ways. First, the active one is generally the one on top of all the others—though not always. Some applications, such as the Clock, have a command that lets them stay on top all the time, even when not active. But Windows also colors the active window differently. If you are using the Windows Default color scheme the active title bar is blue with white text, while inactive windows have white bars with black text. You can also modify the color of the inactive windows' borders, although the Default scheme doesn't do so (see Chapter 8 for more information).

You must be able to move from one application's window to another. Like anything else in Windows, there are several ways to do so:

- **Click** on another window.
- Press **Alt-Tab**.
- Press **Alt-Shift-Tab**.
- Press **Alt-Esc**.
- Press **Alt-Shift-Esc**.
- Use the **Task List** dialog box.
- Create a keyboard **shortcut**.

If the window you want to move to is visible, you can just click on it and it becomes the active window: It is moved to the front, above the currently active window. A quick way to move to the last window in which you worked is simply to press **Alt-Tab**. Pressing Alt-Tab displays a panel in the center of the screen (see Figure 5.6). This panel shows the icon, application name, and filename of the last window in which you worked. If you release the keys, that other window becomes the active window: It is moved to the top of the windows.

You don't have to release the keys as soon as you see the first panel. Instead, you can continue pressing **Tab** (while you hold down **Alt**) to see each window's panel

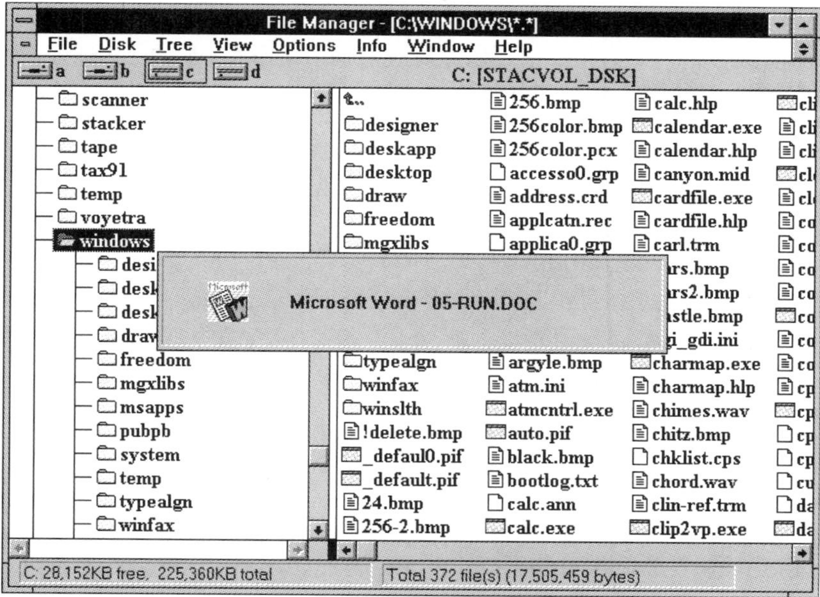

Figure 5.6 The Alt-Tab application-title panel

in turn. Release the mouse button when you see the one you want. You can also press **Alt-Shift-Tab** to move through the windows in the *opposite* direction. Instead of seeing the last window you used, you will see the one you *haven't* used since all the others. This is also useful when you press **Alt-Tab** quickly and accidentally fly right by the one you want to open. Without releasing Alt, press and hold **Shift** and press **Tab** again to reverse the direction.

▼ ***Note*** The Control Panel's Desktop dialog box lets you turn off this type of "Fast 'Alt+Tab' Switching," as it's called. See Chapter 8 for more information.

The ubiquitous **Esc** key also works while you are using Alt-Tab. If you begin Alt-Tabbing through the windows and decide you *don't* want to swap, just press **Esc** and then release **Alt** to return to the application in which you were working.

You may also press **Alt-Esc** to jump to another window. In some ways this is quicker than Alt-Tab. If you only have one open application (together with Program Manager), Alt-Esc is probably the quickest way to jump between windows, because it immediately makes the other window the active one: It doesn't display a panel first. However, if you have several applications open this method may be confusing, because it doesn't automatically display the last window in which you worked. Rather, it takes you to the "next" window in a difficult-to-understand sequence. However, pressing **Alt-Esc** several times cycles you through all the windows one by one, in the same way Alt-Tab does.

If you have many open windows, it's often faster to use the **Task List** dialog box (see Figure 5.7). Press **Ctrl-Esc** or select the **Switch To** option from the **Control menu.** If the desktop is visible between windows, you may also double-click on any clear space. The Task List dialog box appears, listing all the open windows, including Program Manager. Double-click on the one to which you want to move, or use the **Down Arrow** to highlight it and press **Enter.** You can also select a name and click on the **Switch To** button.

▼ ***Note*** The Task List may not open if your computer is short of memory.

The quickest way to jump between windows—assuming you have a good memory—is to create a shortcut key for each application with which you work. (You may at least want to create shortcuts for the ones you use the most.) You learned how to create shortcuts—using the Program Item Properties dialog box—in Chapter 4. These shortcuts will open applications when you are in Program Manager, but they may also be used to jump between open applications.

The only problem with these shortcuts, of course, is that it's easy to use conflicting key-combinations. You have to make sure that the combination you

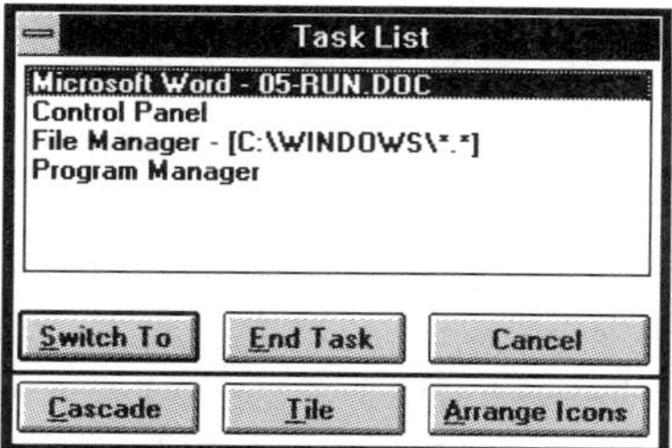

Figure 5.7 The Task List dialog box

assign to an application is not the same as one used for a macro or keyboard shortcut in any of the applications in which you may be working when you want to swap to the application with the shortcut! If there is a conflict, Windows will override the application in which you are working, and switch to another window instead of carrying out the normal operation.

Managing the Desktop

Look at the Task List dialog box again (in Figure 5.7). You will notice it has six buttons at the bottom. You've already seen what Switch To does. Here's what the other five do:

End Task Closes the selected application.

Cancel Closes the Task List dialog box. You can also press **Esc**.

Cascade Cascades the application windows in the same way that Program Manager's Windows | Cascade command cascades group windows.

Tile Tiles the application windows in the same way that Program Manager's Windows | Tile command tiles group windows.

Arrange Icons Arranges the application windows in the same way that Program Manager's Windows | Arrange Icons command arranges the group-window icons. This will arrange the icon positions even if the windows are currently open.

Closing Applications and Windows

You've already seen how to close Program Manager, and the vast majority of Windows applications use the same methods: Select **Close** from the Control menu, **double-click** on the Control menu, select **File | Exit**, press **Alt-F4**, or use the Task List dialog box (press **Ctrl-Esc** or select **Switch To** from the Control menu).

Notice that the Task List dialog box lets you close an application without displaying its window first. This is especially useful when you have several applications you want to close. Simply press **Ctrl-Esc**, click on the first, and click on End Task; then repeat for each of the other applications.

If you try to close an application with an open, unsaved file, Windows displays a message box asking if you want to save the file before you close. You will be able to click on **Yes** (to save the file and close the application), **No** (to close the application without saving the file), and **Cancel** (to keep the application open, so you can return to the file and make changes before you save it).

If you close Windows itself, it will close each application for you. In other words, you don't need to close each open application window. Just close Program Manager and let Windows do the rest. Again, if you have open files, Windows asks if you want to save them before closing. You may not be able to close Windows if you have open applications that are DOS applications. You won't be able to use the Task List dialog box to close them. You must go to the application itself and close it using its own exit command. Read Chapter 7—there is a way that you can, in certain circumstances, override this restriction (using the **Allow Close When Active** option in the PIF Editor).

Some Windows applications may have a different command for exiting. File|Close is occasionally used by software publishers to close their applications, although it's nonstandard (File|Close should close the application file, not the application itself). Some applications may even allow you to build macros that will let you close Windows by clicking on a button or selecting a menu option.

Application Compatibility

Although applications designed for Windows 3.0 and 3.1 will run in Windows 3.1, as will most DOS applications, there's a large category of Windows applications that will *not* run in Windows 3.1: those created for versions earlier than 3.0. In addition, there are a few compatibility problems with applications created for 3.0.

All Windows applications contain an internal version number (a "mark") that Windows can read when you try to run the program. Because there are so many differences between Windows 3.1 and 2.*x*, when you try to run an application designed for an early version of Windows it will warn you that you may have problems. You can continue and run the program, but you may cause Windows to crash. However, Windows 3.1 is less likely then 3.0 to crash, and Windows doesn't really know if the old application will cause problems; it has simply read the version and warned you that there *might* be problems.

You can continue if you wish, ignoring the problem. You can also use a utility to change the version number in the program. You may be able to obtain a program such as MARK30 from a bulletin board or shareware catalog. These programs change the version mark to indicate Windows 3.0, so the warning message doesn't appear. That doesn't mean the program will run any better.

Although much was made of the fact that Windows 3.0 applications are compatible with Windows 3.1, this isn't entirely true. You may run into problems with your 3.0 applications. Open the help file called APPS.HLP to find information about problems with a number of applications. The problems range from minor to serious, and this help file tells you which version you need and, in some cases, how to fix problems that may occur. You can read this help file by double-clicking on the name APPS.HLP in File Manger, or by opening any Help window and using the File | Open command. APPS.HLP is in the WINDOWS directory (see Chapter 10 for more information about Help).

Application Problems

If you used Windows 3.0, you are probably familiar with the term "Unrecoverable Application Error" or "UAE." Windows 3.0 would just crash and you would have no idea why. Perhaps it would just freeze up, and you would have to reboot your computer. Or maybe just one or two applications would close automatically, but the rest of the system remained unstable—so you had to reboot anyway.

A Microsoft representative recently told a seminar audience that they wouldn't get *any* UAEs in Windows 3.1. He could *guarantee* it, he said, "because they're not called that anymore." Jokes aside, Windows 3.1 is much more stable than its predecessor. That's not to say you won't have problems now and again, and you may even have applications lock up. But the problems probably won't affect the whole system.

If an application locks up, press **Ctrl-Alt-Del**. You will see a DOS-type screen providing you with three options; you can press **Esc** and return to your application, press **Enter** and close the application, or press **Ctrl-Alt-Del** to reboot your computer. You won't often want to use the last option, because you will lose any data you have in other, functioning applications. Instead, all you need to do is press **Enter**. Windows will then try to close the locked application. If it can't you will have to reboot. If it can, you should save your data in all the other applications. You may then want to restart Windows, although it will usually be stable enough to continue.

Windows also has a special troubleshooting application called Dr. Watson. This can monitor your system, and it may be able to keep a record of what happened when an application crashed. This won't help you much, but it may be of use to the software publisher's technical support line. See Appendix D for more information.

Installing New Application Software

Windows has a serious problem with the way it handles the installation of new programs. When you install a new program, the installation procedure may carry out any or all of these operations:

- Install files in new directories
- Install files in the WINDOWS and SYSTEM directories
- Replace files in the WINDOWS and SYSTEM directories (with new drivers, for instance)
- Modify the AUTOEXEC.BAT and CONFIG.SYS files
- Modify the WIN.INI and SYSTEM.INI files
- Add new icons and program groups to Program Manager

This is rarely a problem if you work with just a few applications. It can be a nuisance, though, if you work with many—for instance, if your job is to evaluate software for your company, or if you write software reviews for publication.

This ability of Windows installations to modify so much can lead to problems in several situations. First, if you want to remove a program, it's difficult to know exactly what to remove—which files in the WINDOWS directory, which entries in WIN.INI. Second, if you have operating problems with Windows or its applications, it's sometimes difficult to find the cause because you are not exactly sure what belongs to which program.

There are a few things you can do about this problem. Always make a backup of CONFIG.SYS, AUTOEXEC.BAT, WIN.INI, and SYSTEM.INI before you install a new program. Then, after installing the program, compare the files—the backups and the new ones—looking for changes. You can compare simply by looking at the files, or use a utility that compares documents. (Major Windows word processors have built-in file-comparison commands.)

When you find changes, mark them. In CONFIG.SYS and AUTOEXEC.BAT you can add a remark line before each change by starting the line with **rem**. In the .INI files you can do this by starting the line with ;. For instance, enter a line that says something like **rem This added by *applicationname***. If you don't want to add these remarks to the .INI files, simply keep a written record of the changes made by the application. (If you add a lot of applications, too many notes in the .INI files can make Windows open slowly.)

You can also compare the WINDOWS and SYSTEM directories before and after installation, by creating a directory document. For instance, in a DOS window (which you will learn about in Chapter 7), type **dir/a/o c:\windows > windows.txt** to create an ASCII file listing the WINDOWS directory. Do this before and after the installation, then compare the documents to find out which new files were installed.

There is a quicker way to do all this. Use the freeware program INCTRL, which produces an installation report for you. You can find this program in PC Magazine's PCMagNet, or perhaps on other bulletin boards or from colleagues.

 **Tip** When you install a new program, experiment with different types of mouse clicks. Many applications have special shortcuts that work when you point at a window component and click in some manner. For instance, double-clicking on the color palette in Paintbrush displays the Edit Colors dialog box; double-clicking on Word for Windows' status bar displays the Go To dialog box; double-clicking on File Manager's Drive-icons bar displays the Select Drive dialog box. Experiment also with Ctrl-double-clicks and Shift-double-clicks.

6

Application Basics

Windows 3.1 comes with several programs that are referred to as the Windows *accessories*. These applications include a word processor, an illustration program, a communications program, a database, a clock, and a calculator.

Americans spend billions of dollars each year on unnecessary software. Computer users buy expensive word processors, when all they want to do is write simple memos. They buy expensive graphics programs, when all they need is to create very simple charts and pictures. They buy expensive, confusing databases, when all they need is to store a few addresses.

If you get to know the Windows accessories, you may find that you can save a little money. Write, for instance, has many basic word processing features. It won't create indexes for you or insert electronic bookmarks. If you really need those features, you must look elsewhere. But if you want to create good-looking documents, with a variety of fonts, graphics, headers and footers, and automatic page numbering, you may find Write is all you need.

As for Write, so for some of the other accessories. Perhaps you can keep your address book in Cardfile. It's not the most sophisticated database or electronic address book you can get, but it is the cheapest—it's free once you have Windows. If you only occasionally need to use your modem, perhaps you should save money and use Terminal instead of buying a communications program.

Computers are seductive. They can do so much that we sometimes forget the time and expense needed to get them to do it all. Sometimes simple applications such as Windows' accessories are more efficient in the long run, when you consider the cost of buying and learning their more sophisticated cousins. So take a look at the accessory programs—you may find something you can use.

These are the Windows accessories:

- **Write** A word processor
- **Paintbrush** A paint program
- **Terminal** A modem communications program
- **Recorder** A macro builder, to automate procedures you use frequently
- **Calculator** An electronic calculator
- **Calendar** An appointment calendar
- **Cardfile** A simple database program, based on "cards"
- **Character Map** A program that helps you use special characters in other applications
- **Clock** A clock
- **Games** Minesweeper and Solitaire
- **Notepad** A simple text editor, for creating and editing ASCII files
- **Sound Recorder** A program for recording and editing sounds
- **Media Player** A multimedia program for operating CDs and playing multimedia files
- **Object Packager** Helps you place objects from one application into another

These accessories are described in detail later in this book. Before we get into the specifics of each one, however, we are going to explain some common features—features that are also common to many Windows applications you may buy or already own.

Certain procedures are common to most Windows applications. That's one of Windows' strengths, that common procedures use common methods. Learn how to do something in one application, and you know how to do it in all. These procedures are the same—or very similar—in a number of Windows' accessories and many third-party applications:

- Opening files
- Saving files
- Closing files
- Closing the application
- Selecting a printer and printing
- Undoing mistakes
- Cutting, copying, and pasting
- Creating headers and footers (common to several Windows accessories, but not third-party applications)

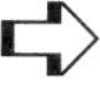

Tip You may sometimes find that when you try to work in a document—enter text into a word processor, for instance—nothing seems to work. Your computer may simply beep, or perhaps a menu will open. You have probably accidentally pressed the Alt key, activating the menu bar. Press **Esc** (several times if you have opened a menu or a dialog box). Then begin working again.

Opening Files

Most applications—Windows accessories and Windows applications written by other software publishers—have a **File | Open** command. This command lets you open the file that holds your data. If the application is a word processor, the file contains a document (a memo, letter, book, and so on). If the application is a database, the file contains the database records (addresses, for instance).

When you select File | Open you see a dialog box similar to the one shown in Figure 6.1. This is the Open dialog box that appears when you use the command in Write, Windows' word processor.

You must first make sure the Open dialog box is showing the correct disk drive. The **Drives** drop-down list box will usually show the hard drive on which you have loaded Windows, so if you want to open a file on a floppy drive or another hard-disk drive, you must select that drive. Click on the down arrow and then, when the list box drops down, click on the drive you want. (If you are using the keyboard, press **Alt-V** to move to the list box; press the down arrow to open it; use the arrow keys to highlight the disk drive you want; then press **Enter**.)

The Open dialog box shows the directories on the selected disk drive. Notice that immediately under the Directories title is a pathname. This tells you the

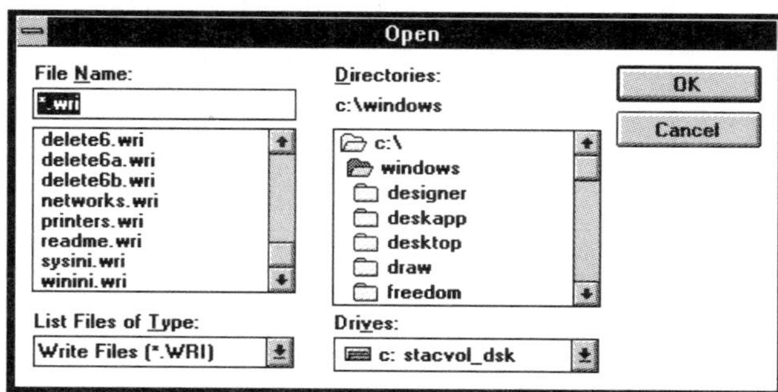

Figure 6.1 Write's Open dialog box

current directory, the one for which the files are listed in the files list box (under the File Name text box). In Figure 6.1 the Open dialog box shows

```
c:\windows
```

which means that the files in the files list box are in the WINDOWS directory.

You can see the same information graphically inside the Directories list box. Each directory, including the root directory, has a small icon of a file. The first two in Figure 6.1 (`c:\`, the root directory, and `windows`) appear to be open, while all the other icons are closed. This means that the WINDOWS directory—which is in the root directory—is open, and all the other directories listed are subdirectories of WINDOWS that are not open.

To open another directory so you can see what files are in that directory, double-click on the directory entry in the list box. Or press **Alt-D** to move to the list box, use the arrow keys to highlight the directory you want to open, and press **Enter**. Figure 6.2 shows the list box after you have opened the SYSTEM directory. This directory has no subdirectories, so no more icons are shown below it.

You can move back up the directory tree, closing subdirectories and viewing the contents of their parent directories in the same way. Just double-click on the parent directory, or select the directory and press **Enter**. These new Open dialog boxes are a great improvement over Windows 3.0's because you can move directly back up the directory tree to any branch. However many subdirectories you have open, for example, you can always double-click on the c:\ to move directly to the root directory. (For a discussion of directories and the directory tree, see Chapter 9.)

When you first open this dialog box, which directory is selected? Generally, the same directory as the executable file is stored in. For instance, WRITE.EXE, the Write program file, is stored in the WINDOWS directory, so the Open dialog box shows that directory. Word for Windows is normally saved in a file named WINWORD, so its Open dialog box will normally show that directory.

However, you can change the *working directory*, or *startup directory* as this is known. In Chapter 4 we explained how to change the working directory while

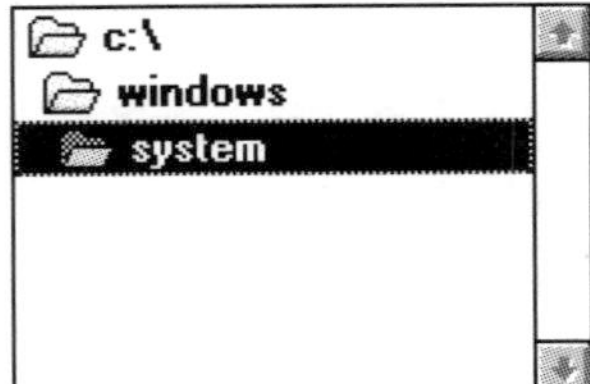

Figure 6.2 The Directories list box after opening the SYSTEM directory

creating application icons. And some applications have internal commands to change the working directory. Word for Windows, for instance, has a Tools | Options command that lets you modify the WIN.INI file.

Once you have selected the directory in which the file you want is saved, the list box under the File Name text box displays the files in that directory. It doesn't usually display all of them, however. When the dialog box first appears it shows the application's standard extension in the **File Name** text box; Figure 6.1 shows *.WRI, because that is the extension used by Write files. This means "display all the files with the .WRI extension."

Below the File Name list box is a **List Files of Type** drop-down list box. You can select another file type from this box. For example, Write lets you open Word for DOS and Text files. Select Word for DOS and the File Name text box changes to *.DOC. Select Text files and it changes to *.TXT. When you select from this list box, however, you are usually doing nothing more than changing the extension in the File Name box. If you select the *.DOC extension, for instance, Write will still examine the file you select to see what the format is: It won't automatically assume it's a Word for DOS file and try to open it accordingly.

You can modify the File Name entry to anything you want, then click on OK to change the file-list specification. For instance, you could change it to *.BKP if you want to list all the backup files (or *.BAK if you want to list backup files from applications other than Windows Write). You could enter P*.WRI, to tell the application to list all files beginning with P and ending with the .WRI extension. The asterisk replaces multiple characters, or even none. For instance, the application will list files named P.WRI, P1.WRI, PETER.WRI, PLACE.WRI, and so on. You can specify a single character by using a question mark. P?.WRI will list only P1.WRI, not the others because they have too few or too many characters.

When you have finally listed all the files, you can now select one to open. Double-click on the filename in the list, or click once and click on OK. You can also press **Alt-N** to move to the File Name text box, **Tab** to move to the list of files, and the arrow keys to select the file. Then press **Enter**.

All of Windows' own applications use this type of Open dialog box. However, some third-party applications use a different type. Most are similar, so you can probably figure them out easily. Also, Windows' own applications vary slightly. For instance, the Calendar's Open dialog box has a Read Only check box. If you select this box you can open the file but not modify it. We explain variations in these dialog boxes in the appropriate chapters.

Saving Files

There are two ways to save a file. You can use the **File | Save** command to save a file with the current filename, or the **File | Save As** command to save it with a new name or a different format. If you have just started work in a file—so it hasn't been saved yet—both these commands are the same. Even if you select File | Save, you will still see the Save As dialog box (as in Figure 6.3).

This dialog box is similar to the Open dialog box. You can select the disk and directory in which you want to save the file. You also have a File Name text box—if you are saving a file for the first time this box will be empty when the dialog box opens.

The files list box contains the existing files in the selected directory. You can click on a name in the list (in some applications the names are dimmed, in others they are normal) to put that name in the File Name text box. You can then modify the name, or continue and save the new file over the old one. For instance, you could click on LETTER07.WRI, and then change the name to LETTER08.WRI.

There is also a **Save File as Type** drop-down list box in this dialog box, but it works differently from the Open dialog box; it changes the File Name extension, and thus changes the list of files. But in most cases it also changes the format in which the file will be saved. In the case of Write, selecting Text Files will make Write save the file in ASCII format instead of the normal .WRI format. (Probably the only case this is not so is for applications that include a *.BAK format in the list. Selecting this format changes the file extension, but the file is saved in the usual format.)

If you are using Save As to save an existing file with a new name or format, selecting an option from the Save File as Type box doesn't normally change the extension in the File Name text box. You must do this yourself, especially if you don't want to save the new format over the existing file.

You can also use the same wildcards (* and ?) in the Save As dialog box as you do in the Open dialog box, so you can list exactly the files you want. Of course you have to type a real name into the text box before you can save. Windows applications use the same name format as DOS applications. The name may have eight characters, a period, and a three-character extension. You can't include spaces in the name or use the following names: CON, AUX, COM1, COM2, COM3,

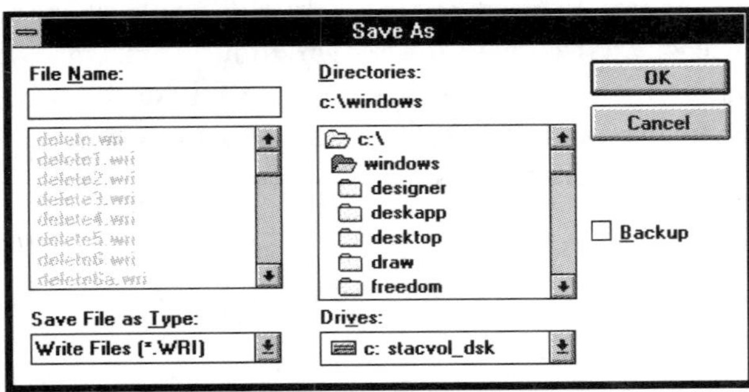

Figure 6.3 Write's Save As dialog box

COM4, LPT1, LPT2, LPT3, PRN, or NUL. Nor can you use any of these characters: " / \ [ ] : ; | = , . ? * (except that a period must go between the name and extension).

Some dialog boxes also have a Backup check box. This has no effect if it's the first time you are saving a file; but if the file has been saved once before, this option makes a backup copy at the same time it saves your file. This is how it works. The application changes the existing, already saved file's extension, normally to .BAK (Write uses .BKP for its backup files). It then saves the current information in the application window in a file with the same name but the normal file extension (in the case of Write, with a .WRI extension). The next time you save, the first backup file is removed and the normal file (.WRI in this case) is renamed with the backup extension. Then the current information is saved with the normal extension. In this way you always have a copy of what the file looked like immediately before you saved it.

So if you damage a file in some way, you can always go to the backup file and retrieve the previous data. (You can open the file in the normal way: type *.BAK—or *.BKP for Write—in the Open dialog box's File Name text box.) You can only go back one step, because a new backup file is created for each item you save.

Not all applications let you make backups. Write does, but Paintbrush and Notepad do not, for instance. Also, the exact manner in which the backup works varies. Some third-party applications always make backups, unless you tell the application not to. Write, however, only makes a backup when you tell it to, so if you use the File | Save command it won't make a backup. This is almost certainly a bug, and reduces the usefulness of this feature.

▼ ***Note*** Don't confuse this type of backup with "backing up" your data. All important files should be saved on another medium—floppy disks, tape, removable hard disks, or whatever—and stored away from your computer.

Most Save As dialog boxes have a default extension, the extension that will be used if you don't enter one. For instance, if you are saving a file in .WRI format, you don't have to enter the extension in the File Name text box; Write will add it for you. However, Windows Sound Recorder has a bug; if you don't add the extension it won't add one. And if the file doesn't have an extension it won't appear in the file list the next time you try to open a file (unless you type *.* into the File Name text box).

In most cases, when you use the File | Save As command the application loads the new file. For instance, if you use the Save As dialog box to save FILE1.WRI as FILE2.DOC, Write will change the title bar to FILE2.DOC. When you continue working you will be modifying FILE2.DOC, not FILE1.WRI.

Once the file has a name, you can save information quickly by selecting **File | Save**. No dialog box appears; the application simply saves the file with its current name and format.

Important Get into the habit of saving frequently, so you won't lose data if your system crashes or an application locks up. Although Windows' own applications don't have Save shortcuts, many applications do, so it's easy to press **Ctrl-S** or **Shift-F12**, for instance, every now and then.

Closing Files

There are several ways to close application files. Generally you can select **File | New**. The application closes the file and opens a blank workspace in which you can begin a new file. Or you can select **File | Open**. This displays the Open dialog box, from which you can select a file. When you open the file the current one is closed.

However, some third-party applications allow you to keep several files open at one time. You might have several word processing documents or several spreadsheets open (each in its own *document window*). Thus using File | New and File | Open does not close a file. To close the file you will usually select **File | Close** (this varies among applications; a few even use File | Close to close the application itself).

These are the ways you can close a file:

- Select **File | New** to close the existing file and begin a new one.
- Select **File | Open** to open an existing file and close the current one.
- In applications with multiple document windows, select **File | Close**.
- In applications with multiple document windows, **double-click** on the document window's Control menu.
- In some applications with multiple document windows, press **Ctrl-F4**.

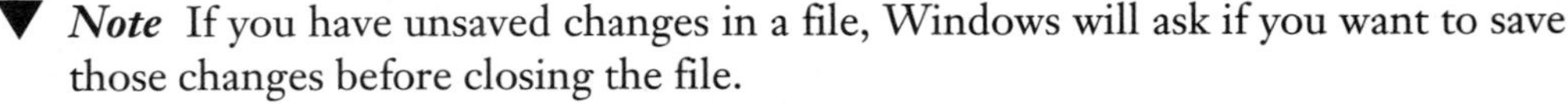

Note If you have unsaved changes in a file, Windows will ask if you want to save those changes before closing the file.

Closing the Application

You can close applications in the same way you close Windows itself. You may select **File | Exit**, double-click on the Control menu, or press **Alt-F4**. For more information and other methods, see Chapter 5.

Creating Headers and Footers

Several of Windows' own applications have a common **File | Page Setup** command that lets you set the page margins and enter a header and footer. The Page Setup dialog box (shown in Figure 6.4), is used by Notepad, Calendar, and Cardfile.

The default settings shown in this figure print the filename as the header and the page number (Page *n*) as the footer. You can type any text you want in the header and footer text boxes—up to 40 characters—including the following codes:

Code	***Enters . .***
&d	The current date
&p	The page number
&f	The filename
&l	The text following the code is aligned at the left margin
&r	The text following the code is aligned at the right margin
&c	The text following the code is centered
&t	The current time

You can mix codes and text. For instance, typing

```
&l&d&cProject Schedule&rSheet &p
```

produces

```
7/6/92                Project Schedule                Sheet 1
```

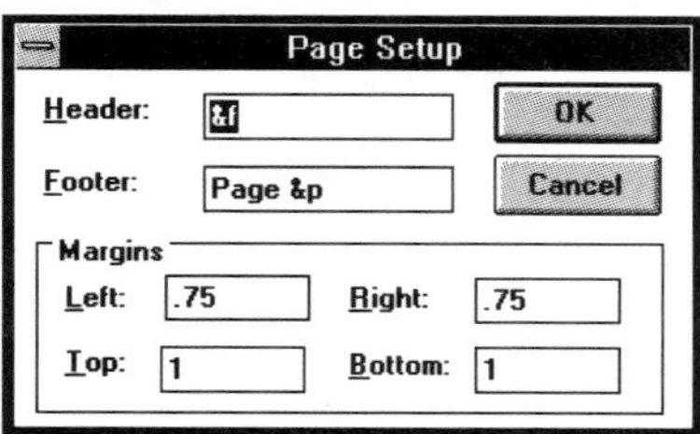

Figure 6.4 The Page Setup dialog box

Remember to leave spaces between the text and codes wherever you need them (between Sheet and &p, for instance). If you enter a line of text with no codes, the text is automatically placed in the center of the page.

The margins are measured in inches—unless you selected the metric system in the Control Panel's International dialog box, in which case the margins are in centimeters. The margins determine how close the document text will be to the edges of the paper; if you are including a header or footer, you must also allow space for them. They print within the margin, so if you make the top or bottom margin too small, you can actually cause the document text to print *over* the header or footer.

Selecting a Printer and Printing

When you install Windows you can load several printer drivers. You can also use the Control Panel to add more at any time. You could have several printers hooked up to your system, so how does an application know which one to use?

As you will see in Chapter 8, in Control Panel's Printers dialog box one of the printers is selected as the *default*. This is the printer that all applications will assume you want to use, unless you select another printer. However, you may select another printer by using an application's **File|Print Setup** command. Once you have selected a new printer, each time you use the File|Print command the information is sent to that printer.

Windows' own applications save only the new printer information as long as they are open. If you close and reopen them, they will again assume that you want to use the default printer. Some third-party applications are a little smarter; if you change the printer the application saves the information in an initialization file, so it knows which printer to use the next time you open the application.

Select **File|Print Setup** in any of Windows' own applications to see a Print Setup dialog box like the one shown in Figure 6.5. (Other applications will display different dialog boxes, but the principle is the same.) The two option buttons at the top let you decide whether you want to use the default printer—the one set up in the Control Panel's Printers dialog box as the default—or whether you want to select another one.

If you want to select one of the other printers, click on the Down Arrow on the **Specific Printer** drop-down list box (the option button is automatically selected when you do so). Then select the printer you want to use from the list. You can also press **Alt-P** to move to the drop-down list box, press the down arrow to open it, and use the arrows to highlight the printer you want. Then press **Enter** to select that printer and close the dialog box, or **Tab** to move to another option in the box.

The other options available in the dialog box depend on the printer you select. Figure 6.5 shows some typical options. You can select the page **Orientation**,

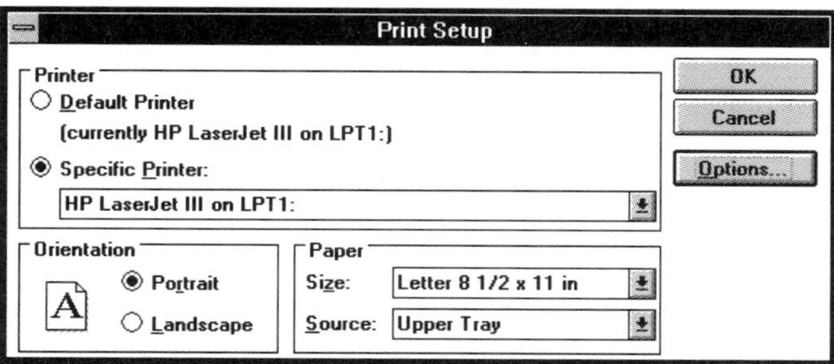

Figure 6.5 The Print Setup dialog box

Portrait or **Landscape**. Notice that when you click on one of the option buttons the sample page containing the large A moves to demonstrate the orientation you selected.

You may also be able to select a **Paper Size** and **Source**. And if the **Options** button is enabled you can click it to see another dialog box. This dialog box will either be the printer driver's Setup dialog box, or the driver's Options dialog box, if it has one. See Chapter 11 for more information about these dialog boxes.

When you finally click on the OK button, you have told your application which printer should be used the next time you select the **File | Print** command, the command that almost all applications use for printing. Selecting this command does one of two things: It sends the information in the file directly to the printer, or it displays another dialog box asking for information about the print job, similar to that in Figure 6.6. Most of Windows' own applications use the first method, although Write displays a Print dialog box, as do most third-party applications.

The top line in this box shows you to which printer Write is going to send your document. If you have more than one printer, you should always glance at this line to make sure you have selected the correct one (if you haven't, close this dialog box and select File | Print Setup).

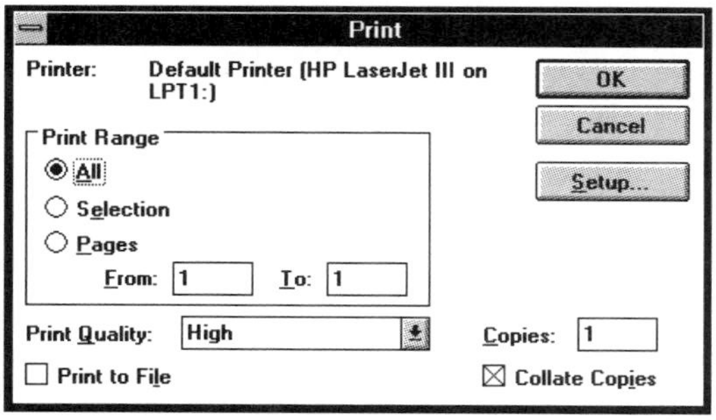

Figure 6.6 Write's Print dialog box

You have three print-area choices. You can print the entire document by selecting **All**, the default; you can print only the text or graphics you selected in the document before opening this dialog box (**Selection**), or you can specify the pages you want to print (**Pages**). If you select the Pages option, enter the page numbers in the **From** and **To** text boxes (both will already display 1).

The options in the **Print Quality** drop-down list box depend on the selected printer—the list box may not be available. You may have options such as High, Medium, Low, and Draft. Selecting a low quality will speed up the printing. However, graphics may be omitted in some modes, and in other modes they will be of a low quality.

The **Copies** text box lets you tell the application how many printouts you want. If you select more than one copy of a multiple-page document, you may want to make sure the **Collate** check box is selected, so that each document is printed complete (rather than all page 1s, then all page 2s, and so on).

Finally, the **Print to File** check box tells the application to create a print file instead of actually printing the file. This file can be printed later, or on a different machine. For instance, if you want to create a PostScript printout but don't have a PostScript printer, you can use the PostScript print driver to create a print file, then take the file to a colleague's computer and print it there. If you select this option, when you click on OK the application asks you for an Output File Name. You will enter a filename (and path if you wish), and Write will create the file. Then you can print the file at another time, by using a batch printing utility, or by using this DOS command:

```
copy c:\pathname\filename lpt1
```

If you are printing a non-PostScript files to a non-PostScript printer, add `/b` to the end of this command.

Undoing Mistakes

Almost all Windows programs have an **Edit|Undo** command. This undoes the last editing command. For instance, if you type a sentence and then decide you want to remove it, you can select Edit|Undo. Select Edit|Undo again, and the sentence reappears (it undoes the undo). If you make a mistake using a painting tool in Paintbrush, use Undo to remove the work you have just done. You can use the Undo shortcut—**Alt-Backspace** or **Ctrl-Z**—instead of selecting from the menu.

Most operations can be undone, but there are always some that cannot. For instance, if you make changes to a card in Cardfile and then go to the next card, you cannot use undo to remove those changes—you can only do so while still in the card. And in Paintbrush, once you have selected another tool, you cannot undo actions done with the previous tool (even if you haven't yet used the new tool). Different applications have different rules, but in general you will find undo a very useful editing tool.

Cutting, Copying, and Pasting

One of Windows' most important features is the ability to cut, copy, and paste information. Windows uses a *Clipboard* onto which text and images are placed when you cut or copy them. Once on the Clipboard the text or image can be pasted down in another place in the document, in the application's other documents, or in a completely different application's documents.

For instance, if you want to copy a block of text from one word processing file to another, select the text then select **Edit | Copy**. The text is now in the Clipboard. Open the other document and place the cursor where you want the text to be placed. Select **Edit | Paste** and Windows copies the text from the Clipboard into the document. The text remains on the Clipboard, so you can continue making as many copies as you want.

You can also copy text and graphics between applications. For instance, you can copy a picture in Paintbrush and paste it into Write, or text in Write and paste it into Notepad. Of course some applications will not accept graphics. You can't copy a picture into Calendar for instance.

Keyboard shortcuts for these commands are as follows:

Edit | Cut	**Ctrl-X** or **Shift-Del**
Edit | Copy	**Ctrl-C** or **Ctrl-Ins**
Edit | Paste	**Ctrl-V** or **Shift-Ins**

As you can see, there are two keyboard shortcuts for each command (just as there are two shortcuts for the Undo command). The ones on the right are the original ones, but Windows has gradually been introducing the new ones. Most applications will work with either set. To copy part of a Paintbrush image, for instance, you can press **Ctrl-C** or **Ctrl-Ins**. However, there are some third-party applications that will *not* use the new shortcuts. Micrografx Designer and Windows Draw, for instance, have been using these keyboard combinations for other operations for a long time, so you cannot use them for cut, copy, and paste.

There's an important advantage to the new set of shortcuts—it doesn't matter if your Num Lock is turned on. With the old set, if you use the Del and Ins keys on the numeric keypad you must make sure the Num Lock key is turned off.

 **Tip** You can even copy and paste from and to text boxes in dialog boxes. For instance, you can copy a filename from the Rename dialog box in File Manager and paste it into the Copy dialog box. Generally, double-clicking on a single-line text box selects the text. Then press **Ctrl-C** to copy. Or place the cursor in the text box and press **Ctrl-V** to paste.

Chapter 27 contains more information about using the Clipboard, including instructions on copying between DOS and Windows applications.

Object Linking and Embedding (OLE)

Many applications now have a feature called Object Linking and Embedding. This lets you paste "objects"—text, pictures, numbers, music, speech, and so on—from one application (the server) into another (the client) while retaining a "connection." If the object is *embedded* it is still connected to the original application. You can edit the object from the application in which it is embedded, usually by double-clicking on it. The server application opens automatically, and when you make your changes and close the server, the object in the client is updated automatically.

A *linked* object has a connection to a particular file. For instance, you may have one file from which you have pasted copies into several documents. By creating a linked object, all those copies are updated automatically whenever you modify the original file.

If an application is a client—that is, if it is able to receive OLE objects—it has more menu options (the last seven options at the end of this chapter). See Chapter 28 for a detailed description of OLE.

Common Menu Options

The following menu options are common to several of the Windows accessories, and many other Windows applications as well.

File | New Clears the window and displays a new document, so you can start a new file. If the current file hasn't been saved, the application asks if you want to do so.

File | Open Opens an existing application file.

File | Save Saves the file. The first time you save you will see the Save As dialog box so you can select a directory and filename.

File | Save As Lets you save the file with a new name, or in a different directory.

File | Print Prints the file on the printer selected in the Print Setup dialog box.

File | Page Setup Sets page margins and creates a header and footer.

File | Print Setup Selects the printer on which you wish to print your files.

File | Exit Closes the application. If you have unsaved changes, the application asks if you want to save the file first.

Edit | Undo (Ctrl-Z) Undoes the last operation, to correct a mistake.

Edit | Cut (Ctrl-X) Cuts the selected text or picture and places it into the Clipboard.

Edit | Copy (Ctrl-C) Copies the selected text or picture into the Clipboard.

Edit | Paste (Ctrl-V) Copies the text or picture from the Clipboard into the application. If the data is coming from an OLE server, the data is automatically pasted as an embedded object.

▼ ***Note*** The following seven options are OLE (Object Linking and Embedding) commands; they are explained in Chapter 28.

Edit | Paste Special Lets you select different types of paste procedures: OLE embedded, OLE link, or non-OLE (normal).

Edit | Paste Link Pastes an object from the Clipboard into the document and creates a link to the original application.

Edit | Links If the document contains linked objects, lets you modify or remove OLE links.

Edit | *application name* Object Lets you edit the selected linked or embedded object. If the selected item is a package, this menu option is replaced by the following two:

> **Edit | Package Object | Activate Contents** Opens the application that created the object in the selected package so you can view, listen to, or edit the object.
>
> **Edit | Package Object | Edit Package** Opens the Object Packager so you can edit the selected package.

Edit | Insert Object Opens an OLE *server* application so you can create an OLE object and paste it into the document. Some applications have an Insert | Object command instead.

7

Running DOS Applications

Working with Windows doesn't mean you have to throw out all your old DOS software. You can use Windows to run your DOS programs, in windows or full screen. You won't get all the advantages of using Windows applications, but you'll still get some. You can copy some types of data between DOS and Windows applications, multitask both types of applications (if you are running in 386 Enhanced mode), open DOS applications from Program Manager icons, use shortcut keys to swap in and out of the DOS windows, and so on.

When you start a DOS program, Windows looks for a PIF (Program Information File) with the same name. A PIF tells Windows how to run a DOS application: how to handle multitasking, whether to run the DOS application in a window, how to handle memory, and other such details. For instance, if you run a DOS program named DOCEDIT.EXE, Windows checks for a file called DOCEDIT.PIF. If Windows finds the PIF file, it uses the specifications to run the application. If it can't find the PIF file, Windows simply uses the default settings, saved in a file called _DEFAULT.PIF.

If you run DOS programs with Windows you probably won't need to change PIF file settings, but you should read this chapter nonetheless. It will give you an idea of how you may be able to improve the application's performance—and that of the system in general—and suggest changes you might have to make if you have problems.

Creating an Icon

You can run DOS programs from a program icon in Program Manager in the same way you use an icon for a Windows program. The main difference is that you want to specify a PIF, if available, rather than the program's .EXE .BAT or .COM file. You'll learn about PIF files later in this chapter.

There are three ways to setup an application: by using the Setup procedure, by using the Program Manager File | New command, and by dragging an icon from File Manager. The advantage of the Setup procedure is that it will automatically associate the program with an appropriate PIF file, if it can. However, the procedure is not always able to create an icon, and you may have to use one of the other methods.

You use the same methods for DOS applications as you do for Windows methods. However, you can specify (or drag) a PIF file instead of an .EXE, a .COM, or a .BAT file. Your application may have loaded a PIF file automatically, or you may have to create one.

Creating and Modifying PIFs

In some circumstances you may need to create your own PIFs or modify an existing one. To find out which PIF is being used by an application (or if a PIF is being used at all), hold the Alt key and double-click on the program icon in Program Manager. The Command Line text box will name the PIF. You may want to modify a PIF if the application isn't running well, or simply to add a keyboard shortcut to open the application.

PIF Editor

You can create or modify a PIF using the PIF Editor. Double-click on the PIF Editor icon in the Main group (if you upgraded from Windows 3.0, the PIF Editor remains in the Accessories group). Or select **File | Run** and run **PIFEDIT**. The window you see depends on whether you are running in Standard or 386-Enhanced mode. The PIF file has options that are related to each mode. You can enter the options for both modes, regardless of the mode in which you are running; simply select the other mode from the **Mode** menu in the PIF Editor window. Some of the options are specific to one mode, some are common to both modes. For instance, entering a Program Filename or selecting shortcut keys in one mode window changes the other, whereas entering Optional Parameters does not.

If you want to edit a PIF, select **File | Open**, and select a PIF. Windows places its PIF files in the WINDOWS directory; some DOS applications may provide PIF files in their own directories. If you are going to create one, make your changes and then use the **File | Save** command to save them in a PIF file. (We explained how to use the File | Open and File | Save commands in Chapter 6.) You should use the same name as the executable file. For instance, if you are creating a PIF for an application called DRAW.EXE, call the PIF file DRAW.PIF. In some cases you may want more than one PIF for an application, and then you will have to use different names for one or more. You may want to run the application in different ways at different times; for instance, you may want different extended memory settings, allow pasting to the Clipboard sometimes but not others, use different startup parameters, and so on. You can create different PIFs, then create an icon for each one.

If you then want to create another PIF, select **File|New**. This resets the PIF back to the default settings (the same ones found in the _DEFAULT.PIF file).

Modifying 386 Enhanced Mode Options

The window shown in Figure 7.1 appears if you are using 386 Enhanced mode, or if you open the PIF Editor in Standard mode and then select **Mode|386 Enhanced**. Let's take a look at all the options in this window.

PROGRAM FILENAME

Enter the name of the program you want to run. If the program is not in the WINDOWS directory, include the pathname. If the program is an .EXE or a .COM file, you don't need to include the extension (but if you don't, when you save the file Windows displays a message saying you have the wrong extension). You must include an extension if it is a DOS batch (.BAT) file. Incidentally, if you want to run a program file that doesn't have an .EXE, a .COM, or a .BAT extension, you can build a DOS .BAT file (a batch file) and run it with a DOS command within that file, then create a PIF that calls the batch file.

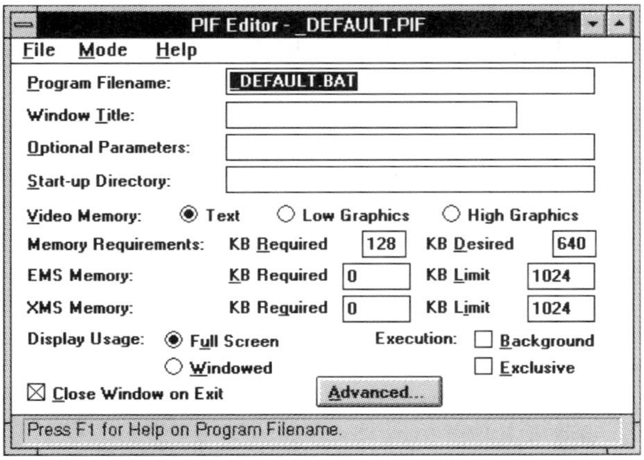

Figure 7.1 The PIF Editor window

WINDOW TITLE

Unlike Windows applications, you can modify the name in the windows' title bar and the icon's label. This entry has no effect if you open the application by double-clicking on the icon. It only works if you double-click on the file in File Manager, or use File | Run in either File Manager or Program Manager. When you double-click on the icon, the entry in the Description line of the Program Item Properties dialog box is used. There is always an entry in this line, so your entry in the PIF file is always overridden. Make the entry in the Program Item Properties dialog box the same as in the PIF file, so Windows always uses your special title.

If you don't enter anything in this text box, Windows just uses the program's filename.

OPTIONAL PARAMETERS

Many programs have *switches* or *optional parameters* that you use when you start them. These may be instructions or filenames. For instance, the display-monitor test program DisplayMate uses the optional parameter `c` to set the menu colors to white and black. You would enter `/c` in the text box. You can enter up to 62 characters—see your application's documentation for information. By the way, if you use the File | Run command in File Manager or Program Manager, these parameters are not used.

Of course this entry is optional, you only use it if the application you are going to run needs it. And if you plan to run the application in both 386 Enhanced and Standard modes, you must enter the appropriate parameters in each window; they are not automatically copied.

If you would like to be able to enter the parameters each time you open the application, simply type ? in this text box. When you use the PIF to start, the application, Windows will display a dialog box in which you can type the parameters and continue.

START-UP DIRECTORY

You can enter the pathname of the directory you want to be current when Windows opens the application. For instance, let's say you have a word processor that stores its document files in a directory called C:\WORD\DATA. When you start the program and then use its command for opening a document, you will find you are in the C:\WINDOWS directory. But if you enter C:\WORD\DATA in the Start-up Directory text box you will be in the correct directory.

There are two things to remember when using this option. First, if you start the program by double-clicking on the icon, the Start-up Directory entry is overridden by the Working Directory entry in the icon's Program Items Properties dialog box. Second, many applications let you enter a default directory into their setup information, so the Start-up Directory is irrelevant.

If you don't enter anything in this text box—or in the Working Directory text box in the icon's Program Items Properties dialog box—the current directory will be the WINDOWS directory.

▼ ***Note*** You can use DOS environment variables in any of the preceding text boxes. For instance, if you include `set abc=c:\temp` in your AUTOEXEC.BAT file, you can place C:\TEMP in the Start-up Directory by entering `%abc%`. The environment variable must be set before you enter Windows. See the SET command in your DOS documentation for more information.

VIDEO MEMORY

The video memory options determine how much memory Windows will assign to the application's video when it starts. Most DOS applications work only in text mode. Others let you select a graphics mode. Text mode is quicker than graphics mode, of course, but graphics mode is needed to display pictures and sometimes to get more text on the screen.

The video memory options determine how much memory will be available for the application. If you select **Text**, Windows assigns 16 KB. **Low Graphics** assigns 32 KB, enough for CGA (Color Graphics Adapter) and Hercules video modes. **High Graphics** assigns 128 KB, enough for EGA (Enhanced Graphics Adapter) or VGA (Video Graphics Array). If you select a lower mode than you need, you may be able to switch to a higher mode, but if the memory isn't available the application may not display correctly, if at all. If you select a higher mode than you need, Windows can assign the unused memory to other applications. However, if you change the application's graphics mode during a session, the needed memory may not be available.

If you want to make sure that as much memory is available as necessary, select High Graphics, and the **Retain Video Memory** check box in the Advanced Options dialog box (which we will look at in a moment). This makes sure that Windows doesn't release the memory to other applications.

MEMORY REQUIREMENTS

The Memory Requirements options determine how much conventional memory (the first 640 KB in your computer) are used for the application. This isn't real conventional memory. This is *virtual* memory, extended memory that Windows makes appear as if it were conventional memory so the DOS program can run. (For instance, you can have several DOS programs each using 640 KB of conventional memory, although obviously your machine doesn't have that much.)

KB Required is the minimum amount of conventional memory needed to start the program. Windows will give the program more, if it can, but if it doesn't have the KB Required available it won't even start the program. You may have to close some other applications. A setting of –1 means "all the conventional memory," (a setting you will probably never want to use), while 0 means "no minimum requirement." You can enter any value up to 640. The lower the value you enter here, the more you leave for other applications.

The **KB Desired** is really the KB limit, the maximum that Windows will assign to that application. Neither of these amounts is the same as that usually listed by an application in its "System Requirements." Such requirements usually include enough memory to run DOS itself in addition to the application. You can enter a number from –1 to 640, with –1 equivalent to "all that is available." If you enter a number that is too low, the program won't be able to start.

EMS AND XMS MEMORY

Some DOS applications require EMS (Expanded) or XMS (Extended) memory. (Windows doesn't actually use EMS memory in 386 Enhanced mode, but it simulates it when needed.) In both cases the **KB Required** setting is the minimum amount required to make the application start. This can usually be left at 0, even if the application needs that type of memory for some procedures; few applications require it to run.

The **KB Limit** is the maximum amount of virtual expanded or extended memory that Windows will provide to the application. Some applications will take all the expanded memory they can, even if they are not going to use it, so entering a number in here stops the application from stealing memory, making it unavailable to other applications. If you enter –1 the application can use all that is available—you will probably never need this setting. If you enter 0 it won't get any.

Note that for both XMS and EMS the KB Limit is set to 1024 by default. That doesn't matter if the application doesn't try to use that sort of memory. But if you are running an application that can use expanded memory but won't need to, set the value to 0 so it won't waste memory.

DISPLAY USAGE

You can make Windows run a DOS application **Full Screen**—that is, so you can't see any window components—or **Windowed**, in a window with borders, title bar, scroll bars, and so on. A window will use more memory, but you will have a few of the usual advantages; you will be able to size and move the window, and use the

Control menu. You will also be able to copy and paste text. Whatever you select here you can change once the application is running by pressing **Alt-Enter**.

EXECUTION: BACKGROUND

The Execution: Background check box is a very important setting. If you select this option the DOS application will run while it is not the active application. A number of settings—such as the Scheduling options in the Control Panel's 386 Enhanced dialog box (described in Chapter 8), and the Multitasking Options in the Advanced Options dialog box (which we will look at in a moment)—control the way Windows multitasks DOS applications. But by default DOS applications are *not* multitasked. As soon as you swap from the DOS application to another one, or to a Windows application, Windows stops running the original application—it simply freezes until you return.

The _DEFAULT.PIF file has this check box turned off, and if you look at the other PIF files loaded on your system you will probably find that *none* of them have it turned on. So if you want your application to continue running—to continue printing, for instance, while you do something else in another application—make sure that this option is turned on. Of course if you are running an application with Exclusive selected, the Background check box selection has no effect—the application will not run.

Also, the Control Panel's 386 Enhanced dialog box has an option called "Exclusive in Foreground." When this is selected, all processing time is given to the Windows applications while one of them is the active application, overriding any PIF setting. That is, *none* of the DOS applications can run in the background, even if they have "Execution: Background" selected.

EXECUTION: EXCLUSIVE

If you select the Exclusive option, Windows will suspend all other activities while the application is the active one, allowing it more memory and processing time. This will make the application run more quickly. Windows will even suspend other DOS applications for which you selected the Execution: Background option. There's one case when other applications will continue running—Windows applications continue if the DOS application is running in a window instead of full screen.

▼ ***Note*** The Exclusive and Background settings can be changed while a DOS application is running, if it is running in a Window. Select Settings from the Control menu.

CLOSE WINDOW ON EXIT

Selecting the Close Window on Exit check box makes sure that the application's window is closed when the application finishes. This is the default; it is the setting you will use most often. There may be times that you want the window to remain after the application has finished, in particular with applications that carry out a particular operation and then close. For instance, if you use the program PKZIP to compress data files, it usually runs full screen, carries out the compression, and then closes the screen.

You could create a PIF for PKZIP and deselect the Close Window on Exit check box. Then, when PKZIP has finished it will remain on the screen, although the title bar will show "Inactive." If it was running full screen, Windows automatically creates a window for it. You can now view the results of the compression (PKZIP lists the files it compressed and the percentage compression). You won't be able to use the window, though. When you have finished with it, select Close from the Control menu.

The Advanced 386 Enhanced Options

There are more options for running an application in 386 Enhanced mode. Click on the **Advanced** button to see the dialog box in Figure 7.2.

BACKGROUND AND FOREGROUND PRIORITY

The Background Priority is an indication of how much processing time the application will get when it is running in the background. (Remember that it won't run

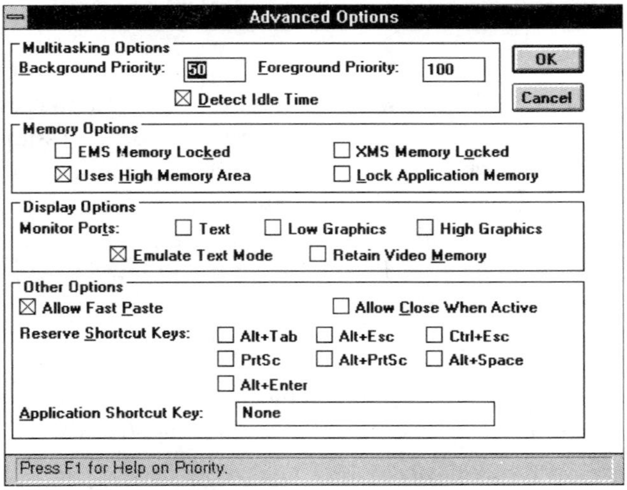

Advanced Options
Multitasking Options
Background Priority: 50
Foreground Priority: 100
OK
Cancel
☒ Detect Idle Time
Memory Options
☐ EMS Memory Locked
☐ XMS Memory Locked
☒ Uses High Memory Area
☐ Lock Application Memory
Display Options
Monitor Ports: ☐ Text ☐ Low Graphics ☐ High Graphics
☒ Emulate Text Mode
☐ Retain Video Memory
Other Options
☒ Allow Fast Paste
☐ Allow Close When Active
Reserve Shortcut Keys: ☐ Alt+Tab ☐ Alt+Esc ☐ Ctrl+Esc ☐ PrtSc ☐ Alt+PrtSc ☐ Alt+Space ☐ Alt+Enter
Application Shortcut Key: None
Press F1 for Help on Priority.

Figure 7.2 The Advanced Options dialog box

in the background unless you selected the Execution: Background option in the PIF Editor window.) The Foreground Priority indicates how much processing time it will get when it is the active application. In both cases the numbers are not milliseconds or bytes or any other real measurements. They are part of a calculation that includes the other DOS applications you have running and the Scheduling and Minimum Timeslice values you entered into the Control Panel's 386 Enhanced dialog box.

Windows uses all these values to calculate how much processing time it must provide to each DOS application and how much to the Windows applications (as a group). We explain this calculation in Chapter 8. Right now you should know that you can enter a number from 0 to 10,000, with a high number providing more resources to the application. Also, remember that selecting Execution: Exclusive gives the application *all* the resources while it runs as the active application, so the Foreground Priority setting will be meaningless.

▼ ***Note*** These priorities can be changed while a DOS application is running, if it is running in a Window. Select Settings from the Control menu.

DETECT IDLE TIME

The Detect Idle Time option should normally remain selected. It tells Windows that if the application is not doing anything, the processing time may be given to another application. This helps speed up the system in general—letting other applications run more quickly—but in some cases may cause problems with an application, especially a communications program that you are running in the background. (Windows may think the application is idle, when it is really just waiting for a response from the "other end.") Turn this option off also if the application is having problems operating.

MEMORY OPTIONS

The Memory Options check boxes determine how Windows will handle system memory. If you select **EMS Memory Locked**, **XMS Memory Locked**, and **Lock Application Memory**, Windows will not swap the EMS, XMS, and conventional memory to disk. (Windows can normally swap memory to disk to free up memory for other uses.) This will improve the application's performance but may slow down other applications, because there will be less memory available for them.

Selecting **Uses High Memory Area** lets Windows use the High Memory Area (HMA) for this application. The HMA is the first 64 KB of extended memory, between 1024 KB and 1088 KB. You can generally leave this turned on; if the memory is available, Windows will use it, if it isn't, there's no harm done. Remember that in 386 Enhanced mode we are using "virtual machines." Each DOS application is running in its own "DOS machine," with its own memory, and, therefore, its own HMA. However, Windows only makes a virtual HMA available to each virtual machine if the HMA is available when you open Windows. If, for instance, you are loading DOS 5.0 "high" it is occupying the HMA—and will occupy the HMA on each virtual machine.

MONITOR PORTS: TEXT, LOW GRAPHICS, HIGH GRAPHICS

Some DOS applications are able to bypass the system BIOS (Basic Input-Output System) and access the display adapter directly. If it does this while running in Windows, it may cause display problems when switching to and from applications. When you switch back to such a program Windows may not be able to restore its screen.

You can get around the problem by telling Windows to monitor the ports. You don't want to do this unless you really have to, because it can slow down the system's performance, particularly switching between applications. If you have problems though, you will have to select one of these options. You want to use the lowest you can, because the higher you go the more memory is used (Text being lowest and High Graphics being highest). Most DOS applications will work fine without any monitoring.

EMULATE TEXT MODE

This option is normally selected, and you will usually leave it so. It tells Windows to run the application in the 80-column, 25-line MDA (Monochrome Display Adapter) mode. It won't work with all applications, but when it does it will speed up the application. In rare cases it may garble the text or stop the application from running altogether.

RETAIN VIDEO MEMORY

Selecting Retain Video Memory ensures that Windows does not release any of the memory you assigned to the application for use in controlling the display (using the Video Memory options in the PIF Editor window). This means that even if the application is not using the memory, the memory will remain assigned to it and cannot be used by another application. This makes sure that if you run the application in graphics mode and then switch to text mode, the memory will still be available when you switch back to graphics mode.

If you don't select this option, and if your system is low on memory when you try to change back to graphics mode, the application may disappear, partly or completely. On the other hand, retaining video memory is locking up memory that might be needed by other applications.

ALLOW FAST PASTE

Windows lets you paste data into DOS windows. It has two methods, one fast and one slow, and it can usually figure out the best method to use. In some cases, it will try to fast paste into an application that cannot accept it, and nothing happens. If you find you can't paste into your application, turn the Allow Fast Paste option *off*. You can learn about pasting into DOS applications in Chapter 27.

ALLOW CLOSE WHEN ACTIVE

As you have already learned, you can close a Windows application by simply clicking on its Control menu, or by selecting Close from the Control menu. You can also close Windows, and the Windows applications will close automatically.

Windows doesn't normally let you do this with DOS applications. Windows can't monitor DOS applications closely, so it doesn't know if the application contains data that hasn't yet been saved. So if it automatically closed a DOS application you might lose important data. You must usually close a DOS application by using its normal Exit or Quit command.

In some cases, it wouldn't matter if Windows did close the application for you. For instance, if you have a DOS application such as Collage Plus' Show, which simply displays graphics files, you may not care if Windows closes it automatically. You don't add data through Show, so you are not going to lose anything. Select Allow Close When Active to let you close an application if it doesn't have data files.

RESERVE SHORTCUT KEYS

Many DOS applications use shortcut key combinations that Windows uses for various procedures. Windows will normally take precedence. That is, if you use a shortcut key combination that both Windows and the application use, Windows uses it, not the application. You can tell Windows to ignore the combination—and let the application use it instead—by selecting the appropriate check box. These are the combinations, with the way Windows uses them:

Alt-Tab Switches to the last-used application.

Alt-Esc Switches to the next application in sequence.

Ctrl-Esc Displays the Task List dialog box. If the application is full screen, Windows displays the last-used application, with the Task List dialog box above it.

PrtSc If the application is in a window, this copies a picture of the full screen into the Clipboard. If it is running full screen, this copies a "text" picture into the clipboard.

Alt-PrtSc If the application is in a window, this copies a picture of the window into the Clipboard. If it is running full screen, this copies a "text" picture into the clipboard.

Alt-Space Opens the Control menu. If the application is full screen, it changes to a window first.

Alt-Enter Toggles the application between full screen and a window.

The first time you reserve a shortcut, the setting is automatically reserved in the Standard mode. But the next time you change the setting, it is not automatically changed in the other mode. Thus an application may operate differently according to the mode in which you are working.

Some of these keystrokes you simply don't need, so you can save some memory by disabling them. If you are going to run the application in a window, you don't really need the commands used to open the Control menu or swap to other applications; you can use your mouse to do that. Also, you won't need Alt-Enter because you can use the Control menu to swap to full screen, although without Alt-Enter you won't be able to swap back. If you only want to run full screen or in a Window, you won't need Alt-Enter anyway. And you could disable two of the swapping commands (Alt-Tab, Alt-Esc, or Ctrl-Esc) and just use one of them. Then you won't need Alt-Spacebar either, because you can use the remaining swapping command and then open the Control menu with the mouse. Also, if you don't plan to take "snapshots" of the screen or window, you won't need the PrtSc or Alt-PrtSc commands.

Remember that reserving a shortcut for an application restricts its use while the DOS application is minimized and the icon selected. For instance, if you have reserved Alt-Tab, you won't be able to use Alt-Tab to move from the icon to another application.

APPLICATION SHORTCUT KEY

You have already seen (in Chapter 4) how you can assign a shortcut key to an application, so that you can quickly swap directly to that application, or even open the application if Program Manager is active. The Advanced Options dialog box Application Shortcut Key is very similar, with some important differences. First, you have a different choice of keystroke combinations. Here are the rules:

- The combination *must* include Alt, Shift, or Ctrl.
- You can combine Alt, Ctrl, and Shift.
- You cannot use Esc, Enter, Tab, Spacebar, Print Screen, or Backspace.
- Unlike the Program Item Properties shortcuts (which allow only three- and four-key shortcuts), you can create two-key shortcuts.

Place the cursor in the box and then press the combination (don't type it). For instance, press **Ctrl-1**, don't actually type C t r l - 1.

Another important difference is that this keystroke combination cannot be used to actually open the application, only to switch to it from another application. (If you set a shortcut in the icon's Program Item Properties dialog box you can start the application by displaying Program Manager and pressing the shortcut.) Finally, any shortcut you enter here will be overridden by the shortcut in the Program Item Properties dialog box—as long as you start the application using the icon. If you start the application using the File | Run command, or by double-clicking on the filename in File Manager, Windows lets you use the shortcut you entered in the PIF. Remember though, if you accidentally use the icon's shortcut while in Program Manager, you will open the application again, unless you place the same shortcut in both places.

▼ *Note* Remember that the shortcut you enter here overrides all other application shortcuts. For instance, if you use the shortcut Alt-E, it will no longer open an application's Edit menu. Rather, it will switch between applications.

The Standard Mode Options

You can also set the PIF options for the Standard mode. You only need to change these settings if you are going to run the application in Standard mode; you can ignore them otherwise. If you are running in Standard mode, the window you see in Figure 7.3 is the one that opens automatically. If you are in 386 Enhanced Mode, select **Mode | Standard**. Windows will display a message box asking if you are sure you want to change to the Standard mode settings. Click on OK.

Some of these options are the same as in the 386 Enhanced mode. The **Program Filename**, **Window Title**, **Start-up Directory**, and **Close Window on Exit** are set the same in both modes. The **Reserve Shortcut Keys** settings are initially the same, but you can make different selections in the Standard window and the changes are not transferred back to the 386 Enhanced window's Advanced Options. (The first time you select a check box—in either of the modes—the settings are transferred to the other mode. The next and subsequent times you change that check box, the setting is not transferred.) Also, some of the options are not available in Standard mode; Alt-Spacebar and Alt-Enter won't work in Standard mode anyway, because DOS applications cannot run in windows (they only run full screen).

The **Optional Parameters** are set differently in each mode, also. Entering parameters in one mode will not automatically enter them into the other mode.

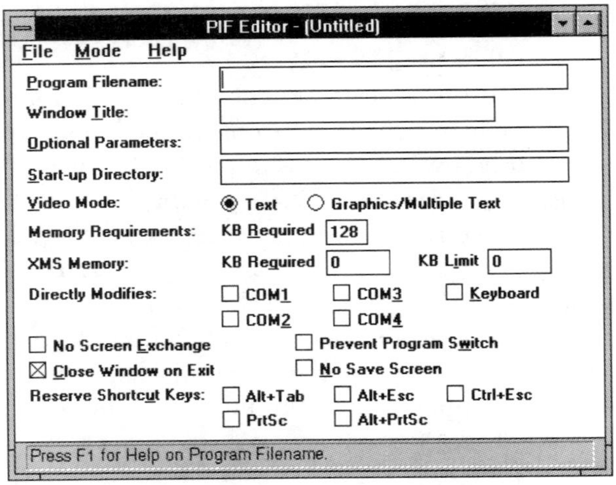

Figure 7.3 The Standard mode PIF Editor window

You may want to run an application in graphics mode in Standard, and text mode in 386 Enhanced, for instance. Let's take a look at the other options.

VIDEO MODE

The Video Mode determines how much memory should be assigned to displaying the application on the computer's monitor. These are similar to the Video Memory settings in 386 Enhanced mode. Text mode assigns enough memory to run the application in text mode. Use this if the application doesn't use graphics. Graphics/Multiple Text mode is for applications that use graphics, or have multiple text screens (such as applications that let you have more than one document open at once). In either case, the display needs more memory.

If you find an application—which you thought used Text mode—is having problems when you try to switch back to Windows, change the setting to Graphics/Multiple Text. When you assign memory to a DOS application, you are making it unavailable to Windows applications. Windows applications won't run while a DOS application is active (in Standard mode), but Windows has to keep the application's screen display in memory for when it can switch back. That's why it may have problems if you don't assign enough memory.

MEMORY REQUIREMENTS

The KB Required Memory Requirements setting is the minimum amount of memory that must be available before Windows will try to start the application. If you don't have that much, it will display a message saying it can't start. If the program needs more than the amount you assign here, Windows will still provide it, as long as it's available.

As we said earlier, this isn't the amount of memory listed in a program's documentation as the "minimum requirement." That usually includes enough to run DOS, plus some. You will normally leave this setting at 128, the default.

XMS MEMORY

The XMS Memory options let you assign Extended memory to applications that use the Lotus/Intel/Microsoft/AST eXtended Memory Specification. The **KB Required** is the amount of memory needed to start the program. Unless the application *must* have extended memory to run, leave this set to 0. Increasing the value increases the time taken to switch to and from the application. The **KB Limit** is the maximum amount of memory that Windows will let the application use. A setting of 0 prohibits the application from using XMS memory, and –1 lets it use as much as it wants. That's not usually a good idea, because it may take much more than it really needs. It may also slow down your system dramatically, so if you want your application to use extended memory, enter a maximum value rather than using –1.

DIRECTLY MODIFIES

The Directly Modifies options make Windows reserve the COM ports and keyboard for the DOS application while it is the active application. If the application uses a COM port, select it so that Windows will maintain only that application's COM-port states. If you select Keyboard, Windows allows only the application's keystrokes: you won't be able to use any Windows keystrokes. You won't be able to press Print Screen or Alt-Print Screen, for instance, to copy the screen to the Clipboard. Nor will you be able to use any of the task-switching keystrokes.

In fact if you select *any* of these check boxes—including the COM check boxes—you won't be able to switch back to Windows once the application is running. Your only option is to close the application. Selecting these options saves a little memory, though.

NO SCREEN EXCHANGE

The No Screen Exchange check box disables the Print Screen and Alt-Print Screen keystroke combinations so that you cannot copy data from the screen to the Clipboard. If you never need to use this feature, select this check box, because it saves a little memory.

PREVENT PROGRAM SWITCH

You can save a little more memory by selecting the Prevent Program Switch check box. Windows won't let you switch back to Program Manager as long as the application is running. The only way to get back is to close the application. As with the Directly Modifies options, this may be a little inconvenient—you won't have any of the benefits of running in Windows—so you probably won't want to use it often.

CLOSE WINDOW ON EXIT

The Close Window on Exit option is similar to that in 386 Enhanced mode. In fact the setting is transferred, so selecting it in one mode changes it in the other. As we mentioned earlier, clearing this option is useful for batch files and applications that run and then close themselves. There are some important differences, though. First, DOS applications do not run in windows in Standard mode, they only run full screen. With this check box cleared, if the application is running in Text mode when you exit the application (or when the application closes itself), you will see a small message—Press Any Key To Exit—at the bottom of your screen. If it is in Graphics mode you won't see the sign, but you can still press a key to clear the window.

NO SAVE SCREEN

You can save memory and speed up switching between applications by selecting the No Save Screen check box. Windows won't save the application's display. Unfortunately you won't be able to use this very often. You should use this only if the application can save its own display, or if it has a convenient redraw command so you can re-display the screen when you return. Otherwise you are likely to be faced by a blank screen when you switch back to the application.

Running Your Applications

You can start a DOS application in the same way you start a Windows application. Remember that even if you haven't named a PIF in an icon's Program Item Properties dialog box, Windows will look for one. First it will check the same directory as the program file, and if it can't find it there it looks in the current directory, WINDOWS directory, SYSTEM directory, and then all the directories listed in the DOS PATH statement (in your AUTOEXEC.BAT file). If it can't find a PIF with the same name as the executable program file, then Windows uses the default PIF settings.

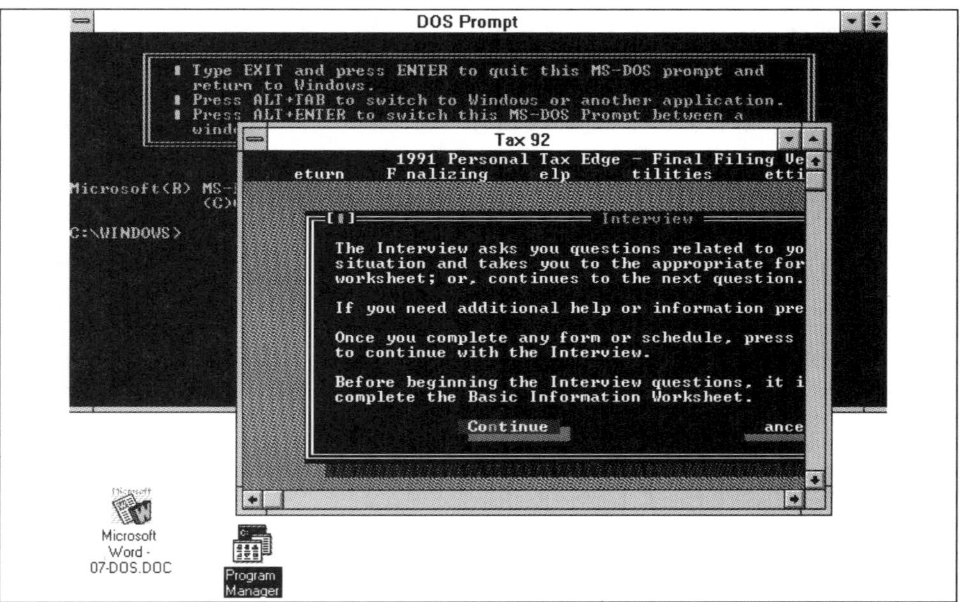

Figure 7.4 DOS applications running in windows

For this reason alone you should probably create a PIF file for each application, place it in the same directory as the executable file, and specifically name it in the Program Item Properties dialog box. That way you will always be sure that Windows is using the correct PIF.

When you start a DOS application, it will either run full screen or in a window. A full screen application looks just as it would in DOS. You won't see any Windows components: no borders, scroll bars, minimize and maximize buttons, and so on. When running in a window, though, the application does have these components (see Figure 7.4). As you've already seen, if you are running in 386 Enhanced mode, the PIF determines whether the application will be full screen or in a window (by default it's full screen). In Standard mode, DOS applications run only full screen.

By the way, you can **minimize** DOS applications in two ways. If the application is full screen, simply swap to another application. Windows automatically places the icon on the desktop at the bottom of your screen. If the application is running in a window, click on the minimize button or select Control|Minimize.

Running in 386 Enhanced Mode

The best mode for running DOS applications is 386 Enhanced mode. This mode lets you run DOS applications in the background if you wish, and makes the transfer of data between DOS and Windows applications—or between two DOS applications—much easier. It also allows you more flexibility in modifying the way in which each DOS application runs, by setting up the PIF file before you begin and by changing settings while running the program. It also lets you run applications that require expanded memory, even if your computer doesn't have expanded memory—something Standard mode can't do.

Take a look at the DOS windows in Figure 7.4. There are some differences, of course, between these windows and ones used by a Windows application. First, of course, there's no menu bar, although there is a Control menu. Notice also that the DOS Prompt window is "maximized." (You can tell because the maximize button has *two* arrows on it, meaning it will *restore* the window.) DOS windows don't necessarily fill the screen when maximized. Their maximized size depends on the font size you are using, as we shall see in a moment. The DOS Prompt window has a border still visible at the bottom of the window, but it can't be used, even to reduce the size of the window, until you restore the window.

To change from a full screen to a window, press **Alt-Enter**. You can press Alt-Enter to change back to full screen, also, or use the **Control | Settings** command, which we will get to in a moment. With the application running in a window, you can open the Control menu. You may find that your mouse won't work in a window—we'll explain why in a moment—but it should still be able to open the control menu. If it can't, press **Alt-Spacebar** to do so.

The DOS window's Control menu has all the usual options for moving, sizing, and switching to another application. It has three more at the bottom: Edit (for copying, pasting, and scrolling), Settings (for modifying the way the program runs in Windows), and Fonts (for selecting a font size).

You will learn about cutting and pasting in Chapter 27, but you need to know about the **Control | Edit | Scroll** command. When you select this command you can use the arrow keys to scroll through the DOS window. When you have finished scrolling, press **Enter**, and you can continue using the program. (The title bar changes to say "Scroll *application name*," to remind you that you are in scroll mode.) While Scroll is turned on you won't be able to change to full screen. If you have a mouse, use the scroll bars instead—it's much quicker.

CHANGING THE SETTINGS

Select **Control | Settings** to see the dialog box shown in Figure 7.5. You have already seen most of the options in this dialog box. The **Display Options** let you change between **Window** and **Full Screen**. You will have to use these if you disabled the Alt-Enter shortcut combination.

The **Tasking Options** are the same as the Execution settings in the PIF file; **Exclusive** suspends other applications while this one is the active one, *except* that

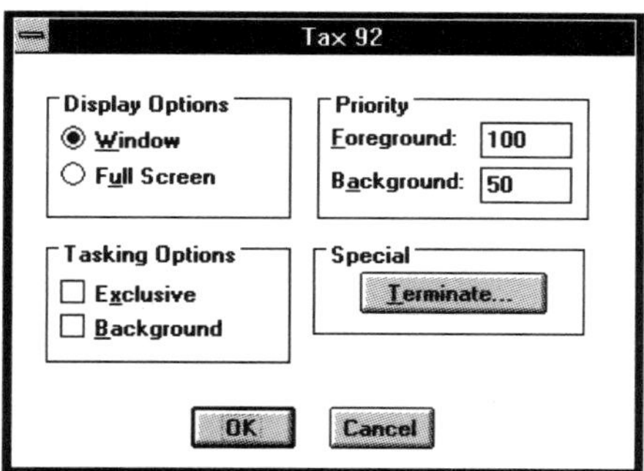

Figure 7.5 The Settings dialog box

Windows applications will continue running if this one is in a window, rather than full screen. Use this option to speed up the application. **Background** means that the application will continue processing even when it is not the active application. Use this option when you want to let the application continue a procedure—printing a document, for instance, or downloading a file from another computer—while you do something else.

These settings are useful because they let you temporarily modify a setting. You may not want an application to normally run in the background, but now and again you may wish to print a file while you work in another application, so you can use the Settings box to change it while you do so.

The **Priority** text boxes are the same as those at the top of the PIF Editor's Advanced Options dialog box. **Foreground** determines the amount of processing time given to the application when it is the active one. Increase the number to speed it up. If the application is running as Exclusive in full screen, this has no effect, because it's going to get all the resources anyway.

Increase the **Background** setting to improve the application's performance while another one is active. For this to work the Background Tasking Option must be selected, and you can't be working in an application that has a Tasking Option set to Exclusive.

All these settings are temporary. The next time you open the application Windows will use the settings in the PIF file, so if you want to use these settings in the future change them using the PIF Editor.

The last option in this dialog box is the **Terminate** button. This is a last resort for closing an application, if the program has "locked up," for instance. It's not the ideal way to close an application, because you may lose data. If even the application's Control menu has locked up, you will have to close the application by pressing **Ctrl-Alt-Del**.

Microsoft recommends that after using the Terminate option you close Windows and reboot your computer, in case DOS has become unstable.

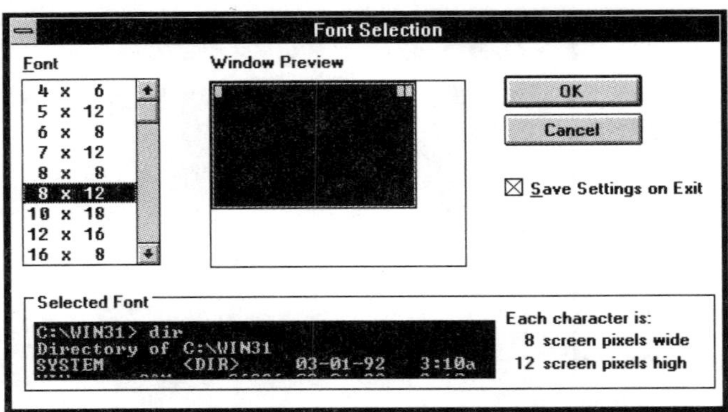

Figure 7.6 The Font Selection dialog box

CHANGING FONT SIZES

You can change the font size used in a DOS window. You may want to do so to make the text more legible, to fit more on the screen, or to change the DOS window's size (because modifying the font changes the maximum size of the window).

Select **Control | Fonts** to see the dialog box shown in Figure 7.6. This box is not the same as the Font dialog boxes you will see in Windows applications. It limits you to a few specific font sizes, measured in pixels. For instance, 8 x 12 means 8 pixels wide and 12 high. The **Selected Font** area at the bottom of the dialog box shows you what the selected font looks like. The **Window Preview** area shows you the effect of the font on the window's size. The font size affects the actual size of the maximized window. As you select a size from the **Font** list box, the Window Preview changes to show you how much of the screen will be covered when the window is maximized. Notice that the sample window has borders; if a border isn't visible, part of the window is off the screen, so you will have to scroll to reach it.

Notice that the **Save Settings on Exit** check box is automatically selected. This makes Windows automatically save these settings—for this specific application—in a file named DOSAPP.INI. The next time you open the application it will use the same font, so you can set up each DOS application differently. If you only want to change the window temporarily, make sure this check box is not selected.

CLOSING DOS APPLICATIONS IN 386 ENHANCED MODE

When you are ready to close a DOS application, you should use the application's own Close or Exit command. This makes sure that it is closed properly and you don't lose any data. Generally, if you try to close a DOS application using any other method, Windows tells you to close the application first. However, as you learned earlier, you can select the **Allow Close When Active** check box in the PIF

Editor's Advanced Options dialog box to let you close the DOS application using Windows commands.

You will be able to double-click on the Control menu, select **Control | Close**, or open the Task List dialog box, select the DOS application, and click on **End Task**. And if you close Windows, you will be able to close the DOS application from a dialog box—without Allow Close When Active selected Windows would tell you to go to the application and close it properly first. You won't be able to use the Alt-F4 shortcut that can be used with Windows applications, however.

Running in Standard Mode

Running DOS applications in Standard mode is similar to running them in 386 Enhanced mode, with a few important exceptions. First, you can run a DOS application only full screen—you can't use a window, so you can't get to the Control menu, either.

Also, while you obviously can't double-click on the Control menu to quit the application, you *can* close it by selecting the application name in the Task List dialog box and clicking on End Task. You can also close it by opening the Control menu while the application is minimized and selecting Close, or even by selecting the icon and pressing Alt-F4. You can only use these methods in 386 Enhanced mode if you specifically set the PIF file to allow it.

However, before you close Windows you must close the DOS application; unlike 386 Enhanced mode the Standard won't let you just click on OK in a dialog box to close the application.

There are a few other things you must know about Standard mode. First, if your program needs expanded memory and you have a 286 computer, you must have an expanded memory board in the computer—Windows can't simulate expanded memory in this mode. However, if you have a 386 or 486, EMM386 will let you simulate expanded memory in Standard mode (in 386 Enhanced mode Windows can simulate expanded memory automatically). See Appendix A for more information.

Also, Standard mode uses *application swapfiles*. These are temporary files that store one application's information when you swap to another application. Obviously you must have enough room on your hard drive to store these files. If you don't, you will see "out of memory" messages, and you won't be able to run any more DOS applications.

Mouse Problems

You won't always be able to use your mouse in a DOS application. There are two main problems (assuming that the mouse is running in Windows applications):

The mouse may not work in DOS applications regardless of whether they are running full screen or in a window, or it may work in full screen but not in a window.

First, you must make sure that a mouse driver was loaded in DOS before opening Windows. This is normally done with a command in the CONFIG.SYS or AUTOEXEC.BAT command. In fact, if you are having problems you should exit Windows and make sure that the mouse works in DOS applications running outside Windows. Experiment with the DOS 5.0 EDIT program, for instance. If it doesn't work, check your mouse's documentation and get it running. You may also have a hardware problem or IRQ (Interrupt Request line) conflict. Try to resolve these problems in DOS, using your mouse's documentation and technical support.

Once the mouse is running outside Windows, it should also run in a full-screen DOS application running in Windows. If it doesn't, you may be running an incompatible TSR (Terminate and Stay Resident) or "pop-up" program from your AUTOEXEC.BAT file. Try removing such programs.

Once you have the mouse running in a full-screen application, there's still a good chance it won't run in a DOS window. That's because the driver isn't compatible with Windows 3.1. Windows 3.0 didn't let you use a mouse in a DOS window, and 3.1 needs a special driver to do so. If you use a Microsoft Mouse, you need version 8.2, which is included on the Windows disks. You can expand MOUSE.SYS and MOUSE.COM using the procedure described in Chapter 1. For other mouse drivers, contact your manufacturer. Also, read the README.WRI file in the WINDOWS directory for more information.

If the mouse runs in a full-screen DOS application, and you know you have an updated mouse driver, there's still one more reason it may not run in a window; your display adapter may not allow it. In particular a 16-color, 800 x 600 driver may not work. Try the new Windows 3.1 Super VGA driver instead. Load a new driver using Windows Setup (double-click on the Windows Setup icon in the Main program group). If you can't find a suitable driver, you may need to contact your display's manufacturer.

Using the DOS Prompt

You can open a DOS prompt—in a window or full screen—to do just about anything you want. You can start a program directly from the DOS prompt, run batch files, carry out various DOS commands, and so on.

DOS Prompt

To open DOS, double-click on the DOS Prompt icon in the Main program group. Or Select **File | Run** in Program Manager and run **DOSPRMPT**. This will run the DOSPRMPT.PIF file, which in turn calls the DOS COMMAND.COM executable file. (If you upgraded from Windows 3.0, 3.1 may not run DOSPRMPT.PIF, because Windows 3.0 used COMMAND.COM directly. Open the Program Item Properties dialog box and change the Command Line to DOSPRMPT.PIF.)

You can run the DOS prompt like any other application. If you are running in 386 Enhanced mode you can run it in a window, for instance, and you may change the font used. You can modify the DOSPRMPT.PIF file in any way you wish. When you are ready to close the DOS prompt, type **EXIT** and press **Enter**.

Warning Do not use the following commands from the DOS prompt: **CHKDSK** with the **/F** switch, **UNDELETE**, and **CHCP**. Also, don't run disk "optimization" or "defragmentation" programs. You must quit Windows before using any of these.

Each DOS window you run is separate from the others. It is running on a "virtual" machine. For instance, if you use the DOS SET command in one DOS window, it has no effect on other DOS windows, or on DOS itself. Or if you change the current directory in one window, the others remain unchanged.

Tip Place `DOSPromptExitInstruc=Off` in the [386Enh] section of SYSTEM.INI to remove the instructions box at the top of the DOS Prompt window. See Appendix B.

Memory-Resident Programs

A memory resident program is one that remains in your computer's memory even though you can't see it on your screen. Also known as TSRs (Terminate and Stay Resident), such programs include device drivers, network drivers, and "pop-up" programs (which remain in memory waiting for you to "call" them).

If you want a memory-resident program to be available to Windows in general, you must load it before you open Windows. Then it is available to all Windows programs, and each time you open a DOS application it is available to that program also. For instance, if you are running on a network, you must start the network shell before starting Windows.

The problem with loading memory-resident programs before Windows is that you are using up valuable memory, in many cases for programs you won't use. If you only have one or two applications that need a memory-resident program, don't load it until *after* you have loaded Windows. Use a batch file that loads the memory-resident program and then loads the application you want to run. The memory-resident program will be available only to that one DOS application, no others. (There's also a way to load memory-resident programs immediately before loading Windows so they are available to Windows applications only—WIN-START.BAT. See Appendix A for more information.)

Windows has a special way to handle "pop-up" programs. These are programs that remain in memory until you need them. For instance, you might have a DOS calculator or envelope addresser that sits waiting while you work in another application. When you are ready to make a calculation or print an envelope, you press the special "hot-keys" and the program pops-up. You can then use the program and close it again, so it sits waiting until the next time you need it.

When you load a pop-up program—by double-clicking on it in File Manager, using the File | Run command, or by using an icon you have created for it—Windows loads a special utility to manage it. You can then activate the pop-up by pressing the appropriate hot keys. Simply leave the application in the window and jump back to it when you need it. You won't actually pop it up, you will simply swap to it using the normal Windows keystrokes for swapping applications. For instance, Figure 7.7 shows APPBK, a pop-up appointment book.

When you are ready to close the application, remove the pop-up from the screen as you would normally (often by pressing **Esc**), then press **Ctrl-C** and Windows closes the application's window.

Some pop-up programs may use Windows' keyboard shortcuts. If so, create a PIF file and reserve the shortcut keys for use by the pop-up. Or select another combination to run the pop-up, if it lets you do so.

There may be cases when you want an application and a pop-up to run in the same window. For instance, you may want to run a screen-snapshot program along with an application so you can take snapshots of the application's screens. Don't load the memory-resident snapshot program by itself. Once it's loaded, Windows

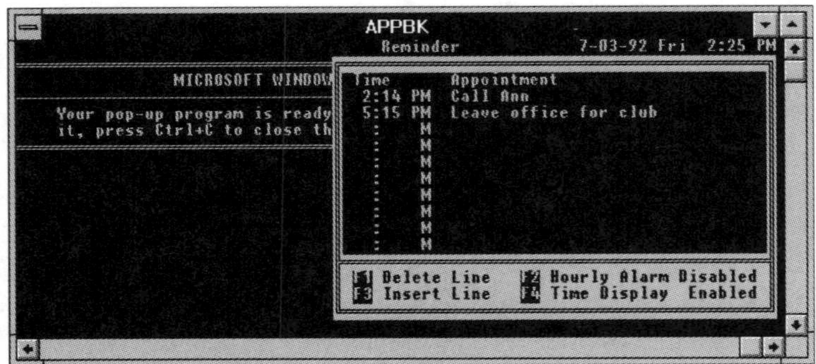

Figure 7.7 The pop-up utility APPBK running in a window

won't let you load another program. Instead, load the DOS prompt using the DOS Prompt icon. *Then* load the memory-resident snapshot program and load the application you want to work with.

You can also create a batch file to do the same thing, loading the pop-up first and the application second. For instance, create a batch file called NEWS.BAT with these lines:

```
c:\pop\appbk.exe
c:\newspapr\news_db.exe
```

When you run this batch file—from an icon, File Manager, or whatever—Windows will load the pop-up called APPBK and then load the program called NEWS_DB.EXE. You can then run the pop-up at any time by pressing the appropriate hot keys: Alt-R, for instance. You can use Notepad to create batch files.

▼ ***Note*** Some memory-resident programs won't run very well in a virtual DOS machine. You may need to use the LocalTSRs= command in the [NonWindowsApp] section of SYSTEM.INI to get them to run.

Problems Running a DOS Application

If you can't get a DOS application to run, here are a few things to try, one at a time.

1. If you get "out of memory messages," try the following:
   a. Close other applications.
   b. Run applications full screen instead of in a window.
   c. Turn off Background Execution in other application's PIFs or Background Priority in their Settings dialog boxes (from the Control menu).
   d. Turn off the desktop's pattern and wallpaper (see Chapter 8).
   e. Clear the Clipboard (see Chapter 27).
   f. Free disk space if you don't have much free (Windows may not have enough room for the temporary files).
2. If the application won't start, try selecting High Graphics Video Memory, and Retain Video Memory in the Advanced Options; try a higher value in the Memory Requirements KB Desired; try turning off the Detect Idle Time check box in the Advanced Options check box.
3. If you have problems switching back to a DOS program, try selecting one of the Monitor Ports options in the Advanced Options dialog box. Or increase

the memory assigned with the Video Mode (Standard mode) or Video Memory options.

4. If you can't switch from the application back to Windows in Standard mode, increase the memory assigned with the Video Mode options.
5. If Windows switches back to a DOS application very slowly, turn off the Monitor Ports options in the Advanced Options dialog box.
6. If the text is garbled in the DOS application, or if the application won't run at all, try turning off Emulate Text Mode in the Advanced Options dialog box.
7. If—in 386 Enhanced mode—the application doesn't run well in graphics mode in a window, run it in text mode.
8. If, when you use the application's mode commands to change from text to graphics mode, the screen disappears or becomes distorted in some way, try selecting a higher Video Memory option in the PIF Editor window and Retain Video Memory in the Advanced Options dialog box.
9. If you try to run a graphics program in a window and get a message saying you can't run the application "while another high resolution application is running full screen," the window may be referring to Windows itself. That is, you may get the message even if there are no other DOS applications running. Try assigning more memory. Also, check to see if you are using version 7.04 of the Microsoft Mouse driver MOUSE.COM. If so, add `/Y` after MOUSE.COM in your AUTOEXEC.BAT or CONFIG.SYS file. (To see what version you have, type **MOUSE.COM** and press **Enter** at the DOS prompt.)
10. If running an application that uses EMS or XMS memory, make sure it's not hogging all the memory. Set the limits in the PIF file to 0 or a low number.

▼ ***Note*** The Control Panel's 386 Enhanced dialog box contains settings that affect the way in which DOS applications run. See Chapter 8 for more information.

Part 2

Managing Windows

8

Customizing Windows: The Control Panel

The Control Panel is an apt name for the application that controls the way Windows functions. Using the Control Panel you can modify the colors used on the desktop or in applications; add and remove fonts; configure printers, communications ports, the mouse, and your keyboard; adjust date, time, currency, and number formats; change the time and date; add "wallpaper" to your desktop and turn on an automatic screen saver; modify the way 386 Enhanced mode works; configure networks; and set up multimedia devices.

Starting Control Panel

Start Control Panel by clicking on the Control Panel icon in the Main program group. Or select **File | Run** and run **CONTROL**. Figure 8.1 shows the Control Panel. Your Control Panel may look slightly different; the MIDI Mapper and Network icons only appear if you installed the appropriate driver, and the 386 Enhanced icon only appears if you are running Windows on a 386 with at least 2 MB of memory. In some rare cases other icons may be added to the Control Panel by the Windows applications you install.

Double-clicking on an icon displays a dialog box that lets you change related settings. For instance, if you want to change the color of a window's work area, select the Color icon. To set up a printer select the Printers icon. These icons are duplicated in the **Settings** menu. That is, for each icon, there is a corresponding menu option. Control Panel's Exit option is also in this menu.

You may also open a dialog box by pressing the **arrow** keys to move to an icon and then pressing **Enter**. Notice also that the message bar at the bottom of the Control Panel "window" describes the function of the selected icon. You can close any of the dialog boxes by pressing **Esc** or using the Control Menu.

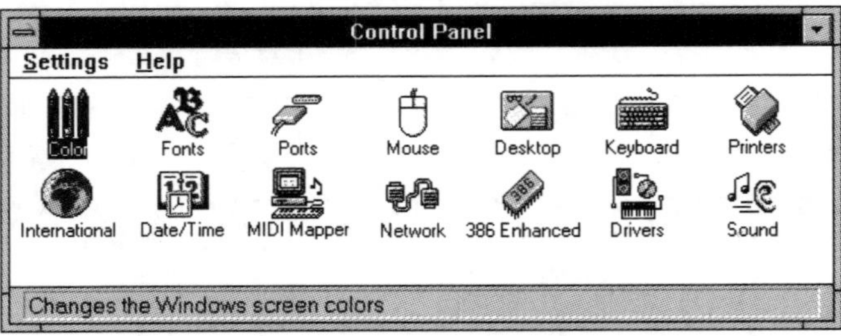

Figure 8.1 The Control Panel

▼ ***Note*** We are not going to cover all these settings in this chapter. For information on Printers, see Chapter 11; and for MIDI Mapper see Chapter 26.

Customizing Colors

Almost any color you can see on your screen can be modified using the Color dialog box. The menus, text, workspaces, scroll bars, dialog boxes, desktop—all these items and several more can be modified. Perhaps, for instance, you would like to change your word processor to a dark background and light text. Maybe you are doing "snapshots" of a program you are documenting and want to modify the colors to get closer to a black-and-white format. Or maybe you simply want to jazz up your screen a bit.

The Color dialog box (shown in Figure 8.2 as it appears after you have clicked on the Color Palette button) lets you choose from dozens of predefined color schemes or create your own.

Changing Screen Elements

When you select a scheme from the **Color Schemes** drop-down list box the example screen shows the effects. Most of these schemes are just for "fun," but some have a specific purpose. The three **LCD** schemes are intended for use with LCD displays: Try all three to see which works best. You may have to adjust a switch on your LCD screen to allow the screen to use the colors. The **Plasma Power Saver** scheme is intended for plasma displays, and saves power by using dark colors.

If you don't like any of the schemes, you can create your own. Click on the **Color Palette** button to open the right side of the dialog box. The palette lets you assign a specific color to a specific element listed in the **Screen Element** drop-

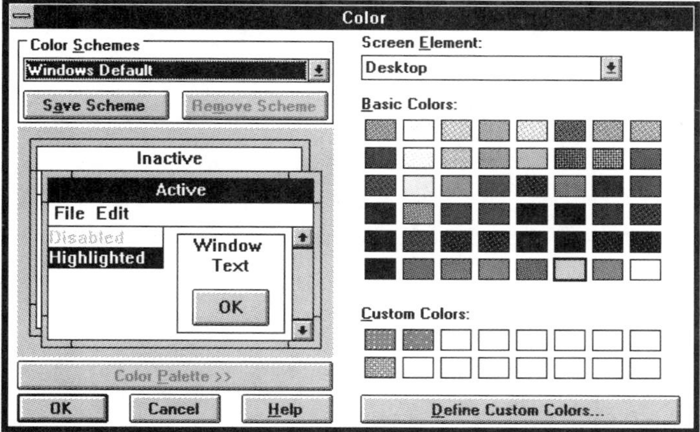

Figure 8.2 The Color dialog box after clicking on the Color Palette button

down list box. Select the element then click on the color in the **Basic Colors** palette. The sample screen will change to show you the effect of your selection.

Tip Instead of selecting an element from the drop-down list box, click on the element in the *sample screen*.

These are the elements you can modify:

Desktop The desktop area on which all windows and icons sit. If you are using a pattern or "wallpaper," that color will not be used.

Application Workspace The background of dialog boxes and some windows. Not necessarily the area in which you work.

Window Background The window background and some text boxes and drop-down list boxes. For instance, you could change the color of a word processor's background with this option. Some applications won't let you change their background colors.

Window Text The text in the work area (not menus, list boxes, and so on) and the color of the dots in the desktop pattern (if used). Use this option to change the color of text in a word processor.

Menu Bar	The window's menu bar.
Menu Text	The text in a menu bar.
Active Title Bar	The title bar in the active window.
Inactive Title Bar	The title bars in all inactive windows.
Active Title Bar Text	The text in the active title bar.
Inactive Title Bar Text	The text in the inactive title bars.
Active Border	The active window's border.
Inactive Border	The inactive windows' borders.
Window Frame	A thin line around each border.
Scroll Bars	The scroll bars in windows and dialog boxes.
Button Face	The face of a button, scroll box, down arrow in drop-down list boxes, and some status bars, tool bars, and ruler bars.
Button Shadow	The shadow used by the components colored with the Button Face choice.
Button Text	The text used by the components colored with the Button Face choice.
Button Highlight	The highlight used by a button when selected, generally a line along the top and left sides of the button. This includes some other components colored with the Button Face choice.
Disabled Text	Text on an inactive item, such as an inactive button or menu option.
Highlight	The highlight in a menu or list box.
Highlighted Text	The highlighted text in a menu or list box.

Some of these elements can only use solid colors—generally the "thin" elements such as text and the Window Frame, but also the Window Background. If you select a mixed color, Windows will select the nearest solid color, the one that your display can produce. Most displays are fairly limited. Standard VGA uses only 16 solid colors, for instance. Some displays can use 20, 256, or even several million. If you have only 16 solid colors, you can still create colors by a process called *dithering*. Windows mixes pixels of two or more colors together, simulating another color. Depending on your display's dot pitch and the degree of mixing required, dithered colors range from appearing almost solid to very grainy, as you can see by the palette in the Color dialog box. There are 48 colors in this palette, but it may be difficult to decide which are the 16 solid ones.

Tip Use solid colors to speed Windows screen redraws. Also, making the Active and Inactive Borders the same color may speed up Windows.

Creating Custom Colors

You can create up to 16 new colors. Click on one of the colors in the palette, then click on the **Define Custom Colors** button to see the Custom Color Selector dialog box (see Figure 8.3). The **Color | Solid** box will show the color you selected.

Notice the small cross hairs (known as the **color refiner cursor**) inside the color box. You can drag this cursor around the box to select the color you want. As you move it the color is displayed in the left side of the **Color | Solid** box. The right side of this box shows the nearest solid color. Remember that some screen elements can't use a dithered color. The Solid color is the one that Windows will apply to the element if you select the dithered color.

If you double-click on the right side of the Color | Solid box, or press **Alt-O**, the color refiner cursor moves to the solid color and the entire Color | Solid box fills with the solid color. Notice the vertical luminosity bar on the right side of the dialog box and the **small triangle** pointing at the bar. Drag this triangle up and down the bar to adjust the amount of the three primary colors mixed together. If you move the triangle to the top of the bar the settings in the **Red**, **Green**, and **Blue** incrementer boxes are set to 255, producing white (an equal mixture of the three primary colors). Move the triangle to the bottom to set each number to 0, providing black (an absence of color). With all three colors set to 255 or 0, it

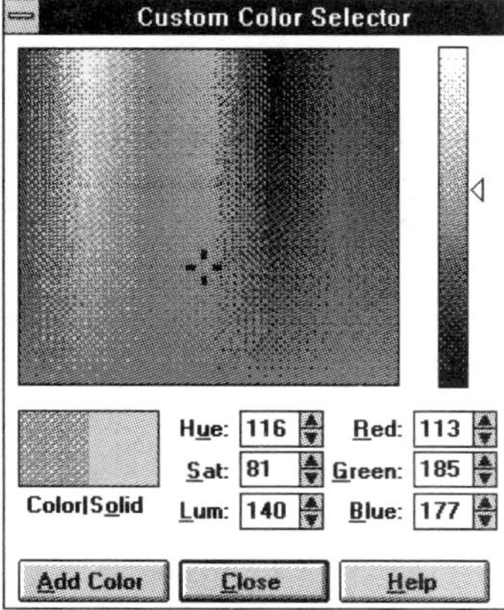

Figure 8.3 The Custom Color Selector

doesn't matter what you do with the color refiner cursor. It will have no effect: The color remains white or black. You can also adjust the numbers directly, using the incrementer arrows or by simply typing a number.

The **Lum** incrementer bar duplicates the action of the small triangle pointing at the luminosity bar. When the triangle is at the top the luminosity value is 240, at the bottom it is 0. The **Hue** and **Sat** (Saturation) incrementer duplicate the action of the color refiner cursor. Adjusting hue is the same as moving the cursor horizontally, and adjusting saturation is the same as moving it vertically.

As you can see, all these components interact. You will probably use the color refiner cursor and luminosity triangle and ignore the incrementer boxes. Move the triangle up and down to increase and decrease the lightness, and move the cursor around to modify the color. When you've got a color you want, click on **Add Color**. The color will appear in one of the **Custom Color** boxes at the bottom of the Color dialog box.

You can leave the Custom Color Selector open while you work in the Color dialog box—just move it out of the way. If you want to see the settings for a color in the Color dialog box palette, press and hold **Ctrl** and **click** on the color, then return to the Custom Color Selector box.

You can replace one of the Custom Colors by clicking on the color in the Color dialog box, and then clicking on Add Color in the Custom Color Selector. (You cannot replace any of the Basic Colors.) Be careful when you click on the Add Color button. The color will be placed in the Custom Colors box you clicked on *or* the one immediately after the last one you changed. So make sure you don't accidentally copy over a color you wanted to keep.

When you have finished, click on the Custom Color Selector's Close button. You can now apply the custom colors to various screen elements. The Custom Colors you add will be saved as soon as you click on the OK button.

Saving New Color Schemes

If you create a new color scheme, click on the **Save Scheme** button. Type a name in the dialog box that appears—you can include spaces—and click on the OK button. The name will appear in the Color Schemes drop-down list box. You don't have to give a color scheme a name: You can simply close the dialog box, and Windows uses the currently selected colors; but if you later select another scheme, you will not be able to return. You can also remove a scheme. Select it and click on the **Remove Schemes** button, then click on Yes in the confirmation dialog box. You can remove any of the color schemes except Windows Default.

Finally, click on the Color dialog box OK button to close it. The Windows components will change to the selected colors.

Working with Fonts

You can use the Fonts dialog box (shown in Figure 8.4) to add and remove Windows fonts. A font or typeface is a style of characters. For instance, the TrueType font named Arial is a "sans serif" font; that is, it doesn't have *serifs*, the small extensions at the end of letters. (Times New Roman is an example of a *serif* font, a font that *does* have serifs.) Fonts are discussed in more detail in Chapter 11.

You can buy other Windows fonts. You may get many other TrueType fonts "bundled" with other applications or buy the fonts themselves. You may also add Windows-compatible fonts through other methods. For instance, you can add Type 1 PostScript fonts using Adobe Type Manager. The Control Panel's Fonts dialog box is used to load only TrueType and Windows vector and raster fonts.

The **Installed Fonts** list box contains all the Windows fonts that are currently loaded. If you click on one of the fonts you can see what the font looks like in the **Sample** list box. You have both scalable and nonscalable fonts. You can use a scalable font in any size you wish; if you select a scalable font the Sample box only shows one version of it. If you select a nonscalable font, the Sample box will show all the different versions. For instance, in Figure 8.4 we have selected MS Sans Serif, which may be used only in the specified point sizes (8, 10, 12, 14, 18, and 24 points). Use the scroll bar to move through all of them.

Notice that under the Sample box a message tells you the type of font you have selected. In Figure 8.4 we can see that the MS Sans Serif is a "screen or plotter font." You can view this on the screen, or print it on a plotter, but it may not print on a printer. If you try to do so Windows will have to substitute another font, one that *can* be printed, and you may not like the result. (It probably will be able to

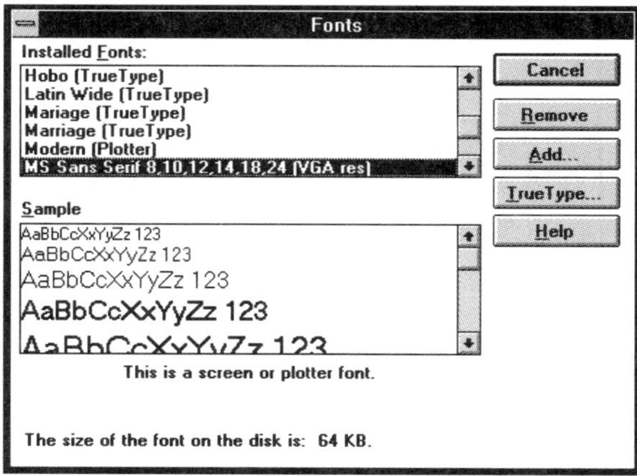

Figure 8.4 The Fonts dialog box

print on a dot-matrix printer.) The TrueType fonts can be printed on any Windows-compatible printer.

Finally, at the bottom of the dialog box you can see how much disk space the font is taking up. This can be useful if you are cleaning your hard disk and deciding on what you can delete to make more room.

TrueType Options

TrueType fonts have a number of advantages. Most important, they generally look the same on the screen as when printed, unlike printer fonts, and they look the same on different devices (allowing for the different resolutions and print quality of the various devices). They are also scalable, so you can print any size you want—with nonscalable fonts you can only print specific sizes. TrueType fonts can be used on the Macintosh, so documents created with Word for Windows, for instance, should look the same if you load them into Word on the Macintosh.

Click on the **TrueType** button to see the dialog box shown in Figure 8.5. You can deselect **Enable TrueType Fonts** to turn off TrueType fonts—they won't be available to any of your applications (by default TrueType fonts are enabled). If they are enabled, you can select the **Show Only TrueType Fonts in Applications** check box to make sure that the only fonts your Windows applications will display are TrueType. Not only will this remove the other fonts that came with Windows, but it will disable Type 1 PostScript fonts that were loaded with Adobe Type Manager and your printer's cartridge, or soft fonts. If you have a good set of TrueType fonts, you may want to disable all the others so you don't run into problems working with incompatible fonts.

Adding and Removing Fonts

You can install screen and TrueType fonts using the Fonts dialog box. You may have to install screen fonts if you have installed new printer or soft fonts. A screen font is simply a font that displays text that matches what the associated printer font will print.

Click on the **Add** button to see the Add Fonts dialog box (Figure 8.6). Select the directory in which the fonts are loaded. If you are loading them directly from a

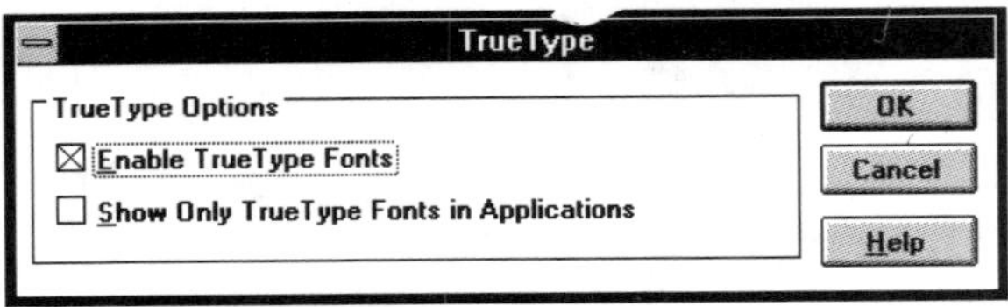

Figure 8.5 The TrueType dialog box

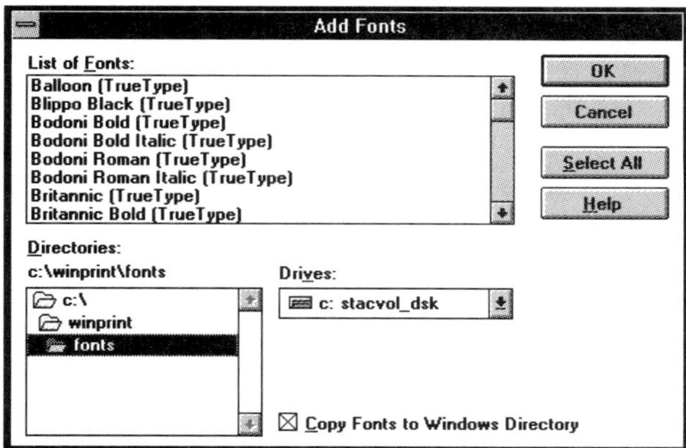

Figure 8.6 The Add Fonts dialog box

floppy disk, select the disk drive from the Drives drop-down list box. The Add Fonts dialog box automatically reads the directory, looking for font files that it recognizes. It won't, for example, recognize Type 1 PostScript files, but it will recognize fonts with the .FON or .FOT extension.

Select the fonts you want to load. If you want all of them, click on **Select All**. Otherwise just click on each one while holding the **Ctrl** key, or click on one, hold **Shift**, move to another and click again to select both fonts and all those in the list between the two. You may also point to the list, hold the mouse button down, and drag the pointer across the fonts. If you are using the keyboard you can select only a contiguous group by pressing **Shift** while you press the **Down Arrow**.

If you want to copy the font files from the directory to the WINDOW\SYSTEM directory (which you will if you are loading from floppy disks or a network drive), make sure the **Copy Fonts to Windows Directory** check box is selected. If the fonts are in another directory on your hard disk, you can deselect this option to save disk space. When you click on OK, Windows adds the fonts and enters the appropriate information into the WIN.INI file.

Fonts are strangely addictive. In the United States millions of dollars worth of fonts are bought on a whim: It's easy to build a disk-full of fonts you rarely use. Most people need only a small number of fonts, and you may eventually realize that you have far more than you need. Rather than leaving them where they are, you should remove them to free up memory (fonts can be real memory hogs).

In the Fonts dialog box, select the ones you want to remove and click on **Remove**. Windows displays a dialog box naming the first font and asking you to confirm that you want to delete it. Before doing so you can click on the **Delete Font File From Disk** check box if you wish. This will do exactly what it says, remove the actual font file from your hard disk. If, when you installed the font, you used the Copy Fonts to Windows Directory option, deleting the font files will simply delete the version in the SYSTEM directory. If the font originally came from another directory on your hard drive, it will still be there. On the other hand, if you didn't copy the font from its original directory, you will be deleting the original.

Decide, then, if you want to delete the file. If you have the font stored on another disk somewhere and are short of disk space, you may want to do so. You can then click on **Yes** to delete the first font, or click on **Yes to All** to delete all the fonts you selected without seeing the confirmation box for each one.

▼ ***Note*** Do not delete the MS Sans Serif font. This is used for dialog box and windows fonts, and Windows will have to substitute another, less legible, font if you remove it.

Configuring Serial Communications Ports

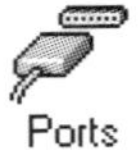

Most computers have two serial communications ports, COM1 and COM2. These are actual connectors on the back of the computer to which you can attach a variety of devices: printers, modems, faxes, mice, and so on. In fact COM1 is usually connected to a mouse.

Your computer may also have two other serial ports, COM3 and COM4, especially if you have an internal fax or modem. The Ports dialog box, shown in Figure 8.7, lets you select which port you want to configure. Select a port and click on the **Settings** button (or double-click on the port) to see the Settings dialog box (shown in Figure 8.8), which lets you adjust the settings for the selected port.

Before you adjust the settings, you will have to refer to the documentation that comes with the device you have connected to the COM port. You don't need to adjust these settings for a port with a mouse connected to it, nor for a modem (you will adjust the settings in your communications program—such as Windows Terminal—according to the system you are connecting to.) You probably only need to

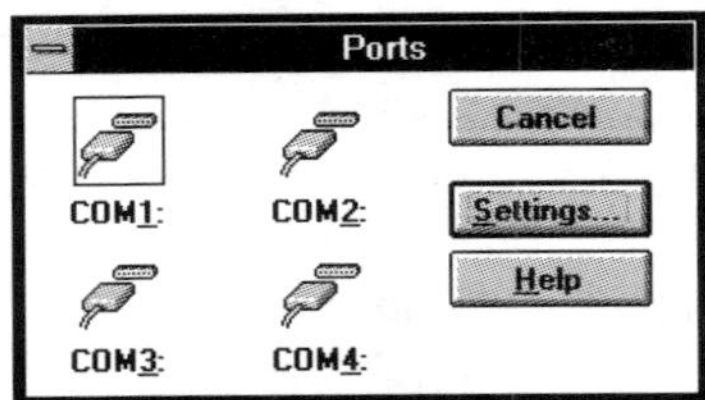

Figure 8.7 The Ports dialog box

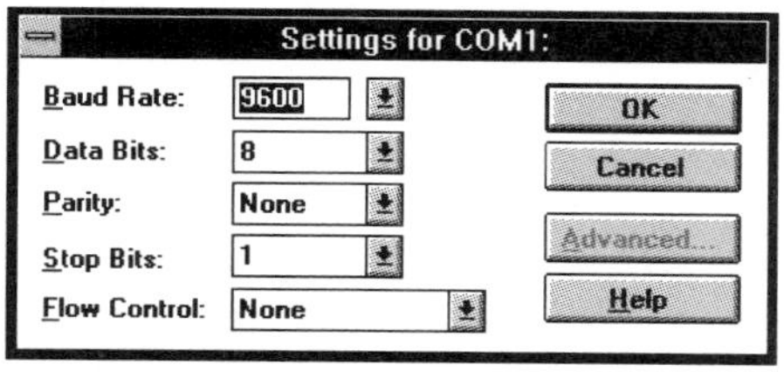

Figure 8.8 The Settings dialog box

adjust these settings if you have a serial printer or other device connected to a COM port. Select the following information from the drop-down list boxes:

Baud Rate The speed at which the device transmits data.

Data Bits The number of bits of data in each byte, generally 7 or 8.

Parity The type of parity check used. A parity check uses the eighth bit in a packet to carry out simple error checking, to confirm that the character was received correctly. (The eighth bit is mathematically related to the first 7 bits. If that relationship is no longer apparent when they arrive at your computer, the communications program knows there has been an error.) If you are using 8 data bits, you must use a Parity of None.

Stop Bits The amount of time between transmitted characters.

Flow Control Flow control is used to control data transfers between computers; it refers to the method used to ensure that data is transmitted only when the other computer is capable of receiving it. The Xon/Xoff method uses a software signal: If either computer is receiving data faster than it can handle it, it sends a message stopping the transmission. When it has caught up it sends another message to continue. The Xon/Xoff method is the most common. In rare cases you may use a Hardware method or None.

These settings are overridden by the settings in a communications program. For this reason you don't need to set up a modem in the Ports dialog box. You will do so when you build a settings file in Windows Terminal. See Chapter 14 for more information.

If you are using more than two COM ports, you may need to adjust the advanced settings: the Base I/O Port Address and the Interrupt Request Line (IRQ). It's unlikely that you will ever need to adjust these settings if you have only two COM ports unless you connect a device that for some reason doesn't use the standard settings. If you have four COM ports, though, you may have to adjust some of the ports' settings to avoid hardware conflicts. Just click on the **Advanced** button to see the Advanced Settings dialog box.

▼ ***Note*** If the Advanced button is disabled, check to see that the comm= line in the [boot] section of SYSTEM.INI says comm=comm.drv. If it doesn't, another application has loaded a different communications driver. Try to figure out which program and then call that program's technical support line. If the comm= line is correct, check to see that the COMM.DRV file in the WINDOWS\SYSTEM directory is dated 3/10/92 or later. If it isn't, the driver wasn't updated. Expand the driver from the installation disks. (See Chapter 1 for instructions on expanding disks.) However, if all your communications ports are working well, you don't need to get to the Advanced settings.

IRQs are used by various computer components to communicate with the computer's processor. In addition to the COM ports, devices such as the floppy disks, hard disks, math coprocessors, parallel printer ports, and system clock all need IRQs. Optional devices such as sound cards, network cards, internal faxes and modems all need IRQs.

Most PC-compatibles use an ISA (Industry Standard Architecture) bus that doesn't allow devices to use the same IRQs, so each device either must have its own IRQ or may share an IRQ with a device that won't be working at the same time. These are the default settings used by an ISA machine and assumed by Windows:

Port	***Address***	***IRQ***
COM1	03F8	4
COM2	03E8	3
COM3	02F8	4
COM4	02E8	3

Notice that COM1 and 3 are assigned to the same IRQ, as are COM2 and 4. This allows you to use COM1 and 2 at the same time—probably the most common setup is a mouse on COM1 and a modem on COM2. If you want to use COM3 the same time you use COM1, or COM4 the same time you use COM2, you will have to assign a different IRQ.

You need to know two things: the IRQs automatically assigned by your computer, and the IRQs you assigned when you installed other devices. You can use Microsoft Diagnostics to check IRQ settings. Windows automatically installs this program; see Appendix D for more information. You can also look in your computer's manual. You should be able to find a table that shows the IRQs. Some of these you obviously won't want to use but others will be shown as "spare" or "reserved." In most systems IRQs 10, 11, 12, and 15 are free. IRQ 5 is usually assigned to LPT2, a second parallel printer port; if you have only one parallel printer, you can probably use this IRQ. If you don't have a math coprocessor you may be able to use IRQ 13.

Check to see if the IRQs that your computer is not using are assigned any other devices. For instance, if you have installed a sound card, it will be assigned to a particular IRQ. You can check which one by reading the documentation, or by running the setup program, or by using Microsoft Diagnostics. In the case of a Windows-compatible multimedia device, you may be able to access a setup dialog box by double-clicking on the device name in the Drivers dialog box. (See more information later in this chapter.) When you have found an IRQ you can use, select that IRQ from the drop-down list box. You probably won't need to select a Base I/O Port Address.

MCA (Micro Channel Architecture) and EISA (Extended Industry Standard Architecture) machines *can* share IRQs. When you install Windows on one of these machines COM-port sharing is turned on by default. When you install on an ISA machine it is turned off by default. In rare circumstances an ISA machine may have software or hardware that also allows port sharing. If so, you can modify the [386 Enh] section in SYSTEM.INI. Add this

```
ComIrqSharing=true
```

(See Appendix B for more information about the .INI files.)

Adjusting the Mouse

The Mouse dialog box, shown in Figure 8.9, lets you configure your mouse in several ways. Perhaps the most important is the **Mouse Tracking Speed**. Use the scroll bar to adjust how far you have to move your hand to move the mouse pointer a certain distance across the screen. This is not really a "speed." Rather, it's the ratio between hand movement and pointer movement. The "faster" you set it, the less you need to move your hand, but the movements must be more precise. Experiment by selecting a speed and then trying the mouse.

The **Double Click Speed** really *is* a speed, the speed with which you must click the mouse button twice to effect a "double-click." Try a setting, then double-click on the **TEST** box. If you get the double-click test just right, the box will change color each time you double-click on it.

You probably noticed that each time you click a mouse button inside the Mouse dialog box, the **L** or **R** near the buttons flashes. These characters inside boxes represent the mouse buttons. This may be a bit confusing, but the button on the

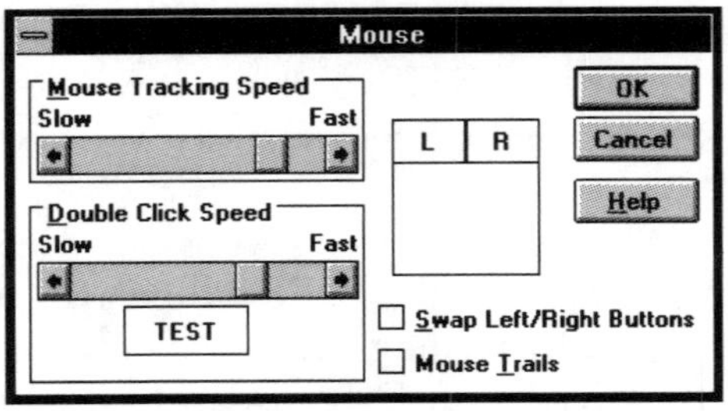

Figure 8.9 The Mouse dialog box

left, which is probably the L button), is the dominant button, the one that you click for most operations.

▼ ***Note*** If you used the mouse tutorial (in Program Manager) and swapped the mouse buttons, the R will be on the left side.

If you click on the **Swap Left/Right** buttons check box, the characters swap positions. (You now probably have the R on the left.) Still the character on the left indicates the dominant button. If the character is an R, it means you will click the right button to carry out most operations; if it's an L, you will click the L button. This lets left-handed people swap buttons to make using the mouse more comfortable. The change is immediate as soon as you click on the check box. That means you will have to click the other button to carry out any operation. To swap the buttons back you must click on the check box with the other button.

Incidentally, some companies sell left-handed mice, mice that are pre-wired to automatically convert between left and right. If you have one of these, clicking the right button will make the L flash and clicking the left button will make the R flash.

The last option, **Mouse Trails**, makes Windows display a "trail" of "ghost" mouse pointers that follow the actual pointer. You may want to use this option if you are using an LCD screen, or if you are creating a demonstration macro with Windows Terminal. In either case the pointer will be easier to see. However, you can only use mouse trails if you are using an EGA, VGA, or Super VGA display driver. As soon as you select the Mouse Trails check box you will be able to see the ghosts.

Tip You can adjust the number of "ghost" pointers using the Mouse-Trails= line in WIN.INI. See Appendix B for more information.

Customizing the Desktop

The Desktop settings are a mixture of items that could be placed firmly in the category of neat stuff, along with others of a more practical nature. You can decorate the desktop with patterns or pictures, for example, or use a "screen saver" to display an animated picture on your screen while you are not using your computer. While screen savers are more amusing than useful (few modern screens need saving from "burn-in"), you can use a password to add a modicum of security, or enter a message to let people know where you are. You can also modify the application-swapping method used by windows, adjust the distance between icons and window positions, and change the cursor blink rate. Figure 8.10 shows the Desktop dialog box.

Patterns and Wallpaper

You can place either a pattern or wallpaper on your desktop, the area on which all windows and icons sit. (There's a mixing of metaphors here, of course—wallpaper is not normally placed on a desktop—but those are the terms Microsoft uses.) A pattern is made up by grids 8 pixels square. Windows simply repeats each 64-pixel grid over and over to fill the desktop. Wallpaper, on the other hand, is a .BMP bitmap file that is either placed in the middle of the desktop or repeated to fill the desktop.

You can select a pattern from the **Pattern Name** drop-down list box near the top of the Desktop dialog box. Windows has over a dozen patterns, but you can create your own. Select one then click on the **Edit Pattern** button. As you can see

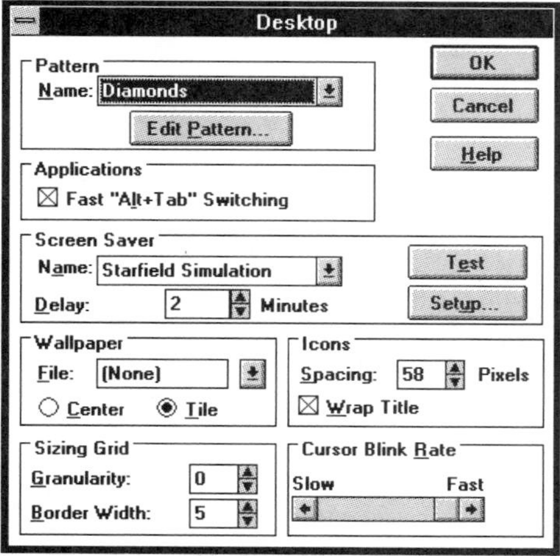

Figure 8.10 The Desktop dialog box

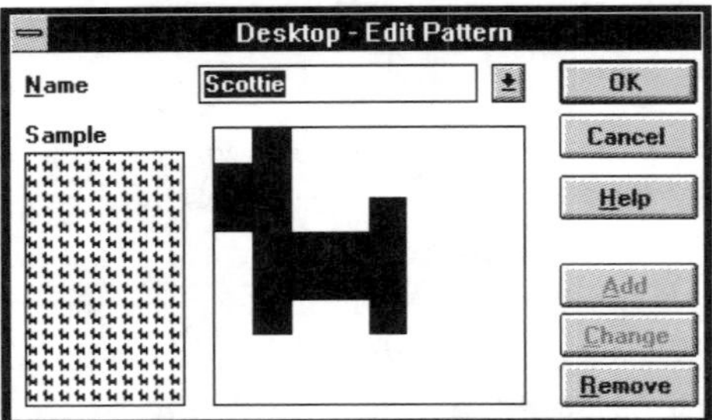

Figure 8.11 The Desktop – Edit Pattern dialog box

from Figure 8.11, the Desktop – Edit Pattern dialog box shows you the selected pattern, along with a sample of the pattern repeated about 150 times. (If you selected **None** from the drop-down list box, the dialog box shows a blank grid.)

You can now modify the pattern shown in the grid. Click to change a pixel's color, or press the mouse button and drag the pointer across an area. Figure 8.11, for instance, shows a Scottie-dog pattern. By clicking on the squares beneath the dog's legs, you could extend them (creating a llama or something). With the Windows Default color scheme these colors are black dots on a gray background. You can change the colors using the Color dialog box. The gray background is the Desktop color, and the black dots are the Windows Text color.

When you have created the pattern you want, click on the **Change** button to modify the pattern you originally selected. Or type a new name in the **Name** drop-down list box and click on **Add** button. Notice that you can select one of the other patterns from the Name drop-down list box and then edit that pattern. You can also delete a pattern using the **Remove** button.

When you have finished editing, click on the **OK** or **Close** button. It doesn't really matter which, as long as you clicked on the Add or Change button first, if you want to save your changes.

Editing patterns is a case when you must have a mouse, because you can't do it with the keyboard. However, these patterns are saved in the Windows SYSTEM.INI file, so if you have nothing better to do one afternoon you could try to decipher the codes and *type* a new pattern in.

The picture selected in the **Wallpaper File** text box sits on top of the pattern. The pattern may appear around the edges of the wallpaper, and if you have a small wallpaper file in the center of the screen—instead of tiled—the rest of the desktop will show the pattern. Also, the labels on icons sitting on the desktop change to show the pattern.

Click on the arrow next to the text box to see a drop-down list box, which lists all the .BMP files in the WINDOWS directory. These are Windows Paintbrush format files, which means you can create your own wallpaper quite easily. With a little imagination you can take art from just about any Windows graphics program, regardless of the format, and, using Paintbrush as an intermediary, create a .BMP file that you can use as wallpaper. You could even create a series of messages that you can leave on your computer while you are away. See Chapter 13 for more information. If you want to use a .BMP file that is not in the WINDOWS directory, type the full pathname and filename into the text box.

 **Tip** Create a calendar in Paintbrush at the beginning of each month, with important dates marked. Then use the calendar as your desktop's wallpaper.

Click on **Center** to put one picture of the wallpaper file in the center of the desktop. Click on **Tile** to repeat the picture as many times as it takes to fill the desktop.

As neat as wallpaper may be, it takes up more memory than a pattern or a solid-color desktop. If you are having problems with your computer's memory, dump the wallpaper!

Application Switching

Windows 3.1 has a new way to handle Alt-Tab switching. As you've already seen, when you press **Alt-Tab** (and keep holding Alt down), a gray box appears on your screen, showing you the icon and name of the next application, and a filename if applicable. This new system is much quicker than the one used by Windows 3.0, in which a window's title bar appeared instead of the gray box. Because the title bars might be in different areas of the screen, and because the text is relatively small, the old method made it difficult to quickly recognize the window you want.

By default the **Fast "Alt+Tab" Switching** check box is selected in the Desktop dialog box. If you prefer the old method for some reason, you can turn off fast switching.

If you "Alt-Tab" out of a DOS application, the old type of switching is used, even if Fast Alt+Tab Switching is selected—you will see the window's title bars instead of the gray box.

Using Screen Savers

There's a burgeoning market in programs called "screen savers." You can buy programs that will replace what is displayed on your screen with something else if you don't press a key or move the mouse for a defined number of minutes. Your screen may display flying toasters or dancing pigs, ant farms or submarine journeys.

Screen savers are meant to save your display from "phosphor burn," a discoloration of the display's phosphor due to showing the same or a similar image for long periods. It's doubtful if the primary purpose of these programs is to save anyone's screen, though. Today's monitors simply don't suffer from phosphor burn to the same degree they used to, and screen savers are even being used on LCD screens—which don't have phosphor—and the more "advanced" screen savers include sounds! In any case, you can always turn your screen off or turn down the brightness.

The primary reason for the success of screen savers is the "neat stuff" factor. People like the idea of having an aquarium on their monitor, or making their windows break up into a complicated puzzle.

Windows has now got into the act and provides five fairly simple screen savers:

Blank Screen Just what it sounds like, a blank screen, making your computer look like it's turned off.

Flying Windows Small dots that seem to move toward and past you, becoming the Windows logo as they get close.

Marquee A message that scrolls across a black screen.

Mystify Geometric patterns that spin around your screen.

Starfield Simulation A Star Trek-like star field that you seem to be flying through.

Select the one you want to use from the **Screen Saver Name** drop-down list box. Select **None** to turn off the screen savers. You can test a screen saver by selecting it and clicking on the **Test** button. End the test by moving the mouse or pressing a key.

You can enter a time in the **Delay** incrementer from 1 to 99 minutes. This is the time that Windows will wait after your last keystroke or mouse movement before displaying the screen saver. You can also customize all the screen savers but Blank. You can add a password to them and adjust speeds and quantities. All this setup information is saved in the CONTROL.INI file in the WINDOWS directory.

For instance, Figure 8.12 shows the dialog box that appears if you select the Marquee option and click on **Setup**. The Marquee screen saver lets you type a message that will be displayed on your screen while you are away. The message will scroll across the screen from right to left. Type the message into the **Text** text box, up to 254 characters long. You can use any ANSI characters you want, and even include unusual characters using Character Map or the Alt- codes, if you know them (see Chapter 19 for more information about special characters).

Click on the **Position Random** option button to let Windows decide where on the screen to put the message. Each time the message scrolls it will be at a different level. If you click on the **Centered** option button instead, the message will always

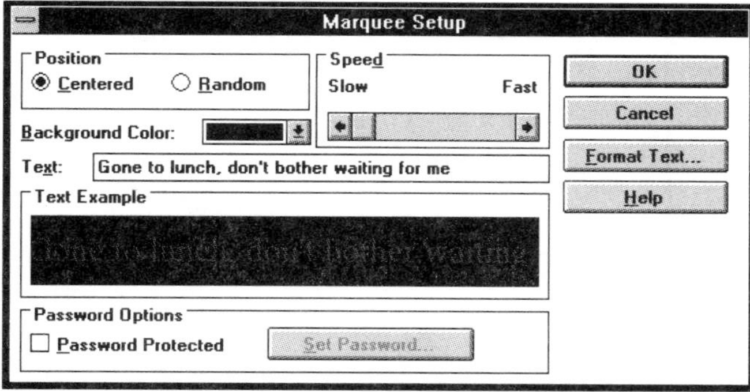

Figure 8.12 The Marquee Setup dialog box

scroll past in the middle of your screen. (While working in the dialog box you may want to click on Centered, or you may not be able to see the text in the **Text Example** box.)

The **Speed** scroll bar lets you adjust how fast the message runs past, and you can select a color from the **Background Color** drop-down list box. All the changes you make will be reflected in the sample.

To modify the text itself, click on **Format Text**. You will see the dialog box shown in Figure 8.13. This is similar to many font-selection boxes you will see in various Windows applications. You can select the font you want to use from the **Font** list box, and select from the **Font Style** and **Size** list boxes also. You can type any size you want into the Size text box—you are not limited to only the sizes in the list. (Click on another option in the dialog box to see the new size in the **Sample** box.) However, the larger the text the more flicker you will get. Over 150 or 180 points probably causes too much flicker. You can also select **Underline** or **Strikeout**, and a text color from the **Color** drop-down list box.

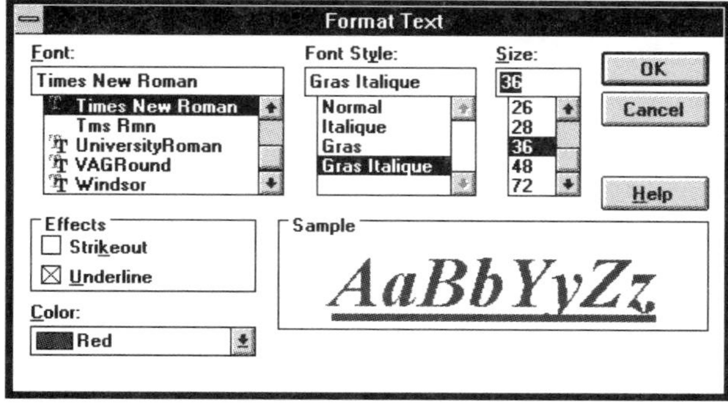

Figure 8.13 The Format Text dialog box

Using Passwords

All the screen savers but Blank let you use a password. Click on the **Password Protected** check box to turn it on, then click on **Set Password** in any of the Setup dialog boxes to see the Change Password dialog box (see Figure 8.14). Type the **New Password**, up to 20 characters long. You can include any characters you want, and even spaces. And Windows regards uppercase and lowercase as the same: If you enter ABC, you will be able to type ABC or abc when you need to use your password. As you type the text box displays asterisks, not the actual password, so someone looking over your shoulder would be unable to read it. Then press **Tab** and type the password again, into the **Retype New Password** text box. This confirms that you really typed what you thought you typed.

Having entered a password, you will not be able to remove a screen saver and return to your work without entering your password into a dialog box that Windows displays. Enter the wrong password, and Windows will tell you to try again.

You don't have to create a real password, even if you select the Password Protected check box. Don't bother to click on the Set Password button and enter a password. This creates a sort of "null" password: Windows will still prompt you for the password when you try to remove the screen saver, but you will be able to press **Enter** to remove the password dialog box. This still offers a small amount of security—an intruder might try to type a password and will only be able to enter if he or she leaves the dialog box empty and presses **Enter**. That lets you use a "password" without having to actually remember one. That may sound absurd, but you shouldn't take the screen saver's password seriously anyway. By itself it's a *very* insecure system, as we shall see in a moment.

In Figure 8.14 you can see the **Old Password** text box. This lets you change your password. Simply type the old one and click on OK to delete the password. Or press **Tab** and type a new one, then press **Tab** and type the new one again.

You can only have one password at a time. That is, all the screen savers use the same password, and if you change the password in one Setup box it affects all of them. You can turn off a password by deselecting the **Password Protected** check box in any of the Setup dialog boxes.

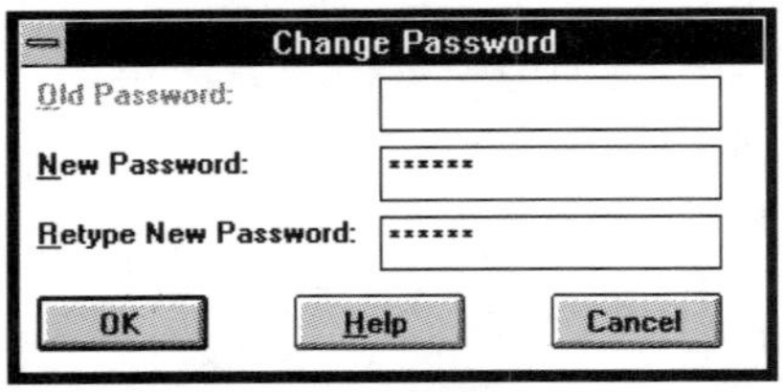

Figure 8.14 The Change Password dialog box

What if you forget your password? You will have to reboot or restart your computer, then reenter Windows. Once you are in Windows you can open the **CONTROL.INI** file with Notepad. Search for the **Password=** line (in the **[ScreenSaver]** section). This line shows you a scrambled version of the password you entered. Don't bother modifying the password here, or you won't be able to use either the original or new one. Rather, delete the line, then close the file and return to the Desktop dialog box and enter a new password. With this line gone Windows will let you enter a new password without knowing the old one.

As you can see, this is not the best method of securing your system. A simple reboot allows anyone to get around the password, and they can even open CONTROL.INI to remove the password you are using (and enter their own if they wanted!). The screen saver password is only a way to stop the most casual of "intruders" from getting to your data.

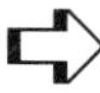

Tip You can quickly add another level of security by renaming WIN.COM (it's in the WINDOWS directory). Then an intruder who restarts your computer could not type WIN to start Windows again. Make the file Hidden (see Chapter 9) to make the modified file a little harder to find.

If you are serious about data security, don't rely on the screen saver password only. You should buy a real data security program, one that will not allow an intruder to do anything once they have rebooted your system.

Other Screen Saver Options

Here are the options you can modify for the other screen savers:

FLYING WINDOWS	
Warp Speed	The speed at which the windows fly toward you.
Density	The maximum number of windows on the screen at any time, from 10 to 200.

MYSTIFY	
Shape	Mystify has two different polygons, Polygon 1 and Polygon 2. Select one, set its options, then select the other and set its options. Both are four-sided polygons.

Active	The polygon selected in the Shape drop-down list box will be included in the screen saver display only if this check box is selected.
Lines	Determines the number of copies of the polygon that the screen saver will display, from 1 to 15.
Two Colors	Uses the two colors you select from the drop-down list boxes to the right of the option button. The polygon will alternate these two colors. If you select black as one of the colors the polygon will disappear at times.
Multiple Random Colors	Windows picks the colors for you.
Clear Screen	Blanks the screen before drawing the polygons. If this option isn't selected, the polygons are drawn on top of the current window, eventually covering it.

STARFIELD SIMULATION	
Warp Speed	The speed at which the stars fly toward you.
Starfield Density	The maximum number of stars on the screen at any time, from 10 to 200.

None of the screen savers will work if you are currently displaying a DOS program. You can get more screen savers from Microsoft in the Microsoft Entertainment Packs. Additional screen saver files must be placed in the SYSTEM directory, or in any directory included in your DOS path (in your AUTOEXEC.BAT file).

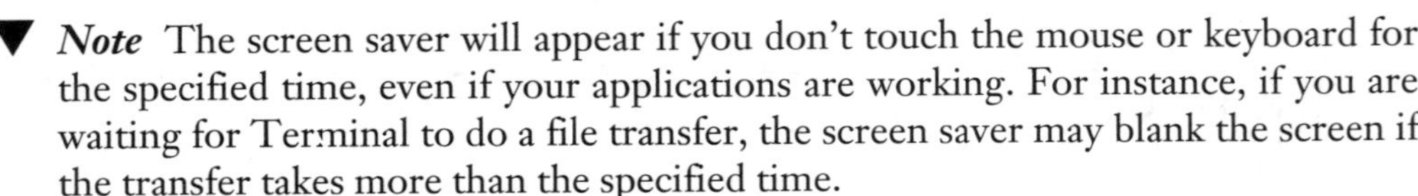

▼ *Note* The screen saver will appear if you don't touch the mouse or keyboard for the specified time, even if your applications are working. For instance, if you are waiting for Terminal to do a file transfer, the screen saver may blank the screen if the transfer takes more than the specified time.

Icon Spacing

The **Icons** area of the Desktop dialog box lets you adjust the amount of horizontal space between icons: the program-group icons in Program Manager, the application icons inside the program groups, directory-window icons in File Manager, and the icons on the desktop.

Simply select an icon spacing (measured in pixels) from the incrementer box. When you click on the OK button, you will not see an immediate effect, except in Program Manager's program-group windows, *if* the **Options | Auto Arrange** option is selected. Otherwise, select a program group and select **Windows | Arrange** to rearrange the application items according to the new measurements. Or select **Options | Auto Arrange** to adjust *all* the program groups at once.

To adjust the program-group icons in Program Manager, select one of the icons and select **Windows | Arrange**. Program Manager readjusts all the icons. These icons are not affected by the Options | Auto Arrange command. This means that you can select a very wide spacing, close the Desktop dialog box, arrange the program-group icons, then go back to Control Panel and select a much tighter spacing for the program icons inside the program-group windows.

The icons on the *desktop* will automatically adjust as you open new ones. Or double-click on the desktop itself to see the Task List dialog box, then click on the **Arrange Icons** button.

You can also make long icon titles wrap onto two or more lines. These titles often overlap onto each other, so wrapping them can make them much easier to read. Simply select the **Wrap Title** check box.

▼ ***Note*** The WIN.INI file lets you adjust other icon features. The IconTitleFaceName= and IconTitleSize= lines change the font and font size used by the icon titles. IconVerticalSpacing= changes the *vertical* spacing between icons. See Appendix B for more information.

The Sizing Grid

The Sizing Grid controls the position of windows on the desktop. Enter a value from 0 to 49 in the **Granularity** incrementer. Each number actually represents 8 pixels. Thus, a value of 5 creates a grid with 40-pixel increments. Enter 0 to allow you to place a window anywhere on the screen. A value of 1 or more makes the windows "snap" into a grid position when you move them. A large value makes the screen quite difficult to work with, unless you have a very large screen and high resolution.

Granularity has no effect on Program Manager's icons, or on icons sitting on the desktop. It affects only open windows.

Changing Window Borders

The Sizing Grid area also has an incrementer box called **Border Width**. This adjusts the size of the border around nonmaximized windows. Select a value from 1 to 50. High values will produce very thick, "clunky" borders, while a value of 1 or 2 almost completely removes them, and may make sizing windows by dragging the borders a little difficult. A value of 3 to 5 is usually fine, depending on the size of your screen and the resolution you are using. The border width value does not affect the size of dialog-box borders.

The Cursor Blink Rate

You can adjust the rate at which the text insertion cursor will blink in applications. Use the scroll bar to adjust the speed, and look at the sample cursor to the right of the scroll bar. Any time the scroll bar is selected you may use the **Right** and **Left arrows** to move the scroll box. The change is immediate, so you can even look at the cursor in another Windows application to see the effect, without closing the Desktop dialog box first.

The Keyboard Settings

The Keyboard dialog box lets you set up the keyboard repeat, the manner in which the keyboard repeats a keystroke if you hold down a key. As you can see in Figure 8.15, the dialog box has two scroll bars. Adjust the **Delay Before First Repeat** to adjust how long you must hold down the key before it begins repeating. Use the **Repeat Rate** scroll bar to adjust how fast the keyboard repeats the characters. Then place the cursor in the **Test** text box, and press and hold a key. You will see exactly how the repeat will operate.

Printer Settings

You will use the Printers dialog box to prepare Windows for printing, telling it what printers are installed and to which ports they are connected. We have discussed this subject in detail in Chapter 11.

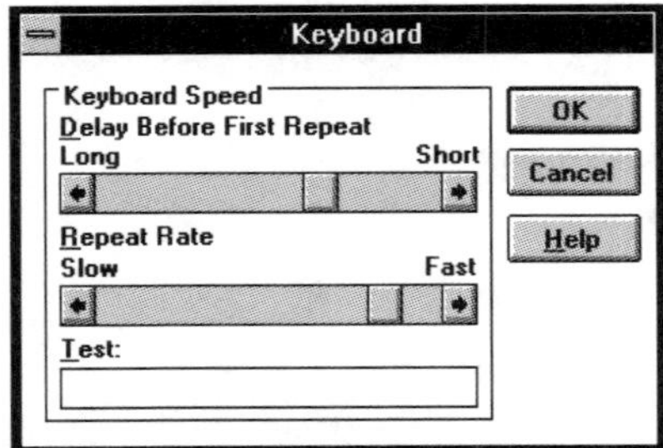

Figure 8.15 The Keyboard dialog box

International Settings

International

The International dialog box (see Figure 8.16) lets you select various items that vary depending on the language you are using and the conventions of the country in which you are working. You can select the correct keyboard layout, the language, the units of measurement, and formats used for currency, dates, times, and numbers. Windows provides this information to any Windows application that wants it. It's up to the application's publisher to use the information. Thus, while a few programs may use the date format, for instance, not all do.

Begin by selecting the country in which you are working from the **Country** drop-down list box. When you do so, Windows automatically adjusts the settings in the Measurement drop-down list box, the List Separator, and the Date, Currency, Time, and Number Format areas of the dialog box. It also changes the default page size used by your printers. These settings will probably be correct, but you can override them if you wish.

Now select an option from the **Language** drop-down list box. Your selection affects the way in which some Windows applications will carry out language-dependent operations, such as sorting lists of words (taking into account the various special characters that may be used in a particular language), or converting the case of text. This option has no effect on the language of the words displayed by Windows (in dialog boxes and menus, for instance). If that's what you need, you must buy a foreign language version of Windows from Microsoft.

The **Keyboard Layout** drop-down list box defines the characters that are produced by your keyboard, letting you type special characters and symbols used by some languages. The **Measurement** drop-down list box lets you choose between the Metric and English units of measurement. This information is used by some applications to set page-margin units, for example.

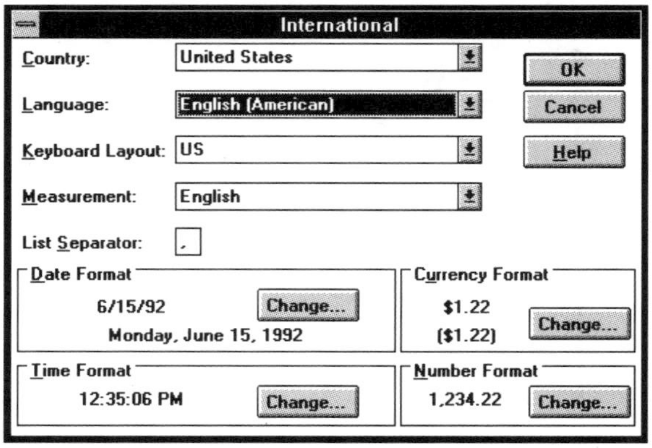

International
Country: United States
Language: English (American)
Keyboard Layout: US
Measurement: English
List Separator: ,
OK
Cancel
Help
Date Format
6/15/92
Monday, June 15, 1992
Change...
Currency Format
$1.22
($1.22)
Change...
Time Format
12:35:06 PM
Change...
Number Format
1,234.22
Change...

Figure 8.16 The International dialog box

You can also enter a **List Separator**, the character you want certain applications to use when separating words or numbers appearing in a list. This character is usually a comma (in English) or a semicolon, although you can enter whatever you wish. Few applications use this information.

Date Format

The Date format determines how some—but not all—Windows applications format the date. Windows Calendar, for instance, doesn't use the format you enter here, and many other applications also do not (they may let you select the format in the application itself). Microsoft Money uses the short format but not the long format.

If you don't like the Date Format that the International dialog box is using, click on the **Change** button in that area to see the dialog box shown in Figure 8.17. This dialog box shows two different formats, a **Short Date Format** and a **Long Date Format**. First, in the **Short Date Format** area click on an option button to select in which **Order** the day (D), month (M), and year (Y) should be placed. While the United States uses MDY, Great Britain and the Commonwealth countries (such as Canada and Australia) use DMY, and some countries use YMD.

Type a character into the **Separator** text box. This is the character that separates the day, month, and year in the short date. It's usually a /, though it can be whatever character you want, a dash or colon, for example.

The three check boxes make Windows display a zero in front of single-digit days and months (**Day** and **Month Leading Zero**), and display all four year digits instead of just two (**Century**).

In the **Long Date Format** area you can also select an **Order**. As you do so the drop-down list boxes below change order. Then you can select the format of the day, month, and year from the drop-down list box. You can use the entire day or

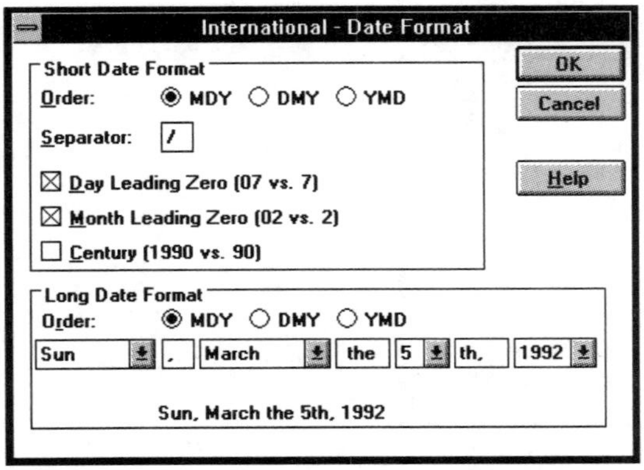

Figure 8.17 The International – Date Format dialog box

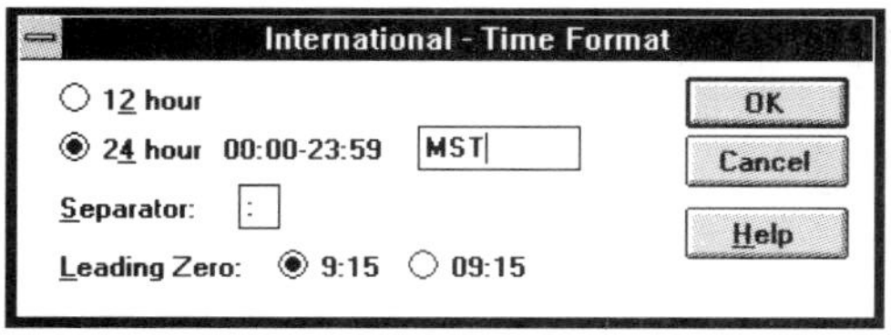

Figure 8.18 The International – Time Format dialog box

an abbreviated day; a single digit, a digit with a leading zero, and abbreviated month or full month; and a four-digit or two-digit year.

Between each element in the long date you can enter a special separator. This can be a single character, or, as in Figure 8.17, special terms. You could put a comma between the day and month, "the" between the month and date, and "th," between the date and year, for example, creating a date such as "Monday, June the 15th, 1992." (Of course, "th," will be wrong for six or seven days each month!)

Time Format

The time format is similar to the date format, in that some applications will use it and some won't. Windows Calendar *does* use the time format you enter here. Click on the **Change** button in the **Time Format** area to see the dialog box shown in Figure 8.18. Select either **12 hour** or **24 hour**. If you select 12 hour you will see two text boxes, one saying **AM** (for before noon), and the other **PM** (for after noon). You can, of course, modify these (to am and pm, for instance, or the notation used in a different language).

If you select **24 hour**, the dialog box shows only one blank text box. You can type any notation you wish in here, such as MST (Mountain Standard Time). You can also enter a **Separator** (a colon or dash, for instance), and a **Leading Zero**, which places a zero before any single-digit hour. It will display 09:15:57, for instance, rather than 9:15:57. The time will *always* have leading zeros in front of single-digit minutes and seconds, even if you don't select the leading zero option.

Currency Format

The Currency Format is used by some applications that work with monetary units, such as spreadsheets and accounting packages. Click on the **Change** button in the **Currency Format** area to see the dialog box shown in Figure 8.19. The **Symbol Placement** drop-down list box lets you place the currency symbol immediately in front of the number, immediately after the number, and in front or after the number but separated by a space.

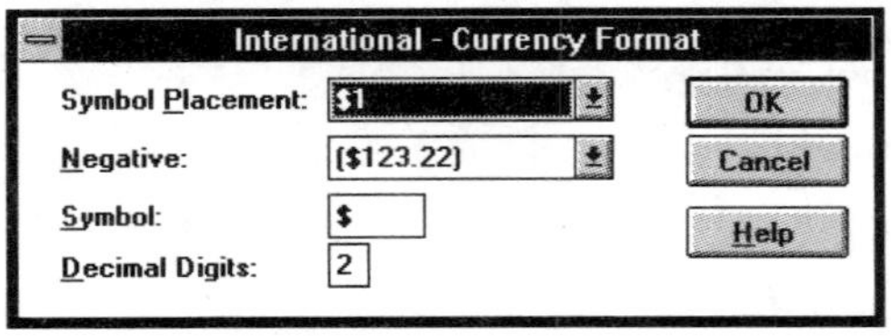

Figure 8.19 The International – Currency Format dialog box

The **Negative** drop-down list box provides a number of different ways to show a negative value, using dashes, parentheses, spaces, and the currency in different orders. And you may type any character you wish into the **Symbol** text box (the preceding drop-down list boxes change to use the new symbol as soon as you move the cursor from the Symbol text box). Finally, you can change the **Decimal Digits** value to whatever you wish. Changing this doesn't necessarily modify the value in an application, only the way the value is displayed. For instance, if you are using a Decimal Digits value of 0, when you type 13.55 into an accounting package it will be displayed as 14 (because it is rounded up). But the calculations using that number will probably use the actual number, 13.55.

Number Formats

The Number Format is used by some applications that work with numbers. Windows Calculator does *not* use this format. Click on the **Change** button in the **Number Format** area to see the dialog box shown in Figure 8.20. The **Symbol Placement** drop-down list box lets you place the currency symbol immediately in front of the number, immediately after the number, and in front or after the number but separated by a space.

The **1000 Separator** lets you enter the character that should be used for separating groups of three digits in a number. While Americans commonly use a comma, some countries use a period. Likewise the **Decimal Separator** varies between countries: some use a period, some a comma. You can also select how many **Decimal Digits** should be included in a number, and whether a **Leading Zero** should be included in decimal fractions.

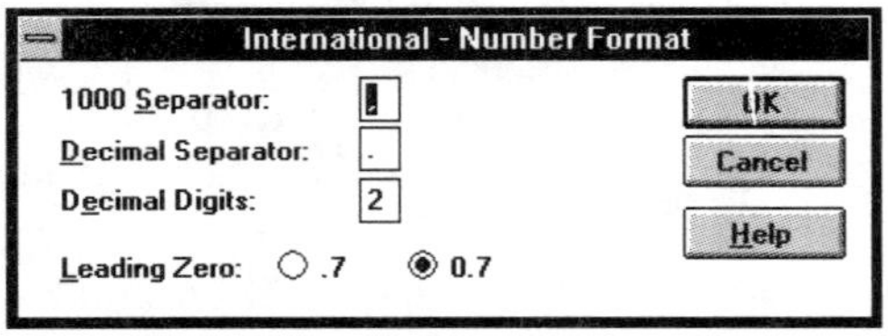

Figure 8.20 The International – Number Format dialog box

Changing the System Date and Time

The Date & Time dialog box (shown in Figure 8.21) lets you change the system date and time. This date and time is used in many ways. Calendar uses it to automatically display the current date. When you save files in any application they are "time and date stamped." And the Clock displays the system time. But the date and time is not only used in Windows applications: you are actually changing the DOS time, so when you leave Windows your DOS applications will use the new date and time. Incidentally, your computer probably keeps the date and time correct automatically. Most PCs have a built-in clock these days, so unless your computer has a hardware problem or a dead battery, it constantly updates the time, even when your computer is turned off.

You can change any part of the date or time by simply placing the cursor on it and clicking on the incrementer buttons. Or, you can type a new value. Notice that the clock is updated constantly, so you can set the time to the nearest second. Notice also that the date and time formats are those that you selected in the International – Date and Time Format dialog boxes.

MIDI Mapper Settings

If you have installed a MIDI device, the MIDI Mapper icon will appear in the Control Panel. This lets you build an interface between software using Windows' General MIDI specifications and the MIDI generator you have connected to your computer. For more information about MIDI Mapper, see Chapter 26.

Optimizing 386 Enhanced Mode

The 386 Enhanced icon only appears in Control Panel if you have a 386 or 486 computer with at least 2 MB of RAM. The 386 Enhanced dialog box (see Figure 8.22) is used to determine how Windows will run in 386 Enhanced mode.

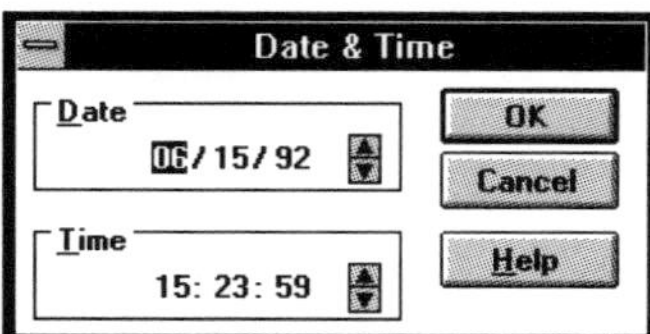

Figure 8.21 The Date & Time dialog box

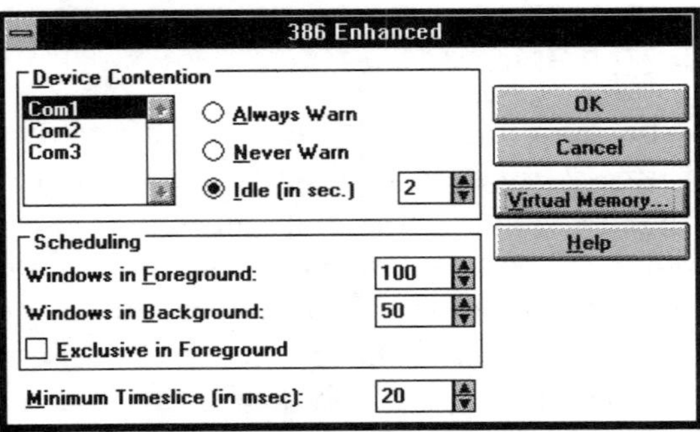

Figure 8.22 The 386 Enhanced dialog box

The **Device Contention** area lets you tell Windows what to do if two or more programs—one of which is a non-Windows application—try to use a serial port at the same time. For instance, if a DOS program and a Windows program both try to use your modem at the same time, what should Windows do? (It doesn't have this problem if both applications are Windows applications, as it can assign a priority to each one.)

Select a serial device from the list box, then select one of the option buttons. Here are your choices:

Always Warn A message will appear warning you that a program is trying to use a busy device, and asking you which application should have control. An example of the message is shown in Figure 8.23.

Never Warn Allow applications to use a device without warning you. In other words, you are simply ignoring any device contentions. If one does occur, the results will be unpredictable.

Idle The application will wait, then try to use the device again. No message will be displayed. You can specify in the incrementer box how many seconds the application should wait, from 1 to 999. This is the default selection. Don't make the time too short, or an application may lose the port if it pauses. But if you make the time too long, applications may have unnecessarily long delays trying to use a port.

Serial-device contention problems are not very common unless, perhaps, you have a serial printer. More likely are parallel-device conflicts in which you print from a DOS and a Windows program to the same printer (most printers are parallel devices). Unlike Windows 3.0—in which you could control parallel-device contention with SYSTEM.INI settings—Windows 3.1 does not attempt to control parallel device conflicts.

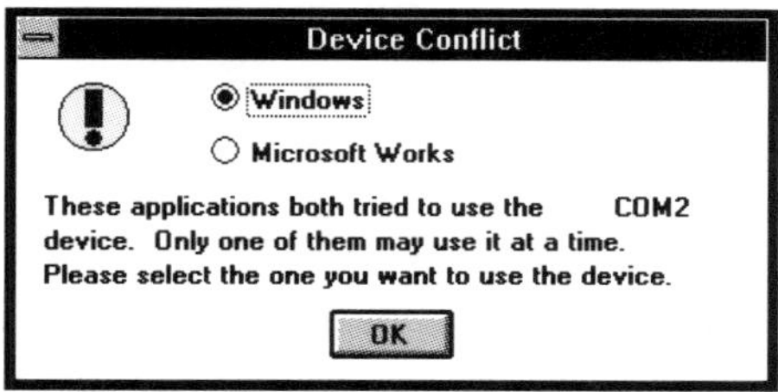

Figure 8.23 The Device Conflict dialog box

The **Scheduling** and **Minimum Timeslice** options specify how Windows handles *multitasking*, the simultaneous operation of two or more applications, when one of them is a DOS application. Actually Windows doesn't really operate more than one application at a time, it just does some quick juggling to make it look that way. Windows runs an application for a few milliseconds at a time, and then jumps to another application and runs that for a while, then it jumps to another, and so on. The result is that it appears to be working on several applications at once.

How does Windows decide which application to work on at any time? Well, it works on Windows applications as needed. When a Windows application sends a message, Windows itself acts on it. It receives messages from the multitasked programs continuously, and acts on each in the order in which it is received.

But if you are also multitasking DOS applications, Windows can't operate in the same way. DOS applications expect complete attention from the CPU; they can't operate using the same message system. Instead, Windows stops working with Windows applications periodically and gives its full attention to DOS applications for a short while, then jumps back to the group of Windows applications.

The **Windows in Foreground** option tells Windows how long it should work with the Windows applications before jumping to the DOS applications, if the active application is a *Windows* application. The **Windows in Background** option tells Windows how long it should work on the Windows applications before jumping to the DOS applications if the active application is a *DOS* application. These numbers are *not* milliseconds. Rather, they are used in a complicated calculation that includes the Background and Foreground Priority settings in the DOS applications' PIFs (as described in Chapter 7) to calculate how many timeslices are assigned to Windows applications before Windows dedicates processing time to a DOS application.

▼ ***Note*** By default, DOS applications do *not* run while they are in the background. A DOS application will do so only if you are using a PIF file that specifically allows it to (the "Execution: Background" check box must be selected). See Chapter 7 for more information.

For instance, you have three Windows applications running, one of which is the active window. You also have two DOS applications running in the background, each of which has a Background Priority setting of 50. Assume also that the Windows in Foreground setting is 100. To calculate the amount of time assigned to the various applications, Windows divides the Windows in Foreground value by the sum of the Windows in Foreground value plus the total of the DOS Background Priority values.

In our example that is 100/(100+50+50), which is the same as 1/2. That means that for every three timeslices, one will be assigned to the Windows applications and two to the DOS applications. The three Windows applications will "share" those two timeslices, with Windows assigning time to each application as it receives messages. What is a timeslice? That depends on the number in the **Minimum Timeslice** incrementer box. By default it is 20 milliseconds, but it can be any value from 1 to 10,000 milliseconds (10 seconds).

If a DOS application is in the foreground, a similar calculation is done, dividing the Windows in Background value by the sum of Windows in Background plus the Foreground Priority value for the DOS application (from the PIF) and the Background Priority value for any other DOS applications running.

How does all this affect the way Windows runs? It means that the more DOS applications you have running, the less time is available to all Windows applications. It also means that running a DOS application as the active application reduces the time available to all Windows applications.

What values, then, should you use for **Minimum Timeslice**, **Windows in Foreground**, and **Windows in Background**? You don't normally need to change them. Remember that all these values only come into play if you are running both Windows and DOS applications at the same time. If you rarely or never run DOS applications, you don't need to adjust these values. If you don't turn on "background execution" in your DOS applications' PIFs, these settings have no effect anyway. If you want to experiment, consider the following:

Minimum Timeslice	The shorter the time, the smoother Windows seems to switch between Windows and DOS tasks, but, paradoxically, the slower it completes tasks, because it wastes time switching. Longer times allow Windows to get more done each time it works in an application, but will appear less smooth.
Windows in Foreground	The larger the value, the more priority given to Windows applications if any of them are running as the active application, reducing the time given to DOS applications.

Windows in Background The larger the value, the more priority given to Windows applications when a DOS application is active, reducing the time given to DOS applications.

Remember also that the priorities you assign to the DOS applications in their PIFs have an affect on the overall calculation. See Chapter 7 for more information about running DOS applications.

There's a check box in the 386 Enhanced dialog box labeled **Exclusive in Foreground**. If you select this check box *all* the processing time is given to Windows applications if one of them is the active application. If you have any DOS applications running, they stop when a Windows application is active.

Click on the **Virtual Memory** button to see the Virtual Memory dialog box. Then click on the **Change** button to enlarge the dialog box, as shown in Figure 8.24. This dialog box lets you do two things: create or modify a *swapfile*, and turn on *32-bit disk access*.

Windows' 386 Enhanced mode uses a special file on your hard disk as a **swapfile**. Windows can swap information from memory to the swapfile when necessary. For instance, if you have 4 MB of memory, but are multitasking several applications and require 6 MB, the swapfile can provide the extra 2 MB. This hard-drive space used to simulate memory is known as *virtual memory*. It lets you run more applications, although they will run more slowly than if you were using real memory.

The swapfile may be a *temporary* file named WIN386.SWP, which Windows creates when it begins running, modifies in size as needed, and deletes when it

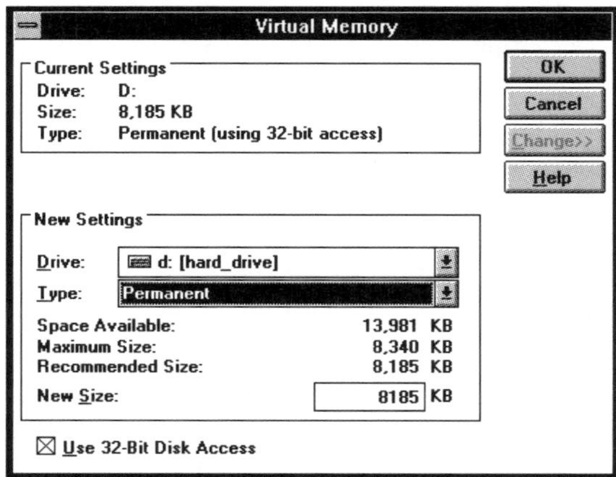

Figure 8.24 The Virtual Memory dialog box after clicking on the Change button

closes. A *permanent* swapfile comprises two parts, a read-only file in the WINDOWS directory called SPART.PAR, and a hidden file called 386SPART.PAR, in the root directory of the chosen hard-disk drive. (SPART.PAR is a small file that tells Windows where to find the actual swapfile.) A permanent swapfile is the ideal, if you have enough disk space. Windows will place the file in an unfragmented area of your disk drive, whereas if you are using a temporary swapfile Windows has to use what it can get at the time—the swapfile may be broken up and spread around the hard disk, slowing access and, therefore, reducing system efficiency. Making a swapfile permanent ensures that the disk space is always available, because no other files can be written into the area. On the other hand, a permanent swapfile permanently uses the hard-disk space: Even when you are not running Windows you won't be able to use the space.

The Windows installation program will automatically create a swapfile, but you can view and adjust the settings in the Virtual Memory dialog box. (When you run Windows in Standard mode it creates temporary *application swapfiles*, one for the Windows applications and one for each DOS application you are running.)

The **Current Settings** area of the dialog box shows you how your swapfile is currently set up. In Figure 8.24 you can see that the swapfile is in the root directory of drive D: (that's where the 386SPART.PAR file is). The file is 8185 KB, and it's a permanent swapfile. You can also see that 32-bit access is turned on (more about that in a moment).

You may want to change the swapfile settings for a variety of reasons. Perhaps you have an application that requires a very large swapfile, as some high-resolution printing applications do, an application that needs a lot of memory, or run many applications at the same time. Perhaps you are running short of disk space, and want to reduce the swapfile. (Better still, delete unnecessary files and back up rarely used files.) Maybe you have been using a temporary swapfile but now have enough disk space to create a permanent one. Or you may want to stop Windows using *any* hard disk space, though you may reduce system speed and run into memory problems if you don't have much RAM.

Select the type of swapfile you want from the **Type** drop-down list box: **Permanent**, **Temporary**, or **None**. If you selected Permanent or Temporary, you can then select, from the **Drive** drop-down list box, the disk drive on which you want to place the swapfile. The file will be created in the root directory. You cannot put a permanent swapfile on a network drive, so if you have a diskless workstation you can't create one.

If you have more than one hard-disk drive, use the one with the most unfragmented space, or, if more than one has sufficient space, select the faster drive. However, the position of the drive also affects speed. Ideally the drive should be the same as the Windows drive. If that isn't possible, the closer to the Windows drive the better: If Windows is on drive C:, use D: rather than E:.

▼ ***Note*** If you are using a disk compression system, such as Stacker, don't place swapfiles on the compressed drive. In fact, the Drives drop-down list box probably won't include the compressed drive.

Windows shows you the **Space Available** on the selected disk drive. That space is probably not all available for a *permanent* swapfile, though—it's simply the amount of free space on the drive. The permanent swapfile can only be in *contiguous* space on the disk drive. Remember, you can't break up a permanent swapfile. If you selected Temporary from the Type drop-down list box, you will see the **Recommended Maximum Size**. Temporary swapfiles vary in size, as needed, but this is the largest it can be and is the largest contiguous block of disk space on that drive.

If you selected Permanent, you will see **Maximum Size**, which is the largest unfragmented area on the disk. If it's not large enough, delete unused files and use a disk "optimization" or "defragmentation" utility. You could also copy files and directories to another disk, even temporarily, to join fragmented disk sectors into larger, unfragmented blocks. (File Manager lets you move entire directories—subdirectories and all—very quickly.)

You will also see **Recommended Size** if you selected Permanent. This number is based on the amount of free, contiguous disk space, and the amount of RAM. If you have a lot of disk space available, Windows will recommend from one and one-half to two times your RAM. If you have 4 MB of RAM, Windows may recommend between 6 and 8 MB, but it won't recommend a size larger than approximately 50% of the Space Available, regardless of the amount of RAM you have.

The **New Size** text box automatically displays the recommended swapfile size. If you click on OK now, that will be the size Windows uses. Of course you can enter a different value if you wish. You might want to reduce the temporary swapfile size. Remember, Windows automatically selects the largest contiguous block as the maximum temporary swapfile size, but you can reduce the number to make sure you always have disk space available on which to save files, even if the swapfile is full. If you have a permanent swapfile, you may want to reduce the size—to save disk space. You might also increase the size in some circumstances if you want to multitask a lot of programs, or if you have programs that use a lot of memory. Some programs even specify a minimum swapfile size. If you enter a value that is too large, Windows immediately replaces it with the maximum usable size.

The last option in this dialog box is the **32-Bit Disk Access** check box. When you installed Windows it checked your disk drive to see if it is compatible with the Western Digital WD1003 disk controller. If it is, Windows added the 32-Bit Disk Access check box to the Virtual Memory dialog box. (Most IDE controllers, and some other types, are WD1003-compatible.) 32-Bit Disk Access (also known as

FastDisk) bypasses the ROM BIOS when reading and writing, accessing the hard-disk controller directly. This means faster reading and writing, and also allows you to run more non-Windows applications or DOS prompts.

▼ ***Note*** The 32-Bit Disk Access check box doesn't appear if Windows thinks your disk-drive controller is not WD1003-compatible. If you are sure it is, you can enter the following lines to the [386Enh] section of the SYSTEM.INI file:

```
32BitDiskAccess=on
device=*INT13
device=*WDCTRL
```

Running with 32-Bit Disk Access turned on when your controller is not completely compatible may cause problems, including a loss of data. If you are not sure, and want to test the operation, back up all your data first. You might also check with your controller's manufacturer to see if the controller is fully compatible. Also, the power-saving features used by some laptops may cause 32-Bit Disk Access to malfunction. You should leave it turned off on such a machine, unless it conforms to the "APM" (Advanced Power Management) specifications. And Windows may *incorrectly* believe your disk is WD1003-compatible. If you are having problems reading and writing files on your disk, try turning the feature off to see if the problems go away.

Important You may see a message similar to "Incompatible hardware/software installed" or "Unable to load KRNL386.EXE" if you are using 32-Bit Disk Access and it finds a virus on your hard drive.

When you have finished making your selections, click on the **OK** button. If you entered a permanent swapfile size that is larger than the recommended size, Windows displays a dialog box saying that it won't be able to use the swapfile area above the recommended size. Microsoft has stated that this is a *bug*, and that Windows *will* use all the swapfile.

Windows asks you if you are sure about the settings you have made. It then tells you it has created a new swapfile, and finally lets you restart Windows. If you don't need to use the swapfile immediately you can click **Continue**. If you need it right away, click the **Restart Windows** button. (You will have the chance to save your work in any open applications.)

Working With Drivers

The Drivers dialog box (Figure 8.25) lets you add new device drivers, generally multimedia devices, but also devices such as digitizing tablets or light pens. Any device connected to your computer requires a driver, a program that tells Windows how to use the device. Some drivers are automatically installed, such as those for the keyboard, display, and mouse, during the installation procedure. You can install new drivers using the Windows Setup procedure. (See Chapter 1.) To install a driver for a printer, plotter, typesetter, or slide scanner, you use the Printers dialog box. But to install other drivers you use the Drivers dialog box.

Drivers are installed in the WINDOWS\SYSTEM directory, and referenced in the CONTROL.INI file. Windows installs a few drivers automatically, as you can see when you open your Drivers dialog box. When you install a new device, though, you should always check with the manufacturer to see if you have the latest driver.

To install a new driver, click on the **Add** button. The Add dialog box displays a list of the drivers on the Windows installation disks. If the driver you want is included, double-click on it, or click once and click on OK. Windows searches the WINDOWS\SYSTEM directory for the driver, and if it finds it, displays a dialog box asking if you want to use the **Current** driver or install a **New** one. Why does it do this? Because you may have removed the driver. "Removing" a driver removes the reference to the driver in the CONTROL.INI file, but not the file itself. So you have the option of using the old driver or installing a new one. Click on the appropriate button to see a dialog box that tells you which disk you need, and tells you to place the disk in the A:\ drive. If you are using the B: drive or any other drive, replace A:\ with the correct drive letter (and pathname, if necessary).

Now, when you click on the OK button, Windows adds the driver. It may then display a Setup dialog box of some kind, depending on the specific driver. For instance, Figure 8.26 shows the MPU-401 Compatible Setup dialog box that appears when you install the Roland MPU-401 driver. (The MPU-401 is a MIDI

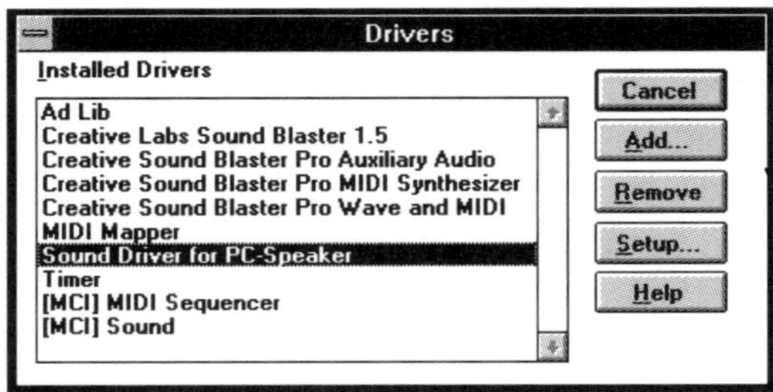

Figure 8.25 The Drivers dialog box

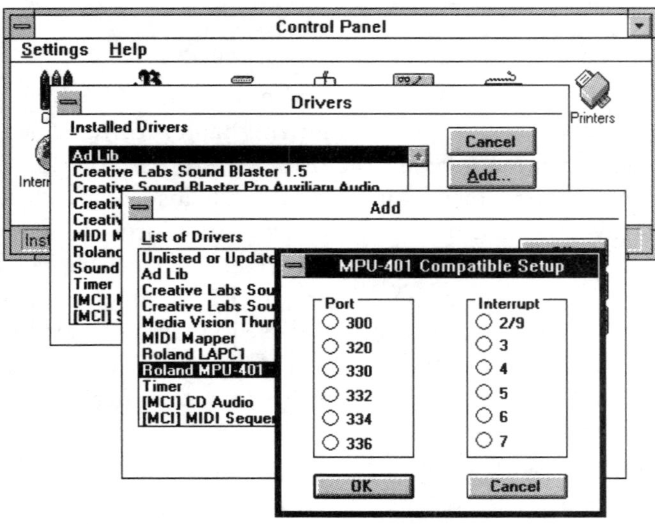

Figure 8.26 The MPU-401 Compatible Setup dialog box displayed after installing the MPU-401 driver

device.) Select the correct option (see your device's installation instructions), and click on OK.

▼ ***Note*** If you install the MPU-401 driver, Windows displays an error message telling you that a "configuration or hardware problem has occurred." This is a bug. It appears because you haven't yet set the Port and IRQ Interrupt, which you can do as soon as you click on the OK button in the error message box.

Windows then gives you the chance to restart. You should click on the **Restart Now** button if you need to use the new driver right away, or **Don't Restart Now** if you don't need it yet.

If the driver you want is not listed, you must select the **Unlisted or Updated Driver** option in the Add dialog box. The Install Driver dialog box prompts you for the name of the directory in which the driver is stored. If you are not quite sure where you placed the driver—perhaps you copied off a floppy disk or bulletin board and onto your hard drive and you don't recall the directory name—or if the pathname is too long to type, click the **Browse** button and use the Directories list box.

Windows won't recognize the device driver itself. It's looking for a file called OEMSETUP.INF, a small text file that tells Windows the name of the driver. In fact OEMSETUP.INF may refer to several drivers, so when you click on the OK button in the Install Driver dialog box Windows displays the Add Unlisted or Updated Driver dialog box, allowing you to choose the driver you want to install.

▼ ***Note*** Whenever you install a driver provided by a device manufacturer, they must also provide the OEMSETUP.INF file.

When you select the driver you want Windows checks the SYSTEM directory to see if the driver is already on your hard drive. If it finds the driver, it displays a dialog box asking if you want to use the **Current** driver or install a **New** one. If you are installing an updated driver, you will want to click on the New button. Once again, a Setup dialog may appear, and after you make your selections you can restart Windows or continue without restarting.

Adjusting Setups

Some, but not all, of the drivers let you set up certain characteristics, often the IRQ (Interrupt Request line) or a port number. You saw in Figure 8.26 an example of a Setup dialog box. For more information about the various options, see the driver's documentation, or ask the manufacturer's technical support line. And for a discussion of selecting free IRQs, see the information on configuring serial ports earlier in this chapter.

You can also modify a driver's setup information after installing it. Just double-click on the driver in the Drivers dialog box, or click once and click on the **Setup** button. Figure 8.27 shows the PC-Speaker Setup dialog box, displayed when you double-click on the **Sound Driver for PC-Speaker** option in the Drivers dialog box. (This is the SPEAKER.DRV driver, available directly from Microsoft or from a bulletin board—see Chapter 14 for information on downloading files from Microsoft.)

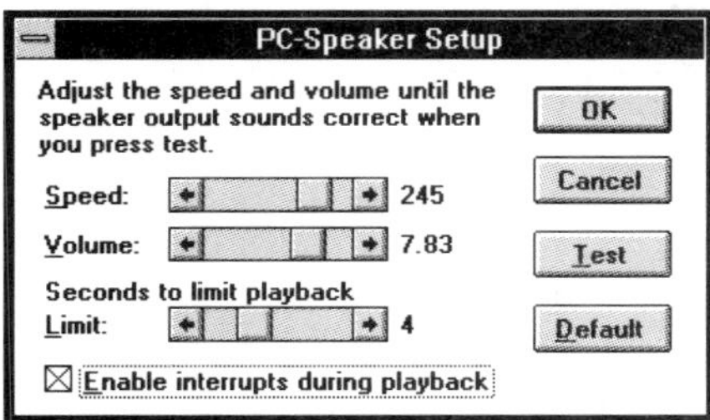

Figure 8.27 The PC-Speaker Setup dialog box

This dialog box lets you adjust the **Speed** with which the PC's internal speaker will play sounds; the **Volume** of those sounds; and a **Limit** to how long it will play a sound. You can also click on the **Enable interrupts during playback** to make sure the mouse and serial communications ports will operate while a sound is playing.

Click on the **Test** button to play the Default Beep sound. (You will learn more about sounds in a moment.) The Test button will be disabled if the Default Beep has been set to None in the Sounds dialog box.

Removing Drivers

You can also remove drivers. Select the one you want in the Drivers dialog box and click on **Remove**. Windows prompts you to confirm that you want to remove the driver. You must restart Windows for the change to take effect. Removing a driver does not actually remove the driver from your hard disk—it simply removes the reference to it from the [drivers.desc] section of the CONTROL.INI file. To remove the file you should find the line in the CONTROL.INI file (see Appendix B for information), note the name of the file it refers to, then delete the line and the file itself.

Associating Sounds and Events

The Sound dialog box (see Figure 8.28) lets you associate a variety of different .WAV sound files with several different events. Windows provides four .WAV files: CHIME, CHORD, DING, and TADA. You can modify these sounds or record new ones using Sound Recorder, or you can buy sounds from various software or shareware vendors. To play these sounds you either need a driver for your internal speaker (such as SPEAKER.DRV, available from Microsoft) or a

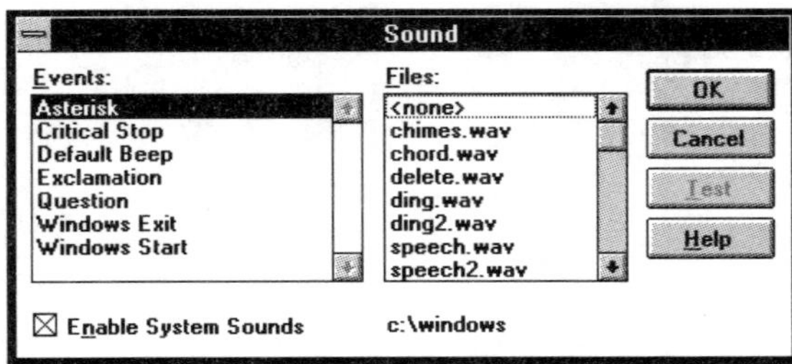

Figure 8.28 The Sound dialog box

sound card and associated driver. To record new sounds you will need a sound card that allows you to record as well as play.

The Sound box lets you select a particular event and associate a sound with it. You can select the sound you want played each time you open or close Windows (**Windows Start** and **Windows Exit**). The other events vary depending on the application you are working in. Most applications use the **Default Beep**, for instance, when you make a mistake (such as click the mouse outside a dialog box). Few applications currently make use of the other events, but undoubtedly more will soon.

To associate a sound with an event, simply click on the event, then click on the sound with which you want to associate it. The Windows .WAV files are in the WINDOWS directory, but you can use the **Files** list box to select files in any directory you wish. The Windows-supplied sounds are, quite frankly, nothing to write home about. However, with the right equipment you can record anything you want, or you may buy more interesting sounds. Be warned: Before you spend money on Star Trek and Monty Python sounds, the novelty of having your computer speak to you in this fairly limited way may wear off very quickly. On the other hand, if you feel inferior to your Macintosh-owning friends, you may feel you need sounds just to "keep up with the Joneses."

If you assign an event to **none** in the Files list box, the ordinary system beep is used instead of a .WAV sound, except in the case of the Windows Start and Exit sounds. In these cases, associating them with **none** ensures that they don't play any sound. You can test a sound by clicking on Sound and then clicking on the **Test** button. Or double-click on the sound file or the event associated with it. If nothing happens, you probably don't have the necessary driver or hardware installed. Finally, the **Enable System Sounds** check box lets you control all system sounds but the Windows Start and Windows Exit sounds. When you deselect the option, the sounds associated with the other five events won't play.

The Network Settings

Network

You can use the Network dialog box to carry out various procedures, depending on the type of network with which you are working. You may be able to change your user ID and password, send messages to people, sign on and off the network, and so on.

Figure 8.29 shows an example of what you might see when you open a Network dialog box. In fact, by the time you read this even the illustrated dialog box may be out of date. The actual dialog box depends both on the type of network with which you are working and the version of that network's Windows driver.

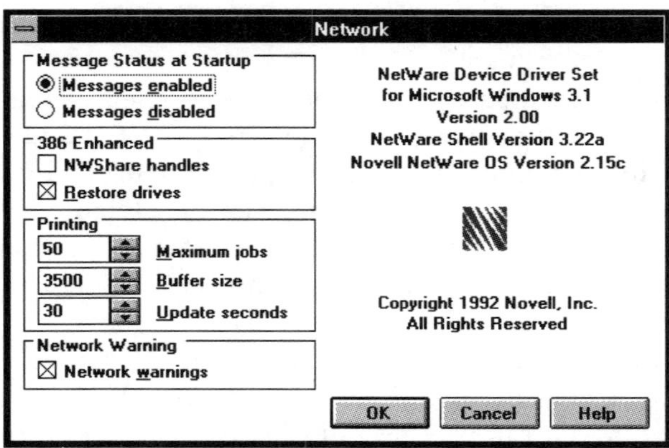

Figure 8.29 A Novell NetWare Network dialog box

As an example, here are the dialog box options for this Network:

Message Status at Startup You can enable or disable messages from network stations. If disabled, you won't get any messages except broadcast messages and others from the file server console. Those from other users, for instance, will not get through. (This is NetWare's CASTOFF command.)

NWShare Handles Changes to the drive mapping in each MS-DOS window is usually independent of the others. If you select this option, changing one affects the others. You may need to do this if you are running a NetWare 286 server.

Restore Drivers If turned on, network directories that you map to a drive (in File Manager) will be lost when you close Windows.

Printing: Maximum Jobs The maximum number of print jobs that Print Manager can display at once, up to 250.

Printing: Buffer Size This allocates memory for the display of print job information in Print Manager, up to 30,000 bytes. Assign at least 14 bytes for each Maximum Jobs value.

Printing: Update Seconds How often the Print Manager should update the network queue information.

Network Warnings If this is turned on, you will see a warning when you open Windows if the network shell isn't loaded, if the shell is an earlier version than the one this network driver was intended for, or if memory is insufficient to run the shell. You should normally leave this turned on.

For help, use the box's Help system, talk to the network administrator, or call the manufacturer's technical support line. Also, read the NETWORKS.WRI file in the WINDOWS directory.

9

Files and Directories: File Manager

While File Manager is not as sophisticated as some file-management programs, it's probably easier to use than most. File Manager won't let you print a list of the files in a directory, or let you view the contents of a file. However, it's a great improvement over the Windows 3.0 File Manager. Although purists might complain about its relative lack of features, it contains all the most important commands that you will need. You can rename files and directories, create new directories, measure disk space, move, copy, and delete files, and so on. You can even "prune and graft" directories, moving an entire "branch" from one place in the directory tree to another, or even onto another disk drive.

Starting File Manager

Start File Manager by clicking on the File Manager icon in the Main program group. Or select **File | Run** and run **WINFILE**. A typical File Manager window is shown in Figure 9.1. (Yours will probably look slightly different.) File Manager generally contains one or more *directory windows*. In Figure 9.1 you can see two directory windows, one on top of the other. Each window can display a directory on any of the computer's disk drives (or, if connected to a network, any network drive).

Each directory window has two main parts. The left side shows the directory "tree," a list of all the directories on the selected drive. You can select a directory from the tree so that the right side of the directory window shows the contents of that directory. (You can use the first three View menu options to modify a directory window, displaying only the directory tree or only one directory at a time. More about this later.)

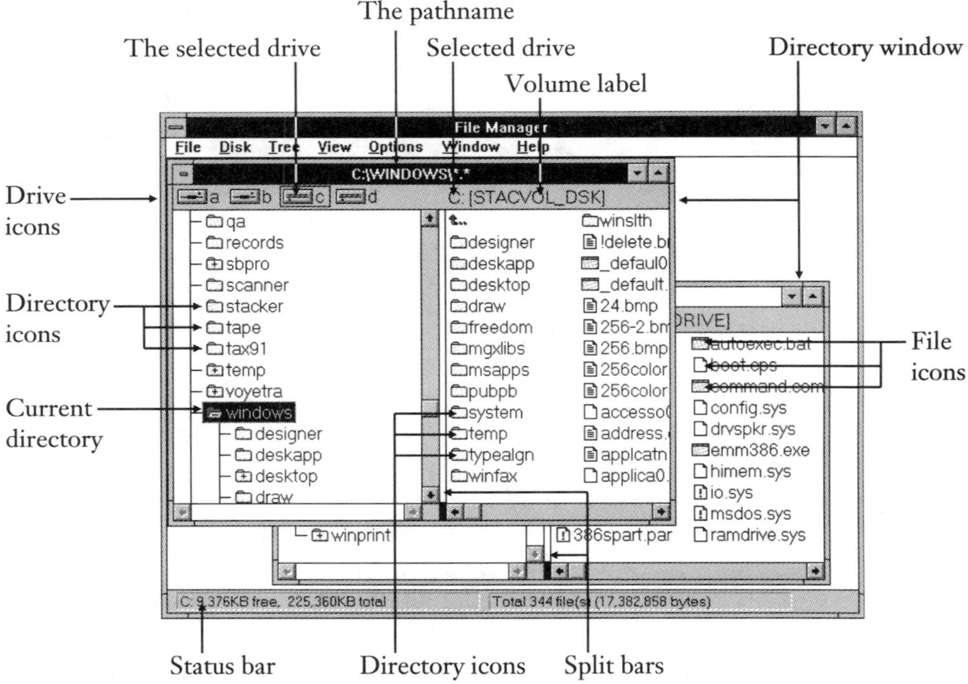

Figure 9.1 A typical File Manager window

Notice that in Figure 9.1 some of the directory icons have **+** or **–** signs on them. These indicate expandable and collapsible directories. If a directory has a + sign on it, that directory contains subdirectories (it is "expandable" because we can open up that "branch" of the directory tree to see the subdirectories). If a directory icon has a – sign on it, it has already been expanded and is displaying its subdirectories. In Windows 3.0 these + and – signs were displayed by default, but with Windows 3.1 you must use the **Tree|Indicate Expandable Branches** command to display them.

The right side of the directory window displays the contents of the directory selected on the left side of the directory tree. You will notice that the directory displays a variety of different icons, as shown in Figure 9.2.

You can use the **parent directory** icon (the arrow) to move back up the directory tree. Double-clicking on this icon (or selecting it and pressing **Enter),** displays the contents of the current directory's parent directory. The **subdirectory** icon takes you the other way; double-clicking on it displays the contents of that subdirectory. The **hidden** or **system** file icon indicates a file with a file attribute of Hidden or System, files such as the Windows swapfile (386SPART.PAR) or DOS system files. The **program**, **batch file**, or **PIF** icon indicates a file that has an .EXE, a .COM, a .BAT, or a .PIF extension, all files that start applications or, in the case of batch files, carry out DOS commands.

Parent directory

Subdirectory

Hidden or system files

Program and batch files and PIFs

Document files

Unknown files

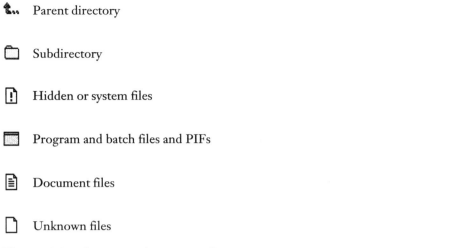

Figure 9.2 The icons shown in a directory

Document file icons indicate files whose extensions have either been associated with a particular application (we'll discuss associations later in this chapter) or are included on the Documents= line in the WIN.INI initialization file (see Appendix B for more information). For instance, files with a .TXT extension are associated with Notepad, so Windows knows they are document files. Finally, the **unknown file** icon indicates a file that Windows doesn't recognize as fitting in any of the other groups: It doesn't recognize the extension and the file is neither hidden nor a system file.

At the top of each directory window you can see the **drive icons**. These show the available drives on your computer or network. The one that is currently displayed in the directory window has a box around it. On the right side of the window you will see the selected drive and volume label: for instance `C:[HARD_DRIVE]` means that drive C: is shown and that its volume label is HARD_DRIVE. The directory window's title bar indicates the full pathname of the selected directory. It also uses a file specification to indicate which files are being displayed. For instance, `C:\WINDOWS\*.*` means that all the files in the WINDOWS directory are displayed. If it showed `C:\WINDOWS\P*.EXE`, all the .EXE files beginning with P would be shown. We will explain how to use the **View | By File Type** command to specify which files you want shown.

At the bottom of the File Manager window is a **status bar**. This shows information concerning disk space and the number of files. If the highlight is on a directory in the left side of the directory window—in the tree—the status bar shows the drive letter, the amount of free space on that drive, the total size of the drive, the number of files in the selected directory, and the total size of those files. If the highlight is in the right side of the directory window—in a directory—the status bar shows the number of selected files and their total size, and the number of files in the directory and their total size.

A Quick Word about Directory Trees

If you have been using computers for a while, you are probably already familiar with the idea of a directory "tree." Each disk drive has what is known as the *root directory*. This directory can be thought of as being at the bottom of a tree of branching directories and *subdirectories*. The root directory has no name; it is indicated by a backslash. C:\ refers to the root directory on drive C:. D:\ is the root directory on drive D:, and so on.

The root directory can contain files and subdirectories. And each of those subdirectories can have their own files and subdirectories. For instance, the WINDOWS directory is a subdirectory of the root directory. The SYSTEM directory is a subdirectory of the WINDOWS directory. DOS uses *pathnames* to describe a file's position in the directory tree. The pathname C:\WINDOWS\SYSTEM\HPPCL5A.DRV refers to a file called HPPCL5A.DRV, which is stored in the SYSTEM directory, which is a subdirectory of the WINDOWS directory, which is a subdirectory of the root directory.

This directory system lets you categorize files according to their use. You can segregate each program's files from those of all other programs. You can keep program files apart from data files, and you can even keep different types of data files in different directories. In one sense the more directories you have the easier it is to categorize your files. However, there are drawbacks to using too many directories. The structure becomes unwieldy—moving through the structure in File Manager or in an application's File Open dialog box becomes very slow, for instance. Also, if you have too many levels of branches your computer will take more time to find files when it is reading and writing to a disk. So, as a general rule, keep the directory tree as simple as you can. It's better to add more subdirectories to the root directory than to add lots of levels to a branch.

File Manager displays the tree structure in the directory window, with the root directory at the *top* of the window. Let's see how you can select a disk drive and move through the drive's tree.

Selecting a Disk Drive

The first time you use File Manger it will display one directory window, with the drive on which you installed Windows shown. You can select another disk drive in several ways:

- **Click** on the icon (at the top of the directory window), representing the disk drive.
- Press **Ctrl-*n***, where *n* is the drive letter.

- Press **Tab** or **F6** once or twice to move the drive icons, press the **arrow** keys to select the drive, then press **Spacebar**.
- Select **Disk | Select Drive**, then double-click on a drive in the Select Drive dialog box.
- **Double-click** on the drive-icon bar, then double-click on a drive in the Select Drive dialog box.
- **Double-click** on the icon representing the disk drive to open another directory window and select that drive.
- Press **Tab** or **F6** once or twice to move the drive icons, press the **arrow** keys to select the drive, then press **Enter** to open another directory window and select that drive.

Whichever method you use, File Manager begins reading the selected drive. If you press **Esc**, File Manager stops and displays what it has found so far. Press **F5** to make File Manager read the drive again.

Moving Around the Directory Tree

Once you've got the drive you want, you need to select the directory. How, then, do you navigate through the directory tree? When you select a drive the highlight is on that drive's current directory or, if you have just opened File Manager, on the directory it was on the last time you saved the settings (we'll discuss how to save settings later). You can display the contents of another directory by selecting the directory. Move the highlight onto the directory by **clicking** on it. If you are using the keyboard, use these keystrokes to move the highlight:

Up and Down Arrows	Up or down the screen, one directory or subdirectory at a time
Home or Backslash (\)	To the root directory
End	To the last directory in the screen
Right Arrow	To the first displayed subdirectory of the highlighted directory (the same as the Down Arrow)
Left Arrow or Backspace	To the subdirectory's parent directory. If on the first level of subdirectories, it moves the highlight back to the root directory.
Page Up	Up one screen
Page Down	Down one screen

Ctrl-Up Arrow	To the previous directory at the same level
Ctrl-Down Arrow	To the next directory at the same level
any character key	To the next displayed directory or subdirectory whose name begins with the typed letter. Continue several times to go to the last occurrence and back to the first occurrence.

 **Tip** The Home and End keys are useful even if you are using the mouse, as they save scrolling through a long directory tree.

Expanding and Collapsing Directories

We mentioned in the previous list that some of the keystrokes move you to the next *displayed* directory. Not all the directories are displayed when you first open File Manager or select a new drive. Only the root directory and the first level of subdirectories are shown. If your directory icons don't show + and – signs to indicate expandable and collapsible branches, the first thing you should do is select **Tree | Indicate Expandable Branches**. Now, as you move through the directory tree, you can see which directories contain subdirectories, and *expand* the branches to get to the subdirectories. (There is one disadvantage of turning on these indicators—File Manager will take a little longer to read the directory tree.)

There are two ways to expand a branch. You can expand "one level"—that is, display all a directory's subdirectories but not all the subdirectories in each subdirectory. Or you can expand an entire branch to display all a directory's subdirectories on all levels.

In Windows 3.0 you could simply click once on the directory icon to expand one level. Unfortunately with Windows 31. you must double-click on the icon. Or you can use the arrow keys to move to the directory and then press **Enter** or **+**. You can also place the highlight on the directory and select **Tree | Expand One Level**.

To expand an entire branch, select the directory and then press *, or select **Tree | Expand Branch**. To collapse a branch—that is, to remove all of a directories subdirectories from view—double-click on the directory, or select it and press – or **Enter**. Or you can select **Tree | CollapseBranch**.

Incidentally, you can quickly expand the entire tree to display all the subdirectories on the disk in one of three ways: Select **Tree | Expand All**, press **Ctrl-***, or place the highlight on the root directory and press *. You won't want to do this often, though, because it takes some time to read the entire tree, especially if you have a lot of directories.

Moving Through the Directory Contents

Once you have selected the directory you need, you can move to the right side of the directory window—the directory contents—to work with the files. Move to the right side by pressing **Tab** or by **clicking** anywhere in the contents area.

What can you do with the contents? Notice that the contents side has both directory and file icons. To see the contents of the *previous directory*, double-click on the parent directory icon (the arrow in the top left corner of the contents); select the icon and press **Enter;** or press **Backspace** regardless of which icon is selected. To see the contents of a *subdirectory*, double-click on a subdirectory icon, or select the icon and press **Enter**. Using these commands you can get to any directory in the tree—you don't need the directory tree view at all (it's just easier to use).

Use these keystrokes to move around in the contents (remember that when the highlight lands on a file or directory you have "selected," it and can carry out an operation on it):

Up or Down Arrow	To the previous or next file or directory
End	The last file or directory in the list
Home	The first file or directory in the list
PgUp	The file or directory at the top of the previous screen
PgDn	The file or directory at the bottom of the next screen
any character key	To the next displayed file or directory whose name begins with the typed letter. Continue several times to go to the last occurrence and back to the first occurrence.

Sorting Files

What, exactly, will you see in the directory contents? When you first open File Manager the directories and files will be sorted in alphabetical order (with the directories first). The name is the only information displayed for each file—no file size, time, or date.

Of course File Manager lets you modify the file sorting and information by selecting options from the View menu. You can sort the files in alphabetical order according to the file *extension* by selecting **View | By Type**. Thus, all the files with .EXE extensions will be grouped together, all with .DOC will be together, and so on. Within each group the files will be sorted in alphabetical order according to the filenames.

You can look at the files in the order of their size, with the largest at the top, by selecting **View | By Size**. Or you may display them in chronological order, with the most recent file at the top, by selecting **View | By Date**. If you want to switch back to viewing them in alphabetical order (by name), select **View | By Name**

Incidentally, most of these commands also affect the directories. They will be sorted into alphabetical order (By Name) or chronological order (By Date). They will even be placed in alphabetical order according to extension if you select By Type (yes, directories can have extensions, as in `DIRCTORY.NEW`). However, if you select By Size, the directories are simply placed in alphabetical order by name.

These options are very useful, as they help you look for particular types of information. If you are looking for a document file you created sometime last May, sort by date. If you are removing files to make more space on your hard drive, sort by size. If you are looking for a particular document file but are not sure of its exact name, sort by type.

Viewing File Data

You can tell File Manager exactly the type of information you want to see. The available information is the file's size, a time and date stamp, and four DOS *attributes.* Attributes are single characters that describe an important characteristic of a file. If the file is **Read Only** (R) it can be read by an application, but it cannot usually be modified or deleted (although File Manager can delete Read Only files). If the file has the **Archive** (A) attribute it means it needs archiving. The DOS XCOPY and BACKUP commands—and most backup programs—remove this attribute when you back up the file. The next time the file is modified, though, the A attribute is added again. So the attribute is a handy way for you (and, more important, for a backup command or program) to tell if the file has been backed up, or if it has been modified since the last time it was backed up.

The **Hidden** (H) attribute makes the file "invisible" to normal viewing. The file won't appear if you use the normal DOS DIR (directory) command, for instance, although you can use a switch to view it. It won't appear in a File Open dialog box. And many file-management utilities won't display the file unless you specifically tell them to include hidden files. Hidden files cannot usually be erased, at least by DOS's DEL or ERASE commands, which is why the IO.SYS and MSDOS.SYS files are hidden. (However, File Manager will let you erase hidden files.) Some software uses hidden files and directories as a copy protection system; other programs hide files as a way to protect essential data. If you hide a directory, DOS will be unable to see it—if you use the DIR command the directory won't be listed, for instance. File Manager will be able to see it, though.

The final attribute is **System** (S). System files are also hidden files (in fact IO.SYS and MSDOS.SYS are actually system files). But system files are an archaeological relic, left over from the CP/M operating system that predates DOS, and

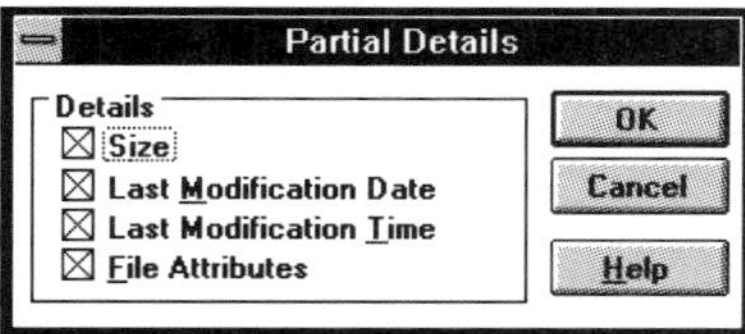

Figure 9.3 The Partial Details dialog box

the concept is not used in DOS. System files are simply another form of hidden files.

There are three options on the View menu that let us specify the data we want to see. The default is **View | Name**. You will see the file's icon and name, but nothing more. Select **View | All File Details** to see all the information, including the file's size, time and date, and attributes. Or select **View | Partial Details** to see the dialog box shown in Figure 9.3. You can select the information you want to see: Size, Last Modification Date, Last Modification Time, and File Attributes. Figure 9.4 shows three directory windows, each displaying the same directory but different information (you will learn how to work with multiple windows and remove the directory tree in a moment).

If you don't need to view the details of all files all the time, you may want to keep the **View | Name** option selected all the time. Then, when you want to view the

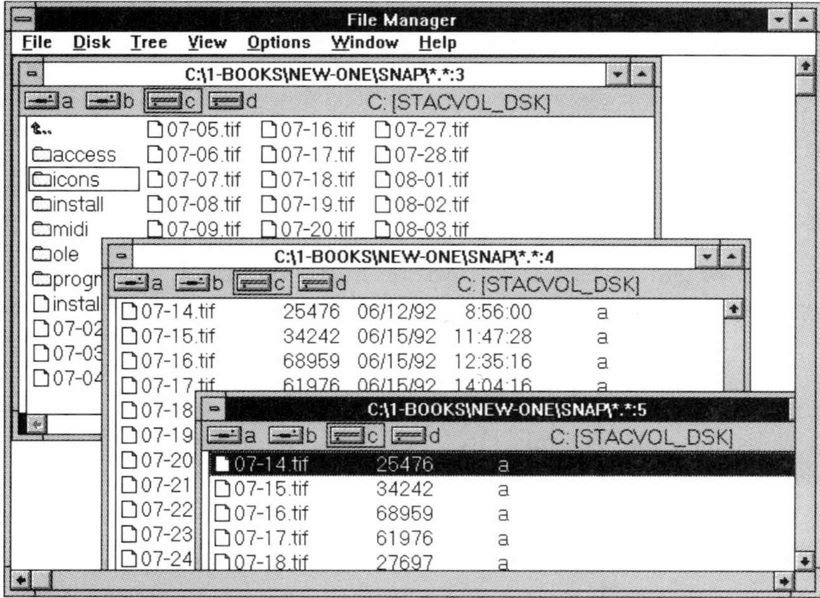

Figure 9.4 Three directory windows, each displaying different file details

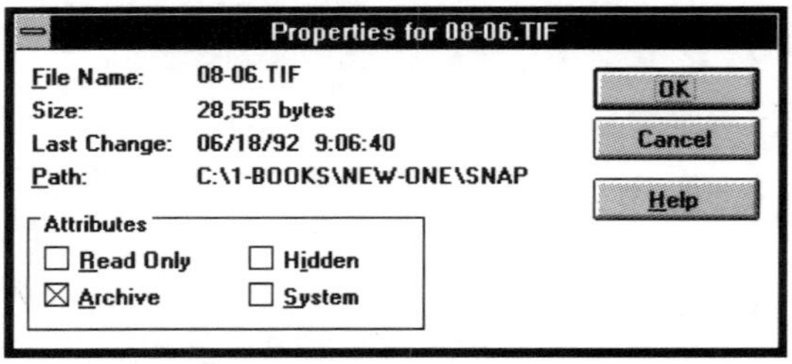

Properties for 08-06.TIF

File Name: 08-06.TIF
Size: 28,555 bytes
Last Change: 06/18/92 9:06:40
Path: C:\1-BOOKS\NEW-ONE\SNAP

Attributes
☐ Read Only ☐ Hidden
☒ Archive ☐ System

OK
Cancel
Help

Figure 9.5 The File Properties dialog box

details of a particular file, click on it and select **File | Properties**. The Properties dialog box appears (see Figure 9.5). This shows you all the information pertaining to that file. If you are working on a network the dialog box may appear slightly different.

Tip Here's a quick way to display a file's properties: hold **Alt** and double-click on the filename. Or hold **Alt**, and press **Enter**.

Updating the View

There are occasions when File Manager doesn't display the correct information. For instance, if you select a floppy-disk drive, File Manager reads the drive and displays the contents. If you then place a different disk in the drive, the display is now wrong.

If you select a drive and immediately select the **View | By File Type** command, File Manager will stop while selecting the file specifications and then continue when you click on OK, but the displayed directory may not display the correct information.

You can update the view at any time by simply selecting the drive again, by pressing **F5**, or by selecting **Window | Refresh**. This is not very quick, though, because it reads all the displayed directories on the tree.

Tip There's a much quicker way to update a single directory. Just click on another directory, then click on the directory you need to update.

Omitting Files from the Contents

You've seen how to sort files and how to specify the file information that should be shown, but there's one more way to specify the contents. You can tell File Manager to omit certain files from the list. By default, File Manager shows you all the files in the selected directory except the hidden and system files (so that you can't accidentally delete these files). But let's say, for instance, you are looking through a directory for a specific .BMP or .DOC file. Rather than view all the files, why not narrow the search a little?

Select **View|By File Type** to see the dialog box shown in Figure 9.6. By clicking on the check boxes you can tell File Manager to include or omit certain file types and directories. For instance, if you only want to see program files, select that option and deselect all others.

Remember the file icons we showed you earlier? File Manager uses the same information to decide if it should include certain files. It assumes that .EXE, .COM, .BAT, and .PIF files are program files. Document files are those that have been associated with an application, or whose extension appears in the Documents= line in WIN.INI. System and hidden files are those with the S or H attribute. And "other files" are those that are neither program nor document files. Of course if you select the **Show Hidden/System Files** option, hidden and system files will only be displayed if they fit the other criteria. For instance, if you select both Show Hidden/System Files and Documents, IO.SYS would not be displayed, even though it is a system file, because it is not a document file. However, hidden *directories* are *always* visible. There's no way to remove them from File Manager's view—although DOS's DIR command won't be able to see them. (unless you use the /a switch). Figure 9.7 shows the effect of displaying only document files in the WINDOWS\SYSTEM directory.

Tip If you use the directory tree to navigate through your hard drive, you may want to omit the directories from the contents.

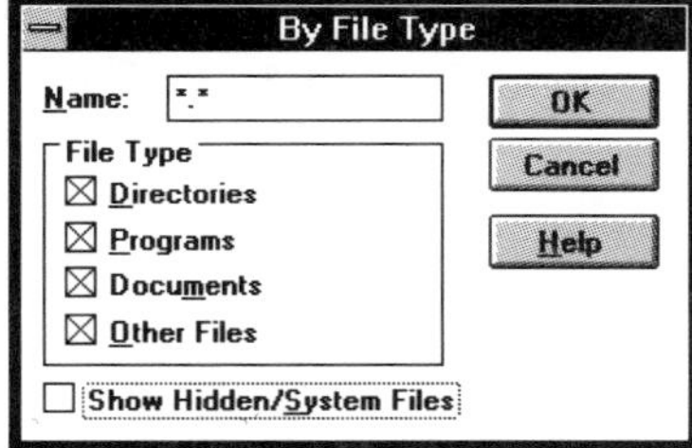

Figure 9.6 The By File Type dialog box

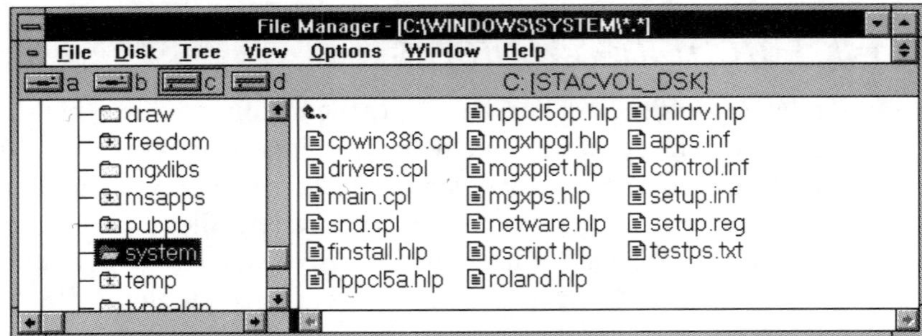

Figure 9.7 The WINDOWS\SYSTEM directory with only document files displayed

Notice also the **Name** text box at the top of the By File Type dialog box. This lets you be even more specific about the type of files you want to view. For instance, selecting the Programs option displays all .EXE, .COM, .BAT, and .PIF files, but if you only want to view .PIF files, type ***.PIF** into the Name text box.

If you only want to view .PIF files beginning with D, type **D*.PIF**. If you want to see all files with extensions that begin with C, type ***.C***. It's important to note, though, that the Name text box depends on the File Type selection you make. For instance, if you type ***.DOC** into the Name text box, select Programs, then deselect all the other check boxes, you won't see any files, because no program file has a .DOC extension.

The asterisk is a *wild card*, but you can also use the ? as a wild card. The asterisk replaces one or more characters. Thus *.* means "any filename and any extension." The question mark replaces just one character. Thus ?.? would mean "any one-character filename and any one-character extension."

The question mark is useful when you want to specify certain files with similar names. For instance, you want to view the files 92_01OD.DOC through 92_09OD.DOC. You could enter **92_0?OD.DOC** to view all of them. Of course you could also type **92_0*OD.DOC**, but that's not as precise; because the asterisk can replace multiple characters, you would also see a file named 92_08XOD.DOC.

When you use the Name text box, the directory window's title bar changes. Instead of displaying C:\WINDOWS\SYSTEM*.*, for instance, it might now show C:\WINDOWS\SYSTEM*.TXT. The title bar doesn't change if you leave the *.* in the Name text box and select a single File Type check box.

Tip If you have been using the Name text box and now want to display all the files, you don't need to retype the *.*. Simply select **View | By File Type**, press **Del**, and press **Enter**.

There's one danger with omitting certain files from the view. You may forget you have done so. If a directory appears to have fewer files than you thought it should have, glance at the title bar to see if you have changed the *.* at the end of the pathname. If not, quickly open the By File Type dialog box and make sure all the check boxes are selected.

Again, remember that hidden files are hidden for a reason, to protect them from accidental damage, which is why File Manager doesn't automatically display them. However, you may find it useful to be able to see everything in each directory, and File Manager won't delete or move a hidden file without warning you first. (We'll discuss these warnings—or confirmations—later in this chapter.)

Working with Multiple Windows

File Manager lets you use several windows at the same time (dozens, if you wish). This is especially useful when moving files from one disk drive to another, or from one end of the directory tree to another. There are several ways to add a new window:

- Select **Window | New Window**.
- **Double-click** on a drive icon.
- Press **Tab** or **F6** once or twice to move the drive icons, press the **arrow** keys to select the drive, then press **Enter**.
- Point at a directory in the directory tree, hold **Shift**, and **double-click**. A new directory window opens, displaying only the directory, not the tree.
- Highlight a directory in the directory tree, hold **Shift**, and press **Enter**. A new directory window opens, displaying only the directory, not the tree.

Whichever method you use, File Manager opens a new window using exactly the same settings as the one from which you selected the command. It will be the same size, displaying the same directory, and have the same configuration—the View options will be the same, for instance.

▼ ***Note*** If a directory is selected in more than one window, a number will appear after the pathname in the directory window's title bar.

Once you have a new window you can modify it. You can select the drive and directory you want and set up the file sorting and viewing options just as you want them. You can also modify the size. Notice that the directory windows have

maximize and **minimize** buttons. If you maximize one window, *all* will be maximized. And if a window is maximized, you must restore it first (click on the **restore button** or select the **Restore** option from the control menu) before you can minimize it. Use the directory window's borders or Control menu to modify its size.

▼ ***Note*** If you are using the keyboard, open a directory window's Control menu by pressing **Alt-hyphen (-)**. Use the standard **Alt-Spacebar** method to open File Manager's Control menu.

You can also modify the way the windows are displayed inside the File Manager window using the Window menu options. Use the **Window | Cascade** (**Shift-F5**) command to place the windows one on top of the other, each one a little lower down the window than the previous one, so all the title bars are visible. Or use **Window | Tile** to give each window equal space (and to leave room at the bottom of the window to display the directory-window icons). This is useful when you have only two windows open and are moving files from one directory or disk to another. In some cases you can press **Shift** while you select **Window | Tile** (or press **Shift-F4**) to arrange the windows so that they are side by side, rather than one on top of the other. This doesn't always work, though, depending on the number of directory windows.

In some cases tiling windows will remove the contents side of the directory windows if there's not enough room to view both sides. However, you can use the first four **View** commands to change this, as we explain a little later in this chapter. Of course if any windows are minimized they are not affected by the Tile or Cascade commands. Figure 9.8 shows an example of two tiled directory windows, as might be used to copy files between the hard drive and a floppy drive.

To move between directory windows, use these methods:

- **Click** on the window if a portion is visible.
- Press **Ctrl-Tab** or **Ctrl-F6** to cycle through the windows.
- Open the **Window** menu and select the window you want from the list.
- Press **Alt-hyphen (-)** to open the directory window's Control menu, and type **t** to move to the next window.

Of course you can close directory windows in the normal way, using the **Control** menu, by typing **Ctrl-F4**, or by double-clicking on the Control menu. And you can use the **Window | Arrange Icons** command to line up all the icons evenly.

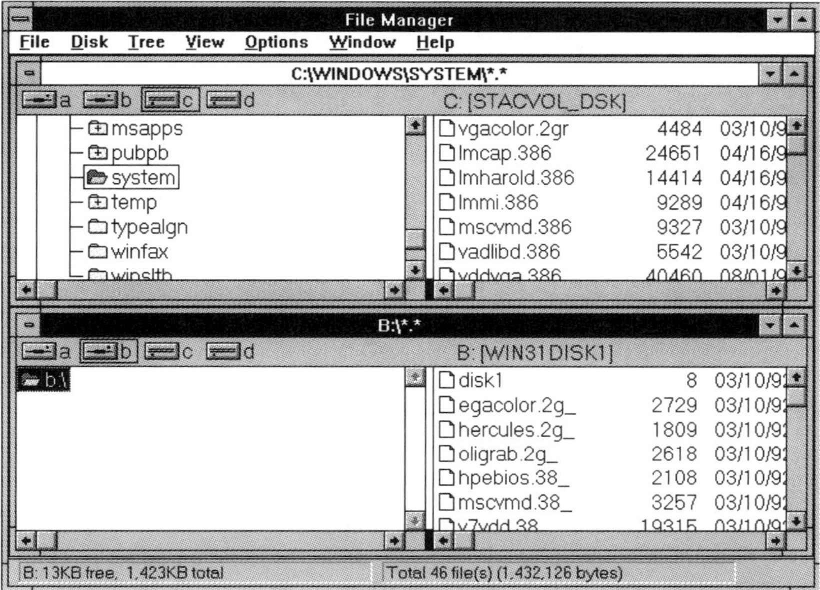

Figure 9.8 Two tiled windows

Selecting Files

The whole purpose of File Manager is to get to the *files* in a directory. Once you have got to a directory you can select one or more files—and directories—and carry out a variety of operations. There are a number of ways to select files or directories in the directory list:

- Select a single item by **clicking** on it or by pressing the **arrow keys** to move the highlight to it.
- Select a group of consecutive items by **clicking** on the first, holding **Shift**, and **clicking** on the last in the group. Or select the first, hold **Shift**, and press the **arrow key** to move to the last.
- Select a group of nonconsecutive items by holding **Ctrl** while you **click** on the items. Or press **Shift-F8**, use the **arrow keys** to move to each item, and press **Spacebar** to select each one; press **Shift-F8** again to finish the selection procedure.
- Select two or more groups of consecutive items: **click** on the first, hold **Shift**, and **click** on the last in the group. Then press **Ctrl** while you click on the first

in the next group, and press **Shift-Ctrl** while you click on the last item in that group. Or, hold **Shift** while you press the **arrow keys** to select the first group, then when you reach the last item press **Shift-F8**, use the **arrow keys** to move to the first in the next group, press **Shift** and the **arrow keys** to select the next group, and press **Shift-F8** again.

- Select a group of items using the Select Files command.
- Select all the files in a directory by pressing **Ctrl-/**.

Select **File | Select Files** to see the dialog box shown in Figure 9.9. This box lets you quickly select a type of file, according to the wild cards you enter. For instance, if you want to select all the files with the PIF extension, type ***.PIF**. If you want to select all the files named DELETE, type **DELETE.***. If you want to select all the files named DELETE and a number (DELETE1, DELETE2, DELETE3, and so on), type **DELETE*.***. You can also use a ? as a wild card, as we explained earlier in this chapter. If you want to select a specific file with this method, type the file's name, including the extension. When you have entered the name or wild cards, click on the **Select** button.

You can use the Select Files dialog box to combine several selections. The dialog box remains displayed until you click the **Close** button. You could select all the *.TXT files, then all the *.BMP files, and then close the dialog box.

Removing Files from a Selection

You can also click on the **Deselect** button to remove files from the selection. For instance, let's say you want to move all the files from the directory except the *.CRD files. Use the **Ctrl-/** method to select all the files, then select **File | Select Files**. Type ***.CRD** and click on **Deselect** and then **Close**.

There are other ways to remove a file from a group selection:

- Hold **Ctrl** and click on the file.
- Press **Shift-F8**, use the arrow keys to move to a file, and press **Spacebar**. Then press **Shift-F8** to end the mode.
- Remove the highlight from all files (but one) by pressing **Ctrl-**.
- **Click** on a file to select that file and deselect all others.

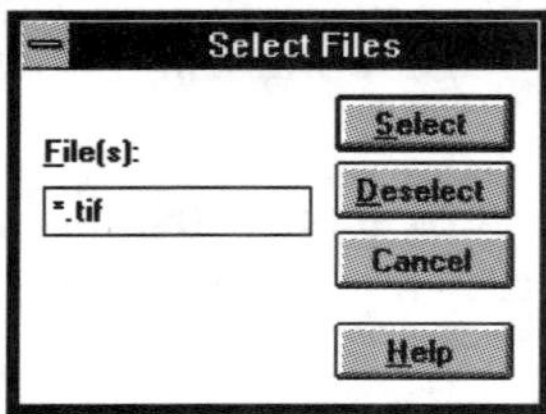

Figure 9.9 The Select Files dialog box

Carrying Out Operations

Once you've selected a file, directory, or group you can carry out a variety of operations. You can move, copy, delete, rename, start a program, view data, create a subdirectory, and so on. You can carry out most basic DOS file-management commands. In some cases File Manager has some commands that DOS does not. For instance, you can rename or move directories, which you can't do in DOS.

Moving and Copying Files and Directories

You can move or copy a single file or directory, or a group of files and directories (use the methods we described earlier to select a group). You can move the object to another directory, or a directory on another disk drive entirely. Use these techniques:

- **Drag** to another directory and release the mouse button to move.
- Hold **Ctrl** and **drag** to another directory to copy.
- **Drag** to a drive icon or a directory on another drive to copy.
- Hold **Alt** and **drag** to a drive icon or a directory on another drive to move.
- Select **File | Copy** or press **F8** to copy.
- Select **File | Move** or press **F7** to move.

Notice that when you drag files or directories to a directory on the same disk, File Manager will *move* them, unless you held the Ctrl key while you dragged (release the mouse button before Ctrl). However, if you are dragging to another disk, File Manager automatically *copies* unless you hold the Alt key.

When you move or copy by dragging the files, File Manager displays a confirmation box (see Figure 9.10), asking you to confirm the operation. Later in this chapter we'll explain how to stop these boxes appearing, but you may want to keep them when you first begin working with File Manager, in case you get mixed up and copy instead of moving, or vice versa. Just click on **Yes** to complete the operation.

When you select one of the File commands, you see a dialog box (like the Copy dialog box in Figure 9.11) that asks for the directory to which you want to move the file or directory. Simply type the name of the directory and click on **OK**. You can

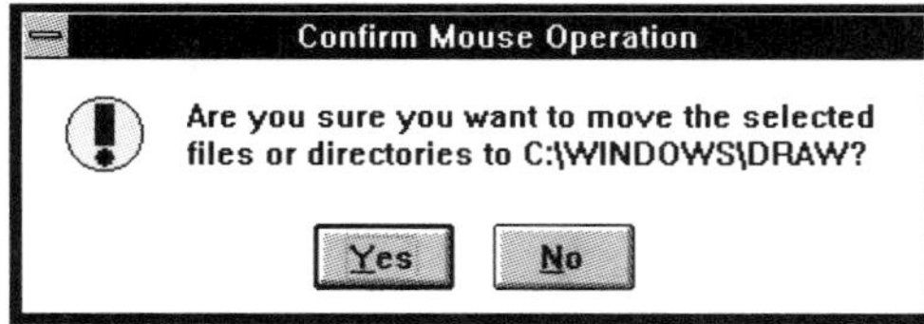

Figure 9.10 A file-move confirmation box

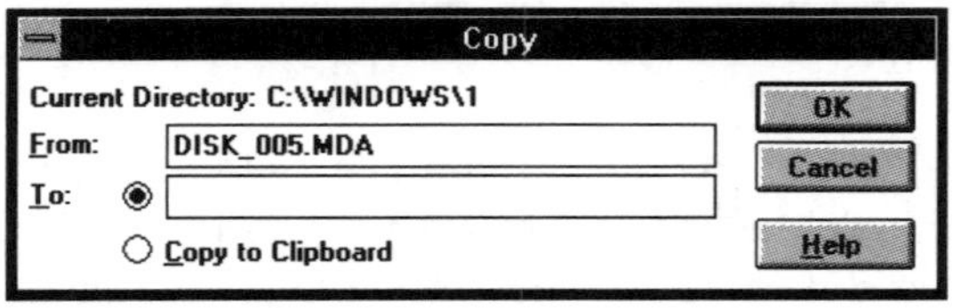

Figure 9.11 The Copy dialog box

rename a file—though not a directory—while you move it, by typing the new name at the end of the pathname.

You can create a **new directory** while you move or copy. For instance, if you are copying directory 1 into directory A, type **C:\A\B** and click on **OK** to copy 1 into a new subdirectory called B. If you are moving a file, you will have to enter the filename at the end of the pathname, or File Manager will assume you are giving it a new filename. For instance, to move file X.DOC to a new directory B in directory A, you can't just type **C:\A\B**, or File Manager will place X.DOC in directory A, and rename the file B. Instead, type

```
C:\A\B\X.DOC
```

Notice at the bottom of the Copy dialog box an option button labeled **Copy to Clipboard.** If you click on this option and leave the **To** text box blank, the file is copied into the Clipboard so it can be embedded or linked into an OLE client application, or into Object Packager. See Chapter 28 for more information.

Whichever method you use to move or copy files, if the file is going to be placed in a directory that has a file of the same name you will see a warning box, as shown in Figure 9.12. You can click on **Yes** to replace the file, but if others in the group match existing files you will see the dialog box again. Or you can click on **Yes to All** to automatically replace all the files without having to see a confirmation dialog box each time.

The ability to move and copy directories—something DOS can't do—lets you rearrange your directory tree. This is sometimes called "pruning and grafting" because you are "pruning" a branch and "grafting" it back onto the tree elsewhere.

Figure 9.12 The Confirm File Replace dialog box

When you move or copy a directory all the files and subdirectories—and the files in those subdirectories—go with the selected directory.

Caution If you copy or move a directory to a directory with a subdirectory of the same name, you will *not* see a warning. Instead, the files are automatically merged into the subdirectory.

Incidentally, if you try to *move* a system, hidden, or read-only file, File Manager asks you to confirm the operation (even if you are not copying a file onto another with the same name).

Note also that File Manager's Move command is not the same as moving a file using DOS. In DOS you have to actually copy the file, then delete the original, which means that the "moved" file is actually a new file. And that means that its archive bit has been turned on; so the next time you use a data-backup program and select the option to save only updated files, the moved file is saved. When you use File Manager's Move command, though, File Manager won't turn on the file's archive bit, unless it was on before you moved the file.

Deleting Files and Directories

You can delete files and directories just as easily as moving or copying them. To delete files, select them and then press **Del**, or select **File | Delete**. The Delete dialog box appears (shown in Figure 9.13), listing the files you selected. Click on **OK** and you will see a Confirm File Delete dialog box, showing the name of the first file. Click on **Yes** to delete that file and view the next Confirm File Delete dialog box. Or you can click on **Yes to All** to delete all the selected files without viewing the confirm box each time.

DOS makes you delete all the files in a directory before you can remove the directory itself. With File Manager you can delete them all at once. Select the directory and press **Del**. You will see the Delete dialog box again, showing just the name of the directory (not its files). Click on **OK**, and File Manager displays a dialog box asking you to confirm that you want to delete the directory. Click on

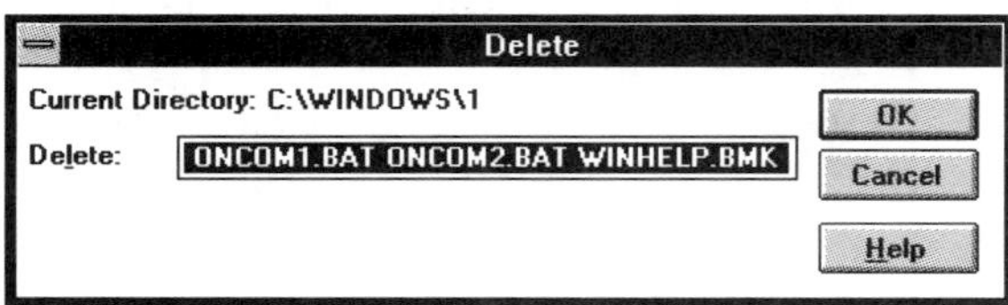

Figure 9.13 The Delete dialog box

Yes to All to make sure you won't see any more confirmation dialog boxes for all the subdirectories. Then you see another confirmation dialog box for the first file in the first directory. Click on **Yes to All** again, so you won't see any more confirmation boxes. Later in this chapter we will tell you how to get rid of all these confirmation dialog boxes.

Of course if you click on the **No** button in any of these confirmation boxes, File Manager won't be able to complete the operation. As long as just one file or subdirectory exists in a directory, that directory can't be removed. In some cases the Yes to All button will be disabled; Windows *never* lets you delete a hidden, system, or read-only file without confirming the operation first, even if you turn off the delete confirmation dialog boxes.

Remember also, if you delete a file accidentally it may be recoverable. DOS 5.0 has an UNDELETE command, as do many file utilities (File Manager itself cannot undelete files, though).

Renaming Files and Directories

File Manager lets you rename files and, unlike DOS, even directories. Simply select the file or directory and select **File | Rename**. Type the new name into the To text box and click on **OK**. If you enter too many characters—remember, DOS limits you to eight characters in the name and three in the extension—File Manager truncates the extra characters. For instance, type

```
THISFILE123.DOCS
```

and File Manager names it THISFILE.DOC.

You probably already know that DOS limits the sorts of filenames you can create. Windows still uses DOS for basic file management, so in addition to the "8 plus 3" character limitation, you can't use any of these characters: **. " / \ [ ] : ; | = , ? ***

Nor can you place spaces in the name, or use the following names: CON, AUX, COM1, COM2, COM3, COM4, LPT1, LPT2, LPT3, PRN, or NUL.

You can do *multiple* renames. Say, for instance, you have a number of graphics files named after a chapter number and illustration number. For instance, 08-03.TIF means the third illustration in Chapter 8. What do you do when Chapter 8 becomes Chapter 7, and you have 20 illustrations to change? You select all 20 files, then in the Rename dialog box you type **07-??.TIF**. All the files will be renamed appropriately, with the fourth and fifth characters remaining the same. But what if some files had two characters for the illustration number while some had only one (08-1.TIF and 08-10.TIF, for instance)? You could use the asterisk wild card, and type **07*.TIF**. All the characters in the name, beginning at the third, would remain the same.

You can also use this method to change a group of files to the same extension. For instance, if you have several files with extensions such as .DOC, .ASC, and .WPB, but you want them all to be .TXT, enter ***.TXT** into the To text box.

Creating New Directories

You've already seen how you can create a new directory while copying or moving files, but of course you can also create a new directory directly, in the same way that DOS uses the MKDIR command. Select the directory in which you want to place the new one—select the disk drive letter at the top of the tree if you want the new directory in the root directory—then select **File | Create Directory**. Type the name into the Create Directory dialog box and click on **OK**.

You can also type a new path into the Create Directory dialog box, in which case you don't need to select the directory first.

Starting Programs

You can start applications directly from File Manager. In fact, you never have to use Program Manager if you don't like it. Use these methods for starting applications:

- **Double-click** on a .EXE, .COM, .PIF, .BAT, or document file.
- Hold **Shift** and **double-click** on a .EXE, .COM, .PIF, .BAT, or document file to run the application minimized.
- **Highlight** a .EXE, .COM, .PIF, .BAT, or document file and press **Enter** (or select **File | Open**).
- **Highlight** a .EXE, .COM, .PIF, .BAT, or document file, hold **Shift**, and press **Enter** (or select **File | Open**) to run the application minimized.
- **Drag** a document file onto its associated application file.
- Select **File | Run** and type the filename (including the pathname if the file isn't in the selected directory).
- **Drag** a document file onto the associated application's **desktop icon** or **title bar**.

To start an application by double-clicking on a document file or dragging the document file onto the application file, icon, or title bar, the document extension must be *associated* with an application. For instance, .TXT files are associated with Notepad, so double-clicking on a .TXT file starts Notepad and loads the file. By default, all files that have document icons are associated with an application. (However, the Documents= line in the WIN.INI file lets you add the documents icon to files that are not associated with applications.) We'll explain later in this chapter how to associate files.

Some applications let you drag an icon from File Manager onto the application's title bar or desktop icon to load the file (if you drag it onto the icon, the application loads the file but remains minimized). Make sure you don't place the icon into the workspace itself, or it may be loaded as an embedded OLE object. Many applications won't let you use this method.

When you select **File | Run** you see the Run dialog box (see Figure 9.14). Type the name of the application file you want to start or the document file you want to load into the associated application. Include the pathname if the file is not in the selected directory. If you type the name of the application, a space, and the name of the document file that is not associated with the application, File Manager opens the application, loads the document file, and automatically creates an association for future use.

If you would like the application you are starting to run minimized—as an icon at the bottom of the screen—select the **Run Minimized** check box before clicking on OK. You can also make File Manager automatically minimize each time you start an application, regardless of the method you use. Select **Options | Minimize on Use**.

Tip Some people prefer a directory tree interface over Program Manager. If you would like to dump Program Manager and make File Manager appear each time you open Windows, change the shell= line in the SYSTEM.INI file to read

```
shell=winfile.exe
```

See Appendix B for more information on working with .INI files.

Printing Files

If a document file is associated with an application, you can print it in one of two ways:

1. Select the file and select **File | Print**.
2. **Drag** the file onto **Print Manager**.

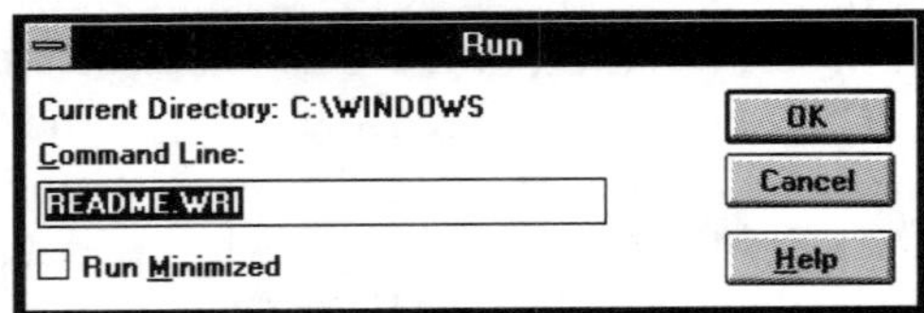

Figure 9.14 The Run dialog box

Not all files can use these methods. You can print .TXT files in Notepad like this, but not .BMP files in Paintbrush. Also, you can print only one file at a time using these methods. To print by dragging onto Print Manager, you must first make sure Print Manager is open. It can be any size, even minimized if you wish.

Changing File and Directory Attributes

DOS has a command called ATTRIB that lets you change the file attributes. We discussed attributes earlier in this chapter: They are read-only, archive, system, and hidden, and each is represented by a single letter (r, a, s, h, respectively). You can change a file's property by selecting it and selecting **File | Properties**. Or hold **Alt** while you double-click on the file, or select the file and press **Alt-Enter**. You will see the Properties dialog box that we described earlier (it's shown in Figure 9.5). Select the check box you want, and click on **OK**.

Use this method to change a group of attributes at the same time. If you want to change a whole group to read-only, for instance, select them all, then select the **File | Properties** command, select Read Only, and click on **OK**. If one of the check boxes is shaded, that means some of the selected files have that attribute and some don't.

You can change directory attributes. If you make a directory hidden, for instance, it will disappear—the DOS DIR command won't find it unless you use the /a or /h switch and it won't appear in File Open dialog boxes, for instance. File Manager will always display hidden directories regardless of the Show Hidden/ System Files setting in the By File Type dialog box.

Printing a Directory List

Many features should be added to File Manager, but one of the most important is the ability to print a list of all the files in a directory. There's an easy way to do this, though. Go to Program Manager and double-click on the DOS Prompt icon. When you see the prompt, change to the directory you want to print. For example, type

```
cd c:\abc\cde
```

and press **Enter** to go to the subdirectory CDE in directory ABC. (See your DOS manual for information about changing directories.) When you get to that directory, type

```
dir >lpt1
```

and press **Enter**. This will print a list of the contents on the printer connected to lpt1.

You can even create an ASCII file containing the directory list. For instance, type

```
dir >dir.txt
```

to create a file called DIR.TXT.

To make the list include all the hidden and system files, use the /a switch (dir/a > dir.txt).

Changing the View

Instead of displaying a split directory window with the directory tree on the left and the directory contents on the right, you may display only the tree or only the contents. Select **View | Tree Only** to remove the directory contents, or **View | Directory Only** to remove the directory tree.

> **Tip** Here's a quicker way to change the view: Place the pointer on the split bar (the bar to the right of the directory tree's scroll bar). The pointer changes to a two-headed arrow. Now drag the split bar off the screen to the left (to remove the directory tree) or to the right (to remove the contents list). Or, to remove the directory tree, simply hold **Shift** and double-click on a directory icon.

The directory tree is convenient (it makes finding the right directory easy), but you don't need it: You can do everything with the contents view, because it includes subdirectory icons, as you saw earlier. On the other hand, if you display only the directory tree you will eventually need to change view to see the files in a directory. You can do so by selecting one of the **View** options, or by holding **Shift** while you double-click on a directory icon to open a new directory window (or highlight the directory and press **Shift-Enter**).

If you want to display both sides of the directory window again, select **View | Tree and Directory**. Or select **View | Split**, drag the split bar into position, and click the button. You can adjust the split bar between the two sides to give more space to one side or the other. Simply **drag** the split bar to one side. If you are using the keyboard, select **View | Split**. When you see the black vertical bar, move it into position with the **arrow keys** and press **Enter.**

Disk Commands

File Manager provides certain important disk commands. You can format a floppy disk, make a system disk, and copy the contents of one disk to another. You can also change any disk's volume label, even your hard disk.

Copying Disks (DISKCOPY)

To copy the contents of one disk to another (the DOS DISKCOPY command), select **Disk | Copy Disk**. If you have two floppy-disk drives, a dialog box with two drop-down list boxes displays the floppy-disk drive letters. In the **Source In** box select the disk drive containing the floppy disk with the data you want to copy. In the **Destination In** box select the disk drive with the floppy onto which you want to copy that data. You can copy data only between the same type disk drives. You can't copy from a 3 1/2-inch drive to a 5-inch drive, for instance, or from a low-density 5-inch drive to a high-density 5-inch drive. And the disks must be the same type. Again, you can't copy from a low-density to a high-density disk, or vice versa.

You can, however, copy from drive A: to drive A:, or B: to B:. File Manager will simply tell you when to swap disks. When you click on **OK**, File Manager warns you that using this command will delete all the data on the destination disk. (This confirmation box is one that can be removed, using the methods we describe later in this chapter.) When you click on **OK**, another box appears telling you to insert the disk into the source drive. Click on **OK** and the operation begins. File Manager will tell you when to swap disks.

Changing the Volume Label (LABEL)

The **Disk | Label Disk** command lets you change any disk's volume label (this is similar to the DOS LABEL command). A volume label is a name assigned to a disk. A disk *drive* always has a name, of course—A:, B:, or whatever—but the disk itself can be given a name also. If you look in a directory window's drive-icon bar, you can see the disk-drive letter and the volume label next to it. This volume label is often no more than reference, but in some cases it is essential. Some installation programs, for instance, check a floppy disk's volume label to see if the correct disk is in the drive. Type up to 11 characters into the Label Disk dialog box and click on **OK**. Make sure you selected the correct disk before you use this command.

Formatting Disks (FORMAT)

The **Disk | Format Disk** command displays the Format Disk dialog box (see Figure 9.15). This box lets you prepare a floppy disk for use. All floppy disks must be formatted before they can be used; they can either be formatted by the manufacturer or the user. A file allocation table (FAT) and root directory are created, and bad areas on the disk are marked. If you format a used disk, the existing data is removed.

Select the drive containing the disk you want to format from the **Disk In** drop-down list box. Then select, from the **Capacity** drop-down list box, the size of the disk. For instance, if you have a 3 1/2-inch disk drive you will see two options, 1.44 MB (high density), and 720K (low density). Don't do a high-density disk format on a low-density disk, or vice versa. File Manager may let you do so, or when you click on **OK**, it may stop and display a message telling you you can't continue.

You can also enter **Label** if you wish, the volume label we just mentioned. Type up to 11 characters. If you select **Make System Disk**, File Manager automatically makes the disk a *system* or *boot* disk after formatting. This is the same as the DOS FORMAT command's /S switch. We'll discuss system disks in a moment. The last option, **Quick Format**, lets you select the *type* of format.

If you *don't* select Quick Format, File Manager does an *unconditional format*. This is the same as DOS 5.0's FORMAT /U command (the same type of format that all the previous versions of DOS carried out automatically). Formatting a disk like this creates a new boot record, root directory, and FAT. It also checks the entire disk for bad sectors and destroys all the existing data. If you format a disk like this, you won't be able to recover any data using DOS 5.0's UNFORMAT command (even if you used DOS 5.0's MIRROR command to save recovery information, since the mirror information is destroyed). Use this type of format for new disks, for disks with which you have been having problems, or if you want to make absolutely sure the data is not recoverable.

If you *do* select Quick Format, File Manager does a DOS FORMAT /Q. This creates a new FAT, boot record, and root directory, but it doesn't check for bad

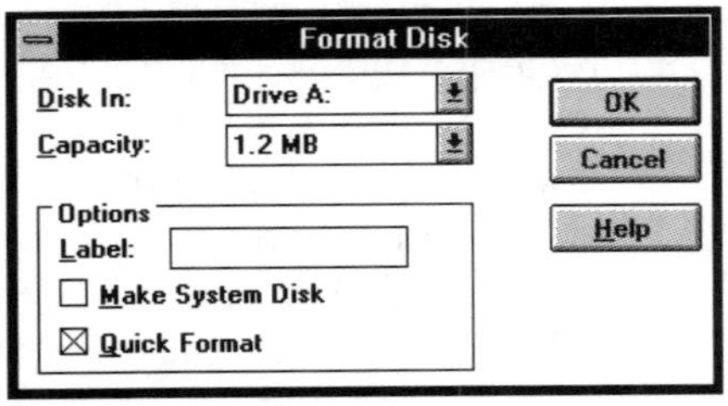

Figure 9.15 The Format Disk dialog box

sectors or delete the data. If you use the MIRROR command you can easily recover the data with the UNFORMAT command. And even if you don't use the MIRROR command, you *may* still be able to recover data, although you will probably have to use an Undelete utility other than DOS 5.0's. This is a very quick way to format a disk. Use this to quickly format a disk you have already been using and know to be good. File Manager won't let you quick-format an unformatted disk. Instead, it will ask if you want to continue with a normal format.

▼ ***Note*** If you are not using DOS 5.0, you may still be able to recover some data from a disk formatted with Quick Format by using a disk utility such as Norton Desktop.

If you have DOS 4.01 or later and booted your computer from a floppy disk, File Manager will not be able to format a disk in that drive.

Creating a System Disk (SYS)

A *system* or *boot* disk contains the files needed to start your computer. Placing these files on a floppy disk lets you get your computer running if your hard disk ever "crashes," or if essential files on the hard disk are damaged. The Make System Disk command is similar to the DOS SYS command.

If you have two floppy-disk drives, when you select **Disk | Make System Disk** you see a dialog box asking to which disk drive you want to copy the files. Generally, you want to copy the files onto a disk that will fit in the A: drive, because that is the drive that is used to boot from. When you click on OK (or as soon as you select the command, if you only have one floppy drive), File Manager copies the IO.SYS, MSDOS.SYS, and COMMAND.COM files.

File Manager will be unable to use a disk if there is some damage to one of the first sectors. It may not be able to work if there are already some files on the disk, because it needs to place the files in the first sectors.

Tip After you have created a system disk, copy important .INI files onto it (WIN.INI, SYSTEM.INI, PROGMAN.INI, CONTROL.INI). If these files are ever damaged, you can copy them from the system disk back into the WINDOWS directory. Also copy the CONFIG.SYS and AUTOEXEC.BAT files (from your hard drive's root directory). And if you use some type of disk compression system—such as Stacker—copy the essential compression files in case they are damaged (such as STACKER.COM and SSWAP.COM).

In a rare case—if you upgraded your DOS from IBM DOS to MS DOS 5.0—the system disk may get the wrong files (IBMBIO.COM and IBMDOS.COM instead of IO.SYS and MSDOS.SYS). Remove these hidden files from your hard drive's root directory and try again, or use the DOS SYS command.

Searching for Files

As the data on your hard disk grows, you will undoubtedly "misplace" files now and again. File Manager makes it easy to track down missing files, using the **File | Search** command. When the Search dialog box appears (see Figure 9.16), enter the file you want to find in the **Search For** text box. If you know the exact name, just type it in, extension and all. If you are not exactly sure of its name, you can use wild cards. For instance, `*.TXT` will search for all files with the .TXT extension. `P*.TXT` searches for all files beginning with P that have the .TXT extension. `PILOT??.*` finds all files with PILOT as the first five characters of the name, two other characters at the end of the name, and any extension.

You can further narrow the search using the **Start From** text box. Initially this text box will display the selected directory, but you can specify any directory you want. Then use the **Search All Subdirectories** check box to determine exactly what will be searched. For instance, if the Start From text box shows `C:\`, and the Search All Subdirectories check box is selected, File Manager will search the entire disk—all directories and subdirectories—for the specified file. If the check box is *not* selected, File Manager only searches the root directory. Of course you can search any branch on the directory tree. Make sure `C:\WINDOWS` is in the Start From text box to search that directory, and select the check box to include all the WINDOWS subdirectories.

Click on **OK** to begin the search. You can press **Esc** at any time to stop the search and display what has been found so far. When the search is complete, or if you stop it early, a **Search Results** directory window appears, displaying all the matching files (see Figure 9.17). You can work with these files in the same way you can in a normal directory window. You can copy, move, rename, and delete files, or view file information. If you try to rename, though, you must include the full path, not just the new name. You can do so quickly by selecting the text in the

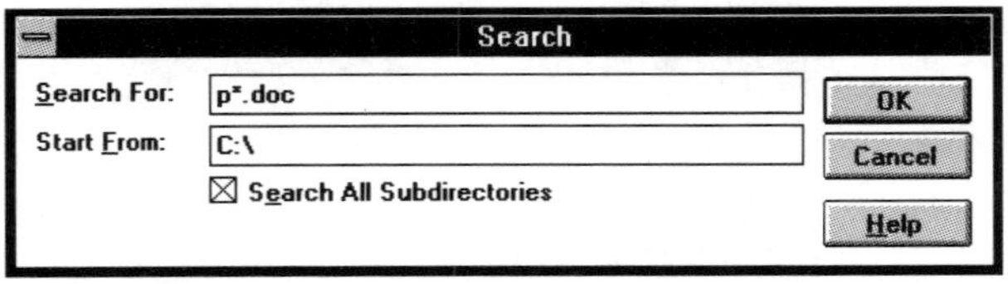

Figure 9.16 The Search dialog box

Search Results: C:\P*.wri

c:\maxwin\pressrel.wri	5632	01/12/92	2:01:50	a
c:\windows\printers.wri	44928	03/10/92	3:10:00	
c:\wrk\printers.wri	44928	04/06/92	0:00:00	
c:\x-window\printers.wri	44928	03/10/92	3:10:00	a

Figure 9.17 The Search Results directory window

From text box, pressing **Ctrl-C** to copy it, pressing **Tab** to move to the To text box, and pressing **Ctrl-V** to paste it.

Whenever you make any changes you will see a message box asking if you want to update the Search Results window. If you click on Yes, File Manager repeats the search completely. Click on **No** to continue working with the files without waiting for a new search. Press **F5** while in the Search Results window to repeat the search.

Tip Occasionally search your hard drive for these files: *.TMP, ~*.*, WIN386.SWP, *.BAK, and *.BKP. The first three are temporary files that should be removed when you close Windows but sometimes are left when your system or an application crashes. The *.BAK and *.BKP files are backup files, which some applications create automatically whether you want them or not. Delete all the temporary files, and all the backup files you don't want to keep.

Warning Do not delete temporary files from your current Windows session. Use the **View | All File Details** to check the date and time.

Associating Files with Applications

Windows uses a system of *associating* file extensions with applications. For instance, the .BMP extension is associated with Paintbrush, .REC is associated with Recorder, and .WAV is associated with Sound Recorder. These associations are used in a variety of ways. You have already seen how you can print a file by dropping it into the Print Manager or by selecting File | Print. The file must be associated with the application you want to print it. You've also seen how double-clicking on a filename will load that file into its associated application.

Tip Associate the extension .ME with Notepad so when you load software you can quickly open the READ.ME files into Notepad by double-clicking.

In an earlier chapter you learned how you can create an icon in Program Manager using a filename instead of an application name if the file is associated with an application. Associations are also used in Object Linking and Embedding (see Chapter 28) so you can click on an object placed in a *client* application to load the object into its associated application.

When you installed Windows, it automatically associated these extensions and applications:

.BMP	Paintbrush
.CAL	Calendar
.CRD	Cardfile
.HLP	Windows Help
.MID	Media Player
.MSP	Paintbrush
.PCX	Paintbrush
.REC	Recorder
.REG	Registration Info Editor
.TRM	Terminal
.TXT	Notepad
.WAV	Sound Recorder
.WRI	Write

As you install more Windows programs, the list of associations will grow. For instance, Word for Windows associates itself with .DOC files. Micrografx Designer associates itself with .DRW files. You may want to change associations for several reasons:

- You have a program that doesn't automatically associate its files with itself.
- A new program you install changes an association to one you don't want.
- You want to change an existing association to another application. For instance, you could make .TXT and .WRI files load into Word for Windows, or .PCX files load into Publisher's Paintbrush.

To change an association, select **File | Associate**. The dialog box shown in Figure 9.18 appears. The **Files with Extension** text box shows the extension of the file that was selected immediately before you chose the command, but you can type a different extension into here if you wish. The **Associate With** text box shows the

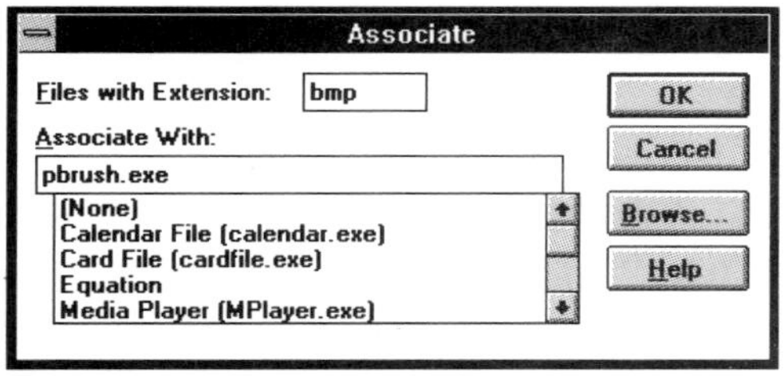

Figure 9.18 The Associate dialog box

application with which the extension is associated. If you want to remove the association, select **(None)** from the top of the drop-down list box. Or, if you want to modify the association, select an application name.

The application with which you want to associate the file may not be listed in this dialog box. Only applications already associated with a file are included. If you want to create a completely new association, click **Browse** to see a typical Browse dialog box, like that used when you create icons in Program Manager. Find the application you want and click on the OK button.

When you finally click on the OK button in the Associate dialog box, the association is saved in the [Extensions] section of the WIN.INI file. Files that have been associated with an application use the document icon in the directory window, the small "page" with four horizontal lines. You can give other file types this icon also, without associating them with an application, by modifying the Documents= line in WIN.INI (see Appendix B for information). Files provided with the icon in this way won't work like associated files.

 **Tip** You can associate a document file with an application file at the same time you load it. Select the document file, then select **File | Run**. When the Run dialog box appears, press **Home**, then type the name of the application (with its pathname if it's not in the same directory), leave a space, and click on OK. File Manager opens the application, loads the document file, and creates the association for future use.

If you move an application file that has been associated with a data-file type, the next time you try to run the data file, Windows won't be able to find the application. Instead it displays a dialog box asking where the application is. When you enter the information, Windows doesn't modify the [Extensions] section of the WIN.INI. Instead, it saves it in the [Programs] section so it can use the information in both sections to find the application the next time it needs it.

More Customization Options

We've already covered a number of ways you can customize File Manager. You can select a particular directory, of course, tell File Manager to display the + and – symbols that indicate expandable and collapsible branches, and modify the view. But there are a few more ways you can customize File Manager: You can remove the status bar, turn off the confirmation messages, and modify the font.

To remove the status bar from the bottom of the File Manager window, select **Options | Status Bar**. You probably won't want to do this, however, because the status bar contains quite useful information, such as the amount of disk space taken up by the selected file and the amount of free space on the current disk.

Removing Confirmation Messages

As you've seen, File Manager has many confirmation messages. When you use the mouse to move or copy files, when you delete or replace files, and when you carry out Disk commands, you will see a dialog box that prompts you to confirm the operation. After you've been using File Manager for a while you may want to stop these boxes from appearing. Select **Options | Confirmation** to see the Confirmation dialog box (Figure 9.19).

Deselect the procedures for which you don't want to see a confirmation dialog box. Most of these options are obvious. The Mouse Action option refers to copying and moving files or directories by dragging them with the mouse, and the Disk Commands refers to formatting and copying disks.

Changing the Font

By default File Manager uses a lowercase, 8-point, MS Sans Serif font for all the text in the directory windows: the filenames, directory names, disk-drive letters, pathname, and disk volume label. This font is not always ideal, especially if you are using a small, high-resolution monitor, in which case 8 points may be too small to read. You can change the font File Manager uses, though. Select **Options | Font**.

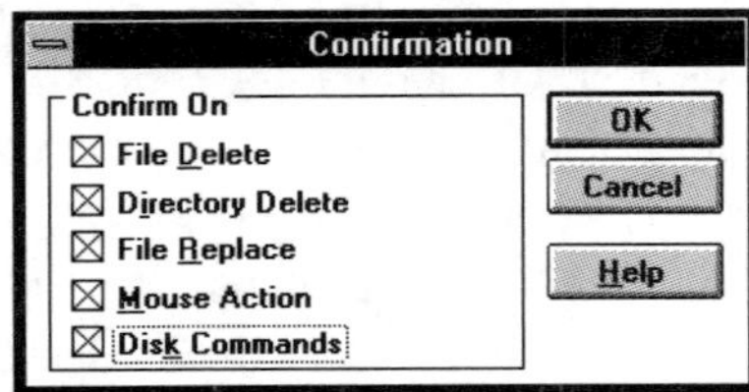

Figure 9.19 The Confirmation dialog box

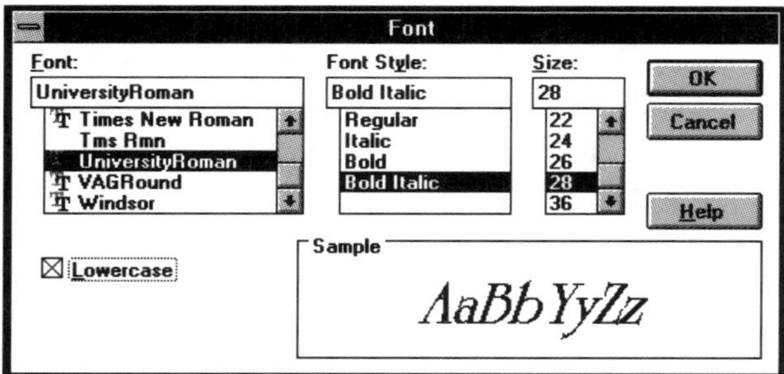

Figure 9.20 The Font dialog box

The Font dialog box (see Figure 9.20) lets you select from a list of the Windows-compatible fonts. You can also select a font style (regular, bold, italic, and bold italic) and a font size, from 4 points (probably totally illegible), to 36 points (probably monstrous). The suitability of a font size depends on the monitor and display mode you are using. The higher the resolution, the smaller the characters. The larger the monitor, the larger the characters. Thus, a high resolution on a small monitor makes small text *very* small.

The Size list box doesn't list all the sizes from 4 to 36, but you can type an intermediate size into the text box if you want. You can also deselect the **Lowercase** check box to change the text to uppercase, the normal for file-management utilities and, indeed, even for DOS. If you try lowercase for a while, you will probably find it easier to read than uppercase.

 **Stupid Computer-Trick Tip** Change a colleague's File Manager to a non-TrueType symbol font such as Zapf Dingbats. File Manager won't let you use the WingDings TrueType font.

Saving Settings

When you have set up File Manager just the way you want it, you can save your settings so that it works the same the next time you open it. Take a good look at the options available to you, and think about what would be most useful. You could set up a directory window for each network drive and then minimize them. Then you could set up an open window for your computer's hard-disk drive, and a few icons for your hard drive, with different settings: one for the Windows directory, one for a data directory showing all file details, and so on.

If you now save your settings, the next time you open File Manager all will look the same. To view a particular directory on a particular drive all you have to do is double-click on the appropriate directory-window icon, for instance. All the file sorting and viewing options will also be as you set them up before saving.

There are two ways to save your settings. The first method, standard, is to make sure there is a check mark next to the **Options | Save Settings on Exit** command. If there is, the next time you close File Manager your settings will be saved automatically. You may not want that, though, because each time you select a different directory or drive, or choose different file sorting or viewing options, the new settings will be saved automatically, unless you remember to turn off the menu option first.

Perhaps a better method is to press and hold **Shift** and then select the **File | Exit** command. File Manager won't close, but it will save your settings. Now make sure there is no check mark next to **Options | Save Settings on Exit**, and your settings will remain until you choose to modify them.

Drag and Drop

File Manager has a feature called "drag and drop." This means that you can carry out various operations by dragging an icon onto another object and releasing it. You have already seen examples of this. For instance, you can copy and move files by dragging them from one directory to another. Here's a more complete list:

- Drag files or directories to **move** or **copy** them.
- Drag a document file onto **Print Manager** to **print** the document.
- Drag a document file onto the associated **program-file icon** to **load** the program and open the file.
- Drag a document file onto the associated program **window's title bar** or **desktop icon** to load the file.
- Drag a program or document file onto **Program Manager** to create a program icon that starts the program and loads the file.
- Drag a file onto an **OLE client** to place an embedded object in an OLE "package."
- Drag a file created by an OLE server onto an **OLE client** while holding Shift-Ctrl to place a linked object in an OLE "package."

Working with Networks

Figure 9.21 shows an example of File Manager working on a network. As you can see, it has a lot of "drives." Notice that each type of drive icon is a little different. As usual it has floppy drives A and B, and a floppy drive C. The other icons

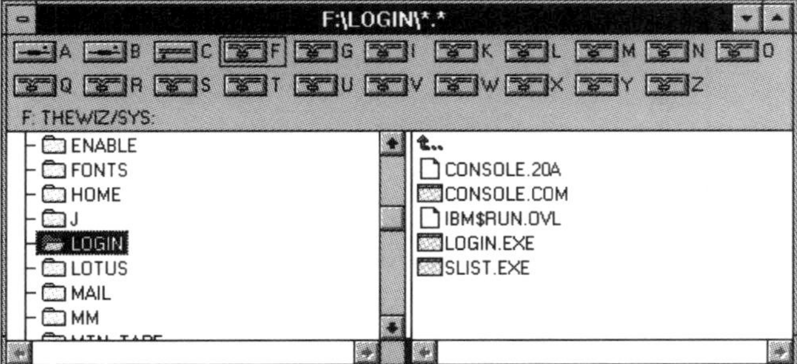

Figure 9.21 A directory window showing network "drives"

represent network drives. A network drive, however, is usually simply a directory on the network server. Representing it as a drive makes navigating through the server's hard drive much easier.

File Manager has a network command that lets you connect to network drives, but each network works a little differently, and each user on a network may have different "rights." Select **Disk | Network Connections** to see a dialog box similar to that shown in Figure 9.22. This box lets you assign network directories to a "drive" in File Manager. Remember that network drives are not usually actual drives—they are simply directories assigned as drives (in the same way DOS lets you use the SUBST command to pretend that a directory is a drive).

Suppose you want to assign the network server's directory ENABLE\DATA to the "drive" H (you want to *map* the directory to the drive). You would replace LOGIN in the **Path** text box with ENABLE\DATA, and then click on the **Map** button. The entry in the **Data drives** list box would change to H: [THEWIZ/SYS:] ENABLE\DATA. (In this case THEWIZ/SYS is the network server and volume.) Notice that you can also click on the **Set Root** button to create a "fake"

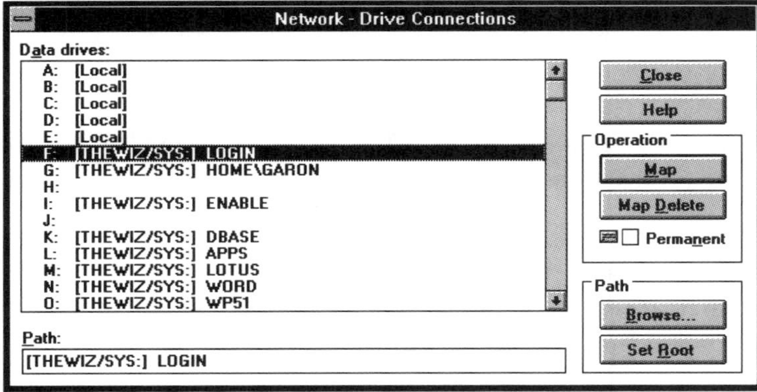

Figure 9.22 The Network – Drive Connections dialog box

root in the directory shown in the Path text box. This is not really the server's root directory; rather it is a directory that allows you to use it as if it were a root directory of the network drive. (This is the same as the NetWare MAP ROOT command.)

If you want to make a permanent connection, select the **Permanent** check box before clicking on Map. That way the directory will be mapped to that drive the next time you open Windows. You can also remove a mapped directory by selecting it in the Data drives list box and clicking on **Map Delete**.

Instead of entering a directory in the Path text box, you could click on the **Browse** button to see the Browse Connections dialog box, in which you can select another server, volume, and directory.

File Manager Modifications

File Manager can be modified by third-party programs. For instance, Norton Desktop for Windows adds various capabilities to File Manager, including an Undelete option in the File menu and a Norton menu on the title bar. Also, Microsoft's Windows Resource Kit contains an "extension" to File Manager called *File Size Information*. This automatically adds a menu to File Manager (**Info**). You can select a directory and then choose the **Info | Show File Size Information** command to see the total size of all the files in the directory and its subdirectories.

File Manager's Menu Options

Here's a summary of File Manager's menu options:

File | Open (Enter) Starts the selected application. If the file is not executable, File Manager checks the file's associated executable file, runs the program, and loads the file. If a directory is selected, File Manager expands or collapses one level of subdirectories.

File | Move (F7) Lets you move a file or directory.

File | Copy (F8) Lets you copy the selected file or directory to the same or another directory, or to the Clipboard.

File | Delete (Del) Deletes the selected file or directory.

File | Rename Lets you rename the selected file or directory.

File | Properties (Alt-Enter) Lets you set a file's attributes (Read-Only, Hidden, Archive, and System), and displays information about the file.

File | Run Lets you start an application and load a file into its associated application.

File | Print Lets you print a file, if that file is associated with an application.

File | Associate Associates a file extension with an application so you can use commands such as File | Open, File | Run, and File | Print on a document file.

File | Create Directory Lets you create a new directory.

File | Search Lets you search your hard disk—or floppy disk—for a specific file or file type.

File | Select Files Lets you select multiple files at once by entering a file criteria.

File | Exit Closes File Manager.

Disk | Copy Disk Does a DOS DISKCOPY, copying information from one floppy disk to another.

Disk | Label Disk Lets you add, modify, or remove a disk volume label.

Disk | Format Disk Lets you format a floppy disk.

Disk | Make System Disk Creates a DOS system disk, which contains the DOS files necessary to boot your computer.

Disk | Network Connections Lets you connect to or disconnect from network drives. This option may be called Connect Network Drive, Disconnect Network Drive, or something similar.

Disk | Select Drive Lets you select the drive you want to display in the current directory window.

Tree | Expand One Level (+) Displays a directory's first-level subdirectories.

Tree | Expand Branch (*) Displays all the subdirectories—at all levels—of the selected directory.

Tree | Expand All (Ctrl-*) Expands the entire directory tree, displaying all the directories and subdirectories on the tree.

Tree | Collapse Branch (-) Collapses the tree below the selected directory so its subdirectories are not displayed.

Tree | Indicate Expandable Branches Places a special mark on directory icons that have subdirectories. When the directory is not expanded, a + appears on the icon. When it is expanded, a – is shown instead.

View | Tree and Directory Places two panels in the current directory window: The one on the left shows the directory tree, the one on the right shows the files in the selected directories.

View | Tree Only Displays only one panel in the current directory window, showing the directory tree (no files).

View | Directory Only Displays only one panel in the current directory window, showing a single directory.

View | Split Displays a black vertical bar used to place the border between the two panels in the directory window.

View | Name Makes the file list display only filenames.

View | All File Details Makes the file list include all information about each file: size, date, time, and attributes.

View | Partial Details Lets you specify what information you wish to see about each file.

View | Sort by Name Makes the file list place the files in alphabetical order by name.

View | Sort by Size Makes the file list place the files in order according to size.

View | Sort by Type Makes the file list place the files in alphabetical order by file extension.

View | Sort by Date Makes the file list place the files in chronological order.

View | By File Type Lets you select what type of files should be included in the list.

Options | Confirmation Lets you decide which commands should display a confirmation dialog box before carrying out the operation.

Options | Font Lets you select a different font and style for the File Manager.

Options | Status Bar Lets you remove the status bar from the bottom of the File Manager.

Options | Minimize on Use Makes the File Manager change to an icon when you start an application from its file list.

Options | Save Settings on Exit Makes File Manager save its settings when you close it.

Window | New Window Opens a new directory window so you can view another disk or another directory.

Window | Cascade Places the open directory windows one on top of the other. The lowest in the stack is in the top-left corner of the File Manager window, and each subsequent document window is offset toward the bottom-right corner.

Window | Tile Places the open directory windows so none are hidden and each has equal space.

Window | Arrange Icons Lines up the directory-window icons tidily at the bottom of the File Manager window.

Window | Refresh Searches the current drive and re-displays the file and directory information.

Window | 1. *pathname* Makes the named directory window the active one.

Tip You might feel that some of the menu options that don't have keyboard shortcuts really need them. Get used to thinking of the Alt-underlined letter method as a keyboard shortcut. Thus the shortcut for File | Create Directory becomes Alt-FE, and that for File | Search Alt-FH.

10

Finding Help

Windows has a sophisticated Help system that any Windows application has access to. Some publishers include next to no Help information, while others include context-sensitive F1 help, Help buttons in every dialog box, a detailed index and glossary, and so on. In general, you will see a Help menu in almost all applications and most device driver-dialog boxes.

The Help system is especially useful in device drivers. There are so many different drivers that they are rarely explained in any paper documentation. Most, however, have Help screens that explain the various dialog box options.

Windows applications all have Help screens (with the exception of the Clock, which is too simple to need it). They tend to vary somewhat; some allow you to access Help from open dialog boxes, others, such as Paintbrush, do not. Also, some of the Help information is a bit sketchy in places and very helpful in others.

▼ ***Note*** Some Windows applications use their own Help system instead of taking advantage of the Windows Help system.

There are a number of ways to open the Help window, depending on the application:

- Select an option from the **Help** menu.
- Click on a **Help** button in a dialog box.
- Press **F1** to see "context sensitive" help: information about the open dialog box, menu selection, or selected tool (in some graphics programs, for instance).

Clicking on the Help button or pressing F1 in a dialog box takes you directly to information about that dialog box, or pressing F1 after selecting a command or tool takes you straight to information about the selection.

Tip You can also open Help files by double-clicking on the .HLP filename in File Manager, because the .HLP extension is associated with the WINHELP.EXE application.

It's important to understand that when you open Help, you are opening one Help document file. Windows loads a program called WINHELP.EXE and then loads the appropriate file, in the same way you might open a word processor and load a file. That means there are limits to the Help system. While the Help windows have special tools that let you search for information within the current file, you can't search for data in another file until you load it.

This is a problem only in a few situations. It means that you can't open the Help window from the menu bar and then find information about a specific device driver (instead you must open the device driver's dialog box—usually from the Print Setup dialog box—and open Help from there). Also, some applications have more than one Help file for the application itself. For instance, Windows Draw has one Help file for its clip art library and another for everything else. Thus, you can't open the Help window from the menu bar and search for information in the clip art help file.

▼ ***Note*** You can only have one Help window open at a time. If one is already open and you open another application's Help, the original screen is replaced with the new one. Also, when you close an application the associated Help window is automatically closed also.

The Help Menu

The Help menu varies among applications. These are the typical options (the ones marked with an asterisk are found in Windows' own applications):

***Help | Contents** Displays a list of topics available in the current Help file.

Help | Help Index Also displays a list of topics. The term Contents is probably more accurate because the information is rarely a true index.

***Help | Windows Tutorial** In Program Manager you can select this option to use an interactive tutorial. Other applications may also have tutorials.

Help | Getting Started Similar to a tutorial, provides basic information to get you started with a specific application.

Help | Windows Basics Some applications may explain how to use Windows' basic tools.

Help | Previews Similar to a tutorial, some applications show you what the program can do. The intention is to whet your appetite rather than teach you.

***Help | Search for Help On** Displays the Search dialog box that lets you go directly to a specific subject.

***Help | How to Use Help** Displays information on how to use the Help system. This may be Windows' generic "how to use help" information (stored in WINHELP.HLP), or the application's own instructions.

Help | Current Topic Context-sensitive help, the same as selecting, say, a dialog box option and pressing F1.

Help | Read Me An application's installation "read me" information, generally information that didn't make it into the documentation before the product shipped.

Help | About *applicationname Displays a dialog box that contains information about the application, generally the version number, sometimes the programmers or publisher, technical support information, serial number, and so on. Windows' own About dialog boxes also provide mode and memory use information.

Let's begin by using the Help | Contents command.

Using the Help Window

If you select **Help | Contents** (or **Help | Index** in some applications), you will see a list of topics. The Figure in 10.1 shows the Help window displayed if you select Help | Contents in Program Manager. Notice the list of underlined topics. These are *jumps*, special text (sometimes graphics), which, when clicked on, display another screen of information.

These are the Help buttons:

Contents Takes you back to the Help Contents window, even if the particular application calls it an "index."

Search Lets you search for information about a particular topic.

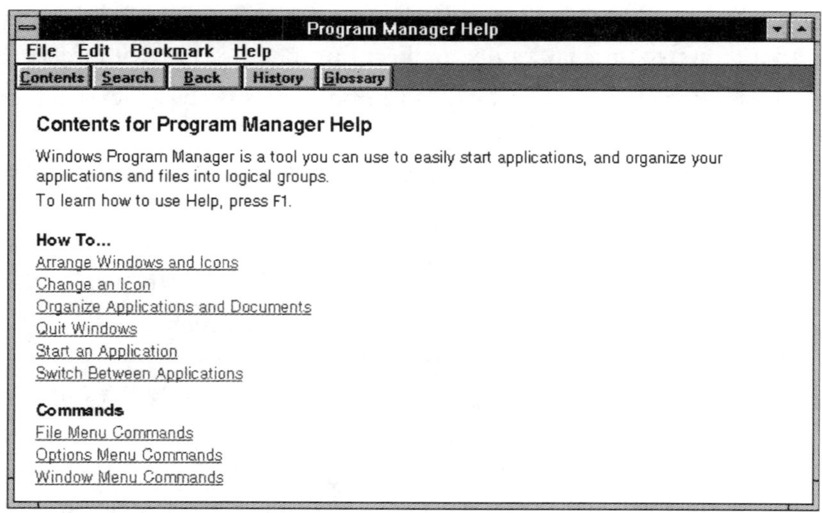

Figure 10.1 The Program Manager Help Contents window

Back	Displays the Help window you viewed immediately before the current one. This button lets you trace your route back through the information.
History	Displays a list of all the Help windows you have viewed since you opened Help so you can quickly jump to the one you need.
Glossary	Displays a list of Windows terms. This button appears only in the Windows Help windows, or in the How to Use Help window. It doesn't appear in other applications' Help windows.
<<	View the previous topic in a series. If you are viewing the first one in the series, this button is disabled. Windows itself doesn't use this (or the next) button, but many Windows applications do.
>>	View the next topics in a series. If you are viewing the last one, this button is disabled.

Moving Through a Help Window

Help windows contain text and sometimes graphics. They also contain *jumps*, pieces of text or graphics used to display more information. A jump may change the displayed screen to show different information, or display a little pop-up box with information.

To view all the text in a Help window, use the scroll bars to scroll through the window, or the following keys:

PgDn	Down one screen
PgUp	Up one screen
Ctrl-Home	To the top of the screen
Ctrl-End	To the bottom of the screen
Up Arrow	Up one line
Down Arrow	Down one line
Tab	Moves a highlight to the next jump
Shift-Tab	Moves a highlight to the previous jump

Remember that you can size or maximize the Help window to make the text easier to use.

 **Tip** Pressing **Ctrl-Tab** momentarily highlights all the Help screen's jumps, the text or graphics that lead to other screens or display pop-up information.

Using Jumps

There are three types of jumps: solid underlined text, dotted-line underlined text, and graphics. Select any jump by **clicking** once, or by pressing **Tab** to move the highlight to it and pressing **Enter**. If you click on a solid underlined text, the window changes to display another Help screen. If you click on text underlined with dots, a small pop-up box appears, displaying a definition or short piece of information.

 **Tip** You can change the jump color, and the color of other Help components, using the [Windows Help] section in WIN.INI. See Appendix B for more information.

Windows itself doesn't use graphics in the Help windows, but many other applications do. The effect of these may vary. In some cases you may see a definition, in others a whole new Help screen. You can tell if text or an object is a jump by pointing at it. If it is, the pointer changes into a small pointing hand. The picture in Figure 10.2 is actually a combination of various jumps. Click on a

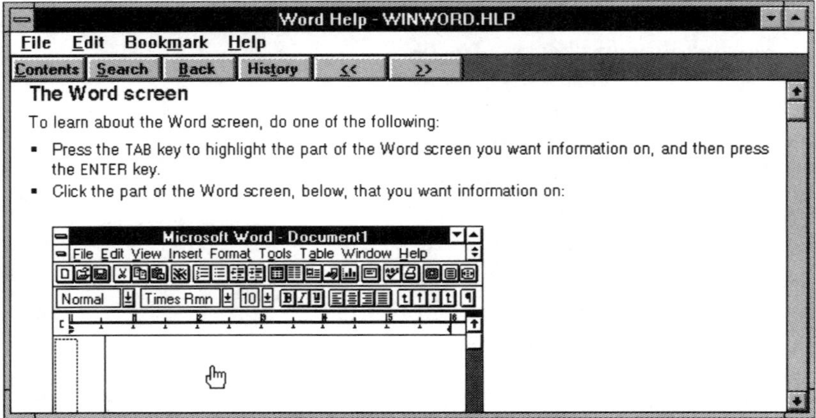

Figure 10.2 A graphic jump in Word for Windows' Help

different portion to view different information. If you don't have a mouse, you can find out if a graphic is a jump by pressing **Ctrl-Tab** to momentarily highlight it.

Moving Between Help Screens

Using jumps isn't the only way to navigate through the Help system. You can move between Help screens (or "pages") by clicking the **Contents** button (to return to the Contents or Index screen); clicking the **Back** button (to return to the previous screen); by clicking on **Search** (to use the Search dialog box); clicking the **History** button (to use the History window); or by clicking the chevron buttons (**<<** and **>>**) to move through a series of related topics.

The **Back** button lets you return along the path you've come since you began working with the Help window. You can even return to a previous screen in a different file (perhaps you opened another file, or selected Help from another application). The chevron buttons (**<<** and **>>**) don't appear in the Windows Help windows, but many other Windows applications use them. They let you move through a series of related topics. For instance, in Word for Windows pressing >> in the "Parts of the Word Screen" information screen displays "The Word Screen," then "Document Control Menu," then "Header/Footer Bar," and so on. Pressing << would take you back through the series.

You can also use the **Bookmark** menu to go directly to bookmarks you have set in a Help file. If you haven't set any, the Bookmark only has one option, Define, which is used to set a bookmark. We'll talk about setting bookmarks later in this chapter.

Using the History Window

The History window lets you jump back to any Help screen you have viewed since the last time you opened Help. As you can see in Figure 10.3, the History window lists all the screens, with the most recent at the top. If you change the Help file—by selecting another one using the File | Open command, or by using the Help commands in another application (remember, only one Help window is open at a time, so selecting from another application is the same as changing the Help file)—the previous applications will be named in front of the Help screen name. In the illustration you can see that we had been working in Word for Windows (WINWORD) before using a Program Manager Help command.

You can use the border to drag the History box out a bit, to make the titles more legible (it will be the new size the next time you open it). To jump directly to one of the listed screens, double-click on it, or use the **arrow keys** and press **Enter**. If you select a screen in another Help file, that file loads automatically.

There's no simple way to keep the History dialog box visible, unfortunately—no Always on Top command, for instance—although you could size the windows to make it readily available.

Searching for Information

You can try to go directly to the information you need by doing a search. Click on the **Search** button to see the dialog box shown in Figure 10.4. Begin by typing a word in the top text box, or select directly from the list. If you type a word, the highlight in the list automatically moves to the first matching entry in the list. When you find a subject you want to investigate, press **Enter** or click on **Show Topics**. A list of related topics is displayed in the bottom list box. Double-click on the one you want to view, or select it and click on **Go To**. The Search dialog box disappears, and the screen you selected appears in the Help window.

The next time you click on the Search button, the same subject will be highlighted. Just press Enter to display the list of topics again.

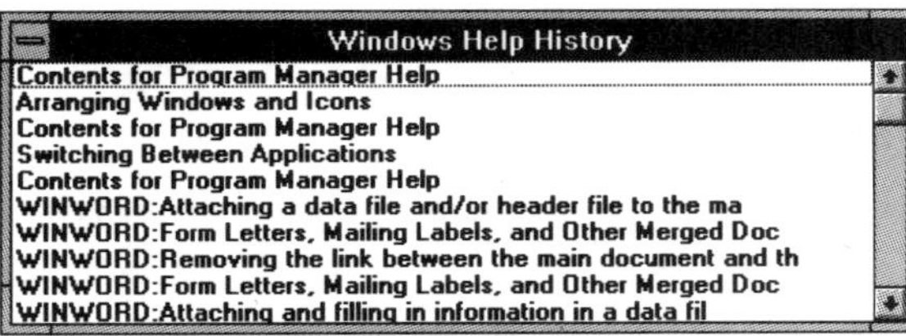

Figure 10.3 The History dialog box

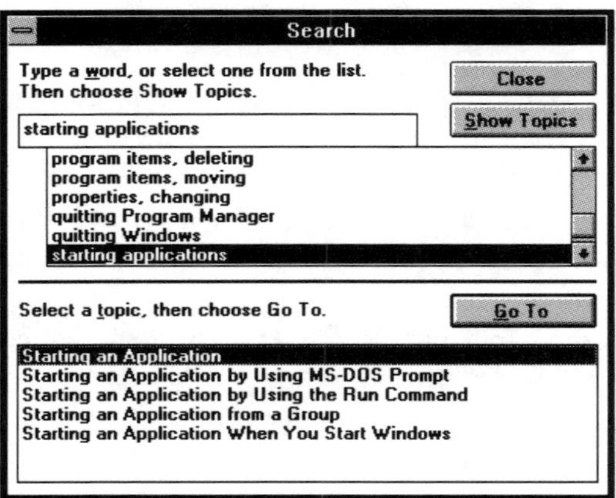

Figure 10.4 The Search dialog box

▼ *Note* Some applications, such as Program Manager, have a **Search for Help On** option in their Help menus, letting you go directly to the Search dialog box without opening a Help window first.

Printing Help Screens

You may occasionally want to print a Help screen. Simply select **File | Print Topic** and the information is sent directly to the printer. You can select a specific printer using the **File | Print Setup** command. This displays a dialog box from which you can choose a printer. If you don't choose one, the information goes to the default printer. You can find more information about selecting printers in Chapter 11.

If you want to print a lot of screens, you may find it easier to copy the information from the Help window to a word processor, format it, and then print it.

Copying Text from Help

If you ever want to copy a portion of text from a Help window, select the **Edit | Copy** command. The Copy dialog box appears (see Figure 10.5), displaying all the screen's text in a list box. If you want to copy the entire text, simply click on the **Copy** button. If you only want part of the text, select it by dragging the mouse across the text, or by pressing **Shift** while you use the **arrow keys** (most of the Notepad keystrokes work in this text box). Then click on **Copy**. The dialog box

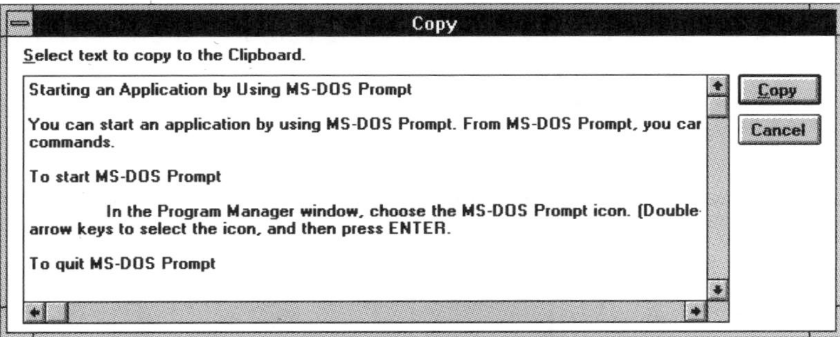

Figure 10.5 The Copy dialog box

closes and the text is copied to the Clipboard. You can now copy the text into another application (or even into an Annotate dialog box; see later in this chapter).

Adding Your Own Notes

You will sometimes find the help information to be a little sparse. Perhaps you find mistakes in the text, or want to add information to make the existing text clearer. Well, you can add your own notes to any Help screen. Just select **Edit|Annotate** to see the Annotate dialog box (Figure 10.6). Type your note. It doesn't have to be concise, go into detail if you wish: You can enter over 2000 characters. When you have finished, click on **Save** and the dialog box closes. A paper clip symbol appears in the top left corner of the screen. This paper clip is a new "jump."

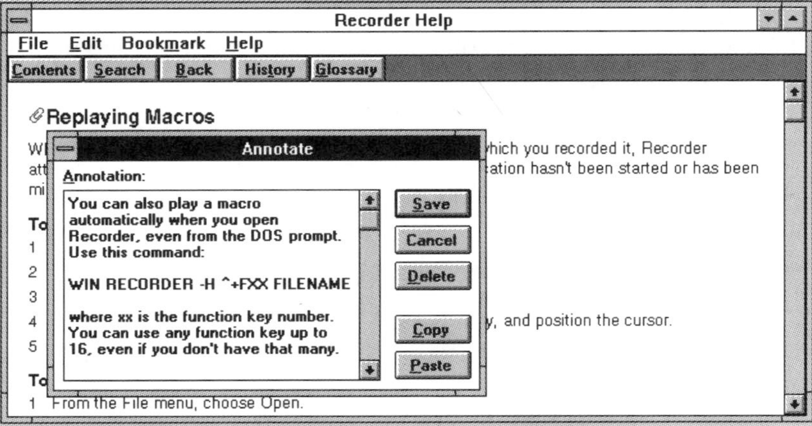

Figure 10.6 The Annotate dialog box, with the paper clip icon in the top left of the Help window

▼ *Note* The Annotate box is rather thin, but you can drag the border to make it wider so it's easier to read your notes.

Now, whenever you want to view the contents of the Annotate box, simply click on the paper clip once. Or press **Tab**—the highlight moves to the paper clip—and then **Enter**. The Annotate box appears with the same size it had when you closed it the last time. (The box will be this size wherever you open it from now on, until you change the size again.) Use the scroll bars to move through your notes, and when you have finished, click on **Cancel**.

Notice the other buttons in this dialog box. Click on **Delete** to remove the annotation completely (if you only want to remove parts, edit the text directly and click on **Save**). The **Copy** button copies the text you have selected or, if you haven't selected any, it copies *all* the text. And the **Paste** button lets you paste the text from the Clipboard into the annotation, so you can copy text from a word processor. (You can't copy graphics.)

Using Bookmarks

Unfortunately, the Jump and Search topics are not always specific enough to find exactly what you want. You may sometimes have to dig a little to get the information you need. Once you have found it, if you are likely to need to refer to the information again, you can set a bookmark on it.

Select **Bookmark | Define** and the dialog box shown in Figure 10.7 appears. It will display the topic name in the **Bookmark Name** text box and a list of the current bookmarks below it. Type a new name into the text box and click on **OK**.

The name is added to the Bookmark menu. Now you can jump directly to that screen by selecting the name from that menu, from anywhere within that Help file. If you are in another Help file at the time, you will have to open the correct file first (we'll explain how later), and then use the Bookmark menu.

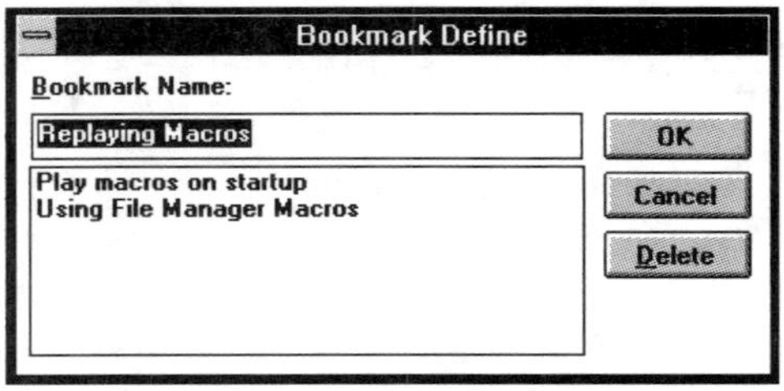

Figure 10.7 The Bookmark Define dialog box

Using the Glossary

Some Help windows—but not all—have a Glossary button. (All of Windows' own applications have it, most others don't.) Click on this button to see a small window with an alphabetical list of Windows terminology, everything from *active* to *wrap* (see Figure 10.8). Click on one of the terms to see a definition in a pop-up box.

Other applications may have their own glossaries. For instance, Word for Windows has a Definitions page that lists terms related specifically to that application. Once opened, the Glossary window is independent of the Help window, so you can leave it open even when you close the Help window.

Keeping Help Visible

Windows Help is an independent application to some degree. So when you click on another window, or use one of the window-swapping techniques (Alt-Tab, for instance), the Help window is placed behind other windows. If you use the **Help | Always on Top** command, though, the window will not be obscured by any other window, even by the active window (except by another "always on top" application, such as Windows Clock).

If you size the Help window to where it takes up as little room as it can while still being usable, and use Always on Top, you can keep the window visible and quickly accessible while you work.

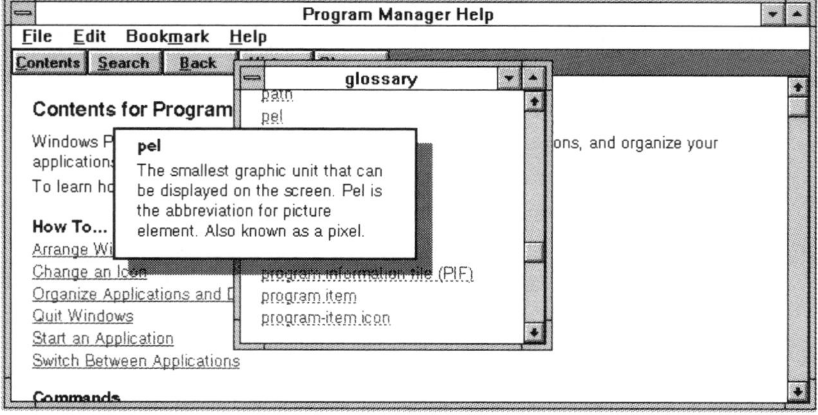

Figure 10.8 The Glossary Window, with a pop-up definition shown

 **Tip** When you are learning a new program, keep the Help screen next to the application screen so you can quickly find the information you need. If you want to make the Glossary stay on top, open it with File | Open rather than the Glossary button, and then select Help | Always on Top. (It's called **GLOSSARY.HLP**.)

Opening Other Help Files

You can open any Help file using the **File | Open** command. A typical Open dialog box will appear. You use this in the same way you would search for an application file in Program Manager's Browse dialog box, or as you would search for a word processor file. You can open any .HLP file. When you do so the current file is closed, but you can still use the Back, History, and chevron buttons to return to screens you were viewing in those Help files. You won't be able to Search for information in the earlier files, though, or use the Bookmark menu to jump to them.

Closing Help Windows

Close a Help window the same way you close any other window—double-click on the Control menu, select Close from the Control menu or **File | Exit**, or press **Alt-F4**. Also, if you close the application associated with the current Help file, the Help window closes automatically.

When the Help window closes, it saves the current size and position in the WIN.INI initialization file, so it will be in the same place the next time.

11

Printing and Fonts

Windows provides a common system for printing. Unlike DOS, in which each application handles printing differently, Windows has a system in which all applications have access to all the printer *drivers*. (A driver is a program that "translates" the information from your applications into information that your printer can understand.) Furthermore, all printer drivers can print through the Print Manager, an application that *spools* files to the printer and manages the *print queue*.

Spooling is a procedure used to free an application more quickly. Depending on the size of the print "job," the type of printer, and the amount of memory it has, a printer is often unable to receive information as quickly as the application can send it. So instead of the information being sent directly to the printer, it may be sent to a special spooling application (in Windows that application is Print Manager), which saves it in a file and sends it on to the printer as quickly as the printer can take it. In the meantime, the application from which the data comes—the word processor or spreadsheet, for instance—can go back to work.

This chapter explains how to install and connect your printer drivers, how to print from an application, and how to work with Print Manager. We will assume you have connected the printer correctly to your computer.

▼ ***Note*** What is a printer? Windows treats a variety of devices as printers. It doesn't matter if you are sending the information to a dot matrix printer, a laser printer, a Linotronic typesetter, a plotter, or a slide recorder; all these objects are treated the same way. Each has a driver and is configured using the Control Panel's Printers dialog box. Even some fax programs load a driver this way, so you can "print" (send) a document to your fax machine.

When you installed Windows you had the chance to install printer drivers and connect them to a port. You can add new printer drivers or change the existing ones to a different computer port, using the Printers dialog box. (You don't use the Windows Setup to add printer drivers.)

You can add and remove drivers, set up driver options, and connect a driver to a physical port from the Printers dialog box. You can get to this dialog box from two places: The **Print Manager** or the **Control Panel**. The Options | Printer Setup command in the Print Manager was added to Windows 3.1 when Microsoft realized that new users assumed—quite understandably—that if you wanted to do something with a printer you would use Print Manager. However, going into the Printers dialog box this way disables one function—the ability to turn off Print Manager. So we are going to open the Printers dialog box from the Control Panel.

Working with Printer Drivers

To get to the Printers dialog box, open the Control Panel by double-clicking on the Control Panel icon in the Main program group, or select **File | Run** in Program Manager and run **CONTROL**. When the Control Panel opens, double-click on the Printers icon to see the Printers dialog box (shown in Figure 11.1).

The Printers dialog box shows you a list of the **Installed Printers**, the printer drivers that are loaded already. This list box also shows to which port each device has been connected. At the top of the list box you will see the **Default Printer**. This is the printer that all Windows applications *assume* you want to use. Most applications let you select another printer—using the File | Setup command—but unless you do so they automatically use the default printer. In some applications selecting a printer makes that printer the default printer for that application only. In other words, the next time you open the application it will automatically assume you want to use the printer you selected last time. However, Windows' own applications do not do this. Each time you open them they assume you want to use the Control Panel's default printer, even if you selected a different one using Print

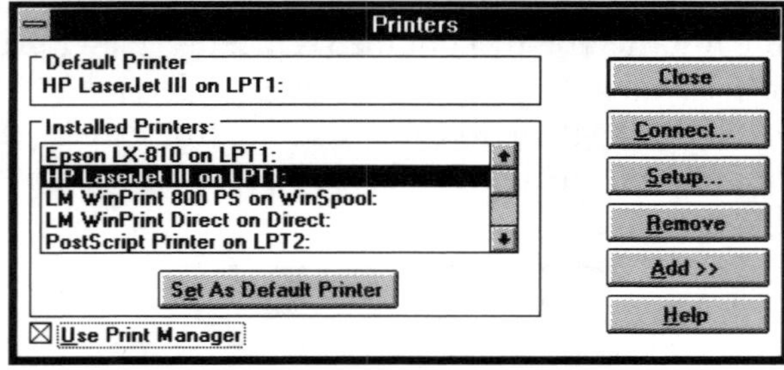

Figure 11.1 The Printers dialog box

Setup the last time you worked with the application. To change the default printer in the Control Panel, select the printer in the Installed Printers list and click **Set As Default Printer**.

Notice also the **Use Print Manager** check box at the bottom. When this is selected, all print jobs are spooled to the Print Manager. If it isn't selected, print jobs go directly to the printer, bypassing Print Manager; you won't even be able to open Print Manager. We discuss *why* you might want to turn off Print Manager later in this chapter when we describe ways to make printing more efficient.

Adding Printer Drivers

If you want to add a printer driver, click on **Add**. The dialog box is enlarged, displaying a box listing the drivers included on the Windows installation disk set (see Figure 11.2). Select the driver you want to install from the **List of Printers**. What do you do if your printer isn't listed? Your printer may be able to "emulate" one of the printers in the list; dot-matrix printers often emulate the Epson printers, and laser printers often emulate the HP LaserJet. Check your documentation. If the printer doesn't emulate another, check with the manufacturer and Microsoft to see if a driver is available. If you are a non-U.S. customer, use the following procedure described under "Installing New and Unlisted Drivers" with the Additional Non-USA Printer Drivers disk. Your final option is to use the Generic/Text Only option in the List of Printers. Use this if you have a daisywheel printer or if there isn't a driver for your printer. You won't be able to print graphics if you use this driver. If you are installing a PostScript printer, see the discussion about PostScript next.

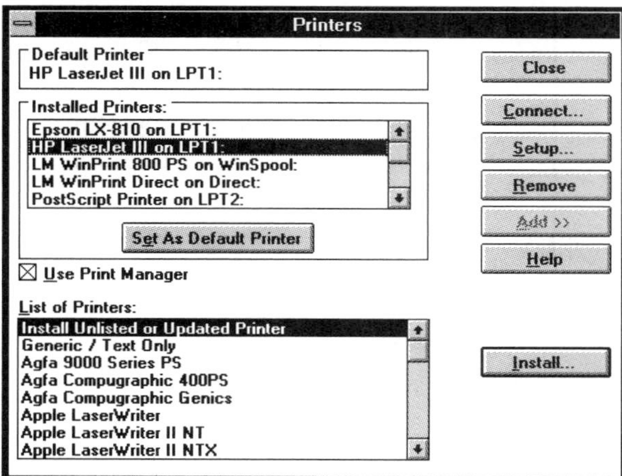

Figure 11.2 The Printers dialog box after clicking on Add

Once you have selected a driver, click on the **Install** button. Windows first looks in the WINDOWS\SYSTEM directory to see if the driver is already loaded—if, for instance, you had it on your system previously and removed it. If the driver is there, it is loaded automatically.

If the driver is not in your SYSTEM directory, a dialog box prompts you to place the disk in drive A: (see Figure 11.3). This dialog box will tell you the name of the driver you need and the disk on which it is stored. You may have to change the disk drive to B:, and you can use the Browse button to select another directory. If you have downloaded an updated driver from an on-line database—CompuServe or the Microsoft Download Service, for instance—you can select the directory into which you placed the file. When you click on **OK** in the Install Driver dialog box, Windows finds the driver for you and adds its name to the Installed Printers list. (In a few cases Windows may ask you to insert another disk for associated font files, for instance.)

INSTALLING POSTSCRIPT DRIVERS

PostScript drivers are a special case because many printers are PostScript-compatible. While the List of Printers includes a PostScript Printer entry, you should not normally select this. Instead, select the name of your particular printer or the name of the printer with which your system is compatible. For instance, if you are printing on a QMS ColorScript 100 or an Olivetti PG 308 HS PostScript model, select the particular printer from the list, not PostScript Printer.

If you are using a printer that has a PostScript cartridge installed, find out which printer the cartridge "emulates" (often the Apple LaserWriter), and select that particular printer. If the cartridge doesn't emulate a particular printer, select the PostScript model of the printer in which the cartridge is installed. For instance, if it is installed in an HP LaserJet IID, select HP LaserJet IID PostScript.

Most PostScript drivers use the same PSCRIPT.DRV file. The file is modified to act slightly differently when you select a different printer. So if you have three different PostScript "drivers" loaded, you may have only one driver file controlling all three versions. This also means that once you have loaded one PostScript

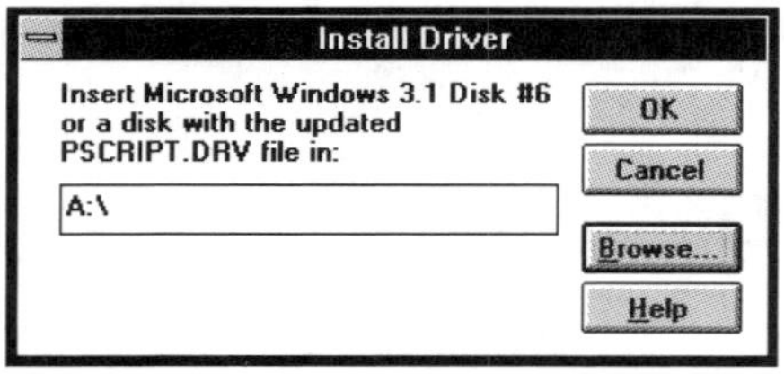

Figure 11.3 The Install Driver dialog box

driver, you may not need the installation disks to load another—Windows simply modifies the existing file.

If you do select the **PostScript Printer** option, Windows loads an Apple LaserWriter Plus PostScript driver. You might select PostScript Printer if you want to use the driver as a PostScript export translator rather than a printer driver. By printing to a file (which we discuss later in this chapter), you can create an .EPS (Encapsulated PostScript) file from any Windows application that can print. The .EPS file can then be imported—as a graphic—into applications that can accept that form of .EPS file (there are different types of EPS, so some applications may not accept it).

INSTALLING NEW AND UNLISTED DRIVERS

If you have a printer driver already loaded, you can't use this method to load an updated driver, because Windows automatically scans the SYSTEM directory for the driver—it will simply add the same one again. Or if you are loading a driver that isn't on the Windows installation disks, you won't be able to select it from the List of Printers. (Some printer manufacturers may be able to provide you with a Windows driver even if their product's driver wasn't included in the original installation set.) Instead, select the first option in the List of Printers, **Install Unlisted or Updated Printer**. When you click on **Install**, Windows doesn't bother checking the SYSTEM directory—instead it displays a slightly modified Install Driver dialog box; this one doesn't tell you the name of the driver or tell you to install a particular Windows installation disk. Just type the disk letter of the drive in which you have placed the driver disk, or click on the Browse button to select a particular directory.

Windows looks in the named directory and then displays the dialog box shown in Figure 11.4. Double-click on the driver you want to install, and Windows copies the driver to the SYSTEM directory and adds its name to the Installed Printers list.

Removing Printer Drivers

If you no longer need a printer driver, remove it by selecting it from the list of Installed Printers and click on Remove. When Windows asks you to confirm, click on **Yes**. Why bother to remove drivers? Apart from cleaning up the "clutter," drivers take up space in your WIN.INI initialization file, and the less Windows has to read from this file the quicker it can start.

If you ever need the driver again, you can get it back easily enough. Its name is removed from the WIN.INI file, but the file itself remains on your hard disk.

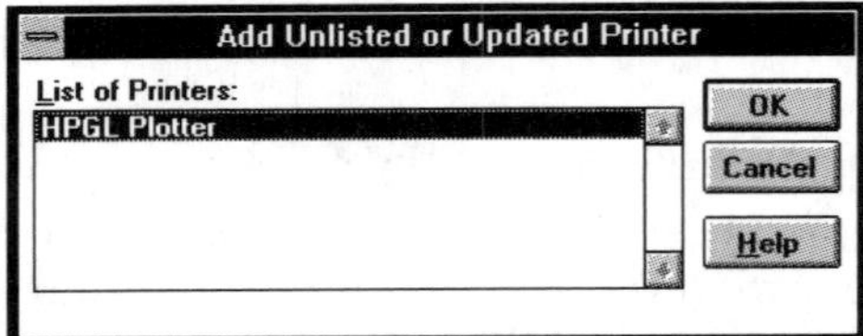

Figure 11.4 The Add Unlisted or Updated Printer dialog box

Driver files are usually stored in the WINDOWS\SYSTEM directory. Select the driver you want to reload from the List of Printers, click on **Install**, and Windows searches SYSTEM and automatically loads the driver.

To see what drivers you have in that directory, use the procedure we have just described for loading an updated printer driver. In the Install Driver dialog box type

```
C:\WINDOWS\SYSTEM
```

(or whatever the correct path is) and click on **OK**. Windows displays a list of drivers. Just double-click on the one you want to reload.

To completely remove a driver you must delete its file in the SYSTEM directory. These files have a .DRV extension and are usually—but not always—quite obvious. PSCRIPT.DRV is the PostScript driver, for instance, and MGXPJET.DRV is the Micrografx PaintJet driver. Rename the file, then use the procedure just described to see a list of the drivers in the SYSTEM directory. If the driver is no longer in the list, delete the renamed file.

Connecting Drivers to a Port

When you install a printer driver, Windows automatically connects it to LPT1, your default printer port. However many printers you add, they are all connected to LPT1. However, if you add the *same* printer several times, each one is added to a different port: LPT1, then LPT2, LPT3, COM1, and so on. You can continue adding the same printer until you run out of ports (including "virtual" ports, which we will learn about in a moment).

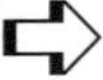 **Tip** Load multiple drivers if you have the same type of printer connected to more than one port. For instance, if you are connected to two PostScript printers, load two PostScript drivers and connect each one to a different port.

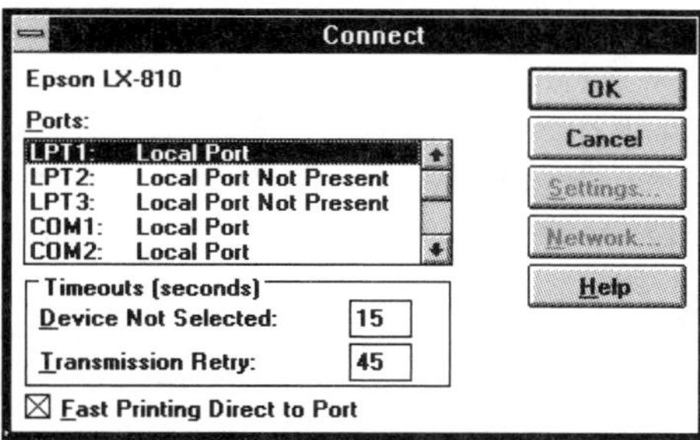

Figure 11.5 The Connect dialog box

You can change the port to which a printer is connected. If you have just loaded a new driver, and the printer is connected to LPT2 instead of LPT1, select the printer in the Installed Printers list and click on **Connect**. The Connect dialog box appears (shown in Figure 11.5). Select the port to which you want to connect the printer. You have a number of options.

LPT1, 2, and 3 — Parallel ports. If one of them doesn't actually exist on your computer, the list box will say Not Present.

COM1, 2, 3, and 4 — Serial ports. If one of them doesn't actually exist on your computer, the list box will say Not Present.

EPT — A special port used for the IBM Personal Pageprinter.

FILE — A print-to-file port. If you select this port, Windows prompts you to enter a filename each time you print.

LPT1.DOS and LPT2.DOS — If you print to one of these ports, Windows doesn't recognize the port as a hardware port. Instead it sees the port as an MS-DOS device. In effect Windows creates a print file called LPT*x*.DOS. DOS sees the name LPT*x* and redirects it to the parallel port. This can be used when you are having problems printing on networks. (The EPT port works in a similar manner.)

LPT1.OS2 and LPT2.OS2 — If you upgraded from Windows 3.0, instead of LPT*x*.DOS you will see LPT*x*.OS2, because the ports were originally used for printing in OS2. (Actually the three-letter extension doesn't matter—you can change it in WIN.INI to anything you want.)

▼ ***Note*** Some applications may automatically add port settings for you. For instance, the WinJet800 adds two ports, Direct:= and WinSpool:=.

If you select a COM port, click on the **Settings** button to see the Settings dialog box, where you set up serial-communications parameters. You can enter the parameters to match the printer. You can also click on the Advanced button to change the device to which you are connecting. This is the same dialog box that is opened when you double-click on the Ports icon in the Control Panel. (You can find more information in Chapter 8.)

You won't normally need to adjust the **Timeout** settings. They should work in most situations, but if you are sending complicated documents to a PostScript printer or to a busy network printer you may need to change them. The **Device Not Selected** timeout is the time it takes Windows to decide if the printer is working—if it is off-line, turned off, or disconnected. If Windows can't get the printer to respond within this time, it displays a message. The **Transmission Retry** timeout is the time Windows will wait when the printer pauses. If a printer can't accept any more information it tells Windows to stop transmitting, processes what it has, and tells Windows to begin again. If a printer pauses more than 45 seconds (or 90 seconds for a PostScript printer), Windows displays a message telling you that the printer can't accept more information. These numbers may need to be increased for network and PostScript printers. Don't change them when you first install a printer—change the values later if you have problems.

There's also a **Fast Printing Direct to Port** check box at the bottom of the Connect dialog box. This should normally be selected. Windows 3.1 can bypass DOS, so Print Manager sends its information directly to the port, unaffected by DOS printing interrupts. This is the fastest way to print. But in some cases you will need those interrupts: Printing on a network that isn't supported by Windows; printing through an electronic switch box that uses DOS interrupts to control printing; using a terminate and stay resident (TSR) program that controls printing through a COM port; or using any other kind of printer software that uses DOS interrupts. If any of these cases apply, deselect this check box.

CONNECTING TO A NETWORK PRINTER

If you are connected to a network, you can click on the **Network** button to select a network printer instead of a hardware port. Figure 11.6 shows a typical Network Connections dialog box. This dialog box varies depending on the network you are working with, so see the network's own documentation and use the Help system for more information.

In the example shown, you would select a network queue from the **Available Queues** list box, then click on the **Connect** button. If you want to make this a permanent connection so that it's available the next time you open Windows, click on the **Permanent** check box before the Connect button. You can also disconnect from a queue by selecting it and clicking on **Disconnect**.

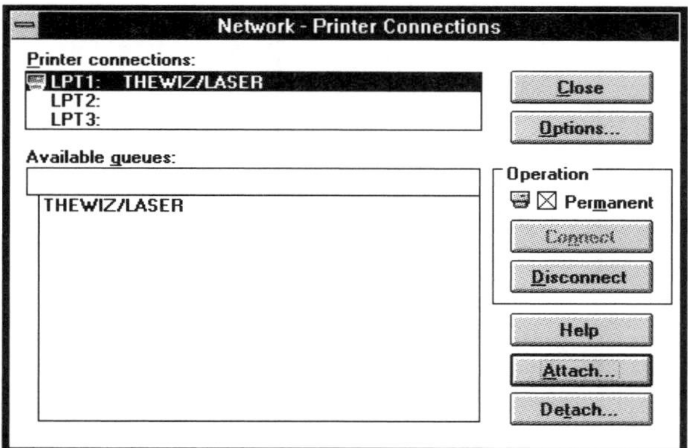

Figure 11.6 A Network-Printer Connections dialog box

This dialog box also lets you select another file server, so you can use a printer on that server. Click on the **Attach** button, and when the dialog box comes up select the server you want and enter a user name and password. You can also click on **Detach** to see a dialog box that will let you detach a network server.

Notice also the **Options** button. If you select the printer connection and click on that button you will see a dialog box that lets you determine how the print job will be handled. You can add a "Banner," for instance, a sheet of paper that identifies a print job as yours (useful on networks with many people sharing a printer). You can also place a blank sheet between print jobs, and select the type of form on which you want to print your work.

▼ *Note* You can also get to the Network Connections dialog box from the Print Manager. Select the Options | Network Connections command.

Setting Up the Printer Driver

Once you have connected your printer driver to a port, click on the **Setup** button in the Printers dialog box. (You should always check the setup after connecting a driver to a port, even if you have been using it on another port.) You will see the selected Printer's Setup dialog box. Of course the actual box you see depends on the printer you selected. Figure 11.7 shows one of the HP LaserJet's Setup dialog boxes (the LaserJet is the most popular Windows printer).

You should set up the options in the way you will normally use them. You can always come back and change them later, or change them from your applications, using the File | Print Setup command. Most of the options in these Setup dialog

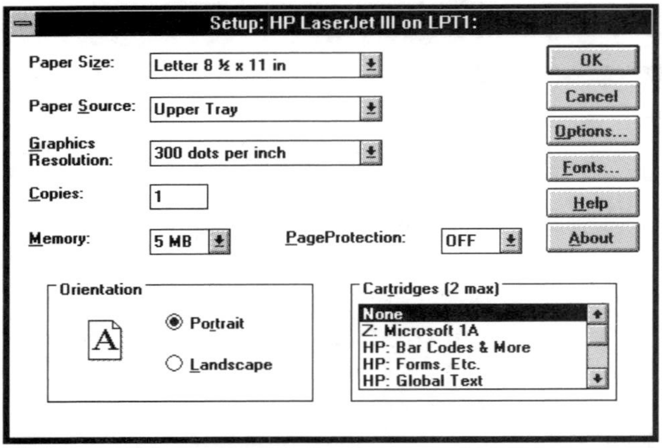

Figure 11.7 The HP LaserJet III's Setup dialog box

boxes are quite obvious, but you may need to click on the Help buttons to read about some of them. Let's take a look at the LaserJet's options:

Paper Size The paper size you are using. The default size depends on the country you selected in the Control Panel's International dialog box, but you can select a different one.

Paper Source The bin from which the paper is fed. You can also select Manual, in which case printing pauses each page so you can feed a sheet.

Graphics Resolution The higher the resolution, the slower the printing. You may want to use a low resolution while printing drafts, a high resolution for the final copy.

Copies The number of copies of each page. It is often quicker to tell the printer to print multiple copies than to tell your application. The application may send multiple copies of the page to the printer, whereas if you use the Copies option in the Setup dialog box the printer only has to receive the page once and just repeats it several times.

Memory The amount of memory your printer has.

Page Protection If you have 2 MB or more of memory you can tell the printer to create each page in memory before sending the paper through the printer. This ensures that complicated pages are not printed with missing information. Select the page size you are using (LTR is letter, 8.5 x 11). You must also set up the printer to use Page Protection. See your documentation.

Orientation The orientation of the printing on the paper. Portrait is the standard method—the pages are taller than they are wide. Notice that as you select an option button the page to the left changes to indicate the orientation of the text on the paper.

Cartridges The font cartridges you have installed in your printer. Selecting a cartridge makes those fonts available to your applications.

Many Setup dialog boxes also have an **Options** button. In the case of the LaserJet, clicking on the Options button displays the dialog box shown in Figure 11.8. Some of the options are disabled if they are not available on your specific model. These are the options in the LaserJet III's Options dialog box.

Gray Scale The type of gray scaling used by the printer. A gray scale is the way dots are used by a printer to simulate gray images. The Photographic Images option provides smooth transitions between different shades of gray. The Line Art Images option provides sharp transitions. The HP ScanJet Images option uses a special halftone designed for use with images from the HP ScanJet.

Duplex Printing Some printers have a duplex printing feature, letting you print on both sides of the paper. The Long Edge and Short Edge options are combined with the Portrait and Landscape options to tell the printer how to print the page on the back of the paper.

Output Bin Some large printers have output bins to catch the printed pages.

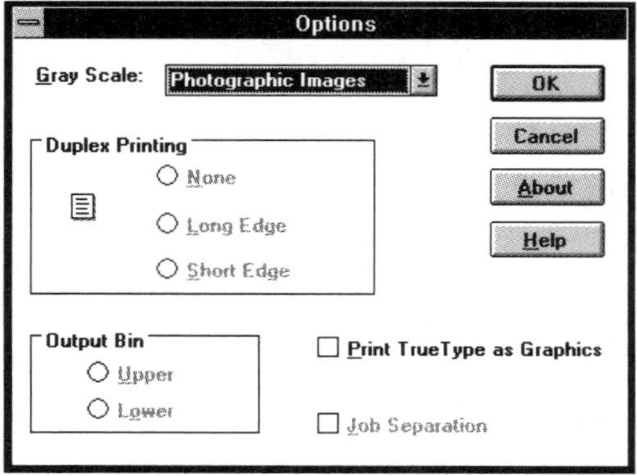

Figure 11.8 The LaserJet III's Options dialog box

Print TrueType as Graphics This option makes Windows send a single graphic image to the printer for each page, rather than individual characters. You may have to do this if you have only 1 MB of memory in your printer and you are printing TrueType fonts and pictures—or several TrueType fonts—on the same page.

Job Separation Some printers let you shift each print job slightly when the paper is deposited in the output bin so you can quickly separate different documents.

The Setup dialog boxes often have other buttons, such as these:

Fonts Displays a dialog box that lets you install new printer fonts. We are going to discuss fonts later in this chapter.

About Displays a box showing the driver's version number, date, and copyright information.

Help Opens the Help window and displays information about the driver.

More Displays more setup options.

Many printer drivers have similar options, and some have entirely different ones. You may see such options as *dithering*, *intensity control*, *print quality*, *pen color*, *device*, *carousel*, and so on. There are too many options to cover here, so use the Help button to read each option's description, or call the device's manufacturer for a recommended setup.

Note Printer drivers are updated continuously, to improve efficiency and fix bugs. You can download new drivers from CompuServe and other on-line services, get them from Microsoft, or get them from your printer's manufacturer.

When you have finished using the printer's Setup dialog box, click on **OK** to close it. Then configure another printer in the Printers dialog box or click on **Close** to finish.

THE POSTSCRIPT DRIVER

As mentioned earlier, most PostScript printers use the PSCRIPT.DRV driver. This has several options that are worth covering. The Setup dialog box is quite straightforward. You can select a paper source, paper size, copies, and orientation. But when you click on the Options button you see the dialog box shown in Figure 11.9.

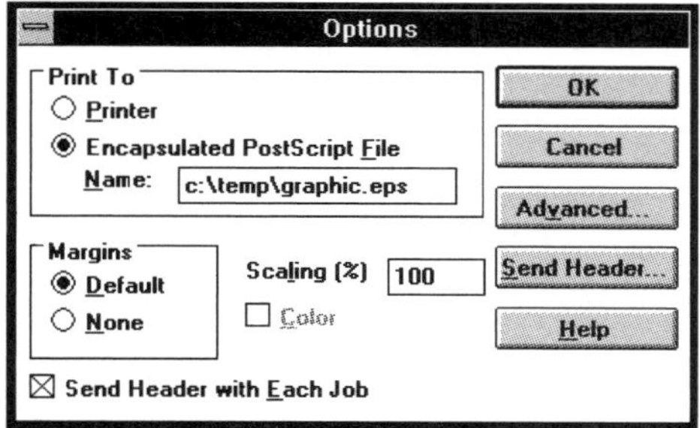

Figure 11.9 The PostScript Options dialog box

The PostScript driver can be used for two purposes: to print on a PostScript printer, and to create an .EPS file that can be exported to compatible applications. The driver effectively allows any Windows application to *export* to .EPS. You can do this by creating a print file instead of printing the document. "Printing-to-file" is explained in more detail later in this chapter. For now, let's look at the PostScript options.

Printer Sends print jobs to the printer.

Encapsulated PostScript File Creates a print file instead of actually printing the data.

Name If you selected the second option button, you can enter a path and filename in the Name text box. If you don't do so, Windows asks you for a filename each time you "print."

Margins Selecting None sets the printing area to the total page size while selecting Default sets the printing area to the total area on which the printer can print. The printing area affects the position of the margins set in your application.

Scaling Lets you increase or decrease the size of the image sent to the printer, letting you fit more or less on the paper. This may be useful when creating a print file that you are going to import as an EPS graphic.

Color If your printer can print in color, select the check box to use colors; deselect it to use gray scales.

Send Header with Each Job Sends the header each time you print. This is normally selected and is recommended if you are printing on a network printer. If you don't send a header with each job, use the Send Header button.

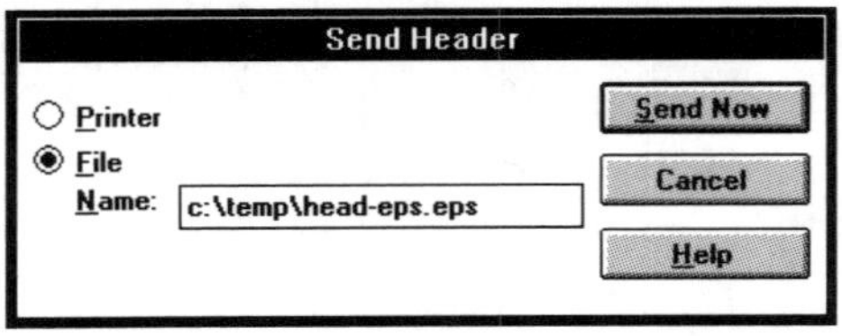

Figure 11.10 The Send Header dialog box

A header contains information that the PostScript printer needs to set it up so it can handle your print jobs. That header information can be sent when you turn your printer on or each time you send a print job. The ideal, perhaps, is to send it once; that way the individual print jobs print a little quicker. However, you have to be sure that the header information is still in the printer when you send each print job. If you are using a network printer, the header information could be changed by another user. Also, if you are creating print files, you have two options: create the file with the header so you don't have to worry about sending a header first, or create the file without the header, in which case you must send the header before you can print the file. You may want to use the second option if you are creating a number of print files. A print file without a header is about 10 KB smaller. You can create a header, create all the print files, then print the header first, followed by all the print files.

To create a header, click on the **Send Header** button. The dialog box shown in Figure 11.10 appears. If you want to send a header directly to the printer, make sure **Printer** is selected and then click **Send Now**. You can now send print to the printer without headers. If you want to create a header file, select **File**, enter a name in the check box, and click on **Send Now**. You must print the header file before the print files. (See a discussion of printing print files later in this chapter.)

The Options dialog box also has an **Advanced** button. Click on this to see the dialog box in Figure 11.11. This dialog box lets you specify how a PostScript printer will work with TrueType fonts, assign memory, and create graphics. Not all the options are available for all printers.

TRUETYPE FONTS	
Send to Printer as	Lets you specify how to use TrueType fonts. **Adobe Type 1**: The default option sends small TrueType fonts as raster graphics (just like a Paintbrush picture), while larger characters (generally over 15 points) use the printer's resident Adobe Type 1 fonts. This is normally the most efficient method.

Bitmap (Type 3): Downloads all fonts as Type 3 fonts. Use this only if your printer has problems working with Type 1, which may happen in rare cases. Quality will improve but it will print more slowly.

Native TrueType: This option is available only for "true image printers" that recognize TrueType fonts. Only a few PostScript printers—such as some new Apple Laserwriters—can use this option. It's the recommended option if present. TrueType fonts are sent to the printer without conversion.

Use Printer Fonts for all TrueType Fonts — Use this option if your printer cannot accept downloaded fonts. The printer will use the closest matching internal fonts. Using printer fonts speeds printing, so you may want to do this even if your printer can use TrueType fonts.

Use Substitution Table — Use this option if your printer cannot accept downloaded fonts and you want to specify which fonts it may use. Click on the Edit Substitution Table to match TrueType fonts with printer fonts.

MEMORY

Virtual Memory KB — Determines how much of the printer's memory is used to handle TrueType and soft fonts. If a document has several different fonts and isn't printing properly, try reducing this number to clear the memory more often. You can find a recommended value for this setting by printing a special test file. At the DOS prompt type

```
c:\windows\system\testps.txt lpt1
```

to send the test document to LPT1. A page is printed showing the recommended value.

Clear Memory per Page — Select this check box if you are having problems printing a document with several TrueType fonts per page. The printer will clear its memory after each page. (Printing will slow down.) If you've set virtual memory correctly, you shouldn't need to use this option.

GRAPHICS	
Resolution	The higher the resolution the slower the printing. This option is combined with the next two to adjust the quality of graphics.
Halftone Frequency	The number of lines per inch in halftones. The lower the resolution, the fewer lines per inch can be used.
Halftone Angle	The angle of the lines used in the halftone. Modifying the angle produces different effects.
Negative Image	Inverts the gray scales: The black becomes white, white becomes black, and light gray becomes dark gray.
Mirror	Creates a mirror image of the document's graphics.
All Colors to Black	Used when printing color images on a black-and-white printer to make very light colors appear.
Compress Bitmaps	Compresses graphics when sending them to the printer, slowing printing but releasing the application faster.
Conform to Adobe Structuring	Creates a document that may be used by applications that can work with the Adobe Document Structuring Conventions (DSC).
Print PostScript Error Information	Prints a page containing an error message whenever you have PostScript errors.

PostScript Type 1 fonts are scalable fonts, resident in most PostScript printers. Type 3 fonts are bitmap fonts, set at a particular point size. They can be scaled, but the characters may not look very good. As you can see from the previous tabulation, in most cases TrueType fonts are sent to the PostScript printer in two formats: The large fonts are sent as Type 1, and the small ones are sent as Type 3. You can change the point size at which Windows makes that decision. By default, fonts 15 points or smaller are sent as Type 3, larger than 15 points are sent as Type 1. You can change this by adding the

```
MinOutlineeppem=
```

line to WIN.INI. Read the PRINTERS.WRI file in your WINDOWS directory.

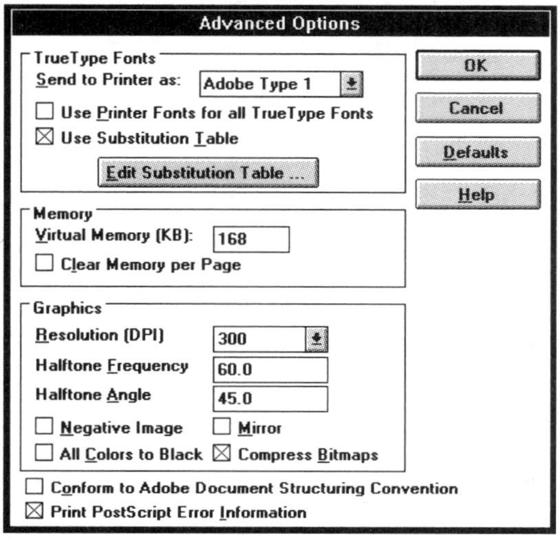

Figure 11.11 The PostScript printer driver's Advanced Options dialog box

BUILDING YOUR OWN PRINTER DRIVER

If you have a dot-matrix printer for which there is no Windows driver, you can set up your own using the Generic/Text Only driver. However, you will not be able to print graphics with this driver. (This driver is also used to print to daisywheel printers—you won't need to change the setup.)

Select the Generic/Text Only driver in the Installed Printers list box and click on **Setup**. The dialog box shown in Figure 11.12 appears. Then click on **Add** to see the Add dialog box (shown in Figure 11.13). In the **New Printer Name** text box type the name of the printer for which you are creating a driver. Then enter the various printer codes. You can get these from your printer's documentation.

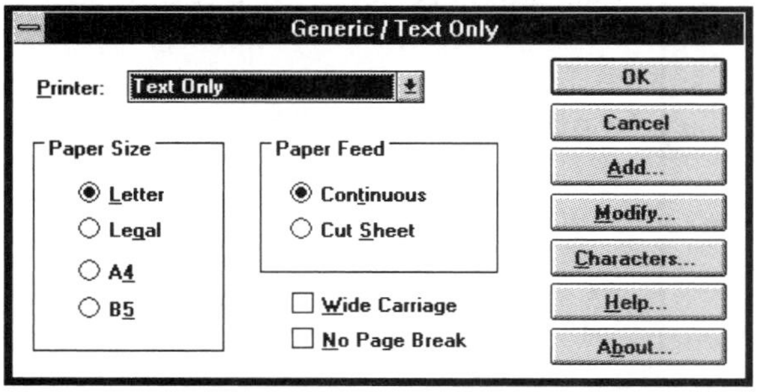

Figure 11.12 The Generic Text Only printer driver setup dialog box

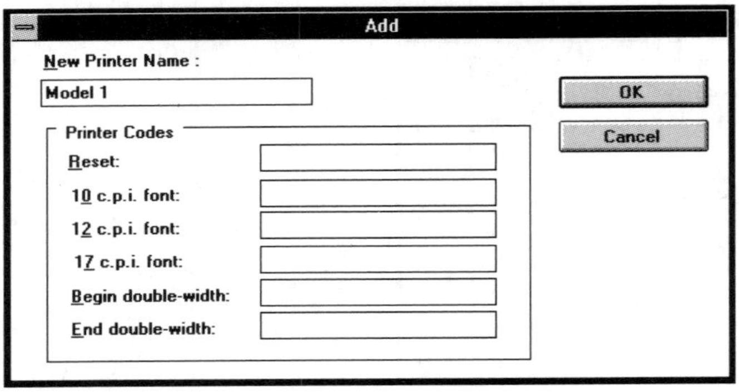

Figure 11.13 The Add dialog box

For instance, if you want to enter the code Esc Ctrl-K A, place the cursor in the text box, press **Esc**, press **Ctrl-K**, and press **A**.

When you've entered the control codes, click on **OK** and then click on **Characters** in the Generic/Text Only dialog box to see the Characters dialog box. The **On Screen** list box shows all the Windows extended (special) characters. Select a character and the **On Printer** text box shows you what will be printed when the Windows character is sent to the printer. You can change this, entering a character that your printer is able to print. Check your documentation for the code. Most dot matrix printers have an extended character table. Find the character in the table and enter its position in the table into the On Printer text box.

When you have set up the control codes and characters, select the options in the Generic/Text Only dialog box itself. You can select a page size and the type of paper feed. If you want to print more than 80 characters across a page select Wide Carriage, and if you want to print continuously—without page breaks—select No Page Break.

You can create several printer drivers this way. When you want to use one, select the Print Setup dialog box in the application, select the driver in the list, click on **Setup**, and then select the specific printer from the Printer drop-down list box. The font sizes you entered will be available in your application, although they probably won't look correct on your screen ("what you see is probably *not* what you will get").

Use this driver's Help system for more information.

Printing from Applications

Printing from a Windows application is simple. In most cases you will just select the **File | Print** command. In some applications the current file is sent directly to the printer. In other applications a dialog box appears in which you can make certain selections—the number of copies, the orientation, the numbers of the pages you want to print, and so on. (This is described in more detail in Chapter 6.)

When you print a document it will be "spooled" to the Print Manager. You will see a message box telling you that the document is printing. While this dialog box is displayed you cannot work in the application, although you can work in another one. Once the document has gone to Print Manager the message box disappears, and you can continue working in the application even though the printer may not have begun printing.

There's another way to print: using File Manager. You can drag a file icon from File Manager onto the Print Manager window or icon. If the file is "associated" with an application—and if that application supports "drag and drop" printing—that application will open and will automatically load and print the file. (See Chapter 9 for more information.)

DOS programs running in Windows do not use Windows' print-management features. They simply print directly to the printer port, as they would if you were running them in DOS. Also, by default DOS applications do not run while they are in the background. A DOS application will print in the background only if you are using a PIF file that specifically allows background operations. (See Chapter 7 for more information.)

Warning If you have a DOS application printing at the same time a Windows application is trying to do so, you will get a device-contention problem. While Windows can mediate problems with serial communications ports, it can't do anything about parallel ports, so print errors will occur. (See Chapter 8 for information about serial-port device contention.)

Note Once you have sent a print job to the Print Manager and your application is no longer displaying a dialog box telling you it is printing, you can close your application. The print job will still print.

SELECTING ANOTHER PRINTER

When you print from an application, it automatically uses the printer selected as the Default Printer in the Printers dialog box. If you want to use another one, select **File | Print Setup** to see the Print Setup dialog box. There are two types: one that shows you a list of printers (see Figure 11.14) and one that contains setup

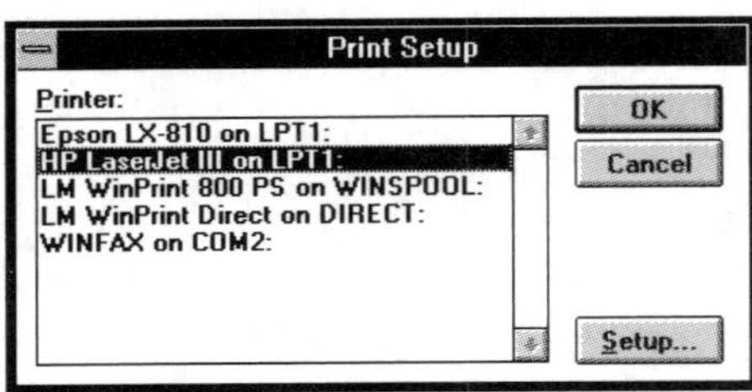

Figure 11.14 The simple Print Setup dialog box

options (see Figure 11.15). The one you will see depends on the application you are working with.

The type of Print Setup dialog box shown in Figure 11.14 lets you select the printer you want and click on **OK** to return to your application and print. You can also select the printer and click on **Setup** to go to the printer driver's Setup dialog box—the same dialog box that you see when you click on Setup in the Control Panel's Printers dialog box.

The dialog box shown in Figure 11.15 has more printer options. You can change the options or select another printer. You can also click on the Options button, but what you see depends on the type of Setup dialog box the selected driver uses. If the Setup dialog box has an Options button, you will see the Options dialog box. If it *doesn't*, you will see the Setup dialog box. This type of Print Setup dialog box is used by all of Windows' own applications and some other Microsoft products. Most other applications use the simple type shown in Figure 11.14, but that may change. The Print Setup dialog box with more options has some advantages—you can change some of the most important options right there—but it does mean that in some cases you will have to go to the Control Panel to change some other options, such as Graphics Resolution or Copies. The options in this Print Setup dialog box are described in Chapter 6.

Print Setup
Printer
Default Printer
(currently HP LaserJet III on LPT1:)
Specific Printer:
HP LaserJet III on LPT1:
Orientation
Portrait
Landscape
Paper
Size: Letter 8 1/2 x 11 in
Source: Upper Tray
OK
Cancel
Options...

Figure 11.15 The Print Setup dialog box with options

> **Important** Some applications have a bug in their Print Setup dialog box procedures. Settings you enter in the printer driver's Setup dialog box don't "stick." That is, if you close the box then reopen it, the setting you made has changed back to its original setting. If this happens, use the Control Panel to make changes to a driver's Setup dialog box.

Printing Problems

The amount of space available on the disk holding the TEMP directory determines how many print jobs you can have in the print queue. When there's no room to create temporary files, Print Manager will display a message that you have insufficient disk space. The TEMP directory is normally a subdirectory of the WINDOWS directory.

Print Manager will also display a message if there's a problem with your printer. Your printer may be turned off, out of paper, disconnected, or off-line. Print Manager can't always figure out the problem (for instance, if it is turned off you will see a message saying it is off-line or not connected). Figure 11.16 shows an example of one of the message boxes you will see.

The message boxes appear over the application in which you are working—you don't have to open Print Manager to see them. And they are a great improvement over the Windows 3.0 message boxes. You can fix the printer problem (add paper or turn it on, for instance) and click on the **Retry** button to continue. No need to go to Print Manager to get started again.

Printing to File

The feature known as "printing to file" lets you create a file on a disk instead of printing pages on a printer. Printing to a file is much quicker than actually printing, so you can print to a file to save time, then print the file later when you have

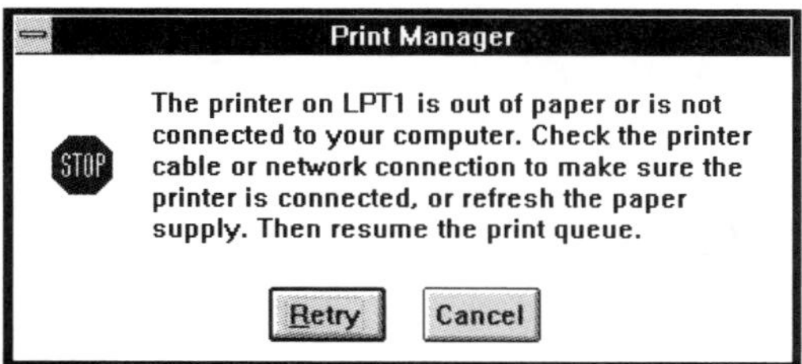

Figure 11.16 A Print Manager message warning you of print problems

more time. You can also print the file on another computer that is connected to a different device.

For instance, let's say you want to produce a color slide of your work. If you have a common application you can probably just give the application file to a service bureau that owns a film recorder. However, if they don't have the application you are working with, you could use a film-recorder driver—instead of your normal printer driver—to create a print file. You could then give the print driver to the service bureau, and they could print the file using a batch-printing utility or the DOS COPY command.

Maybe you want to print a PostScript file but you don't have a PostScript printer. Create a print file with the PostScript driver, then take the file to a computer that is connected to a PostScript printer and print it from there. A more common use is to simply print files later when you aren't using your computer. You can place all the print files in a special directory, then use a single DOS command to print them all before you leave your office in the evening, for instance.

Tip Creating a PostScript print file is like exporting a PostScript image. The file can be imported into some applications as a PostScript image.

There are several ways to print to a file. Individual applications may let you do so, some printer drivers let you specify a filename instead of a port, and Windows provides a special print-to-file port. You can also add your own print-to-file ports to WIN.INI.

USING PRINT DIALOG BOXES

Some applications—such as Write—have a check box in their Print dialog boxes that let you send the print job to a file. The check box is usually named **Print to File**. If you select this check box, when you begin printing you will see a dialog box like that shown in Figure 11.17. Simply enter the name of the file and the drive and directory in which you want to place it. (If you don't enter a pathname it is

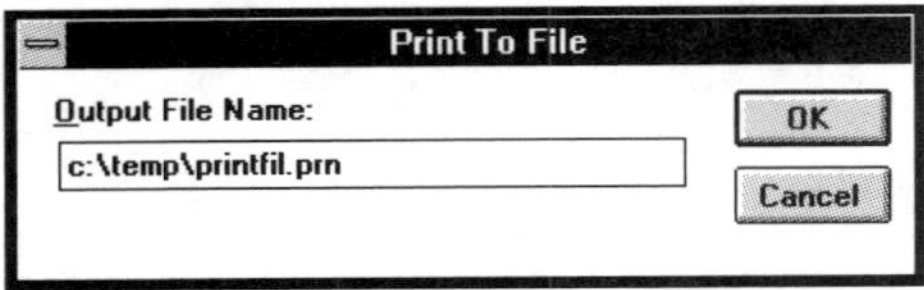

Figure 11.17 Write's Print to File dialog box

automatically placed in the current directory, the one in which you last saved or opened a file.) Include a file extension only if you want one; it isn't necessary.

▼ *Note* When you select a Print to File check box, remember to deselect it the next time you want to print!

USING PRINTER DRIVERS

Some printer drivers—in particular the PostScript ones—also have a print-to-file option. In Figure 11.9 earlier in this chapter we showed you the dialog box that appears when you click on the **Options** button in the Windows PostScript driver. Select the Encapsulated PostScript File option button, then type a path and filename. Again, include the extension if you need one.

If you want to print several files, leave the Name text box empty so the application will prompt you for a filename each time you print a file. If you select the print-to-file option in the printer driver and also in Write's Print dialog box, the Print dialog box will override the driver. In other words, if you entered a name in the driver's Name check box, it will be ignored. (This is not the case in some other applications.) Thus, using the driver's print-to-file option is most useful when printing from an application that doesn't have a print-to-file check box in its Print dialog box.

▼ *Note* There's a bug in Write that prevents you from using this method directly. If you select the Encapsulated PostScript File option button using Write's Print Setup command (or even by clicking on the Setup button in the Print dialog box and then the Options button in the Print Setup dialog box), the printer driver will not save the setting. However, you can set it from another application or from the Control Panel, then go to Write and print using the driver. You can also use the Print to File option in Write's Print dialog box.

THE PRINT-TO-FILE PORT

Windows provides a port called FILE. You can connect a printer to this port in the Connect dialog box that we saw earlier. Then, when you print to that device—from *any* application using *any* driver—you will see a Print to File dialog box in which you can enter the path and filename. This feature is useful if you need to use various applications to create print files in a specific format. For instance, you print a lot of PostScript files, but your computer is not connected to a PostScript printer.

ADD YOUR OWN PORTS

You can add your own print-to-file "port" to the WIN.INI file, then connect a printer to that port. For instance, if you add the line

```
PRINTFIL.EPS=
```

to the [Ports] section of the WIN.INI file and connect a printer to that port, every time you print with that printer it creates a file called PRINTFIL.EPS. The advantage of this is that you don't have to add a filename each time you print. The disadvantages are that you can't specify a pathname, and that you will overwrite the PRINTFIL.EPS file each time.

Incidentally, the WIN.INI file already has a port set up like this. It's called EPT, and is intended for use by the IBM Personal Pageprinter. If you don't have one of these printers you can print directly to the EPT print file. Also, note that when you add a print filename of your own, don't put a colon between the filename and the = sign (most of the ports do have the colon, but print files shouldn't). (For more information about WIN.INI, see Appendix B.)

PRINTING THE FILES

Here's an easy way to print your print files. In DOS, change to the directory in which you have placed the print files. Then use this command:

```
copy filename lpt1 /b
```

where lpt1 is the port to which your printer is attached. If you are using a PostScript printer, omit the /b switch. You can, of course, use wild cards to print several or all of the files. For instance,

```
copy *.* lpt1 /b
```

prints all of the files. Or try

```
copy *.prn lpt1 /b
```

to print only those files with the .PRN extension, or

```
copy 05-*.* lpt1 /b
```

to print all of the files whose names begin with 05-.

Using Print Manager

Print Manager

When you print a document to a local printer—one connected directly to your printer—the Print Manager icon appears at the bottom of the screen (it will be obscured if you can't see the desktop). You can double-click on it or use any of the other window-swapping procedures to open it. If you are printing to a network printer—one available through a local area network—Print Manager may not automatically open (depending on the setting in the Network Options dialog box, which we will describe later). You can open it by double-clicking on the Print Manager icon in the Main Group. Or select **File | Run** in Program Manager and run **PRINTMAN**. You can open Print Manager at any time, not just when you are printing. You can then set up options or configure printers. The only time you won't be able to open Print Manager is when the Use Print Manager check box is not selected in the Control Panel's Printers dialog box.

Although you can install and configure printer drivers with the Print Manager, its primary purpose is to control the printing of your files. Print Manager controls your print jobs even if you never bother to look in on it.

▼ ***Note*** The **Options | Printer Setup** command displays the Printers dialog box. This is the same as the Printers dialog box displayed when you double-click on the Printers icon in Control Panel, except that it has no Use Print Manager check box.

When you send a job to the printer from one of your Windows applications, it is "spooled" to the Print Manager. That is, the application does all it has to do to print the document, passes it on to the Print Manager, and goes on with work. The information is saved in a temporary file—or several temporary files—on your hard disk, in the TEMP directory that should have been created when you installed Windows. (TEMP is normally a subdirectory of WINDOWS.)

The Print Manager, meanwhile, sends the information to the printer. While Print Manager is doing its job, you can continue working in the application from which the print job came, or perhaps another application. This is known as "background printing." However, with the default setting it's not all it should be. Background printing can slow your system down drastically. If you have a slow processor, you may find that working in an application while printing in the background is totally impractical. You may be able to improve performance, as we shall see later.

▼ ***Note*** While spooling through the Print Manager is intended to cut down on unproductive computer time, the time it takes to print the file is a little longer. When print speed is more important than working while you print in the background—or if you find background printing makes foreground processing too sluggish—turn off the Print Manager in the Control Panel's Printers dialog box.

There's another advantage to using Print Manager: You can print several documents from a variety of applications and not have to wait for the printer to finish

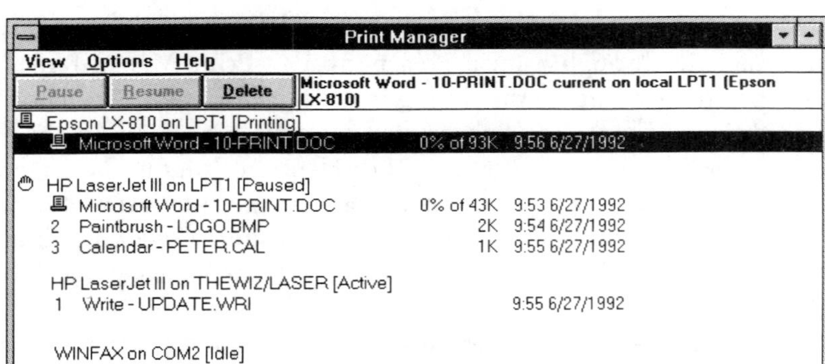

Figure 11.18 The Print Manager

each file before selecting the Print command. The documents go into a "print queue," which Print Manager controls. As we noted earlier, only Windows applications go into this queue: DOS applications go directly to the printer port. Thus, while DOS applications can interfere with each other if you try to print from two or more at the same time—or a DOS application can interfere with a Windows application—thanks to the print queue you can print from several Windows applications at the same time with no problems.

Figure 11.18 shows the Print Manager with a few print jobs in its queues. Print Manager can show both *local* queues and *network* queues (in the illustration the HP LaserJet III on THEWIZ/LASER is a network queue, as it doesn't mention a port). We will discuss network queues in more detail later.

The Print Queue

The print queue displays the following information:

- The name of each printer configured in the Printers dialog box.
- The port to which the printer is connected. In the case of a network printer, the printer path is shown instead of a port.
- The status of the printer: *Idle* (not in use), *Printing*, *Paused* (you clicked the Pause button), *Active* (a network printer that is printing), or *STALLED* (Print Manager is unable to print, perhaps because the printer is off, off-line, disconnected, or out of paper).
- The title of each print job below the appropriate printer (the application and filename).
- A printer icon to show the print job is printing, or a number indicating the position in the queue.

Three other pieces of information may be displayed, depending on the View menu options:

1. If View | Print File Size is selected, the size in kilobytes of each print job's temporary print files in TEMP directory, an indication of how long a print job will take.
2. If View | Print File Size is selected, the percentage of the job that has been completed.
3. If View | Time/Date Sent is selected, the time and date that you sent the print job to the printer.

Notice also that the area to the right of the buttons—immediately below the menu bar—provides information about the selected printer (not necessarily the one printing). If it's a local printer, it shows if it is printing or idle. If it is a network printer it may show more information, such as the current print job and the network path.

Windows doesn't provide Print Manager just to let you view the queue. You can also manipulate the print jobs: You can stop printers, remove print jobs, and shuffle them into different positions.

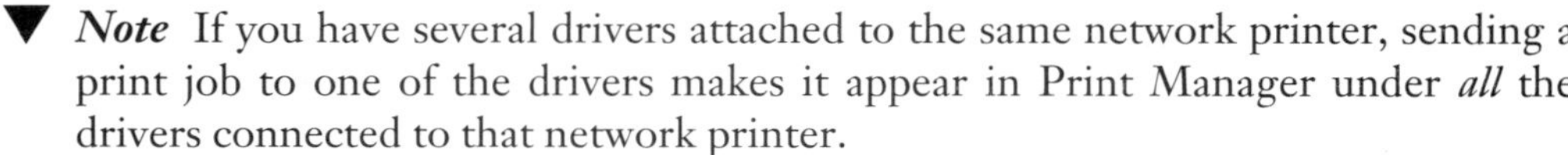

▼ ***Note*** If you have several drivers attached to the same network printer, sending a print job to one of the drivers makes it appear in Print Manager under *all* the drivers connected to that network printer.

Controlling Print Jobs

You can temporarily stop a printer from working if you need to. You may, for instance, want to put a different type of paper in the printer. If you are sharing a printer with another computer—using a switch box between the printer and computers—you could also stop printing, let the other computer print, and resume.

Simply select the printer you want to stop—click on the printer name or press the up and down arrows to highlight it—and then click on the **Pause** button. Click on **Resume** when you are ready to continue. You can pause a printer at any time, even when you are not printing. Print Manager will store the print jobs you send to that printer and wait until you click the **Resume** button to begin printing. You can't pause a network printer, but you can select the print job and click on **Pause**.

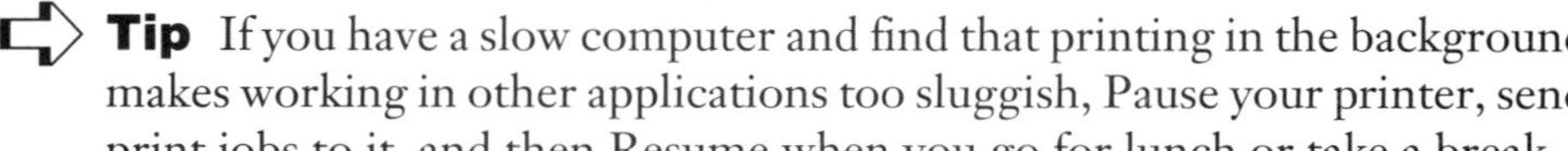

Tip If you have a slow computer and find that printing in the background makes working in other applications too sluggish, Pause your printer, send print jobs to it, and then Resume when you go for lunch or take a break.

You can also remove print jobs from the queue. Perhaps you have just realized you forgot to add something to a document, or just noticed a mistake. Select the print job this time (not the printer name), and click on **Delete**. Print Manager will ask you to confirm that you want to delete the document. Make sure the dialog box names the correct file (that you didn't select the wrong one from the list). You can even delete a file while it is printing. Print Manager won't send any more pages to the printer; however, the printer may have several left in its memory, so it may continue printing for a while.

You can delete the entire print queue by closing Print Manager. Double-click on the Control menu or use **File | Exit**. When you delete a print file or the entire queue, you may need to reset your printer, especially if you are printing graphics. Part of the graphic may have reached the printer, and it's waiting for the rest, so the next time you print you get the graphic on top of another page.

You may occasionally want to **move** print jobs in a local queue (you can't do so on a network queue). Perhaps you have sent a number of print jobs to Print Manager, or a few large ones. Now you realize that you need to see the last print job as soon as possible. You can move it into second position so it will print next, or shuffle it into any other position. The only restriction is that you cannot move a print job to (or from) the beginning of the queue (even if you paused the printer before sending any print jobs to it). To move a print job, just **drag** it with the mouse and release the mouse button when it's in the position you want. The pointer changes to a thick vertical arrow when you are dragging print jobs. When you release the mouse button the print job is moved *in front* of the one you are pointing to. If you don't have a mouse, highlight the print job, hold **Ctrl**, and use the **Up** and **Down arrows** to move it.

Changing Print Priorities

Print Manager lets you change print priorities, the amount of processing time that should be assigned to printing. (You cannot adjust each print job independently—you are adjusting Print Manager itself.) If you select **Options | Low Priority**, Windows assigns most of its processing time to the applications and only a little to Print Manager. If you select **Options | High Priority**, Windows gives most time to Print Manager.

Low Priority — Your documents print slowly.

Your applications pass the print jobs to Print Manager more quickly, so you can return to work.

Your applications runs smoothly, with minimal jerkiness, while Print Manager prints in the background.

Medium Priority — A compromise between Low and High Priority.

High Priority Your documents print quickly.

If Print Manager is already printing when you send a document from an application, the application takes a long time to send it, so you must wait longer to continue working.

Using your application while Print Manager prints in the background may be difficult; there may be a lag in the keyboard and mouse response.

The effects of these priorities depend on the machine you are using. If you have a 486 with a fast hard drive, you may not notice any problems using High Priority. If you have a 286, though, you will probably find High Priority makes it difficult to use your application, due to the lag in keyboard and mouse response. (You may even find Low Priority is difficult.) How much difference do these priorities make? For example, if Print Manager is already printing and you print a document from an application, you may be able to continue working after 20 seconds if you are using Low Priority. Print the same file with High Priority set, and you may have to wait 90 seconds.

Dealing with Messages

Some printers may need to send messages to tell you, for example, to put paper in the manual sheet-feed slot. You can tell Print Manager how to handle such messages. If you want Print Manager to display a message even if you are working in another application, select **Options | Alert Always**. To make Print Manager flash its title bar or icon, select **Options | Flash if Inactive**. When you open or select the Print Manager window it displays the message. Of course you may not be able to see the icon or window. To simply ignore any message that arrives when the Print Manager is not the active window, select **Options | Ignore if Inactive**.

You will probably never see any of these messages. The "paper out" or "printer off-line" type messages always appear, regardless of your selection in the Options menu. And some printers will simply send an "off-line" message when you have to place paper in the manual sheet feed, so you will see an "off-line" message whatever your selection.

Printing on a Network

If you are using network printers, the information about the printers is sent to Windows by the network. The information received depends on the type of network. Some, for instance, will not send a list of the print jobs currently in the network queue. This information is periodically updated; you can force an update by pressing **F5** or selecting **View | Refresh**. The time and date shown for a print job is the network time and date, not your computer's time and date, so it may not be what you expect.

▼ *Note* For information about your specific network, read the NETWORKS.WRI file in the WINDOWS directory. You can open this file in Windows Write. The network dialog boxes also have Help buttons. Click on these buttons for specific information.

CONNECTING AND DISCONNECTING NETWORK PRINTERS

We explained earlier how to connect to a network printer by clicking on the Network button in the Connect dialog box. (Display the Connect dialog box by clicking on Connect in the Printers dialog box.) You can also connect to a network printer using the **Options | Network Connections** command. You will see the same dialog box and carry out the same procedures.

You can use this same dialog box to disconnect from a network printer. Select it in the **Current Printer Connections** list box, and click on **Disconnect**. Some networks let you reconnect to a network printer from which you have disconnected. Click on the **Previous** button. When the Previous Network Connections dialog box appears, double-click on the one you want to reconnect to, or select it and click on **Select**.

VIEWING NETWORK QUEUES

In the same way Print Manager manages Windows' print queue, networks also manage print queues. The network gets print jobs from different computers and assigns them a place in the queue. Some networks let you view the queue, although you won't be able to modify it. Select the network printer whose queue you want to see, and then select **View | Selected Net Queue**. You will see the dialog box shown in Figure 11.19.

Your network may also let you view queue information for printers you are not connected to. Select **View | Other Net Queue**. When the Other Net Queue dialog box appears enter the printer path in the **Network Queue** text box, then click on **View**. The list box shows the print jobs currently pending. You may want to do this to find a printer that isn't busy. If you decide you want to use this printer you must first use the **Options | Network Connections** command to connect to the printer.

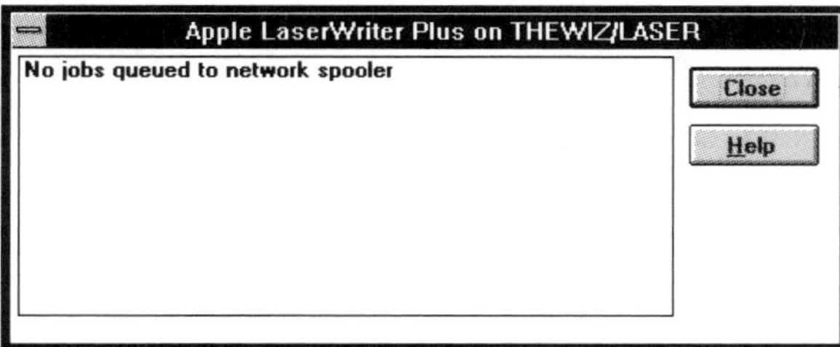

Figure 11.19 The Network Queue dialog box

CHANGING NETWORK SETTINGS

Select **Options | Network Settings**. Deselect the **Update Network Display** check box if you don't want Print Manager to periodically update the status of the print jobs in a network queue.

By default Windows sends print jobs directly to the network printer, bypassing Print Manager. Print Manager will not open automatically, although you can open it and view the print jobs, and even pause them. However, if you deselect the **Print Net Jobs Direct** check box network print jobs will go through the Print Manager, and the Print Manager icon will automatically appear when you send a print job.

Closing Print Manager

As we said earlier, you can ignore Print Manager most of the time. When you print a job, Windows loads Print Manager and places the icon at the bottom of the desktop. If you are printing on a network printer it doesn't bother with the icon. When the printing has finished, Print Manager automatically closes. If you have opened Print Manager—even if you then minimized it—you will have to close it. Close Print Manager as you would any other application.

Print Manager's Menu Options

Here's a quick summary of Print Manager's menu options and buttons.

View | Time/Date Sent Includes the time and date that each job was sent to the printer in the queue information.

View | Print File Size Includes the size of each print job's temporary files in the queue information. It also includes the percentage of the print job that has been completed.

View | Refresh (F5) Asks the network for an updated status list of the print jobs being sent to the network.

View | Selected Net Queue Displays information about the selected network queue.

View | Other Net Queue Lets you view information about a network queue that your computer is *not* connected to.

View | Exit Closes Print Manager.

Options | Low Priority Assigns more processing time to your applications, less to Print Manager.

Options | Medium Priority Assigns processing time equally among applications and Print Manager.

Options | High Priority Assigns more processing time to Print Manager and less to your applications.

Options | Alert Always Always displays special printer messages, even if Print Manager is not active.

Options | Flash if Inactive Flashes the icon or title bar if Print Manager is not active when it receives a special message.

Options | Ignore if Inactive Takes no action if Print Manager is not active when it receives a special message.

Options | Network Settings Lets you make the network update queue information and make print jobs bypass Print Manager.

Options | Network Connections Lets you connect to a network printer.

Options | Printer Setup Displays the Printers dialog box so you can install, set up, and connect printers.

These are the buttons:

Pause Stops sending data to the selected printer or stops the selected network print job.

Resume Resumes sending data to the selected printer after you clicked **Pause**.

Delete Removes the selected print job from the print queue.

More Efficient Printing

How can you make Windows print your work more efficiently? That depends on your hardware and what you want to do. Do you want to get the paper out of the printer more quickly and not worry about working while printing in the background? Or can you wait for the paper but want to continue working without the sluggish keyboard and mouse response so typical of background printing? Try some of these tips.

- Windows prints faster with the Print Manager turned *off* (in Control Panel's Printers dialog box). You won't be able to work in the application while printing, but you will be able to use other applications.
- The slower the disk on which the TEMP directory is located, the slower the printing will be. So if the TEMP directory is on a slow drive, you may not notice much difference by turning off Print Manager. (A short document may print in one minute with Print Manager, 50 seconds without, for instance.) You may be able to increase print speed by moving the TEMP directory to your fastest disk drive. (See Appendix A for information about the TEMP directory.)
- Better still, put the TEMP directory on a RAM disk. You probably don't want the TEMP directory on a RAM disk if you run in Standard mode though (see Appendix A for details).
- Some applications let you have two or more copies of the application open at the same time. The first copy will be unavailable while it is printing directly to Print Manager, but you can work on another document in the other copy.
- Put more memory in your printer (or add a print buffer). Your printer may be able to accept most print jobs as fast as the application can send them. If you are not using Print Manager the job will print faster and release your application sooner. If you are using Print Manager, the job is finished sooner, so Print Manager won't slow down your other applications so long.
- For the same reasons, use a faster printer. The faster the printer, the sooner Print Manager finishes work—and stops slowing down other applications.
- Use Print Manager's Options | Low Priority commands to let you work while printing in the background. You will be able to use your application sooner, and you won't notice near as much slowdown in the keyboard and mouse. However, the actual printing will take a long time.
- Use Options | High Priority to print quickly. Your application will be locked up longer, and even when it frees up the keyboard and mouse, actions may be "jerky."
- Check to see if your application has a "background printing" feature (as does Ami Pro 2.0). This uses an internal spooler, which may be more efficient than Print Manager.
- Turn off the Collate feature in the Print dialog box, if available (with some applications you must turn it off *and* change the Printer Setup dialog box to multiple copies). Instead of sending each page several times, Windows sends it once, and your printer prints several copies. You must then spend time

putting the pages in order. This may be worthwhile only if the pages contain lots of complicated graphics.

- Make sure you select the Fast Printing Direct to Port check box in the Connect dialog box, opened from Control Panel's Printers dialog box. (In a few cases, explained earlier, this check box must be unselected.)
- If you are using a network, bypass Print Manager. Select Options | Network Options and select the Print Net Jobs Direct.
- Make sure your printer is correctly set up. For instance, if your printer can be used either serial or parallel, make sure you use a *parallel* cable (it's *much* faster).
- If you use 386 Enhanced mode and run DOS applications at the same time as printing from Windows applications, read the information in Chapter 7 on setting up processing priorities. See also Control Panel's 386 Enhanced dialog box in Chapter 8.

Working with Fonts

You can use a variety of different types of fonts with Windows 3.1. Three basic types come with Windows.

1. **Raster or Bitmap**—Stored in files as bitmaps, an array of dots. They cannot be changed in size (scaled) or rotated.
2. **Vector or Plotter**—Stored as a set of lines drawn between points, described mathematically. They can be scaled. Some applications such as PageMaker can switch to vector fonts for large characters. They print slowly.
3. **Outline (TrueType)**—Windows 3.1 has outline fonts built into the Graphics Device Interface (GDI). They can be scaled and rotated.

Fonts are also often described as *screen fonts* (those used to display characters on your computer's screen) and *printer fonts* (those used to print characters). There are three types of printer fonts: *device fonts* (stored in the printer itself or in a font cartridge or other add-on hardware); *printable screen fonts* (Windows' screen fonts can be printed on dot matrix printers); and *downloadable soft fonts* (font files on your hard disk that are sent to the printer when needed). Each TrueType font works as both a screen font and downloadable soft font, so the font you see on your screen matches the one sent to your printer. (In some cases the TrueType font on your screen won't look like the one sent to the printer, especially at small sizes or when zoomed out on a page.)

The fonts you can use depend on the type of device you are working with. HPPCL printers (those using HP's Printer Command Language, such as the LaserJet) cannot use the Windows screen fonts, and many devices—in particular plotters—cannot work with downloadable fonts.

▼ ***Note*** If your computer has less than 2 MB, your TrueType fonts may not work well. Select another type of font instead.

The fonts that come with Windows 3.1 are shown here.

TRUETYPE FONTS

Scalable, will print on dot matrix, HPPCL, and PostScript printers that accept downloadable fonts. Will not print on plotters.

Arial (with Bold, Italic, Bold Italic)
Courier New (with Bold, Italic, Bold Italic)
Symbol
Times New Roman (with Bold, Italic, Bold Italic)
Wingdings

RASTER FONTS

Screen fonts, used for dialog boxes, title bars, icons, and so on. Will also print on dot-matrix printers.

Courier, 10, 12, 15 points
MS Sans Serif, 8, 10, 12, 14, 18, 24 points
MS Serif, 8, 10, 12, 14, 18, 24 points
Small, 2, 4, 6 points
Symbol, 8, 10, 12, 14, 18, 24 points
System, size depends on display
Terminal, size depends on display

▼ ***Note*** You won't get all of these screen fonts. The ones installed depend on the type of display adapter you are using.

VECTOR FONTS

Scalable, will print on plotters, HPPCL printers, and PostScript printers that accept downloadable fonts. Will not print on dot-matrix printers.

Modern
Roman
Script

In addition to the fonts provided by Windows, other fonts are available to your applications:

Third-party outline fonts Outline fonts sold by other companies. The most common of these are the Type 1 PostScript fonts that work with Adobe Type Manager. Other products include Bitstream's Facelift and Atech's Publisher's PowerPak. These fonts come with special utilities to load them and usually include a matching screen font for each printer font.

Internal printer fonts Most printers have built-in fonts. When you select the printer driver the fonts automatically become available to your applications. (The driver must be the default printer in the Printers dialog box, or you must select the driver using File|Print Setup in an individual application.)

Cartridge printer fonts Loading a cartridge into your printer makes more fonts available. Many cartridges are already listed in the driver's Setup dialog box; simply select the cartridge and both the printer and screen fonts are available automatically. If the cartridge is not listed, use the installation program that came with the cartridge. If it doesn't have one—and you are installing the cartridge in an HPPCL-compatible printer such as a LaserJet or DeskJet—use the HP Font Installer.

Printer soft fonts You can buy more soft fonts for many printers. These should be loaded using the printer driver's font installer. We are going to describe the HP Font Installer as an example.

Vector fonts If you buy new plotter or vector fonts, install them using the Control Panel's Fonts dialog box.

TrueType fonts Hundreds of different TrueType fonts are available. You can buy these from other companies or find them in shareware catalogs and on bulletin boards. Install them using the Control Panel's Fonts dialog box.

Screen fonts If your printer driver or cartridge does not automatically provide screen fonts, you may be able to get matching screen fonts from the manufacturer. Install them using the Control Panel's Fonts dialog box.

▼ *Note* For information on the Control Panel's Fonts dialog box, see Chapter 8.

The HP Font Installer

If you want to load downloadable soft fonts onto your printer, your printer's driver may have a special utility to help you. Figure 11.20 shows the dialog box used by the HPPCL printer drivers, such as the LaserJet and DeskJet drivers. This box is displayed by clicking on the **Fonts** button in the driver's Setup dialog box.

You can install screen fonts for cartridges and soft fonts with this dialog box. Some printers let you install only cartridge fonts.

Begin by clicking on the **Add Fonts** button. A dialog box prompts you for the disk and directory in which the fonts are saved. When you click on **OK** the Font Installer searches the directory for compatible fonts and lists them in the **Source** list box (as shown in Figure 11.20). The Add Fonts button changes to **Close Drive**.

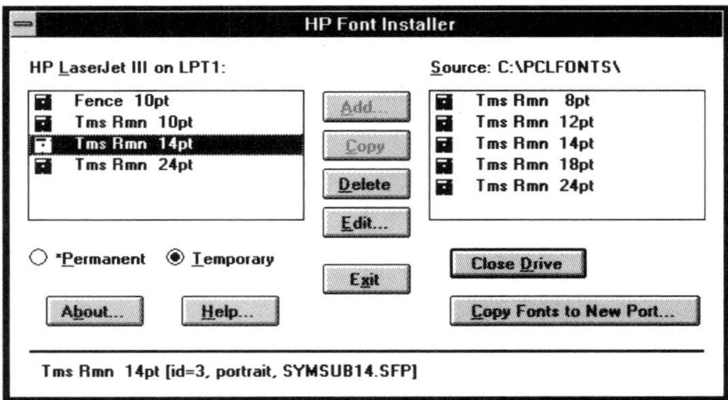

Figure 11.20 The HP Font Installer

If these are not the fonts you want, click on **Close Drive** to change it back, click on **Add Fonts**, and try another directory.

When you find the fonts you are looking for, select the ones you want to use. Click on each one, or use the arrow keys to move to each one and press **Spacebar**. Then click on the **Add** button. A dialog box appears, asking where to copy the fonts. If the fonts are already on your hard disk, you can enter that directory so the installer doesn't make unnecessary copies. If you are loading the fonts from floppy disks, you will probably want to use the default PCLFONTS directory.

When you click on **OK**, the fonts will be installed and displayed in the list box on the left. You may see the Edit dialog box first (see Figure 11.21) if the Font Installer doesn't recognize the file. You must enter a font name (don't worry about the family). If all the fonts you selected have the same name (just different sizes, for instance), click on the **Edit Mode** check box to change all the fonts at once. Then click on **OK** to install the fonts.

▼ ***Note*** You may find that if there is one font that Font Installer cannot recognize it doesn't install any. You may have to go back and try the other fonts again.

Now you have to decide the type of downloading you want to use. These fonts must be downloaded to your printer, so they are available when you use them. Once downloaded they are stored in the printer's memory. You can make them either **Permanent** or **Temporary**. Permanent fonts are loaded into the printer when you close the dialog box or each time you boot your computer. Temporary fonts are downloaded only when you use them. This may slow printing a little, but it frees printer memory for other purposes, such as printing graphics. If you are not

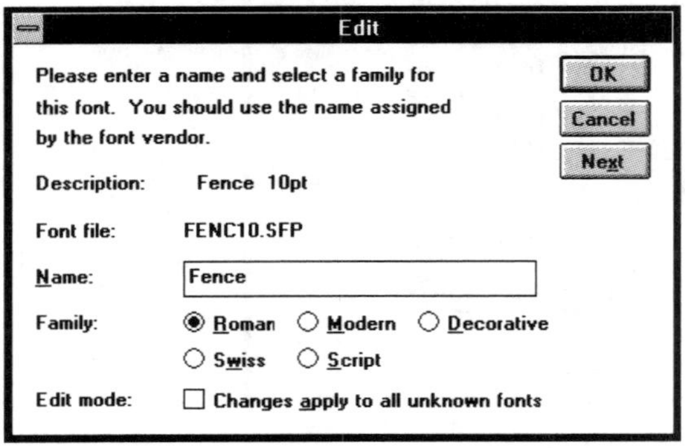

Figure 11.21 The Edit dialog box

going to use the fonts much, why waste the printer's memory? Select the fonts—one at a time—and click on the option buttons below the list.

Finally, click on the **Exit** button. The Font Installer displays the Download Options dialog box with two check boxes. If you have made some of the fonts Permanent and want to download the fonts immediately—so you can use them right way—select the **Download now** check box. If you want to download the fonts to your printer each time you boot your computer, select **Download at startup**; Windows will add the necessary information to your AUTOEXEC.BAT file. Of course your printer must be on-line before you boot your computer.

You can select both check boxes—or you can *clear* both options. The fonts won't be downloaded and a line won't be added to the AUTOEXEC.BAT file, but you can return to the Font Installer later and download them.

If you have just installed cartridge fonts, when you close the HP Font Installer you must then select the cartridge from the Cartridges list in the Setup dialog box.

EDITING AND DELETING FONTS

You can edit or delete a font by selecting it from the left side of the Font Installer and clicking on the **Edit** or **Delete** button. (You may find that you cannot use keyboard shortcuts to activate these buttons. Doing so may crash the Font Installer.)

When you edit a font you see the dialog box we showed you in Figure 11.21. (Select one font at a time when editing.) You can change the font name if you wish. You will need to do so if you have more than one font using the same name. You can change the ID number but will probably never need to do so. This is the ID number (`SoftFont`*n*) used in the WIN.INI file. (This font information is loaded into the section related to that particular device, such as the [HPPCL5A,LPT1] section, for instance.) You can also change the download type (permanent or temporary) and the font family.

Delete a font by selecting it and clicking on the Delete button.

COPYING FONTS TO ANOTHER PORT

If you have another HP printer on a different computer port, or if you move the printer, you can use the **Copy Fonts to New Port** button to use the same fonts on the other printer. A dialog box asks which port; select the port and click on **OK**. Then select the fonts from one of the list boxes (not both). Click on the **Copy** button if you want to use the fonts on both ports or the **Move** button if you want to remove them from the original port—if you moved the printer, for instance.

Finally, click on the **Copy Fonts to New Port** button. All this procedure does is modify the WIN.INI settings for each port.

Using Your Fonts

Once you have installed the fonts correctly, they are automatically available to your Windows applications. If a font has a matching screen font, "what you see is normally what you get." The font you see on the screen is the same as the one that will be printed on the paper. There are some exceptions, however. TrueType fonts don't always look correct on your screen at small sizes. Bold text, for instance, doesn't always look bold.

If you don't have matching screen fonts, Windows selects the closest it can find. It will usually look very similar to the font that will be printed and should create the correct line lengths and page breaks. In some cases the choice will *not* be close to the printed font, though.

If you try to print a font that cannot be used on your printer, Windows also has to substitute. Again, it may find a font that matches closely, but it may not.

▼ ***Note*** Some applications also load fonts for their own use, fonts that cannot be used by other Windows applications.

Most applications have some sort of indication as to the type of font you are selecting. When you open a font drop-down list box, TrueType fonts are normally indicated by two small T's. Printer fonts, and sometimes other outline fonts such as Type 1 PostScript fonts, are often indicated by a small picture of a printer. Other fonts are raster and vector fonts.

Part 3

Windows' Major Accessories

12

Word Processing: Windows Write

Windows Write is a surprisingly capable word processor. You can work with a variety of fonts, insert graphics from other Windows applications, enter headers and footers, set tabs, and carry out a number of typical word processing procedures. You may find that Write has all the features you need, especially if you only write simple letters and memos.

Start Write by clicking on the Write icon in the Accessories program group. Or select **File | Run** and run **WRITE**. Write's window opens, ready for you to begin typing your document (see Figure 12.1).

Entering and Editing Text

You can see in Figure 12.1 that Write has an *insertion* point to indicate where the text you type will be placed. Like most word processors—but unlike Windows Notepad—the *word wrap* feature is automatically turned on. In other words, when you type to the end of a line, Write automatically makes subsequent text appear on the following line. Each paragraph is a single unit, dependent on the page margins: Adjust the margins, and the line lengths adjust accordingly.

What is the length of a line? By default Write sets its margins to six inches, so once you have typed six inches, the text wraps to the next line. If the Write window is sized so that the full six inches are not visible, the window automatically scrolls to the right as you type, and back to the left when the text insertion point wraps back to the left margin.

You may begin a new paragraph by pressing **Enter**. Generally, Write works in the same way as most word processors. Press **Backspace** to delete the previous character, and **Delete** to delete the next character or the selected text. Notice also

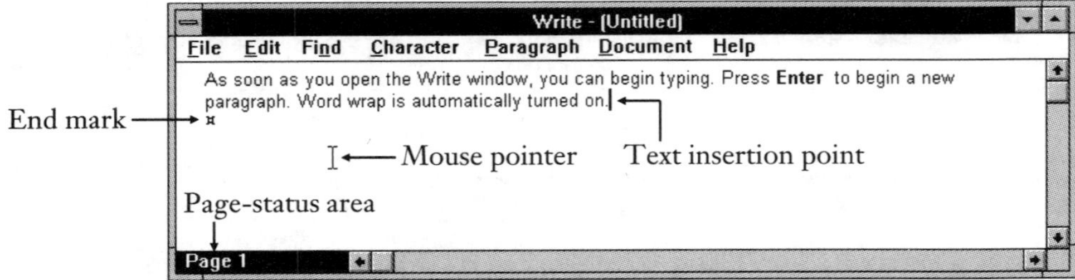

Figure 12.1 The Write window

in Figure 12.1 the *end mark*, which shows you the end of the document (it moves down as you type), and the *page status area*, which shows the number of the page on which the top line currently displayed in the window is found. This page number, however, is not updated continuously. It changes only when you print the document or select the **File | Repaginate** command.

Moving the Cursor

Use the following keys to move the text insertion point in your Write documents. (The 5 key refers to the numeric keypad 5, with Num Lock turned off):

To move to	*Press*
Next word	**Ctrl-Right Arrow**
Previous word	**Ctrl-Left Arrow**
Next sentence	**5-Right Arrow**
Previous sentence	**5-Left Arrow**
Beginning of line	**Home**
End of line	**End**
Next paragraph	**5-Down Arrow**
Previous paragraph	**5-Up Arrow**
Next screen	**PgDn**
Previous screen	**PgUp**
Bottom of window	**Ctrl-PgDn**
Top of window	**Ctrl-PgUp**
Next page	**5-PgDn**
Previous page	**5-PgUp**
Beginning of document	**Ctrl-Home**
End of document	**Ctrl-End**

The next- and previous-page commands will not work until page breaks have been added—you must have used Edit | Repaginate or printed the document.

There are several other ways to move around in the document. You can use the scroll bars, as you learned in an earlier chapter. Drag the scroll box to the end of the bar to move to the end of the document, and to the middle of the bar to move to the middle. Click on the arrows or the bar to move through it line-by-line or screen-by-screen.

You can also search for a specific piece of text—we'll cover that later. Or you can go directly to a specific page by selecting **Find | Go To Page** (or press **F4**). The Go To dialog box appears. Type a page number and click on **OK** to move the insertion point to the top of the page.

Selecting Text

While working in a Write file you will sometimes need to select text by placing the highlight over it. Once selected you can delete it, change the font and font size, modify paragraph settings, and so on.

You can easily select text by pressing **Shift** while you use any of the keystrokes we have just described. For instance, **Shift-Right Arrow** selects the next character, **Shift-5-Down Arrow** selects all of the text from the insertion point to the end of the current paragraph, and **Shift-Ctrl-End** selects all of the text from the insertion point to the end of the document.

You can also use the mouse to select text.

- **Drag** the pointer across the text while holding the mouse button.
- Press **Shift** and click in the text to select from the insertion point to the point at which you click.
- Place the pointer in the **left side of the window**. When it changes to an arrow, **click** the button to select a line. Hold **Shift** and **drag** the pointer to select more lines.
- Place the pointer in the **left side of the window**. When it changes to an arrow, d**ouble-click** to select a paragraph. Hold **Shift** and **drag** the pointer to select more lines.
- Place the pointer in the **left side of the window**. When it changes to an arrow, **double-click** to select a paragraph, but don't release the mouse button the second time. Now **drag** the pointer down, holding the mouse button, to select more paragraphs. Release the button, then hold **Shift** and **drag** the pointer to select more lines.
- Place the pointer in the **left side of the window**. When it changes to an arrow, **click** once to select a line. Move the pointer down the page, hold **Shift**, and **click** again to select all the text between the two places.
- Place the pointer in the **left side of the window**. When it changes to an arrow, press **Ctrl** and **click** once to select all the text in the document.

- **Click** in the text, hold the mouse button, and **drag** the pointer up or down. The page will automatically scroll, line by line, highlighting the text as it goes.
- **Click** in the text. Use the scroll bars to move to another part of the document. Hold **Shift** and **click** again to select everything from the first position to the second.

You can remove the selection highlight by clicking anywhere in the document.

Tip Here's a quick way to **copy text**. Select it, point at the position to which you want to copy it, press and hold **Alt**, and click the mouse button.

Using Hyphens

There are two ways to enter hyphens into your text. You can, of course, type them directly into a word, forcing Write to break the word at the position you define. The problem with this is that documents are dynamic things—they change as you enter new text, select different fonts, modify the margins, and so on.

A better way to enter hyphens is to use *optional* or *conditional* hyphens. You can tell Write to hyphenate a word at a particular position *if it needs to*. If it doesn't need to—if the word is not near the margin—the hyphen won't appear.

Of course you won't hyphenate many words like this. Before you print a document, look at the right edge to see where long words have been forced to the next line, leaving a large gap in the right edge. Place the text insertion point in the long word, where you want the hyphen to be placed, and press **Ctrl-Shift-Hyphen** (-). A hyphen will appear, and if you placed the hyphen in a good position—where the first half of the word is now short enough to fit on the first line—the word will be broken in two pieces. If you later adjust the document's format, or add or remove text such that the hyphenated word is no longer in a hyphenation position, Write will automatically remove the hyphen.

If you try to hyphenate a word that is not in a position to be hyphenated, the line will flash, but no hyphen will appear. However, Write will print the hyphen if it needs to—if, for instance, you add text or adjust formatting to push that word onto the page edge.

Working with Page Breaks

Write does not automatically adjust pages as you type. It treats all the text as if it were on one page, making text entry quicker, because it doesn't have to keep up with page changes. When you print the document Write automatically figures out the page positions, but you may want to make Write do so before you print. You can't use the Go To command until you have repaginated, and you may simply

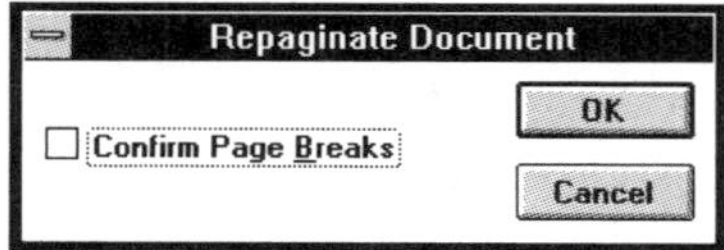

Figure 12.2 The Repaginate Document dialog box

want to know how many pages of text you have entered or make sure the pages break in the correct positions.

You can enter page breaks at any time by pressing **Ctrl-Enter**. Write places a dotted line in the document to indicate the end of the page. If you want Write to enter page breaks for you, or want to enter several at the same time, select **File | Repaginate**. Write displays the Repaginate Document dialog box (see Figure 12.2). If you simply want a quick count of pages, or want to be able to use Go To, click on the **OK** button, and Write places page breaks throughout the document.

If you want to see exactly where Write plans to place these page breaks, however, select **Confirm Page Breaks** before you click on **OK**. You would do this, for instance, before you print a final copy of a document; you want to be able to place page breaks precisely, so you have no *widows* (single lines of text left at the top of a page) or *orphans* (single lines of text left at the bottom of a page). You may also want to adjust positions so that text remains with associated pictures, for instance, or so new headers are at the top of a page.

When Write gets to the first position at which it wants to place a page break, it displays the dialog box shown in Figure 12.3. It also uses a small chevron in the left side of the window to indicate the position at which the page break will be placed;

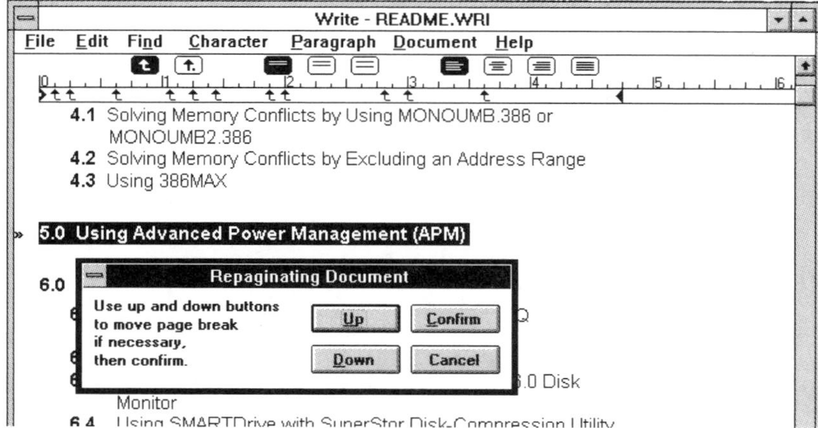

Figure 12.3 The Repaginating Document dialog box

the chevron points at the line that will become the first line on the next page. You can't click on the Down button yet because you can't make Write include more lines than will fit on the page. You can click on the **Up** button, though, to move the highlight up as many lines as you wish, so *fewer* lines will appear on that page. You can then click on the **Down** button to move the highlight down line by line if you decide you've gone too far up the page. The chevron remains on the page, showing you the maximum position. When you click on **Confirm**, Write places a page break immediately before the highlighted line and moves to the next position.

Tip If you get an "out of memory" message while repaginating, save your file and try again. If you still have problems, try closing other windows.

If you repaginate without confirming page breaks, the document will contain the chevrons to indicate page breaks (the chevron points at the first line on each page). If you do confirm page breaks, Write will contain the chevrons as well as dotted lines to indicate where you moved page breaks. (It won't display a dotted line if you accepted the proposed page break instead of moving it.)

You can repaginate a document again. If you do so and select Confirm Page Breaks, Write will ask if you want to **Keep** or **Remove** each page break you positioned previously. If you select Keep, Write moves on to the next position and asks the same thing. If you select Remove, Write removes the page break, moves to the next proposed page break position, and displays the Repaginating Document dialog box, asking you to confirm or reposition the page break.

Searching and Replacing

You can search your document for specific text and replace that text at the same time, if necessary. Select **Find | Find** to see the dialog box shown in Figure 12.4. Type the text into the Find What text box: part of a word, an entire word, several words, or even several sentences. You can enter up to 255 characters, although you will probably never do so: The more you enter, the more likely you are to make a mistake, in which case the search will fail. However, you can paste text into this text box (pressing **Ctrl-V**). You could, for instance, copy a block of text from another Write document—or any other word processor—and paste it into the Find dialog box.

You can use a question mark as a wild card in the specified text. For instance, if you want to find both "1991" and "1992," type **199?**. This is different from the normal use of the ? wild card, though. Usually the ? replaces just one character, but when searching you can use it to replace multiple characters (our example search

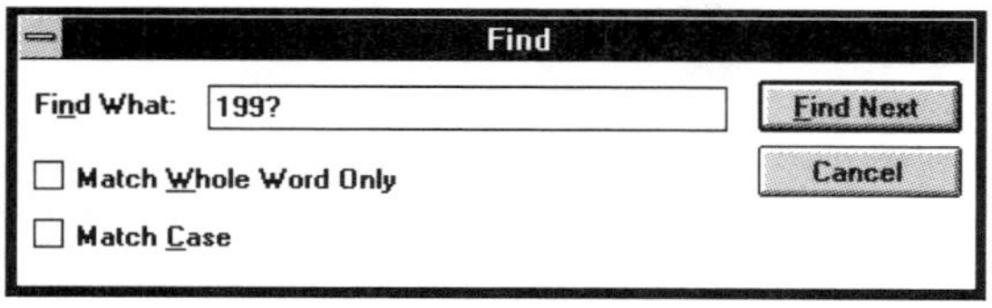

Find

Find What: 199?

Find Next

Cancel

Match Whole Word Only

Match Case

Figure 12.4 The Find dialog box

would also find 199987). Entering **And?** will find all words beginning with And: and, Anderson, android, and androgynous, for instance. (If you want to search for a real question mark, enter **^?**. For instance, to search for When?, type **when^?**.)

You may also search for special characters. Use these codes:

Blank space ^w
Tab ^t
Paragraph mark ^p
Manual page break ^d
Question mark ^?
Optional hyphen ^-
Caret ^^

You can use the check boxes to speed the search a little. For instance, if you want to search for the word NeXT, you can save time by clicking on the **Match Case** check box, so Write will only search for "NeXT" and not for "next." You can also click on the **Match Whole Word Only** check box to tell Write that the text you entered into the text box is a complete word, or several complete words, and not word fragments. For instance, if you are searching for the word "master," click on the check box so Write doesn't bother stopping for "mastered" or "mastering."

When you are ready, click on **Find Next** and Write searches from the current text insertion point toward the end of the document. When it finds the text it stops and highlights it. (Sometimes the highlighted text will be *underneath* the dialog box, so you will be unable to see it. Just use the title bar or Control menu to drag the box out of the way.) You can now click on **Cancel** to remove the Find dialog box, or click on **Find Next** to continue searching.

Write continues searching all the way to the bottom of the document. If the insertion point was not at the beginning of the document when you started, Write automatically moves to the top of the document and searches from there down to the original insertion point. When it has searched the entire document, it displays a dialog box telling you that the operation is complete. Click on the **OK** button, then click on the Find dialog box's **Cancel** button to remove it, or **Find Next** button to continue.

When you find the text you want, you don't have to remove the dialog box to work with it. Just click in the text, or press **Alt-F6**, and make your changes. When you want to continue with the search, click on the dialog box, or press **Alt-F6** again.

Once you have closed the Find dialog box, you don't have to open it again to search for the text. Simply press **F3** (or select **Find | Repeat Last Find**). Of course you will have to select Find | Find again to change the search criteria.

Replacing Text

You can automatically replace text as you search for it. Select **Find | Replace** to see the Replace dialog box (Figure 12.5). Enter the search criteria just as you did in the Search dialog box. But then enter the text with which you want to replace the text that Write finds. For instance, perhaps you want to search for "Mr. Smith" and replace it with "Mr. Smyth," or search for "April 12th" and replace it with "May 15th."

You can also enter special characters. Use those characters we listed earlier for the Search command, except ^w, ^?, and ^^.

▼ ***Note*** When using the special characters in the Replace With text box, always enter them as *lowercase*.

When you are ready, click on the **Find Next** button. Write highlights the first matching text it finds. (As with the Search, the text may actually be underneath the dialog box.) If Write has found text that you want to replace, click on **Replace** and Write changes the text and automatically searches for the next occurrence. If the text isn't what you want to change, click on **Find Next** to go straight to the next occurrence.

At any time you can click on **Replace All** to modify all the matching text everywhere in the document. For instance, if you know that you typed Smith instead of Smyth, and that the document should only refer to a Smyth—no Smiths—you can change all the Smiths at once, without examining each one. When you click on **Replace All**, Write does the complete job for you. It will tell

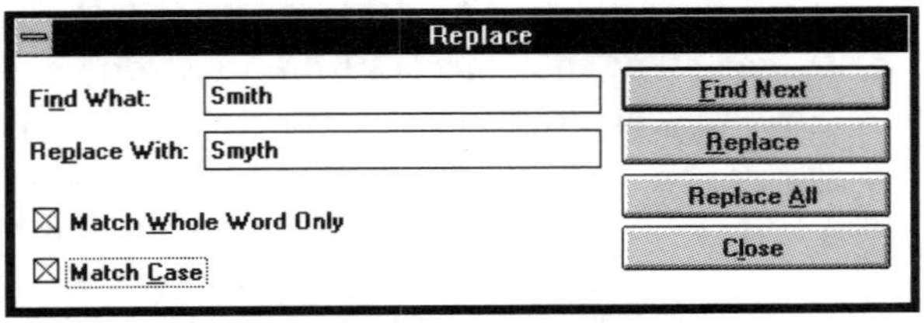

Figure 12.5 The Replace dialog box

you if it couldn't find any matching text, but it won't tell you how many times it made the change.

By the way, you can select a block of text before using the Replace command. The Replace All button will say **Replace Selection**, instead, and clicking on it will replace all occurrences of the selected text in the selection and leave the rest of the document unchanged.

Modifying Characters

You can modify the text characters in various ways. You can select any Windows-compatible or printer font, change the font *style* and size, and superscript or subscript it. You can define text characteristics by selecting the characters you want to change and selecting the change, or by selecting the characteristics and then typing the text. When you type, subsequent text takes the characteristics of the current insertion-point position.

By default Write uses the first TrueType font it can find in your font list (for more information about fonts, see Chapter 11). That may not be suitable, but you can change the font easily, selecting from TrueType, PostScript Type 1, and printer fonts. The printer fonts indicated depend on the printer selected, so if you intend to use printer fonts use the **File | Print Setup** command to make sure you have the correct printer selected—the printer on which you plan to print the document.

Select **Character | Fonts** to see the Fonts dialog box (shown in Figure 12.6). Select a font, style, and size from the various list boxes. Font names preceded by TT are TrueType fonts, and the ones with pictures of a printer are Type 1 and printer fonts. The ones with neither indication are screen or plotter fonts. Notice that when you select a font you will see what it looks like in the sample box, and a

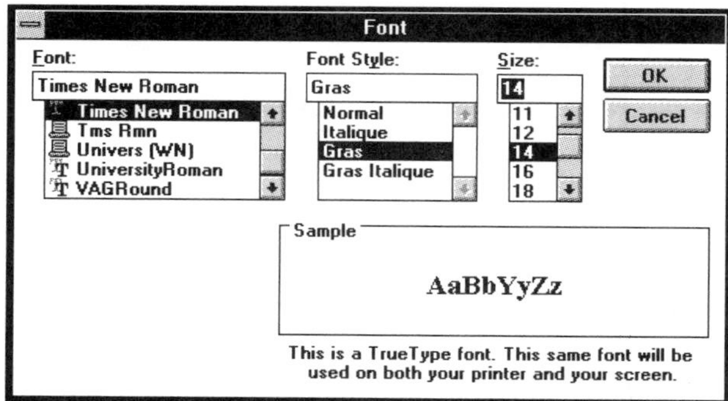

Figure 12.6 The Font dialog box

short description of the type is shown below the sample box. (This sample box is empty if you select a block of text with varying characteristics.)

The Size list box doesn't show all these sizes, however. For instance, it shows 36, 48, and stops at 72. But you can type any other size you wish, as long as it is between 4 and 127. When you click on the OK button in this dialog box, Write makes only the changes you have selected. For instance, if you selected a block of text that contains two different fonts and you change the size—but don't select another font—Write changes the size of all the text, but the fonts themselves remain unchanged.

You don't have to open the Font dialog box to make changes to text style. Select **Character | Bold** (or press **Ctrl-B**), **Character | Italic** (or press **Ctrl-I**), and **Character | Underline** (or press **Ctrl-U**) to select these styles. You can, of course, combine these styles to make underlined-bold text, for instance, or bold-italic text. If you want to convert text back to regular—removing the styles—press **F5** or select **Character | Regular**. To remove just one of the styles, select that one style.

You can create superscript or subscript characters by selecting **Character | Superscript** or **Character | Subscript**. When Write makes a superscript character it reduces it in size slightly, then moves it above the text line a little. When it subscripts it reduces the character and moves it *down* a little. These styles are used in mathematics, scientific notation, and so on. For instance, you might superscript the letters TM to create a trademark sign next to a product name, or a lowercase o to create the degree sign (as in 20°). You can also reduce the character's size a little more if it looks better that way.

Of course you can reduce characters using the Font dialog box, but there's a quicker way. Just select **Character | Reduce Font** or **Character | Enlarge Font**. The font size is modified according to the size list box in the Font dialog box. Small fonts are modified less than large ones. An 11-point font is enlarged to 12 points, a 12-point goes to 14 points, and a 36-point goes to 48 points. If these changes are not what you want, you will have to use the Font dialog box.

Unless the font you have selected has an associated *screen* font, the characters displayed on the screen may not look exactly correct. TrueType fonts have screen fonts, as do Type 1 PostScript fonts loaded using Adobe Type Manager. Many printer fonts may not have screen fonts. Write will do the best it can, substituting a suitable screen font, but it may not get it exactly right.

Modifying Paragraphs

A paragraph is a block of text between *paragraph marks*. Write's paragraph marks are not visible, although you can select them. (Press **Enter**, hold Shift, and press

Backspace; the highlighted area is a paragraph marker.) Certain characteristics are attached to entire paragraphs—to the paragraph's end mark. In the same way that a character can have a font, size, and style, a paragraph can have alignment, spacing, and indentation.

Each time you press **Enter** you end one paragraph and create a new one. The new one automatically has the characteristics of the previous one until you change it. You can change a paragraph's characteristics by placing the insertion point anywhere inside and selecting the new characteristics. You can also select a block of text that includes several paragraphs and then make modifications to all those paragraphs at once.

It's important to understand that paragraph formats are attached to the paragraph mark, not the text itself, with the paragraph using the format that is attached to the mark immediately following it. Thus, if you copy text from one paragraph to another, it conforms to the new paragraph's format, while if you copy a paragraph marker from one paragraph to another, the paragraph to which you copy it takes on the format of the one from which it came.

A paragraph mark may be deleted in three ways: by selecting it and pressing **Del**; by placing the insertion point at the end of the last line in the paragraph (press **End**) and pressing **Del**; or by placing the insertion point at the beginning of the first line in a paragraph (press **Home**) and pressing **Backspace**. When you do so the first paragraph—the one ahead of the mark—takes on the format of the second one, the paragraph after the mark.

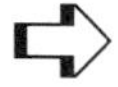 **Tip** Paragraph marks can be copied to the Clipboard. You can then adjust other paragraph formats by pasting the copied paragraph mark to the end of each paragraph and deleting the old one.

First, lets take a look at the ruler. Select **Document | Ruler On** to display the ruler shown in Figure 12.7. The ruler contains nine buttons that let you modify tab formats, line spacing, and alignment, plus a bar in which you can place tabs and adjust margins. The actual ruler—the graduated, numbered rule—shows you the width of the text lines. As you can see from the illustration, by default the lines of text are six inches wide when you are using paper eight-and-one-half inches wide. You can change the margins—and the units—in the Page Layout dialog box (displayed by selecting Document | Page Layout; we'll describe this a little later).

As you will learn in a moment, you can use this ruler by clicking on the buttons to select paragraph formats, or by clicking in the tab bar to place tab markers.

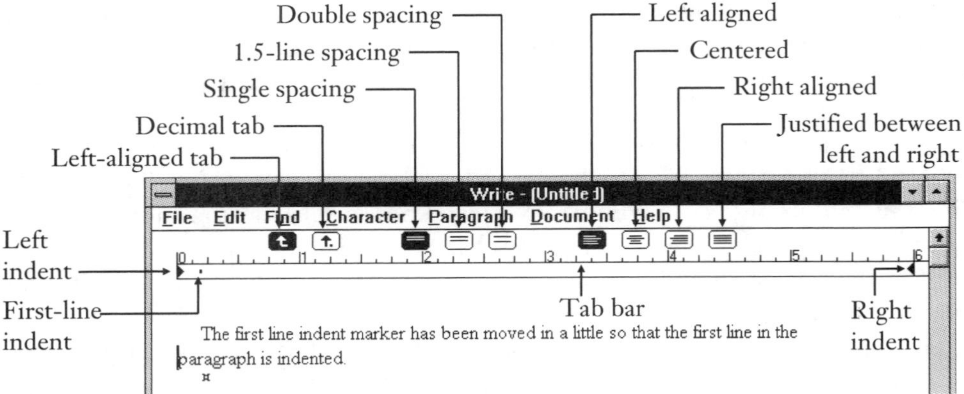

Figure 12.7 Write's ruler

Indenting Text

When you first begin a Write document, the indents are set so that if you type several lines of text, the lines will stretch between the left and right margins. (The margins are set in the Page Layout dialog box, which we will describe later.) You can adjust each paragraph so that it is indented from the margins. For instance, you may want to place a quote inside your text so that its lines are shorter, to make it stand out. You may also want to begin each paragraph with the first line slightly indented, as is common in many documents. The indents are based on the margins. That is, if you later move the margins, the indents will change accordingly.

The easiest way to place indents is to use the ruler. Place the insertion point in the paragraph you want to change, and point to one of the triangular indent markers in the ruler, press and hold the mouse button, and drag the marker along the bar toward the center of the page.

▼ ***Note*** You cannot create *negative* indents; that is, you cannot adjust the text to flow into the page margins as you can with some word processors.

When you first try to select the left indent marker you will instead grab the first-line indent marker, the little square. Move this a little way, then drag the triangle into position and reposition the first-line marker. This first-line indent marker shows where the first character in the paragraph will be placed; so if you want to indent paragraphs, all you need to do is drag this square in a little. If you want to create a hanging indent, however, the first-line indent marker will be outside the left indent marker.

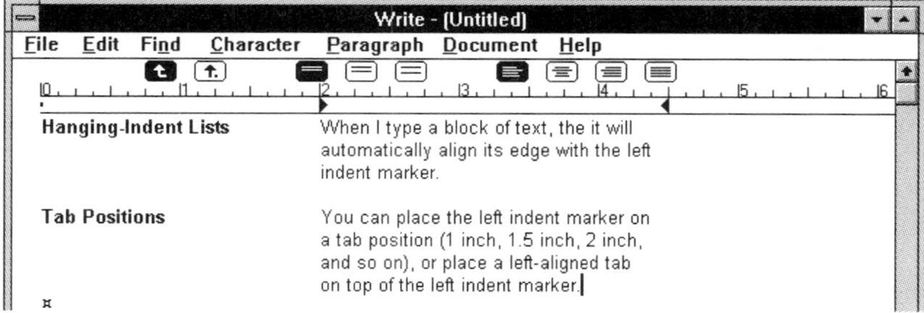

Figure 12.8 A hanging-indent list

If you want to create a **hanging indent list** (such as that in Figure 12.8), use the following procedure. Place the first-line indent on the left, where you want the list items to be placed. Put the left indent where you want the explanatory text. Either place it on a tab position (a full half inch) or place a left-aligned tab on top of it. Now you can type an item, press **Tab**, and type a block of text explaining the item. The block of text will be placed with its left edge at the left indent.

When you make changes in the ruler, these changes are shown in the Indents dialog box. In fact, if you don't have a mouse you will have to adjust your indents using this box; select **Paragraph | Indents** to see the dialog box shown in Figure 12.9. In the figure the indents are set up to create a hanging indent. The **First Line** is a negative number because the first line is to the left of the **Left Indent**. The **Right Indent** entry shows that the right edge of the text is also indented 1.5 inches from the right margin. If you wanted to simply indent the first line of a paragraph, say, 1 inch, the First Line entry would be 1, and the Left Indent would be 0.

Aligning Text

A paragraph's text may be aligned within the indents in one of four ways (see Figure 12.10).

- Left aligned, so there's a straight edge on the left and a ragged edge on the right
- Centered, so each line is equally spaced from each side

Indents

Left Indent: 2.00"
First Line: -2"
Right Indent: 1.5"
OK
Cancel

Figure 12.9 The Indents dialog box, showing a hanging indent

This text is aligned on the left. This text is aligned on the left. This text is aligned on the left. This text is aligned on the left. This text is aligned on the left. This text is aligned on the left.

This text is centered. This text is centered. This text is centered. This text is centered. This text is centered. This text is centered. This text is centered. This text is centered.

This text is aligned on the right. This text is aligned on the right. This text is aligned on the right. This text is aligned on the right. This text is aligned on the right. This text is aligned on the right. This text is aligned on the right.

This text is justified. This text is justified. This text is justified. This text is justified. This text is justified. This text is justified. This text is justified. This text is justified.

Figure 12.10 Samples of the four types of text alignment

- Right aligned, so there's a ragged edge on the left and a straight edge on the right
- Justified, so each line stretches from the left to the right side, with straight edges on each side

To align text, place the insertion point anywhere in a paragraph and select one of the four options (**Left**, **Centered**, **Right**, or **Justified**) from the **Character** menu. Or click on one of the alignment buttons in the ruler.

Adjusting Line Spacing

The lines in a paragraph can be single-spaced, one-and-a-half-line spaced, or double-spaced. Simply place the insertion point anywhere in a paragraph and select one of the three options (**Single Space**, **1 1/2 Space**, or **Double Space**) from the **Character** menu. Or click on one of the spacing buttons in the ruler (see Figure 12.7).

Setting the Page Layout

You've learned how to format individual characters and entire paragraphs. There's one more formatting "unit," the document. When you first begin typing, Write automatically uses the following settings for the document:

Top and Bottom Margins	1 inch
Left and Right Margins	1.25 inches

Header	0.75 inch from the top of the page
Footer	0.75 inch from the bottom of the page
Start Page Numbers at	1

No header or footer is entered—you must enter the text—but if you do create them, by default they are 0.75 inch from the top and bottom. You can modify these settings. The margins are set for the entire document. If you want to change the text position on the page for a few paragraphs of text, you will use the indentation commands we have just described.

Select **Document|Page Layout** to see the Page Layout dialog box (Figure 12.11). The **Start Page Numbers At** text box shows from which number Write will begin when calculating the page number to place in the page status area at the bottom of the window and the page number printed in headers or footers.

You can also set the margins. You might want to adjust the top and bottom margins to allow for several header lines, or reduce the rather large left and right margins. Finally, the **Measurements** option buttons let you change from inches to centimeters. The default setting depends on what is selected in the Control Panel's International dialog box, English or Metric. If English is selected, then inches are the default.

Setting Tabs

When you set tabs, you do so for the entire document. Unlike more sophisticated word processors, Write doesn't let you set up tabs for individual paragraphs. Write's default tabs are set every half inch across the page—even if you are working in centimeters. (These tabs are not visible, however.)

The easiest way to set up new tabs is to use the ruler. Simply click on the type of tab you want to use, then click in the tab bar where you want to set them. You can set up two types, left-aligned tabs (the text begins at the tab point) and decimal tabs (the decimal point in a number is set at the tab point, with the numbers to the left of the decimal point appearing to the left of the tab point). Use left-aligned tabs when you want to create a column with each line beginning at the tab. Use a

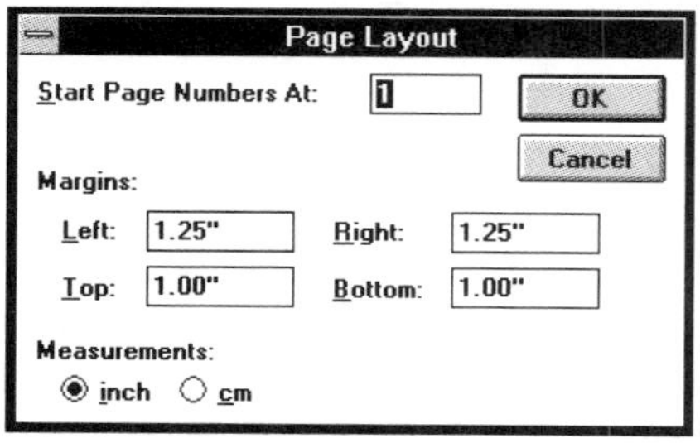

Page Layout
Start Page Numbers At: 1 OK
Cancel
Margins:
Left: 1.25" Right: 1.25"
Top: 1.00" Bottom: 1.00"
Measurements:
inch cm

Figure 12.11 The Page Layout dialog box

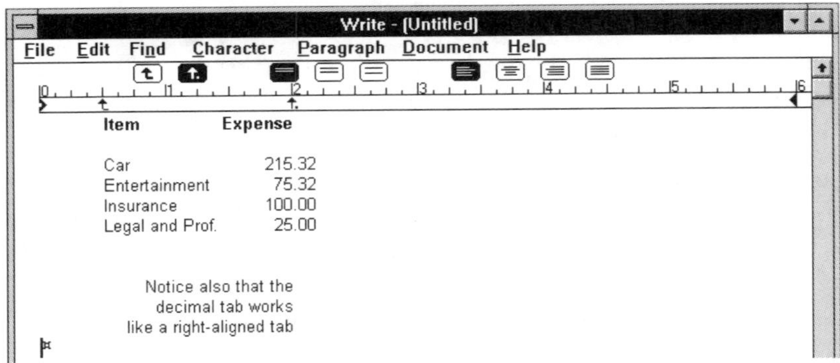

Figure 12.12 Using tabs

decimal tab to create a column of decimal numbers. (See Figure 12.12 for an example of both types.)

Tip You can use the decimal tab to set up *right*-aligned text, as long as you have no more than one period in each line at the end of the line.

Once you have placed tabs in the tab bar, you can move them by dragging them along the bar. You can delete them by dragging them *off* the bar.

Incidentally, once you place a tab in the tab bar—or enter a tab into the Tabs dialog box, which we will look at in a moment—Write's preset tabs up to that point are removed. For instance, if you set a tab at four inches, all the preset tabs up to that point (0.5, 1, 1.5, and so on) are no longer effective. The tabs *after* the one you placed are still active, unless you place another tab after the first.

When you place tabs in the tab bar, Write automatically enters the information into the Tabs dialog box—which you must use if you don't have a mouse. Select **Document | Tabs** and the dialog box appears (Figure 12.13). You can set up to 12 tab points. Just type the positions into the **Position** text boxes, and select the **Decimal** check box for the decimal tabs. You can move between the Position text boxes and Decimal check boxes by pressing **Tab**; select the check box by pressing the **Spacebar**.

By the way, when you use a decimal tab, the number or text isn't immediately placed in the correct position. You will type, pause, and then a second or two later Write places the text with the first period it finds immediately under the tab position or, if it can't find a period, it places the last character in each line against the tab point. (If you used the Control Panel's International dialog box to change the decimal point to a comma, Write will look for a comma instead of a period.)

Tabs
Positions: 0.5 2
Decimal:
Positions:
Decimal:
OK Cancel Clear All

Figure 12.13 The Tabs dialog box

Creating Headers and Footers

If you want to create a header or footer—text that appears in the top or bottom of each page—select **Document | Header** or **Document | Footer**. Write removes all your text from the window and displays a dialog box like that shown in Figure 12.14. It also places the text insertion bar in the window, in the top-left corner. Notice also that the title bar changes to read HEADER or FOOTER.

Type the text you want to appear in the header or footer. You can add tabs if you wish, but those tabs will affect the entire document, not just the header or footer. You can also use all the normal paragraph- and character-formatting commands, so you can make the text bold and centered, for instance. To move back to the dialog box, click on it or press **Alt-F6**.

If you want to enter a page number in the text, place the insertion point where you want it and click on **Insert Page #**. For instance, you could type **Page 16-** and then click Insert Page #. Write will insert "(page)." When you print the document the appropriate number will appear on each page. You can type as many lines in the header as you wish, as long as you adjust the settings so that it fits. You can adjust the **Distance from Top/Bottom** text box to move the header or footer closer to the bottom, but remember that most printers won't print all the way to the edge.

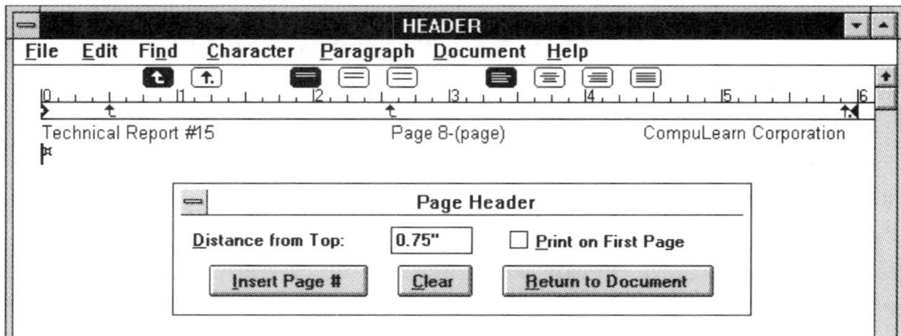

Figure 12.14 Creating a header

You may be able to enter 0.25 inch, though. Also, if you enter too many lines of text the header or footer will be pushed down or up so that it overlaps the main document text. You can change the Top and Bottom margins to give more room for the header.

If you want the header or footer on the first page of the document, click on the **Print on First Page** check box. Because headers and footers are often omitted from the first page—where they are not usually needed—Write leaves this check box unselected by default. To remove the text from the header or footer and start over, or to remove a header or footer you no longer want to use, click on the **Clear** button.

When you've finished setting up your header or footer, click on **Return to Document**. Write removes the header and replaces the document text. If you want to view or edit the header or footer, select the command from the Document menu again.

Moving and Sizing Pictures

Windows Write lets you place pictures in a document. These pictures may be simple copies, embedded copies, or linked copies. The easiest way to place a picture in Write is to use the **Edit|Copy** command in another application—say, Windows Paintbrush—and then use **Edit|Paste** in Write (or press **Ctrl-V**). The picture will be copied into the document and placed on the left margin. You can move it into position using the various indentation and alignment tools we have already looked at. For instance, use **Paragraph|Centered** to put it in the middle of the page.

If the application from which you copied the picture is an Object Linking and Embedding (OLE) *server* application, when you paste the picture into Write an *embedded* copy is created. That means you can double-click on the picture to open the original application and automatically load the picture. You may then edit the picture and close the application so the picture in Write is updated. (You may also select the picture, then select **Edit|Edit *applicationname* Object** instead of double-clicking on the picture.)

You can create a *linked* copy if you wish: In this case the copy in Write is linked to the original file. Make a change in the original file, and the copy in Write is automatically updated. We have discussed Object Linking and Embedding in more detail in Chapter 28.

Once in your Write document, a picture can be moved, sized, selected, copied, and pasted. To **move** the picture, select it and then select **Edit|Move Picture**. (To select the picture with the keyboard, place the cursor next to the picture, hold Shift, and press an arrow key to move the cursor across the picture.) The pointer changes to a square, and a dotted line appears around the picture. You can now drag the picture left or right (or use the arrow keys) and click the mouse button (or press **Enter**) when it's in position. You may press **Esc** while moving the picture to cancel the operation. If you want to move a picture *vertically*, copy and paste it to a different line.

When you move a picture using the Edit|Move Picture command you are actually setting its left-alignment position, the position it will have when you click on the left-align button in the ruler or select Paragraph|Left. You can also place it in the middle of the page using the centered button (Paragraph|Centered), or on the right margin using the right-align button (Paragraph|Right). The justified button (Paragraph|Justified) has no effect. To place the picture more precisely, use the Paragraph|Indent command, or drag the left-indent marker in the ruler.

You can also change the **size** of a picture. Select the picture then select **Edit|Size Picture**. A dotted line appears around the picture, and the pointer turns into a square. Now move the pointer to the side or corner you want to drag. As the pointer reaches an edge it "grabs" the edge; you can now drag it in or out (or use the arrows to move it). If you grab a lower corner, you can adjust the image both vertically and horizontally at the same time. When you've got the picture the size you want it, click the mouse button (or press **Enter**).

While you are sizing the picture you will see size information in the page-status area. For instance, 2.0X/2.5Y means that the picture is twice its original width and 2.5 times its original height. You can use these numbers to make sure you are sizing the picture proportionally. Also, you can limit distortion by sizing in full units only (2.0, not 2.5) and by not modifying the size too much. The more you change the image, the greater will be the distortion.

Incidentally, as you size the picture you can drag the pointer across the edges of the window to make Write automatically scroll the window for you, so you can make the picture larger than the visible workspace.

Importing and Exporting Files

Write usually opens and saves files with the .WRI format. However, you can open or save files with other formats.

Word for MS-DOS The format used by Microsoft's DOS word processor, Word. It uses a .DOC extension, but this is not the same as the Word for Windows format. (Word for Windows can read it, though.) If you want to read a Write document into Word for Windows, there's no need to convert it when saving it—Word for Windows can read Write documents.

Word for MS-DOS/ Text Only — This is the same format as the Word for MS-DOS, but with all the formatting information stripped out, so all you get is the text.

Text File — An ASCII text file, which can be read by Notepad or almost any word processor. Use this format to export to programs that cannot read Write or Word files, or to create DOS batch files or edit Windows .INI files. Write saves the file with a .TXT extension, though you may enter a different one if you wish. You can also open ASCII files even if they don't have a .TXT extension: enter, for instance, *.*, *.DOC, or *.ASC in the Open dialog box's File Name check box.

3.0 Write — This option appears only if the file you want to save contains pictures. Saving the file in this format strips the pictures out, so you can open the file in Windows 3.0. (The pictures remain displayed in the window until you close the file, but won't be there when you reopen.)

Word for Windows (and others) — You can open Word for Windows files (and possibly other formats). The text will be loaded into Write, but you will not get the text formatting commands. Instead you will see various special characters that you can simply delete.

To open one of these formats, select File|Open, then put the appropriate extension in the File Name text box. You can select an extension from the List Files of Type drop-down list box. If you want to open a Word for Windows file, or try some other format, you won't find the file type named in the List Files of Type list box, but you can select the Word for DOS entry to place .DOC in the File Name text box.

When you try to open a non-Write file, you will see the dialog box shown in Figure 12.15. You can convert the document into Write format or leave it unconverted. (The file on your disk is not converted, just the information placed in memory.) These two buttons give you four options.

- Click **Convert**, then use File|Save to save the original file in Write format.
- Click **Convert**, then use File|Save As and assign a new name to save in Write format while leaving the original file untouched.

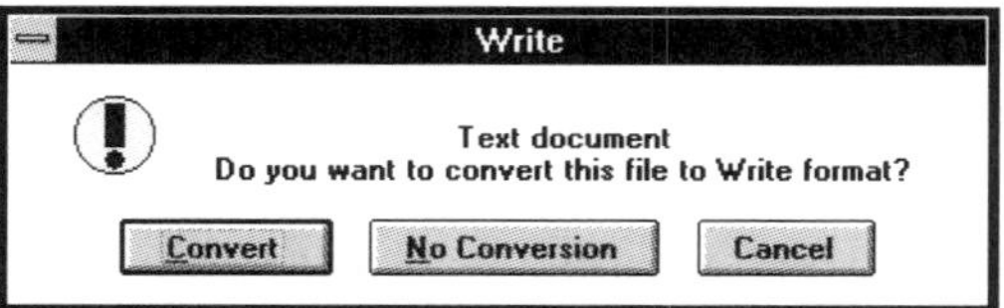

Figure 12.15 The conversion dialog box

- Click **No Conversion**, then use File | Save to save in the file's original format (only with Word for DOS and ASCII files).
- Click **No Conversion**, then use File | Save As and select the Write format to save in Write format while leaving the original file untouched.

Only convert files you want to save in Write format. If you are opening a WIN.INI file, for instance, you should *not* convert the file, because it must remain in ASCII when you save it. If you choose not to convert a file, it will remain in its original format when you save it. For instance, you open a Word for DOS file without converting it. You can edit this file, and each time you use the File | Save command it is saved in Word for DOS format. You can, however, use the File | Save As command to save it in Write format. If you save a file that contains pictures in another format, Write will have to remove the pictures.

Write's File Backup System

Like many applications, Write will create backup files for you. Simply select the Backup check box in the Save As dialog box when you save a file. However, it's important to note that Write does *not* automatically make a backup each time you save the file—you must select the Backup check box every time you wish to create a backup, which rather reduces the effectiveness of this feature. (This is almost certainly a bug.)

Write makes .WRI backups with the .BKP extension. If you are saving a file in the Word for DOS format, the backup will have a .BAK extension (not the *first* time you save a Write document in Word format, however—only when you save a file that is already in Word format, because the original Write file is regarded as the backup).

The Menu Options

Here's a summary of Write's menu options.

File | New Clears the window and displays a new document, so you can start a new file. If the current file hasn't been saved, Write asks if you want to do so.

File | Open Lets you open an existing document file.

File | Save Saves the file. The first time you save you will see the Save As dialog box so you can select a directory and filename.

File | Save As Lets you save the file with a new name or in a different directory.

File | Print Prints the file on the printer selected in the Print Setup dialog box.

File | Print Setup Lets you select the printer on which you wish to print your files. Each time you open Write, it automatically selects the default printer selected in the Control Panel's Printers dialog box.

File | Repaginate Places the page breaks in the correct positions.

File | Exit Closes the application. If you have unsaved changes, the application asks if you want to save the file first.

Edit | Cut (Ctrl-X) Cuts the selected text or picture and places it into the Clipboard.

Edit | Copy (Ctrl-C) Copies the selected text or picture into the Clipboard.

Edit | Paste (Ctrl-V) Copies the text or picture from the Clipboard into the application. Data coming from an OLE server is automatically pasted as an embedded object.

▼ ***Note*** The following seven options are OLE (Object Linking and Embedding) commands; they are explained in Chapter 28.

Edit | Paste Special Lets you select different types of paste procedures: OLE embedded, OLE link, or non-OLE (normal).

Edit | Paste Link Pastes an object from the Clipboard into Write and creates a link to the original application.

Edit | Links If Write contains linked objects, lets you modify or remove OLE links.

Edit | ***application name*** **Object** Lets you edit the selected linked or embedded object. If the selected item is a package, this menu option is replaced by the following two:

> **Edit | Package Object | Activate Contents** Opens the application that created the object in the selected package so you can view, listen to, or edit the object.
>
> **Edit | Package Object | Edit Package** Opens the Object Packager so you can edit the selected package.

Edit | Insert Object Lets you open an OLE *server* application so you can create an OLE object and paste it into Write.

Edit | Move Picture Lets you move a picture horizontally.

Edit | Size Picture Lets you shrink or enlarge a picture.

Find | Find Lets you search for specific text.

Find | Repeat Last Find (F3) Searches for the text you entered earlier using Find | Find.

Find | Replace Lets you search for specific text and replace it with other text.

Find | Go to Page (F4) Lets you move quickly to a specific page.

Character | Regular (F5) Removes from the selected characters boldface, italic, underline, superscript, or subscript.

Character | Bold (Ctrl-B) Changes the selected characters to boldface.

Character | Italic (Ctrl-I) Changes the selected characters to italic.

Character | Underline (Ctrl-U) Underlines the selected characters.

Character | Superscript Raises the selected characters above the normal text position and reduces their size.

Character | Subscript Lowers the selected characters below the normal text position and reduces their size.

Character | Enlarge Font Increases the font size.

Character | Reduce Font Decreases the font size.

Character | Fonts Lets you select another font and font size.

Paragraph | Normal Changes the selected paragraph to Write's default settings.

Paragraph | Left Aligns the selected paragraph on the left.

Paragraph | Centered Aligns the selected paragraph in the center.

Paragraph | Right Aligns the selected paragraph on the right.

Paragraph | Justified Justifies the selected paragraph so the text has straight edges on both the left and right sides.

Paragraph | Single Space Sets the line spacing to normal for the selected paragraph.

Paragraph | 1 1/2 Space Places a half-line space before each line in the paragraph.

Paragraph | Double Space Places a full-line space before each line in the paragraph.

Paragraph | Indents Lets you set left, right, and first-line indents for the selected paragraph.

Document | Header Lets you enter a header.

Document | Footer Lets you enter a footer.

Document|Ruler On Turns on the ruler, with which you can set tabs and select paragraph formatting.

Document|Tabs Lets you set tabs by typing measurements into a dialog box.

Document|Page Layout Lets you enter a starting page number and page margins.

13

Illustrations: Windows Paintbrush

Windows Paintbrush is a simple *paint* program that creates bitmap images. Bitmap images are made of many colored dots known as *pixels*: When you draw a line you are actually turning on the pixels along the line. Once the line is created the program doesn't really know it's a line, it just knows that the pixels along the line have been "turned on." That means, also, that once created a bitmap's resolution is set. Display the picture on a screen with a higher resolution, and the picture remains the same resolution as before. Because the program doesn't know what each dot represents, it has no way to increase resolution by turning some of them off. It wouldn't know which ones to modify. Instead, it simply colors enough pixels to color the same area of the screen as before.

A *draw* program, on the other hand, draws images mathematically. The program knows the line is a line, because a mathematical equation tells it so. It only "turns on" the dots necessary to create the line, so the higher the resolution of the screen on which the picture is being displayed or the printer on which it is printed, the fewer dots are needed.

You can use Paintbrush for play—to create computer art for your own pleasure—or create pictures you can use in your documents: sketches of equipment, maps, diagrams, and so on. You can even add text as labels and headings.

Starting Paintbrush

Start Paintbrush by clicking on the Paintbrush icon in the Accessories program group. Or you can select **File | Run** and run **PAINTBRUSH**. Paintbrush opens with a blank drawing area, as shown in Figure 13.1. The large blank area inside the window is the *drawing area*, the space in which you will paint your pictures. At the bottom is the *palette*, from which you can select the colors with which you will

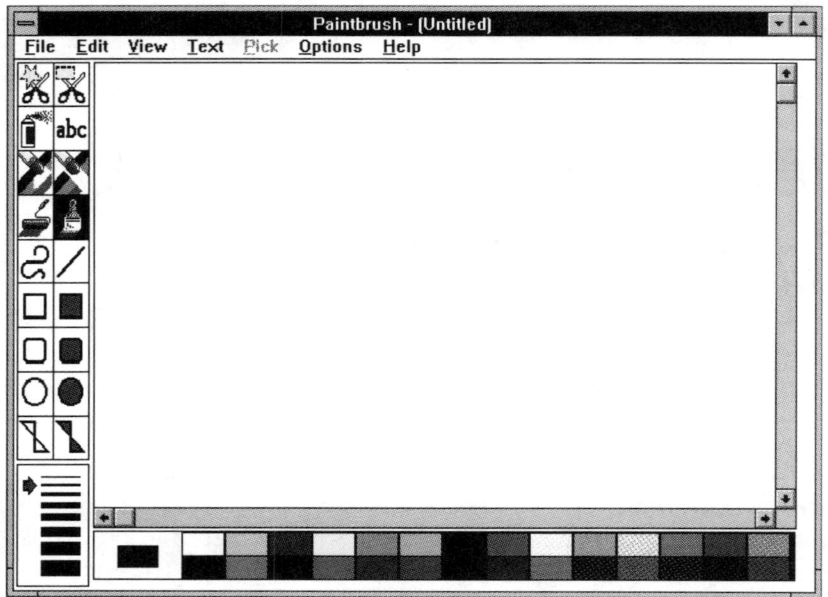

Figure 13.1 The Paintbrush window

draw. At the left side of the palette is the *linesize box*, which lets you select the width of the various painting tools. Above the linesize box is the *toolbox*, from which you will select the painting tools.

To use Paintbrush efficiently you need a mouse. If you don't have a mouse, you will still get a pointer in Paintbrush. It is possible to use the keyboard to duplicate mouse actions using these keyboard combinations.

This combination. . .	*Does this. . .*
Ins	Duplicates clicking the left mouse button.
F9-Ins	Duplicates double-clicking the left mouse button.
Del	Duplicates clicking the right mouse button.
F9-Del	Duplicates double-clicking the right mouse button.
Tab	Moves the pointer counterclockwise through the drawing area, Toolbox, Linesize box, and Palette. Then use the arrow keys to point to an option and press **Ins** to select it.
Shift-Tab	Moves the pointer clockwise though the drawing area, Toolbox, Linesize box, and Palette. Then use the arrow keys to point to an option and press **Ins** to select it.

These keys move the pointer in the drawing area.

This combination. . .	*Does this. . .*
Arrow Keys	Moves the mouse cursor in the drawing area.
Ins-Arrow Key	Moves the mouse cursor while holding the mouse button.
PgUp	Moves up one screen.
PgDn	Moves down one screen.
Home	Moves to the top of the drawing area.
End	Moves to the bottom of the drawing area.
Shift-Up Arrow	Moves up about 10 pixels.
Shift-Down Arrow	Moves down about 10 pixels.
Shift-Home	Moves to the left edge of the drawing area.
Shift-End	Moves to the right edge of the drawing area.
Shift-PgUp	Moves left one screen
Shift-PgDn	Moves right one screen.
Shift-Left Arrow	Moves left about 8 pixels.
Shift-Right Arrow	Moves right about 8 pixels.

▼ *Note* The keystrokes for moving the pointer don't work well while you are zoomed in on pixels. You can use the Arrow keys to move the pointer, but the other movement keys do not work properly.

We will describe mouse actions throughout this chapter: If you don't have a mouse, refer to the previous table to find the keyboard equivalents.

Preparing the Drawing Area

When you open Paintbrush it automatically selects a drawing-area size based on the video mode Windows is running in. For instance, if you are running VGA, Paintbrush will create a drawing area that is 6.67 inches wide and 5 inches high. It will use 96 pixels per inch, so the total pixel size will be 640 by 480—the same resolution as VGA. If you use a different video mode, Paintbrush will use different settings. For instance, if you are using 1024 by 768 resolution, Paintbrush may use 120 pixels per inch and make the drawing area 8.53 inches by 5.95 inches, giving a total of 1024 by 714.

The size that Paintbrush selects for you may not be large enough—or may be too large—for the work you are planning. Select **Options | Image Attributes** to see the Image Attributes dialog box (shown in Figure 13.2). This dialog box shows you the width and height of the drawing area, the units that these are measured in (inches, centimeters, or *pels*—pixels), and whether the image will be in color or black and white.

Paintbrush's image size can be a little confusing. Paintbrush is really measuring the image's *dimensions in pixels*. A bitmap is made up of thousands of pixels, the pixel being the smallest area in the bitmap that Paintbrush can modify. Try this: Type **one** into the Width text box, and then click on the **Pels** option button. The number in the Width text box will change to show you how many pixels per unit Paintbrush will use. For instance, you may find that Paintbrush is using 96 pixels per inch. Therefore, if your image is 5 inches wide, it will be 480 pixels wide.

The image size, however, does not translate into screen size. An image that is 5 inches wide will probably not be 5 inches wide on your screen. It can be the same as the *print size*. When you print your image you will have two options: To print at Paintbrush's resolution (in this case, 96 pixels per inch), or to print at the printer's resolution, which will be much higher. If you print an image using Paintbrush's resolution a 5-inch image will be 5 inches on the paper. But an image printed using the *printer's* resolution will be far smaller. If you have a 300-dpi printer, a 5-inch, 96 pixel-per-inch image will be 1.6 inches wide. If it has a resolution of 800 dpi, the image will be a little over half an inch wide. (Dpi means "dots per inch," which is the same as pixels per inch.)

Paintbrush's printed images often appear very "grainy." Large text, for instance, looks jagged rather than smooth. You can improve the resolution dramatically by calculating image size according to your printer's resolution. If you want a high-resolution 2-inch image on a 300-dpi printer, you should set the drawing area to 600 dpi wide. Then, when you print the image, you will choose the **Use Printer Resolution** check box in the Print dialog box. However, read the information about halftones later in this chapter in the section on printing. If you are creating a black-and-white image, using Printer Resolution improves the picture's resolution. (If you are printing a color image on a black-and-white printer, however,

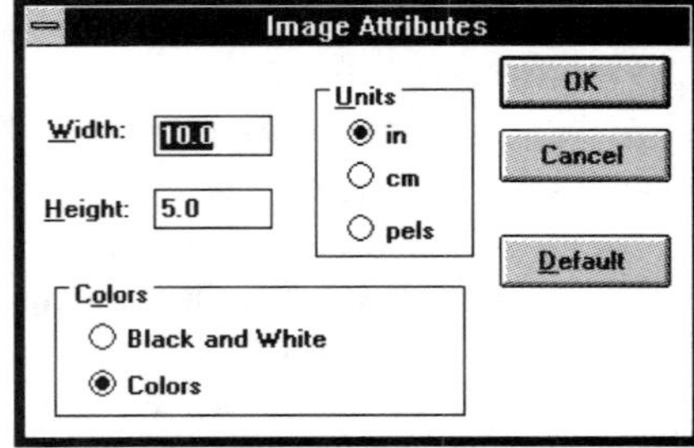

Figure 13.2 The Image Attributes dialog box

Printer Resolution will change the shades of gray used to simulate the colors—the final effect may be a murky image.

There are significant problems with creating an image for a printer-resolution output. Because there are so many more pixels in the image, it will appear much larger on the screen. If Paintbrush is using 96 pixels per inch and you have calculated the image size for a 300-dpi printer, the image will be three times larger. If you are working with an 800-dpi printer, the image will be more than eight times the size. Much of the drawing area will be pushed off-screen, and you will need to use the scroll bars to reach it. Also, the file will be much bigger, which takes up more disk space and, more important, slows down Paintbrush during some operations. Unfortunately Paintbrush doesn't make working with large images very easy, so you will have to decide how important high resolution really is.

The Image Attributes dialog box also lets you choose whether to create a black and white image or a color image. By default Paintbrush selects **Color**, but unless you need color you should select **Black and White**. Color images use up much more disk space and can slow down Paintbrush and any applications into which you paste them.

Clicking on the **Default** button in this dialog box returns the page to its default size: It does *not* change the units or colors.

When you finally click on the **OK** button in the Image Attributes dialog box, Paintbrush will give you two chances to change your mind. First it displays a message box asking if you want to begin a new session with the new settings. If you click on **Yes**, it then asks if you want to save changes to the drawing area. This message box may appear even before you paint anything. You can save, continue without saving, or cancel the operation entirely.

There's another important thing you should know about changing image attributes. The new drawing area will be filled with the background color you selected immediately before opening the Image Attributes dialog box. For instance, if you select blue as the background color, when you create a new drawing area the entire area will be filled with blue. If you change the image attributes between color and black-and-white, you may have to replace the background color. (You will learn of various methods to change the background color later.)

▼ ***Note*** Your image will probably be distorted on the screen, stretched down so it appears taller than it will when printed. For instance, a square will probably not appear square on the screen. Instead it will look like a rectangle that is slightly taller than its width.

Paintbrush can work only with the *visible* drawing area. Anything you do to the portion of the drawing area outside the visible area will be ignored. For instance, if you paste a very large object—larger than the visible area—into the drawing area, the parts of the object that fall outside the visible area will be lost. If you move an area of the picture outside the visible drawing area, the portion that is placed outside will be lost.

The Color Palette

You need to understand how to select background and foreground colors before you can use the drawing tools, so let's take a quick look at the color Palette. The palette comprises 28 blocks of various colors and a special box on the left side indicating the selected colors (see Figure 13.3). To select a **foreground color**, point at the color you want and click the **left** mouse button. To select a **background color**, point at the one you want and click the **right** mouse button. If you are working with a black-and-white image the palette contains black, white, and 26 grays. These are not genuine grays on most monitors—Paintbrush simulates the grays by mixing white and black pixels, a process called *dithering*.

▼ ***Note*** If you have to use the keyboard, press **Tab** three times to move the pointer from the drawing area to the palette; use the **arrow keys** to move the pointer to the color you want; press **Ins** to select the foreground color and **Del** to select the background color; press **Tab** to move back to the drawing area.

The Selected Colors box shows your choices. The color in the middle is the foreground color, and the area around the center box indicates the background color. How, then, are these colors used? That depends on the tool or procedure.

Foreground color

- The color of objects drawn with the Curve, Line, Box, Rounded Box, Circle/Ellipse, and Polygon tools
- The color of the *fill* inside the Filled Box, Filled Rounded Box, Filled Circle/Ellipse, and Filled Polygon tools

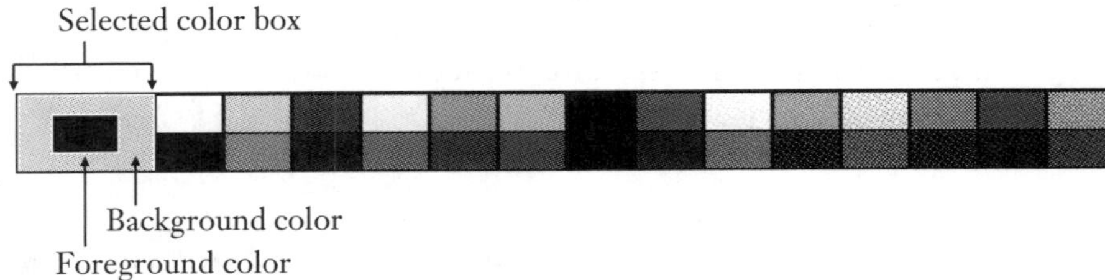

Figure 13.3 The color palette

- The color of the paint placed on the drawing area by the Airbrush, Paint Roller, and Brush tools
- The color of text
- The color that will be replaced by the Color Eraser tool (it will be replaced with the current background color)

Background color

- The color of the *outline* drawn with the Filled Box, Filled Rounded Box, Filled Circle/Ellipse, and Filled Polygon tools
- The color placed on the drawing area by the Eraser tool
- The color with which the foreground color is replaced by the Color Eraser tool
- The color with which the selected area is painted when you turn on Pick | Clear and use one of the Pick menu procedures
- The color with which a selected area is replaced when you remove it by dragging it away or by using the Edit | Cut command

---

 **Tip** When you open Paintbrush the drawing area is white. Here's a quick way to fill the drawing area with a color before you begin painting. Point at the color you want to use, and click the *right* mouse button. Then select **File | New**, or **double-click** on the **Eraser** tool in the Toolbox (third down in the right column). If you want to change the color of the drawing area after you have begun painting, use the **Paint Roller** or **Color Eraser** tool.

There's an important distinction between *background* and *drawing-area* colors. The drawing area initially takes the background color, but you can select another background color at any time to create a particular effect while painting. So it's probably easier to think of background and drawing-area colors as different.

You can remove the Color Palette from the window—enlarging the drawing area slightly—by selecting **View | Palette.**

The Tools

Paintbrush has 18 painting and editing tools. These let you apply "paint" in different ways, select parts of the drawing, replace colored areas with other colors, and erase areas. Figure 13.4 shows the toolbox with each tool labeled.

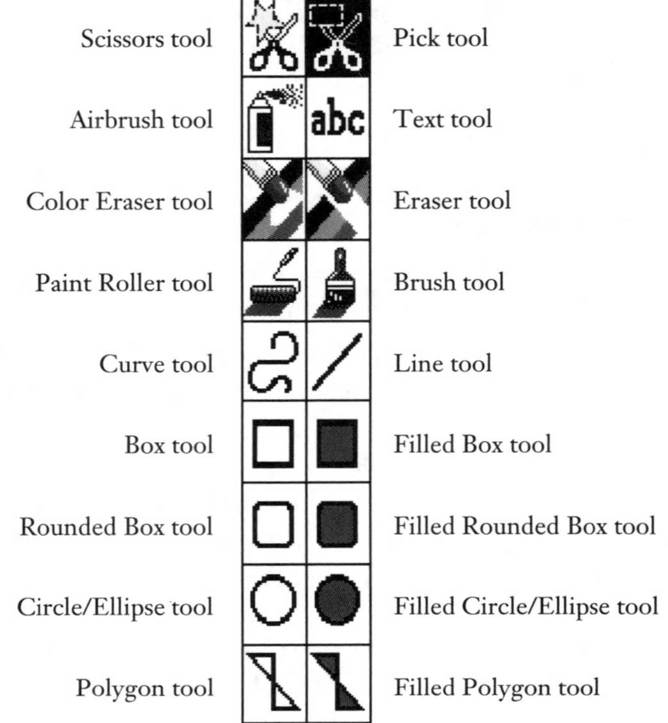

Figure 13.4 The Toolbox

Scissors tool	Selects an area of the painting so you can modify it in some way.
Pick tool	Selects a square or rectangular area of the painting so you can modify it in some way.
Airbrush tool	"Sprays" paint onto the drawing area.
Text tool	Lets you type text into the drawing area.
Color Eraser tool	Changes one color to another when you drag the tool over an area.
Eraser tool	Replaces all the areas over which you drag the tool with the background color.
Paint Roller tool	Fills a closed area with the foreground color.
Brush tool	Applies paint wherever you drag the tool.
Curve tool	Draws curves.
Line tool	Draws straight lines.

Box tool	Draws empty boxes using the foreground color as the outline.
Filled Box tool	Draws boxes using the foreground color as the outline and filling them with the background color.
Rounded Box tool	Draws empty boxes with rounded edges using the foreground color as the outline.
Filled Rounded Box tool	Draws boxes with rounded corners using the foreground color as the outline and filling them with the background color.
Circle/Ellipse tool	Draws empty circles and ellipses using the foreground color as the outline.
Filled Circle/Ellipse tool	Draws circles and ellipses using the foreground color as the outline and filling them with the background color.
Polygon tool	Draws empty polygons (multi-edged objects) using the foreground color as the outline.
Filled Polygon tool	Draws polygons using the foreground color as the outline and filling them with the background color.
Undo tool	There's a special Undo tool that doesn't appear in the Toolbox. It's activated by pressing **Backspace** and lets you selectively undo areas you have just painted.

Select a tool by pointing at it and clicking. If you have to use the keyboard, press **Tab** once to move the pointer to the Toolbox, use the **arrow** keys to select the tool, press **Ins** to select the tool, and press **Tab** three more times to move back to the drawing area.

When you select a tool the pointer will change. Usually it will become a large cross. Some of the tools, however, have special pointers. The Color Eraser is a square with a cross inside. The Eraser's pointer is a hollow square. In both cases the size of the square depends on the size selected in the Linesize box in the bottom-left corner of the window.

The Brush's pointer depends on the shape selected in the Brush Shapes dialog box (**Options | Brush Shapes**). The Paint Roller pointer looks just like the Paint Roller icon. And the Text tool is an insertion bar, similar to that used in many word processors.

The Linesize Box

The size of most of the tools depends on the selection you make in the Linesize box (Figure 13.5). The thicker the line selected here, the thicker the lines created by

Figure 13.5 The Linesize Box

the painting tools. Simply click on the bar closest to the line size you want to use. If you have to use the keyboard, use the **Tab** and **arrow** keys to point to the size you want and press **Ins** to select it.

Tip You can make more space in the visible drawing area by selecting **View | Tools and Linesize**. Both the Toolbox and Linesize box disappear. Use the same command to retrieve them when you need to select a new tool or line size.

The Painting Tools

The painting tools place colors (or shades of gray) on the drawing area. Each tool places the paint in a different way, allowing you to create a variety of effects. Select a tool by clicking on the icon in the Toolbox. Then move the pointer to the drawing area, press and hold down the mouse button, and drag the pointer to paint. (When you use the Paint Roller you will simply point and click, not drag.)

Note If you are used to working with *drawing* programs, one characteristic of a *paint* program will take some getting used to. Once drawn, an object is no longer an object, it is simply a collection of pixels on the page. While a draw program will allow you to select a line or square, for instance, by clicking on it, a paint program will not. Paintbrush allows you to select only *areas*, not objects.

Some of the painting tools let you *abandon* a drawing before you finish it by clicking the **right mouse button**. For instance, if you are dragging the Box tool you can click the right button before you release the left button. The box that you have drawn so far will be removed, so you can begin again. This feature works only with the Line, Curve, Box, Rounded Box, Circle/Ellipse, and Polygon tools and any of the Filled-object tools. You can use the Edit | Undo command with any tool.

Let's start with the simplest drawing tool.

THE LINE TOOL

The line tool draws single lines. Click on the line tool, place the pointer where you want your line to begin, and drag the pointer to where you want it to end. A thin black line appears while you drag the pointer, but when you release the button Paintbrush paints the line with the correct line size and foreground color.

You can make sure you paint only horizontal, vertical, or 45-degree lines by holding **Shift** while you drag the pointer. You will find that Paintbrush automatically moves the line in the direction closest to the pointer. If you release the Shift button, the line is free again to go in any direction, so make sure you release the mouse button *before* the Shift button.

THE CURVE TOOL

You can draw curved lines using the Curve tool. Place the tool where you want the curved line to begin, hold the mouse button and drag the tool to where you want it to *end*, and release the mouse button. Then hold the button again and move the tool: The line will curve toward the tool, so you can move it around until you have the curve you want.

Release the mouse button, then press and hold it again. The curve will jump a little toward the tool. You can now adjust the curve to get it back into position, or move the tool to create a second curve in the line. If you experiment with this, you will find you are able to create a variety of different types of curved lines, from simple waves to sharp "cusps." (See Figure 13.6 for some examples.)

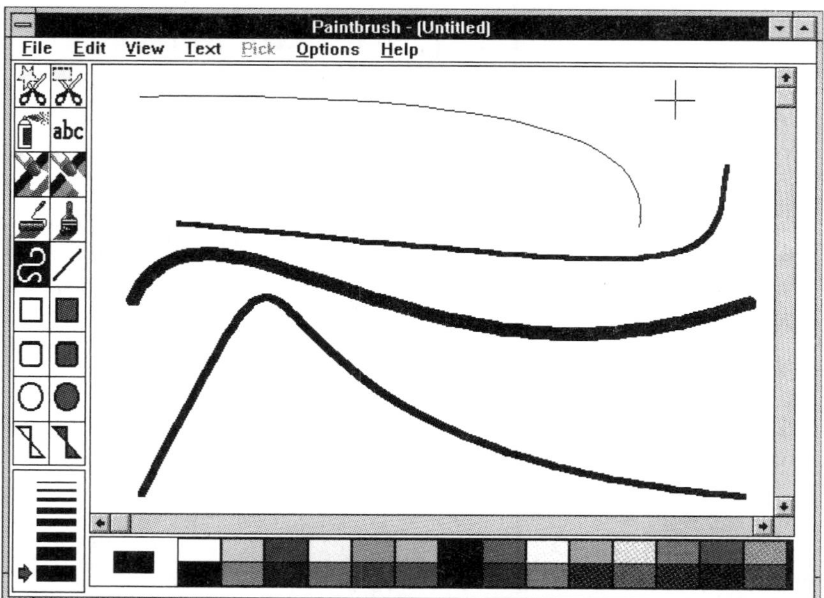

Figure 13.6 Drawing a curve (top), and some examples of completed lines drawn with the Curve tool

When you release the mouse button again, Paintbrush paints the line with the correct line size and foreground color. If you click the **right button** any time up to this point, the curve is removed, so you can begin again.

THE BOX, ROUNDED BOX, AND CIRCLE/ELLIPSE TOOLS

The Box, Rounded Box, and Circle/Ellipse tools all create finished shapes. Simply drag the tool across the drawing area and Paintbrush displays the shape. When you release the mouse button Paintbrush paints the object with the selected line size and the appropriate color. If you are using the *simple* Box, Rounded Box, or Circle/Ellipse tool, the object is unfilled; that is, it is created by drawing its outline, and the outline will take the foreground color. If you are using the *filled* tools, however, the objects are filled with the foreground color—the outlines are created using the *background* color. Thus, if you wish to create a filled object with an outline you must select a background color that differs from the drawing area's color.

The **Shift** key determines exactly the type of object that the tool creates. Press **Shift** with one of the Box tools to create a square, with a Rounded Box tool to create a square with rounded corners, and with a Circle/Ellipse tool to create a circle. You can also abandon an object before releasing the mouse button by clicking the **right button**.

Tip As we mentioned earlier, these objects probably won't look correct on your screen. A square will look like a tall rectangle, a circle like a tall ellipse. However, the *printed* picture should look correct. *All* the objects you paint will be distorted; it's just more obvious with a square or circle. You may want to experiment: Draw a square and measure it on the screen to get an idea of how much distortion you are getting. If you then print it and measure the printed square you will get an idea of the ratio between screen and paper size.

THE POLYGON TOOLS

The Polygon tools let you create multisided objects by drawing a series of straight lines. Begin by drawing a single straight line, as you would with the Line tool. The end of this line will be the beginning of the next. Move the tool to where you want the next line to end, and click the button to draw the next line. You may also press and hold the mouse button down, then move the pointer to adjust the line into the correct position. Continue like this until you have completed the shape you want.

There are two ways to finish the object. The first method is to place the tool on top of the starting point and click the mouse button. Paintbrush allows a little room for error here: It will join the lines if the tool is within a few pixels of the starting point. Make sure you get as close as you can. The second method is to double-click the button. Paintbrush will draw two lines, one from the end of the last line to the current tool position and one from the current tool position to the starting point, closing the object.

The starting and ending points of a polyline *must* meet. You cannot create open polyline objects with this tool. If you need an open polyline object draw a *closed* object and then use the Eraser to remove one line.

As with the Line tool, you can hold **Shift** to limit any of the individual lines to the vertical, horizontal, or 45 degrees. As with the other object tools, the simple Polyline tool uses the foreground color for its outline, and the Filled Polyline tool draws the outline with the background color and fills the inside of the object with the foreground color. The outline is drawn using the selected line size. See Figure 13.7 for examples of objects drawn with the Polyline tools.

THE AIRBRUSH TOOL

The Airbrush tool "sprays" paint onto the drawing area. If you point to the drawing area and click once, Paintbrush places a circle full of colored dots, not a circle of solid color. The circle's diameter is controlled by the line selected in the Linesize dialog box, and the tool uses the foreground color.

If you move the mouse while you hold the button down, Paintbrush deposits a series of circles. If you overlap these circles the color will become solid as the various dotted circles combine with each other. The slower you drag, the denser will be the spray.

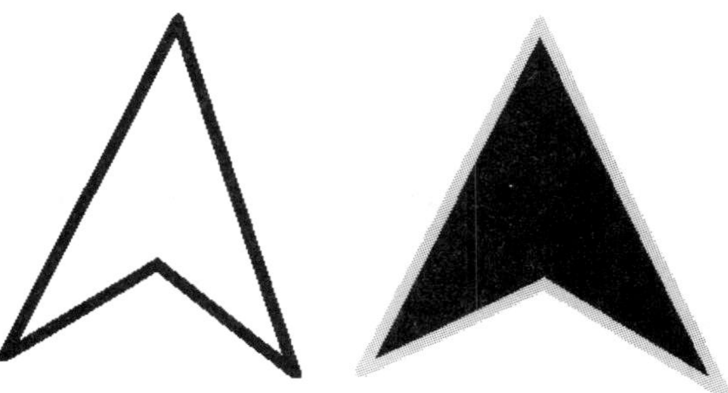

Figure 13.7 Two polyline objects, drawn with the Polyline tool (left) and Filled Polyline tool (right)

If you hold **Shift** while you use this tool, you are limited to horizontal or vertical lines. This works a little differently from the way the other tools use Shift. You must press **Shift** and then start spraying, moving the mouse close to the vertical or horizontal line. Once you have begun you will not be able to change orientation unless you first release Shift.

THE BRUSH TOOL

The Brush is a freehand-drawing tool. The paint is placed wherever you move the pointer while holding the mouse button. The type of line drawn is determined by three things: the selected line size, the foreground color, and the Brush Shape. Select **Options | Brush Shape** to see the Brush Shape dialog box (shown in Figure 13.8). Alternatively, you can double-click on the Brush tool in the Toolbox to open the dialog box; or press **Tab** to move the pointer to the Toolbox, press the **arrow** keys to point to the Brush tool, and press **F9-Ins.**

Double-click on the shape you want, or click once and click on **OK**. (You can also press the arrow keys to select the shape and press **Enter**.) Each of these shapes will give a slightly different effect. With practice and a steady hand you can use the thin-line shapes for drawing calligraphic letters. Figure 13.9 shows examples of each of the different shapes. The line on top was drawn using the brush shape on the left side of the dialog box, and the line on the bottom used the shape on the right of the box.

Pressing **Shift** while using this tool works the same way as it does with the Airbrush tool. Press **Shift** before you press the mouse button, and you will be able to paint only a horizontal or vertical line. You will be unable to change orientation until you release Shift. However, if you move the tool away from the line and then release shift before releasing the mouse button, Paintbrush will draw a line between the line you have just drawn and the tool position perpendicular to the line you have just drawn.

THE PAINT ROLLER TOOL

The Paint Roller tool fills an entire area with just one click of the mouse button. Using this tool is like pouring paint onto an area and letting it flow as far as it can,

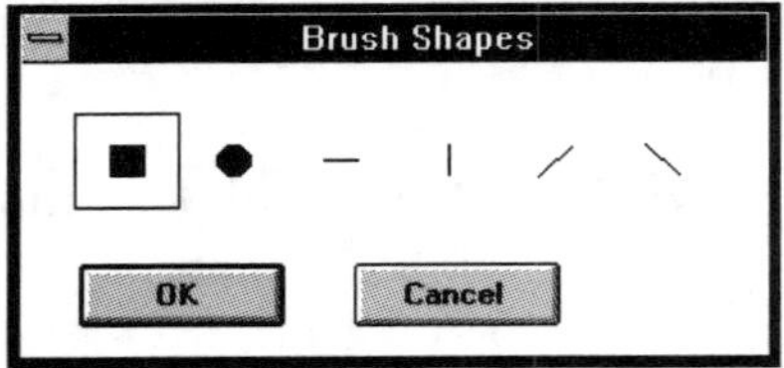

Figure 13.8 The Brush Shape dialog box

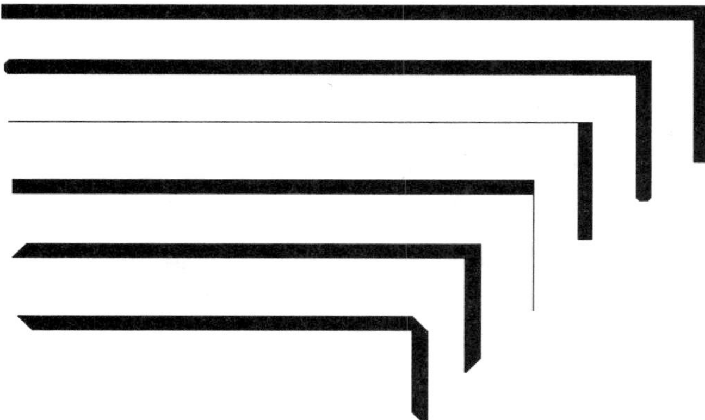

Figure 13.9 The effects of different brush shapes

replacing the original color. The paint you apply will flow in all directions from the area at which you are pointing when you click the mouse button. It only stops when it hits an obstruction—another color or the edge of the visible drawing area. The color applied is the foreground color.

▼ ***Note*** The color will not go off-screen. It will stop at the scroll bars, Toolbox, or menu bar, even if the drawing area is much larger than can be seen on your screen.

For instance, suppose you have one object in the middle of the drawing area. If you select a foreground color, point outside that object, and click the button, the entire drawing area is covered with the new color with the exception of the object in the middle. On the other hand, if you point inside the object in the middle and click, the object itself will fill. It takes only one small opening—just one pixel wide—for the paint to spill out into an area you don't intend (see Figure 13.10). You can use **Edit | Undo** to remove the paint, fix the hole, and try again.

If you look closely at Figure 13.10 you will notice that the Paint Roller tool is a picture of a roller. A sharp point is shown on the lower-left corner of the icon. You apply the color with this point. Because it is so fine, you can place it on quite thin objects, allowing you to replace object outlines.

The Paint Roller will work only if you are trying to replace a solid color, not a "dithered" color. So if you are working on a black-and-white painting, the tool works only when you are replacing black or white, because all the grays are dithered.

A dithered color is one created with dots of two or more colors. Because most monitors are limited to a small number of colors—usually 16, sometimes 64 or

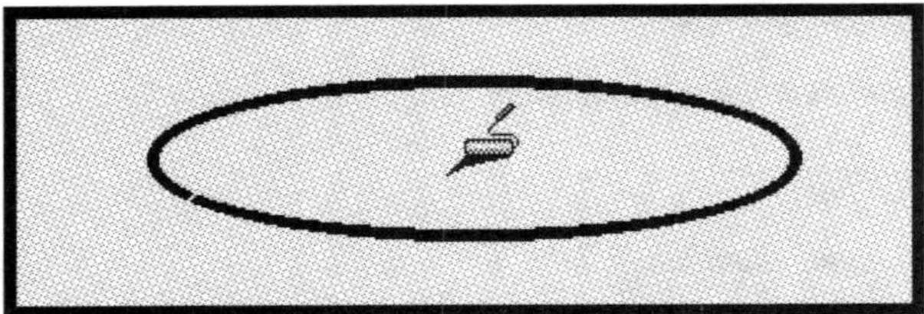

Figure 13.10 An oval filled with the Paint Roller; the paint has spilled through a small gap.

256—Paintbrush may not be able to accurately display some colors. Instead it has to simulate them by mixing pixels of color together. You can often tell if a color is dithered just by looking at it in the palette. If you paint an area with a dithered color and then zoom in on it to the pixel level (using **View | Zoom In**, explained later in this chapter), you will see that the pixels within the color are actually different colors.

The Paint Roller can't work with dithered colors because it regards a pixel of another color as a barrier, the point at which it is supposed to stop filling.

The Eraser Tools

Paintbrush has two different types of tools that "erase" areas: the Eraser and Color Eraser tools. The **Eraser** simply replaces the area over which it is dragged with the background color. You can adjust the size of the tool, according to how precise you need to be, by selecting a different line size.

You may not want to think of this tool as an eraser. It doesn't really erase, it simply replaces one color with another. If the current background color is the same as the drawing-area color, it does appear to erase, because the paint being removed is replaced with the same color as the drawing area's color, as if it has been erased to expose the color below. But the background color is not always the same as the drawing-area color, and you can use this tool to replace the drawing-area color with the new background color—which makes it appear to work like the Brush tool, drawing thick lines across the drawing area.

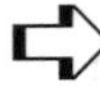 **Tip** Double-click on the Eraser in the Toolbox as a shortcut for **File | New**. Paintbrush will clear the drawing area—letting you save your work first if you wish—and fill the drawing area with the current background color.

The **Color Eraser** tool is a more selective version of the Eraser. With this tool you can specify which color you want to replace and which color you want it to be replaced with. For instance, you have several objects colored blue and you would like them to be green. How can you convert them? You might be able to use the Paint Roller tool to convert each object one by one, but if the blue was a dithered blue the Paint Roller won't work. And the Paint Roller is difficult to use on very thin lines, because if you don't get the point of the roller positioned exactly in the correct position, you modify the wrong item.

The other way to convert the colors is to use the Color Eraser, which will convert from the current foreground color to the current background color. Click on blue in the palette with the left button. Then click on green with the right button. Now drag the tool across the area you want to convert while holding the mouse button. If the tool passes over an area of blue, the tool converts it to green.

You can adjust the size of the tool by selecting another line size—you will usually want the largest size possible, because precise movements are not usually as important with this tool. You don't need to worry about erasing or modifying anything but areas colored with the current foreground color.

Like the Eraser tool, the Color Eraser isn't really an eraser—it's a color converter.

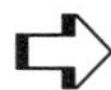 **Tip** To convert *all* the areas of a particular color on the screen, select that color as the foreground color, select the color you want to convert to as the background color, and double-click on the Color Eraser tool in the Toolbox. This will have no effect on the color that is off-screen, on different parts of the drawing area.

Pressing **Shift** while using either of these tools works in the same way as it does with the Brush tool. Press **Shift** before you press the mouse button, and you will be able to move the tool only in a horizontal or vertical line. You will be unable to change orientation until you release Shift. However, if you move the tool away from the line and then release Shift before releasing the mouse button, Paintbrush will "erase" a line between the line you have just erased and the tool position perpendicular to the line you've just erased.

 ***Note*** Paintbrush also has a special Undo tool that works like an eraser. See "Undoing Mistakes" next.

Undoing Mistakes

Like most applications, Paintbrush has an **Edit | Undo** command, but it also has a special Undo tool. If you paint an object and decide you don't like the result, press **Backspace**. The pointer will change to a small square with a cross inside—similar to the Color Eraser tool, but this time the cross is diagonal. Press the mouse button and drag the tool across the area you painted with the previous tool. The new paint—and only the new paint—will be removed.

When you release the mouse button, the tool automatically reverts to the previous tool, but you can press Backspace again to continue with the Undo tool. The size of the tool is dependent on the selected line size—you may want to select a large size so you can undo the paint more rapidly.

The advantage of this tool is that you can selectively undo. The **Edit | Undo** command (**Ctrl-Z**) undoes *all* the work you did with the previous tool, all the way back to the last time you

- selected the tool.
- clicked on a scroll bar.
- used any of the keyboard scroll commands (not including arrow keys).
- switched applications.
- changed window size.

While Edit | Undo undoes everything, the Undo tool lets you select which portions you want to undo.

Later in this chapter we will explain how to edit at the pixel level, modifying a pixel at a time. The Undo tool does *not* work at the pixel level. The **Edit | Undo** command does, but it returns you to normal view, undoing *all* the changes you have made while at the pixel level.

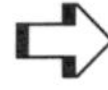

Tip If you are using one tool for a long time, periodically click on the scroll bars. That way, if you have to undo you won't lose any of the previous work.

Painting Precisely

There may be times when you want to use a tool very precisely. For instance, you may want to move an object into exact alignment with another, or draw a line very precisely. Paintbrush doesn't have an alignment feature—a grid or a snap-to-ruler function—but it does let you view the position of the tool, measured to the exact pixel. Select **View | Cursor Position** and Paintbrush places a small box next to the

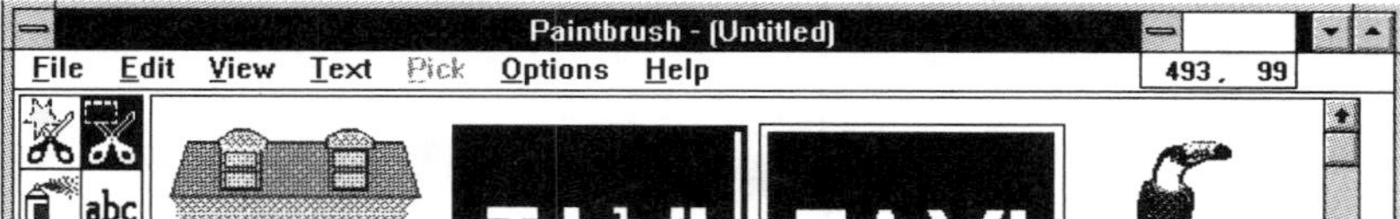

Figure 13.11 The Cursor Position box on the title bar

minimize button on the title bar. Move the pointer into the drawing area and numbers appear in this box (see Figure 13.11). The first number is the number of pixels from the left side of the drawing area and the second is the number of pixels from the top of the drawing area. These are not the distances from the edges of the *visible* drawing area, but the total drawing area.

You can move this box to anywhere but the drawing area. You can place it on the Toolbox or palette, for instance, or even on the desktop or another application, if the Paintbrush window is not maximized. Just drag the title bar to move it, and release the button when it's in position (if you release the button while it's over the drawing area, it jumps back to its starting position).

These coordinates will help you draw and position precisely. For instance, if you have two text characters you want to align, point at the edge of one and check the coordinates. Then use the Pick tool to select the other character. Place the pointer on the edge you want to align, then move the object into position; when the appropriate coordinate matches the other character's position, release the button.

To close this box, select **View | Cursor Position** again, or double-click on the box's Control menu.

 **Tip** You can often work more precisely with the keyboard. Pressing the arrow keys, for instance, moves the tool one pixel at a time.

Working with Cutouts: The Selection Tools

The two selection tools at the top of the Toolbox—the Scissors and Pick tools—let you "cut out" an area so that you can perform another operation. Once you've cut out an area you can use any of these commands.

- **Edit | Cut** to remove the cutout and place it in the Clipboard
- **Edit | Copy** to copy the cutout into the Clipboard
- **Edit | Paste** to paste the cutout from the Clipboard into the drawing area
- **Move** the selected area by dragging the mouse
- **Copy** the selected area by holding Ctrl and dragging the mouse

- **Sweep** the selected area by holding Shift and dragging the mouse, creating multiple copies
- **Edit | Copy To** to copy the area to another file
- **Pick | Flip Horizontal** to turn the area over horizontally
- **Pick | Flip Vertical** to turn the area vertically
- **Pick | Inverse** to invert the colors
- **Pick | Shrink + Grow** to shrink or expand the area

The **Scissors** tool lets you select an area by outlining it with the mouse pointer. Simply click on the tool, move the pointer to the area, press the mouse button, and drag the pointer around the area you want to select. As you drag you will notice that a dotted line appears on the route taken by the pointer.

You don't have to drag the pointer all the way to the starting point. When you release the mouse button Paintbrush will join together the beginning and end of the dotted line by drawing a straight line between the two points. The Scissors tool lets you select an area very precisely, grabbing nothing but the area you want. If you are used to working with a Draw program you will have to get used to the idea that you are selecting an area, not an object. Even if the background is white and your drawings are black, when you select an area you are selecting colors, not objects.

In a drawing program, you can use a selection tool to select an object; however large the area you surround with the tool, you are only selecting objects, not background. Paintbrush can only "think" in terms of colors on a canvas, so you are selecting all the colors in the area surrounded by the dotted line, even areas you might think of as background. If you now drag the area and place it close to another object you have drawn, any of the "background" that overlaps that object will cover it. The Scissors tool helps you avoid this problem by allowing you to limit the extent of the area you select.

The **Pick** tool lets you select square or rectangular areas. Click on the tool then place it at one corner of the area you want to select. Press the mouse button and drag the pointer diagonally across the drawing area. As you do so Paintbrush draws a rectangular dotted-line box. Release the button when you have selected the area you want.

▼ *Note* Paintbrush has no delete command, but you can use **Edit | Cut** to remove an area and place it in the Clipboard.

Cut, Copy, and Paste

The Edit menu has the usual Cut, Copy, and Paste commands. These let you copy part or all of a drawing to the Clipboard so you can paste it into another application, into another Paintbrush file, or into another part of the current picture. Windows lets you have several Paintbrush windows open at once. This makes it easy to copy and paste between Paintbrush files.

If you select an area and then choose the **Edit | Cut** command, the selected area is removed and placed in the Clipboard. The space where it had been is replaced with the current background color.

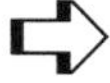 **Tip** Use the Scissors tool like a freehand tool, to draw filled objects with irregular shapes. Make the background color the color with which you want to fill the object, draw the object with the Scissors tool, then cut it to the Clipboard. The cut area will be painted with the background color, without an outline.

If you cut or copy a cutout to the Clipboard and then paste it into the drawing area, Paintbrush will drop it into the top-left corner of the visible area, with a dotted line around it. The surface below the pasted cutout remains in place—when you move the cutout you will see the original area reappear. However, as soon as the dotted line disappears, the pasted cutout is fixed in place and everything underneath it is gone. You must be careful not to click the mouse button except while the pointer is within the dotted-line area. If you click on a different area, select another tool, use any of the keyboard scrolling commands, or click on a scroll bar, the dotted line disappears and the area is set in its new position (you can use Edit | Undo to remove it).

Important When you paste, move, or copy an area, something strange can happen to colors. Any part of the area painted with the current background color becomes transparent. If, for instance, the background color is blue, any blue areas in the cutout become transparent when you move the cutout. However, if you press the **right mouse button** while moving or copying the object, instead of the left button, the background color remains opaque. You can also move an object into place using the **left mouse button**, then press **Del** to recover the color. Or simply select a different background color before you select the cutout area, or before you paste it from the Clipboard.

Incidentally, Paintbrush is an OLE (Object Linking and Embedding) *server*, an application that can provide images that may be embedded or linked in OLE *client* applications. If you cut or copy an image in Paintbrush, and then paste it into an

OLE server, the image is automatically *embedded*. You could paste it into a word processor, desktop publishing program, or spreadsheet, for instance. When you click on the embedded image in the client application, Paintbrush opens automatically, allowing you to edit the picture.

You can also *link* images in OLE clients. When linked an image maintains a connection to the original file; edit the Paintbrush file and the image in the OLE client changes automatically. For more information on OLE see Chapter 28.

When you copy or cut an image to the Clipboard, Paintbrush actually copies it in several different formats, so the application into which you want to paste it can select the appropriate one. In some cases, the receiving application will have trouble reading the Clipboard image. In this case you should try selecting the **Options | Omit Picture Format** command before copying or cutting an area. The picture will be copied as a simple bitmap that the other application may be able to handle more easily.

PASTING LARGE OBJECTS AND WINDOWS SNAPSHOTS

As we mentioned earlier, if you paste an object that is so large it overlaps into nonvisible portions of the drawing area, the overlapping areas are removed. In other words, if you scroll to view the rest of the drawing area you will find that the rest of the picture has gone.

This is especially frustrating if you are trying to take "snapshots" of other Windows applications, perhaps for a program's documentation. Windows has two commands for taking pictures of what is on your screen. Press **Print Screen** and Windows places a picture of everything on your screen into the Clipboard. Or press **Alt-Print Screen** and Windows places a picture of the active window into the Clipboard.

This can be pasted into Paintbrush, but only if you know the trick. First, you must make sure your drawing area is large enough to take the object. The default image size is probably large enough. Make sure that the image size measured in pixels is the same as your video mode. If you are working in VGA it must be 640 by 480. If you are using 1024 by 768, make sure the pixel size of the image is the same. Remember that what counts is the pixel size, not the size in inches or centimeters that is an indication of the print size.

Now, select **View | Zoom Out** (**Ctrl-O**). Paintbrush will show you the entire drawing area. Select **Edit | Paste** (**Ctrl-V**) to paste the image. Paintbrush displays a cross-hatch pattern instead of the actual image. Don't zoom back in on the picture yet. Instead, click on the **Toolbox** and the image appears. Now you can use **View | Zoom In** (**Ctrl-N**) to return to the normal view.

Moving and Copying Cutouts

Once you have defined a cutout you can move it by simply dragging it with the mouse. You can also use the keyboard to move it. Even if you have a mouse you may sometimes want to use the keyboard method because it lets you move cutouts more precisely. Place the pointer inside the cutout, then hold the **Ins** key and use the **arrows** to move the cutout.

Remember though, if part of the cutout is in the current background color that portion will be transparent. If you don't want it to be transparent, move the cutout using the **right mouse button**.

When you move a cutout the area from which you move it is replaced with the *current* background color, *not* necessarily the drawing-area color. For instance, let's say the drawing area is white. You draw a green square, then change the background color to blue. If you now cut a piece of the green square and move it, the hole you leave will be colored blue, not white.

Don't try to push a cutout out of the visible drawing area. Remember that Paintbrush only works on the visible area, so anything you do on the drawing area outside the visible area has no effect. If you push a cutout off the visible area and then click outside the cutout—to fix it in place—you will find that the portion of the cutout outside the visible area has disappeared.

This makes moving objects a long way a little tricky. As soon as you click on one of the scroll bars the dotted line disappears, so you can't move an object in steps, using the scroll bars to move you through the drawing area. Nor can you move objects when the picture is zoomed all the way out (**View|Zoom Out**; you'll learn more about this in a moment). If you want to move part of the drawing from the visible area to another part of the drawing area, use **Edit|Cut** to place the area in the Clipboard, use the scroll bars to move to the area in which you want the cutout, then use **Edit|Paste** to place it.

You can easily **copy** a cutout without using the Clipboard, by the way—leaving the original area unchanged—by holding **Ctrl** before you drag the cutout away. Once you have moved the cutout even slightly, you can release the Ctrl key if you want. Again, if portions of the cutout are in the current background color you can use the **right mouse button** to move the cutout and keep it entirely opaque.

Sweeping Cutouts

Paintbrush has a feature called *sweeping*, which lets you create a trail of copies. Select the cutout as usual, then hold down **Shift** before dragging the object. If you move the cutout slowly, it tends to paint the area it moves across with the color on its trailing edge. For instance, if the cutout is blue on one side and green on the

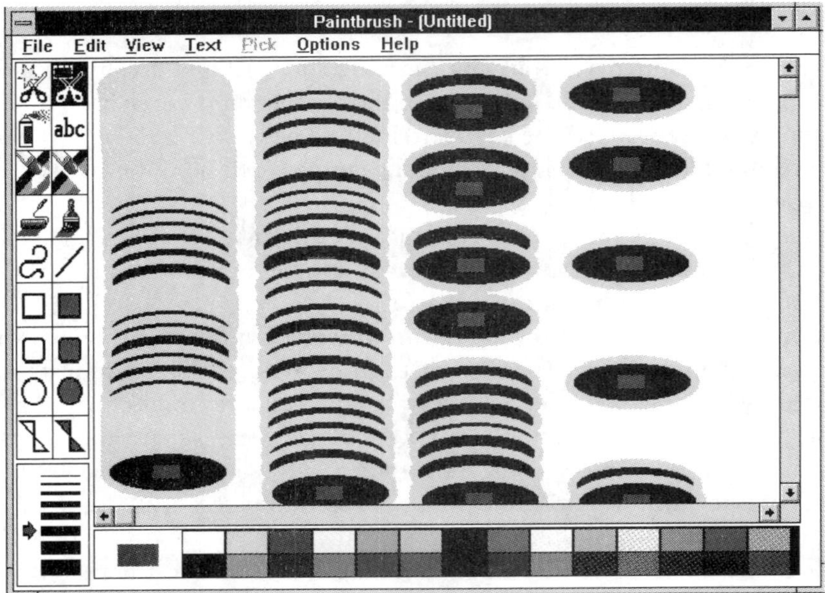

Figure 13.12 The effects of different speeds on sweeping, from slow (left) to fast (right)

other, dragging it slowly so that the green side is at the back will paint the area green. However, if you move the cutout more quickly Paintbrush actually duplicates the cutout (see Figure 13.12). The faster you move the cutout, the more detail the duplicates will have. Slow movements tend to duplicate only the cutout's trailing edge, while faster movements duplicate the cutout's interior or forward edge.

The background color has the same effect on swept cutouts as on moved and copied cutouts. Any portion of the cutout that has the background color will become transparent. If you want to sweep without getting any transparent areas, either select a different background color before beginning or hold the **right mouse button** while you drag the object.

Saving and Pasting Cutouts

A cutout may be saved in a separate file. Select the cutout and then select **Edit | Copy To**. Paintbrush displays the Copy To dialog box, which is the same as the Save As dialog box (see later in this chapter for details). Provide a filename and select a file format, then click on the **OK** button to save it. This creates a genuine Paintbrush file, which can be opened like any other.

 **Tip** Use the Pick tool to select an area for Edit|Copy To, not the Scissors tool. Paintbrush can only save square cutouts, so if you use the Scissors tool it will have to save the surrounding area anyway.

You can also paste a file—whether created in the normal way or by using Edit|Copy To. Select **Edit|Paste From** and you will see a dialog box that is exactly the same as the Open dialog box (described later in this chapter). You can select a file and, if you wish, click on the **Info** button to check its size and format.

When you click on **OK**, the entire file will be pasted into the current drawing area. Of course if the file you are pasting is larger than the current drawing area, it won't all fit. You will have a chance to move it so that the portions off-screen can be moved into the visible drawing area, but when you finally set the pasted picture you will lose some of it. You may want to View|Zoom Out before you use Edit|Paste From.

If the file you are pasting is in color but the current drawing area is black-and-white, Paintbrush will convert the pasted area. Also, if some of the pasted picture is in the current background color, those parts will be transparent when you move it. However, when you get it into position you can press **Del** to change the colors back to opaque (do this *before* you set the area, that is, before you select another tool or click on the scroll bars). Or you can move the area by pressing the **right mouse button**.

The Pick Menu Options

The options in the Pick menu let you do some more advanced editing with cutouts. The Pick menu is not enabled until you have a cutout on your screen—until you have selected an object using the Scissors or Pick tool, or pasted an object into the drawing area. You can change a cutout's size, tilt it, "flip" it around horizontally or vertically, or "invert" the colors. When you size or tilt a cutout you are actually creating a *copy* of the selected area. You can leave the copy in its original position so that it covers the original cutout, or you can carry out the operation elsewhere in the drawing area.

If you want to place the copy away from the original cutout, what happens to the original? That depends on the **Pick|Clear** option. When this option is *not* selected (when there is no check mark next to it), the original cutout remains unchanged. If you select **Pick|Clear** before carrying out an operation, the original cutout will be filled with the current background color. Thus, with Pick|Clear unselected you are making a copy. With it selected you are using the original.

The Clear option has no effect on flipping the cutout or inverting its colors, only on the Shrink + Grow and Tilt commands. Whenever you use the Flip Horizontal or Flip Vertical commands, any area of the object that is uncovered after the operation takes the background color, regardless of the Clear setting.

Sizing Cutouts

You can enlarge or shrink a cutout. However, the resolution of a bitmap suffers when you modify its size. Because Paintbrush doesn't really know what your painting is—it simply sees a mass of colored pixels—it doesn't know how to modify its size. For instance, if you want to enlarge a diagonal line, Paintbrush has no way of knowing which pixels it should color to create a smooth line—it doesn't even know it's a line. Consequently it enlarges everything proportionally. Lines and edges that appeared reasonably sharp now appear jagged. You have the same problem going the other way, shrinking an object. Fine detail tends to be lost and the image distorted.

Of course you might *want* to work with some of these effects, or only want to modify the size slightly. To change a cutout's size, select it using the Scissors or Pick tool. Then, if you want to replace the original cutout with background color, select **Pick|Clear**. Next select **Pick|Shrink + Grow**. The dotted line disappears from the cutout. Place the pointer at one corner of the area in which you want to place the copy, and drag across the area to create a dotted-line box. Simply drag this box until you have the size you want, and release the mouse button. The copy is created and, if you selected the Clear command, the original cutout is replaced with background color. (See Figure 13.13.)

You can also distort the image's proportions—in fact you probably will, using this method. If you want to make sure the copy has exactly the *same* proportions as

Figure 13.13 Creating different size images (the original is in the top-left corner)

the original—the same ratio of one side to the other—hold the **Shift** key down while dragging the tool.

When you have created the first copy, you don't have to stop. You can continue using the tool to create as many as you wish. Each time you drag the tool and release the button a new copy appears. If you want to stop, click on the Toolbox or scroll bars.

Tilting Cutouts

The procedure for tilting cutouts is similar to that used to size them. Select the **Pick | Clear** command if you want to replace the original cutout with background color. Then select **Pick | Tilt**. The dotted-line box around the cutout disappears. Point to where you want the top-left corner of the copy, then press and hold the mouse button. The dotted-line box reappears. Now move the mouse: As you move from side to side the box slants one way or the other. When you release the button, the tilted copy appears. As with the Shrink + Grow tool, you can create as many tilted copies as you wish before clicking on the Toolbox or a scroll bar. See Figure 13.14 for an example of a tilted cutout.

Flipping Cutouts

When you flip a cutout you do not create a copy; the original cutout is flipped in its original position. Consequently the Edit | Clear command has no effect—uncovered areas are always filled with the background color.

You have two flipping choices, of course. You can create a copy that is upside down or reversed. Simply select the cutout with the Scissors or Pick tool, then

Figure 13.14 Cutouts modified using the Pick menu's Tilt, Flip Vertical, and Inverse commands

select **Pick | Flip Horizontal** (to reverse the image) or **Pick | Vertical** (to turn it upside down).

Inverting Cutout Colors

You may "invert" a cutout's colors. Select the cutout and then select **Pick | Inverse**. Black areas become white, white areas become black, and the other colors change to their complementary colors. A complementary color is a sort of "opposite." The complementary color of the primary color red, for instance, is an equal mixture of the other two primary colors, green and blue. The complementary of green is an equal mixture of red and blue, purple. The Impressionists believed that a primary-colored object should have its complementary color in its shadow.

Adjusting the Drawing Area

Paintbrush has four views. The normal view is the one you see when you first open a file, or when you clear the drawing area by selecting new Image Attributes, by selecting File | New, or by double-clicking on the Eraser tool.

You can zoom in on the picture so that you can edit at the "pixel level"; you can zoom out to see the entire drawing area; or you can view the picture without any of the Paintbrush window visible.

Most of your work will be done in the normal view. Unfortunately most commands and procedures cannot be used in the other views, so you will use those views only for limited purposes.

View | Zoom In Lets you see each individual pixel and precisely edit the picture.

View | Zoom Out Lets you see the entire drawing area so you can paste large cutouts and move them into position.

View | Picture Removes the Paintbrush window and fills the screen with the drawing area so you can preview the picture. This view shows more detail than the Zoom Out option.

Drawing with Pixels

You may sometimes need to get right down to the "pixel level" to carry out very precise editing. When you zoom in on the drawing, you are able to see each individual pixel and can change each pixel's color independently of the others. This is especially useful if you are cleaning up an image you have scanned in another application, or if you have created a "snapshot" of a Windows screen and want to remove or edit particular objects. You can even edit icons for use by Object Packager (see Chapter 28).

Select **View | Zoom In**, or press **Ctrl-N**. The pointer changes into a box. Move the box to the area you want to edit and click the mouse button. Paintbrush zooms in so you can see each pixel, as shown in Figure 13.15. Notice the box in the top left that shows you the displayed area in normal view—when you edit pixels you will see what the changes look like in this box. Also notice that you can use the scroll bars to move through the entire drawing area at this magnification.

Only two tools work while you are editing pixels: the Brush and the Paint Roller. The Brush lets you modify individual pixels. Point at a pixel and click the **left mouse button** to apply the foreground color, or click the **right mouse button** to apply the background color. If you hold the button down and drag the pointer, each pixel over which it passes is changed.

Tip When you are editing black-and-white images, set the foreground color to black and the background color to white (or vice versa). Then you can edit any pixel, black or white, without needing to return to the palette to select another color.

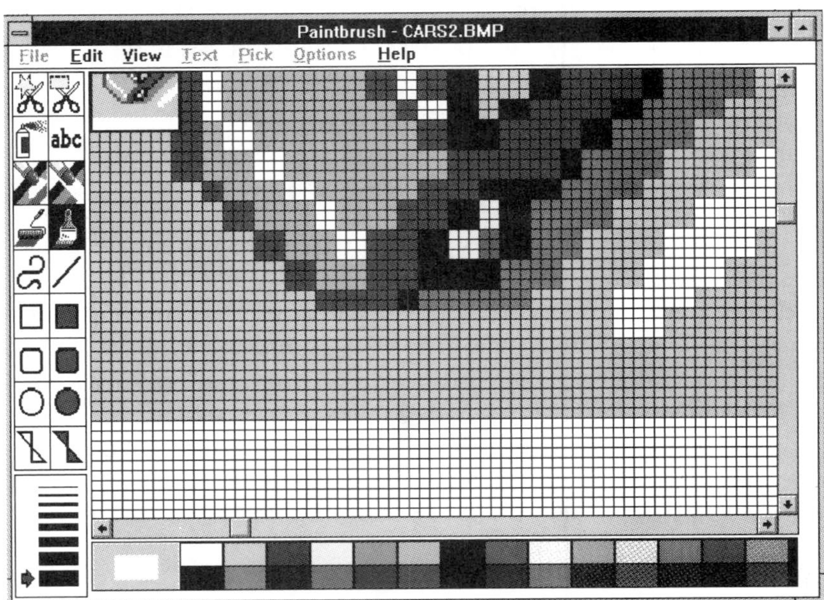

Figure 13.15 The Paintbrush window in pixel-edit mode

The Paint Roller works the same way in the normal view. Select the color with which you want to paint as the foreground color, then click on a pixel. All adjoining pixels of the same color are converted, and the paint continues flowing from pixel to pixel until it reaches a different color or it reaches the edge of the edit area. (By adjoining we mean pixels with touching sides; if only the corners touch the paint will not flow.) The paint will not flow out of the visible drawing area onto the area just off-screen.

When you have finished working on the pixels, select **View | Zoom Out** to return to normal view, or press **Ctrl-O**. You can also return to normal view by selecting **Edit | Undo** (**Ctrl-Z**), or by double-clicking anywhere on the color palette (this also displays the Edit Color dialog box).

Tip It's often difficult to paint single rows of pixels. You may find that your hand swerves off course and colors the pixels to one side. Try this instead. Select the Brush tool and place the pointer on the first pixel in the row. Press and hold **Ins** and then hold one of the arrow keys to move the pointer along the row, painting the pixels as it goes. It will probably miss some, so you can press the opposite arrow key when you get to the end of the row to run back along it.

Editing pixels can be difficult without a mouse because the scroll keys don't work properly at this magnification. You will have to keep zooming in and out to move around the drawing area, whereas with a mouse you can use the scroll bars.

Zooming Out

You may occasionally want to zoom out on the picture so you can move an object. You can't use the selection tools while zoomed out, though, so you should select a cutout in normal view and copy or paste it to the Clipboard. Then select **View | Zoom Out** or press **Ctrl-O**. Paintbrush displays the entire drawing area.

Now paste the cutout back into the drawing area. Paintbrush displays a cross-hatch pattern that you can move to the position in which you want the cutout (see Figure 13.16). Click outside the cross-hatch and the cutout appears.

You cannot copy or sweep cutouts in this view, and you cannot use any other tools. All you can do is paste, move, and undo. When you have finished, press **Esc** to return to the normal view, or select **View | Zoom In** (**Ctrl-N**).

Viewing the Picture

Paintbrush lets you see a preview screen that shows you what your picture looks like without all the clutter of the Paintbrush window in the way. Select

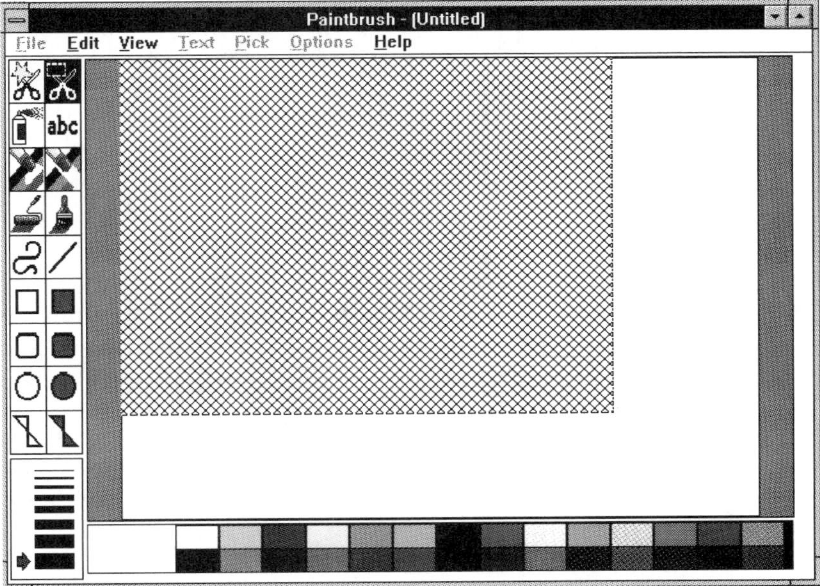

Figure 13.16 Pasting a large object while zoomed out

View | View Picture or press **Ctrl-P**. The Paintbrush window disappears, and in its place you will see the picture full size. If you are using the default image attributes you will be able to see everything in the drawing area. However, if you created a drawing area larger than the default, some parts of the drawing will be missing.

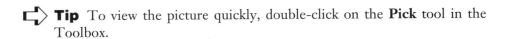

Tip To view the picture quickly, double-click on the **Pick** tool in the Toolbox.

You can't actually *do* anything to the picture in this view, only look at it. When you want to return to the previous view, click the mouse button or press any key.

Working with Text

Unlike some more sophisticated paint programs, Paintbrush lets you work with all the Windows fonts, including Type 1 PostScript and TrueType fonts. It does *not* let you select printer fonts, however.

A word processor or desktop publishing program stores commands that tell the printer which font to use when you print the document. But Paintbrush uses the font as a sort of painting device. Once you have typed text into the drawing area, the characters are no longer text—they are simply a collection of pixels, just like any other painted object.

When you are ready to add text to a painting, select **Text | Fonts**. Paintbrush displays the Fonts dialog box (see Figure 13.17). This box lets you select a font in the same way you might in a word processor. First, select a font from the Font list box on the left. A font with TT next to the name is a TrueType font. The others may be Type 1 PostScript fonts or Windows' other screen fonts.

Notice that when you select a font, Paintbrush shows you what it looks like in the Sample box. You can also select a font style (Normal, Bold, Italic, or Bold Italic) and a font size. The available styles and sizes depend on the type of font you have selected. Printer fonts tend to have few options, while Type 1 PostScript and TrueType fonts allow much more flexibility.

▼ ***Note*** The sample is displayed using the current foreground color. If that happens to be white, the Samples box will be empty.

For instance, if you select a TrueType font you can use *any* font size. You are not limited to the options in the Size list box; type whatever size you want into the text box above the list box. You can also make Paintbrush underline the text or add a "strikeout," a line through the middle. Click on these check boxes to see the effect in the Samples box.

abc

When you have made your selections you are ready to type. Click on the **OK** button to close the dialog box, then click on the **Text** tool. The pointer changes into a text-insertion bar. Point to where you want to begin typing and click the mouse button; a vertical line appears on the drawing area. Begin typing.

You can type only in the visible drawing area. If your text reaches the edge and you continue typing, it will *not* type off-screen. When you click the scroll bar you will discover that the text stopped at the edge. If you typed a character half in and

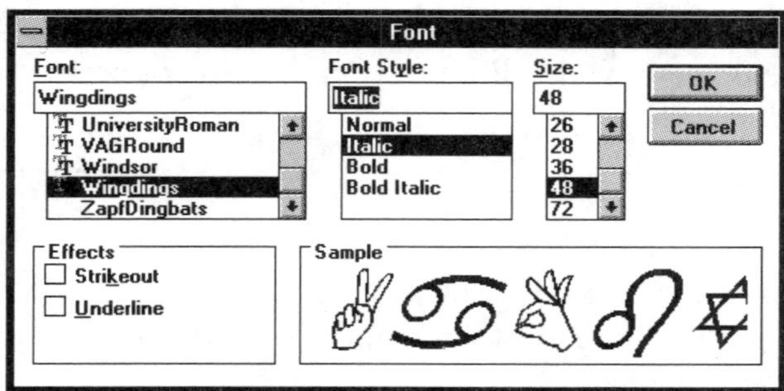

Figure 13.17 The Fonts dialog box

half out of the visible area it will be truncated. Unfortunately, you can't zoom out and then type. And if you use the scroll bar or any of the keyboard scroll commands the vertical bar disappears. This makes working with text a little difficult, but not impossible.

If you press **Enter** while typing, the text tool jumps down to the next line, and moves back to the beginning of the line. If you want to create a long line of text, you could type until the vertical line is almost at the edge of the visible drawing area, click the scroll bar, then place the text bar back in the drawing area and begin again. (Because you probably won't be able to line up the text bar exactly with the existing text, you may have to go back later and line up the two pieces of text.)

You cannot go back and modify individual characters or words. For instance, a draw program might let you highlight a typed character, or even an entire block of text, and modify the text settings. You can't do that with Paintbrush. You can, however, modify the entire line of text as long as the text bar is still visible. You can select another font (using the **Text|Fonts** command), or use any of these commands.

- **Text|Regular** Returns the text to normal, removing bold, italic, underline, shadow, and outline. It will *not* remove a strikethrough.
- **Text|Bold (Ctrl-B)** Makes the text bold.
- **Text|Italic (Ctrl-I)** Makes the text italic.
- **Text|Underline (Ctrl-U)** Makes the text underlined.
- **Text|Outline** Places an outline around the text.
- **Text|Shadow** Places a shadow below the text.

Selecting one of these commands will change the entire line—the text already typed and the text you type subsequently. Also, if you select a color from the palette, all the text is changed. You can also press **Backspace** to delete typed characters. Once you remove the text bar from the drawing area—by scrolling, clicking on the Toolbox, changing view, and so on—the text is set as a bitmap. If you want to change existing text, you will have to retype it.

 **Tip** If you want each character in a line colored differently, use the Paint Roller or Color Eraser tools to modify them when you've finished typing.

The **Text|Outline** creates an outline around the text. The text itself takes the foreground color and the outline takes the background color. The **Text|Shadow** command creates a shadowed effect below the text; the shadow takes the background color. You cannot combine shadows and outlines. Figure 13.18 shows a few examples of text styles.

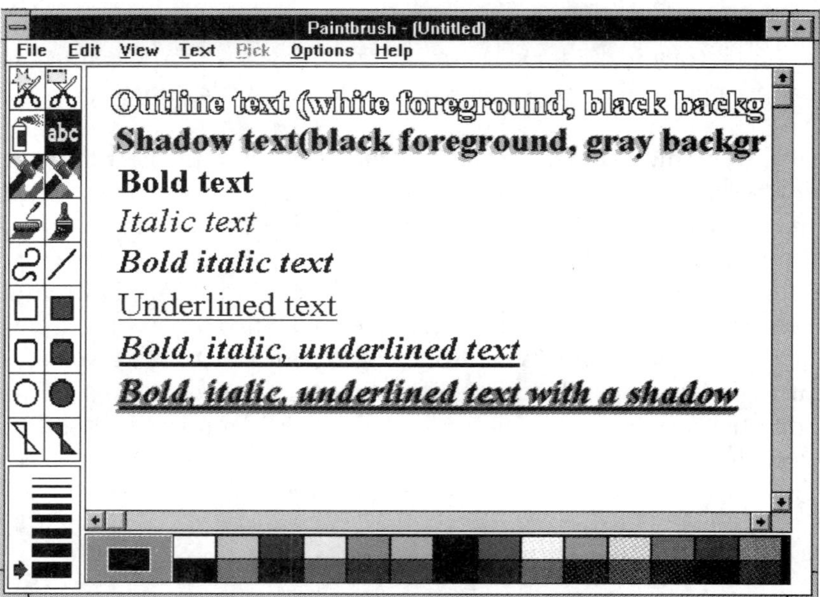

Figure 13.18 Various text styles

Working with Colors

Paintbrush lets you create your own colors and save them as palette files. You will still be limited to the same number of colors or shades of gray—each palette can hold up to 28. To create a color you must edit an existing color. Click on the one you want to edit, then select **Options | Edit Colors**. The Edit Colors dialog box appears (see Figure 13.19).

Tip Here's a quicker way to open the Edit Colors dialog box: Double-click on the color in the palette.

Each color is created using the RGB model. That is, a color is described as a mixture of the three primary colors, red, green, and blue. You can adjust the color by using the scroll bars to add or reduce the amount of each color in the mixture. Or you can type a number in the text box at the end of each scroll bar. Windows uses numbers from 0 to 255 to describe the amount of each color, with 255 being equal to 100%. Thus if all three colors are set to 255, the color is white. If all three are set to 0, the color is black.

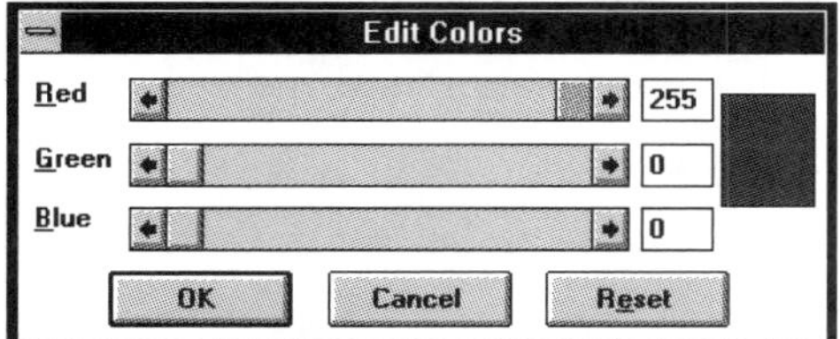

Figure 13.19 The Edit Colors dialog box displaying Red

Why 0 to 255? Because each color is assigned one byte to describe it (8 bits), and the largest number that can be written by one byte is 255. As each pixel is a mixture of the three primary colors, each pixel could be described by 3 bytes. Combining 256 shades of each primary color (0 to 255), gives you a total of 16,777,216 different colors (256^3).

Combining 256 shades of each primary color gives you a total of 16,777,216 different colors. That's a lot of choices, but it's unlikely your monitor can display that many. If you create a color that your monitor can't display, Paintbrush will "dither" the color; that is, it will simulate the color by mixing pixels of different colors.

Paintbrush will let you save your files in four .BMP formats: 2-color (black-and-white), 16-color (the default), 256-color, and 24-bit (or 16,777,216-color). If you use 40 colors in a painting and then save the file as a 16-color image, you are going to lose some of those colors. But again, Paintbrush will simulate the colors it can't save by dithering with pixels of the colors that it *can* save.

The box on the right side shows the color as you are mixing it. When you have the one you want, click on **OK** to replace the color in the palette with the new one. If you later change your mind about this color and want to return to the color that originally held that space in the palette, double-click on the color to open the Edit Colors dialog box and then click on the **Reset** button.

Tip While the Edit Colors dialog box is displayed, you can click on the palette to select another color.

If you want to keep your new colors, you must save them in a new file. Select **Options | Save Colors** and use the Save Color As dialog box to save the palette in a .PAL file. You must remember to do this before you close the application because Paintbrush won't ask if you want to save your new colors.

Paintbrush always opens with the default palette, so if you want to use one of your new ones you will have to open it each time using the **Options | Get Colors** command. Once you have loaded another palette the only way to reload the default palette is to close and reopen Paintbrush. You might want to save the default palette as a palette file so you can reopen it without closing Paintbrush.

File Formats

Paintbrush uses the Windows .BMP file format, a simple bitmap format. By default its art is saved in .BMP files, and this is the format that Windows uses for its wallpaper files (more about this later in this chapter). However, there are several different versions of the .BMP format, and you can save work in .PCX, probably the most common graphics format. You can also open files saved in the .MSP format, an old Windows bitmap format.

Saving Files

As with most Windows applications, you will use the **File | Save** and **File | Save As** commands to save your files. The Save As dialog box is shown in Figure 13.20.

Paintbrush can save its files in the following formats:

- ZSoft PC Paintbrush file (.PCX)
- Monochrome bitmap (.BMP)
- 16-color bitmap (.BMP)
- 256-color bitmap (.BMP)
- 24-bit bitmap (.BMP)

Which one of these formats should you use? Well, most of Paintbrush's wallpaper files are 16-color bitmaps, and if you are working in normal VGA mode that's the default format, the one in which the file will be saved if you don't select another format.

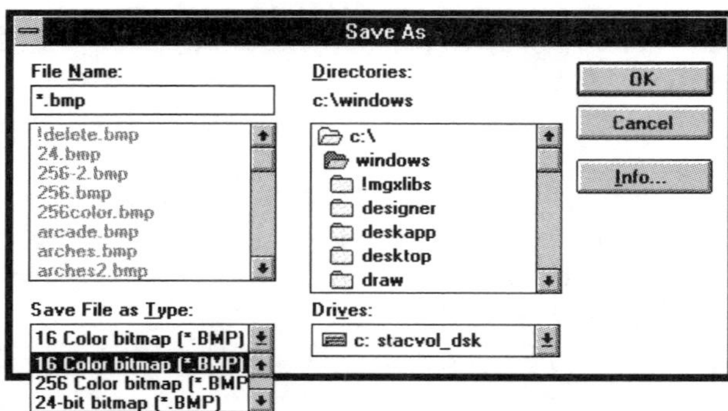

Figure 13.20 The Save As dialog box with the Save File as Type drop-down list box displayed

But you should select the format you need. Use .PCX if you want to use the image with a program that uses that format. The .PCX format is originally from ZSoft's PC Paintbrush line of products and is used by many other applications. If the image is in color, Paintbrush creates a color .PCX file, the number of colors depending on the video mode you are running; for instance, if your monitor is in 16-color mode, the .PCX will be a 16-color image, even if the original is 256-color or 24-bit (16.7 million colors). If the image is monochrome Paintbrush creates a 2-color .PCX file.

If you plan to print an image on a black-and-white printer, create your work in black-and-white and save in the Monochrome format. If you created a black-and-white image, Monochrome is the save-format default. Incidentally, saving color images in Monochrome format doesn't work well. You may lose a lot of detail, so save only black-and-white images in this format.

You need the other two formats only if you will print or display the image on a device that can work with that many colors. A 24-bit image is sometimes known as "true color," because it can work with more than 16 million colors.

It's difficult to work with large numbers of colors in Paintbrush; you would have to create several (or many) different palettes and keep swapping them. You need these high-color formats only if you are going to use the image in another, more sophisticated, paint program.

Another reason for using a simple format is to save disk space. A 24-bit image uses far more disk space than a 16-color image, even if you use the same number of colors in each. For instance, the TARTAN.BMP wallpaper file is 8 KB in Monochrome, 33 KB in 16-color, 67 KB in 256-color, and 197 KB in 24-bit format. It's 13 KB in 16-color .PCX, by the way.

There's an **Info** button in the Save As dialog box. Click on this button to see information about the image. A dialog box will show you the pixel dimensions and the number of colors. This information is more useful when you are *opening* files. The dialog box also shows you the number of "planes." This information is related to the way the file stores the image on disk and won't be of any use to you.

Tip You can also "save" a file in .EPS format by "printing-to-file" using a PostScript printer driver. (See Chapter 11 for more information.)

Opening Image Files

Paintbrush lets you open files in several different formats:

- .BMP (Paintbrush Bitmap files)
- .PCX (ZSoft PC Paintbrush files)
- .DIB (Device Independent Bitmap files)
- .MSP (Microsoft Paint)

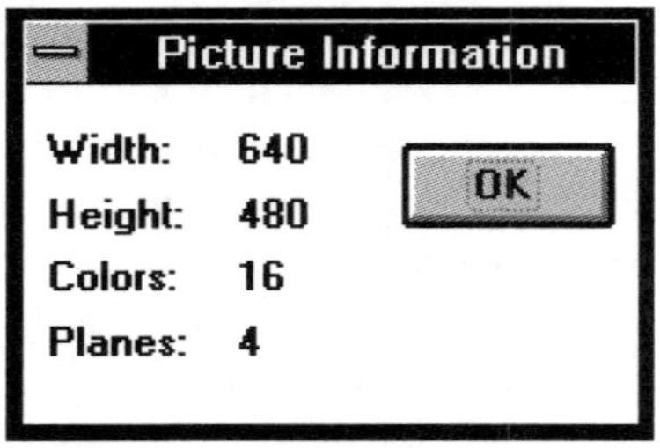

Picture Information

Width: 640

Height: 480

Colors: 16

Planes: 4

OK

Figure 13.21 The Picture Information dialog box

Although you can open and work with .MSP and .DIB files, you cannot save them in the same format. You must save them in one of the standard formats (by default, 16-color .BMP). The .MSP format was used by Microsoft Paint, the paint program provided by Windows prior to version 3.0. The .DIB format is a "device independent bitmap," a new Windows format used by some graphics programs. (It's not truly device independent.)

You won't be able to open all files in these formats, in particular .PCX files. For instance, you may not be able to open a sophisticated .PCX file. Notice the Info button in the Open dialog box. Highlight a file in the File Name list box and click on **Info** to see information about the file. The Picture Information dialog box (see Figure 13.21) shows you the file's dimensions (in pixels) and the number of colors (2, 16, 256, or 16777216, which is a 24-bit image). It also shows the number of "planes." If an image has three planes, Paintbrush probably won't be able to open it.

Importing Art

You've seen how you can open .DIB, .MSP, and .PCX files, and you've learned how to use the **Edit | Paste From** command to merge these formats into an existing file. But you can also import art—even vector images—from just about any Windows application. For instance, let's say you have one of the popular drawing programs that comes with a library of clip art: Micrografx Designer, Windows Draw, Arts & Letters, Corel Draw, and others. You can use these clip art libraries, containing thousands of images in many cases, with Paintbrush.

Simply display the image you want in the other package, select it, and copy it to the Clipboard, change to Paintbrush, and use **Edit | Paste** to copy it into the drawing area. If the image is a vector image (as are the images produced by the programs we named), it is instantly converted into a bitmap and can be edited in the same way you edit your own paintings.

Incidentally, you can find art from a variety of other sources. Word for Windows 2.0 has a 50-image .WMF library. You can display an image in Word, then

Figure 13.22 Clip art images pasted from Word for Windows and Windows Draw. The taxi signs show the difference between enlarging the image in Paintbrush (left) and before importing (right).

copy it to Paintbrush. The result is a high-quality bitmap image. (Figure 13.22 shows sample images from Word for Windows and Windows Draw.) Many other applications have clip art; this is a source you shouldn't overlook when working with Paintbrush. You can also buy clip art disks, commercially or from shareware companies. If you buy .PCX clip art for use with Paintbrush, however, make sure it is compatible. Remember, some .PCX formats are not.

 **Tip** If you import vector-format clip art, modify its size *before* you paste it into Paintbrush so its resolution is not distorted. Once it's pasted into Paintbrush it becomes a bitmap, and modifying its size *will* distort it.

Creating Windows Wallpaper

Windows lets you place a *wallpaper* on the desktop. The desktop is the area of the screen underneath everything else; minimize all the windows and you will see the windows' icons sitting on the desktop. The wallpaper is simply a picture or pattern that may appear on the desktop. (Microsoft mixed their metaphors here—perhaps they should have called wallpaper "tablecloths.") You can use wallpapers by selecting them in the Desktop dialog box, opened from the Control Panel. (See Chapter 8 for more information.)

The wallpaper files are Paintbrush .BMP files. That means you can edit existing wallpaper or create new ones. Most of Windows' wallpaper files are 32 pixels by 32 pixels, but they can be any size you want. Control Panel lets you place the wallpaper in the center or *tile* it so the image is repeated over and over, covering the entire desktop.

You could, for instance, place a scanned photograph on your desktop. Scan it, copy it from your scan program to Paintbrush (or save it in .PCX format and open it in Paintbrush), and save it as a .BMP. (Some scanner programs can save directly into .BMP, so you may not even need Paintbrush.) You could also create a calendar in Paintbrush each month, with important dates marked, and use it as wallpaper. Ideally the file should be in the Windows directory, so Control Panel can find it automatically, although you can also tell Control Panel to look in another directory.

You can also paint your own full-size image, one that covers the entire desktop, rather than tiling the image. Consider your video resolution when you create an image; if you are using 640 by 480 you will want an image of the same pixel size. The default image size will normally—but not always—be the correct one.

Copying Windows Icons

You can paste Windows icons—from any application or the icon-library files—using the Object Packager. Open Object Packager, use the **Insert Icon** button to select an icon, then select **Edit | Copy**. Go to Paintbrush and paste the icon into the drawing area. (For more information about Object Packager see Chapter 28.)

You can now edit this icon—you will probably need to zoom in on it to edit at the pixel level. You can also enlarge the icon, though it will be greatly distorted if you enlarge it more than a couple of times its original size. You may be able to improve an enlarged object by editing it, however.

You can save your modified icon as a .PCX or .BMP file, but you *won't* be able to save it as an icon. In other words, you can't edit it and then use it again as an application icon. Unfortunately you need a special icon editor to modify Windows' icons.

Printing Paintings

You will have a number of options when printing Paintbrush images. You can use the **File | Page Setup** command to set the page margins and include a header and footer (by default the printout will *not* have either). You can also use the **File | Print Setup** to select another printer. Both these commands are described in Chapter 6.

When you are ready to print, select the **File | Print** command. Paintbrush displays the Print dialog box (see Figure 13.23). Notice the Quality settings. Some printers let you print images quickly, with a lower quality. Select **Draft** if you want to do so. If you want the best quality, rather than a shorter print time, select **Proof**. Many printers don't support this feature, in which case you won't notice any difference between the two results.

You can also select the **Number of copies** you want to print and the size of the image. If you type **200** in the **Scaling** text box, for example, the image will be twice its normal size. The **Printer Resolution** check box also affects image size. In fact Printer Resolution and Scaling are related. Printing the image with Printer Resolution selected prints one dot for each pixel in the image. Consequently the image is smaller than the normal resolution—but also sharper, if it's a black-and-white image.

As we explained earlier, your printer's resolution is probably much higher than the default resolution used by Paintbrush. When Paintbrush prints an image from a system with a VGA monitor, it uses a resolution of 96 pixels per inch. Your printer, however, may be capable of printing up 300, 400, or even 800 dots per inch.

A dot is only the same as a pixel if you are printing a black-and-white image. If you are printing a color image on a black-and-white printer, the printer has to create a *halftone*. Halftoning is a complicated subject, and we're not going to discuss it in too much detail. Basically, the printer has to substitute a white, gray, or black for each color. And to print a gray it has to simulate it by printing a halftone, a matrix of dots. For instance, if the matrix contains nine dots the printer could simulate a very light gray by printing one black dot and eight white ones. It could simulate a very dark gray by doing the opposite, printing eight black dots and one white one.

Now, if you print a black-and-white image at printer resolution the printer will produce one dot for each pixel. The image will be smaller than if you had used Paintbrush's own resolution, and consequently it will appear much sharper. If you

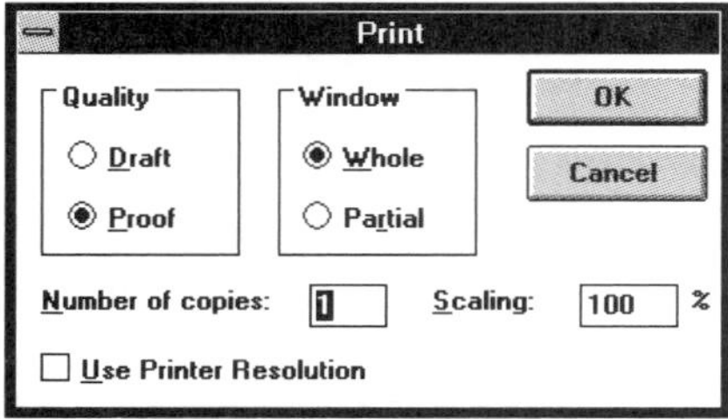

Figure 13.23 The Print dialog box

print a color image on a black-and-white printer using printer resolution, the image will still be small, but it won't simulate the colors very well. It simply doesn't have enough dots to create enough halftones.

Printing at printer resolution reduces the image size, and adding a value above 100% as a Scaling factor increases the image size. The Printer Resolution check box is another way to adjust the Scaling factor to a particular level. If your image has 96 pixels per inch, compared with the printer's 300 dots per inch, a Scaling factor of 313% produces a picture the same size as a nonprinter resolution image. One option reduces the size, the other increases it, and you are back where you started.

The **Whole** and **Partial** options let you print the entire image or a selected portion. If you select Whole and click on **OK**, Paintbrush prints the entire drawing area. If it's too large to fit on one page, it is printed on two or more pages. If you select the Partial option and click on **OK**, however, Paintbrush displays the entire drawing area. You must now drag the pointer around the area you want to print (or press **Esc** to cancel the print operation). When you release the mouse button, Paintbrush begins printing.

The Menu Options

Here's a summary of the Paint menu options.

File | New Clears the window and displays a new workspace so you can start a new picture. If the current file hasn't been saved, Paintbrush asks if you want to do so. You can also double-click on the Eraser tool in the Toolbox to execute this command. The new file will fill the drawing area with the background color.

File | Open Lets you open an existing picture file. You can open several different formats and view information about a file before you open it.

File | Save Saves the file. The first time you save you will see the Save As dialog box so you can select a directory and filename. You can save in five different formats and view information about the current file.

File | Save As Lets you save the file with a new name, or in a different directory.

File | Page Setup Lets you set page margins and create a header and footer.

File | Print Prints the file on the printer selected in the Print Setup dialog box.

File | Print Setup Lets you select the printer on which you wish to print your files. Each time you open the application, it automatically selects the default printer selected in the Control Panel's Printers dialog box.

File | Exit Closes the application. If you have unsaved changes, Paintbrush asks if you want to save the file first.

Edit | Undo (Ctrl-Z) Undoes the last operation to correct a mistake.

Edit | Cut (Ctrl-X) Cuts the selected area of the picture and places it into the Clipboard.

Edit | Copy (Ctrl-C) Copies the selected area of the picture into the Clipboard.

Edit | Paste (Ctrl-V) Copies the picture from the Clipboard into the application.

Edit | Copy To Copies the select portion of the file and places it in a new file.

Edit | Paste From Copies an entire .BMP, .DIB, or .PCX file into the open file.

View | Zoom In (Ctrl-N) Zooms in on the bitmap, down to pixel level. You can modify individual pixels.

View | Zoom Out (Ctrl-O) Zooms out to normal size.

View | View Picture (Ctrl-P) Displays the bitmap full-screen on a white background.

View | Tools and Linesize Displays or removes the Toolbox on the left side of the window and the Linesize box in the bottom-left corner.

View | Palette Displays or removes the color palette at the bottom of the window.

View | Cursor Position Displays a small box that shows the position of the mouse pointer, measured in pixels from the top-left corner.

Text | Regular Removes the boldface, italic, underline, outline, and shadow from the current text. It will not remove strikeout (set with the Text | Fonts command).

Text | Bold (Ctrl-B) Makes the current text bold.

Text | Italic (Ctrl-I) Makes the current text italic.

Text | Underline (Ctrl-U) Makes the current text underlined.

Text | Outline Uses the background color to outline the current text.

Text | Shadow Uses the background color to put a shadow around the current text.

Text | Fonts Lets you select a font, font style, and font size. You can also make the font underlined or strikeout.

 *Note* The Pick menu is disabled until you select part of the drawing, using the Scissors or Pick tool.

Pick | Flip Horizontal Turns the selected part of the bitmap around horizontally.

Pick | Flip Vertical Turns the selected part of the bitmap over vertically.

Pick | Inverse Inverts the colors in the selected part of the bitmap. Black becomes white and white black, for instance.

Pick | Shrink + Grow Makes a copy of the selected part of the bitmap: You can make the copy larger or smaller than the original as you place it in the drawing area.

Pick | Tilt Makes a copy of the selected part of the bitmap: You can slant the copy as you place it in the drawing area.

Pick | Clear When used in combination with the Pick | Shrink + Grow and the Pick | Tilt commands it places the background color into the original selected area.

Options | Image Attributes Displays information about the current image file.

Options | Brush Shapes Lets you select the shape of the "brush" used by the tools.

Options | Edit Colors Lets you modify the colors in the palette.

Options | Get Colors Lets you open a color-palette file.

Options | Save Colors Lets you save your palette changes in a new file.

Options | Omit Picture Format Copies an image to the Clipboard in a simple bitmap format for applications that have problems pasting Paintbrush's images.

14

Communications: Windows Terminal

More and more of us every day find a need for electronic data transmission. Perhaps you want to download software from a bulletin board. Maybe you want to send a message to someone by MCIMail or CompuServe, or research a subject with an on-line database. Perhaps you can dial up your local library's database so you can use their electronic encyclopedia or book index. Or maybe you want to connect your computer directly to another one to transfer files.

You may find that Windows Terminal is all the communications software you need. It doesn't have all the features of a sophisticated communications package, but unless you use your computer for data communications every day it probably has enough.

To dial up—or answer a call from—another computer, you will need a modem. The modem will be connected to one of your computer's serial communication ports and to a telephone line. If you want to connect two computers together directly—without a phone line—you will need a *null modem* cable. The other system also requires some sort of communications software, Terminal or another program.

The Control Panel's Ports dialog box contains information about the serial communications ports, but the settings you enter into Terminal will override these. You need to modify the Ports settings only if Windows incorrectly detects the base port address and the interrupt request line (IRQ). (See Chapter 8 for more information.)

Starting Terminal

Start Terminal by clicking on the Terminal icon in the Accessories program group, or select **File | Run** and run **TERMINAL**. Figure 14.1 shows the Terminal window.

> **Tip** You can make Terminal open and dial a number right away by creating a Windows Recorder macro. (See Chapter 15 for more information.)

The first time you open Terminal you may see the message "The selected COM port is either not supported or is being used by another device." That means Terminal is looking at the wrong COM port. Just click on the **OK** button: We'll sort that out in a moment.

Right now the terminal window is like an empty shell. You can't call a bulletin board or another computer until you have created the communications "settings." You must tell Terminal what number to call, how your computer should work while communicating with another device, how to handle the incoming data, and so on.

The Settings menu contains 11 commands that you will use to set up the communications session, but you won't have to do this each time. Terminal lets you save the information in a settings file. Let's compare Terminal to, say, Windows Write. When you save a Write file, you save the information in the work area, the large blank area in the middle of the window. That information is saved in a .WRI file. The next time you open that file, you will see the same information.

But when you save a Terminal settings file (a .TRM file), you are not saving the information in the work area; you are saving the information you entered into Terminal's dialog boxes, information that tells Terminal how to operate when you

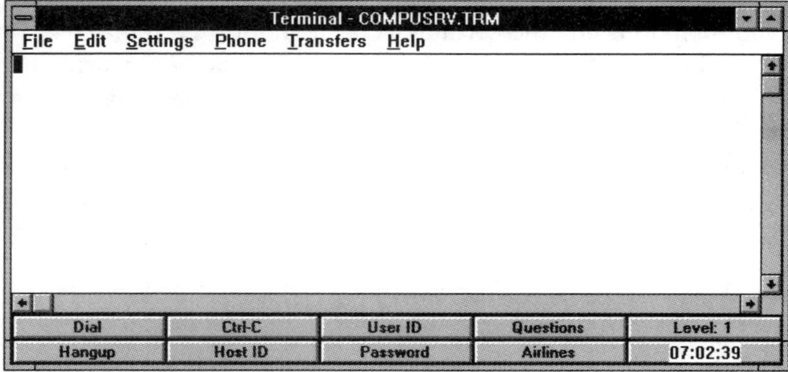

Figure 14.1 The Terminal window

dial up another device. The work area is simply the area in which you type to transmit messages and in which Terminal displays the response from the other end. (That information can be saved, but not in a .TRM file and not with the **File | Save** command; we'll get to that later.)

You will create a separate settings file for each number you want your computer to dial. Of course much of the information will be the same in each file—the only difference is, in some cases, the telephone number.

The Basic Settings

A Settings file contains much information that is optional, but some of the information is essential. If you don't select the correct baud rate or the correct number of data bits, for instance, you won't be able to make a connection with a remote device. Let's start by looking at the information that you must get right. This information should be available from your modem's documentation, the remote device's documentation, or a technical support line.

If you can't find the information—if your documentation doesn't specify it, for instance—the default settings will usually be okay. Some of the settings need to be changed only in very rare circumstances.

The Phone Number

Select **Settings | Phone Number** to see the Phone Number dialog box (shown in Figure 14.2). Type the full number. For instance, if you have to dial a 9 to get an outside line, include 9. If you are calling long distance, include the 1. If you need to pause to wait for dial tone—after dialing the 9, for instance, or if you dialed a long-distance service—type one comma for every two seconds pause. (If your modem is not Hayes-compatible, a comma may cause a different delay length.) You can include dashes and parentheses if you want—they will have no effect on the dialing.

For instance, typing **121-1212** tells Terminal to dial that local number: no access or long distance codes. Typing **9,,121-1212** tells Terminal to dial 9, wait four seconds, then dial the local number. You also can dial long distance or 1-800 numbers this way.

However, if you want to enter a very long number you may have problems, because you have a maximum of 34 characters—*including* dashes, parentheses, and commas. (Actually the dialing "string" sent to the modem can be up to 38 characters, but four of those are already used in the Modem Commands dialog box, which you will learn about later.) For instance, let's say you want to use your long-distance company's phone card to dial from your laptop while you are on business trips. You must dial the 1-800 number, wait for a dial tone, dial the

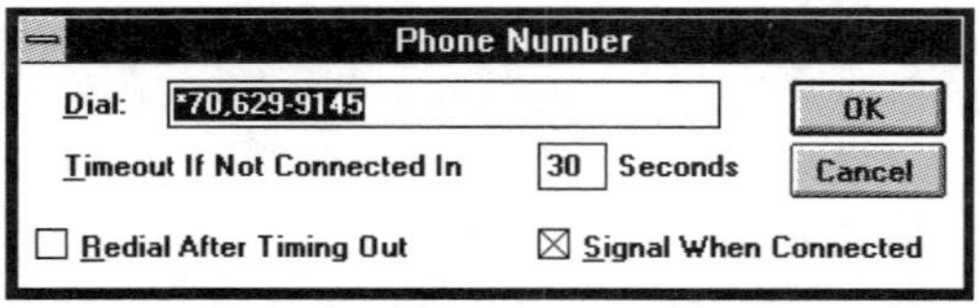

Phone Number

Dial: *70,629-9145 OK

Timeout If Not Connected In 30 Seconds Cancel

Redial After Timing Out ☒ Signal When Connected

Figure 14.2 The Phone Number dialog box

number you want to call, wait for a buzz, and dial your phone-card code number. This alone could be 36 digits (assuming a 14-digit code). Don't include any parentheses or dashes—Terminal doesn't need them. They are only for your benefit when typing or reading the number. That leaves two spaces for commas, which may—or may not—be enough pauses for your long-distance company's system to work. Of course if your code is less than 14 digits, there is more room for commas.

▼ ***Note*** If your phone line accepts only pulse dialing, you must change the Dial Prefix to ATDP (see "Modem Commands," later in this chapter). Your line probably accepts both pulse and tone dialing, even if you have only pulse phones.

You can also dial letters, if you are using tone dial. In other words, you could dial numbers such as 1-800-BUY-HITS. Look in your modem's documentation, and you may find other codes you can dial. You may, for instance, be able to send a code that increases the pause time allowed for a comma, thus freeing more space for other characters and allowing you to dial longer numbers.

If you have call waiting, you may want to enter the code to disconnect it before the telephone number. For instance, in many areas you would dial ***70** to disconnect. If call waiting is turned on, you may lose data when an incoming call is signaled. If you are in the middle of downloading a file, you may have to start again. If you are using a pulse line, this code may be 1170. Call your telephone company for details.

There are three more settings in this box. The **Timeout If Not Connected In** tells Terminal how many seconds it should wait before closing the session if you are not connected. By default Terminal will wait 30 seconds. That time starts as soon as the modem begins dialing, so if you have a long number with lots of pauses, or if you are calling a system that takes a long time to connect, you must adjust the time accordingly.

Redial After Timing Out is a very useful feature. It tells Terminal to try the call again if it times out before you have been connected. If the number you called is busy, Terminal will timeout, then redial immediately. If you select the **Signal When Connected** check box, you will hear the default beep when Terminal connects with another system. This isn't so useful if you are sitting at your computer—you will probably hear the modem make the connection anyway—but you might find it useful if you are letting your computer redial to get through to a busy line and are leaving your computer unattended for a few moments. The default beep itself is not much help (it's quieter than the modem), but you could use the Control Panel's Sounds dialog box to connect a much longer sound to the default beep—music perhaps—so you will hear the signal even if you are not near the computer at the exact moment of connection. (See Chapter 8 for information about Sounds.)

If you use Windows on your laptop during business trips, or if you move to another area code, remember that you will have to modify the area codes used by the phone numbers. Some communications packages let you define your current area code and will make the appropriate adjustments for you, but Terminal simply dials what you tell it to dial.

Terminal Emulation

Select **Settings | Terminal Emulation** to see the dialog box shown in Figure 14.3. This dialog box tells Terminal which terminal type your computer should act like, that is, which terminal it should "emulate." A terminal is a piece of equipment that allows you to communicate with a mainframe computer, usually a monitor and a keyboard. These are the types you can try.

- **TTY (Generic)** This type of terminal can send only the standard alphanumeric characters, the backspace, tab, and carriage return (the Enter key). Use this emulation if you are not sure which one to pick.
- **DEC VT-100 (ANSI)** Use this emulation if the device you are calling expects an ANSI device or a VT-100. To truly emulate a VT-100 you must turn on Scroll Lock. (If Scroll Lock is off, the arrow and function keys do not work as those on a true VT-100 do.)
- **DEC VT-52** Use this emulation if the device you are calling expects a VT-52.

The TTY emulation will work in most circumstances. You may want to try TTY first, unless the other device's documentation or technical support say otherwise.

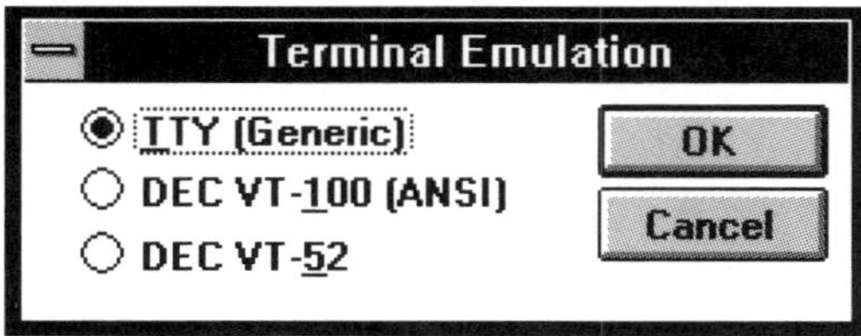

Figure 14.3 The Terminal Emulation dialog box

Terminal Preferences

Select **Settings|Terminal Preferences** to see the dialog box shown in Figure 14.4. This information tells Terminal how to handle the information you transmit and receive. If you are not sure about this information you can usually leave the settings as they are and adjust them later if you have problems. These are the options for Terminal Modes.

Line Wrap	If incoming lines exceed the line length set with the Columns option buttons, Terminal will wrap them onto the next line. If you don't turn Line Wrap on, you will lose the characters that exceed the columns setting. In most cases you will want this turned *on*.
Local Echo	Tells Terminal to "echo" the characters you type back to your computer. Most remote devices these days are "full duplex," which means they echo each character back to your computer. In other words, when you press a key a character is transmitted to the remote device, but it isn't displayed in the Terminal window. The remote device then sends the same character back so you can see it. (It happens so quickly that the character seems to appear when you type it.) In most cases you will want Local Echo turned *off*. If, however, you connect to a remote system that doesn't echo back (a "half duplex" system), you must turn Local Echo on.
Sound	Lets the remote device use your computer's beep.
CR->CR/LF (Inbound and **Outbound)**	Tells Terminal to add a linefeed to every carriage return. A carriage return simply returns the text insertion point to the beginning of the line. A linefeed is needed to move it to the next line. Most remote devices add a linefeed to each carriage return (in the same way the Enter key on your computer does), so in most cases you will want these turned *off*. If the remote device does not do this, you will have to turn the options on.
Columns: 80 or **132**	The number of columns of text that Terminal will receive. If your screen is unable to display the full number, or if you don't have Terminal maximized, you can view the off-screen columns using the horizontal scroll bars. (The Terminal Font setting will determine how many characters you can see without scrolling.) Try to ensure this column's setting matches

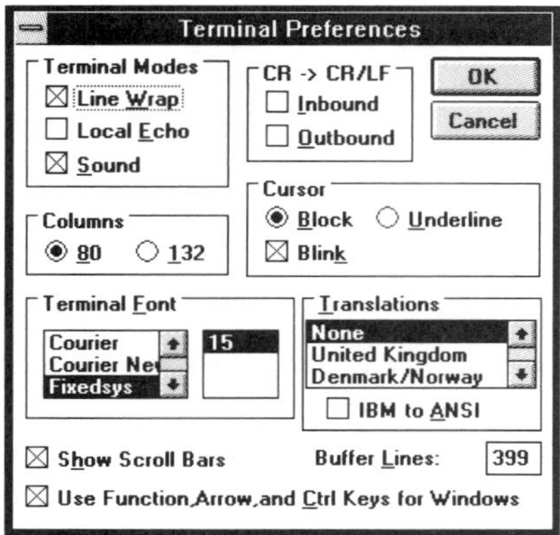

Figure 14.4 The Terminal Preferences dialog box

the number of columns sent by the other device (you can often tell the other device how many to send). If the other device sends more columns, make sure you turn Line Wrap on, or you will lose characters. Most users will want to use the 80-column setting, as it is easier to read.

Cursor: Block or **Underline** — Lets you modify the text cursor that appears in Terminal's window. You can have a Block or a thick underline.

Cursor Blink — Lets you turn cursor blinking on and off.

Terminal Font — Lets you select a font for the Terminal window. You can select both a font and a font size. The default is Fixedsys 15. To see a sample of the selected font click on **OK** and type a few characters.

Translations — If the remote device is using a character set different from the one you specified when you installed Windows (the one specified by Keyboard Layout in the Control Panel's International dialog box), you can select another. The default, None, means the remote device is using the same setting as your system. You will normally leave this set on None.

IBM to ANSI — Select this option if you will be receiving characters from the extended characters set (characters that are normally created in Windows by pressing **Alt**, typing **0**, and typing a four-character code). (See Chapter 19 for information about these characters.) Usually you don't need to worry about this setting.

Show Scroll Bars Lets you remove the scroll bars from the window. But even if you set the columns and the incoming text so entire lines are displayed within the window, you may still want to scroll *vertically* to review lines earlier in the communications session; therefore you will probably want to leave the scroll bars turned on.

Buffer Lines Terminal saves lines of text during your communications session. You can tell Terminal to save 399 lines (if you are in 80-column mode) or 244 lines (in 132-column mode), if you have enough memory to do so. The minimum number Terminal saves is 25, even if you enter a smaller number. You can use the vertical scroll bar to view the saved text and then copy it to another document.

Use Function, Arrow, and Ctrl Keys for Windows By default this check box is selected, meaning that if you use the function, arrow, or Ctrl keys, Windows recognizes them and they are not transmitted to the host computer. When this option is on, you will be able to use the keys to select and copy text from your session. If they are off, you must use the mouse to select and the Edit|Copy command to copy, and you won't be able to use the PgUp and PgDn keys to move around the window or the arrow keys to select text.

Also, if you need to transmit a Ctrl-C (an interrupt), you must turn this option *off* or program a function key to send the Ctrl-C signal (see later in this chapter for information about function keys).

Leave this option on unless you know you will need these keys for communicating with the remote device.

Communications

Select **Settings|Communications** to see the dialog box shown in Figure 14.5. This box determines exactly how the data will be transmitted. The settings in this box depend on how the remote computer and your modem operate; see your documentation or call the on-line service's technical support line. You don't need to understand what *baud rate* or *parity* mean as long as you get the settings correct. These are the Communications options.

Connector Tells Terminal which communications port it should use. This depends on the port to which you connected your modem. If it is connected to the wrong port, you may get a message telling you another device is connected to it, or your mouse pointer may lock up when you leave the dialog box (even if the port wasn't the mouse port). You must select a COM port before you can make any of the other settings. Incidentally, the settings you select here will supersede those in the Control Panel's Ports dialog box.

Baud Rate

The baud rate is a measure of how fast data is transmitted: the larger the number, the faster the transmission. You must select a speed that both your modem and the remote device can work with. Usually you will want to use the fastest speed you can. Some on-line systems base their charges on the baud rate used, so a higher baud rate causes a higher hourly charge. That's usually okay, though, because you can get your work done more quickly with a fast baud rate. However, as a new user you may find it cheaper to use a slower baud rate, because you may spend a lot of time reading menu options and figuring out how to use the on-line service rather than transmitting data.

Important Your modem doesn't usually have to match the remote device's highest baud rate. Most modems operate at a number of speeds. Thus, if the remote modem has a maximum speed of 9600, it will also operate at 4800, 2400, 1200, and so on.

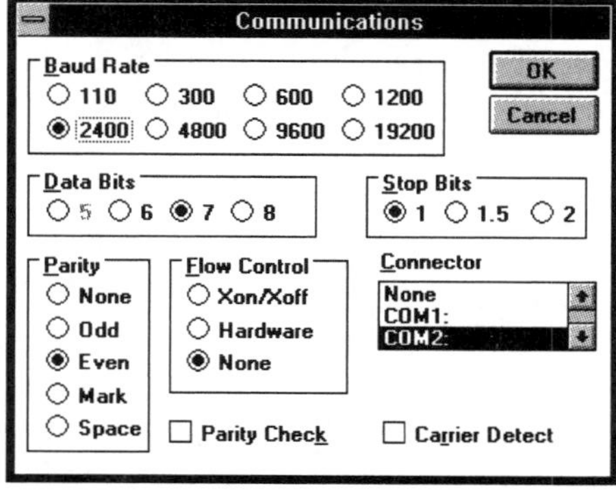

Figure 14.5 The Communications dialog box

Data Bits — The number of bits of data in each "packet" transmitted. This setting is usually 7 or 8.

Stop Bits — The amount of time between transmitted characters.

Parity — The type of parity check used. A parity check uses the eighth bit in a packet to carry out simple error checking, to confirm that the character was received correctly. (The eighth bit is mathematically related to the first seven. If that relationship is no longer apparent when they arrive at your computer, Terminal knows there has been an error.) If you are using eight data bits, you *must* use a Parity of None.

Flow Control — Flow control refers to the method used to ensure that data is transmitted only when the other computer is capable of receiving it. The Xon/Xoff method uses a software signal: If Terminal—or the other computer—is receiving data faster than it can handle it, it sends a message stopping the transmission. When it has caught up it sends another message to continue. The Xon/Xoff method is the most common, so select it if you are not sure. In rare cases you may use a Hardware method or None.

Parity Check — When this feature is selected, each character transmitted with a parity error is shown as a question mark. When it is turned off, each character is displayed as it is received, even if it has a parity error. You might use this when transmitting lots of important numbers, so Terminal will use a question mark instead of a false number.

Carrier Detect — Your modem should be able to detect automatically when it makes a connection with another modem. (When a connection is made Terminal should display the word CONNECT.) However, if all the settings are correct and it *still* can't recognize a connection, try turning on this option.

Many bulletin boards and on-line services use a sort of shorthand for describing the settings you need. For instance, N-8-1 means No Parity, 8 Data Bits, 1 Stop Bit. (If you see a bulletin board advertised, but no settings are indicated, try these settings.) As for your baud rate, if a bulletin board advertisement doesn't indicate a rate, you can probably use any speed up to at least 9600. Use the advertised settings, and leave the options with their default settings.

Modem Commands

Select **Settings | Modem Commands** to see the dialog box shown in Figure 14.6. To send messages from your computer to the remote computer, Terminal must first "talk" with the modem, telling it what it wants to do. This dialog box tells Terminal how to talk to the modem.

You probably will never need to modify the settings in this dialog box: It is set up for working with a Hayes-compatible modem, and most modems these days *are* Hayes compatible. If your modem is not, select the type you have (MultiTech or TrailBlazer), or select None. The correct settings will appear for the MultiTech or TrailBlazer options, but if you select None the text boxes are emptied: You will have to enter the correct settings yourself. (You should find them in your modem's documentation.)

Important If you want to pulse dial, instead of tone dial, change the Dial Prefix entry from ATDT to ATDP. Most phone lines these days use tone or pulse, even if you have only pulse phones.

The first line, Dial (see Figure 14.6), indicates the information that should be sent to the modem when you tell Terminal to dial the call. The prefix information is sent, then the information you entered for the phone number (**Settings | Phone Number**), and then the suffix information. Unfortunately the total (excluding the ATDT or ATDP) cannot exceed 38 characters, so you can't dial a very long telephone number (see the discussion of calling cards earlier in this chapter).

Terminal sends the Hangup command when you select **Phone | Hangup**. This command is usually +++ATH. If it doesn't seem to work, look in your documentation (you may need to look for "disconnect" or "onhook").

Terminal uses the Binary TX (transmission) and Binary RX (receipt) codes to inform the modem when to expect a binary transmission. The last entry, in the

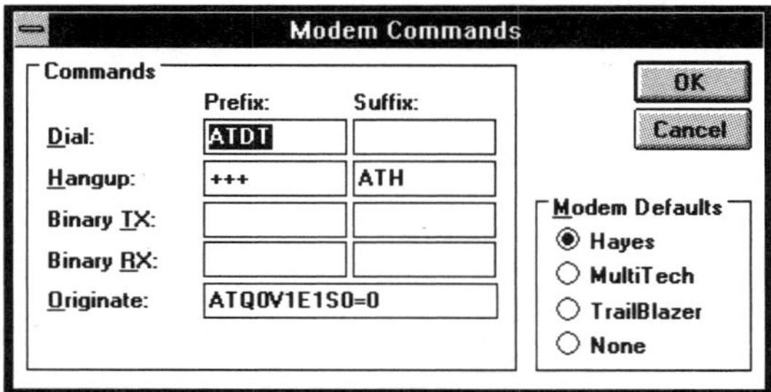

Figure 14.6 The Modem Commands dialog box

Originate text box, is the code that Terminal sends when it's telling the modem to prepare to dial a telephone number.

It's Easier Than It Sounds!

We've just explained many settings, most of which you will probably never need to change. As an example of how you would prepare your computer for dialing a remote device, here's what you would do to dial CompuServe, the nation's largest on-line service. Begin by looking in your CompuServe documentation for the local telephone number, then follow these instructions.

1. Select **Settings | Phone Number** and enter the number. You could enter a code to turn off call waiting, but it's not essential unless you are doing binary or text transfers (which you will learn about later). Click on **OK**.
2. Select **Settings | Communications**. Select the COM port to which your modem is connected. Then select the fastest baud rate your modem can use, 7 data bits, 1 stop bit, Even Parity, and Xon/Xoff Flow Control. Click on **OK**.
3. Select **Phone | Dial** to call CompuServe.
4. When you get the **CONNECT** message, press **Enter**.
5. If you are prompted for a **Host ID**, type **compuserve** and press **Enter**.
6. When CompuServe prompts for your User ID, type the **User ID** they provided you with, and press **Enter**.
7. When CompuServe prompts for your Password, type the **Password** they provided you with, and press **Enter**.

That's it—you're connected to CompuServe. Incidentally, using this method you can't press **Ctrl-C** when you see the CONNECT message, as some of CompuServe's documentation suggests, but pressing **Enter** usually works. If you want to use Ctrl-C, assign ^C to one of the function keys. Or select **Settings | Terminal Preferences** and turn off the "Use Function, Arrow, and Ctrl Keys for Windows" option. If you turn this off, you won't be able to use the arrow keys to select and copy text.

Saving Your Settings

Once you have completed your settings you can save them in a file. Select **File | Save** to see a typical Save As dialog box. Terminal will automatically save the file with a .TRM extension. The next time you want to call the same device, you can simply open this file instead of rebuilding the settings.

▼ *Note* Terminal is a great example of an application for which you might want several Program Manager icons, one for each bulletin board or computer you dial up. In the Program Item Properties dialog box's Command Line text box enter TERMINAL.EXE followed by the name of the .TRM file. For instance, TERMINAL.EXE COMPUSRV.TRM will open a file named COMPUSRV.TRM.

Once you have created some settings files you can use your existing files as templates for other files. If you want to dial up a system that has settings similar to one of your other files, open that file, make the necessary changes (the phone number, at least!), and save it using the **File | Save As** command.

Placing a Call

If you have entered all the settings we have covered so far, you are ready to begin a data communications session. We haven't yet explained how to set up the function keys so you can enter several characters or words with one click of the mouse. Nor have we explained how to prepare your system for transferring text or binary files. (If you want to know about these options before you learn about placing a call, skip forward and return when you have read those sections.) However, you have done enough to call a remote device and to communicate with it using your keyboard.

▼ *Note* You can make Terminal automatically open and dial using Windows Recorder. (See Chapter 15 for more information.)

When you are ready to make a call, simply select **Phone | Dial**. Terminal begins by sending the Originate command to the modem (from the Modem Communications dialog box). Terminal displays the Originate command (and all subsequent commands and text that it transmits in the windows). An OK response appears, and Terminal then sends the Dial Prefix, the number in the Phone Number dialog box, and the Dial Suffix (if any). While your modem is dialing you will see a small dialog box (clicking on this box's **Cancel** button stops the dialing). Then, if all goes well, you will hear the other device answer and see CONNECT followed by a baud rate.

▼ *Note* If you haven't entered a number in the Phone Number dialog box, Terminal displays that box when you select **Phone | Dial**. You can enter a number and click on **OK** to dial.

You may also hear a hissing sound from your modem. Your system is now connected to the other device, and you can continue, following the instructions in your documentation or on screen. Some systems expect a response from you before they continue after CONNECT. Try pressing **Enter** or **Ctrl-C**.

Once connected you communicate by typing. Usually a remote system will prompt you, by displaying a menu of options, for instance. You then type the number or letter corresponding to the option you want to choose, and—usually—press Enter. Using systems such as bulletin boards and on-line information services is reasonably easy. It's just a matter of following directions (although, admittedly, some directions are better than others!).

You can also transmit data to the other system in a few other ways. You can use the **Edit|Paste** command (**Ctrl-V**) to copy the text in the Clipboard into the Terminal window and transmit it immediately. You may be able to paste text in order to send messages to the remote system, depending on how that system operates. You can compose them off-line in a word processor, then dial the system and paste them into Terminal, thus saving on-line time and money. You can only paste text from the Clipboard, not graphics. If you want to send a graphics file, you will have to use a binary transfer, explained later.

The **Edit|Send** (**Ctrl-Shift-Ins**) command may be useful when you want to retransmit something. For instance, if you read an on-line message and decide to forward it to someone else, you can highlight the message using the mouse or the Shift and arrow keys, and then select **Edit|Send**. Terminal transmits all the highlighted text. (If you turned off the "Use Function, Arrow, and Ctrl Keys for Windows" check box in the Terminal Preferences dialog box, you won't be able to use arrow keys to highlight text, although you can use the Ctrl-Shift-Ins keyboard shortcut.) You can scroll back up the window and select text, even though you won't be able to see the bottom of the text, where the text is being transmitted.

Communication Problems?

What if you set up your session and it just doesn't work? Here are a few common problems and their probable solutions.

- Terminal doesn't display anything when you select Phone|Dial. You connected to the wrong **Connector** (**Communications** dialog box).
- Terminal displays ERROR under the Dial Prefix/Telephone Number line and doesn't dial the number. You have too many characters in the **Phone Number** dialog box (or, perhaps, in the Dial Prefix and Dial Suffix text boxes in the Modem Communications dialog boxes).
- Your settings are correct and the modem dials, but it can't make a connection and Terminal doesn't display CONNECT. Try selecting **Carrier Detect** (**Communications** dialog box).

- Terminal displays gibberish ("Åîter cèoice î_íâer!," for instance). Your **Baud Rate, Data Bits, Stop Bits, Parity,** or **Flow Control** choices are wrong (**Communications** dialog box).
- Terminal doesn't display each character you type. Turn **Local Echo** *on* (**Terminal Preferences** dialog box).
- Terminal displays every character you type twice. Turn **Local Echo** *off* (**Terminal Preferences** dialog box).
- Terminal displays all the incoming data on one line, overwriting a line each time a new one arrives. Turn **Inbound CR->CR/LF** *on* (**Terminal Preferences** dialog box).
- Terminal displays a blank line between each incoming line. Turn **Inbound CR->CR/LF** *off* (**Terminal Preferences** dialog box).
- Terminal adds a blank line each time you press Enter. Turn **Outbound CR->CR/LF** *off* (**Terminal Preferences** dialog box).

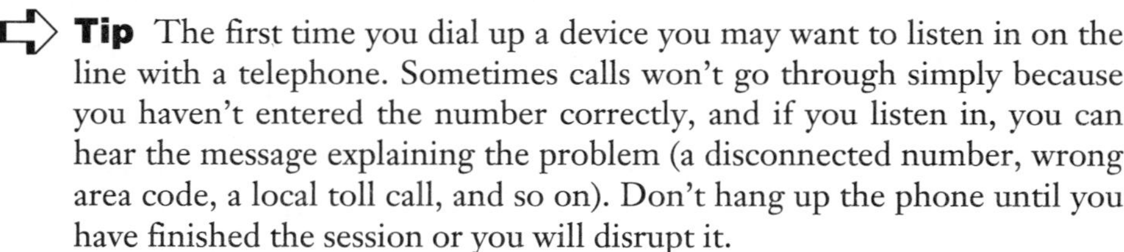

Tip The first time you dial up a device you may want to listen in on the line with a telephone. Sometimes calls won't go through simply because you haven't entered the number correctly, and if you listen in, you can hear the message explaining the problem (a disconnected number, wrong area code, a local toll call, and so on). Don't hang up the phone until you have finished the session or you will disrupt it.

Ending a Session

When you have finished working with a remote device, you should use the correct log-off procedure. You are often expected to type a command such as *off* or *bye*. You should then select **Phone | Hangup** to put the modem "on-hook." If the remote device terminates the session for some reason, or if a "glitch" drops your phone line, you should still use the Phone | Hangup command even though you are not really off-hook.

Don't end communications sessions by selecting Phone | Hangup if there is a proper log-off procedure. The remote device will keep the line off-hook for a while, not realizing that you have gone. In the meantime you have locked up one of its incoming lines, and it is calculating on-line charges as if you were still connected.

When you close Terminal, it will ask if you want to save your settings. If you plan to call the same device again, you should save them so you can use them next time.

Saving Communications Data

There are several ways to save data from a communications session.

- Print it.
- Copy text from the Terminal window to the Clipboard.
- Save text directly to a file.
- Save binary data to a file.

Printing Data

If you want to print the data that appears in your Terminal window—incoming and outgoing data—you can select **Settings | Printer Echo** command. You probably won't want to do this with every session. Rather, you can turn this option on when you need it—before or during a communications session—and then turn it off when you don't.

The data isn't sent to your printer immediately. It is held in Print Manager and isn't printed until you select Settings | Printer Echo again or close Terminal. You can, however, send the data directly to the printer by turning off Print Manager in the Control Panel. If you do turn off Print Manager, the last page of text is not printed until you select Settings | Printer Echo.

If you save your settings after turning on Printer Echo, your next session will automatically send data to your printer. Remember that you can also copy text from the Terminal window into a word processor, or use a receive-text transfer to automatically place all incoming text in a file. (More about these options later.)

Copying Text with the Clipboard

When you type text, or when text arrives from the remote device, Terminal displays it in the window. The lines scroll upward as new lines arrive. They scroll out of the window but they are not yet lost. Terminal saves these lines in its *buffer*, and you can go back to view earlier lines.

You can use the scroll bars to move around in the buffer to find the text you want to select. You can also use these keys.

Move to the top left of the window.	**Ctrl-Home**
Move to the bottom right of the window.	**Ctrl-End**
Move to the left of the window.	**Home**
Move to the right of the window.	**End**
Move up one screen.	**PgUp**
Move down one screen.	**PgDn**

If the "Use Function, Arrow, and Ctrl Keys for Windows" check box is *not* selected in the Terminal Preferences dialog box, you won't be able to use the Ctrl-Home or Ctrl-End commands.

Remember that you can't go back through the session indefinitely. Terminal saves at least 25 lines of the session in its *buffer*, so you can view them in the window. You can tell Terminal to store up to 399 lines. More than that, however, and the text is lost.

You can use the Clipboard to copy text to another application. You can use the mouse or, if the "Use Function, Arrow, and Ctrl Keys for Windows" check box is selected, the Shift and arrow keys to select the text you want to copy. Place the cursor where you want to begin, press and hold **Shift**, and use the **arrow keys** to highlight the text. Then press **Edit|Copy** or **Ctrl-C** to copy the text into the Clipboard. You may then switch to another application and use its Edit|Paste command to paste the text.

The **Edit|Select All** command selects all the text in the buffer (all the text still displayed in the Terminal window) so you can copy it all into the Clipboard and to another application.

Terminal's buffer takes up memory. It rarely becomes a problem, but if you want to free that memory, or if you simply want to remove the text from the window, select **Edit|Clear Buffer**.

Text and Binary Transfers

You can use Terminal's file-transfer commands to save data directly into a file. The text transfer command will save all the text that appears on your screen in an ASCII file on your hard drive. You can also "download" files from the remote system to your computer. You might do this if you want to copy a shareware program from a bulletin board, for instance. Of course you can do the opposite, also, "uploading" files from your computer to the remote computer.

Remember that Windows lets you multitask. You can work in another application while Terminal continues working. For instance, you might be downloading a file from a bulletin board. While waiting, you could open a word processor and write a memo. Modify the word processor's window so that it sits over the Terminal window, allowing you to see the status line. That way you will see when the file transfer is complete.

Tip Move the Terminal window, pushing the horizontal scroll bar and function keys down off the screen. That way the status line will take up only one line at the bottom of the screen, leaving the rest of the screen for your other application.

Caution Do not use a DOS application in Standard mode, or a DOS application that has been set to Exclusive and is running full screen in 386 Enhanced mode. In both cases your communications session will be locked up. An Exclusive DOS application can run in a window, however, without stopping the communications session. (See Chapter 7 for more information.)

File Transfers

There are two ways to transfer files: as *text* or as *binary* files. When you transfer a text file, the individual characters are transmitted, as if you had typed them. For instance, if you are transferring a text file to be used as a message, Terminal has to find the file, open it, convert the binary data to text, and transmit it. You can transmit only ASCII files, which are simple text files that contain standard keyboard characters and a few formatting characters, such as carriage returns and linefeeds. Windows Notepad creates ASCII files, but just about any word processor can do so. Windows Write, for instance, lets you save files in ASCII format.

A file on your hard disk is stored as binary data. Terminal can transmit and receive files in binary format, without converting them first. The files may be graphics, word processing, spreadsheets, or any other DOS file. You can transmit ASCII files as either binary or text files. All others must be transmitted as binary files.

Use text transfer when you are more interested in speed than ensuring against a few errors. Text transfers are good for sending short messages, for instance. Use binary transfers if the file is anything but ASCII, or if you want to be sure the transmitted message is absolutely correct—binary transfers use more accurate error-checking then text transfers.

Text Transfers

Before you transfer a text file select **Settings | Text Transfer** to see the dialog box shown in Figure 14.7. When you first open the box the Standard Flow Control option button is selected, and the dialog box looks as it does in the figure. You can change the setting, though. Figures 14.8 and 14.9 show how the box changes if you select the other options. This text box lets you define how Terminal handles text transfers, and lets you define a transmission-verification method if necessary. These are the various options.

Standard Flow Control Uses the flow control method specified in the Communications dialog box.

Character at a Time Sends the data one character at a time.

Delay Between Characters Lets you specify the delay between characters, in tenths of a second. This slow transmission may ensure a clean copy, but there is no verification.

Wait for Character Echo One character is sent, and then the computer waits for the other system to echo the character back. Terminal can then verify that both characters are the same. Not all systems echo characters reliably, though, so you may want to use the next method.

Line at a Time Sends the data one line at a time.

Delay Between Lines Lets you specify the delay between lines in tenths of a second. This slow transmission may ensure a clean copy, but there is no verification.

Wait for Prompt String One line is sent, and then the computer waits for the other system to prompt for the next line. You can specify the string of characters that should be received as an indication. The default is the carriage return (^M).

Wrap Outgoing Text at Column Use this if the file you want to send uses word wrap rather than a line break or paragraph break at the end of each line, or if the file's lines are longer than the system to which you are sending it can handle. Always enter a number one less than the page width (131 instead of 132, 79 instead of 80), to allow space for an end-of-line marker.

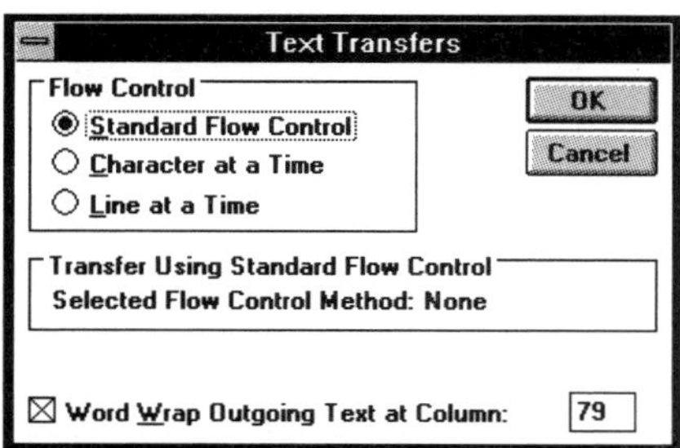

Figure 14.7 The Text Transfers dialog box with Standard Flow Control selected

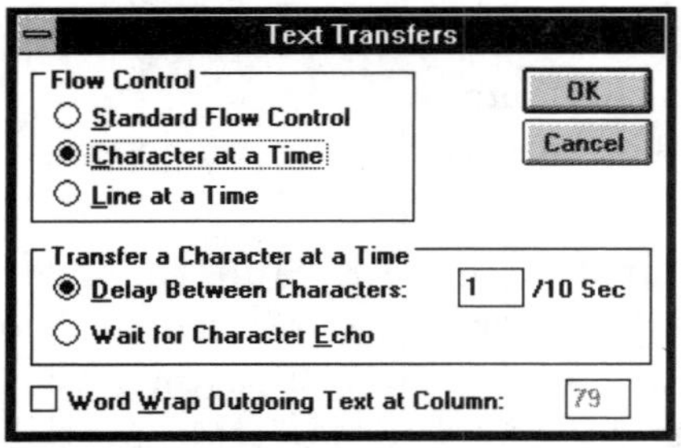

Figure 14.8 The Text Transfers dialog box with Character at a Time selected

The Character and Line methods are slower than the Standard Flow Control option, but you may want to use them if you have trouble with text transfers losing data. You can normally leave these options with their default settings.

RECEIVING TEXT FILES

When we talk about receiving a text file, we really mean receiving text and placing it in an ASCII file. The text may not originally come from a single file—you can use this method to save all the text that you receive, a sort of record of the communications session. Or you can selectively receive—saving information from a database in a file, for instance, or a message you have received.

Select **Transfers|Receive Text File**. The dialog box that appears is a typical file box, like a File Open dialog box. Select the file to which you want to save the data, or simply select the directory into which you want to place it, and type a name in the File Name text box. If you select an existing file you can add the incoming text to the end of the file—click on the **Append File** check box. Or you can copy over the existing file with the new text: Click on **OK** and Terminal asks if you want to replace the existing file. Click on **Yes** and the old file will be replaced with the new text as it is received.

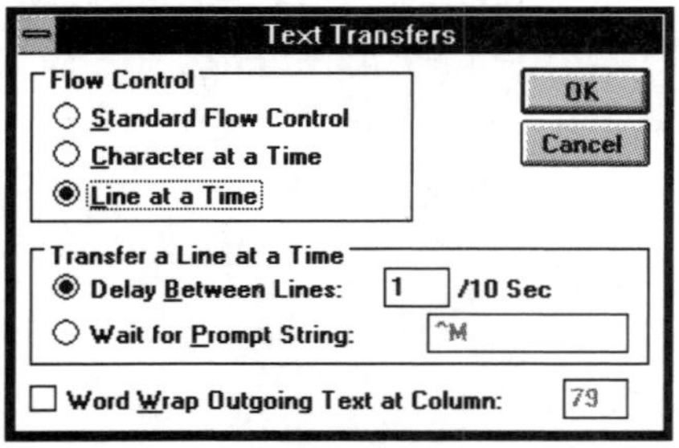

Figure 14.9 The Text Transfers dialog box with Line at a Time selected

Important If you enter a new filename, you *must* include the extension (.TXT usually), or Terminal won't let you continue with the transfer.

You can also select **Save Controls** to make Terminal save all the data it receives, even non-ASCII formatting characters. And **Table Format** tells Terminal to create a table by replacing two or more consecutive spaces with tabs. Use this if you are receiving columns of data.

When you finally click on the **OK** button, Terminal displays a special status bar at the bottom of the window, as shown in Figure 14.10. This shows you the name of the file in which you are saving the text and the amount of text saved so far (in KB). It has two buttons. Clicking on **Pause** stops saving the information but retains the status bar. Pause doesn't stop the text arriving at your computer—it simply tells Terminal to stop saving it. The button changes to **Resume**: Click on it to continue saving the text. This is especially useful when you only want to save portions of the communications session. For instance, you have called your library to look for information on their electronic encyclopedia. You are searching for several things and only want to save the information, not the "conversation" you have with the library's system. You can use the Pause and Resume buttons to select exactly the information you want, clicking on **Resume** when the remote system begins sending relevant information and **Pause** when it finishes.

Clicking on the **Stop** button tells Terminal to stop saving the text entirely. If you want to restart, you must select **Transfers | Receive Text Files** again. If you don't have a mouse, you can use the **Transfers | Pause**, **Transfers | Resume**, and **Transfers | Stop** commands.

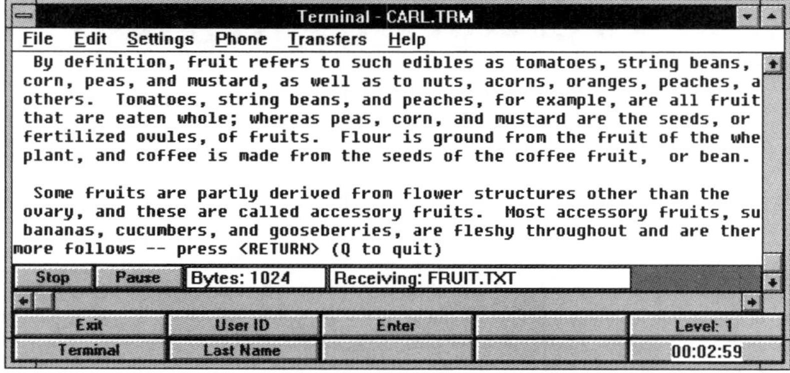

Figure 14.10 The text-transfer status bar while saving text

SENDING TEXT FILES

Sending text files is a simple procedure. When the remote system is ready to receive a file, select **Transfers | Send Text File**. Select the file you want to transmit. You may also select the **Append LF** check box (to add linefeeds to each carriage return), or **Strip LF** check box (to remove linefeeds from each carriage return). You probably won't need to adjust these. Terminal assumes that the receiving system automatically adds linefeeds, so it automatically selects the Strip LF check box. If, when you transfer the text, each line is typed over the previous one, or if the text is double-spaced, you will have to start again and change the Append or Strip settings.

When you have selected the file you want to send, click on **OK**. Terminal displays a status bar at the bottom of the window (see Figure 14.11) and begins transmitting the file. The other computer doesn't know the difference between the text being sent to it and your typing, although of course a text-file transfer is much quicker. Notice the indicator on the status bar that shows you how much of the file has been transmitted. This gives you an idea of how long it's going to take to complete. This status bar also has the **Stop** and **Pause** buttons. Pause stops the text transmission temporarily. The button changes to **Resume**, which you can click to continue. The Stop button stops the transmission entirely. To continue you would have to start over by selecting Transfers | Send Text File. Again, if you don't have a mouse, use the **Transfers | Pause**, **Transfers | Resume**, and **Transfers | Stop** commands.

VIEWING TEXT FILES

You can use the **Transfers | View Text File** to read a text file. The text is scrolled through the Terminal window but is not transmitted. You could use this feature to

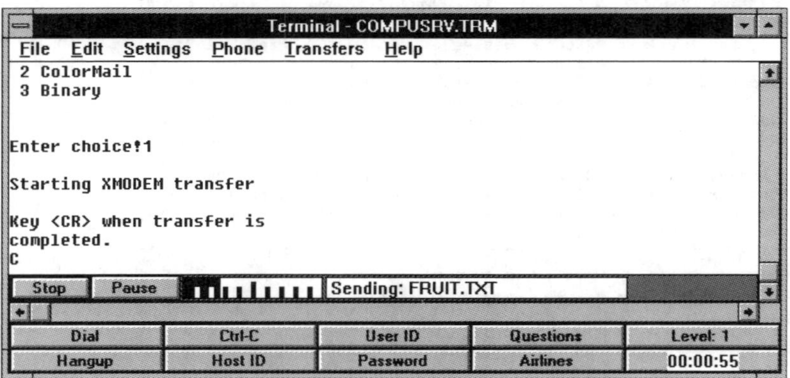

Figure 14.11 The text-transfer status bar while transmitting text

read a text file you have just received, or one that you want to send, to make sure it contains the correct information. (If it doesn't, you will have to use Notepad to edit it: You can't edit it from Terminal.)

The View Text File dialog box has a couple of options. These are used to modify a file that may have arrived with incorrect linefeed/carriage return. If you set the CR->CR/LF options correctly in the Terminal Preferences dialog box you probably won't need to use them. If you select **Append LF**, Terminal adds a linefeed each time it sees a carriage return: Use this if each line overwrites the last. **Strip LF** makes Terminal remove the linefeeds following carriage returns. Use this if the file is double-spaced.

When you click on **OK** Terminal displays the document in the window, wrapping long lines automatically to fit the Column setting in the Terminal Preferences dialog box. Terminal also displays a status bar at the bottom of the window: Use the **Pause** button to stop the scrolling momentarily so you can read the file, then click **Resume** to continue. Click **Stop** to end file viewing at any time. Notice also that the status bar has an indicator showing how much of the file has been viewed so far.

Binary Transfers

If you want to transfer a file that isn't an ASCII file, or if you want to transfer an ASCII file but use more accurate error-checking methods, you must use a binary transfer. For instance, you may want to transfer a piece of clip art from a bulletin board, a shareware program, or a device driver. You can use a binary transfer with any computer file, whether it's a program, word processor, spreadsheet, graphic, or any other kind of file.

Begin by selecting **Settings | Binary Transfers** to see the dialog box shown in Figure 14.12. You can select from two different types of data transmission methods (or *protocols*). **XModem/CRC** uses eight data bits, with a parity set to None. (You don't have to reset your Communications dialog box entries: Terminal automatically makes adjustments during transmission.) This protocol will use a cyclic redundancy check (CRC) method of error checking or, if the remote can't use CRC, a checksum method. **Kermit** uses seven or eight data bits, with parity set to Even, Odd, or None.

These specifics normally won't concern you. Simply find which of the two methods the remote system can support, and select that one. Most systems will

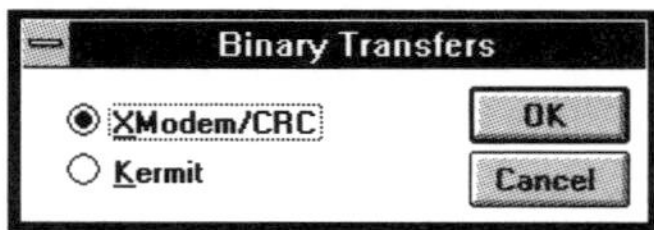

Figure 14.12 The Binary Transfers dialog box

have several options: CompuServe, for instance, can use seven methods, including these two.

RECEIVING BINARY FILES

Working with binary files is similar to working with text files. Select **Transfers | Receive Binary File**. Select the file to which you want to save the data (if you want to overwrite a file), or simply select the directory into which you want to place it, and type a name in the File Name text box. The filename doesn't have to be the same as the file you are receiving—you can enter any name you want.

▼ ***Note*** If you enter a new filename, you *must* include the extension, or Terminal won't let you continue with the transfer.

When you click on the **OK** button, Terminal displays a special status bar at the bottom of the window similar to the one used for text transmissions. It shows the name of the file to which you are saving the data and the amount of data saved so far (in KB). It has only one button, **Stop**, which stops the data transmission entirely. There's no Pause button because you cannot pause and resume binary transfers.

Terminal will wait a short while, but if it doesn't receive any data it assumes there was some problem with the setup and halts the operation. You may have specified the wrong type of binary transfer.

On the other hand everything may be set up correctly and Terminal may receive data, but problems can occur during transmission, perhaps due to a bad line. Terminal tries to complete the transmission. Using the XModem/CRC method it will try up to 20 times to transmit or receive; with Kermit it will make five attempts. These retries are indicated in the status bar. But if Terminal still can't complete the transfer, it cancels the operation.

While receiving a binary file you can minimize Terminal and continue working in another application. When the transfer finishes or fails, the icon will flash. You can also work in another application's window, on top of the Terminal window, so you can view the status bar. (Remember the earlier caution about working with DOS applications.)

Here's an example of a binary transfer. We entered the CompuServe MSL forum (see the end of the chapter for more information about the Windows-related forums) by typing **go msl** and pressing **Enter**.

```
Enter choice number!go msl
```

CompuServe opened the library and displayed this menu:

```
MICROSOFT SOFTWARE LIBRARY
 1 BROWSE thru files
 2 SCAN
 3 KEYWORD list
 4 DOWNLOAD a file
 5 READ a file
Enter choice !1
```

We typed **1** and pressed **Enter** to browse through a list of the files. CompuServe asked two questions, but we pressed **Enter** in both cases.

```
Enter keywords (e.g. modem)
or <CR> for all:
Oldest files in days
or <CR> for all:
```

Then CompuServe began showing a list of all the files in the library. We wanted to see the following file:

```
[76703,714]
S13442.ZIP/binary          04-Jun-92 167107            Accesses: 17
    Title   : TrueType Font Files Spec (1 of 3)
    Keywords: S13442 Q85202 TTSPEC1
    This file contains part 1 of the TrueType Font Files Specifications
    as a Word for Windows 2.0 document.
Press <CR> for next or type CHOICES !choices
```

Notice that the filename is S13442.ZIP. We typed **choices**, pressed **Enter** and saw the following:

```
 1 (REA)  Read this file
 2 (DOW)  Download this file
 3 (DES)  Description
 4 (TOP)  Top Access Menu
Enter choice or <CR> for next !2
```

We typed **2**, for download, and pressed **Enter**. We then saw the following options:

```
Access Protocol Menu
Transfer protocols available -
 1 XMODEM
 2 CompuServe B+ and original B
 3 CompuServe A
 4 DC2/DC4 (Capture)
 5 YMODEM
```

```
  6 CompuServe QB (B w/send ahead)
  7 Kermit
  0 Abort transfer request
Enter choice !1
```

We typed **1**, for XModem, because we had already selected the XModem transfer type with the Settings | Binary Transfers command. CompuServe prepared for transfer and displayed this:

```
Starting XMODEM send.
Please initiate XMODEM receive
and press <CR> when the transfer
is complete.
```

We selected **Transfers | Receive Binary File** and entered the name TTYPE.ZIP (remember, no need to use the file's original name). When we clicked on **OK** the transfer began. When it was completed, we simply pressed **Enter** and continued with the CompuServe session. It's that simple.

Incidentally, notice that the file is a "zip" file, a compressed format. Most files on bulletin boards are compressed to save time and money when you transfer them. This file needs the PKUNZIP utility to uncompress it. Other files may be executable files that automatically uncompress themselves when you run them. PKUNZIP is a popular shareware utility that you can get from a variety of sources, such as shareware catalogs, colleagues, or the bulletin boards.

SENDING BINARY FILES

Sending binary files is just as simple as receiving them. When the remote system is ready to receive a file, select **Transfers | Send Binary File**. Select the file you want to transmit and click on **OK**. Terminal displays a status bar at the bottom of the window, similar to the one used for text transfers, and begins transmitting the file. The status bar contains the name of the file you are transmitting, an indicator that shows you how much of the file has been transmitted, and a Stop button.

Using Function Keys

Terminal lets you use "function keys" at the bottom of the page, as you saw in Figure 14.1. You can assign commands to these keys, then carry out the commands by clicking on the "key" with the mouse, or by pressing **Ctrl-Alt-*functionkey***. To operate the function key on the top left you would press **Ctrl-Alt-F1**, for instance. (You can use these key sequences even if you have turned off the "Use Function,

Arrow, and Ctrl Keys for Windows" option in the Terminal Preferences dialog box.) When you save your settings file these function key commands will be saved, so you can use a different set for each device you communicate with.

The top row of keys is controlled by F1 through F4, the bottom row by F5 through F8. You can use these keys to carry out complicated log-on procedures, or enter "navigation" commands to help you find your way through a bulletin board or on-line service. Not only do these keys make working on-line easier, but they can also save you money: The more quickly and efficiently you enter commands, the less time you spend connected, and the lower your "connect" and long-distance charges.

Select **Settings | Function Keys** to see the dialog box shown in Figure 14.13. This box lets you assign a label and command to each function key: The first four lines are for the top row (F1 through F4), and the rest are for the bottom row. Notice the **Key Level** area. You can assign four different function-key levels, a total of 32 different commands. (When you are in a communications session, you can click on the **Level** button on the top row of function keys to change the level with which you are working.)

Notice also the **Keys Visible** check box. When this is selected the keys will be visible at the bottom of the Terminal window. If they are not visible you can still use the Ctrl-Alt-*functionkey* method, but you won't be able to see the labels or click on the buttons with the mouse. Incidentally, deselecting the Keys Visible check box does not immediately remove the keys, but the next time you open the settings file the keys will not be visible. However, the **Settings | Show/Hide Function Keys** commands override the Keys Visible check box, so you can always view or remove the function keys regardless of the Keys Visible setting. (The difference is that the Keys Visible setting is stored in the settings file and the Settings | Show/Hide Function Keys selection is not.)

To add a command, simply enter a Key Name, up to 17 characters, that will be displayed on the function key. Then type the command. You can use alphanumeric characters and any of these codes.

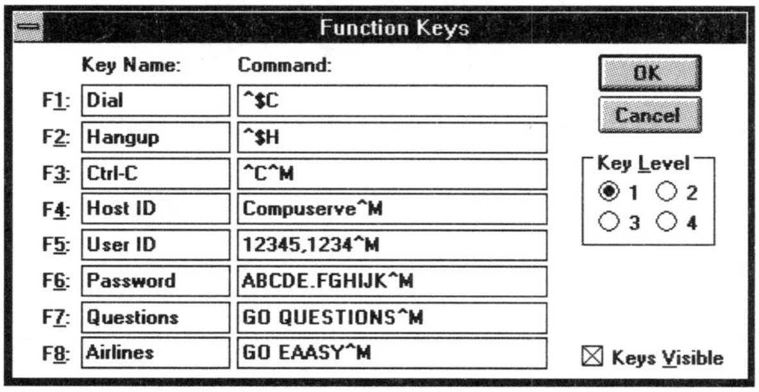

Figure 14.13 The Function Keys dialog box

Code	*Purpose*
^A to ^Z	Sends a control code (A to Z).
^C	Sends a Ctrl-C (often used to cancel operations).
^M	Sends a carriage return.
^J	Sends a linefeed.
^H	Sends a backspace.
^G	Sends a bell.
^$D*nn*	Pauses *nn* seconds before continuing.
^$B	Sends a 17-millisecond break code.
^$C	Dials the phone number (same as Phone | Dial).
^$H	Hangs up (same as Phone | Hangup).
^$L1 to ^$L4	Moves to another function-key level.
^^	Sends a caret (^).
^@	Sends a Null character.
^[*n*	Sends an escape-code sequence where *n* is the code or codes.

What, then, could you program on these keys? You might want to put an entire dialing and log-on sequence on one key. Here's how the sequence might go for connecting with an on-line service.

```
^$C^$D11^C^$D03userid^M^$D02password^M
```

This dials the telephone number you entered into the Phone Number dialog box (**^$C**); waits for 11 seconds for the call to be put through and a connection made (**^$D11**); sends a Ctrl-C (**^C**); waits for three seconds to be prompted for a user ID (**^$D03**); types the user ID and a carriage return (***userid*^M**); waits for two seconds to be prompted for the password (**^$D02**); and then types the password and a carriage return (***password*^M**).

▼ ***Note*** Don't include a password in a function-key command unless you are absolutely sure of the security of your computer. Ideally passwords should never be written down. Realistically, we all know they are. Limit your risk by making sure the password is not written where another person can find it—including in a Terminal function key if other people have access to your computer.

Timing is important when creating a sequence like this. Make the pauses too short and the commands are issued before the remote computer can understand them. Make the pause too long and the command may be misunderstood or ignored. If the remote computer with which you are working is not fairly consistent with its timing, you may find it easier to break the log-on sequence into several steps, each on its own key. Including the dialing in the string leaves a lot of room for error because the speed of phone connections can vary greatly. Also a dial-up service may vary its log-on procedure slightly from day to day, making the function-key command unusable at certain times.

Unfortunately you can put only 42 characters on a function key, so you may have to put a full log-on command on two keys. You might put the dialing on a separate key (or just use the menu option) and create a function key that you can click as soon as you see CONNECT.

You can also put navigation codes on function keys. For instance, on CompuServe you can jump around the system using a GO *name* command. If you want to go to the Health forum, for instance, you would type GO GOODHEALTH and press **Enter**. It's much easier to name a function key Health and type GO GOODHEALTH ^M into the Command text box.

You might want to put various control-key commands on function keys. These commands vary among on-line systems. For instance, Ctrl-U might delete everything you have typed since you last pressed **Enter**. You could label a key Delete and put ^U on the function key. On some systems Ctrl-S might halt the information being sent by the other system and Ctrl-Q resume the flow. You could label two keys Halt and Resume and put ^S and ^Q on them, respectively.

You could also put "addresses" on function keys. If you want to send a message by MCIMail or CompuServe, it's quicker and easier to click on a function key than look up the person's "address."

Tip Before dialing an on-line service, plan what you will do once connected. Then assign commands to the function keys so you can use your on-line time and money more efficiently.

Using the function keys is simple. When you come to a place in your communications session where you need to use the key, simply click on it with the mouse. Or press **Ctrl-Alt-*function key***. The keyboard method works only with the current level, the keys that are displayed at the bottom of the window or—if the keys are not visible—the level shown in the Function Keys dialog box.

To use one of the keys on a different level, click on the Level key. The next level is shown each time you click.

Tip If you don't have a mouse, you can't activate the Level button to change levels. Instead, type **Alt-S K Alt-L** to see the Function Keys dialog box and move to the Key Level area. Then use the arrow keys to select the level you want and press **Enter**. Terminal will display the selected level. Or assign the ^$L*n* codes to, say, F8, so pressing **Ctrl-Alt-F8** always moves to the next level.

The key in the bottom-right corner is the **timer** key. By default it shows the current time (the time set in the Control Panel's Date & Time dialog box). But if you click on it, or select **Settings | Timer Mode**, it changes to show a digital stop watch and begins counting. If you then dial a number, the timer is reset to zero as soon as a connection is made. You can reset it to zero any time by selecting Settings | Timer Mode again. You can also see the clock by clicking on the key, and return to the timer by clicking again. (There's no way to use the keyboard to swap between the timer and clock except by resetting the timer with the Settings | Timer Mode command.)

The timer can be a useful reminder of the amount of time you have spent in the current session racking up on-line and phone charges. Incidentally, the timer will run even if the function keys are not shown. Of course you will have to use **Settings | Show Function Keys** to see the elapsed time.

Unusual Communications Sessions

Terminal is a simple communications program designed for sessions in which you dial another device and carry out fairly simple procedures. There are two procedures for which it isn't designed but which you may be able to carry out: receiving calls dialed from the remote device and connecting two computers together directly, without using a modem.

Receiving Calls

Terminal is not set up to receive calls from other systems. However, you may be able to trick it into doing so. Prepare all the settings as normal, then try one of these options.

- In the **Settings | Modem Commands** change the Originate text box to **ats0=1**. Remove all text from the Dial Prefix and Suffix text boxes. Click on **OK**, then use Phone | Dial to dial a number (any number, even a 1). You can click the **Cancel** button after the modem has received the message (no need to wait 30 seconds). The modem should go into auto-answer mode and automatically answer the next incoming call after one ring. You can use **ats0=2** to set two rings, and so on.
- Wait until the remote system calls you. You will see RING in the Terminal window. Then type **ata** and press **Enter**. The modem should answer the incoming call.
- Use your modem's software or hardware switches to change it to "auto-answer." When another system calls, the modem should automatically answer the call and make a connection.

If your modem isn't Hayes-compatible, it may use different codes. (Check your documentation for information about "auto-answer.") If these tricks don't work, you will have to purchase a more sophisticated communications package if you need to receive data calls.

Connecting without a Modem

You can connect your computer to another without using a modem or phone line. You could, for instance, connect your desktop computer to a laptop and transfer files from one to the other. This is a quicker method than copying files onto floppy disks.

Setting up such a session is quite simple. You will need a null modem cable connected between the two computers. Null modem cables are usually quite short, so you will have a null modem connected to one computer, a standard serial cable connected to the other, and the two cables connected together.

You must then set up both computers accordingly, making sure both use the same settings. Remember to select the correct communications port in the Communications dialog box. You will also want to select **Local Echo** and turn on **CR ->CR/LF** in the Terminal Preferences dialog box.

When you are ready to begin the session, press **Enter** twice (there's no number to dial). You can then continue typing information that will appear at the other terminal and using the file transfer utilities to transfer data.

The Microsoft Forums on CompuServe

CompuServe is probably the world's largest on-line information service. Many product manufacturers maintain *forums* on CompuServe, areas that ordinary users can access to ask questions, view information, and download files. CompuServe uses navigation commands that comprise the word GO and the name of the forum you want to enter. These are the current commands for entering Windows-related forums.

GO WINNEW	Windows New Users Forum
GO WINADV	MS Windows Advanced Forum
GO MSKB	MS Knowledge Base (covers all Microsoft products)
GO MSL	MS Software Library
GO WINAPA	Windows 3rd Party A Forum (third party software developers)
GO WINAPB	Windows 3rd Party B Forum
GO WINAPC	Windows 3rd Party C Forum
GO MULTIMEDIA	Multimedia Forum

GO WINSDK	MS Windows SDK (Software Developer's Kit) Forum
GO MSWIN32	Microsoft WIN32 Forum (for software developers)
GO WINEXT	MS Windows Extensions Forum (for software developers)

There are also about 30 other forums related to specific Windows applications and shareware and software companies that sell Windows software. The MS Knowledge Base may be very useful. This contains much of the same information used by Microsoft's technical-support people to answer questions. You can use this when technical support is closed or during the day to save money: You'll pay connect charges, but you won't pay long-distance charges or be put on hold. And in many cases you will get a more complete answer to your questions.

You can download files from these forums, such as text files explaining how to carry out certain procedures, updated software drivers for various products, and Windows shareware programs. For instance, you could do a binary transfer to get a copy of SPEAK.EXE, the compressed file that contains a driver for your computer's internal speaker (allowing you to use .WAV sounds without installing a sound board).

For more information, simply type GO WINNEW at any CompuServe prompt. If you are not a CompuServe member, call 1 (800) 848-8990. You can also download the latest device drivers from the Microsoft Download Service at (206) 936-6735 or (206) 637-9009, from GEnie, or from various user-group bulletin boards on the APCUG network.

There's a new bulletin board you may also want to try, WIX (the Windows Magazine Information Exchange), a system dedicated solely to Windows. Dial 1-800-695-4882. When prompted enter WIX. When asked for your name, enter WINMAG. You can then register online. Or call 1-800-695-4775 to speak to a representative.

Terminal's Menu Options

Here's a summary of Terminal's menu options.

File | New Clears the Terminal window, allowing you to create a new settings file. If you haven't saved the previous settings, Terminal asks if you want to do so.

File | Open Lets you open an existing settings file.

File | Save Saves the current settings.

File | Save As Saves the current settings in a new settings file.

File | Print Setup Selects a printer for use by the **Settings | Printer Echo** command.

File | Exit Closes Terminal. If you haven't saved the current settings, Terminal asks if you want to do so.

Edit | Copy (Ctrl-C) Copies the selected text to the Clipboard.

Edit | Paste (Ctrl-V) Pastes text from the Clipboard to the Terminal window and transmits it to the remote device.

Edit | Send (Ctrl-Shift-Ins) Transmits the text selected in the Terminal window.

Edit | Select All Selects all the text in the Terminal window so you can copy it to the Clipboard.

Edit | Clear Buffer Clears the buffer, removing all the text from the window.

Settings | Phone Number Lets you specify the telephone number you want to call.

Settings | Terminal Emulation Lets you specify which terminal type the program should operate like during communications sessions.

Settings | Terminal Preferences Lets you specify how to handle incoming and outgoing data.

Settings | Function Keys Lets you assign commands to the function keys and to "keys" at the bottom of the window.

Settings | Text Transfers Lets you specify how Terminal should transfer ASCII text files.

Settings | Binary Transfers Lets you specify how Terminal should transfer files in binary format.

Settings | Communications Lets you set up the communications protocol.

Settings | Modem Commands Lets you modify commands sent to the modem.

Settings | Printer Echo Turns Printer Echo on and off so you can print the communications session.

Settings | Timer Mode Turns the timer on and off. If the function keys are displayed, the bottom-right key shows the elapsed time.

Settings | Show/Hide Function Keys Shows or removes the function keys from the bottom of the window.

Phone | Dial Dials the telephone number entered at Settings | Phone Number.

Phone | Hangup Tells the modem to hang up.

Transfers | Send Text File Lets you select a text file for transmission.

Transfers | Receive Text File Tells Terminal to wait for the remote system to send a text file.

Transfers | View Text File Lets you view a text file to make sure it's the one you want to send.

Transfers | Send Binary File Lets you select a binary file for transmission.

Transfers | Receive Binary File Tells Terminal to wait for the remote system to send a binary file.

Transfers | Pause Tells Terminal to pause a text transfer.

Transfers | Resume Tells Terminal to resume a text transfer.

Transfers | Stop Tells Terminal to stop a text or binary transfer.

15

Macros: Windows Recorder

Recorder is an accessory that lets you create Windows macros, files that automatically run various procedures. Why might you want to do so? You could create a demonstration, for instance, to teach users how to work with a new Windows application. You could also automate certain routine tasks. For instance, Microsoft Money 1.0—a simple accounting package—lets you create customized reports. It doesn't let you save those reports, though, so each time you want to create a specific report you must customize it all over again.

You could use Recorder to automate the report-building procedure, so that when you want to view that type of report all you need to do is press two keys or double-click on a report name. You can also use Recorder to open Terminal, load a file, and begin a communications session. Or you can use it to open several applications at once. You can also use Recorder as a sort of "glossary," similar to the ones many word processing applications have; and you can "store" long paragraphs in Recorder and use a macro to insert the stored text into a document.

You may have used other applications' macro systems. For instance, Word for Windows lets you create macros by recording keystrokes or by writing a script using a complicated macro language: You are, in effect, writing a macro *program*. Recorder is much simpler than this. There are no programming commands to learn; it simply *records* your keyboard and, if necessary, mouse actions, and plays them back when you tell it to do so.

You can then save a number of macros in a macro file. You might have one file for spreadsheet macros, one for word processing macros, one for accounting macros, and so on. Recorder is especially useful for creating macros for Windows applications that don't have their own macro language or macro generator. You can use Recorder to make simple applications more capable, by creating complicated formats with one command, for instance. One thing Recorder *can't* do for you is work with DOS applications.

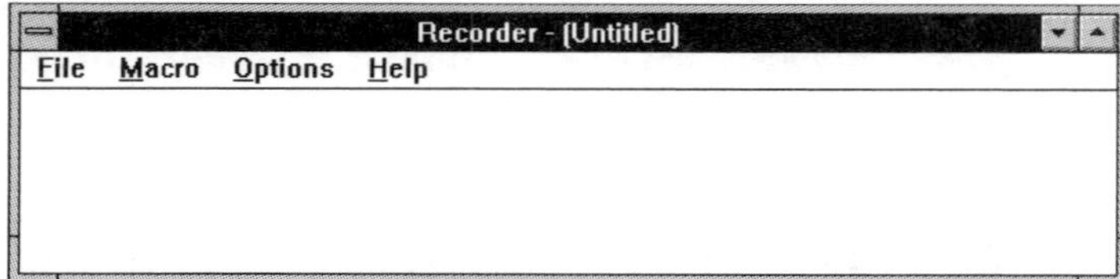

Figure 15.1 The Recorder window

Starting Recorder

Start Recorder by clicking on the Recorder icon in the Accessories program group. Or select **File | Run** and run **RECORDER**. The Recorder window that opens (as shown in Figure 15.1) is, initially at least, a blank window with a menu bar. As you create macros the names will appear in a list in the window.

Recording a Macro

To begin recording a macro, open both the application you want to work with and Recorder. Go to the application, then swap back to Recorder. Then select the **Options** menu, and make sure there is a check mark next to **Control + Break Checking**. You will probably use Ctrl-Break to stop recording, so if this option is turned off you may have problems.

Next select **Macro | Record** to see the Record Macro dialog box (shown in Figure 15.2). You must enter either a macro name or a shortcut key. You can type

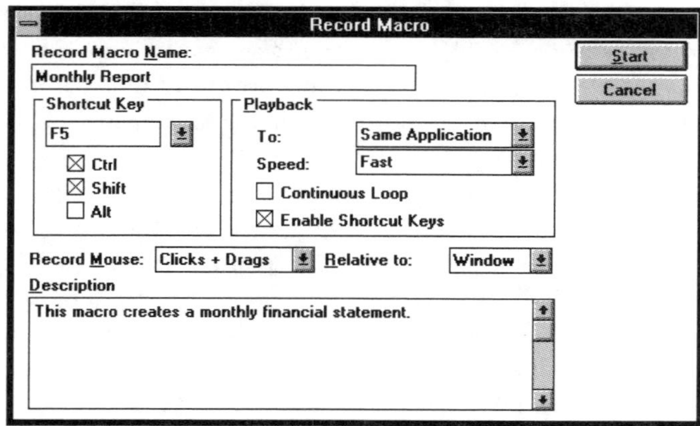

Figure 15.2 The Record Macro dialog box

up to 39 characters in the **Record Macro Name** text box. You will probably want to enter a descriptive name, such as "4th quarter estimates," "Check book summary," or "New demo." When the macro is completed, this name will appear in the Recorder window's list. You will be able to run the macro by selecting its name from the list.

You can also select a **Shortcut Key** to be combined with **Ctrl**, **Shift**, and **Alt** (select these by clicking on the check boxes). You can type any character into the Shortcut Key box, or click on the down arrow and select one of the special keys from the drop-down list box—such as the F keys, Num Lock, Down (down arrow), Caps Lock, and so on. You will be able to run the macro by pressing the shortcut keystrokes any time Recorder is open and the appropriate macro file is loaded, even if Recorder is minimized. That means you must make sure you don't create conflicting keyboard shortcuts. Make sure you don't choose a shortcut that is used by

- the application in which you are creating the macro.
- a Program Manager application icon.
- another Recorder macro in the same file.

Next, choose your Playback options. You can choose an option from the top drop-down list box to define where the macro may be used. **Same Application** means the macro will start only in the application in which you record it, the most common setting. You can, in rare circumstances, select **Any Application** to allow the macro to work in any application. You could, for instance, use Recorder to type a long phrase for you and allow it to do so in several different applications: Notepad, Windows Write, and Cardfile.

You must also select a **Speed**. You will normally want to select **Fast** so the macro gets its work done quickly. But if you are creating some type of demonstration macro, or if you want to watch the macro as it works—to make sure everything is working correctly—you can select **Recorded Speed** to run the macro at the same speed at which you recorded it. Whichever you choose, you can always change the speed later.

The **Continuous Loop** check box makes Recorder repeat the macro over and over until you press **Ctrl-Break**. This is a useful feature for a demonstration at a trade show, for instance.

 **Tip** To make sure nobody stops your demonstration, you can select **Options|Control + Break Checking** just before running the macro. Recorder won't recognize the Ctrl-Break, so the only way to stop the macro is by turning off or rebooting the computer.

The **Enable Shortcut Keys** allows you to "nest" macros by using a macro's shortcut key sequence in another macro. For instance, you build one macro that opens an application, opens a file, and goes to a specific page. The macro could then "press" a shortcut-key sequence that runs another "nested" macro, one that types a long paragraph perhaps. Of course you must create the nested macro before you can create the one that runs it. And if you modify the nested macro, you are also modifying the macro in which it runs.

You now have three **Record Mouse** options. We advise that you select **Ignore Mouse**, unless you really have to use one (if you are demonstrating a program, for instance). It's much safer to build macros using the keyboard because commands are carried out regardless of the position of a window's various components. For instance, if you record a macro with a window maximized, then run the macro with the window half the screen size, the mouse actions would be incorrect. If you must use a mouse, you can use **Clicks + Drags** (which records the mouse movements only when the mouse button is pressed), or **Everything** (which records all mouse actions). In both cases the keyboard is also recorded.

▼ ***Note*** Because mouse movements depend on the video resolution, you can't record mouse actions on one system and use the macro on a system running a different video mode. Also, if you record a macro with one keyboard setup and then run it on a different country's keyboard setup some keys may not operate as you expect.

The last drop-down list box, **Relative To**, affects the macro only if you have selected one of the mouse options. **Window** means that Recorder records the mouse coordinates relative to the top-left corner of the current window. **Screen** means it records the mouse coordinates relative to the top-left corner of the screen. If you use the Window option, the position of the window when you play the macro doesn't matter, although the size does. Because mouse movements will be related to the top-left corner, you can move the window to a different part of the screen and the mouse will still work correctly. Modify the window's size, though, and you have a problem. A window component that was, say, 200 pixels from the left side of the window may now be 400.

If you select the Screen option, both the window's size and position affect the playback. Move the window, and its components are no longer in the same position relative to the top-left corner of the screen.

Incidentally, these last two options—Record Mouse and Relative To—are the only ones that can't be changed once the macro has been recorded. All the other settings may be modified, using the **Macro | Properties** command.

The final component of the Record Macro dialog box is the **Description** box. You can type a detailed explanation of what the macro does. In fact you can type as much as you want in this box. For instance, if your macro enters a paragraph or two—or a page or two—of text into a document, you could use the Clipboard to copy the same text into the Description box.

Now you are ready to begin recording your macro. Click on **Start**. The dialog box disappears, and Recorder is minimized. Terminal returns you to the last application you were in before entering Recorder (this is why we told you to go to that application and then swap back to Recorder before opening the Record Macro dialog box). Carry out the operation you want to record. Wherever possible, use keyboard shortcuts rather than the mouse. Press **Alt-F** to open File menus, for instance, and the **arrow keys** and **Enter** to select an option. Then the position of the window won't matter.

If you are creating a demonstration, the speed at which you carry out operations is important. You don't want to do it too fast, nor too slow. In fact it might take several practice sessions to get it just right.

Don't select from list boxes while creating a macro if at all possible. Rather, type the entry you need in the associated text box. That way the macro will still work even if the contents of the list box change their order (if, for example, the box now contains more or fewer filenames).

Incidentally, if you need to include a Ctrl-Break in a macro, you will have to turn off **Options | Control + Break Checking** before you select the **Macro | Record** command; and also remember to turn it off before running the macro. Leave the Recorder icon visible so you can click on it to end recording.

Stopping Recording

When you have finished your procedure, you can use one of two methods to stop recording: You can press **Ctrl-Break**, or, if the Recorder icon is visible, you can click on it. Either way the Recorder dialog box appears (see Figure 15.3). Once this box appears recording has stopped, and nothing you do will be recorded. You could go to another application and carry out some procedure—go to File Manager and look for a specific file, for example—then return to the box and continue.

Select **Save Macro** to stop recording and save the procedures you have recorded. Select **Resume Recording** to remove the box and continue where you

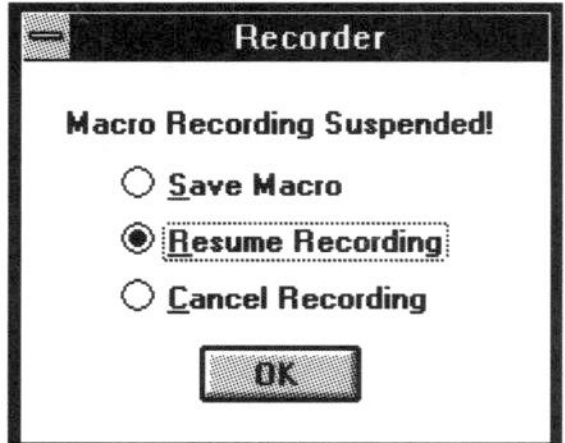

Figure 15.3 The Recorder dialog box

were in the procedure, or **Cancel Recording** to stop the recording entirely. You will lose all the work you have done and will have to start all over again if you still want to create the macro. By the way, double-clicking on these option buttons is the same as clicking once and clicking on **OK**.

If you are recording mouse actions, don't use the mouse to stop the recording. And even if you aren't recording mouse buttons, don't use the mouse if it means you have to use a keyboard method to see the icon first. If you are not recording mouse movements, however, you could use the mouse to minimize applications so you could get to the Recorder icon. Remember that all keyboard actions will be recorded and can't be removed.

Saving Files

Each time you record a macro, Recorder adds it to the list in its window. You should then select **File | Save** to save the macro in a file. Group macros according to when you are likely to use them. You might have a file of spreadsheet macros, a file of word processing macros, another with database macros, and so on. Macro files are saved with the .REC extension.

You can also merge macro files. Open the first file, select **File | Merge**, and select the file you want to merge with. When you click on **OK** Recorder copies the macros from that file into the current one. Use **File | Save** or **File | Save As** to save the changes. Figure 15.4 shows Recorder with a list of macros. Notice that the scroll bar appears on the right side if necessary, and that the macros are not in alphabetical order: They are stored in the order in which they were created.

Tip You can sort macros into alphabetical order using a rather laborious process of copying, merging, and deleting files.

Recorder - APPLCATN.REC
File Macro Options Help
ctrl+shift+P Business Profit & Loss
ctrl+shift+L Liquid Assets
ctrl+1
ctrl+2
ctrl+3
ctrl+4
ctrl+Scroll Lock Snapshot
Account #3
ctrl+alt+Q Last Quarter

Figure 15.4 The Recorder window with a list of macros

Using Your Macros

If you want to use a macro, the first thing you must do is open Recorder and open the appropriate macro file. You may want to create a Program Manager application icon for each Recorder file. For instance, if you have a Recorder file with macros that work only in Microsoft Money, copy the Recorder icon (by holding **Ctrl** and dragging the icon) and place it next to the Microsoft Money icon. Then hold down **Alt** and double-click on the copy. In the Program Item Properties dialog box type the name of the macro file (MSMONEY.REC, for instance) after RECORDER.EXE. Click on **Run Minimized**, then close the dialog box.

Now, when you want to work in Money, hold **Shift** and double-click on the Recorder icon first. Windows will open Recorder and minimize it at the bottom of your screen. Then double-click on the Money icon to open the application and begin. You can now start an icon by pressing the shortcut keys. You can also use any of the window-swapping methods to display the Recorder window and select a macro. Just click on the one you want, then select **Macro | Run**. Or you can double-click on the macro name.

If you recorded the macro to be played back to the "Same Application," Windows moves to that application regardless of the one in which you were before you selected the macro. For instance, if you recorded a macro for Write, you can press the shortcut keys while you are in Program Manager if you wish—Recorder will go to Write and run the macro. If you recorded an "Any Application" macro, Recorder will run it from the application that is active at the point at which you pressed the shortcut, or the application that was active immediately before you went to Recorder.

▼ *Note* If you create a "Same Application" macro and that application is not present, Windows may seem to "lock up." It will eventually begin running again, but you can press **Ctrl-Break** to continue immediately.

▼ *Note* The **Options | Shortcut Keys** command lets you turn off the shortcut-key method of starting macros. Use this if you are working with an application that uses the same shortcut keys. You can also use the **Macro | Properties** command to change a macro's shortcut key so it doesn't conflict with others.

You can halt a macro at any time by pressing **Ctrl-Break**, as long as the **Options | Ctrl-Break Checking** option has a check mark next to it. Recorder displays a dialog box asking you to confirm the cancellation. The Ctrl-Break

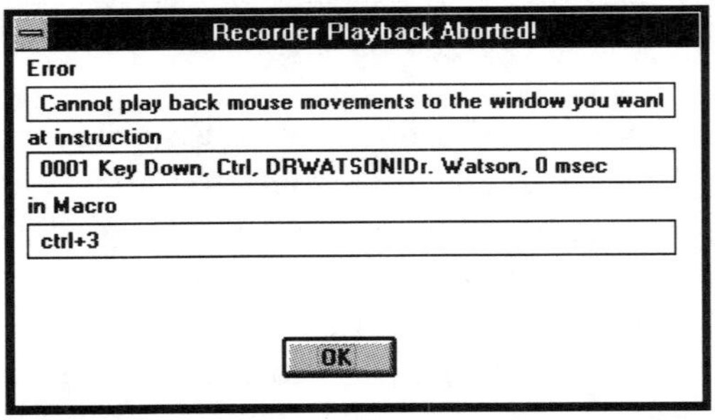

Recorder Playback Aborted!
Error
Cannot play back mouse movements to the window you want
at instruction
0001 Key Down, Ctrl, DRWATSON!Dr. Watson, 0 msec
in Macro
ctrl+3
OK

Figure 15.5 The Recorder Playback Aborted! dialog box

Checking option is on by default every time you open Recorder. If you turn it off, there's no way to stop the macro: While the macro is running, your keyboard and mouse are locked up. You can't do anything but wait or restart your computer (you could press **Ctrl-Alt-Del** twice to reboot).

There's another Recorder Option menu command that affects what happens when you run a macro. By default Recorder will minimize automatically each time you run a macro. If you select **Options | Minimize on Use**—to remove the check mark—Recorder will not minimize.

Sometimes you will run into problems with your macro. Recorder may stop the macro and display a dialog box like the one in Figure 15.5. All you can do is click on **OK**, try to figure out where you went wrong, either creating or running the macro, and try recording it again. Also, if the macro swaps into a full-screen DOS application, it will stop running; it will continue if you swap back to a Windows application.

A macro can't be repaired; you must recreate it. But you should find out what you did wrong so you won't do it again. Look for the following:

- You were in the wrong application window when you pressed the shortcut keys.
- You were in the wrong application window when you swapped to Recorder.
- The application window was minimized, although you recorded the macro with it open.
- You are recording mouse movements, but the window is a different size.
- You are recording mouse movements relative to the screen, but the window is in a different position.
- The macro works with more than one application, but they are not all open, or they are not in the correct positions.
- Your macro selects from a list box, but the contents of the list box are different from when you created the macro.

- Your macro calls a file that no longer exists.
- You have changed the configuration of your application since creating the macro. You have moved or modified menu options or menu keyboard shortcuts, for instance.

Managing Macros

Once you have created a macro you cannot edit it. If you need to change something, you must rerecord it. You can, however, modify the macro's properties. Highlight the macro and then select **Macro | Properties**. You will see the Macro Properties dialog box, which is very similar to the Record Macro box you saw earlier.

You can change any of the original settings except the Record Mouse and Relative To settings. You can change the macro's name, for instance, or give it a new keyboard shortcut. You could also turn the Continuous setting on and off.

You can also change the recording defaults. Select **Options | Preferences** to see the Default Preferences dialog box. You can select the Playback To, Playback Speed, Record Mouse, and Relative To settings. These simply change the way the Record Macro dialog box is set up the next time you create a macro. It has no effect on existing macros. These settings are saved when you close Recorder.

You can also delete a macro from the file's list. Simply click on the macro name and then select **Macro | Delete**.

Starting Macros Automatically

You can run a macro automatically when you open a macro file. For instance, if you want to run a macro when you open Windows, put the Recorder icon in the Program Manager's StartUp group (it should be the last icon in the group, starting from the top left of the window—and remember to save your Program Manager settings). You can adjust the icon's Command Line to automatically run a macro that can open an application, or run a macro on another application opened by the StartUp group.

Use % to represent Alt, ^ to represent Ctrl, and + to represent Shift. For instance, in the Command Line type

```
recorder -h ^+n filename
```

This will run the macro that has the shortcut Ctrl-Shift-*n*. The *n* can be any key you want, even a fake function key (you may use any function key up to F16, even if you only have 10 or 12 function keys). For instance, if you want to run the macro Ctrl-Shift-F16 in a file named ACCOUNTS.REC, type

```
recorder -h ^+F16 accounts
```

You can use this command from DOS when you first open Windows. You could have a batch file for each macro you may want to run when you start Windows, and put

```
win recorder -h ^+n filename
```

in each batch file. One batch file could be used to automatically start a communications session, another might be used to open a particular group of applications, and so on.

▼ ***Note*** You can't go the *other* way. That is, you can't use Recorder to completely close Windows, although you can get as far as the "This will end your Windows session" dialog box.

Menu Options

Here's a summary of Recorder's menu options.

File | New Clears the window so you can start a new recorder file. If the current file hasn't been saved, the application asks if you want to do so.

File | Open Lets you open an existing recorder file.

File | Save Saves the file. The first time you save you will see the Save As dialog box so you can select a directory and filename.

File | Save As Lets you save the file with a new name or in a different directory.

File | Merge Merges the current recorder file with another, adding the other macros.

File | Exit Closes Recorder. If you have unsaved changes, the application asks if you want to save the file first.

Macro | Run Runs the selected macro.

Macro | Record Lets you select the settings and begin recording a macro.

Macro | Delete Deletes the selected macro.

Macro | Properties Displays the settings used by the selected macro.

Options | Control + Break Checking Lets you use Ctrl-Break to stop recording a macro. When turned off you can wait for a macro to end, but the only way to stop it is to reboot or restart your computer.

Options | Shortcut Keys Lets you use the macro shortcut keys to run macros.

Options | Minimize on Use Makes Recorder automatically minimize when you run a macro.

Options | Preferences Lets you set several defaults that control how the macros are recorded.

Part 4

Windows' "Desktop" Accessories

16

Calculator

Windows Calculator is a combination of two calculators: the simple Standard Calculator and the sophisticated Scientific Calculator. But the Windows Calculator has a slight advantage: You can copy and paste numbers between Calculator and your other Windows applications. If you are working in a word processor and need to make a calculation, you can highlight a number, copy it, paste it into Calculator, perform the calculation, and copy the result back to the word processor. You can even type calculations into your word processor and copy them into Calculator to run them.

Starting Calculator

Calculator

Start Calculator by clicking on the Calculator icon in the Accessories program group. Or you can select **File | Run** and run **CALCULATOR**. The first time you open Calculator it starts in Standard mode, as shown in Figure 16.1. (Thereafter Calculator always opens in the mode in which it was closed.)

The calculator is an unusual window in that its size cannot be modified. You cannot maximize it or use its border to adjust its size. You can, however, minimize it. (Maximize and Size appear in the Control menu, but they are always disabled.) At the top of the calculator is a text box that works like the LCD on your pocket calculator, displaying the numbers. Below that is a small box that displays an M when a number is stored in memory. The other items are the calculator's keys.

You probably already know how to use the Standard calculator: It works pretty much the same way as a pocket calculator. You can use both the keyboard and mouse. However, remember that the numbers on your *numeric* keypad work only

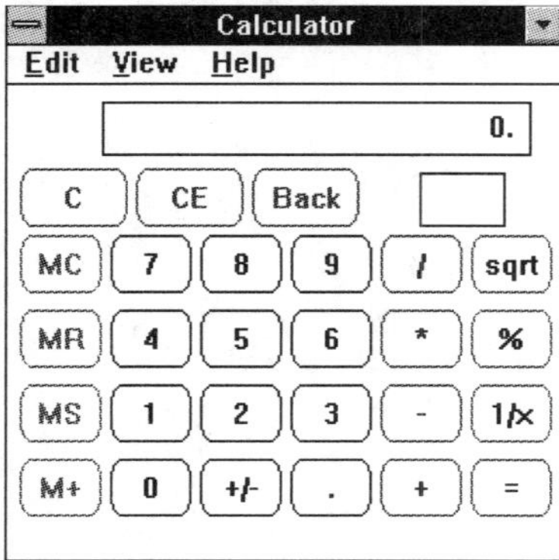

Figure 16.1 The Calculator window in Standard mode

if the Num Lock is *on*. Otherwise they work as cursor movement keys. You will probably find it easiest to use both mouse and keyboard together: the numeric keypad to enter the numbers, and the mouse to click the function keys.

Let's begin by looking at the Standard calculator's keys.

Calculator Button	*Keyboard*	*Function*
0 – 9	**0 – 9** on qwerty keypad, or numeric keypad if Num Lock is on	Enter numbers into the long text box at the top of the calculator.
.	. or ,	Decimal Point: Enters a decimal point.
/	/	Division: Press if you want to divide the current number by another.
*	*	Multiplication: Press if you want to multiply the current number by another.
–	–	Subtraction: Press if you want to subtract a number from the current one.
+	+	Addition: Press if you want to add a number to the current one.
=	= or **Enter**	Equals: Performs the operation between the previous two numbers.

Calculator Button	*Keyboard*	*Function*
sqrt	**@**	Square Root: Finds the square root of the displayed number.
%	%	Percent: Applies the displayed number, as a percentage, to the one entered before, according to the operator entered between them. For instance, "500 * 8 %" multiplies 500 by 8%.
1/x	**r**	Reciprocal: Finds the reciprocal of the displayed number. For instance, if 200 is displayed, the reciprocal is 200/1, or 0.005.
+/–	**F9**	Change Sign: Changes the displayed number from positive to negative, or vice versa.
C	**Esc**	Clear Calculation: Removes the current calculation and places 0 in the box.
CE	**Del**	Clear Entry: Removes the displayed number. The calculation is still active, though, so you can enter a new number and continue.
Back	**Backspace** or **Left Arrow**	Deletes the last digit in the displayed number. If the number is the result of a calculation and has a decimal point, it deletes all the decimal places.
MC	**Ctrl-L**	Memory Clear: Removes the value from memory.
MR	**Ctrl-R**	Memory Recall: Displays the number stored in memory.
MS	**Ctrl-M**	Memory Store: Stores the displayed number in memory, writing over any existing number.
M+	**Ctrl-P**	Memory Plus: Adds the displayed number to the number stored in memory.

▼ *Note* You can type either **.** or **,** to enter a decimal point. By default a **.** is displayed, even if you typed **,** , but you may change the character in the Control Panel's International dialog box.

Here are a few examples of the buttons that must be clicked to carry out operations.

To do this . . .	*Click these . . .*
100 divided by 15	100 / 15 =
100 plus 15	100 + 15 =
3% of 237	237 * 3 % (then click **C** to clear the calculation)
237 divided by 3% of 237	237 / 3 % =
237 multiplied by 3% of 237	237 * 3 % =
237 plus 3%	237 + 3 % =
237 minus 3%	237 – 3 % =
reciprocal of 1/237	237 1/x
square root of (132 plus 5)	132 + 5 = sqrt
square root of 137	137 sqrt

After carrying out an operation that does not end with =, clear the calculation, just to be sure it has ended. For instance, 237 + 3 % gives you 3% of 237. But the calculation isn't over because Calculator now wants to add 3% of 237 to 237. Clearing the calculation ensures that it has ended and will not interfere with the next.

Using Memory

You can place the displayed number into memory. Simply click on **MS** or press **Ctrl-M** and Calculator places the number into memory overwriting any other number currently stored. You can also add a number to the one already stored by clicking on **M+** or pressing **Ctrl-MP**. When Calculator has a number in memory, an M appears in the small text box to the right of the Back key. Whenever the value stored in memory is 0, the M is removed.

When you want to use a number you have stored, simply click on **MR** or press **Ctrl-R**. You can recall a number in this way at any time instead of typing a number. For instance, "237 * MR =" multiplies the number in memory by 237.

You can also clear the memory by clicking on **MC** or pressing **Ctrl-L**. There's no real need ever to clear memory, because you can always use **MS** to write over the memory. The number in memory is *not* stored when you close the Calculator.

 **Tip** If you need to store *two* numbers, use the Clipboard as an additional memory. Select **Edit | Copy**, then, when you are ready to use the number, select **Edit | Paste**. If you need many more memories, you can use the Statistics Box in the Scientific Calculator to store dozens of numbers.

Working with Other Applications

You can use Windows' Clipboard to copy numbers to and from other Windows applications. Some applications—such as Microsoft Money—actually integrate Calculator directly. In Money, for instance, you can open Calculator using a menu option, so there's no need to go to Program Manager first.

If you have a number on which you want to perform a calculation, simply highlight it in the source application and select **Edit | Copy**. (If you want to replace that number with the result of the calculation, use **Edit | Cut** instead.) Incidentally, many Windows applications let you quickly select a number by double-clicking on it, but they often include the space after the number. That's okay, Calculator will remove the space when you paste the number.

 ***Note*** Do not include commas in large numbers. Calculator will read 10,000 as 10.0.

Go to Calculator and select **Edit | Paste** (or press **Ctrl-V**). Windows copies the number into the top text box. If there is already a number in the box, the pasted number will be appended. So if the number in the box is 123 and you paste 987, you will end up with 123987. You may need to clear the display before pasting the number. (However, if you are in the Scientific Calculator and change the number system before pasting, the existing number is replaced by the pasted number.)

As you will learn in a moment, the Scientific Calculator has four number systems: hexadecimal, decimal, octal, and binary. Before you paste a number you must select the number system you want. Calculator will not convert the number. For instance, if you paste 237 while in hexadecimal, it will assume that it is 237 hex, which is actually 567 decimal. And if you try to paste 237 while in binary your computer will beep at you, because 237 is not an acceptable binary number.

Perform the calculation with the pasted number, then select **Edit | Copy** (or press **Ctrl-C**). Return to the application and use **Edit | Paste** to place the result in the document.

You can type entire equations in another application and paste the completed equation into Calculator. For instance, if you paste *84*3=* Calculator will perform the calculation and display 252. Calculator has some special codes you can include.

If you paste *84*3=:m*, Calculator will perform the calculation and then enter the result into memory. Paste *84*3=:m22–2*:R=* and Calculator subtracts 2 from 22, then multiplies the result by the number stored in memory. The final display will show 5040.

Leave spaces between numbers and operators if you wish, but there's no need. Here are the special codes you can use.

:letter	Combining a colon with a letter reproduces the Ctrl-*letter* keyboard shortcut. For instance, **:s** is the same as Ctrl-S in the Scientific Calculator, which opens the Statistics Box. However, :l is *not* the same as Ctrl-L (Clear Memory), for some reason. Use :c instead.
:number	Combining a colon with a number reproduces the F-key. For instance, **:5** is the same as F5, which converts a number to a hexadecimal number in the Scientific Calculator.
:c	Memory Clear (Ctrl-L)
:m	Memory Store (Ctrl-M)
:p	Memory Plus (Ctrl-P)
:r	Memory Recall (Ctrl-R)
:q	Clear Calculation (Esc)
:e	Exp, Scientific notation in the Scientific Calculator's decimal mode (x). (Pasting this function may not work correctly.)
****	Dat key in the Scientific Calculator (Ins).

▼ ***Note*** Unfortunately there are some bugs in the copy-and-paste feature. Occasionally pasting a number automatically carries out an operation, and clearing the calculation and starting over seems to have no effect—pasting again may cause the same calculation. For instance, pasting 10000 into the Scientific Calculator might result in 0.005236133250254 being displayed, or pasting a number into the Standard Calculator may automatically calculate the reciprocal.

The Scientific Calculator

The Scientific Calculator carries out simple mathematical, scientific, and statistical calculations. It can work in four number systems—hexadecimal, decimal, octal, and binary—and convert numbers among these systems.

Select **View | Scientific** to change to Scientific mode. This calculator works in the same way as the Standard one; you can click on the buttons or use keyboard equivalents. When you start the Scientific Calculator it is *always* in decimal mode, regardless of the mode it was in when you closed it last. Figure 16.2 shows the Scientific Calculator.

Notice the three boxes below the option buttons on the right side of the Calculator in Figure 16.2. These boxes show **stat**, **M**, and **(=2**. You've seen the M before, in the Standard Calculator. It shows that there's a value stored in the memory. The stat indicates that the Statistics Box is open—you'll learn more about that in a moment. And the (=2 shows that the equation has two open parentheses. When you enter a closed parenthesis, the indicator will change to (=1. Enter another and the indicator is removed.

Using Scientific Functions

The Scientific Calculator has many more functions than the Standard Calculator, so we've broken them down into mathematical functions, logical operators, and trigonometry.

▼ ***Note*** The following tables don't show keys that we have already explained for the Standard Calculator.

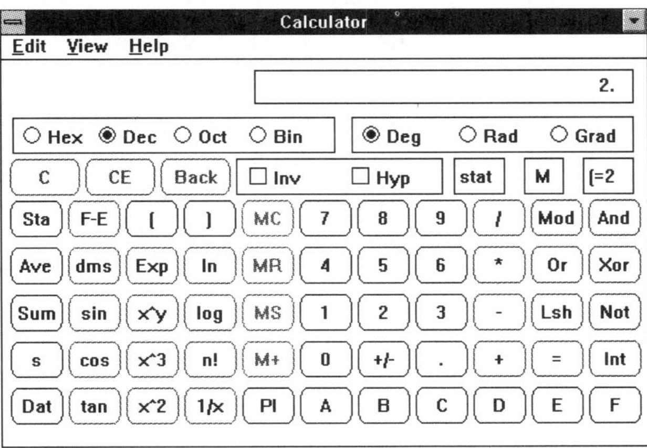

Figure 16.2 The Scientific Calculator.

MATHEMATICAL FUNCTIONS

Calculator Button	*Keyboard*	*Function*
Inv	i	Modifies various calculations (shown in the tables) to find the inverse of the normal calculation. After the calculation Inv automatically turns off.
Exp	x	Lets you enter numbers in scientific notation. The exponent may not exceed +307. You can use this function only with decimal numbers.
F-E	v	Switches between scientific and normal notation. You can use this function only with decimal numbers. Numbers over 10^{15} are automatically displayed in scientific notation and cannot be converted.
Int	;	Removes the fractional portion—leaving the integer portion—of a decimal number.
Inv Int	i ;	Removes integer portion—leaving the fractional portion—of a decimal number.
PI	p	Displays the value of pi, 3.14159265359.
Inv PI	i p	Displays the value of 2 * pi, 6.28318530718.
x^y	y	Calculates x raised to the y; *10 x^y 3* = displays 1000.
Inv x^y	i y	Calculates the yth root of x; *10 Inv x^y 3* = displays 2.154434690032.
x^2	@	Squares the displayed number.
Inv x^2	i @	Calculates the square root of the displayed number.
x^3	#	Cubes the displayed number.
Inv x^3	i #	Calculates the cube root of the displayed number.
ln	n	Calculates natural (base *e*) logarithm.

MATHEMATICAL FUNCTIONS *(continued)*

Calculator Button	*Keyboard*	*Function*
Inv ln	i n	Calculates natural (base *e*) logarithm raised to the power of the displayed number.
log	l	Calculates the common (base 10) logarithm.
Inv log	i l	Calculates 10 raised to the power of the displayed number.
n!	!	Calculates the factorial of the displayed number, the product of all the whole numbers from 1 to the displayed number; 4 n! displays 24, which is 1 x 2 x 3 x 4.

LOGICAL OPERATORS

Calculator Button	*Keyboard*	*Function*
Lsh	<	Shift bit register left. Click **Lsh**, enter the number of bits, and click on **=**.
Inv Lsh	i <	Shift bit register right. Click **Lsh**, enter the number of bits, and click on **=**.
Mod	%	Calculates the modulus (the sum remaining) after dividing one number by another. For instance, 52 Mod 3 is 1.
And	&	Bitwise AND.
Or	|	Bitwise OR.
Xor	^	Bitwise exclusive OR.
Not	~	Bitwise inverse.
(	(	Begins a parenthetical calculation. You may have up to 25 levels of parentheses in a calculation. The current number of open parentheses is shown in the (= text box (the third box down from the top on the right side; see Figure 16.2).
)	)	Ends a parenthetical calculation.

TRIGONOMETRY

Calculator Button	*Keyboard*	*Function*
Deg	**F2**	Sets trigonometric calculations to degrees.
Rad	**F3**	Sets trigonometric calculations to radians.
Grad	**F4**	Sets trigonometric calculations to gradients.
dms	**m**	Converts the displayed number to degrees-minutes-seconds.
Hyp	**h**	Sets the calculation to find the hyperbolic sine, arc sine, cosine, arc cosine, tangent, or arc tangent. After the calculation Hyp automatically turns off.
Inv dms	**i m**	Converts the displayed number to degrees.
sin	**s**	Calculates the sine of the displayed number.
Inv sin	**i s**	Calculates the arc sine of the displayed number.
Hyp sin	**h s**	Calculates the hyperbolic sine of the displayed number.
Hyp Inv sin	**h i s**	Calculates the arc hyperbolic sine of the displayed number.
cos	**o**	Calculates the cosine of the displayed number.
Inv cos	**i o**	Calculates the arc cosine of the displayed number.
Hyp cos	**h o**	Calculates the hyperbolic cosine of the displayed number.
Hyp Inv cos	**h i o**	Calculates the arc hyperbolic cosine of the displayed number.
tan	**t**	Calculates the tangent of the displayed number.
Inv tan	**i t**	Calculates the arc tangent of the displayed number.
Hyp tan	**h t**	Calculates the hyperbolic tangent of the displayed number.

TRIGONOMETRY *(continued)*

Calculator Button	*Keyboard*	*Function*
Hyp Inv tan	**h i t**	Calculates the arc hyperbolic tangent.
Inv cos	**i o**	Calculates the arc cosine of the displayed number.

Using Statistical Functions

Calculator has several simple statistical calculations. You can average a set of numbers, average the numbers' squares, calculate a standard deviation and an inverse standard deviation, sum a group of numbers, and sum the squares of a group of numbers. These are the keys you can use to make statistical calculations.

Calculator Button	*Keyboard*	*Function*
Sta	**Ctrl-S**	Opens the Statistics Box.
Dat	**Ins**	Copies the displayed number into the Statistics Box.
Ave	**Ctrl-A**	Calculates the average of the numbers in the Statistics Box.
Inv Ave	**i Ctrl-A**	Select the Inv check box before averaging the numbers to find the average of the squares.
s	**Ctrl-D**	Calculates the standard deviation with the population parameter as n–1.
Inv s	**i Ctrl-D**	Select the Inv check box before the standard deviation calculation to use the population parameter n.
Sum	**Ctrl-T**	Sums the numbers in the Statistics Box.
Inv Sum	**i Ctrl-T**	Select the Inv check box before summing the numbers to find the sum of the squares.

Begin by clicking **Sta** to open the Statistics Box (see Figure 16.3). The Statistics Box is a type of dialog box, but it allows you to work in the Calculator while it remains open. It has a list box that contains numbers that you send to it from the Calculator (by clicking on the **Dat** button) and four buttons. **Ret** switches you back to the Calculator. You can use **Ret** and the Calculator's **Sta** button to jump between the two (you can also use **Ctrl-Tab**, or any of the other Windows-switching methods—just click on the calculator, for instance).

The **LOAD** button copies the number you have selected in the Statistics Box to the Calculator—it will replace the currently displayed number. The **CD** deletes the selected number, and the **CAD** clears the Statistics Box of all numbers. At the bottom of the dialog box is a note indicating the number of entries in the box: "n=8" means that the Statistics Box contains eight entries. The Statistics Box remains open until you close Calculator or close the box itself using the Control menu.

How do you use this box? Let's say you want to make a series of calculations and average the result of each calculation. Click on **Sta** to open the Statistics Box. Move the Calculator and the Statistics Box so you can view both. If you have a small screen they may have to overlap: Try putting them in opposite corners, and even pushing the edges off-screen a little.

Make your first calculation, then click on **Dat** to copy the result to the Statistics Box. Do the rest of the calculations, each time copying the result using the Dat button. When you are ready to calculate the average, click **Ave**, and the Calculator displays the average of all the numbers stored in the Statistics Box.

Averages can distort information. The average of 1 + 2 + 1 + 500 is 126, a number that may be meaningless. A standard deviation indicates the amount that individual members in a group vary from the average: A large number indicates that some members vary greatly; a small number shows that most of the members

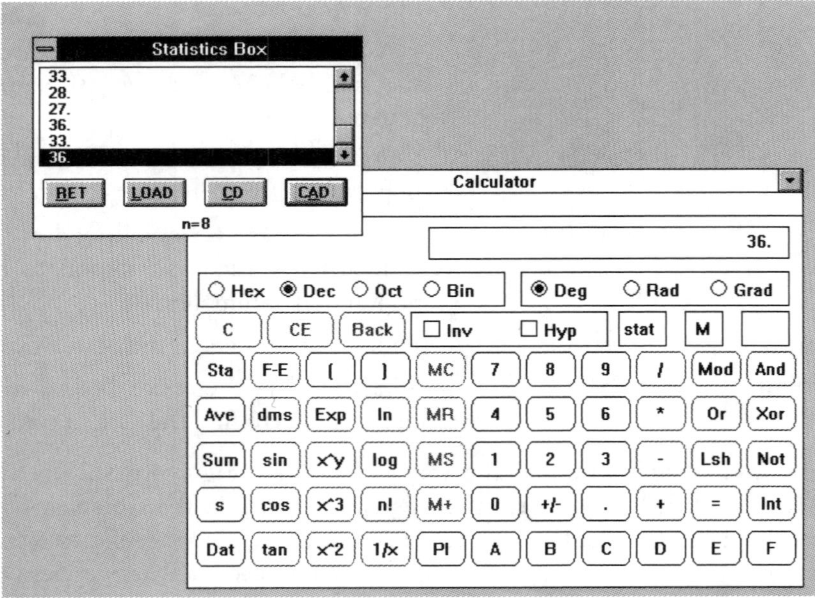

Figure 16.3 The Statistics Box and the Calculator

are close to the average. You can do two types of standard deviations, *n weighting* (or *population weighting*), and *n–1 weighting*. The first method is commonly used when you are checking the standard deviation for an entire group, while the second is used if you are estimating standard deviation by sampling a portion of the group. However, if the sample is more than 30 numbers, the difference will be minor.

To use n–1 weighting, simply click **Sta** and the Calculator displays the *estimated* standard deviation. Instead of dividing by the total number of entries in the Statistics Box (n=), the Calculator uses the total minus one. To use n weighting, click on the **Inv** check box first, then click **Sta**. The Calculator displays the *population* standard deviation.

You can also sum the numbers in the Statistics Box (click on **Sum**); calculate the squares and sum those (select **Inv** and then click **Sum**); or square the numbers and average the squares (select **Inv** and then click **Ave**).

Working with Different Number Systems

The Scientific Calculator can use four numbers systems: decimal (base 10), which we use in everyday life; hexadecimal (base 15); octal (base 8); and binary (base 2). Hexadecimal, octal, and binary are commonly used in computer programming. You can work in any of these number systems or convert numbers from one to another. Seven option buttons near the top of the Calculator control number modes.

Calculator Button	*Keyboard*	*Function*
Hex	**F5**	Selects hexadecimal mode or converts a number to hexadecimal.
Dec	**F6**	Selects decimal mode or converts a number to decimal.
Oct	**F7**	Selects octal mode or converts a number to octal.
Bin	**F8**	Selects binary mode or converts a number to binary.

The following three option buttons appear only when Hex, Oct, or Bin are selected. If Dec is selected, the Calculator displays Deg, Rad, and Grad in their place.

Calculator Button	*Keyboard*	*Function*
Dword	**F2**	Displays the full hexadecimal, octal, or binary number.

Calculator Button	*Keyboard*	*Function*
Word	**F3**	Displays the lower 16 bits of the current hexadecimal, octal, or binary number.
Byte	**F4**	Displays the lower 8 bits of the current hexadecimal, octal, or binary number.

To work in a particular system, click on the **option** button and then use the Calculator as normal. Inappropriate keys will be disabled (although they won't be dimmed). Numbers 2 through 9 and the letters are disabled in binary, for instance.

Converting a number is simple. Enter the number, then click on the option button of the system to which you want to convert the number. Calculator automatically changes the number in the display to the appropriate one. For instance, enter 236 in the decimal mode. Click on **Hex** to see EC, **Oct** to see 354, and **Bin** to see 11101100. Only decimal mode accepts decimal places, so when Calculator converts numbers from decimal to one of the other modes it *truncates* the decimal places; that is, it does not *round* the number, it *removes* the decimal places and then converts the number.

As we mentioned earlier, you can copy and paste using any of these number systems as long as the number you are pasting is valid for the selected number system. You can't paste 123 into binary, or EF into decimal, for instance.

17

Calendar

Windows' Calendar helps you keep track of your important appointments and even sets alarms if you need an audible reminder. It also lets you view any day and date from 1980 to 2099, which is useful for those of you into long-term planning. It's not the most sophisticated of calendar programs, but if all you need to do is keep a simple list of dates and appointments, and print out simple lists and calendars, it may be enough for you.

Starting Calendar

Calendar

Start Calendar by clicking on the Calendar icon in the Accessories program group. Or select **File | Run** and run **CALENDAR**. The Calendar automatically opens in Day view, as shown in Figure 17.1.

The information you enter into the calendar is stored in a file in the same way a word processor saves text in a file. You can have several calendar files. Perhaps one for business and one personal, or one for everyone who uses the computer. Calendar automatically opens in a blank calendar. The first time you use Calendar you will want to enter appointments and then use the **File | Save** command to create a Calendar file. (Calendar's files have the .CAL extension.)

Calendar lets you open .CAL files as *read-only* files. For instance, an office might have one .CAL file for important company dates. Anyone in the office could open the file as read-only, with just one person authorized to make changes. (Actually, you can make changes, but you won't be able to save them. Instead, Calendar will let you create a new file.)

To open a read-only file, select **File | Open**, click on the Read Only check box, and open the file. Of course this isn't a particularly effective security measure, as it

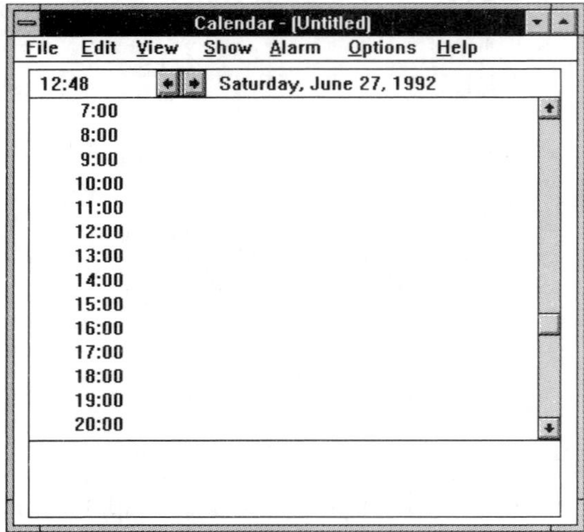

Figure 17.1 The Calendar window in Day view

is voluntary. If someone wants to modify the file they can open it without making it read-only, and if they don't want to modify it they are unlikely to do so accidentally. If you want to keep a file safe, it's better to set it as read-only using File Manager. But then, a user could use File Manager or DOS to change its attributes.

Tip Calendar doesn't automatically open your calendar file. Create an icon in Program Manager (or edit the existing icon) with the command line *filename*.cal. When you double-click on the icon Calendar will open and load *filename*.cal for you. Create as many of these icons as you want, one for each Calendar file if you wish.

The Day view contains a column of times on the left side, starting at midnight, and working down the list in one-hour increments. (You can change this default setting, as you will learn in a moment.) When you open the file 7.00 is shown in the top line, but you can scroll up to see earlier times. The time in the top left—in the bar with the arrow buttons—is the current system time, and the date to the right is, initially, the current date. Remember that you can change the time and date in the Control Panel.

Notice the scratch pad at the bottom. You can enter short notes here; you can fill the scratch-pad box and no more. There's only one scratch pad for each day, not for each time you select. You can get to the scratch pad by clicking the mouse in it or by pressing **Tab**.

Calendar always opens in this Day view, and it always opens displaying the current day.

Selecting Dates and Views

Of course you can change the view. Notice the arrow buttons between the time and the date. To see the previous day, click on the **Left Arrow**, or press **Ctrl-PgUp**, or select **Show | Previous**. To see the next day, click on the **Right Arrow**, or press **Ctrl-PgDn**, or select **Show | Next**. To return to today, select **Show | Today**.

You can also select any day you wish, from the beginning of 1980 to the end of 2099. Select **Show | Date** or press **F4** to see the Show Date dialog box (see Figure 17.2). Enter the date and click on **OK**, and Calendar displays that day. The date you enter is in the format selected in Control Panel. If you haven't changed the Control Panel settings, you can use any of these formats.

To see this date	*Use any of these formats*
August 1, 1992	8/1/92 08/01/92 8-1-92 08-01-92

You can also enter all four of the year digits. If you want to see any year other than 1980 through 1999, you *must* enter all four year digits. For instance, type **1/1/2004**, not **1/1/04**.

If you would like to see an entire month at a time, select **View | Month**, or press **F9**, or double-click on the date in the status bar. Figure 17.3 shows a Month view. You can switch back by selecting **View | Day**; by pressing **F8**; by double-clicking on the date in the status bar; by double-clicking on one of the days; or by using the **arrow keys** to move to a date and pressing **Enter**. The highlighted day on the monthly calendar is the selected day—in other words, the notes in the scratch pad

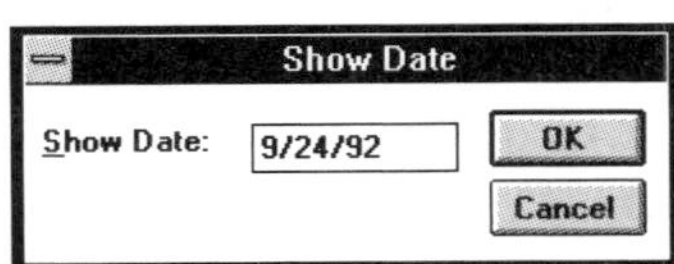

Figure 17.2 The Show Date dialog box

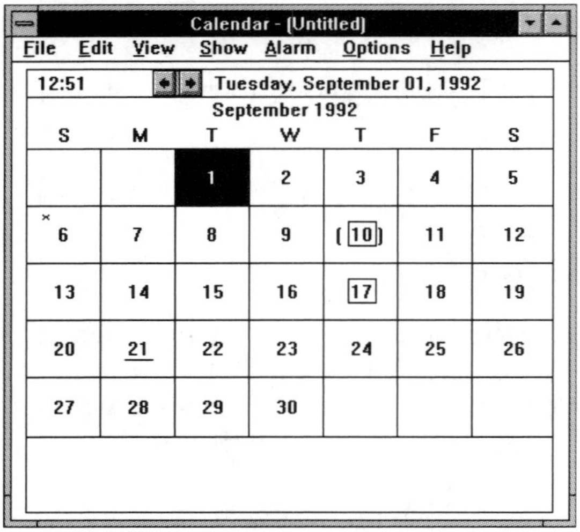

Figure 17.3 The Month View with several days "marked"

are associated with that day, and if you select the **Options | Mark** command, you can mark that day. Also, if you press **F8** or select **View | Day**, you will see the Day view for the highlighted day. Today's date is indicated with angle brackets (> 7 <, for example).

The date selection tools work in a similar manner in the Month view. Notice that the month view also has arrow buttons, although clicking them selects the next or last *month*, of course. And the **Show | Previous** and **Show | Next** commands display the previous and next months.

Entering and Removing Appointments

Entering an appointment is simple. Display the day in which you want to enter the appointment. Then point at the appropriate time and click the mouse button. Or use one of these keys:

To move to	*Press*
The first entry	**Ctrl-Home**
Twelve hours from the first entry	**Ctrl-End**
Down one entry	**Down arrow** or **Enter**
Up one entry	**Up arrow**
The next screen	**PgDn**
The previous screen	**PgUp**

To move from the scratch pad into the appointment area, press **Tab**. If the appointment area doesn't contain the time you want—perhaps you want to set an appointment for 10:45—you can modify it. We'll explain how in a moment.

Now that you have selected the time you want, type a line describing the appointment. Although you can view only 33 characters at a time, you can enter 80 characters. The extra characters will be printed when you print your calendar, and you will be able to read them by selecting the entry and moving through the text using **Left Arrow**, **Right Arrow**, **Home**, **End**, **Ctrl-Left Arrow**, and **Ctrl-Right Arrow**.

You can use the Edit commands to enter text into the appointment entries or the scratch pad. For instance, you can copy text from another Windows application—names and telephone numbers from the Cardfile, for instance—and paste them using **Edit | Paste**. Or if you have a repetitive appointment, you can enter one, copy the text, and paste it into the others.

Using Alarms

No electronic calendar would be complete without an alarm. You can quickly set an alarm for any appointment by placing the insertion point on the line and selecting **Alarm | Set** or pressing **F5**. Calendar places a small bell on the left side of the line (as shown in Figure 17.4). You can *remove* an alarm in the same way.

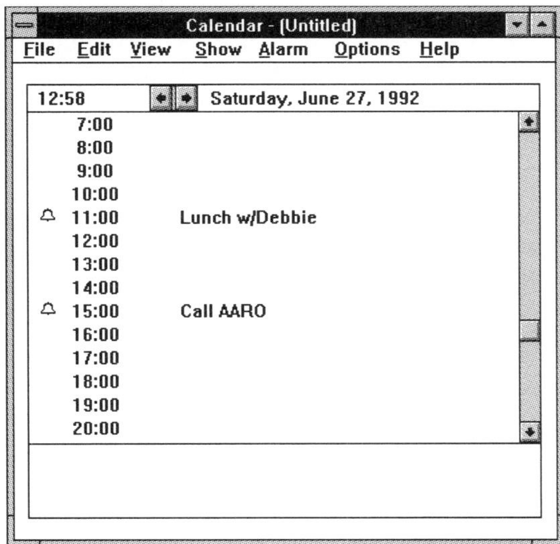

Figure 17.4 The Alarm message box

Alarm Controls

Early Ring (0 - 10): 0 OK

☒ Sound Cancel

Figure 17.5 The Alarm Controls dialog box

How will the alarm work? That depends on the settings in the Alarm Controls dialog box (see Figure 17.5) displayed by selecting **Alarm | Controls**. By default the alarm will *not* have an **early ring** and *will* **sound**. However, if you turn off system sounds in the Control Panel's Sounds dialog box, your computer will not beep even if Sounds in the Alarm Controls box is enabled.

When the appointment time is reached, Calendar will make your computer beep several times. If the Calendar window is active, it will display a box (see Figure 17.6) showing you the appointment time and the notes you made for that appointment entry. If Calendar is covered by another application, you won't see this box, so use **Alt-Tab** or **Ctrl-Esc** to move to the Calendar. If the Calendar is not active, but the title bar is visible, you will notice the title bar flashing; and if its icon is visible in one corner of the desktop, it will appear and disappear. Click once on the title bar or icon and the message box pops up. Either way, you should turn off the alarm by clicking the **OK** button in the Alarm message box.

Tip You can make the alarm use a different sound—music perhaps, or someone screaming at you if you really want to. If you have the necessary hardware and driver, you can use the Control Panel to associate any sound with the Default Beep. Of course that same sound will be used by other programs in various situations. (See Chapter 8 for more information.)

Of course you must have Calendar running for the alarm to go off. If it isn't open the alarm will sound when you open it—as long as you open it on the day for

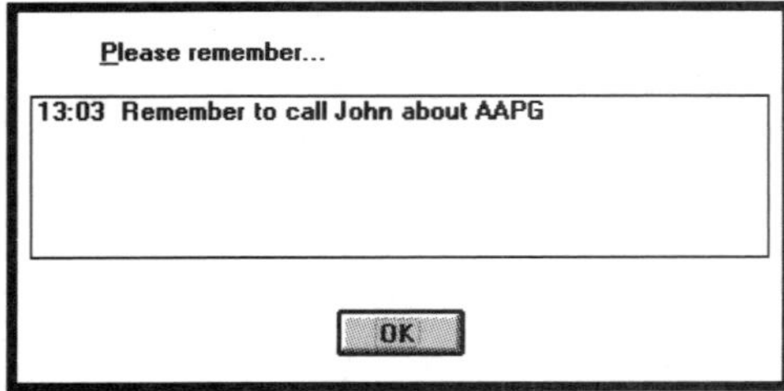

Figure 17.6 The Please Remember message box

which the alarm is set. For some reason, however, the Alarm message box will not appear until you go to another application and then return to Calendar.

You can turn off the alarm's beep by clicking on the Sounds check box in the Alarm Controls check box, but you may not want to do so. If the Calendar is completely obscured by other windows when the alarm goes off, the only indication is the beep. Windows does not automatically display the Alarm message box.

You can also set an alarm to go off up to 10 minutes ahead of time by entering a number in the Early Ring text box in the Alarm Controls check box. For instance, if you have to meet someone in your building's lobby at 2:00 PM, you might want to set the alarm a few minutes early to give you time to get there.

Incidentally, the Alarm Controls affect *all* alarms, not just the currently selected alarm. So if you create an alarm and then set a two-minute early ring, all your alarms will ring two minutes early until you reset the Controls.

Marking Dates

You can *mark* any day so that a special symbol will appear on that day in the Month view. You could mark a day and then put an explanatory note in the scratch pad at the bottom of the window. For instance, you could use one symbol for company holidays, another for family occasions (birthdays, anniversaries, and so on), and yet another for special events.

Select **Options | Mark** or press **F6** to see the Day Markings dialog box (shown in Figure 17.7). Click on each symbol you want to place on the selected day. These symbols are not very clear. The first symbol places a box around the date. The second puts the date in parentheses. The third places a dot in the bottom-left corner. The fourth places an x in the top-left corner, and the fifth underlines the date.

You can place all five marks on one day if you wish. And you can remove a mark in the same way you placed it: Select the day, press **F6**, click on the mark you want to remove, and click on **OK**.

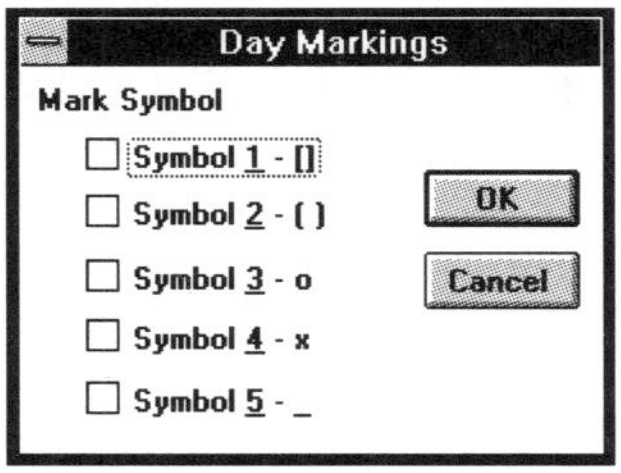

Day Markings
Mark Symbol
Symbol 1 - []
Symbol 2 - ( )
Symbol 3 - o
Symbol 4 - x
Symbol 5 - _
OK
Cancel

Figure 17.7 The Day Markings dialog box

Figure 17.8 The Day Settings dialog box

Modifying the Day View

Calendar's day view may not be quite what you need. By default it has one entry for every hour of the day, and when you first open the calendar it displays the 7:00 AM entry. But what if you want to begin the day earlier, or if you need more frequent appointment entries?

Select **Options | Day Settings** to see the Day Settings dialog box (shown in Figure 17.8). You can select an interval: If the default hourly entry is not enough, you can have an entry every 15 or 30 minutes instead. You can also select the 12- or 24-hour format. (In other words, if you select 24-hour format, 2:00 AM will be shown as 14:00.) And you can enter a starting time in the format *hours:minutes*. This is the first appointment entry that will be displayed when you open the file.

When you change the day settings, you change the entire file. That is, all the days will conform to the new settings. If you have already made appointments at time intervals that you have now removed, Calendar will save those appointments. Effectively the appointments become **special times**.

Perhaps one entry an hour is enough for you—but now and again you want to be able to set an appointment between the hours. Calendar lets you enter special times. Select **Options | Special Time**, or press **F7** to see the Special Time dialog box (shown in Figure 17.9). Type the time you want in the format *hours:minutes*. Then click on the AM or PM option button. (If you are using the 24-hour format, the AM and PM option buttons are disabled; so enter the special time in 24-hour format too.)

When you click on the **Insert** button, Calendar inserts an entry for the time you selected and places the cursor in the entry so you can begin typing immediately. Incidentally, if you get a message telling you the time is "not a special time," it just means you tried to create an entry for a time that already has one, such as 2:00 PM.

Figure 17.9 The Special Time dialog box

You can remove a special-time entry by selecting it, pressing **F7** to see the Special Time box, and clicking on **Delete**. You can also remove all the special times (and appointments) by using the **Edit | Remove** command, as we explain next.

Removing Appointments

The **Edit | Remove** command displays the Remove dialog box (see Figure 17.10) and lets you remove appointments from one day or a range of days. When the dialog box appears, it displays the current date in the From text box. If you now click on the **OK** button, all the appointments for that day are removed—you don't need to enter a To date. All Special Times are removed also, even if you haven't entered appointments for those times.

If you want to remove appointments from a range of dates, you can enter a date in the To text box. You can also enter a date in the From text box if you want to remove appointments from dates before the selected one.

Printing the Calendar

Calendar uses the same Page Setup procedure as Notepad and Cardfile. So see Chapter 6 for more information about setting margins and creating headers and footers.

When you want to print your appointments, select **File | Print**. The Print dialog box is just the same as the Remove dialog box you saw a moment ago. The From text box displays the selected date: Click on **OK** if you want to print only the selected day's appointments. Or type a later date in the To text box if you want to print a range. You can also enter an earlier date in the From text box if you wish.

When Calendar prints your appointments, it begins with the day and date and then prints the appointments in a list. All the text you entered is printed, and if you set an alarm for an appointment, an asterisk is printed on the left side of the line. After each day's appointments, Calendar prints all the text in that day's scratch pad. Then it prints the next day's information. (It doesn't print each day on a new page.)

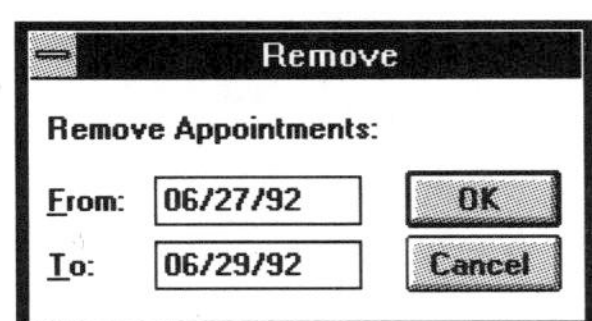

Figure 17.10 The Remove dialog box

Menu Options

Here's a summary of Calendar's menu options.

File | New Clears the window and displays the current date so you can start a new file. If the current file hasn't been saved, Calendar asks if you want to do so.

File | Open Lets you open a Calendar file.

File | Save Saves the file. The first time you save the file you will see the Save As dialog box so you can select a directory and filename.

File | Save As Lets you save the file with a new name or in a different directory.

File | Print Prints the file on the printer selected in the Print Setup dialog box.

File | Page Setup Lets you set page margins and create a header and footer.

File | Print Setup Lets you select the printer on which you want to print your Calendar files. Each time you open Calendar, it automatically selects the default printer selected in the Control Panel's Printers dialog box.

File | Exit Closes Calendar. If you have unsaved changes, Calendar asks if you want to save the file first.

Edit | Cut (Ctrl-X) Cuts the selected text and places it into the Clipboard.

Edit | Copy (Ctrl-C) Copies the selected text into the Clipboard.

Edit | Paste (Ctrl-V) Copies text from the Clipboard. You cannot paste images into Calendar.

Edit | Remove Removes all the appointments from a range of dates.

View | Day (F8) Displays a single day.

View | Month (F9) Displays an entire month.

Show | Today Displays today's date. In Month view it moves the highlight to today's date.

Show | Previous (Ctrl-PgUp) Displays the previous day or month, depending on the selected view.

Show | Next (Ctrl-PgDn) Displays the next day or month, depending on the selected view.

Show | Date (F4) Lets you select a specific date to view.

Alarm | Set (F5) Enabled only in Day view. Sets an alarm at the selected time.

Alarm | Controls Lets you decide if alarms will be audible and if they will occur a few minutes before the selected time.

Options | Mark (F6) Places a marker on the day. You can mark a day while in Month or Day view, but the mark itself will appear only on the day in Month view.

Options | Special Time (F7) Enabled only in Day view. Lets you add a line for a specific time.

Options | Day Settings Lets you define the Day view: the earliest time on the page, the intervals, and whether the times should be in 12-hour or 24-hour format.

18

Cardfile

Cardfile is a simple database. As you can tell from its name, Cardfile is based on the popular system that uses cards to store information. You can buy small plastic boxes, tabbed dividers, and cards from many office-supply stores. Sales people use this to store the names and addresses of prospects, freelancers use them to store information about prospective clients, and many people use them instead of an address book, storing information about family, friends, colleagues, and clients.

Cardfile is an electronic version of the plastic and paper card file. You can store a small amount of information about anything you wish on electronic "cards" stored in a file on your hard disk. Each card represents one *record*, but, unlike more sophisticated databases, each record has only two *fields*. That is, all the information on the card is grouped into one small indexed field and one large field, with no way to break it down into separate categories of information (such as Name, Street, Address, and so on).

If you've seen Cardfile in previous versions of Windows, you may want to take another look. Windows 3.1's OLE (Object Linking and Embedding) has made Cardfile into a much more powerful application. You can now load entire spreadsheets, documents, pictures, songs, speeches, calendars, and so on. You could, for instance, build a database of your stamp collection and include a picture of each of your most valuable stamps. Or you could build a database of speeches, and make Cardfile play them by double-clicking on an icon.

Opening Cardfile

Cardfile

Start Cardfile by clicking on the Cardfile icon in the Accessories program group. Or select **File | Run** and run **CARDFILE**. Figure 18.1 shows the Cardfile window.

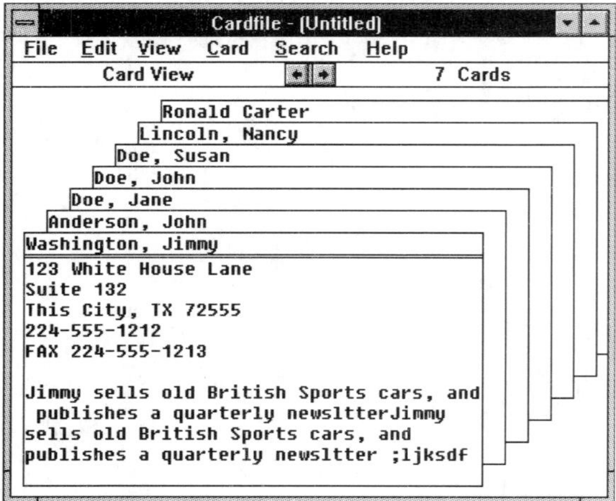

Figure 18.1 The Cardfile window

Cardfile automatically opens a blank card and places the insertion point in the top-left corner so you can begin entering information immediately.

The size of the cards is fixed and unfortunately is not very large. You can type only enough text to fill the card—Cardfile won't accept any more. (As you will learn later, you can use OLE to place much larger amounts of text on a card.) Cardfile displays as many cards as it can in the window, so increasing the window size will display more cards. As you can see from the figure, the cards are placed as in a stack: The one on top is completely visible while the others show only their top lines (the index lines).

There's a status line below the menu bar. This tells you what view you are in (there are only two views, card view—as shown—and list view, which shows a list of the index lines). It also tells you how many cards are stored in the file. There are two scroll arrows in the middle of this status bar: Clicking them moves the stack so you can view the last card (left arrow) or next card (right arrow).

Entering Information

Before you begin typing information into the card, you may want to create the index entry. This is the information that appears on the top line of the card. In Figure 18.1 the index entries are names. Not only does putting information in the index line save precious space in the card, but it allows you to view a list of subjects and quickly find the card you are looking for. Press **F6** or select **Edit | Index** to see the Index dialog box. Type the entry and click on **OK**. An entry may be up to 39 characters long. Remember that the entry will be indexed alphabetically starting with the first character—thus it makes more sense to enter "Washington, Jimmy" than "Jimmy Washington." Also, if you want to index by a number, remember that while 10 will appear after 02 in an indexed list, it would appear *in front* of 2 because Cardfile begins by looking at the first digits.

Tip You can quickly display the Index dialog box—to enter or edit an index entry—by double-clicking on the top card's index line.

Now you can begin typing to enter the information into the card. You might think of this as a "freeform" file record. You can enter the information in any format you wish. You might type a street address on one line, the suite number on the next, and the city, state, and zip on the next. On the other hand, you might want to string all this information together, especially if you intend to add some notes to the bottom of the card.

Unfortunately, what you see is what you get: You can't add more text to the card than you can see, which seriously limits the amount of information that can be stored.

Tip You can store very large amounts of text or data in a card—from virtually any application—using OLE. See later in this chapter for more information.

Cards are like simple word processing documents, and the usual keyboard commands work. You can type up to 40 characters on each line, and the text automatically wraps to the next line if you continue typing. Here are the keyboard commands you can use.

Home	Moves the cursor to the beginning of the line.
End	Moves the cursor to the end of the line.
Left and **Right Arrows**	Moves the cursor left or right, one character at a time.
Up and **Down Arrows**	Moves the cursor up or down, one line at a time.
Ctrl-Left or **Right Arrow**	Moves the cursor left or right, one word at a time.
Shift-Arrow	Selects the text in the direction of the arrow.
Shift-Ctrl-Left or **Right Arrow**	Selects the text, one word at a time, to the left or right.

Shift-Home	Selects the text from the cursor to the beginning of the line.
Shift-End	Selects the text from the cursor to the end of the line.
Del	Removes the character to the right.
Backspace	Removes the character to the left.

▼ *Note* The **Ctrl-Home**, **Ctrl-End**, **PgUp**, and **End** combinations are used for moving through the card stack, not within a card.

You can, of course, use the **Edit | Copy**, **Edit | Cut**, and **Edit | Paste** commands to move and copy text between cards. You can even use them to copy text from a card to its index line, and vice versa.

Cardfile also lets you quickly delete or duplicate a card. Select **Card | Delete** to remove a card from the stack (Cardfile will prompt you to confirm that you really want to remove it). Select **Card | Duplicate** to make an exact copy of the card.

Working with Pictures

Cardfile also lets you store pictures, one per card. You might want to store maps, sketches, even scanned photographs or company logos. Cardfile works well with images copied to the Clipboard from Paintbrush, but other applications also may be able to provide Cardfile with images. Figure 18.2 shows an image pasted from Publisher's Paintbrush (a distant cousin of Windows Paintbrush).

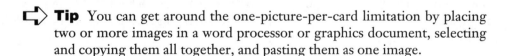

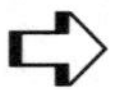 **Tip** You can get around the one-picture-per-card limitation by placing two or more images in a word processor or graphics document, selecting and copying them all together, and pasting them as one image.

Before you can paste a picture you must select picture mode using the **Edit | Picture** command. Then go to the application that contains the image you want to paste and copy it to the Clipboard. Return to Cardfile, move the card you want to use to the front, and do one of the following:

- Press **Ctrl-V.**
- Select **Edit | Paste**.
- Select **Edit | Paste Link**.
- Select **Edit | Paste Special**, click on **bitmap**, and click on **Paste**.

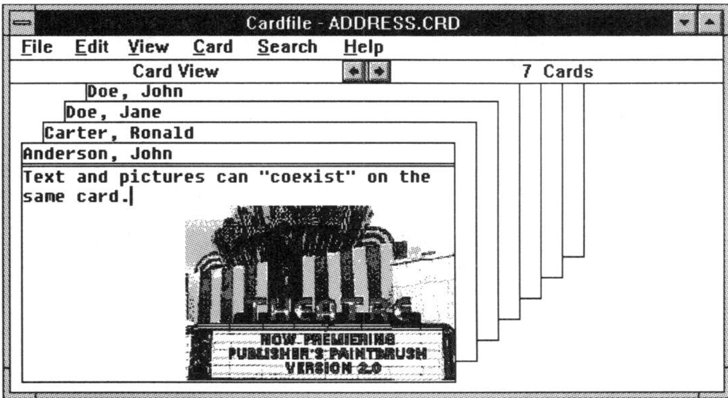

Figure 18.2 A Publisher's Paintbrush picture pasted into Cardfile

Cardfile is an OLE *client* application. That means it can accept OLE images from OLE *servers*. The subject of OLE is discussed in detail in Chapter 28. For now, all you really need to know is that OLE provides a way to create a connection from data pasted into an application to the application in which it was created.

Paintbrush is an OLE server. When you paste an image from Paintbrush into Cardfile you automatically *embed* the image. That means the image is still "connected" to Paintbrush. If you double-click on the picture (while Cardfile is in Picture mode), Paintbrush will automatically open and load the picture. (You can also select **Edit | Paintbrush Picture Object**.) You can then make changes, close Paintbrush, and the picture in Cardfile will automatically be updated. If you have a Paintbrush image in the Clipboard—or an image from another OLE server—and press **Ctrl-V** or select **Edit | Paste**, that image is automatically embedded.

▼ *Note* Some graphics applications, even though they are OLE servers, may not be able to display their images in Cardfile. Instead they will usually display the application's icon—click on the icon to view the picture. This icon is known as a *package*. As OLE functions depend on how the software publisher wrote the application, some OLE servers may not be able to work with Cardfile at all, or they may place an "invisible" package in the card.

You can also *link* images to the source file. If you use the **Edit | Paste Link** option, the picture is pasted into the card and a link is created. Now, if you double-click on the image Paintbrush will open and load the original file. You can make changes, close Paintbrush, and both the image in the card *and* the original file will be changed. If you want to create a link, you must save the image in the original application *before* you copy it to the Clipboard.

▼ *Note* Each card can accept only one image or OLE package, even if that OLE package contains text, not pictures.

You may want to paste an image in the old, non-OLE way, with no connection to either the application or the source file. If so, select **Edit | Paste Special**. The Paste Special dialog box appears (see Figure 18.3). Usually you will not select the first option in the list box. You will normally select one that says "bitmap" or "device independent bitmap." If you are pasting a Paintbrush image, select bitmap. (If you are working with another OLE server you may have to check the application's documentation.) Next, click on the **Paste** button. The picture is pasted into the card, but it is not embedded or linked. If you double-click on it now, nothing happens.

There's a lot more to OLE. We are going to discuss its impact on Cardfile a little more at the end of this chapter. (Chapter 28 explains OLE in detail.)

Once you have an image pasted into the card, you can move it around. Cardfile always pastes the picture into the top-left corner, but you can move it in any direction. In fact you can move it *out* of the card so just a portion of the picture is visible on one edge or corner. (You can then drag it back into the card whenever you want to view it.) That way, the picture will not obscure your text.

Move the picture by simply dragging it. If you don't have a mouse you can use the arrow keys to move it around. As soon as you select Picture mode the arrow keys are active. There's no need to select the picture first. The arrow-key method can be very slow, however.

▼ *Note* If you choose not to move the picture off the card, your text will be obscured by the picture when you display the card. If you are in picture mode, drag the picture out of the way, read the text, and replace the picture. If you are in text mode, point at the top of the picture, press and hold the mouse button, and drag the pointer down. The text under the picture will be uncovered.

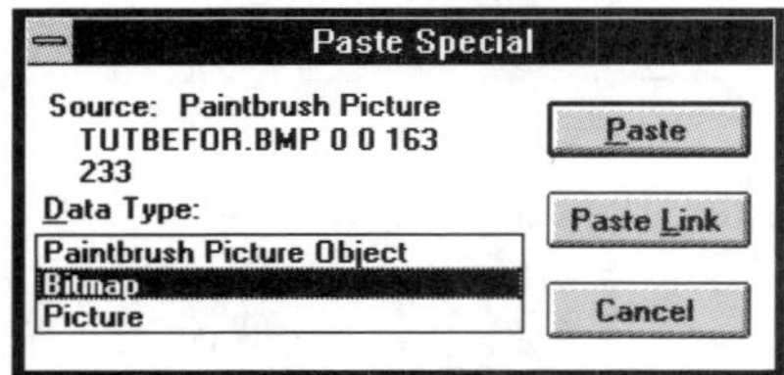

Figure 18.3 The Paste Special dialog box

If you want to wrap text around a graphic, paste the picture first, then enter the text. You will have to use the Tab and Space keys to leave a space in the text where the picture is. While you are typing the graphic will be blanked out from that line, but it will reappear when you return to the card later.

Adding a Card and Saving Data

When you are ready to add the next card, press **F7** or select **Card | Add**. The Add dialog box appears. Type the index entry into this box and click on **OK**. A blank card appears with the index-entry filled in. Continue adding data to the card.

Incidentally, before you move to the next card, it's possible to restore the card you have been working in to its previous state. This is a type of Undo command, though it undoes much more than usual. Select **Edit | Restore** and Cardfile removes all the information you have added or edited. Once you've moved to the next card, it's too late. However, data is not saved on the hard disk each time you move to another card. You must select **File | Save** or **File | Save As** to save the information. That means, of course, that it *is* possible to restore information by closing the file without saving, and then reopening. (You'll lose all the changes since the last time you saved, which might be more than just one card.)

Cardfile's Save As dialog box (displayed using **File | Save As**) lets you save cards in a format that Windows 3.0 can read. Select "3.0 Card File (*.CRD)" from the Save File as Type drop-down list box. When the file is saved in this format any embedded or linked objects are automatically converted to ordinary pasted objects (*static* objects as they are sometimes known). And color pictures are converted to black and white.

Using List View

Cardfile also has a list view. Select **View | List** and Cardfile displays a list of the index entries (see Figure 18.4). This "stack" works a little differently. Rather than moving the cards around in a circle, you move the highlight down the list. You can use **Up Arrow** and **Down Arrow** to move through the list. **Ctrl-Home** and **Ctrl-End** work in the same way as in the card view, highlighting the first or last card in the stack. **PgUp** and **PgDn** work slightly differently here, moving through the list one screen at a time. The list view still has the arrows in the status line, which move the highlight to the next or previous card.

When you find a card you want to view select **View | Card** and Cardfile displays the stack with the selected card on top. If you point to an entry in the list and **double-click**, Cardfile opens the Index dialog box.

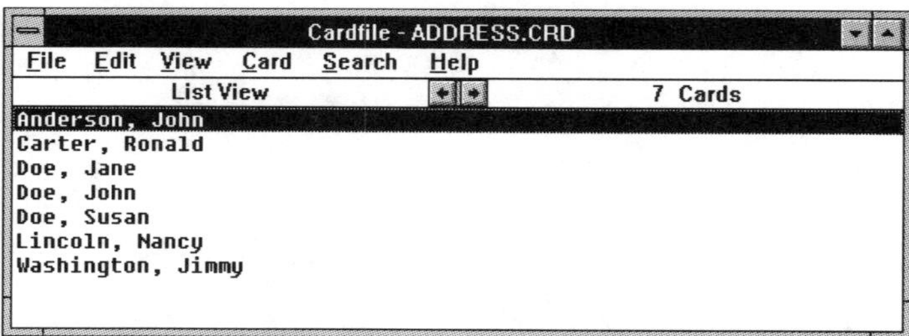

Figure 18.4 The Cardfile in list view

Searching the Card Stack

The cards are placed in a stack. When you move from card to card you are cycling cards through the stack in the same way you would with a real stack of cards. If you are looking at card 1 and want to see card 2, card 1 goes to the bottom of the stack, exposing card 2. Then card 2 goes to the bottom and card 3 appears on the top, and so on.

There are a number of ways to move through the stack of cards to find a particular card.

- Press **PgUp** to move to the next card in the stack.
- Press **PgDn** to move to the previous card in the stack.
- Click on the **Left Arrow** in the status bar to move to the previous card in the stack.
- Click on the **Right Arrow** in the status bar to move to the next card in the stack.
- Click on an **index line** to view that card.
- Press **Ctrl-Home** to move to the first card in the index.
- Press **Ctrl-End** to move to the last card in the index.
- Press **F4** or select **Search | Go To** to use the Go To dialog box.
- Select **Search | Find** to use the Find dialog box.
- Press **Ctrl-Shift-*first index letter*** to move to the first card beginning with that letter.

Cardfile sorts cards in index-entry order, numerically and alphabetically. The easiest way to move through the cards is to click on the arrows in the status line or use the PgUp and PgDn keys.

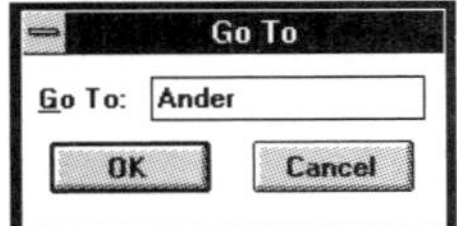

Figure 18.5 The Go To dialog box

Tip Here's a quick way to move through the stack. Place the pointer on the *second* index line, the one behind the card at the front. Click the mouse button repeatedly. Each time you click, the second card is moved to the top and the first card cycles around to the bottom of the stack.

If you want to move to the general area of the stack that holds the card you want, press **Ctrl-Shift-** and the first letter in the index entry. For example, pressing **Ctrl-Shift-W** will move you to the first card with an index entry beginning with W. You could then press **Ctrl-Shift-W** again to move to the *next* card whose index begins with W. This method won't work with numbers, by the way, only letters.

When you press **F4** or select **Search | Go To** Cardfile displays the Go To dialog box (see Figure 18.5). Type part of the index line you want to find. For instance, if the indexed name is Anderson, you could enter just Ander. Click on **OK** and Cardfile searches from the currently displayed card to the bottom of the stack and displays the first card whose index line includes the characters you entered.

You can also search the cards themselves. For instance, you might find a phone number on your phone bill but not remember whose number it is. You could search the entire stack of cards for the number. Select **Search | Find** to see the Find dialog box (shown in Figure 18.6). Enter the text you are looking for, or just a portion of the text.

If you select the **Match Case** check box, Cardfile will search only for text capitalized just as you typed it. For instance, if you type "NeXT" it would ignore

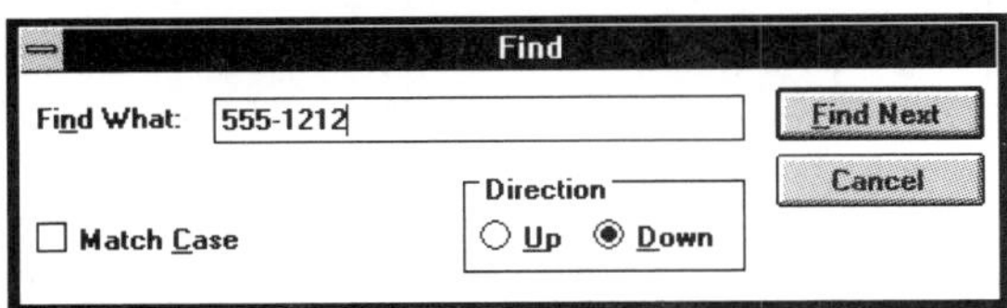

Figure 18.6 The Find dialog box

"next." You can also tell Cardfile in which direction it should search, up or down the stack of cards. Searching "down" means searching from the displayed card (on the top of the stack) through toward the bottom of the stack. Searching "up" means starting with the card on the bottom of the stack and searching toward the top.

Clicking on **Find Next** begins the search. Cardfile will display the first card in which it finds the specified text and will highlight the text. The Find dialog box remains open, so if the displayed card is not the one you want, click on **Find Next** and Cardfile will move to the next one that matches the search text. On the other hand, you can click on **Cancel** to close the dialog box, work in that card, and search for the same text again without opening the dialog box—just press **F3** or select **Search | Find Next**.

By the way, you can use Find only in card view, not list view. Go To works in either view, as does the Ctrl-Shift-index letter method.

Dialing Your Telephone

If you have a Hayes-compatible modem connected to the same line as your phone, you can make Cardfile dial your telephone for you. Select the card containing the number, then select **Card | Autodial**, or press **F5**. Cardfile searches the card for a number with four or more digits and then opens the Autodial dialog box, which displays the number that Cardfile found. Of course this might not be a telephone number, or it might not be the one you want to use (Cardfile uses the first one it finds in the card). You can replace the number with another one if you wish. By the way, you must enter *all* the digits that have to be dialed, and no more. Unlike some sophisticated dialers, Cardfile cannot figure out if it needs to add a 1 before a number, for instance, or to drop an area code if it's a local call.

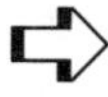

Tip Before you press **F5**, highlight the number you want to dial. Cardfile will place that number in the Autodial dialog box. Or, when entering text into a card, place the phone number in the top-left corner so Cardfile isn't confused by other numbers, such as street numbers.

You can enter a prefix if necessary. For instance, you might need to dial a 9 to get an outside line, or dial *70 to turn off call waiting. Make sure you enter the prefix *and* select the **Use Prefix** check box. The first time you use Autodial, click on **Setup** to extend the dialog box and see the setup options (shown in Figure 18.7). Make sure the **Dial Type** is correct (select Tone if your phone "beeps" when you press a key, or Pulse if it "click-click-clicks"). The **Port** will probably be correct if you have already used other Windows programs with your modem. Otherwise, make sure the correct COM port is selected.

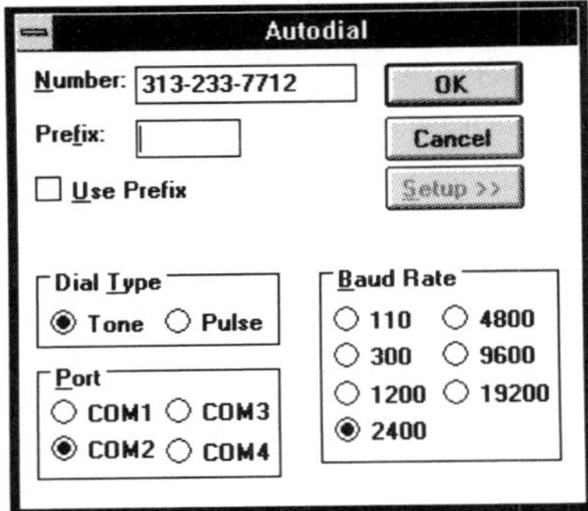

Figure 18.7 The Autodial dialog box showing its setup options

Finally, select the correct baud rate for your modem. The baud rate setting may not have much effect in this situation—it's normally used to control transmission of data—but some modems may need this setting to dial. Many will dial with whatever setting you select.

When you click on **OK** Cardfile displays a small message box telling you to pick up your phone, and then it begins dialing the call. Pick up your phone, but do *not* click on the OK button in the message box yet. As soon as you do so the modem disconnects, so wait until the modem has finished dialing before clicking.

Merging Files

You can join two Cardfile files together, merging all the cards into one database. You might want to merge two address files—for example, your business and personal files. Open one of the files, then select **File | Merge**. The File Merge dialog box appears, which is a typical "Open File" box. Find the file you want to merge with and double-click on it. Cardfile adds the cards in that file to the open file.

You can now save the file. If you want to maintain the current file, use **File | Save As** to create a totally new file. The file you merged from remains unchanged.

Incidentally, you can also split files into two smaller ones. Open the first, then use **File | Save As** to create a copy. Then use **Card | Delete** to remove the cards you don't want, open the original file, and delete the cards that are now stored in the new one.

Printing Cards

You can, of course, print your cards. Use **File | Print** to print the displayed card (the command is not available when you are in list view), or use **File | Print All** to print all the cards in the file. Select card view before printing if you want to print the entire contents of each card, or list view if you want a list of the index entries. Printing all the cards in card view puts several cards on each sheet of paper, not one card per page. Each card is printed as it appears on your screen, including graphics. If you adjust the margins, you can get up to four cards on one $8\frac{1}{2}''$ x 11" sheet of paper. (Use 0.75 for both the top and bottom margins.)

You can also add a header and a footer to the printout. See Chapter 6 for more information on page and printer setup.

Cardfile and OLE

As we mentioned in the introduction to this chapter, Cardfile is much more powerful now that it has OLE to work with. Object Linking and Embedding lets you place the contents of one application into any OLE *client*. Cardfile is a client, so it can accept OLE *packages*, icons that represent data. Double-clicking on a package "plays" the information. If it's a sound, you will hear that sound. If it's a picture, the application that created the picture will open and you will see the picture. The information doesn't necessarily have to come from an OLE server, though; any Windows document file can be placed in a card, so double-clicking will open the original application. You can even drag DOS application files from File Manager onto a card, so a DOS application will run when you double-click on the OLE icon.

OLE expands Cardfile's capabilities enormously. You can embed text files, for instance, that let you store large amounts of text, much more than the capacity of the card itself. You can add sounds, spreadsheets, calendar files, complicated graphics that cannot normally be displayed on a card, photographs, forms, even data communication files that automatically open Windows Terminal. Anything you can create in another application can be embedded in a card. And anything that can be created in an OLE server application can be linked to a card.

For instance, if you copy text from a word processor, then paste it into a card while text mode is selected, Cardfile pastes simple text. Select **Edit | Picture** and *then* paste the text, however, and a package is pasted into the card. If you are using, say, Word for Windows, you will see the Word icon. This icon represents the text. Double-click on the icon to open Word and display the text. (The text formatting may have changed slightly.) In this way you can paste documents into Cardfile that are tens or hundreds of times larger than the amount that can be held as simple text.

If you would like to go directly to a data communications session from a card, open both Cardfile and File Manager and drag a .TRM file to a card. When you double-click on that card, Terminal will open and load the .TRM file—you can immediately dial and connect to the other computer or bulletin board.

If you are interested in working with OLE, you should read Chapter 28, which explains OLE in detail. OLE is very powerful and fairly simple to use—once you understand the various methods.

Cardfile's Menu Options

Here's a summary table showing Cardfile's menu commands.

File | New Closes the current file and displays a new card so you can start a new file. If the current file hasn't been saved, the application asks if you want to do so.

File | Open Lets you open an existing Clipboard file.

File | Save Saves the file. The first time you save you will see the Save As dialog box so you can select a directory and filename.

File | Save As Lets you save the file with a new name, in a different directory, or in Windows 3.0 format.

File | Print Prints the selected card on the printer selected in the Print Setup dialog box. Available only in card view.

File | Print All Prints all the cards in the file.

File | Page Setup Lets you set page margins and create a header and footer.

File | Print Setup Lets you select the printer on which you wish to print your files. Each time you open the application, it automatically selects the default printer selected in the Control Panel's Printers dialog box.

File | Merge Copies the cards from another file into the current one.

File | Exit Closes the application. If you have unsaved changes, Cardfile asks if you want to save the file first.

Edit | Undo (Ctrl-Z) Undoes the last editing operation to correct a mistake. Undo will remove only the last character typed, not the last word.

Edit | Cut (Ctrl-X) Cuts the selected text or picture and places it into the Clipboard.

Edit | Copy (Ctrl-C) Copies the selected text or picture into the Clipboard.

Edit | Paste (Ctrl-V) Copies the text or picture from the Clipboard into the application. If the data is coming from an OLE server, the data is automatically pasted as an embedded object.

Edit | Paste Link Pastes an object from the Clipboard into Clipboard, and creates a link to the original application.

Edit | Paste Special Lets you select different types of paste procedures: OLE embedded, OLE link, or non-OLE (normal).

Edit | Index (F6) Lets you add an index entry to the top line of the card. The card will be filed in index-entry order.

Edit | Restore Removes all the changes you have made to the card since you last opened or saved the card.

Edit | Text Turns on text mode so you can enter text.

Edit | Picture Turns on picture mode so you can cut, copy, paste, or move a picture.

Edit | Link If the card contains a linked object, lets you modify or remove the OLE link.

Edit | *application name* Object Lets you edit the selected linked or embedded object. If the selected item is a package, this menu option is replaced by the following two:

> **Edit | Package Object | Activate Contents** Opens the application that created the object in the selected package so you can view, listen to, or edit the object.
>
> **Edit | Package Object | Edit Package** Opens the Object Packager so you can edit the selected package.

Edit | Insert Object Lets you open an OLE *server* application so you can create an OLE object and paste it into Clipboard.

View | Card Displays the card selected from the list.

View | List Displays a list of index entries, one for each card.

Card | Add (F7) Saves the information in the displayed card and displays a blank one.

Card | Delete Deletes the selected card.

Card | Duplicate Makes a copy of the selected card.

Card | Autodial (F5) Lets you automatically dial the first telephone number in the selected card or dial the highlighted number. You may also enter a number to dial.

Search | Go To (F4) Lets you quickly move to a particular card by specifying the Index text.

Search | Find Lets you search all the cards for the specified text.

Search | Find Next (F3) Lets you search the cards for the specified text again, without reentering the text.

19

Character Map

Character Map is a mini application that helps you use special characters in your Windows applications. Most typeface sets contain special characters, and they are quite easy to use. Each has a code, and most Windows applications have a simple method for inserting special characters. Generally, you turn on Num Lock, press and hold **Alt**, type **0**, and then type the character's three-digit code. The problem, of course, is knowing which code each character uses.

Opening Character Map

Character Map

Start Character Map by clicking on the Character Map icon in the Accessories program group. Or select **File | Run** and run **CHARMAP**. Figure 19.1 shows the Character Map window. When it first opens it displays the Symbol typeface, but you can select any typeface on your system. The next time it opens it will display the typeface that was selected when you closed the application.

The Character Map shown in Figure 19.1 is displaying the special characters in the Wingdings TrueType typeface. You can select any of your Windows fonts from the Font drop-down list box in the top left, whether they are TrueType, Type 1, screen, or vector fonts. If you are using the keyboard, press **Alt-F** to move to the list box, then press **F4** to open the list box. (If you use the down arrow it may take a very long time, as it will try to display each font the highlight passes over.) Then type the first letter of the font you want to view and use the Down Arrow to select the specific font.

If you want a better look at a character, point at it and hold the mouse button down—Windows enlarges the character for you. Or press **Tab** until the highlight moves into the grid (you will see a dotted line around one of the boxes), and then

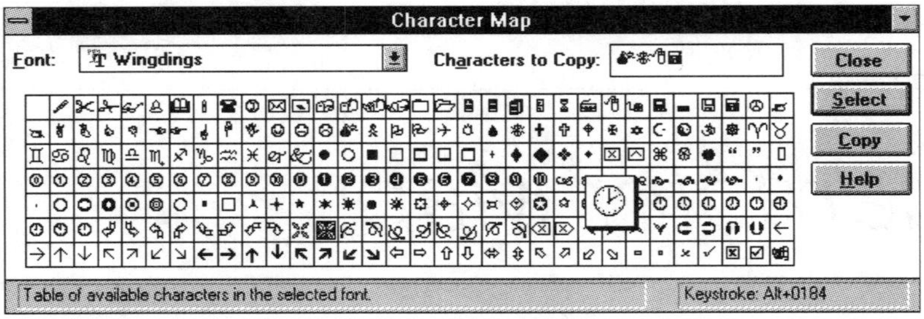

Figure 19.1 The Character Map showing the enlargement of a character

use the arrow keys to move to a character. Each box on which the highlight lands is automatically enlarged.

When you find a character you want to use, double-click on it, or click once and click on **Select**. The character is added to the text box in the top right of the window. You can select as many characters as you want. You can also place the cursor into this text box so you can delete characters, insert spaces between them, or even *type* characters.

Notice the information at the bottom right of the box. When you select a character, this will show you how to create that character *without* opening Character Map. It will tell you the code used to create the character, or the key you must press on your keyboard to create it. This information might be useful if you want to create macros, for instance, so you can insert certain special characters without opening Character Map.

When you have all the characters you need, click on **Copy**—the characters are placed in the Clipboard. Go to the application into which you want to place the characters and use the **Edit|Paste** command. Windows will place the characters into the application. In some cases they may change font. For instance, if you are pasting Wingdings characters into an application, they may be converted to the application's default font. Just select the characters and apply Wingdings font again.

You can only paste these special characters into Windows applications. That doesn't mean you can't use special characters in DOS applications. Some DOS applications let you work with special characters: See your application's documentation to find out how.

Using Special Characters

There are a number of reasons to use special characters. Perhaps the most important reason is to replace "typewriter" style characters with real "typesetting" characters. For instance, which looks better—1/2 or $\frac{1}{2}$? How about (c) or ©? Using the

Table 19.1 Typewriting vs. Typesetting Characters

Character	Typewriter	Typesetting	Usual ANSI Code
Single quotes	' '	‘ ’	145 and 146
Apostrophe	'	’	146
Double quotes	" "	“ ”	147 and 148
Bullet	o	•	149
En dash	-	–	150
(used to indicate a range as in “40–50 rpm”)			
Em dash	--	—	151
(used to indicate a break in the sentence, as in “I’ll be there—wearing green—at noon.”)			
One half	1/2	½	189
One quarter	1/4	¼	188
Three quarters	3/4	¾	190
Copyright sign	copyright	©	169
Registered trademark	reg.	®	174
Trademark	TM	™	
Cent	cent	¢	162
Plus or minus	+/-	±	177
Spanish question mark		¿	191
Division sign	/	÷	247
English pound sign	pound	£	163
mu	mu	µ	181
(12th Greek letter, means micro)			

correct characters makes a document look more professional. Table 19.1 lists a few common characters that you may want to use, available in most normal text fonts (such as Times New Roman).

There are many other special characters you may want to use. You can select accented characters for foreign names and words. For instance, you can type “niño” instead of “nino,” or “Günther” instead of “Gunther.”

Another reason to use special characters is to add highlight elements to a document. For instance, Wingdings has a number of computer-related characters.

If you are writing a training or user manual, you might use the mouse character in the margin next to mouse-related instructions. Remember, you can enlarge the character so it really stands out. You can use these unusual characters in all sorts of ways. Use a ♣ or □ to indicate the end of a chapter or newsletter article, for instance. Or use an arrow or bullseye as a bullet in a list. Use a check mark in a simple checklist, and try putting characters such as petal shapes together as border elements. Take a look at all the special characters you have available, and you'll come up with ideas of your own.

20

Clock

Windows Clock is a simple application that shows you the time and, if you wish, the date. The clock is a window, so you can maximize it, minimize it, or have it any size in between. Several features make it quite convenient. You can keep the clock "Always on Top," so you can see the clock while working in other applications. And even the clock *icon* will display the time, so you can display the time without taking up much room. (The clock displays the hours and minutes in the icon and the month and day—if you turned on the date—in the title.)

Clock displays the system time, of course. You can change system time using DOS's TIME command, or Control Panel's Date & Time dialog box.

Starting Clock

Start Clock by clicking on the Clock icon in the Accessories program group. Or select **File | Run** and run **CLOCK**. The Clock window opens, as shown in Figure 20.1.

The default clock is analog and doesn't show the date. As you'll see in a moment, you can make it digital, add the date, and even change the font. Select **Always on Top** from the Control menu if you want the clock to be visible all the time. You can then size and move the clock to place it over an area of your application in which you don't need to work—the title bar, for instance. (You can reduce the clock so it's about the same height as a title bar, see Figure 20.2.) This command is on the Control menu so that it's always accessible, even when the clock is minimized.

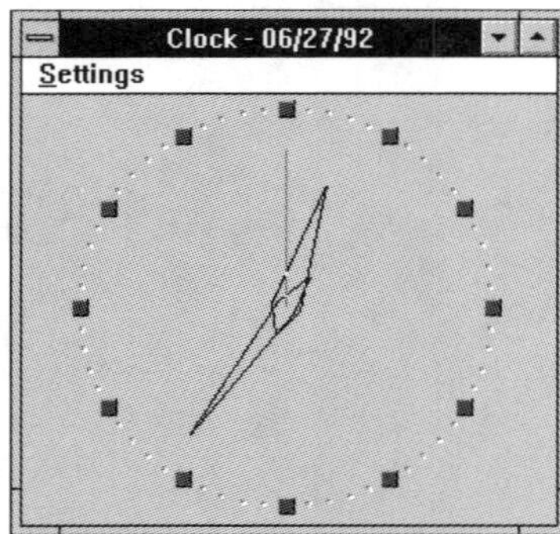

Figure 20.1 The Clock window showing the standard analog face, a second hand, and the date

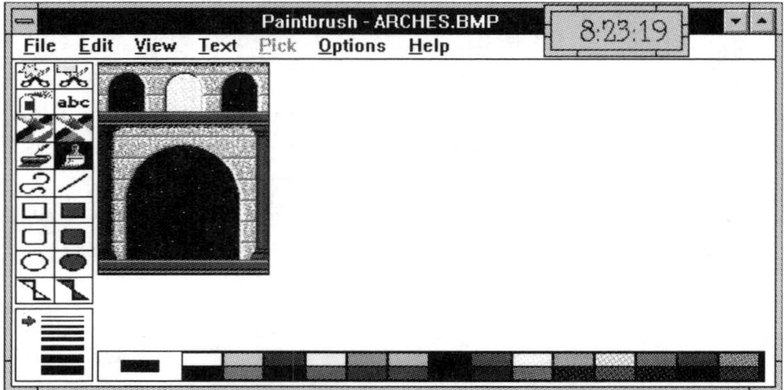

Figure 20.2 The clock placed on Paintbrush's menu bar

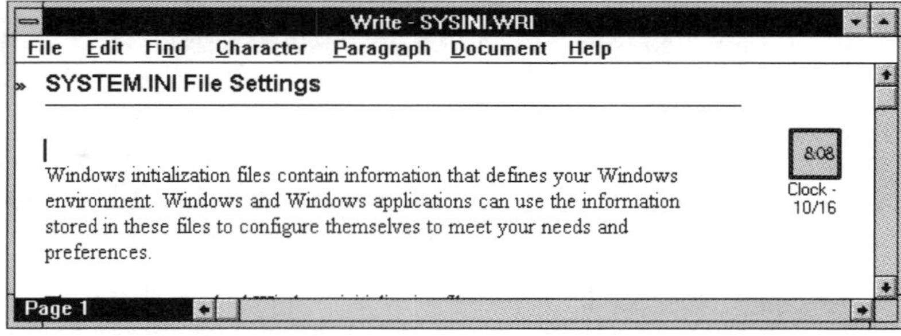

Figure 20.3 The clock icon visible on top of Write while working on a document

Tip If you use a "virtual desktop" such as More Widows, Big Desk, or TopDesk, you may want to run several clocks at the same time so it's always visible. Windows 3.1 won't let you run more than one clock at a time. However, you can make a copy of CLOCK.EXE (or several copies, if you wish). Name the copy CLOCK2.EXE, and give it an icon in Program Manager. The only potential problem with this system is that when you reopen the clocks they will all have the same settings.

Customizing Clock

The most obvious change you can make is to select **Settings | Digital** to select the digital clock (see Figure 20.4). Although the illustration shows the time in a raised or embossed font, that style is used only when the clock is large enough to be displayed appropriately. You can also remove the title and menu bars. Selecting **Settings | No Title** removes the title bar. You can also press **Esc** or double-click anywhere in the clock face (not on the title bar) to toggle the bars on and off. The **Settings | Seconds** and **Settings | Date** commands adds the seconds and date to the clock. In the digital clock the date appears below the time. In the analog clock it appears in the title bar.

Modify Clock's size like any other window. Use the minimize and maximize buttons, the Control menu, the borders, or double-click on the title bar. You can also move the clock around the window. The easiest method is by dragging the title bar, but if you have removed the title bar you can drag the clock face itself.

You can even modify the font, selecting any Windows-compatible font except Wingdings and Symbol. You can, however, select another special-character font,

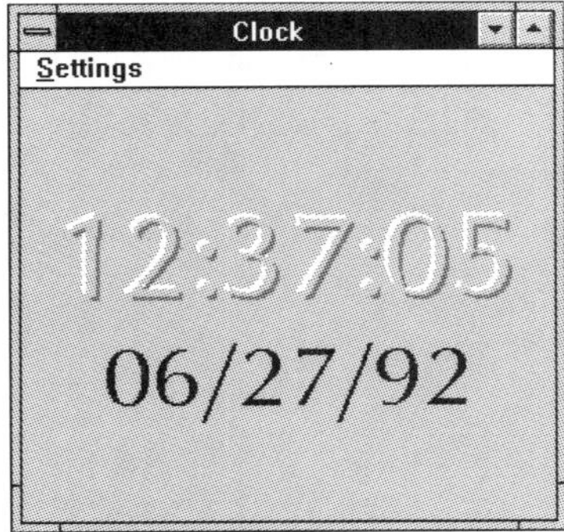

Figure 20.4 The digital clock with the time and date

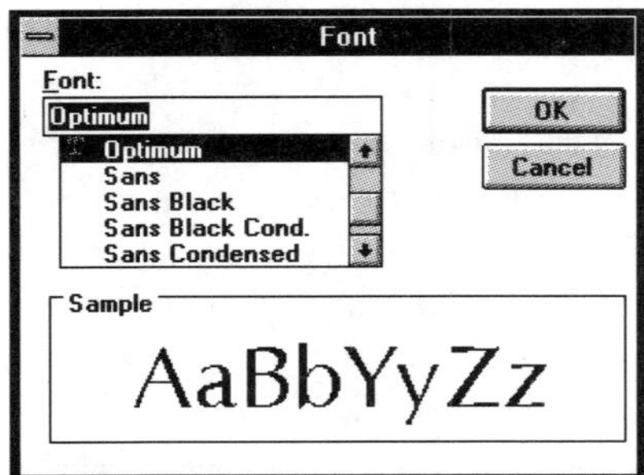

Figure 20.5 The Font dialog box

such as Zapf Dingbats. (This won't help you tell the time, but it might be amusing if you are looking for a stupid Windows trick to play on a colleague.) Select **Settings | Font** to see the Font dialog box (shown in Figure 20.5). Select a font from the list: Windows shows you an example of what that font will look like in Figure 20.5.

The settings are saved each time you close the Clock so it will look the same the next time you open it. Use the Control menu to close the Clock like any other window. If you have removed the title and menu bar, you won't be able to press Alt-Spacebar to open the Control menu, but you can press Ctrl-Esc and use the Task List dialog box to close it so it will open without a title bar the next time you start it.

Tip Are you stuck in the clock? Windows won't let you switch to other applications while you've got the clock maximized? Turn off Always on Top in the control menu!

21

Games

Many people seem to think computers were designed for games, with work a secondary concern. However, Windows doesn't pay much attention to pure entertainment. Microsoft sells "Windows Entertainment Packs," and, perhaps to whet your appetite, Windows provides a taste of what is available.

In the Games program group you will find just two simple games, Minesweeper and Solitaire. It's popular to suggest that these are not simply entertainment, but provide a way to "practice basic skills," and take a "relaxing break." Perhaps you should tell your boss that the next time you're caught goofing off!

Minesweeper

Start the Minesweeper game by double-clicking on the Minesweeper icon in the Games program group. Or select **File | Run** and run **WINMINE**. The Minesweeper "window" appears (see Figure 21.1). This is not a typical application window. You can move and minimize it, but you cannot maximize it. The only way to modify its size is by selecting the **Game | Custom** option.

The game comprises a grid with "mines" hidden randomly under some of the squares. You must uncover all the squares that do not have mines, leaving the mined squares covered. You have up to 999 seconds to accomplish this—the maximum time that the LEDs (light-emitting diodes) on the right side can display. (You can continue playing after 999 seconds, but Minesweeper won't time you.) The LEDs on the left side of the window indicate the number of hidden mines.

Figure 21.1 The Minesweeper window

Your first move is pure luck. Point at a square and click. One of three things will happen.

1. **A mine is uncovered** The game's already over—you exploded.
2. **A number appears** The square you clicked on doesn't have a mine, but it is next to one that does. The number indicates how many adjoining squares contain mines. For instance, if the square shows 4, four of the eight surrounding squares contain mines.
3. **Blank and numbered squares are uncovered** If the square you clicked on doesn't contain a mine, Minesweeper uncovers all the adjoining ones that don't have mines and are not next to a square that has one. Minesweeper continues uncovering squares until it reaches some that are next to mines. (These squares display a number, indicating how many mines they are next to.) Large areas of the board can be uncovered in this way.

In Figure 21.2 we clicked on the square at the fourth column, fourth row. Minesweeper uncovered three contiguous empty squares and the surrounding squares that are next to mines.

Figure 21.2 These squares were uncovered with one click on the fourth column, fourth row

Think of each number as the center of a nine-square grid. If the number is on the side of the window, parts of the grid are missing, but that just makes it easier. For instance, if a square in one corner shows 3, it means all the surrounding squares contain mines (because there are only three surrounding squares).

You can mark a square with a flag by pointing at it and clicking the **right mouse button**. Once marked you cannot uncover it by clicking on it with the left button. This is simply a way to remind yourself of where you believe the mines are, and to avoid accidentally clicking on one. It also subtracts one from the mine count in the top left LEDs. Remember that you may have incorrectly flagged a square, in which case the mine count will be wrong.

There's a command called **Game | Marks (?)** that toggles on and off the ability to use a special marker. If a check mark appears next to the option in the menu, you can place a question mark on a square by clicking the **right button twice**—the first time places the flag, the second replaces it with a question mark. This is a way to mark a mine without adjusting the mine count LEDs. However, a question mark doesn't protect a square. You can click on it with the left button to uncover it.

You can remove a question mark by pointing at it and clicking the right mouse button again. If the Game | Marks (?) option is selected you can remove the flag from a square by clicking twice. You only need to click once if the option isn't selected. The question mark is useful for testing scenarios. Place the question marks where you think mines may be, or mark "either/or" locations, and then think through the logic behind your decisions.

Finding Mines

The game, then, is a process of elimination. Once you have some numbers on the board you can decide which squares *must* have a mine and which *cannot* have a mine. The first thing you should do is look for numbered squares that have a matching number of uncovered squares touching—all the uncovered squares must have mines. For example, you can often find squares containing 1, with only one square touching—that square obviously contains a mine. Once you have marked some mines, you can look for squares that *cannot* have mines.

For instance, in Figure 21.3 we quickly found four mined squares. The number 4 has only four uncovered squares adjoining it, so they must all contain mines. That means the two squares immediately below the rightmost flag *cannot* contain mines. Why? Because in the column to the right of the 4 are four 1s. The third 1 down touches the rightmost flag, so the other squares touching the 1 cannot contain mines. We can uncover those squares and find more clues.

We can also tell from this example that the square up and to the left of the 3 must have a mine (so we should mark it). We know this because there are only three squares touching the 3. Consequently, the square above that one cannot have

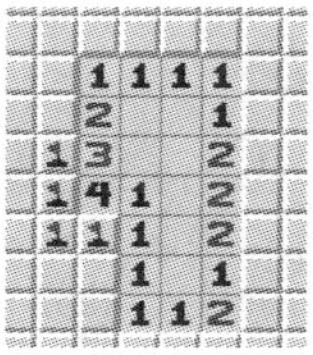

Figure 21.3 An example of mine-sweeping strategy

a mine because there's a 2 touching it, and the 2 touches the square to its left and the 1 to the left of the 3, both of which we know have mines.

Here's another example: In Figure 21.4 we have marked several mines. We know there's a mine at position (a), for instance, because of the 1 in the square diagonally down and to the right. That number 1 means that there is one mine in this square's surrounding squares. As all but one square have been uncovered, we know which square has the mine. The square at (b) has been marked for the same reason. (We have marked both these squares with flags, which look a little like 1s.)

The squares marked at (c) must have mines because of the 2 next to them—they are the only two uncovered squares next to the number 2. We know also that square (d) *cannot* have a mine: The 3 indicates that three of the surrounding squares have mines, and we've already found those, so (d) must be clear.

At times you simply have to take a chance, because there aren't enough clues to lead you to the next square to click on. You can take a shot in the dark, or, if you want to take the game seriously, figure out the squares with the best chance. For example, the Beginner's game board has 64 squares and 10 mines, so wherever you click the first time you have 1 chance in 6.4 of hitting a mine. Now, let's say the first square you click on is a 1. That means the surrounding squares contain one mine. So if you click in a surrounding square you have 1 chance in 3 of hitting a mine if the original square is in a corner, 1 in 5 if it's on the edge but not in the corner, and 1 in 8 if it's inside the board.

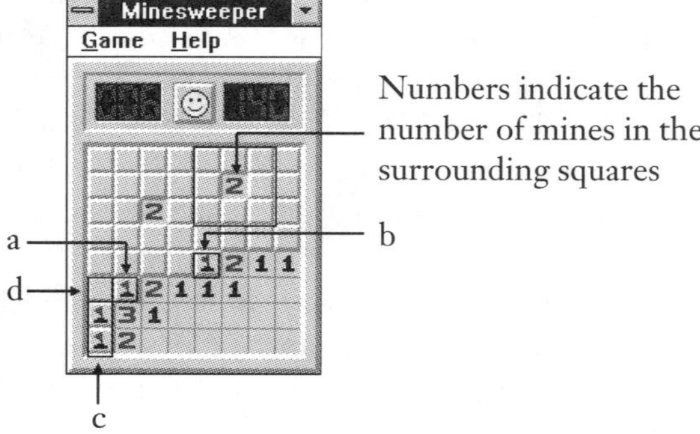

Figure 21.4 Minesweeper with some mines marked

What if you decide to click elsewhere on the board, in a square that is not next to the original one? Well, if the number was a 1, we know there are nine other mines outside the adjoining grid. Using our three examples the chances of hitting a mine would be 1:6.7, 1:6.4, and 1:6.1. (Simply subtract the squares in the grid from 64, then divide by 9.) This means that if you click in the middle of the board and the square displays a 1, you should click on one of the surrounding eight squares because you have a 1:8 chance of hitting a mine, compared with a 1:6.1 chance of hitting one elsewhere.

Of course if the original number was a different number, the calculations change. If the number is a 2, the three chances within the square's adjoining gird are now 1:1.5, 1:2.5, and 1:4, and outside the grid they are 1:7.5, 1:7.3, and 1:7.

Clearing Areas

You can clear mines from an area surrounding a numbered square. For instance, let's say you have uncovered a number and marked the mines around it. There are some squares you haven't marked because you are sure they don't contain mines. You can clear these squares by clicking on each one with the left button. Or you can point at the number, press and hold the left button, then click the right button. Minesweeper automatically uncovers all the surrounding unmarked squares, revealing blanks or more numbers. Of course if you are wrong and Minesweeper reveals a mine, you've just lost the game.

To use this two-button method you must have flagged the correct number of mines in the surrounding squares. If the number is a 3, for instance, you can't use the method if you've marked two mines or four. The question mark has no effect, however.

For instance, take a look at Figure 21.5. In this Intermediate level game we pointed at the 3 in the sixth row, second column from the right, and pressed both mouse buttons. Minesweeper cleared the surrounding squares, but one was incorrectly flagged (the mine with a cross on it). Consequently, the mined square wasn't marked. The mine is on the right of the 3, and its square is colored red when uncovered.

If you hit a mine at any time, the game's over. The mine you hit is uncovered, as are all the mines you didn't flag. A square that you flagged incorrectly will display a mine with a red cross through it.

But what if you win? To win you must uncover all the *unmined* squares within 999 seconds (more than 16 minutes). You don't have to flag the mines (that's for your benefit). When you finally win, the smiley face puts on its dark glasses, and Minesweeper flags any squares that contained mines but weren't flagged. A dialog box may appear asking for your name (if you've beaten the previous record for winning the game in the shortest time). Your name will be entered into the Fastest

Figure 21.5 An unflagged mine exploded when the two-button method was used (row 6, last column on the right).

Mine Sweepers dialog box, displayed by selecting **Game | Best Times**. (You can use the Reset Scores button in this dialog box to set the times back to 999 and remove the players' names.)

Now you can start all over again. (There's no hurry to get back to work.) There are three ways to begin a new game: Select **Game | New**, press **F2**, or click on the **smiley face** (if you've just lost a game the face won't be smiling).

Customizing Minesweeper

You can customize Minesweeper in a number of ways. You can toggle between a color and a black-and-white board by selecting **Game | Color**. Or you can select the game level from the **Game** menu: **Beginner** (64 squares and 10 mines), **Intermediate** (256 squares and 40 mines), or **Expert** (480 squares and 99 mines). Notice, by the way, that the Intermediate board is simply larger—it has the same ratio of mines to squares (1:6.4) as the Beginner board. The Expert board, however, has a ratio of 1:4.9.

If these options aren't good enough for you, select **Game | Custom** to see the Custom Field dialog box. In this you may enter a height of up to 24 squares, a width of up to 30 squares, and up to 667 mines (which is rather pointless). The next time you open Minesweeper, it will still have the last configuration.

Solitaire

Start the Solitaire game by double-clicking on the Solitaire icon in the Games program group. Or select **File | Run** and run **SOL**. Figure 21.6 shows the Solitaire

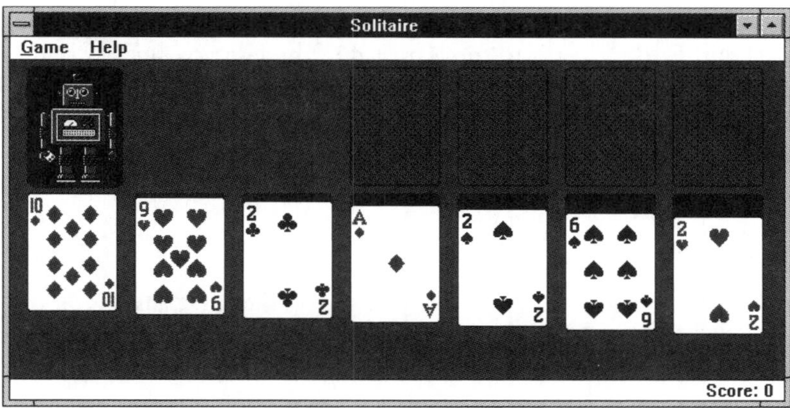

Figure 21.6 The Solitaire window

window. You can maximize this window, if you wish, or use the borders to adjust its size.

The window shows a deck of 52 cards. Windows has dealt 28 of those cards for you, in seven stacks (the *row* stacks): one in the first, two in the second, and so on to stack seven, which contains seven cards. The top card in each stack is faceup; the others are face down. The rest of the cards are in the deck in the top-left corner, face down. There are also four blank decks in the top row. You will try to move stacks from the rows to these *suit* stacks.

The purpose of the game is to place as many cards as possible in the suit stacks, in the appropriate suits, with ace at the bottom and King at the top (ace, 2, 3, 4, 5, 6, 7, 8, 9, 10, Jack, Queen, King). To do that you must use the row stacks as intermediate stacks. Each row stack alternates black and red cards (light and dark cards on a monochrome monitor), running the *opposite* direction, with the King at the bottom. Whenever you can move a card to the suit stacks you should do so. And if you can move a card from the deck to a row stack, or from one row stack to another, you should do so.

Moving Cards

You can move cards using the mouse. Simply point, press, and hold the mouse button, and drag the card to where you want it to go. If the move is improper, Solitaire pops the card back when you release the button. To turn over a face-down card, click once on it.

You can use the keyboard to play Solitaire, but you probably won't want to. It's very slow. Press **Tab** to move the pointer between the face-down deck, the face-up cards from the deck, the suit stacks, and the row stacks. Use the **Left** and **Right Arrow** keys to move between individual stacks. The **Up Arrow** and **Down Arrow** keys move the pointer up and down an individual stack. **Home** moves the pointer to the deck, and **End** moves it to the last card of the last row stack. Press **Enter** or **Spacebar** to turn over a card or deal a card from the deck. To move a card, point at it, press **Enter** or **Spacebar**, then use the arrow keys and press **Enter** or **Spacebar** again.

Playing the Game

When you begin a new game, how do you start? The first thing you must do is check your cards to see if you can move any. If you have any aces, place them on the suit stacks in the top row. If you have faceup cards that are immediately lower than others on another stack—and of a different color—you can move them to the other stacks.

For instance, in Figure 21.6 you can move the ace of diamonds onto one of the suit stacks. None of the other cards can be moved. However, moving the ace exposed a face-down card. Click on the card to turn it over. In this example the card was the 9 of spades, which could immediately be moved to the 10 of diamonds (because the 10 of diamonds is red and one card higher than the 9 of spades).

That exposed another card, in this case the 9 of diamonds. At this point we are stuck because none of the cards can go anywhere. No card has another one that is a different color and one step higher onto which it could be placed. So we click on the deck to deal some cards. The result is as you see it in Figure 21.7.

By default Solitaire deals three cards. (You can customize the program to deal one card at a time; we'll explain that later.) You see all three cards, but you can use only the top one. If you want to use a card lower down, you must find some way to use the top card first. In our example the 8 of spades can go on the 9 of hearts. But

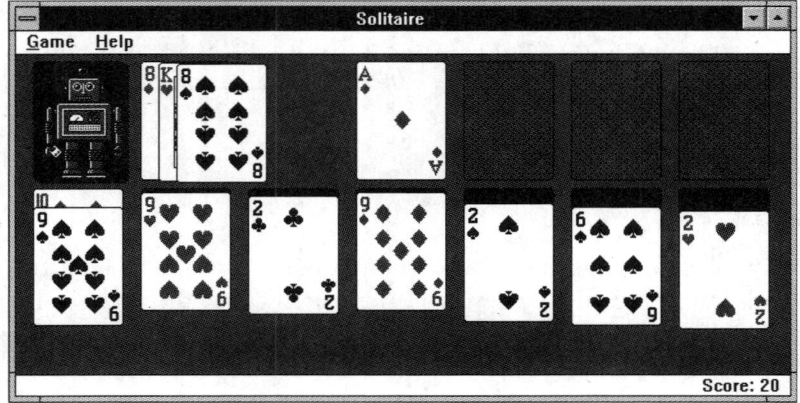

Figure 21.7 Solitaire after making several moves and dealing some cards

the next card is a King. You can place a King only on a blank space in the row or on top of one of the suit stacks. In other words, you must move all the cards out of one of the row stacks, or build a suit stack all the way to the Queen. There's no way to do that right now, so we can't use the King—or the 8 of diamonds below it (which could have gone on the 9 of spades).

▼ ***Note*** If moving cards creates a blank space in the row, only a King may be placed on the blank.

Our only option is to click on the deck again, to deal three more cards. The three new cards appear, covering the other two. This time we get the 8 of hearts (which we place on the 9 of spades) and the 7 of clubs (which we place on the 8 of hearts).

You continue in this way, playing the cards whenever you can and dealing new cards when you can't. As you place cards from the deck onto rows, you will find that cards on other rows can be moved across, extending the stack. As you deal or uncover aces, you will place them on the suit stacks. As your suit stacks grow you will take appropriate dealt or uncovered cards and place them on the suit stacks.

When you run out of cards in the deck, a large green circle appears where the face-down deck was. Click on the circle twice to place the faceup cards back in the deck and draw again. If you see a red cross instead of the circle, you are using the Vegas scoring method and cannot draw again (we'll explain the different scoring methods in a few moments).

You can also move all the faceup cards from one row stack to another. For instance, you have one stack from King down to 9, and another from 7 down to 4. You deal an 8 and place it on the King-to-9 stack. You can now move the 7-to-4 stack over to the other one. You will want to do this for several reasons. First, you want to uncover the cards that are face down in the row stacks so you can use them elsewhere. You also want to make blank spaces in the row, so if you deal a King you can move it to the blank and begin a new stack. And you may sometimes want to get to cards inside row stacks so they can be moved to the suit stacks.

For instance, you have a stack from King to 3. The 5 in this stack is the 5 of clubs, which you can place on the clubs suit stack. So you move the last two cards from this stack (the 4 and 3) to another stack—assuming that a black 5 is available on another stack.

If you ever move a card and immediately regret it, select **Game | Undo** and Solitaire reverses the last move. There's no keyboard shortcut for this: For some reason, Alt-Backspace won't work.

When you have finished a game, you can select **Game | Deal** to begin a new one.

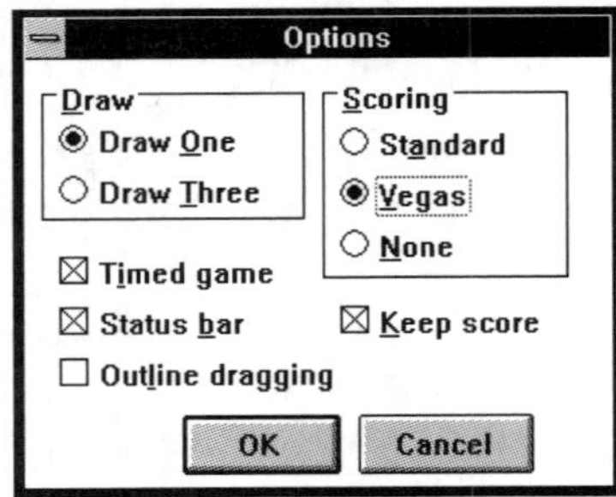

Figure 21.8 The Options dialog box

Drawing and Scoring

You have two drawing methods to choose from. Select **Game | Options**. When the Options dialog box appears (Figure 21.8) select either Draw One or Draw Three. With the first method, each time you draw from the deck you get just one card. With the second you get three cards. If you are using Draw One, a game is regarded as one pass through the deck. With Draw Three a game is three passes through the deck.

You also have two scoring methods to choose from, Standard or Vegas. (The score is shown at the bottom of Solitaire's window, in the status bar.) By default the game uses Standard scoring. Select the Vegas method by clicking on the Vegas option button and click on **OK**. Notice that you can also select **None**, so Solitaire won't keep score.

The **Standard** method bases your score on the cards you move and the time you take. You get points for particular moves, and every 10 seconds Solitaire subtracts two points from your score. Also, if you win—placing *all* the cards in the suit stacks, a rare occurrence—you get a bonus, based on the total time. You can turn off the timing and base the score on the moves only. (Make sure the **Timed Game** check box doesn't have a check mark in it.) These are the points you get in Standard scoring.

Move	*Points*
Move a card to a suit stack	10
Move a card from the deck to a row stack	5
Turn over a card in a suit stack	5
Move a card from a suit stack to a row stack	–15

Move	*Points*
Pass through the deck more than three times (Draw Three option)	–20 points per pass
Pass through the deck more than once (Draw One option)	–100 points per pass

You will never have a *negative* score using the Standard system, by the way. Solitaire will subtract down to 0, but no lower.

Tip Notice that you score for placing a card in a row stack and a suit stack. So if you deal a card that can go in a suit stack, move it to a row stack first, if possible. *Then* move it to the suit stack. You will earn 15 points instead of 10.

When you use **Vegas** scoring you begin each game by wagering $52 (you will see –$52 in the status bar, in red). You must earn more than you wagered. You earn points only when you place a card in a suit stack (5 points each time), and you lose 5 points if you take a card from a suit stack and place it on a row stack. As you earn points your negative score will drop until, if you're lucky, you see a positive number (in black).

You will not be able to pass through the deck more than once (if you are using the Draw One option) or three times (if you are using the Draw Three option) if you use the Vegas scoring method (with Standard you can go through as many times as you want, but you lose points after the initial one or three times).

You can keep a count of your wins (or losses) accumulated during several games while playing with Vegas scoring by selecting the **Keep Score** check box in the Options dialog box. (This option is disabled if you select Standard scoring.) If you use this option, to return to a –$52 you must select either None or Standard in the Option, click on **OK**, then return and reselect the Vegas option.

Note You can't change Draw, Scoring, or Timed Game options in the middle of a game. Each time you change these options Solitaire deals a new game.

Customizing Solitaire

As you can see in the Options dialog box (Figure 21.8), you can turn the status bar on and off by clicking on the **Status Bar** check box. The status bar displays the score (as long as None is not selected as the Scoring method) and the elapsed time (if Timed Game is selected). If you turn off the status bar, but you still have one of the Scoring options selected, Solitaire will still keep score, and you can view the score at any time by turning the status bar back on.

Notice also the **Outline Dragging** check box. When this is turned on, moving a card displays merely an outline of the card until you release the mouse button. There are two advantages to this. First, if you are using Windows on a very slow machine, the outline moves will be quicker than moving the actual card. Second, when you use outline dragging Solitaire will indicate correct moves by changing the color of the card the outline passes over (as in Figure 21.9).

There's a disadvantage to outline dragging, though. Because you are moving only an outline, the card itself remains in position until you release the mouse button. You won't be able to move a card simply to see what's underneath unless outline dragging is turned off.

You can also modify the back of the deck. Select **Game | Decks** to see the Select Card Back dialog box. You have 12 different card backs to choose from: fish, a seashell, Dracula's castle, a robot, flowers, and so on. Double-click the one you want, or select it and click on **OK**. Solitaire will use the selected deck for all subsequent games and automatically select the deck the next time you play.

Tips

Solitaire can get complicated. You have so many places to watch at the same time: Can you place a card directly on a suit stack? Can you move one row stack onto another to expose a card that can be placed on a suit stack? Should you lose points moving a card from the suit stacks to the row stacks so you can use a dealt card?

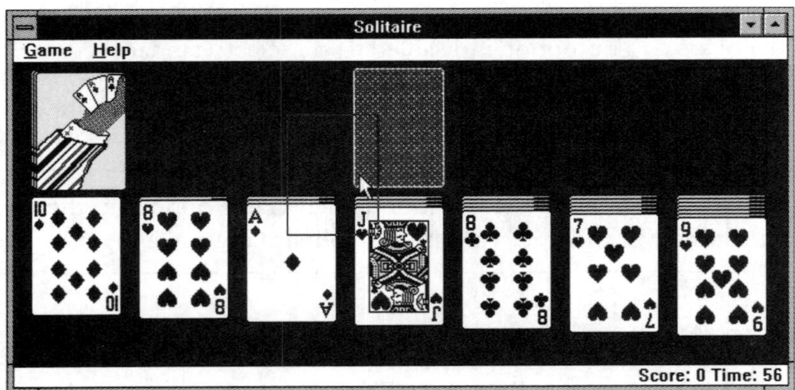

Figure 21.9 Using outline dragging to move a card

The most important thing to remember is to not miss any plays. Each time you place a card in a row stack or move a card to a suit stack, check the other cards to see if you have opened up any opportunities. It's important to uncover the face-down cards on the row stacks as soon as possible and to provide spaces in which you can place Kings.

Here are a few more things to keep in mind.

- You can move a King only to an empty row stack or to the top of a suit stack.
- As soon as you uncover a face-down card in a row stack, turn it over.
- Move cards to the suit stacks as soon as possible.
- You can split row stacks, moving some of the cards to another stack, exposing the cards below.
- You can move an entire row stack onto another row stack—leaving a blank space for a King.
- Once you have four Kings on the board (or enough spaces for all four Kings), don't join stacks together unless absolutely necessary. Once merged, you cannot split the stacks and place the top half back in a blank space.
- If you have a King on top of several face-down cards and a blank space becomes available, you may move the King to the space immediately (freeing the cards below), or leave the space open waiting for another King.
- You may want to move a card from a suit stack to a row stack if it enables you to then use one of the dealt cards. For instance, by borrowing a red 3 from a suit stack you can use a black 2. However, you will be penalized 15 points in Standard scoring, or 5 points in Vegas scoring.

Caution If you've never played any computer games—or if the last computer game you played was an early "ping-pong" game—you may not realize just how addictive such games can be. It's easy to get involved in one of these games, and before you know it you've missed a deadline, forgotten to pick up your kids from school, or overlooked eating, sleeping, or showering.

22

Notepad

Notepad is a simple text editor. It uses ASCII files, so it's perfect for editing Windows' .INI files, AUTOEXEC.BAT, and CONFIG.SYS. You can also use it to create DOS batch files and view README files. Some Windows applications open Notepad automatically, allowing you to use it for keeping simple notes. The Desktop Set, for instance, has an Edit | Notes command that opens a Notepad file and associates the file with an entry in its phone book.

Notepad contains simple text-formatting features—it is by no means a powerful word processor. You can open, save, and close files. You can set up page margins and enter a header and a footer. You can also select a printer and print the document; cut, copy, and paste text; add a time and date "stamp"; turn word wrap on and off; and search for particular words.

The fancy footwork done by real word processors is achieved by using embedded codes, and Notepad simply isn't that powerful. You don't want these codes turning up in .INI files or .BAT files anyway, so if you need more formatting features than Notepad gives you, try Windows Write or use a full-featured word processor.

Starting Notepad

Start Notepad by clicking on the Notepad icon in the Accessories program group. Or select **File | Run** and run **NOTEPAD**. Figure 22.1 shows the Notepad window. Notepad automatically opens a blank text area, so as soon as you open Notepad you can begin typing. Use these keyboard commands.

Start a new paragraph	**Enter**
Leave a blank line	Press **Enter** twice

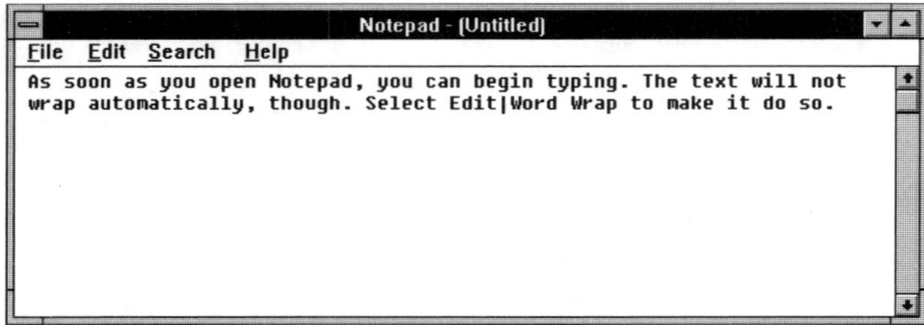

Figure 22.1 The Notepad window

Indent a line	**Tab**
Enter a tab space	**Tab**
Delete the previous character	**Backspace**
Delete the next character	**Del**
Delete next word	**Ctrl-Del**
Delete a block of text	Select the text, then press **Backspace** or **Del**, or select **Edit | Delete**
Move cursor one character	**left** and **right arrow** keys
Move cursor one line	**up** and **down arrow** keys
Move cursor to next word	**Ctrl-right arrow**
Move cursor to last word	**Ctrl-left arrow**
Move cursor to end of line	**End**
Move cursor to start of line	**Home**
Move cursor to end of file	**Ctrl-End**
Move cursor to start of file	**Ctrl-Home**
Select text, character at a time	**Shift-left arrow** and **Shift-right arrow**
Select text, line at a time	**Shift-up arrow** and **Shift-down arrow**
Select all text to start of line	**Shift-Home**
Select all text to end of line	**Shift-End**
Select all text to start of file	**Shift-Ctrl-Home**
Select all text to end of file	**Shift-Ctrl-End**
Select all text in file	**Edit | Select All**

You can also select text by dragging the mouse pointer across it, or by clicking at the beginning of a text block you want to select, pressing and holding **Shift**, and at the end of the block.

Pressing **Tab** moves the insertion point across about eight spaces, letting you indent paragraphs or set up columns of text. You can't change the tab spacing or add intermediate tab points. By default **Edit | Word Wrap** is turned off each time you open Notepad, even if you turned it on the last time you used it. As you type your text into the window, Notepad places it all on one line until you exceed 124 characters, at which point Notepad starts a new line. You can start a new line at any time by simply pressing **Enter**. If you turn Word Wrap *on*, though, Notepad automatically starts a new line when you reach the edge of the Window—so the line's length depends on the window's width. When Word Wrap is on, a check mark appears next to it in the Edit menu and the horizontal scroll bar disappears (Word Wrap remains on even if you open a new file).

We explained how to use the File commands earlier in this book—how to open, close, and save files, and how to select a printer and close an application—so we won't repeat that here. Notepad files use the .TXT extension, and Windows automatically associates that extension with Notepad. So if you double-click on a Notepad file in File Manager, Notepad automatically opens and loads the file. Many applications use the extension .TXT for ASCII files—for README files, for example—so when you load a new application you can easily view these files by double-clicking on them. Windows lets you open several Notepad windows at the same time, so you can work on several different files at once, perhaps copying text from one to another.

We explained the Edit menu's Undo, Cut, Copy, Paste, and Delete commands in Chapter 6. They work just the same in Notepad.

Searching for Text

Notepad contains a simple text-search procedure. Select **Search | Find** to see the Find dialog box (shown in Figure 22.2). Type the text you are looking for into the Find What text box—a word, several words, or just part of a word. If you are looking for a word of a specific case (NOTEPAD rather than Notepad, for instance), click on the Match Case check box, and make sure you typed the text correctly. If you want to search from the current text insertion point *down* the document, click on **Find Next**. If you want to search *up* the file, select Up and then click on **Find Next**.

Notepad begins searching for the text. When it finds the first occurrence, it stops and highlights it. You can now press **Esc** or click **Cancel** to remove the dialog box, or click **Find Next** to continue to the next occurrence. If it is unable to find the text it will display a message. It is important to note that the search feature will not automatically start at the top of the file again. Some word processors' search commands will search from the text insertion point to the end of the file, and then—usually after asking if you want to continue from the beginning—go to the top of the file and start again. If you didn't start at the beginning of the file and want to make sure Notepad searches the entire file, you will have to place the insertion point at the top of the file.

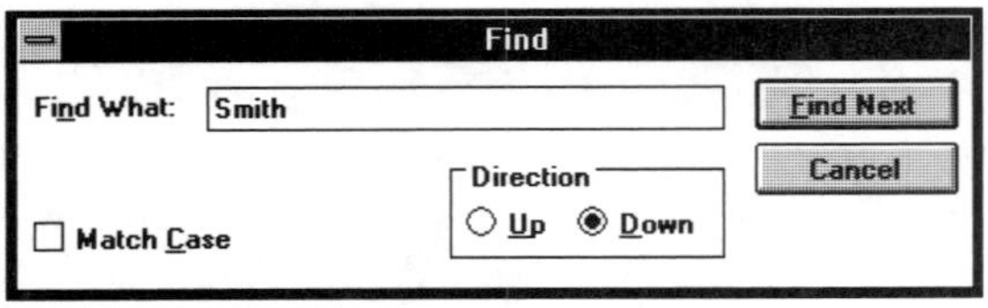

Figure 22.2 The Find dialog box

Once you have closed the Find dialog box, you can search for the text again, without reopening the box, by selecting **Search | Find Next** or by pressing **F3**. In fact, the first time you need to search for text since opening or beginning a file you can press **F3** and the Find dialog box appears.

Creating an Automatic Time Log

Notepad has a special feature that lets you automatically create a time-log document. Each time you open the document Notepad will add the time and date to the last line. You can then make notes—perhaps write down the day's activities.

All you need to do to create a time-log document is type **.LOG** in the first line. It must be uppercase, and the **.** must be in the first column. You can add a time and date stamp to any document by selecting **Edit | Time/Date** or by pressing **F5.**

▼ ***Note*** Use the Control Panel to change the time-log and Edit | Time/Date date formats.

Printing

You can place headers and footers in your document, using the same system Calendar and Cardfile use. (See Chapter 6 for more information.) When you print the document, remember that Word Wrap will affect what it looks like. If Word Wrap is *off*, long lines will still be wrapped to fit them within the margins. If Word Wrap is *on*, the size of the window affects how the text looks on the page—if your window is very narrow, the text will appear in a narrow column on the left side of the page.

Incidentally, Notepad prints the entire file at once—you won't have the option of selecting which pages you want.

 **Tip** If you often need to work in an ASCII file—an .INI or .BAT file, for instance—set up an icon for it. In the Program Item Properties box, type the filename in the Command Line text box (see Chapter 4 for details). If the file is not associated with Notepad, type **notepad** ***path-name\filename***. For example, you could type **notepad c:\autoexec.bat**. Double-clicking on the icon will open Notepad, with AUTOEXEC.BAT already loaded.

Notepad's Menu Options

Following is a summary of Notepad's menu commands.

File | New Clears the window so you can start a new file. If the current text hasn't been saved, Notepad asks if you want to do so.

File | Open Lets you open a Notepad file, or any ASCII file. Notepad is usually unable to open files with complicated text formatting.

File | Save Saves the file. The first time you save the file you will see the Save As dialog box so you can select a directory and filename.

File | Save As Lets you save the file with a new name or in a different directory.

File | Print Prints the file on the printer selected in the Print Setup dialog box.

File | Page Setup Lets you set page margins and create a header and footer.

File | Print Setup Lets you select the printer on which you wish to print your Notepad files. Each time you open Notepad, it automatically selects the default printer selected in the Control Panel's Printers dialog box.

File | Exit Closes Notepad. If you have unsaved text in the window, Notepad asks if you want to save it first.

Edit | Undo (Ctrl-Backspace) Undoes the last changes you made.

Edit | Cut (Ctrl-X) Cuts the selected text and places it into the Clipboard.

Edit | Copy (Ctrl-C) Copies the selected text into the Clipboard.

Edit | Paste (Ctrl-V) Copies text from the Clipboard. You cannot paste images into Notepad.

Edit | Delete (Del) Deletes the selected text.

Edit | Select All Selects all the text in the document.

Edit | Time/Date (F5) Enters the current time and date at the insertion point in the format set in the Control Panel (for example, 11:08AM 6/5/92). This is a static date stamp. Unlike some word processors, Notepad will not update the time stamp each time you open or print a file.

Edit | Word Wrap A check mark appears next to this option if word wrap is turned on. The default is off.

Search | Find Displays the Find dialog box, which lets you search for a string of text.

Search | Find Next (F3) Searches again for the string of text you specified in the Find dialog box, or displays the Find dialog box.

Part 5

Windows' Multimedia

23

Windows and Multimedia

Multimedia. As often as we hear that word these days one would think everyone was using it, but to most of us "multimedia" is a rather vague concept. We know that it refers to the integration of sound, photo-quality images, video, and animation with standard computer text and graphics, but how it all fits together is another story.

Windows 3.1 has brought us all one step closer to multimedia. Without breaking the bank many of us will gradually enter the world of multimedia; we'll add a sound board, perhaps, install an animation program, or add a CD-ROM drive. You don't have to run out and buy a new machine to get started. You don't need a machine sold as a "Multimedia PC" (MPC), nor will you need Windows' "Multimedia Extension." You can add multimedia components piece by piece, as you need (or want) them.

What Can Multimedia Do for You?

Multimedia changes the way you can use a computer. Without multimedia a computer is, to a great extent, a way to produce a nonelectronic copy (usually paper). We create memos, letters, books, spreadsheets, mailing labels, color slides and transparencies, and so on. When the end product *is* electronic, it is usually for a mundane record-keeping purpose, such as recording expenses and calculating taxes—and even then the data is likely to be printed at some point.

But multimedia makes the computer's sounds and images into the end product itself. We can play music, view video film of rare animals, or listen to Beethoven while we read about his life. That's not to say that multimedia "data" cannot be "exported" from the computer—MIDI music can be recorded onto tape, animation sequences can be videotaped, and information from a CD atlas can end up on paper—but the computer becomes not just something to work with, but something to learn from and play with.

Computer games have been around for a while, and they are certainly part of the multimedia puzzle. The more sophisticated the games become the more effort publishers put into the graphics and sound. In fact probably the most common use of multimedia hardware is for play. The characteristics, then, of a multimedia computer are the ability to:

- display high-quality graphics.
- display video images.
- play sounds—voice, music, and special effects.
- record sounds.
- display 2-D or 3-D animated graphics.
- use sound and graphics from a CD-ROM disk.

You can see from this list that multimedia requires both software and hardware, and that many of us already have some of the components. You may have a high-quality video display, an animation program, and a sound board, for instance. Multimedia is not a single, etched-in-stone configuration. It's more of a concept, using your computer for more sound than a simple beep and your display for more than the display of text and simple static images.

Microsoft's Multimedia PC (MPC)

So what is *Multimedia PC* (MPC)? It's a standard established by Microsoft and a number of hardware manufacturers. It specifies the minimum configuration of a PC that will be able to use MPC software. A PC that meets Microsoft's Multimedia PC standard is a machine that has a minimum configuration as follows:

- 386SX or greater
- 2 MB RAM or more
- 30 MB hard disk
- color VGA display
- CD-ROM drive
- Audio board
- Speakers or headphones
- 3.5 inch, high-density floppy-disk drive
- Windows with Multimedia (Windows 3.0 with the Multimedia Extension or, now, Windows 3.1)

The most important specifications are for the CD-ROM and the software. For a computer to fit the MPC specifications, the CD-ROM drive must be able to maintain 150 KB/sec data transfer without using more than 40% of the computer's CPU capacity—this lets the computer handle sound and graphics while reading from the disk.

Late in 1991 Windows released the *Multimedia Extension*. This was a version of Windows that was available to computer manufacturers. A manufacturer could put together a system that contained the components necessary for multimedia, bundle the Multimedia Extension, and sell it as a *Multimedia PC*. The software itself included device drivers, the Media Control Interface (MCI), Sound Recorder, Media Player, and a few other changes. The Multimedia Extension wasn't available to end users—it came with the hardware.

Everything in Multimedia Extension is now included in Windows 3.1. In other words, if you have Windows 3.1, you don't need to buy the Multimedia Extension separately to turn your computer into a Multimedia PC. Of course manufacturers will still sell Multimedia PCs, but now you have the same Windows software that they do. You can add the hardware you want, piece by piece. (Just look for MPC-compatible hardware and software.)

On the one hand, you can start in multimedia, to a limited degree, on a 286. Just add a sound board and a few good games. You can even connect a CD-ROM drive to a 286. If you want to get serious about multimedia, however, you will find you want more than the basic Multimedia PC computer: a 25-MHz 386DX or greater, and at least 4 MB of RAM. A 30-MB hard drive is too small for most Windows users, with or without multimedia. If you are working with graphics and digitized sound, you need a lot of disk space. A 10-minute .WAV file can take up about 7 MB. (MIDI files are much smaller because they *describe* sounds rather than digitally record them.)

A Few Uses for Multimedia

So you can play sounds and graphics on your PC. What good does that do you? Well, here are a few ideas.

- Use a CD-ROM for research, education, and games.
- Add music and speech to your word processing, spreadsheet, and database documents.
- Improve your games with realistic sound.
- Compose and edit music, then play it on a MIDI (Musical Instrument Digital Interface) generator or sound card (see Figure 23.1).
- Copy music from an external device—a tape recorder, for instance—and automatically transcribe and print the score.
- Let your computer teach you how to play piano.

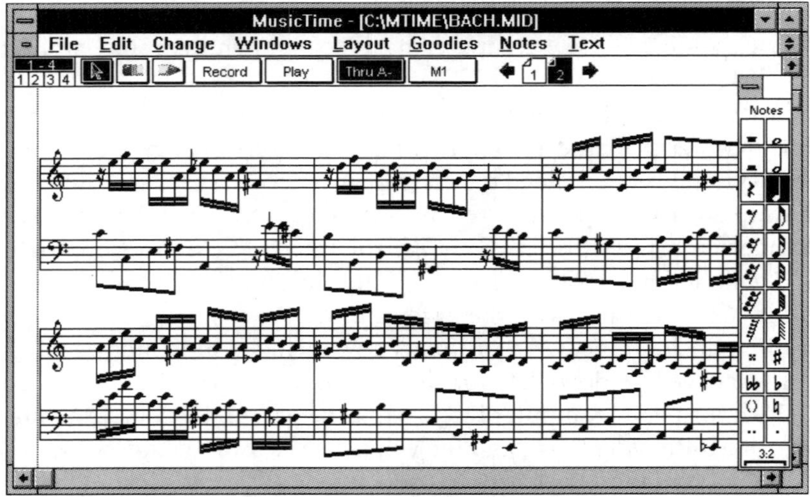

Figure 23.1 MusicTime, an example of "desktop composition and notation"

- Combine music, voice, text, still graphics, and animation to create on-screen training presentations, or copy them to video tape. Or create product presentations for trade shows or storefronts.
- Watch television on your computer display—have a channel running in a window, and swap back and forth.
- Display video images from other sources—cable, VCRs, video cameras, still video cameras—and digitize images.
- Use Kodak's new PhotoCD technology to convert your photographic film, then display your photographs on your computer and combine them into documents. (PhotoCD needs a nonstandard CD-ROM drive, though.)

Perhaps the component getting most attention is the CD-ROM. Because Compact Disks can hold so much information, it's possible for one disk to contain thousands of static graphics, video, sound, and enormous amounts of text. CD-ROM is not providing a new way to view or see data—a CD-ROM is simply a way to store large amounts of information. In fact the information is read from the disk rather slowly when compared with a hard disk, and you can buy programs that load onto your hard disk and combine sound, video, and text—you don't have to use CD-ROM for that. But whereas a hard-disk based program might provide 10 or 15 MB of data, a CD-ROM program can provide about 600 MB. This large storage simply makes multimedia more practical. A small library of CD-ROMs can contain many gigabytes of multimedia information—hours of video and sound, thousands of photographs, warehouses full of books.

Here's a list of the sort of disks available.

- **Magazine Rack** Last year's issues of 342 magazines.
- **U.S. History on CD-ROM** 107 major history books and 1000 illustrations.
- **National Geographic Mammals** An encyclopedia with sound, color photographs, and video.
- **The Bible Library** Nine versions of the bible and 20 biblical reference works.
- **The Grolier Electronic Encyclopedia** Ten million words, 2000 color graphics, and audio recordings of famous speeches.
- **Sherlock Holmes, Consulting Detective** Three interactive games with 90 minutes of video and sound.
- **Multimedia Beethoven** Listen to the music and read the score at the same time, then learn about Beethoven's life and times.
- **Monarch Notes** 200 sets of study notes, with pictures, spoken excerpts, and commentary.
- **Macmillan Dictionary for Children** 12,000 entries, word games, actual pronunciations, sound effects, pictures, and an animated character (Zak), to help children use the system.
- **Great Literature Personal Library Series** The full text of 943 great works, with pictures, music, and spoken passages.

Upgrading to Multimedia

You can upgrade to multimedia step by step. The simplest step is to add a driver for your PC's built-in speaker so you can listen to music and voice. It won't sound very good, but it's free. You can either get the SPEAKER.DRV driver from Microsoft or use one included with some of the commercial sound products now on the market that include libraries of different sounds.

You won't be able to record your own sounds. So the next step could be to buy a simple sound board with recording capabilities. You can purchase such boards for about $100. This will let you hear the sounds your computer plays on speakers or headphones and record your own music and speech files.

A step higher would be a high-quality sound board with an on-board MIDI generator or a MIDI interface so you can create your own music. Or a video interface so you can add TV or other video images. Or how about an animation program for as little as $75. You don't need any special hardware, although a sound board might help.

You can also purchase a CD-ROM drive, or a multimedia "kit," which usually comes with a CD-ROM drive, a sound board, speakers, and a selection of sample CDs. Look for equipment and CDs that comply with the Multimedia PC Specification 1.0—such equipment is usually identified by the MPC logo.

Windows' Own Multimedia Applications

Windows has two of its own—very simple—multimedia applications. Sound Player lets you record, edit, and play sounds. The sound files created by this application can be placed inside other applications (OLE *client* applications). Your word processor can play music, your spreadsheet can include verbal comments.

The other application is called Media Player, which can operate external devices such as CD players or play sound and MIDI files through a sound card. Both these applications are described in the next two chapters. We have also described the MIDI Mapper, a Control Panel utility that appears if you install a MIDI instrument and its software driver.

Windows supports these types of sound:

- **Waveform** Digitized sound files (11 and 22 kHz), using the .WAV extension. Pulse code modulation (PCM) is used to store a digital representation of the wave. These sounds can be recorded and played by Sound Recorder, played by Media Player, and embedded in documents using OLE (Object Linking and Embedding).
- **General MIDI** (Musical Instrument Digital Interface) Synthesized sound files using the .MID and .RMI extensions. MIDI is a standard means of communicating between computers and electronic instruments. MIDI files *describe* sounds rather than digitize them (the file tells the instrument which sound to play, at which note, and for how long) and can be played by the Media Player.
- **Redbook Audio** Standard CD-ROM player audio.

Windows comes with drivers for the following devices:

- Adlib sound card
- Creative Labs Sound Blaster sound card
- Media Vision Thunder Board sound card
- Roland LAPC1 MIDI devices
- Roland MPU401 MIDI devices

If you have one of these devices you can use the Windows driver, but you should always check with the manufacturer to see if there is an updated driver.

24

Sound Recorder

Remember the Sound icon in Windows 3.0's Control Panel? Remember the anti-climax when you opened the Sound dialog box and discovered that all you could do was turn your computer's beep on and off? Well Windows 3.1 has finally taken sound a little further. Not only are a number of Windows programs available for manipulating sounds, but Windows itself lets you associate sounds with various system procedures (see Chapter 8) and use OLE to package sounds in any OLE-client application (see Chapter 28 for more information about OLE).

Windows' own Sound Recorder is a simple sound-editing accessory. You can add or blend sound files together, modify a sound's speed and volume, add an echo, or reverse it. You can also delete portions of it: Combined with the other commands this lets you take pieces from a variety of different sources and put them together in one file. If you have a sound card installed in your computer you can record your own voice or music. You can save the finished product and add sounds to any OLE client application.

You require both a sound driver and sound hardware, but your computer already has the hardware necessary to play sounds. You can use a sound driver to play sounds on your computer's internal speaker. It won't sound great, but it will probably be clear enough for voices to be intelligible. You may find a sound driver in a shareware catalog, or directly from Microsoft. In fact, if you use the CompuServe computer network you can download a driver directly. Download SPEAKER.DRV from the Microsoft Software Library (type **GO MSL** to move directly to this library).

If you install a sound card in your computer, you will be able to hear much clearer music and voices. Make sure your sound card is Windows-compatible—most are—and that a Windows 3.1 driver is available. Some sound card drivers are included on your Windows disks. You must load sound drivers through the Control Panel's Drivers dialog box. (See Chapter 8 for more information.)

▼ ***Note*** Working with digitized sound uses a lot of memory and disk space. A 10-minute sound file will use around 7 MB. The TADA.WAV sound file provided with Windows plays for less than three seconds and takes up 53 KB.

Opening Sound Recorder

Start Sound Recorder by clicking on the Sound Recorder icon in the Accessories program group. Or select **File | Run** and run **SOUND**. Figure 24.1 shows the Sound Recorder window. You can do one of two things when you first open the Sound Recorder: begin recording or load a sound file.

Playing Sounds

Windows comes with several sounds stored in .WAV files in the Windows directory. Select File | Open to display the Open dialog box. This box will display the .WAV files by default. (Sound Recorder will play only Windows .WAV files. It will not play Windows' .MID MIDI files.)

You may remember that these sounds are the same as those displayed in the Control Panel's Sounds dialog box (see Chapter 8). Open one of the .WAV files, and Sound Recorder will display its name in the title bar. Notice also that the Length number in the right side of the window indicates the duration of the sound in seconds. On the left side of the window the Position indicator shows you the position of the scroll box on the scroll bar. A reading of 32.33 means that the scroll box is 32.33 seconds through the file. The scroll box moves through the file while the sound is playing, or you can drag the scroll box to the position at which you want to play or edit. (To move the scroll box with the keyboard, press **Tab** until the highlight is on the box, then press the **Left** and **Right Arrow** keys to position it.)

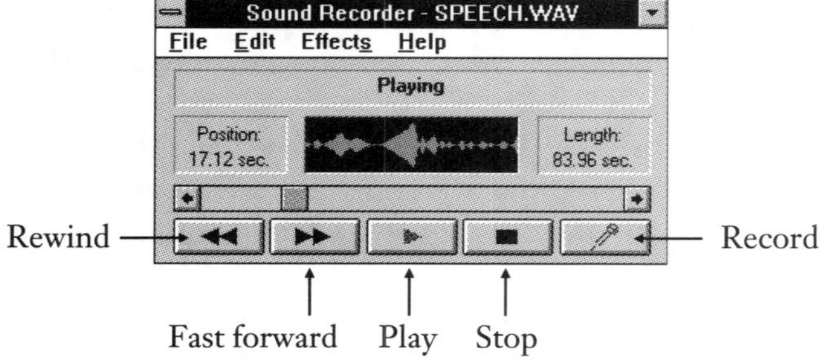

Figure 24.1 The Sound Recorder window playing a file

To play the sound, simply click the **Play** button. (If you are using the keyboard, press **Tab** to move to the Play button and then press **Enter** or **Spacebar**.) The sound begins playing and is displayed graphically in the Wave box in the middle of the widow. The scroll box moves along the scroll bar, indicating the play position, and the Position indicator shows how many seconds have elapsed. The word Playing should appear immediately below the menu bar. (If you are using SPEAKER.DRV, Sound Recorder may not display Playing.)

If you want to stop the sound while it is playing, click the **Stop** button. To return to the beginning of the sound, click the **Rewind** button. Clicking the **Fast Forward** button will move the scroll box to the end of the file and stop the sound playing. (The Rewind and Forward buttons do not move the scroll box through the sound bit by bit—they only move it all the way to the beginning or end.)

▼ ***Note*** Different sound drivers may operate the Sound Recorder differently. For instance, the SPEAKER.DRV driver will not let you stop a sound until it has finished playing.

Recording Sounds

The last button on the right is the **Record** button. This will be enabled only if you have a sound card with recording capabilities, of course. You may be able to record your voice with a microphone, for example, or record music directly from a CD or tape player.

Prepare for recording by either opening a new file or positioning the scroll box where you want to insert the recording. If you move the scroll box all the way to the end of a file, the recorded sounds will be appended, extending the length of the file. If you place the sound box at the middle or beginning of a file, the sound will not be "inserted." Rather, it will record over the existing sound.

When you are ready, click the **Record** button and begin speaking into your microphone, or play your music. After 60 seconds the recording will automatically stop, but you can begin again and record another 60 seconds if you wish. That may seem quite a short recording, but 60 seconds is enough for a voice annotation, and it takes up about 700 KB of disk space! If you reach the limits of your computer's memory you may not be able to record a full 60 seconds. The larger the sound file you are working with, and the less memory you have, the sooner you will reach the limit. Sound Recorder will tell you how long you may record (see Figure 24.2). For instance, if the file is already 58 seconds long and you begin recording from the end, Sound Recorder will tell you that the maximum length of the file is 118 seconds. By watching the Position indicator you will be able to anticipate how soon the recording will end.

Figure 24.2 Recording sounds

Tip If you want to record more than 60 seconds without stopping and starting, "record" 60 seconds (of nothing), save the file, then use the Edit | Insert File command to insert the saved file into itself. Insert as many copies as necessary to create a file of the length you want. Then click the **Rewind** button to move back to the beginning, and start recording.

You can click the **Stop** button at any time to end the recording. You can also click the **Rewind** button to move to the beginning of the file, and the **Forward** button to move to the end of the file. You can even move the scroll box to a different position. While you are using any of these adjustments Sound Recorder will pause recording, then begin immediately. Remember that recording anywhere but at the end of the file records over the existing sound.

▼ ***Note*** You will not be able to record over the .WAV files provided by Windows.

Editing Sounds

Once you have recorded sounds, you can modify them in various ways. You can delete portions, merge or append files, modify the volume, and so on. The **scroll box position** is important while editing because it affects the position at which you make the changes. Click on the scroll bar arrows to move the scroll box one-tenth of a second. Click on the scroll bar between the scroll box and the scroll arrow to move it one second. Click the **Rewind** or **Forward** buttons to move the scroll box to the beginning or end of the file. Or drag the scroll box through the sound. Look at the sound in the Wave box as you move the scroll box to get an idea of where you are.

To move through the scroll bar with the keyboard, press **Tab** to move to the scroll bar, then use the **Home** and **End** keys instead of the Rewind and Forward buttons, or press the **Arrow** keys to move through the scroll bar one-tenth of a second at a time. Press **PgUp** and **PgDn** to move through it one second at a time.

You can delete only from the scroll box position to the beginning or end of the file—in other words, you can't delete a section in the middle of the file. Move the scroll box into position by dragging it, or by playing the sound and clicking the Stop button when it reaches where you want it. Then select **Edit | Delete Before Current Position** or **Edit | Delete After Current Position** to remove the entire sound from the scroll box position to the beginning or end of the file.

▼ *Note* If you want to remove a sound from the middle of a file, place the scroll box at the end of the piece you want to remove and use the Edit | Delete Before Current Position. Then save the file with a new name. Reopen the original file and place the scroll box at the beginning of the piece you want to remove. Then use the Edit | Delete After Current Position. Then use Edit | Insert File command (described in a moment) to insert the new file.

You can merge files in two ways. The **Edit | Insert File** command lets you insert a file at the scroll box position. The file is thereby lengthened. Inserting a 10-second file in the middle of a 40-second file creates a 50-second file. When you select this command, Sound Recorder displays a dialog box from which you can select the file. Click on **OK** and the selected file is inserted into the original file; the scroll box moves to the *beginning* of the inserted portion (so you can click the **Play** button to hear the inserted sound).

The **Edit | Mix with File** command also displays a dialog box, but this time, when you select a file and click on **OK**, Sound Recorder mixes the two sounds together. For instance, if you have a voice file, you could mix it with a music file, effectively providing background music. Mixing files does not necessarily increase the length of the file. Mixing a 10-second file near the beginning of a 40-second file will not increase the length, for instance. However, placing the scroll box at the end of the file and then mixing a file is the same as inserting a file and *will* lengthen the original file.

There are also several special effects you can use. You can increase or decrease the volume by using the **Effects | Increase Volume (by 25%)** and **Effects | Decrease Volume** command (the Decrease Volume command also decreases volume 25%). You can also double or halve the speed of the sound, using the **Effects | Increase Speed (by 100%)** and **Effects | Decrease Speed** commands. You may also add an echo (**Effects | Add Echo**) and even play the sound backwards (**Effects | Reverse**). Incidentally, adding an echo several times increases the "reverberation."

You should know about the **File | Revert** command. This command is a sort of super Undo, letting you remove all the changes you have made since the last time you saved the file. Some changes can be undone easily. If you increased the speed, you can undo by selecting **Effects | Decrease Speed**. If you reversed the sound you can select **Effects | Reverse** again. But if you made a number of changes that you decide you don't like, or if you added an echo, deleted a portion, or inserted or mixed a file, you can select **File | Revert** to remove all the changes.

Here's an example of when you might want to revert to the saved version of the file. You are working with a voice file and want to add music. You mixed a music file, but now find that the music is too loud. You can revert to the saved version, increase the voice's volume, mix the file again, and then reduce the volume again to lower the volume of both the voice and music while keeping the relative volumes the same.

Saving Sound Files

While saving sound files should work in the same way that you save any other file—a Notepad, Write, or Calendar file, for instance—you should be careful not to get stung by a **bug** present in Sound Recorder's Save As command. Unlike most Windows applications, Sound Recorder does not automatically add a file extension for you when you save the file. For instance, if you begin a new file, then select File | Save, the Save As dialog box appears, displaying *.WAV highlighted in the File Name text box. If you simply type a name over the *.WAV and click on **OK**, the file will be saved *without* an extension.

Unsuspecting users can lose .WAV files this way, although the files are still on the disk. If you want to find a file that you may have lost, select **File | Open** and when the Open dialog box appears, select the All Files option from the List Files as Type drop-down list box.

Using Your Sounds

Sounds you create can be used in a variety of ways.

- Play them with Sound Recorder.
- Play them using another application.
- Attach them to system sounds.
- Attach them to application-specific events.
- Place them in OLE client applications.

You can play them directly from Sound Recorder. If you are transcribing a recorded voice, for instance, you can play the sound in Sound Recorder while you type the text into a word processor. If you arrange the windows so that both are visible, you can easily stop and move the sound back a few words. Some other Windows applications are also able to play .WAV files.

As you saw in Chapter 8, you can attach .WAV sounds to system sounds. Instead of beeping, your computer can scream at you, if you so wish. When you open or close Windows you can have Captain Kirk or Scotty informing you of the system status. While few Windows applications make full use of this ability to link sounds to specific events, more are undoubtedly on the way. (Some third-party applications let you assign sounds not only to the basic Windows events—Default Beep, Windows Exit, Windows Start, and so on—but to events specific to particular applications.)

You can also use Windows' OLE (Object Linking and Embedding) to place a sound in another application's file as long as the application is an OLE *client* (an application that is designed to accept OLE objects). Select **Edit | Copy** in Sound Recorder, then move to the other application. You can now *embed* or *link* the sound. An embedded sound is independent of the original sound, while a linked sound remains associated with the original .WAV file—modify that original file, and the sound in the application will be changed also.

To embed the sound simply paste it as normal. Select **Edit | Paste** or press **Ctrl-V**. To link the file select the **Edit | Paste Link** option. If the application doesn't have this option, select **Edit | Paste Special**. (If it doesn't have either of these options it probably isn't an OLE client.) When the Paste Special dialog box appears, notice that one of the buttons is labeled Paste Link. If the button is enabled, click on it and Windows pastes the sound object into the application. If the Paste Link button is disabled, you must select another option from the Data Type list box. When you find an option that enables the Paste Link button, click on the button.

When you paste a sound object into a file, the Sound Recorder icon appears (as you can see in Figure 24.3). As long as the file is on a computer with both Sound Recorder and a sound driver, you can double-click on the icon to hear the sound. You can also click once on the icon, then select **Edit | Sound Object**, or **Edit | Sound Link** to open Sound Recorder and load the sound, so you can edit it. Some applications will use different edit menu options; Windows Write, for instance, has an **Edit | Sound Object | Play** option to play the sound and an **Edit | Sound Object | Edit** command to open Sound Recorder.

If you modify the sound then close the Sound Recorder, one of two things will happen. If it's an embedded object, the object's sound is changed—double-click on the icon to hear the difference. If you linked the object, you have modified both the sound object in the client application and the original file. So if other documents contain sounds linked to the same file, the sounds in those documents will also change.

You can also create a sound directly from the client application. Clients have a menu option named something like **Edit | Insert Object**, or **Insert | Object**.

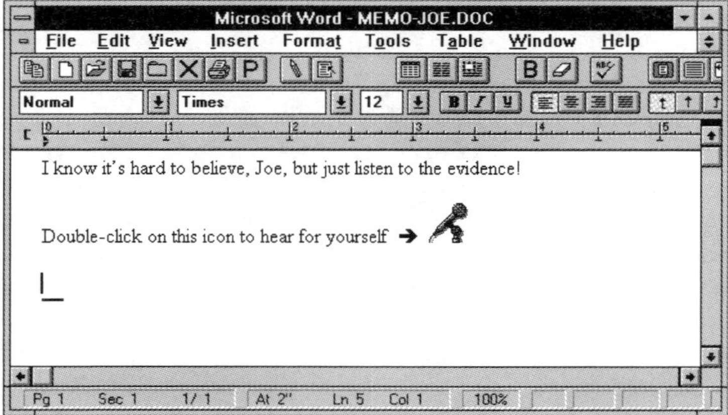

Figure 24.3 The Sound Recorder icon in a Word for Windows memo, indicating a sound object

When you select the option Windows displays the Object dialog box, a list of OLE *servers*—applications that can create OLE objects. If you select the Sound option, Windows opens Sound Recorder automatically.

For instance, let's say you are working in Word for Windows and want to add a sound to a memo—a verbal comment, a piece of music, or part of a speech, for instance. You would select **Edit|Insert Object**, select Sound from the Object dialog box, and click on **OK**. When Sound Recorder opened you would record the sound, or use the **Edit|Insert File** to copy the sound from an existing file. (Don't use the **File|Open** command, or you will open a new file, in effect closing the embedded sound you were creating.) Then, when you closed Sound Recorder, the icon would appear in the memo. You have embedded a sound object that can be played by double-clicking on it.

There's much more to OLE—read Chapter 28 for more information.

Sound Recorder's Menu Options

Here's a summary of Sound Recorder's menu options.

File|New Clears the Sound Recorder so you can begin creating a new file. If the current file hasn't been saved, the application asks if you want to do so.

File|Open Lets you open an existing sound (.WAV) file.

File|Save Saves the file. The first time you save you will see the Save As dialog box so you can select a directory and filename.

File|Save As Lets you save the file with a new name, or in a different directory.

File | Revert Lets you undo all the changes since the last time you saved the file.

File | Exit Closes Sound Recorder. If you have unsaved changes, it asks if you want to save the file first.

Edit | Copy (Ctrl-C) Copies the entire sound into the Clipboard so you can paste it into an OLE client application. The Sound Recorder icon will be displayed in the other application.

Edit | Insert File Inserts another sound file at the current position.

Edit | Mix with File Mixes another sound file with the current file, blending the sounds together.

Edit | Delete Before Current Position Removes all the sounds from the sound file before the current scroll box position.

Edit | Delete After Current Position Removes all the sounds from the sound file after the current scroll box position.

Effects | Increase Volume (By 25%) Increases the sound's volume by 25%.

Effects | Decrease Volume Decreases the sound's volume by 25%.

Effects | Increase Speed (By 100%) Doubles the sound's speed (making it last half as long).

Effects | Decrease Speed Halves the sound's speed (making it last twice as long).

Effects | Add Echo Adds an echo to the entire sound file.

Effects | Reverse Reverses the sound, so it plays backwards.

Help | About A typical about dialog box, but it also indicates the sound driver's capabilities (in the fourth line from the top).

25

Media Player

Windows Media Player is a special application for working with MCI (Media Control Interface) multimedia devices and files. Media Player will operate two types of devices, *simple* and *compound*. A simple device is generally an external device—such as a CD player, VCR, or videodisc player—that does not play a computer file. These devices play whatever is installed—the CD or videodisc that you loaded, for instance.

A compound device is one that plays a computer file. The file may be a MIDI (Musical Instrument Digital Interface) file played on a sequencer or a sound board, for instance, or an animation program.

Opening Media Player

Start Media Player by clicking on the Media Player icon in the Accessories program group. Or select **File | Run** and run **MPLAYER**. Figure 25.1 shows the Media Player window. You can do one of two things when you first open the Media Player: begin recording or load a file.

Like Sound Recorder, the Media Player "window" is not a true window: It cannot be sized or maximized. It can be minimized, however.

Selecting Media Devices

The first step to playing a media device is to select that device. Open the **Device** menu to see a list of the devices for which you have installed device drivers. (See Chapter 8 for more information on drivers.) The Device menu displays a check

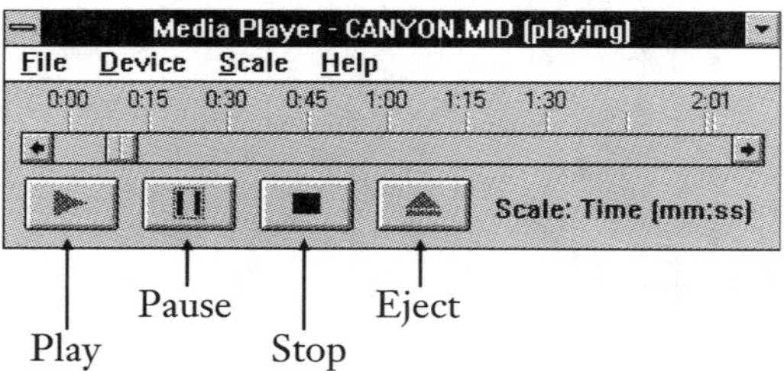

Figure 25.1 The Media Player window playing the Windows sample MIDI file, CANYON.MID

mark next to the currently selected device. Each device with an ellipsis (. . .) after its name is a *compound* device. Selecting one of these devices displays a dialog box from which you can select the file that you want played by that device. Select a file and Media Player displays the filename in the title bar. If a device doesn't have an ellipsis after its name it's a *simple* device. If you select a simple device Media Player displays the device's name in the title bar and waits for further instructions.

You can also use the **File | Open** command to open compound-device files. This command displays a typical file Open dialog box. Select a file type from the List Files of Type drop-down list box. (This list box automatically displays the file type associated with the last compound device you selected from the Device menu.) Selecting a file type and opening a file automatically selects the appropriate device. (File | Open won't be enabled if a simple device is currently selected. If it isn't, select the file using the Device menu.)

Playing Media Devices

Once you have loaded the device—and the file, in the case of a compound device—you can use the buttons on the Media Player to play. These buttons are similar to those found on many electronic devices these days—VCRs, tape recorders, and CD players, for instance. Use **Play** button to begin playing, and the **Pause** or **Stop** button to stop the playing. If the device you are playing has an **Eject** button, you can also use the Eject button on the Media Player to operate the Eject mechanism. In the case of a simple device, when you press **Play** the device begins playing whatever is loaded—the CD, for example, or videodisc. If it is a compound device, it begins playing the selected file.

▼ ***Note*** Once you start a simple device, it will continue playing, even if you close Media Player. A compound device, however, will stop if you close it.

As the device plays, the scroll box in the media player moves along the scroll bar, indicating the playback position. You can move the scroll box using the mouse before you begin playing or even while the device is playing, if you wish. Click on the scroll arrows to make a small move, between the scroll box and the arrows for larger moves, or drag the scroll box to the position you want.

You can also use the keyboard to operate the controls. Press **Tab** to move to the scroll box or buttons. Press the **arrow keys** to move in small jumps, **PgUp** and **PgDn** to move in large jumps, **Home** to move to the beginning, and **End** to move to the end.

You can adjust the scale on the Media Player. Select **Scale|Time** to see the playback length marked with a time scale—minutes and seconds, seconds, or even milliseconds if the playback time is very short. Select **Scale|Tracks** if the device monitors playback position according to predetermined tracks, such as CD players. The Scale indicator in the bottom right shows you the scale type currently in use, and, in the case of a time scale, the units (msec, sec, or mm:ss).

▼ ***Note*** Media Player may not be able to play all files that appear to be compatible. Some .MID files will not work, for instance.

26

Using MIDI Mapper

If you have installed a MIDI (Musical Instrument Digital Interface) generator of some kind and the appropriate software drivers, Windows adds a special icon to your Control Panel—the MIDI Mapper icon. A MIDI generator is a "black box" that creates sounds electronically (some generators are simply the sound-generating electronics removed from an electronic keyboard). Those sounds simulate other instruments, such as drums, pianos, guitars, glockenspiels, and many others.

A MIDI generator may be in a box with a controller, or it may be controlled by another device, such as a keyboard or MIDI sequencer. A sequencer may be another black box device, or it may be a computer program—several MIDI sequencer programs are available for Windows. In other words, a Windows sequencer lets you send instructions to a MIDI generator that will create music. Windows sequencers can also record music and transcribe it into musical notation. When you use a MIDI sequencer program on your computer, you send messages from the computer to the MIDI generator. These messages tell the generator when to turn a note on and off, and on what "instrument" that note should be played. Of course messages can go in the opposite direction, from the generator to the computer, so the computer can record and manipulate the sound digitally, and even transcribe the sound so you can print the musical notation.

The problem is, then, how do the computer and generator know what a message means? They use a series of channels, and each message refers to the duration of a note on a particular channel. But what if the two systems use different channels for different instruments? That's where Microsoft's MPC (Multimedia PC) General MIDI file specifications come in. These describe how to use MPC to create General MIDI files. (General MIDI is the MIDI Manufacturer's Association's guidelines for creating MIDI music.) These specifications describe exactly what each message channel does. The MIDI Mapper is a sort of translator between a General MIDI file and a particular generator. It determines where each General

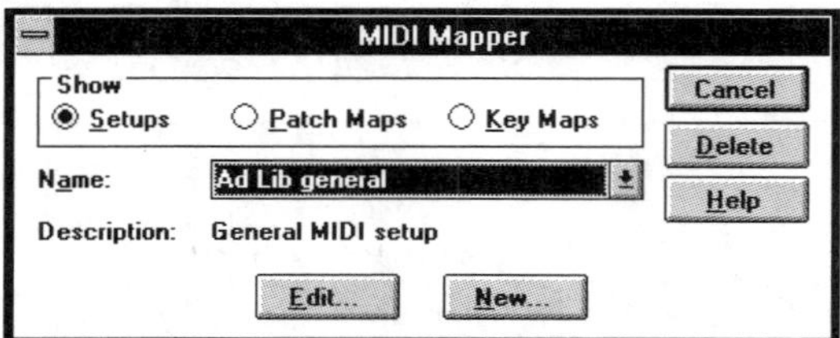

Figure 26.1 The MIDI Mapper dialog box

MIDI channel is routed when a message is sent to a particular generator. To do this it uses *key maps*, *channel maps*, and *patch maps*. If the routing is wrong, the wrong instrument may play, or some sounds may simply not be played at all.

You probably won't need to change the MIDI Mapper. When you install your MIDI driver, the Mapper is adjusted appropriately. You will need to modify the Mapper only if you want to play a non-General MIDI file on the generator, or if you connect a generator that doesn't have a ready-made MIDI Mapper setup. If this is the case you can check your generator's documentation or technical support to find the correct settings for a custom setup. (Your generator's manufacturer may also be able to provide you with a ready-made setup that you can install.)

Begin by double-clicking on the MIDI Mapper icon to display the MIDI Mapper dialog box (see Figure 26.1). This dialog box has three option buttons: Setups, Patch Maps, and Key Maps. When the box appears the Setup option button is selected. That means the Name and Description below refer to the MIDI setup. Clicking on an option button changes the contents of the Name drop-down list box.

Click on **Setup** to see a list of the preconfigured setups for specific generators. These setups determine which MIDI channels are active, to which destination and port MIDI messages are sent, and which patch map will be used, if any. Click on **Patch Maps** to see a list of the patch maps. These ensure that a MIDI instrument message is sent to the correct generator channel at the correct volume; they also may define key maps. Click on **Key Maps** to see a list of the current key maps. These translate source keys into generator destination keys, if necessary.

Selecting a Setup

You must select the correct setup for the generator you will be working with. Select from the Name drop-down list box. Your options depend on the driver you installed, but here are some typical ones.

Ad Lib — An Ad Lib-compatible generator on a sound card; it uses channels 12 to 16 (the base-level channels).

Ad Lib General	An Ad Lib-compatible generator on a sound card; it uses all 16 channels.
Extended MIDI	A General MIDI generator connected to a Sound Blaster-compatible MIDI port. This is the Microsoft authoring guidelines standard; it uses channels 1 to 10 (the extended-level channels).
General MIDI	A General MIDI generator connected to a Sound Blaster-compatible MIDI port. Use this for MIDI files created under the General MIDI guidelines, using all 16 channels.
LAPC1	The Roland synthesizer on an LAPC1 sound card; it uses all 16 channels.
MT32	The Roland MT-32 synthesizer connected to a Sound Blaster-compatible MIDI port; it uses all 16 channels.
Proteus general	The E-mu Systems Proteus/1 synthesizer, connected to a Sound Blaster-compatible MIDI port; it uses all 16 channels.
Proteus/1	The E-mu Systems Proteus/1 synthesizer, connected to a Sound Blaster-compatible MIDI port; it uses channels 1 to 10.

What exactly does a setup contain? It defines the match between source and destination channels (the sound channels coming from the MIDI application, going to the generator) and the name of the generator port used for each channel (so sounds can go to different generators). It also defines the *patch map* used for each channel. A patch map translates an instrument's sound and volume (or keyboard velocity) settings. It may also define various *key maps*, which translate between General MIDI specifications and a generator that works with a different system. A key map makes sure that the correct percussion instrument is played, or that a melodic instrument uses the correct octave.

You can see the way setups, patch maps, and key maps are interrelated. First, select the setup from the Name drop-down list box. Click on **Edit** to see the MIDI Setup dialog box. Look in the Patch Map Name column to see if a patch map is referenced. If not, the setup doesn't use a patch map or a key map. If one *is* listed, press **Esc** to remove the dialog box, click on the **Patch Map** option button, then select the patch map from the Name drop-down list box. Click on **Edit** to see the MIDI Patch Map dialog box. The Key Map Name column shows which key maps are used. (This dialog box has a scroll bar, so you may need to scroll through it to see all the key maps.)

Also, notice that a setup may use more than one patch or key map. For instance, the Proteus General setup uses the Prot/1 and Prot/1 Perc patch maps. The Prot/1 patch map uses six key maps, and the Prot/1 Perc map uses another, different, key map.

Loading a New Setup

If your device isn't included in the setup list, check with the manufacturer. They may have an updated setup file, which will save you creating your own. The file is named MIDIMAP.CFG and is stored in the WINDOWS\SYSTEM directory. Rename the original file (!MIDIMAP.CFG, for instance), or copy it onto a backup disk. Then copy the new one into the directory. Now, when you open the MIDI Mapper, your new setup should be included in the Name drop-down list box.

Customizing a Setup

If your MIDI-device setup isn't included in the setup list and if the manufacturer can't provide a setup file, you will have to create your own setup, defining how each output channel is handled. You will probably need to refer to your generator's documentation for information that the MIDI Mapper will require and set up the generator itself to receive multichannel MIDI messages.

You will begin by creating a *key map* (that defines which keys correspond to which percussion instruments) and two new *patch maps* (for melodic and percussion instruments).

Creating a Key Map

A key map is used to translate General MIDI messages into those that your generator can understand, letting you assign a particular key to a particular sound. A source key that plays a particular percussion instrument, or a melodic instrument at a particular octave, may not match the same key on your generator. The key map matches the keys correctly.

Click on the **Key Maps** option button. The Name drop-down list box now displays the key maps. Click on the **New** button. The New MIDI Key Map dialog box appears. Type a Name and Description, and click on **OK** to see the MIDI Key Map dialog box (shown in Figure 26.2). This box shows the source keys 35 through 50. You can scroll down the list to see keys 51 to 81. (Keys 0 to 34 and 82 to 127 are reserved.) The **Src Key** column shows all the keys that may be included in a MIDI message. The **Src Key Name** column shows the percussion instruments associated with the key. These are the instruments defined by the General MIDI specifications. These first two columns cannot be changed.

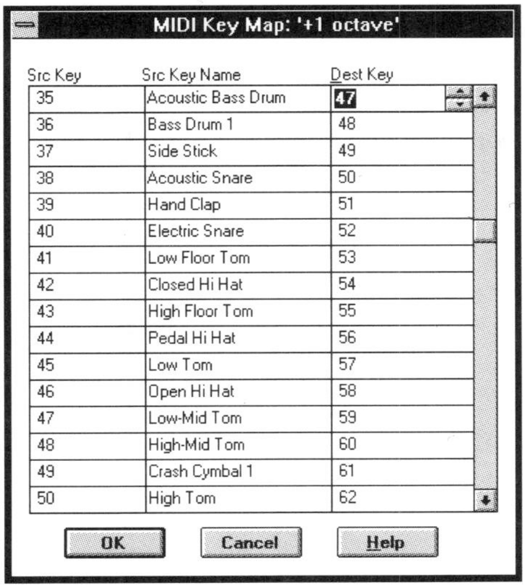

MIDI Key Map: '+1 octave'

Src Key	Src Key Name	Dest Key
35	Acoustic Bass Drum	47
36	Bass Drum 1	48
37	Side Stick	49
38	Acoustic Snare	50
39	Hand Clap	51
40	Electric Snare	52
41	Low Floor Tom	53
42	Closed Hi Hat	54
43	High Floor Tom	55
44	Pedal Hi Hat	56
45	Low Tom	57
46	Open Hi Hat	58
47	Low-Mid Tom	59
48	High-Mid Tom	60
49	Crash Cymbal 1	61
50	High Tom	62

OK Cancel Help

Figure 26.2 The MIDI Key Map dialog box

The only field you can change is in the **Dest Key** column, which shows the destination key that you want the source key to play when the message reaches the generator. You can highlight a number and type over it, or use the arrow keys to select another. (The arrow keys appear on the selected line.)

If you are creating a melodic key map, you can ignore the instrument name in the Src Key Name column.

When you have made your changes, click the **OK** button. You may need to create several key maps. If so create them now, before you move on to the patch maps.

▼ *Note* MIDI Mapper already has some key maps you may be able to work with. The **+1 octave**, **–1 octave**, and **+2 octave** key maps shift the key up or down appropriately. The **55**, **79**, **38**, and **21** key maps translate all the keys to destination key 55, 79, 38, or 21.

Creating the Patch Maps

A patch map translates instruments and volumes, and may also specify a key map to translate source keys into the appropriate destination keys. You may need to create two patch maps, one for percussion instruments and one for melodic instruments.

Click on the **Patch Maps** option button, then click on the **New** button. The New MIDI Patch Map dialog box appears. Type a name and description, then click on **OK** to see the MIDI Patch Map dialog box (shown in Figure 26.3).

MIDI Patch Map: 'MT32'

1 based patches

Src Patch	Src Patch Name	Dest Patch	Volume %	Key Map Name
0	Acoustic Grand Piano	0	100	[None]
1	Bright Acoustic Piano	1	100	-1 octave
2	Electric Grand Piano	3	100	21 / +2 octaves
3	Honky-tonk Piano	7	100	MT32
4	Rhodes Piano	5	100	[None]
5	Chorused Piano	6	100	[None]
6	Harpsichord	17	100	[None]
7	Clavinet	21	100	[None]
8	Celesta	22	100	[None]
9	Glockenspiel	101	100	[None]
10	Music Box	101	100	[None]
11	Vibraphone	98	100	[None]
12	Marimba	104	100	[None]
13	Xylophone	103	100	[None]
14	Tubular Bells	102	100	[None]
15	Dulcimer	105	100	[None]

OK Cancel Help

Figure 26.3 The MIDI Patch Map dialog box with the Key Name drop-down list box shown

---

Tip When you create a percussive patch map, add *Perc* to the end of the name to differentiate it from a melodic key map with the same name (as in MT32 Perc and Prot/1 Perc).

The MIDI Patch Map dialog box lists the 128 General MIDI source patches (0 to 127). If your generator numbers its patches from 1 to 128—rather than 0 to 127—click on the **1 based patches** button, or press **Alt-1**. This adjusts the Dest Patch column accordingly. These are the columns of the MIDI Patch Map dialog box.

Src Patch The source patch. General MIDI specifies 128 patches, numbered 0 to 127.

Src Patch Name The melodic instruments related to the patch. If you are creating a patch map for percussion instruments you can ignore this column.

Dest Patch The destination patch. If your generator uses General MIDI, the destination patch should match the source patch. If not, you can type over the number with another patch number, or use the arrow keys to select one. If you are creating a percussion patch map, change *all* the destination patch numbers to your generator's percussion patch number.

Volume % The volume used by the destination patch, as a percentage of the volume specified by the MIDI message. This is also known as the *keyboard velocity* and is used by generators that can measure the force with which the key is pressed.

Key Map Name The key map to be used by that patch. Select a name from the drop-down list box. If you are creating a percussion patch map, change *all* the destination patch numbers to the same key map. If you are creating a melodic patch map you may find that some instruments match the General MIDI specifications and others don't. Some instruments may play an octave higher or lower than General MIDI, for instance. Select a key map that shifts the destination key appropriately.

Creating a Setup

Now that you have finished your key and patch maps you can create your final setup. For each MIDI source channel you specify the destination channel, the port name, and the patch map name.

Click on the **Setup** option button, then click on the **New** button. When the New MIDI Setup dialog box appears, type a name and description. Click on **OK** to see the MIDI Setup dialog box (see Figure 26.4).

This dialog box lists 16 channels. The number of channels you use depends on the type of generator. Microsoft's General MIDI specifications recognize two types of MIDI setups.

Extended-level generators Use channels 1 through 10, with 16 notes on nine melodic instruments and 16 notes on eight percussion instruments. Channels 1 through 9 are melodic, and channel 10 is percussive.

Base-level generators Use channels 13 through 16, with six notes on three melodic instruments and three notes on three percussive instruments. Channels 13 through 15 are melodic and channel 16 is percussive.

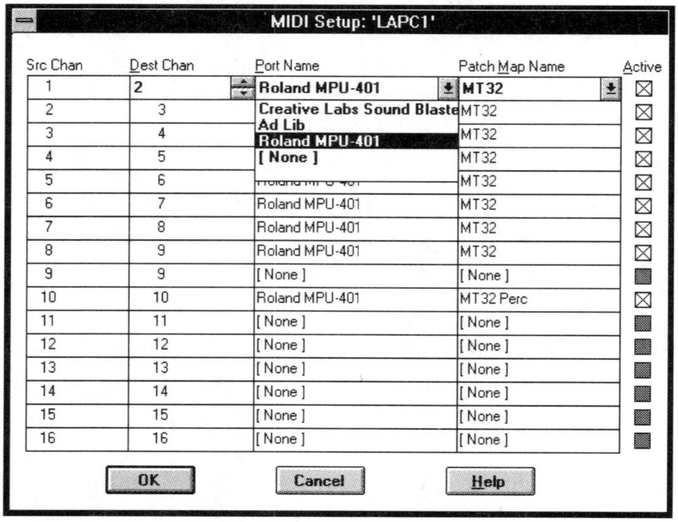

MIDI Setup: 'LAPC1'

Src Chan	Dest Chan	Port Name	Patch Map Name	Active
1	2	Roland MPU-401	MT32	☒
2	3		MT32	☒
3	4		MT32	☒
4	5		MT32	☒
5	6		MT32	☒
6	7	Roland MPU-401	MT32	☒
7	8	Roland MPU-401	MT32	☒
8	9	Roland MPU-401	MT32	☒
9	9	[None]	[None]	■
10	10	Roland MPU-401	MT32 Perc	☒
11	11	[None]	[None]	■
12	12	[None]	[None]	■
13	13	[None]	[None]	■
14	14	[None]	[None]	■
15	15	[None]	[None]	■
16	16	[None]	[None]	■

Creative Labs Sound Blaste
Ad Lib
Roland MPU-401
[None]

OK Cancel Help

Figure 26.4 The MIDI Setup dialog box with the Port Name drop-down list box shown

These are the columns of the MIDI Setup dialog box.

Src Chan Source channels, the information coming from the MIDI application and MIDI file.

Dest Chan Destination channel, the channel your generator will use to play the sounds from the associated source channel. By default the destination channels and source channels match, although you can select another channel.

Port Name The port to which the channel is sent. You can select different ports for different channels. For instance, you might send some channels to a MIDI generator connected to your computer and others to your Ad Lib-compatible sound board.

Patch Map Name The patch map required for the channel. Obviously you must connect a melodic patch map to a melodic channel and a percussive patch map to a percussive channel.

Active When you selected a Port Name, MIDI Mapper automatically selected the Active check box. This simply means that the associated channel will be sent to the generator. You can block a channel by deselecting the check box.

When you've made your selections, click on the **OK** button, and you have created a new MIDI setup.

Important After you create a new setup, patch map, or key map, the MIDI Mapper's Cancel button changes to Close. You must click on this button or your changes will not be saved. Pressing **Esc** or double-clicking on the Control-box menu will *not* save your changes.

Editing and Deleting

You can both edit and delete any setup, patch map, or key map. Select the item in the Name drop-down list box and then click on **Edit** to modify it, or **Delete** to remove it. When you have finished, click on the **Close** button to save your changes.

You won't be able to delete the current setup or a patch map or key map used by the current setup. To do so, select another setup, click on **Close**, then reopen the MIDI Mapper and delete the item.

Part 6

Sharing Data

27

The Clipboard

Windows Clipboard is a special application that is always active. It just sits in the background, waiting for you to use it. In fact you have already seen how to use Clipboard. When you cut or copy text or graphics, the data is placed into it. When you copy the data back into an application, it is copied from the Clipboard. Most of the time you never actually see the Clipboard, although you will learn in a moment how to view its contents.

In this chapter we are going to discuss how to copy data within and between applications, including DOS applications. We will also explain how to work with the Clipboard images, saving them for future use, if necessary.

Copying, Cutting, and Pasting

The simplest way to use the Clipboard is with the Edit|Cut, Edit|Copy, and Edit|Paste commands. Most Windows applications have these commands, and as you've already seen, you can use them to transfer data within or between Windows applications.

Edit | Cut	**Ctrl-X** or **Shift-Del**	Removes the data, placing it in the Clipboard
Edit | Copy	**Ctrl-C** or **Ctrl-Ins**	Copies the data to the Clipboard
Edit | Paste	**Ctrl-V** or **Shift-Ins**	Copies the data from the Clipboard to the document

Select the picture or text you want to copy or cut and use the command—select from the Edit menu or use the keyboard shortcut. The data is placed in the Clipboard. Now you can move to the other application, or to another part of the current document, and use the Paste command to copy the data from the Clipboard into the document. You are only copying from the Clipboard; in other words, the data remains in the Clipboard, so you can paste it as many times as you want, until you Edit|Cut or Edit|Copy something else to the Clipboard.

▼ ***Note*** When you paste data from an OLE (Object Linking and Embedding) *server* into an OLE *client*, that data is automatically *embedded*. (See Chapter 28 for more information.)

You can't copy all kinds of data into all Windows applications. Some applications won't accept graphics, for instance. If you want to know what kind of data an application will accept, check its documentation. However, if you are new to Windows you may be surprised at just how easily different formats are transferred between applications. Any image in the Clipboard can be copied to most word processors and desktop publishing programs, for instance, and you can often copy text into graphics programs. Data exchange is a very important and useful feature of Windows, and most application publishers make their programs accept as many formats as possible. Incidentally, if you try to paste a format that the application cannot accept, it may, instead, paste the icon associated with the application from which the data originally came.

▼ ***Note*** The data remains in the Clipboard only until you place something else there, or until you close Windows. You can save the contents in a file, however, as we'll explain later. You may also buy applications that let you store multiple Clipboard images automatically and then retrieve them from a list.

Notice that these commands have two keyboard shortcuts. Originally Windows used the second set (Shift-Del, Ctrl-Ins, and Shift-Ins). These commands sometimes cause problems, especially with new users; if you use your Ins and Del keys on your numeric keypad, you must make sure that Num Lock is turned off. If you don't, the commands won't function. The new commands don't have this problem—they are always available.

In most Windows applications *both* sets of keyboard shortcuts will work. Some applications still use only the older version and the new commands may have other uses. For instance, in the Micrografx Windows Draw, Ctrl-V is the View Previous command. Some software publishers have been using these new keyboard shortcuts to operate other commands for some time, and it's not easy to change.

Copying Screens and Windows

You can copy a picture of everything on your computer screen—or just a single window—to the Clipboard. This is especially useful if you need to describe what is happening on your screen—perhaps to fax a letter to a technical support line or to illustrate a user manual. To get a picture of the entire screen, simply press the **Print Screen** key. In some cases—if you have an "unenhanced" keyboard—**Print Screen** may not work. Try **Shift-Print Screen** or **Alt-Print Screen** instead.

If you want to copy a picture of just the active window or dialog box, press **Alt-Print Screen**. You can now save this image for later use (we'll explain how to save .CLP images a little later in this chapter) or paste it into an application.

This image is in bitmap format (.BMP), which can be pasted into most Windows applications. You can even paste it into Paintbrush and edit it, removing the parts you don't want, for instance. However, there's a trick to getting the image into Paintbrush. (See Chapter 13 for details.)

If you use one of these commands in a full-screen DOS application, the image will be a "text" image rather than a bitmap. (DOS applications running in windows are copied as bitmaps.) You can then copy this text into a word processor. It may look like garbage to begin with, but if you convert the text to a nonproportional font (one in which all characters are the same size) and reduce the point size so it can all fit between the document's margins, you can set up the text to create a picture of the DOS application's screen. Try using the Courier New TrueType font that comes with Windows. Figure 27.1 shows a text image copied into a word processor, converted to Courier New, and changed to bold.

```
"
···············1991·Personal·Tax·Edge·-·Final·Filing·Version·1.0·······92RETURN¶
····Return····Finalizing····Help·····Utilities····Settings·····Quit¶
____________________________________________________________________________¶
____________________________________________________________________________¶
_______+-[_]----------------------·Welcome·--------------------------+_______¶
_______¦·············································¦_______¶
_______¦·······1991·Personal·Tax·Edge·-·Final·Filing·Version·1.0·······¦_______¶
_______¦·············································¦_______¶
_______¦···········Copyright·1992·by·Parsons·Technology,·Inc.···········¦_______¶
_______¦····················All·Rights·Reserved.······················¦_______¶
_______¦·············································¦_______¶
_______¦·······To·select·any·menu·bar·item·or·button,·hold·down·······¦_______¶
_______¦·······the·[ALT]·key·and·press·the·highlighted·[Letter].·······¦_______¶
_______¦·············································¦_______¶
_______¦····························OK····_························¦_______¶
_______¦·························__________························¦_______¶
_______+-------------------------------------------------------------+_______¶
____________________________________________________________________________¶
____________________________________________________________________________¶
____________________________________________________________________________¶
____________________________________________________________________________¶
·F1·Help··ESC·Exit··Ctrl-R·Move¶
```

Figure 27.1 A "text image" from a DOS application

Remember that you can configure a DOS application's PIF so that the Alt-Print Screen and Print Screen keys do not work in this manner. (See Chapter 7 for more information.)

Sharing Text with DOS Applications

You may use Windows' Clipboard to transfer text to and from a DOS application. If you want to copy selected text from the DOS application, you must be running in 386 Enhanced mode, but you can paste into a DOS application in either mode. (You can copy a screenful of text from a DOS window in Standard mode using Print Screen.) Thus you may use the Clipboard to copy text from a Windows application to a DOS application, and vice versa. You can also transfer text between DOS applications, and even within a single DOS application, in the same way you might transfer text from one part of a Windows document to another, or from one Windows document to another.

Not all of the keyboard shortcuts function in all DOS applications. For instance, you may not be able to use Alt-Spacebar to open the Control menu. Some of the shortcuts may have been disabled in the application's PIF. If one of the shortcuts doesn't seem to work correctly, read Chapter 7 for information about reserving shortcut keys.

Copying Text to the Clipboard

If you want to copy text from a DOS application to the Clipboard, make sure the application is running in a window. (That's why you can use this feature only in 386 Enhanced mode—Standard mode won't let you put DOS applications in windows.) If the application is running full screen, you can normally press **Alt-Enter** to change to a window.

Now select **Control | Edit | Mark**. A flashing block appears in the top-left corner of the DOS window, and the word Mark appears in the title bar. You can use the mouse to select the text you want, or use the arrow keys to move the block to the first character, press and hold **Shift**, and then use the arrow keys to highlight a block of text. If you make a mistake, release Shift and press an arrow key—the block will move back to the top-left corner. Now try again.

Next, press **Enter** or click the **right mouse button** to copy the text onto the Clipboard. Or select **Control | Edit | Copy**. Figure 27.2 shows a block being placed over text in a DOS application file. The text is copied to the Clipboard with a carriage return at the end of each line (it doesn't automatically "wrap" onto the next line). You can now paste this text into a Windows application, a different document in the same application, or another DOS application altogether.

Pasting Text into DOS Applications

There are two ways to paste text into a DOS application. The first, and easiest, method works only in **386 Enhanced mode** because the DOS application must be operating in a window. Place the cursor where you want to place the text, and then select **Control | Edit | Paste**. Windows drops the text into the DOS application (it pastes it into the BIOS keyboard buffer, which then "types" it into the application). It won't wrap the text; it regards each original line as separate and puts a carriage return at the end of each one.

If you are running in **Standard mode**, you can still paste text. Place the cursor where you want to insert the text, then swap to another application: Try using Alt-Tab, Alt-Esc, or Ctrl-Esc. Then find the DOS application's icon and select it—click on it once to open the Control menu, or press **Alt-Esc** until the icon is selected and then press **Alt-Spacebar** to open its Control menu. Select **Paste** from the menu, and Windows reopens the application for you and pastes the text.

If nothing happens when you try to paste data, you may have to adjust the method selected in the application's PIF. By default Windows uses the "Fast Paste" method, but some applications cannot accept data in this format. Use the PIF Editor to modify the setting (see Chapter 7). You can modify this setting only for 386 Enhanced mode.

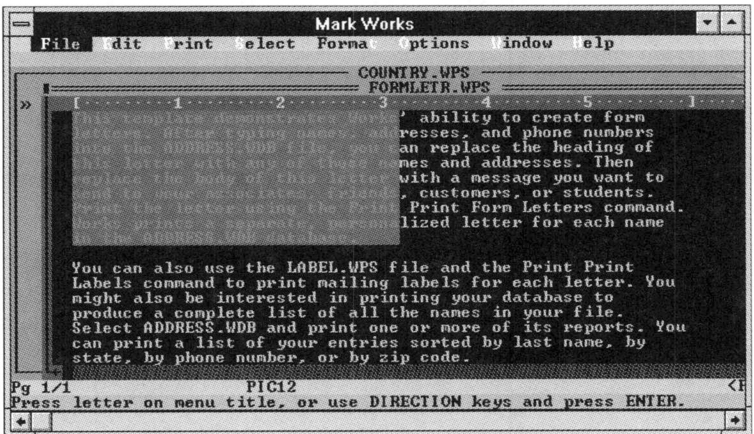

Figure 27.2 Selecting a block of text in a DOS application

Using Clipboard Viewer

You can view the contents of the Clipboard and save Clipboard files in the Clipboard Viewer. Double-click on the Clipboard icon in the Main program group. Or select **File | Run** and run **CLIPBRD**. The Clipboard Viewer appears, as shown in Figure 27.3.

You can save the data in a .CLP file for later use. Select **File | Save As**, select a directory and enter a filename, and click on **OK**. You can open .CLP files later using the **File | Open** command. Why would you want to do this? You might want to save data that you know you will want to transfer to another application later, for instance, or use the Print Screen feature to save "screen shots" and use Paintbrush to edit them later. You could even use this as a way to transfer graphics from one computer to another. For instance, you want to use a piece of clip art in the .DRW format, but your machine doesn't have a program that can display that format. Find a colleague's machine that does have a .DRW program, display the image, and copy it to the Clipboard; save it as a .CLP file and place the file on a floppy disk; open the file in the Clipboard viewer on the other machine; paste the image into the application.

You can clear the Clipboard by selecting **Edit | Delete** or by simply pressing **Del**. You may want to do so to reduce the amount of memory your computer is using, making it available for other applications.

The Clipboard Formats

When you copy something to the Clipboard, the data is saved in a variety of formats, so it may be inserted into various different applications. If you open the

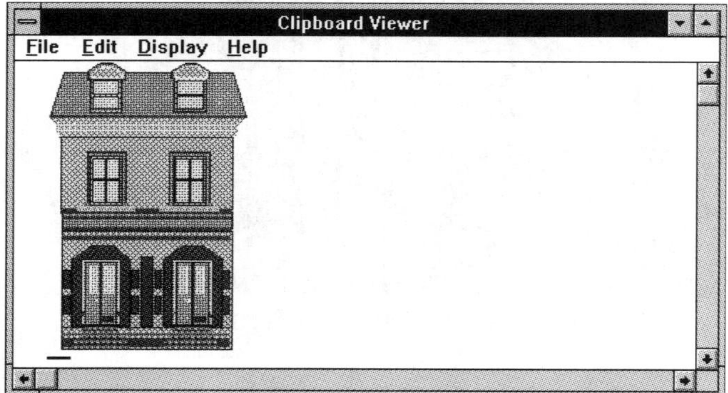

Figure 27.3 The Clipboard Viewer showing a picture in the Clipboard

Display menu you can see a list of the different formats, some of which you may be able to view. Here are a few formats that you may see listed.

Bitmap	A simple bitmap format (.BMP) used by Paintbrush.
DIB Bitmap	A Device Independent Bitmap, another type of bitmap. (Strictly speaking it's not device independent. The name was selected to differentiate the format from the Device Dependent Bitmap used in Windows 1.0.)
Link	Provides enough information to allow the data to be pasted with a DDE link. This data is used only when pasting into a DDE client application.
MGX_DRW	A format used by Micrografx Designer and Windows Draw.
Native	A full description of the data, which can only be interpreted by the source application.
ObjectLink	Provides enough information to allow the data to be pasted with an OLE link. This data is used only when pasting into an OLE client application.
OEM Text	The character set used by DOS.
Owner Display	A full description of the data, which depends on the source application and probably can be read only by the source application.
OwnerLink	Identifies the server application and the class of the linked or embedded object. This data is used only when pasting into an OLE client application.
Palette	The colors used in or available to the image.
Picture	A Windows metafile (.WMF).
Rich Text Format	A text format.
Text	A simple text with no character or paragraph formatting.

You can select **Display|Auto** to return to the format in which the data was originally displayed. Why would you want to display this data in another format? You probably won't. Changing this format has no effect on the way in which the data is pasted into another application. The application receiving the data picks the one it can work with, if any. If you are pasting into an OLE client application, you can use the Edit|Paste Special to select a format. (See Chapter 28 for more information.) This Display menu list may be useful to a developer for debugging a program.

28

OLE and Object Packager

In the previous chapter we explained how to transfer data between applications using the Clipboard. But there's another way to transfer data, available to some applications. You can use a system called Object Linking and Embedding (OLE). Unlike simply copying data from one application and pasting it into another, OLE does more (Microsoft calls it "smart cut and paste"). First, it lets you insert "objects" that you cannot normally paste. In addition to letting you insert text, numbers, and pictures, OLE also lets you insert sounds, application-file icons (which run the application when clicked on), and command icons (which run a DOS command when clicked on). This feature is called *Object* Linking and Embedding because the item you insert is not necessarily what you might think of as *data*.

Second, the item is not simply inserted and left, like a chart or table glued into a notebook. The object retains a connection from the application into which it was inserted—known as the *client*—to the application from which it comes, known as the *server*. There are two basic types of OLE objects, depending on the type of connection: *linked* and *embedded*. A linked object retains a connection to the original file from which the data came. An embedded object retains a link to the application that created the data file, but not the data file itself.

▼ ***Note*** You must have 2 MB of RAM as a bare minimum to use OLE.

Linking versus Embedding

A **linked** object is one that remains linked to the original data file. For instance, you create and save a Paintbrush picture. You then use OLE to place a linked object—your new picture—in Windows Write. The picture in Write is linked to the original Paintbrush file, so changes to that file are shown in Write. You can edit the object in the client by double-clicking on it, or by selecting a special command from the menu bar. Windows opens the server application for you—in this case, Paintbrush—and loads the original file. Make your changes and close the application, and Windows updates both the original file and the object in the client. Both the original file and the object in the client remain the same, and any other documents that have links to that file are automatically updated also.

It's important to note that the objects in the server and client are generally independent objects. For example, some word processing applications "import" graphics by entering a code into a document: The code tells the application the file format and filename of the image and in which directory it can be found. This is a type of linking—changes to the original file are seen in the word processor, but if you move the original file the word processor will be unable to display the image.

OLE linking does not depend totally on this link, because the object is a real object, not a reference code. Remove or delete the original object, and the object in the client remains. However, in some circumstances the object may be removed. For instance, if Word for Windows tries to update a linked object but is unable to find the file to which it is linked, Word displays an error message in place of the object. Windows Write, on the other hand, would simply keep the object without being able to update it.

The second type of connected object is the **embedded** object. In this case there is no link to a file, but there is a connection to the server application. You can still edit the embedded object in the same way you edit a linked object. When you double-click on the object Windows opens the server application, but it doesn't load the original file. Instead, it loads the object itself from the client application. When you make your changes and close the application, the client object is modified—the original file remains unchanged.

The manner in which the object is displayed in the client varies. Often the object itself is displayed. You will see the actual Paintbrush picture, the actual chart from Microsoft Graph, and the actual text from Microsoft WordArt. In other cases you will see an icon instead. For instance, if you insert a **sound**, you will see a small picture of a microphone. If you insert text from Word for Windows into Windows Write or Cardfile you will see the Word icon. These icons are known as *object packages* or simply *packages*. To view or hear an object in a package, you must double-click on it. Windows will play the sound or open the server application so you can view the object. Windows also comes with an accessory called **Object Packager**, which lets you put any type of object into a package. You will learn how to work with this accessory later in this chapter.

What are the advantages of OLE? First, it is easy to modify an object, whether the object is a chart, a memo, a table, or a picture. Without OLE you would need to go to Program Manager, open another application, open the original file, make and save your changes, copy the data to the clipboard, return to the other application, and paste the changed data. With OLE you simply double-click on the object, make your changes, and close the window. All the opening, saving, copying, and pasting is done for you. (Figure 28.1 shows an example—a graph in Windows Write has been opened by double-clicking on it.)

The other advantage is that documents can be kept current very easily. If you produce a monthly report that contains sales figures from a spreadsheet, you can link the numbers in your word processor with the original numbers in the spreadsheet. Changing the spreadsheet automatically changes the numbers in the word processor. You can make sure that illustrations in a hardware manual are the latest, without having to import them. A report showing customers who are behind on their payments can automatically show the latest information from your database.

Some applications work only as servers, some only as clients, some as both client and server, and some cannot work with OLE at all. For instance, not only will Word accept objects from other applications, but it can also provide documents that may be inserted into other applications. Paintbrush, however, will not accept objects from other applications; in other words, it cannot act as a client. The ability of an application to work with OLE—and whether the application will be a client, server, or both—depends wholly on the application's publisher. Several of the

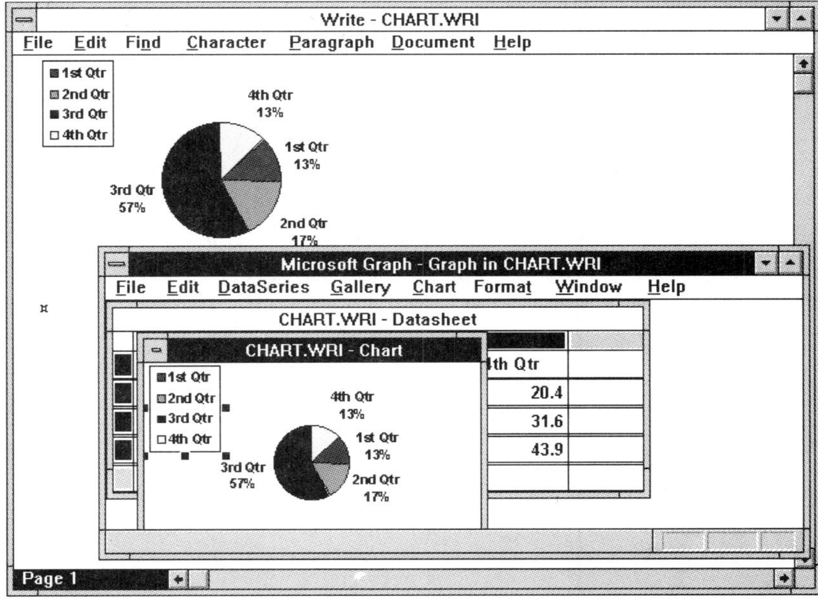

Figure 28.1 Double-clicking on the chart in Write displayed Microsoft Graph

Microsoft Windows mini-applications work with OLE, but if a software company wants its own Windows applications to use OLE it must program them to do so. Some applications will use it, some will not.

Tip If you want to embed an object from an application that is *not* an OLE server into an OLE client, you *can* do so by creating an Object Package. (See later in this chapter.)

The following Windows accessory applications will work with OLE:

- **Cardfile**: client
- **Object Packager**: server and client
- **Sound Recorder**: server
- **Windows Paintbrush**: server
- **Windows Write**: client

A number of other Windows applications already support OLE: Word for Windows, Excel, Windows Draw, and the Microsoft mini-applications Microsoft WordArt, Equation Editor, Microsoft Draw, and Microsoft Graph. By the time you read this, many other OLE applications will be available and more will be on the way.

Tip Want a quick way to find which of your applications act as OLE servers? Go to one that you already know can act as a *client* (Windows Write, for instance), and select the Insert Object command (usually in the Edit menu). Windows displays a dialog box that lists the *types* of object that may be inserted. Some will be obvious—Sound means an object from the Sound Recorder, for example. If you don't know what a listed object is, select it and click on **OK**: Windows will open the server application.

Linking and Embedding Objects

How, then, do you embed or link an object? Unfortunately the menu options are not very clear, and the command names vary between applications, although the actual procedures are the same. You may need to see your application's documentation for specifics. There are several different ways to embed and link objects, so we will look at each one in turn.

Embedding an Object with Insert Object

Use this procedure to embed an object into a client, starting while working in the client.

1. In the client document, place the cursor where you want to place the object. (In Cardfile, simply open a card—the object will always be placed in the upper-left corner.)
2. If you are using Cardfile, select **Edit | Picture**.
3. Select **Edit | Insert Object**. (In some applications this command may be in a different place. Word for Windows uses **Insert | Object**, for example.) The Insert New Object dialog box appears, listing all the types of OLE objects you can work with (see Figure 28.2).
4. Double-click on the object you want to embed. The server application opens.
5. Create the object that you want to embed (the text, picture, sound, chart, and so on). If you want to embed an existing object, do *not* use the application's File | Open command—doing so will break the connection between the client and the server. Instead, use the **Edit | Paste From** (in Paintbrush) or similar command to copy an entire file into the current document. In Word for Windows, for instance, you can use the **Insert | File** command.
6. While creating the object, you can use the **File | Update** command to periodically save your work.
7. When you have finished your object, select **File | Exit & Return** to (in Paintbrush), **File | Exit** (in Sound Recorder), or **File | Close** in some other applications (such as Word for Windows). The server closes, and you return to the client document. Your object will appear in the document. In the case of a sound, a microphone icon will be shown. (Double-clicking on the microphone plays the sound.)

Note that this method does not save the object you created as a separate file. In some applications you may be able to do so by using the **File | Save As** command, as the command may save the file and let you continue working on the embedded object. However, other applications won't let you do this without finishing work

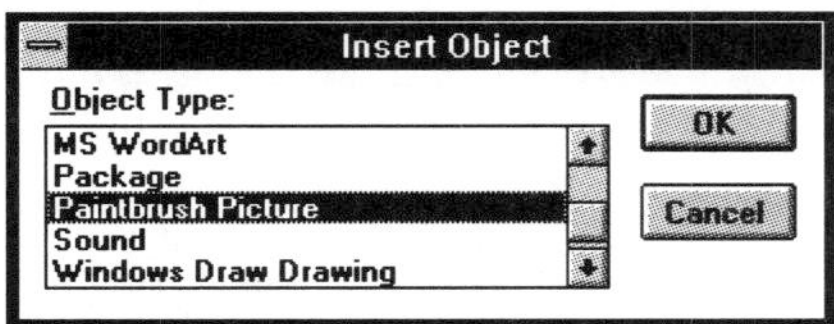

Figure 28.2 The Insert New Object dialog box

on the embedded object first. You can always open it later and save it as a file, or save it as a file and then use the next method to embed it.

Embedding an Object, Starting from the Server

There are a few advantages to starting at the other end, at the server. You can create an object and save it in a file before you embed it. Or you can open an existing file and embed that. You can also embed just one portion of a file—one or two paragraphs, part of a drawing, a few spreadsheet cells, and so on. Follow this procedure.

1. In the server, open or create the object you want to embed.
2. If you wish, save the object using **File | Save**.
3. Select the entire file or just the portion that you want to embed.
4. Copy the object into the Clipboard. Use the **Edit | Copy** command, or press **Ctrl-C** (Ctrl-Ins in some applications).
5. Open the client application and document.
6. Place the cursor where you want to embed the object. (Remember, if you are embedding in Cardfile, you must select **Edit | Picture** first.)
7. Paste the object into the client. Use **Edit | Paste** or Ctrl-V (Shift-Ins in some applications). Windows embeds the object into the client document.

The object may sometimes appear as an icon. For instance, if you paste Word for Windows text into Windows Write, Windows adds an icon, not the actual text. When the application cannot display the format you have pasted, it places the text in a "package" instead. You can view it by double-clicking on the icon, or by selecting it and then selecting the Edit | Edit Word Document Object command.

All you have done with this procedure is to copy and paste from one application to another. We did that before, and simple data was transferred. Text is placed into the receiving application, for example, or a picture; but there is no connection to the application that created the data. The difference here is that if you use applications that are capable of acting as server and client, Windows automatically embeds the object into the client.

This raises a question. If simply copying and pasting from a server to a client embeds a picture, how can you do a simple, nonembedded copy and paste? How, for example, can you paste text into Windows Write, with no connection to Word for Windows? Or how can you paste a picture from Paintbrush into Word for Windows, with no connection to Paintbrush? You can use Edit | Paste Special, which lets you select the format in which the information will be pasted. More about that in a moment.

 *Note* In Cardfile, if Edit | Text is selected, pasting text will not embed an object. If you want to embed a text object you must select Edit | Picture first.

Linking Objects with Paste Link

How, then, do we link an object—create a connection by which the object in the client will be automatically updated if the original in the server is modified? Follow this procedure.

1. In the server, open or create the object you want to embed.
2. Save the object using **File | Save**. If you don't save, you may be able to paste the object into the client, but it won't be linked (because there won't be an original to link to!).
3. Select the entire file or just the portion you want to embed.
4. Copy the object into the Clipboard. Use the **Edit | Copy** command, or press **Ctrl-C** (Ctrl-Ins in some applications).
5. Open the client application and document.
6. Place the cursor where you want to embed the object. (Remember, if you are linking in Cardfile, you must select **Edit | Picture**.)
7. Select **Edit | Paste Link**. The object is pasted into the client.

Some applications don't have an Edit | Paste Link command (Word for Windows, for example). You will have to use the **Edit | Paste Special** command instead. Let's look at that right now.

Working with Edit|Paste Special

Edit | Paste Special displays the Paste Special dialog box (see Figure 28.3 for an example). This box shows you the different formats in which you can paste the data currently stored in the Clipboard. It is available only in OLE client applications. If an application is not a client, there are no alternatives to the simple copy and paste procedure, which automatically selects the format that is used. Paste Special lets you

- Paste an embedded object.
- Paste an object and link it to the original file in the server application.

- Paste an object as if you were pasting between non-OLE applications.
- In some cases, select alternative formats for a non-OLE paste.

The options depend on whether or not the object comes from an OLE server. Let's say you copy text from Windows Write into the Clipboard and open the Paste Special dialog box in Word for Windows. The dialog box will list only Unformatted Text. Because Write is not a server, the text cannot be pasted as an embedded or linked object, so it can be only simple text. If you select an object in Paintbrush, however, and then open the dialog box in Word for Windows, you will see two options: Paintbrush Picture Object and Bitmap. In some cases you may have even more options. For instance, if you copy an image from Micrografx Windows Draw, you see four options: Windows Draw Drawing Object, Picture, Bitmap, and Device Independent Bitmap. Each may work slightly differently in different applications.

Notice, however, that there are two buttons that will place the object into the client: Paste and Paste Link. The **Paste** button has two effects, depending on the item selected from the list. If you select the Object (Paintbrush Picture Object, Word Document Object, and so on), the object is *embedded* into the client. If you select one of the other options, the data is simply copied into the client, as if you had cut and pasted between non-OLE applications.

The **Paste Link** button pastes the object into the document and creates a link to the original file in the server application. However, this button may be disabled if you have selected the Object. If so, select one of the other options. Here's a summary, for example, of your options when pasting a Paintbrush picture.

- Select **Paintbrush Picture Object** and click on **Paste**. The object is embedded in the client.
- Select **Bitmap** and click on **Paste**. The object is copied into the client with no connections; that is, it is not embedded or linked.
- Select **Bitmap** and click on **Paste Link**. The object is linked to the original.

This all may seem a little confusing at first, especially as the terms used in the Paste Special dialog box vary from client to client. For instance, Windows Write displays Word Document Object, Picture, and Text, while Word for Windows

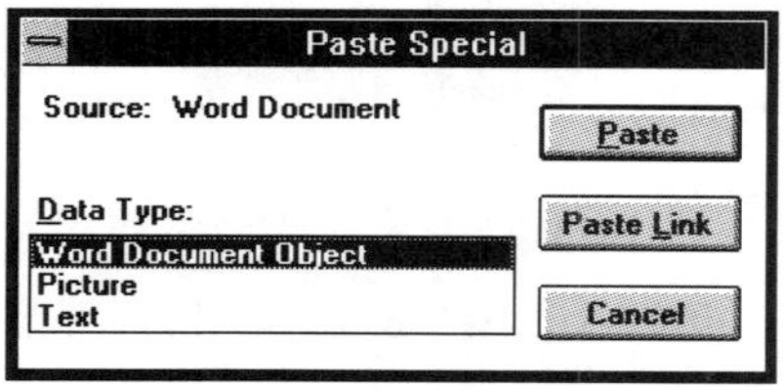

Figure 28.3 The Paste Special dialog box

shows Microsoft Word Object, Formatted Text, and Unformatted Text. But all you need to remember is that, usually,

- The entry that ends with the word **Object** can be *embedded* by clicking **Paste**.
- Other entries can be pasted without embedding by clicking on **Paste**.
- The **Paste Link** button pastes a *linked* object.

Incidentally, in some *vector*-graphics applications you cannot link just one part of a file, even if you select just one part of the file before copying to the clipboard. If you select just a portion of a picture and paste a linked object into another application, the object may include the entire picture, not just the selected portions. In *raster* (bitmap) graphics programs you get only the portion of the picture you selected. Check the application's documentation for details—or try it and see.

Embedding and Linking Objects—A Summary

Using OLE is actually quite simple, if you can just get these different methods straight.

- Embed an object by copying and pasting: copying from a server and pasting in a client *automatically* embeds the picture.
- Embed an object by opening the client and using Edit | Insert Object.
- Link an object by opening the server, copying the object, opening the client, and selecting Edit | Paste Link.
- If the application doesn't have Edit | Paste Link, use Edit | Paste Special and click the Paste Link button.
- To do a non-OLE copy and paste between OLE applications, select Edit | Paste Special, click on the second or subsequent item in the list, and click the **Paste** button.

Object Packages

You have already seen that Windows automatically places some objects inside packages when the client application is unable to display the data it receives from the server. When you place a sound object in a client, or a Word for Windows object in Cardfile or Windows Write, for instance, Windows places a package instead of the object—the package is usually the source application's icon, although you will learn how to change this icon. You can view or hear the object by double-clicking on it. Figure 28.4 shows an example of a packaged object.

You can also use Object Packager or File Manager to create packages. Instead of placing an actual picture or range of data in a document, for example, you can use

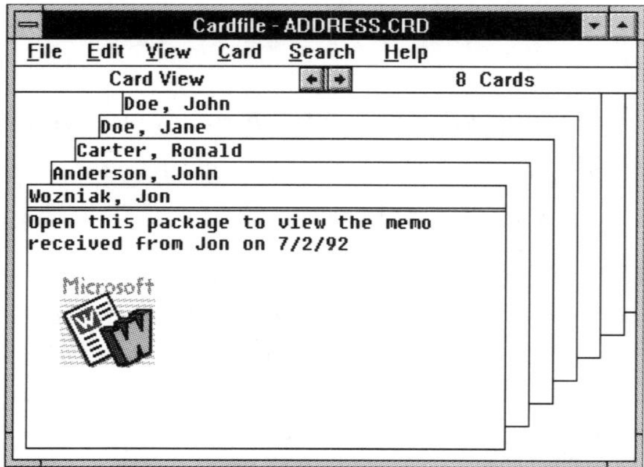

Figure 28.4 A packaged Word for Windows document placed in a Cardfile card

Object Packager to place an icon in the document. Or you can use File Manager to create a linked package.

▼ ***Note*** Strictly speaking, packages are always embedded, but they may contain embedded or linked objects. However, when we refer to a linked or embedded package, we're talking about the end result—the object in the package contains a link to the original file or is simply embedded.

Creating packages is like adding attachments to the end of a paper document. The information in the package does not take up much room in the document. Readers who want to view or listen to the object can double-click on the package. Otherwise they simply ignore it. But an object doesn't have to be information or sound. It can be a DOS command or an executable file. Double-clicking on the package will run the command or program. (The package still takes up disk space, of course, increasing the size of the file into which you paste it. In fact a package takes up more disk space than the object alone.)

Object packaging is an OLE function. You can't place a package in just any application—it must be an OLE client application. You can, however, build packages with objects created in *any* Windows application, not just server applications. There are two rules. First, you can work only with entire files from non-OLE applications. You can't select just a portion of a picture or a block of text, for instance. Second, the file type must be *associated* with an application. This is done using the File|Associate command in File Manager. (It is explained in Chapter 9.) For instance, you can package .TXT files because the .TXT extension is associated with Notepad. Although Notepad is not an OLE application, double-clicking a

.TXT package will open Notepad and display the file. If the file type has no association, the package cannot open.

The Object Packager Window

Open the Object Packager by double-clicking on the icon in the Accessories program group. Or select **File | Run** and run **PACKAGER**. The Object Packager window has two sub windows: the Appearance window and the Content window. The Appearance window shows the icon that you are going to place in the document (how the package will "appear"), and the Content window shows what the package will contain—the picture, text, data, or sound. You can select each window by clicking on it or by pressing **Tab**. Figure 28.5 shows Object Packager after a package has been created.

Why the scroll bars? The package Appearance doesn't have to be an icon. As you will learn in a moment, you can use a picture to represent the icon. If you do so the scroll bars will let you scroll down and across the picture. The Content window usually displays a text description of the package contents. If it is a linked object, the text is the name of the file to which the object is linked. If it is an embedded object, the text is a description of the object.

In one condition, however, you can see a picture of the object. If you use the Clipboard to copy and paste the object from an OLE server application, you can click on the **Picture** option button to display a picture. The picture may be the actual object—it will be if you paste a Paintbrush picture, for instance. Or the picture may be an icon representing the server application. In either case, if part of it is not displayed in the window, the scroll bars will let you view the entire picture.

Creating Packages

As with a normal OLE object, the package may be embedded or linked. There are several ways to package documents using Object Packager or File Manager. Let's look at them one by one.

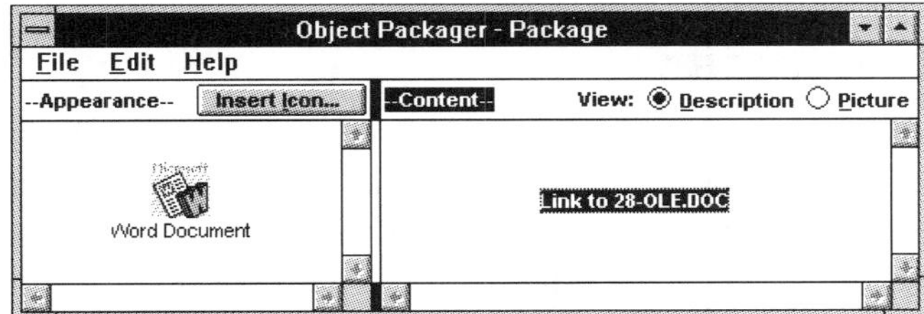

Figure 28.5 The Object Packager window

EMBEDDING AN ENTIRE FILE IN A PACKAGE

Follow this procedure to embed a file in a package.

1. Select the Object Packager's Content window.
2. Select **File | Import**. The Import dialog box appears.
3. Select the file you want to use and click on **OK**. The filename appears in the Content window, and the icon of the application that created the file appears in the Appearance window.
4. Select **Edit | Copy Package**.
5. Open an OLE server application and document.
6. Position the insertion point, and select **Edit | Paste**. The icon is inserted into the document. The file is embedded—it's now a separate copy of the original.

You can change the icon used for the package—you can even replace it with a picture—and change the icon's label. You will learn how to do this later in this chapter.

EMBEDDING OR LINKING PARTIAL FILES

You can use this method to embed or link just part of a file in a package.

1. In the server application, select the object you want to embed or link. (If you are going to link, save the file first.)
2. Go to the Object Packager and select the Content window.
3. Choose the **Edit | Paste** option if you want to embed the object, or the **Edit | Paste Link** option if you want to link it. A description of the object or the filename appears in the Content window, and the icon of the application that created the file appears in the Appearance window.
4. Select **Edit | Copy Package**.
5. Open an OLE server application and document.
6. Position the insertion point, and select **Edit | Paste**. The icon is inserted into the document.

EMBEDDING OR LINKING ENTIRE FILES

You can use this method to embed or link an entire file, using both File Manager and Object Packager. You can embed a non-OLE file using this method, or even embed an executable program file—a Windows or DOS program—that can be run by clicking on the package in the client application.

1. Open File Manager and select the file you want to package.
2. Select **File | Copy**.

3. In the Copy dialog box, click on the **Copy to Clipboard** option button and click on **OK**.
4. Open Object Packager and select the Content window.
5. Choose the **Edit | Paste** option if you want to embed the object, or **Edit | Paste Link** option if you want to link it. The filename appears in the Content window, and the icon of the application that created the file appears in the Appearance window. (If it's a file type that has no associated application, Object Packager's own icon appears.)
6. Select **Edit | Copy** Package.
7. Open an OLE server application and document.
8. Position the insertion point and select **Edit | Paste**. The icon is inserted into the document.

When you Copy to Clipboard from the File Manager, you are copying only the name of the selected file.

DRAGGING FROM FILE MANAGER TO OBJECT PACKAGER

You can embed or link an entire file by dragging it from File Manager onto Object Packager's Content window. Simply size and move the File Manager and Object Packager windows so both are visible, then select the file and drag it over to the Content window.

If the file was created by an OLE server you can create a linked package. Hold down **Shift-Ctrl** while you drag and release the file. (Not all applications will let you link a file this way.)

Again, the file may be an executable file—a Windows or DOS program file.

DRAGGING FROM FILE MANAGER TO A CLIENT

The quickest way to create a package is to drag a file from File Manager directly to the client application. Simply display File Manager and the client application together on your screen. Find the file you want to insert into the client's document. Click on it and drag it over into the client. Release the mouse when the cursor is where you want to place the package.

This sort of package is an *embedded* package. If you want to create a *linked* package, press **Shift-Ctrl** while you drag the file. (You can create a linked package only if the source is a server application, and even then some servers won't let you use this method.)

You can even drag executable files into the client—in which case the program will run when you double-click on the package.

CREATING PACKAGES—A SUMMARY

Here's a summary of the various methods used to create packages.

- Use **File | Import** in Object Packager to create an embedded package.
- Copy an object to the Clipboard from another application. In Object Packager select the Content window and use **Edit | Paste** to create an embedded package, **Edit | Paste Link** for a linked package.
- Use **File | Copy** in File Manager to copy a file to the Clipboard. In Object Packager select the Content window and use **Edit | Paste** to create an embedded package, **Edit | Paste Link** for a linked package.
- **Drag** a file from File Manager to **Object Packager's** Content window to create an embedded object.
- **Drag** a file from File Manager to **Object Packager's** Content window while holding **Shift-Ctrl** to create an embedded object.
- **Drag** a file from File Manager to the **client** to create an embedded object.
- **Drag** a file from File Manager to the **client** while holding **Shift-Ctrl** to create a linked object.

Changing the Icon

The icon in the Appearance window is the program icon of the application that created the file or portion of the file in the package. If you don't want to use the icon, you can use another, or you can use a picture created in Paintbrush or another paint or drawing package. You could, for example, associate music with a photograph or painting.

There are several ways to use a different icon. (You can also change the label that appears under the icon—we'll cover that next.)

- Use **File | Import** to load a file created by the application whose icon you want to use. Then use File | Import again to load the actual file you want to package. The original icon will remain in the Appearance window, but the Content window will display the name of the second file.
- Copy a portion of a file to the Clipboard, then go to Object Packager. Click on the Appearance window. Select **Edit | Paste**, and either the file's icon is displayed or the information from the file itself. For example, if you paste text from Word for Windows, the Word icon is pasted. If you copy a picture from Paintbrush, the actual picture is pasted. If you now import a file, or paste into the Content window, the Appearance window does not change.

- Click on the **Insert Icon** button to see the Insert Icon dialog box, the same box as the Change Icon dialog box described in Chapter 4. Select an icon from the scrolling display, or select another file. The MORICONS.DLL file contains many icons, but you can select an icon from any Windows executable file.

You can also modify an icon using Object Packager as a way to place an icon in a paint program. (This is a quick way to get icons into a paint program for *any* purpose.) Load an icon into Object Packager, using whatever method you wish. Then select the Appearance window, and select Edit|Copy to copy the icon to the Clipboard. Go to Paintbrush and use Edit|Paste to copy the icon into the work area. Make your changes, copy the new icon to the clipboard, return to Object Packager, select the Appearance window, and select Edit|Paste. You won't be able to give this new "icon" a label, however.

Important Do not change the size of the icon once pasted into the client application. Doing so may damage the link.

Changing the Icon Label

When you place an entire file into Object Packager, the filename appears as the icon's label. If you copy just a portion of a file through the Clipboard, the label is the object type and application name. If you use the Insert Icon button to choose a different one, it won't have a label.

You can change or add a label by selecting **Edit|Label**. Type the text you want—up to 39 characters—into the Label dialog box and click on **OK**. Unfortunately the label will be displayed on one line; it will not wrap onto two or more lines.

Creating a Command Package

As we mentioned earlier, a package can contain a DOS command rather than an object. For instance, you might want to run a DOS application or batch file when the user double-clicks on the package. Select **Edit|Command Line**. Type the DOS command or the path and filename of a batch file. Click on OK.

Object Packager does not automatically add an icon when you create a Command Line package, so you must select one before you can copy the package. (See the preceding instructions on Changing the Icon.) Then select Edit|Copy package, and paste the package into the client.

The Object Packager Menus

Before we leave Object Packager, let's take a quick look at a summary of its menu options.

File | New Clears the Object Packager window so you can create a new package.

File | Update This appears only when you open an existing package from a client. It updates the package with any changes you have made.

File | Import Loads a file into the Object Packager. The file will be an embedded object.

File | Save Saves the contents of the package with a new filename.

File | Exit Closes Object Packager.

Edit | Undo Undoes the last change made while creating a package.

Edit | Cut Removes the contents of the selected window and places it in the Clipboard. You can cut the icon in the Appearance window and paste it into Paintbrush so you can edit it. If the object in the Content window originally came through the Clipboard, you can cut it and place it directly in a client as an embedded or linked *object*, rather than a package.

Edit | Copy Copies the contents of the selected window and places it in the Clipboard. (See Edit | Cut.)

Edit | Delete Removes the contents of the selected window.

Edit | Paste Embeds an object from the Clipboard into the Content window. If you paste into the Appearance window, either the icon belonging to the application that created the object is pasted, or the actual picture if it comes from a graphics program.

Edit | Paste Link Places an object from the Clipboard into the Object Packager and creates a link.

Edit | Copy Package Copies the entire package—icon and contents—into the Clipboard. You can then paste it into the client.

Edit | Links Modifies the link between the object in the package and the source. Available only if the object was pasted using Edit | Paste Link (not if it was dragged from the File Manager using Shift-Ctrl). (See discussion of Links later in this chapter.)

Edit | Label Changes the label of the icon in the Appearance window.

Edit | Command Line Lets you enter a DOS command that is run when you double-click on the icon in the client.

Edit | Edit *type* Object Displays the object in its application window, letting you edit it.

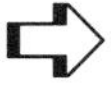 **Tip** You can combine linked and embedded objects in packages. For example, create a Write document. Place various linked or embedded objects or packages in the Write document. Save the file, then place that file in a package. Now the user can double-click on the Write icon to view various objects and packages.

Working with Objects and Packages

Now that you have placed an object or a package into a client-application document, what can you do with it? In many cases you can already see the object—the picture or text, for instance. If the object is in a package you can use a command to open the application so you can view it, or to play a sound. You may also edit the object (or the package that holds it). The commands that you use will vary among applications.

To view, edit, or listen to an embedded object, double-click on it. You can also select the object or package and select an Edit menu option that names the object—something like **Edit | Windows Draw Drawing Object**, for instance, or **Edit | Sound Object**. Some applications have an option called **Edit | Package Object | Activate Contents**. Yet other applications may have no menu option—just double-click.

The application will open automatically, or, in the case of a sound, the sound will play. (In the case of sounds, Windows Write has two options: **Edit | Sound Object | Play** to hear the sound, and **Edit | Sound Object | Edit** to open Sound Recorder and load the .WAV file.) You can now edit the object. When you close the application, the changes are made to the embedded object. Remember, the embedded object is saved in the client document.

If the object is linked, the procedure is similar. Double-click on the object or select it and choose the appropriate option from the Edit menu. This may be an option such as **Edit | Edit Word Document Object**. As with embedded objects, some applications may have an option called **Edit | Package Object | Activate Contents**. Others may have no menu option for packages—just double-click.

Again, the application opens (or the sound plays). With a *linked* object, it loads the *original* file, the one that originally supplied the object. Edit the file, then save the changes. The changes will be saved to the original file and the linked object in the client is updated.

You can edit a package itself—the label and icon, for instance. Select the package and then choose a menu option such as **Edit | Package Object | Edit Package** or **Edit | Package Object**. When Object Packager opens you can make your changes and then close it to update the package in the client application.

▼ ***Note*** If you get a message saying the action cannot be completed, the server may be busy (printing, for instance) or unavailable (damaged, moved, deleted, or locked up).

Managing Links

Windows provides a way to manage the links between a linked object and its source file. You can fix broken links, change the link to another file, tell Windows to immediately update the linked object, and so on. Perhaps the most important features are the ability to turn off automatic updates and to fix the link—if you move, delete, or rename the source file, obviously the linked object cannot be updated until you fix the link.

Select **Edit | Links** to see the Links dialog box; see Figure 28.6. This box varies slightly between applications. The one shown is from Windows Write. The Links box lists all the linked objects in the document—it doesn't include *embedded* objects. For each link it usually shows the name of the server application and the file to which it is linked (and sometimes even the path, or at least part of it). It often also includes identifying information, such as an object number (for a vector-graphics program), bitmap coordinates (for a paint program), or other identifier. However, the identifier will probably never be of use to you; it's used by the application to determine what data is updated.

The last information in this box is the link **Status**: It may be *Unavailable* (meaning the link has broken), *Automatic* (the object is automatically updated in certain events), *Manual* (the object is updated only when you use the Update Now button), or *Internal* (meaning the object and source are from the same application).

It's not always clear which link pertains to which object in the document, because in applications that display the source file's path, you probably won't be able to see the filename. However, you can be sure which link you are working on by selecting the object *before* you open the Links dialog box—the selected link will

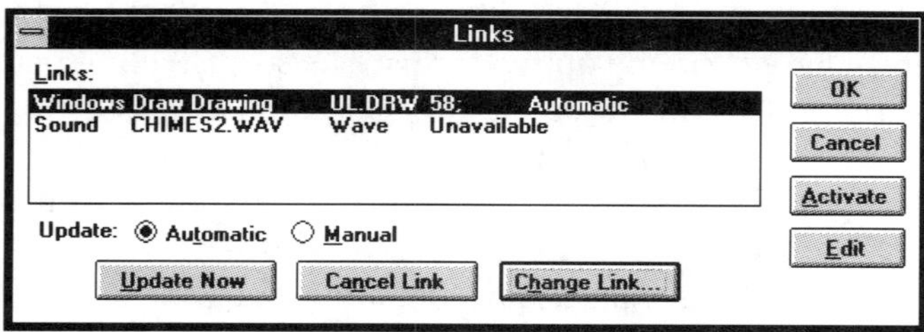

Figure 28.6 The Windows Write's Links dialog box

be highlighted. You can also click on a link in the list and then click on **Change Link**. The dialog box that appears will show you the full path and filename.

Automatic links are updated often, perhaps too often. For instance, each time you open a Windows Write document that contains linked objects, a message asks if you want to "update links now." Click on **Yes** and the object is updated with the latest data from the original file. If any links in the document are set to "manual," they are not updated. You can change a link to a manual update by selecting it in the list box and clicking on **Manual**.

If you double-click on an object to open the server, make changes, and save and close the file, the linked object won't be updated if its link is set to "manual." Usually, the only way to update a manual link is to select the object in the Links dialog box and click on **Update Now**. However, some applications may let you update some other way. Word for Windows, for instance, lets you select the object and press **F9**. Making your links manual will save time—you won't have to wait for your application to update a document's links each time you open it.

The Links dialog box in Figure 28.6 has an **Activate** button and an **Edit** button. In most cases these will do the same thing: open the source file so you can view or edit it. In the case of sounds, Activate plays the sound, and Edit opens Sound Recorder and loads the sound. In some applications the Links dialog box has an **Open Source** button instead. If you want to edit or view the source file, select the link and click on this button. (If it's a sound file, Open Source will probably play the sound, not open Sound Recorder. Use the Edit menu options to open Sound Recorder.) Some dialog boxes also have a **Locked** check box. Select a link and click on **Locked** so the link cannot be updated using any method, even by clicking on **Update Now**.

If you wish to convert a linked object to a simple non-OLE pasted object, select the link and click on **Cancel Link**. The object remains in the document, but it is no longer linked, or even embedded. In the case of a package, the icon remains in the document, but it won't do anything when you double-click on it. Be careful using this feature. Some applications won't ask you to confirm the cancellation, and once canceled the link cannot be fixed (not even using the Change Link button).

If, however, you have moved or renamed a file, you can fix the link by selecting it and clicking on **Change Link**. The dialog box you see will vary. It may be a simple File Open type dialog box, which shows you the current source file and lets you select another. You may select the file you renamed or moved, or even, in some cases, a completely different file (but you won't be able to select a file of a different type—changing a sound file to a graphics file, for instance). Some Links dialog boxes use a different Change Link dialog box, such as the one shown in Figure 28.7. You can enter a new path and filename. You may also be able to change the Item Name, by entering a new range of spreadsheet cells, for instance.

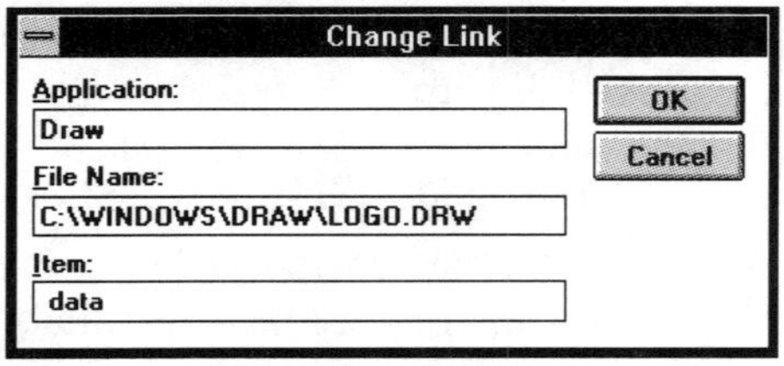

Figure 28.7 Word for Windows' Change Link dialog box

Dynamic Data Exchange (DDE)

You may have heard of Dynamic Data Exchange (DDE). DDE was Windows' first version of data linking. OLE builds on DDE—Microsoft regards it as a more advanced version of DDE. It allows you to both link and embed data (DDE is designed to link data only), and it does so in a simpler, easier-to-use manner. From the programmer's standpoint, OLE is easier to use. Whereas a programming team creating a new Windows application had to add extensive code to implement DDE, adding OLE is much easier. Windows uses its OLE DLL files to do most of the work, so a programmer has to write just enough code to tap into those DLLs. This presumably means that more Windows applications will use OLE than DDE. In fact DDE was never widely used, while OLE seems to be catching on with applications publishers quite fast. And the ability to embed packages with non-OLE objects makes some OLE features available to applications with no special program code added.

DDE is still in use, and in some cases it uses the same dialog boxes as OLE. Microsoft Word for Windows, for instance, uses the Paste Special dialog box to create a DDE link and the Links dialog box to maintain DDE links. DDE is beyond the scope of this book, however. If you want to learn more about the DDE capabilities of your application, check its documentation.

Appendix A

Optimizing Windows

Windows' major drawback is that it imposes a lot of operating "overhead" on your system. The IBM PC-compatible is a text-based machine, and it takes a lot of work to force a graphics-based operating system like Windows on it. One of the first things that new users discover is that Windows can be very slow. A Windows word processor running on a 386 may be slower in many ways than a DOS word processor on a 386SX or even a 286. (The Windows word processor can do much more than the DOS word processor, which is why, we hope, it's worth the trouble.)

This appendix examines ways in which you can improve the performance of Windows: how you can make it faster and multitask more programs by improving memory use.

Preparing CONFIG.SYS

The CONFIG.SYS file is the first file your computer runs when it boots. This file sets up the system configuration and loads device drivers. These are the settings that Windows needs in the CONFIG.SYS file.

- A line that loads HIMEM.SYS, which must appear before any device drivers are loaded into extended memory. This is added by Setup when you install Windows.

  ```
  (DEVICE=C:\HIMEM.SYS)
  ```

  This is the extended-memory manager; it is discussed later.
- A `files=`*nn* line. This tells DOS how many files it may access at one time. Set *nn* to at least 30. Some programs may require more, perhaps as many as 60.

Remember that this isn't simply the number of document files you open, but includes all files of all types that are used while you are running Windows.

- A `buffers=nn` line. This creates a simple cache that DOS uses to store data while it reads and writes from and to the disk. Each buffer uses 532 bytes, so the higher the number you enter, the more memory you use. If you are using DOS 5.0, use `buffers=30`. Otherwise use `buffers=20`. If you are using the SMARTDrive disk cache, use `buffers=10`.
- If your system has an EGA (Extended Graphics Adapter) monitor and you run DOS applications in Standard mode, you need this line:

  ```
  device=c:\windows\ega.sys
  ```

- If you have DOS applications that need expanded memory and your computer has no expanded memory, and if you are running Windows in Standard mode on a 386, you need this line:

  ```
  device=c:\windows\emm386.exe nnn
  ```

  If you are running in 386 Enhanced mode, or if your computer has expanded memory, or if your computer is a 286, you don't need EMM386. However, if you have DOS 5.0 you may be using EMM386 to load programs into upper memory. See your DOS documentation. (We will discuss EMM386 later in this appendix.)
- A shell line such as

  ```
  shell=c:\dos\command.com c:\dos /e:1024 /p
  ```

  (It will almost always show COMMAND.COM.) This defines which command interpreter should be used when you use the DOS prompt. The second path (after COMMAND.COM) is required by DOS 5.0 if the COMMAND.COM file is not in the root directory.

▼ ***Note*** You can find more information about these commands in your DOS documentation.

Preparing AUTOEXEC.BAT

After running CONFIG.SYS, your computer looks for a batch file called AUTOEXEC.BAT. If it finds the file, it runs all the commands in the file. This is what Windows needs in this file.

- A SET statement that sets a TEMP variable. This tells Windows where to save all the temporary files it creates while working. For instance,

  ```
  SET TEMP=C:\WINDOWS\TEMP
  ```

tells Windows to use the TEMP subdirectory of the WINDOWS directory. (This is the default setting that Windows Setup enters in AUTOEXEC.BAT.) You can improve performance by using the fastest drive your system has for the TEMP directory; however, make sure the drive has at least 1 MB of free space, preferably more. If you use a RAM drive, you may be able to assign the TEMP directory to it, to make it even faster. You shouldn't do this if you run in Standard mode, or if you don't have much memory.

If you don't have a TEMP setting, temporary files go in the root directory of the Windows hard disk. If you are working on a diskless workstation, you might set the TEMP to a RAM drive (if you have enough memory; see later in this appendix) or a network drive.

- A PATH statement that tells DOS in which directories to search for executable files if it can't find a file in the current directory. Setup automatically adds the Windows directory to the PATH; this means that whatever the current disk and directory, you can start Windows by typing **WIN** and pressing **Enter**. You don't have to be in the Windows directory. A PATH statement might look like this:

```
PATH C:\WINDOWS;C:\;C:\MOUSE;C:\DOS;C:\PCTOOLS;C:\WINWORD
```

- A line loading the SMARTDrive disk cache, if you plan to use it, such as

```
C:\SMARTDRV.EXE 2048 532
```

This is explained later in this appendix.

Managing Memory

Perhaps the most important thing you can do to improve system performance is to improve memory use. These are the four types of memory you may have on your system.

1. **Conventional Memory** The first 640 KB is considered conventional memory; it is the memory in which DOS applications normally run. Memory usually comes in 1-MB steps these days, and the rest of that 1 MB—384 KB, known as "upper memory"—cannot be used by DOS applications unless you use a special memory manager. The upper memory is used by DOS itself to run system devices, such as your display.
2. **Extended Memory** Memory above 1 MB of RAM is considered Extended Memory. You need extended memory to run Windows properly—at least 2 MB, preferably 4 MB or more. Most DOS applications can't use extended memory unless you use a memory manager. Windows uses a built-in memory manager in 386 Enhanced mode, and uses a memory manager called HIMEM in Standard mode.

3. **Expanded Memory** Some computers have *expanded memory*. This memory requires a special memory board installed in your computer and an expanded-memory manager. Windows and Windows applications do not use expanded memory, although DOS applications designed to interact with the memory manager can use it. If you want to use such DOS applications in Windows, you have a few options. The 386 Enhanced mode cannot use expanded memory, but it can automatically simulate expanded memory by using extended memory—assuming you have enough on your system. A 386 or 486 computer running in Standard mode can also simulate expanded memory by using a memory manager called EMM386. If you want to run an expanded-memory DOS application on a 286, the expanded memory must be present in the computer—Windows can't simulate it.

   You can also configure the memory on some expanded-memory boards as extended memory. If your expanded-memory board can do this, and if you plan to run Windows on a 386 or 486, configure all of the expanded memory as extended memory. If you are using a 286, configure as much as your DOS applications need as expanded memory and the rest as extended.

4. **Virtual Memory** Virtual memory is simulated memory on your hard disk. In Windows the virtual memory is used in the form of *swap files*. When Windows needs more memory but doesn't have enough real memory available, it can swap information from the real memory into the swap files, allowing it to run more applications than it could otherwise. Note that swap files take up disk space and work more slowly than real memory.

Freeing Conventional Memory

You should reduce the amount of conventional memory used before you start Windows. You can do this by removing unnecessary programs from memory. The AUTOEXEC.BAT and CONFIG.SYS files load programs automatically when you start your computer. Edit these files to remove unnecessary programs. You can use Notepad to open these files, or run **SYSEDIT** from File Manager or Program Manager.

▼ ***Note*** Before editing these files, make backup copies so you can restore them if you have a problem.

Don't delete the lines in these files, simply type **rem** at the beginning of each line you want to disable (leave a space between rem and the command). This disables the command (converting it to a "remark" line), but it's still there if you need it later.

It's a good idea to understand all the commands in these files. Work your way through them line by line, consulting your DOS manual if necessary, to figure out what each line does.

MODIFYING CONFIG.SYS

A line that begins with `DEVICE` or `DEVICEHIGH` is loading a **device driver**. For instance,

```
DEVICEhigh=C:\IMAGEIN\MARSDRV.SYS
```

loads a scanner driver for a program called IMAGEIN. If you no longer use this driver or rarely use it, you may want to remove the command. You can always add it again (or remove the rem at the beginning of the line) when you need it.

You can also try reducing the **SHELL=C:\DOS\COMMAND.COM** command's environment space (the /E: switch). By default DOS uses 256 bytes if you don't enter a value. The command line may show a larger value, such as 1024. You can enter any number from 16 to 32768 in 16-byte increments.

Here's a quick way to find out the size of your current environment. At the DOS prompt, type **set >envsize.txt** and press **Enter**. Then type **dir envsize.txt**. You will see the name of the file and the file size in bytes, which will be just a little larger than the environment size. (You can then delete ENVSIZE.TXT.) You might add a little to this number and enter it as the environment size in the SHELL= command. For instance,

```
SHELL=COMMAND.COM /e:300
```

creates a 300-byte environment size. If you reduce the environment size too much, DOS will display the message "out of environment space" when you try to use a SET command.

You can experiment with the **buffers=** line. If you really need to reduce memory use, reduce the number of buffers. Each buffer uses 532 bytes in DOS 5.0. However, reducing buffers may increase the disk access time, so there's a trade off.

If you are using a **LASTDRIVE** command, use the lowest drive possible. For instance, don't use LASTDRIVE=Z if you want only 15 drives. Instead, use LASTDRIVE=O. Setting up drives with LASTDRIVE reserves a bit of memory for each one, so you want to set up as few drives as possible. (By default DOS allows up to drive E, but if you want to use more drives—network "drives" for instance—you need the LASTDRIVE command.)

MODIFYING AUTOEXEC.BAT

The AUTOEXEC.BAT file may load memory-resident programs. But you may not want to load these before you enter Windows; doing so uses more memory each time you open a DOS application, because Windows duplicates your conventional memory when it creates a "virtual DOS machine." Instead, remove the memory-resident program and load it when you need it, inside Windows (see Chapter 7).

Try removing **SET** commands. Some programs automatically add SET commands when you install them. If you are no longer using the program, remove the SET command. The SET command creates *environment variables*, information that can be read by any application. For instance,

```
set temp=c:\windows\temp
```

is used to set up a directory in which temporary files are stored. When a program wants to store its temporary files, it looks at the TEMP environment variable to see where you want them placed. Reducing the number of environment variables you use allows you to reduce the environment space specified by the SHELL command in CONFIG.SYS. Also remove unnecessary PATH statements, those left by programs you no longer use. This not only reduces the necessary environment size, but can also speed up running executable files.

USING WINSTART.BAT

When you start Windows in 386 Enhanced mode, it searches for a file called WINSTART.BAT and executes the commands it contains. You may use this batch file to load executable, memory-resident programs that Windows applications use. If you load a program in AUTOEXEC.BAT, that program will be duplicated in each virtual DOS machine you create (by using the Windows DOS prompt or starting a DOS program), wasting memory. Loading it in WINSTART.BAT instead limits its use to WINDOWS applications, saving memory in any DOS application windows you start.

Simply create an ASCII file called WINSTART.BAT file and place it in the WINDOWS directory. Then transfer the lines from your AUTOEXEC.BAT file. You could use this to load a network shell. The DOS applications wouldn't have access to the network, but the Windows applications would. However, not all programs will run when started from WINSTART.BAT, so it may be a case of trial and error. And you can't load .SYS drivers in WINSTART.BAT—they must be loaded from CONFIG.SYS.

Using the HIMEM.SYS Extended Memory Manager

Windows can use all the extended memory on your system, in both Standard and 386 Enhanced modes. When running in Standard mode, Windows uses HIMEM.SYS to control extended memory. In 386 Enhanced mode Windows disables HIMEM.SYS (and EMM386.EXE) and takes over its memory management functions. However, HIMEM.SYS must still be available or Windows cannot start.

Your CONFIG.SYS file should contain a line starting HIMEM.SYS—which must appear before EMM386.EXE and device drivers and applications using extended memory—such as

```
DEVICE=C:\HIMEM.SYS
```

This is usually all that you need (assuming that HIMEM.SYS is in the root directory; change the path if it isn't).

In rare cases there are some changes you can make, however. You can specify the computer type you are using; you probably need to do so if you have an Acer1100, Wyse, or IBM 7552. HIMEM.SYS should be able to recognize other types; if it doesn't you can specify which one. See your DOS manual for the relevant codes. You can also change the number of extended memory *handles*, determine whether HIMEM.SYS should control the A20 line, turn off shadow RAM, and so on—all things you will probably never need to do, and for which you should check your DOS manual.

▼ ***Note*** Windows comes with a later version of HIMEM.SYS than DOS 5.0. Use File Manager to search for all copies of HIMEM.SYS on your disk, then delete all but the latest one. Make sure that one is in the directory indicated in the CONFIG.SYS file.

Managing Expanded Memory with EMM386

Windows 5.0 uses a program called EMM386 to manage expanded memory, or to load programs into extended memory. Windows can also use this program as an expanded-memory manager. When do you need to use this program? If

- your computer is a 386 or higher,
- you want to operate in Standard mode,
- you have a DOS program that requires expanded memory, and
- your computer has no expanded memory.

EMM386 will let your computer use *extended* memory to simulate expanded memory. This is the only case in which you need to use EMM386 to manage expanded memory in Windows. However, you can also use EMM386 to load programs into high memory, freeing conventional memory. You also need to use EMM386 to simulate expanded memory on a 386 or higher if you load expanded-memory programs from the AUTOEXEC.BAT or CONFIG.SYS file. (See your DOS documentation for details.)

If you have a 286, you can't use EMM386 to simulate expanded memory; so if your DOS program needs it you must have real expanded memory installed, along with its memory manager. If you have a 386 or 486 running in 386 Enhanced mode, you don't need EMM386 because Windows can simulate expanded memory without the help of EMM386.

If you need to use EMM386, add a line like this to CONFIG.SYS.

```
device=c:\windows\emm386.exe
```

Make sure you use the directory that the file is stored in. This example tells DOS that you want 256 KB of expanded memory, the default. The line must be *after* the HIMEM.SYS line but *before* any lines that require expanded memory.

If you want more expanded memory than 256 KB you must state how much. For instance,

```
device=c:\windows\emm386.exe 512
```

provides 512 KB of memory. Use the lowest amount possible to save extended memory for other applications.

You will probably never need to specify anything else; however, there are some other option. You can enable support for the Weitek math coprocessor, specify the location of the 64-KB page frame used by EMM386, or specify memory areas that EMM386 can use or must leave alone. You can find more information about these in the DOS manual.

There are a few options you may want to use.

- **auto**: Activates expanded memory only when a program calls for it.
- **/nohigh**: Stops EMM386 from loading any part of itself into high memory. If there isn't much room left in high memory, this may allow just enough room to load another, larger, program, thus saving conventional memory.
- **l=*nnnn***: Makes sure that *nnnn* bytes of extended memory will always be available.
- **noems**: Turns off expanded memory management, but allows access to the high memory.

For more information about these options and about using EMM386.EXE to load programs into high memory, see your DOS manual.

▼ ***Note*** Windows comes with a later version of EMM386.EXE than DOS 5.0. Use File Manager to search for all copies of EMM386.EXE on your disk, then delete all but the latest one. Make sure that file is in the directory indicated in the CONFIG.SYS file.

Controlling Memory and Processing Used by DOS Applications

The manner in which your system operates when running DOS applications is controlled in several ways. First, each DOS application is controlled by a PIF (Program Information File). By default virtually all PIFs restrain the DOS application from operating while another application is active; however, you can allow multitasking. You can also use the PIF to turn off all background processing while you are using the DOS application and to determine how much memory should be assigned to the program. (You can find more information about PIFs in Chapter 7.)

The Control Panel's 386 Enhanced dialog box also allows you to adjust the way in which Windows assigns processing to applications while a DOS application is running. (For more information, see Chapter 8.)

Upgrade to DOS 5.0

If you are using a version of DOS earlier than 5.0, you should consider upgrading. DOS 5.0 manages memory much better and provides more conventional memory for applications. Some DOS programs will not load into Windows if you are running an earlier version, because they can't get enough memory to start. DOS 5.0 also lets you free more memory by loading programs "high," that is, placing them in the upper memory blocks.

Use a Memory Manager

You can improve memory allocation by using a high-memory manager. DOS 5.0, for instance, lets you load device drivers into high memory—the area between conventional memory (640 KB) and the beginning of extended memory (1 MB). You can use the DEVICEHIGH command in CONFIG.SYS to load device drivers high, and LOADHIGH to load memory-resident programs—such as "pop-up" utilities and some mouse drivers. See your DOS documentation for more information.

Some other memory managers do a better job than DOS 5.0. These programs often make more high memory available—letting you move more programs out of conventional memory—and in addition to loading device drivers and TSRs (memory resident or "terminate and stay resident" programs) into high memory, they may also let you load DOS resources high (FILES and BUFFERS, for instance).

The About Dialog Box and System Resources

If you select **Help|About** in Program Manager or any of Windows' accessory applications, you will see a dialog box like that shown in Figure A.1. This box

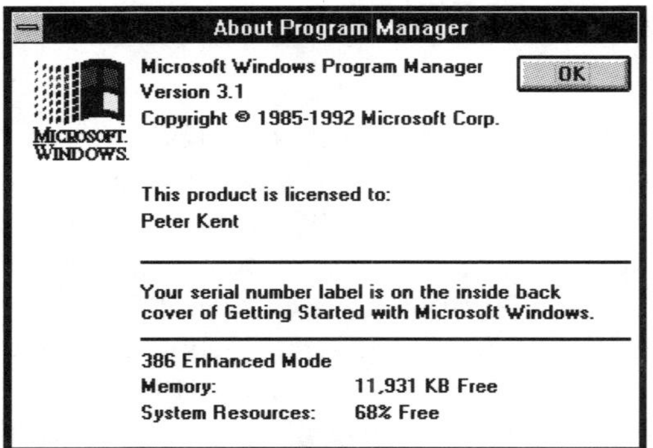

Figure A.1 The About dialog box

shows the mode in which you are operating and the amount of memory you have available. You may seem to have a lot more memory than you really have installed, but this number includes three types of memory: the computer's *conventional* memory (the first 1 MB), its *extended* memory, and its *virtual* memory (the swapfile you created). So if you have a very large swapfile, it will appear that you have a lot of memory. Windows doesn't use a permanent swapfile in Standard mode (it uses temporary swapfiles for DOS applications only), so this number will be lower.

There's another number in this dialog box, the System Resources. This refers to an area of memory in which Windows stores information about each application window you have started: its icons, document windows, menu bar, list boxes, and so on—all the graphical elements that make up the windows. Windows 3.0 had two 64-KB "heaps" that stored this information. Windows 3.1 has three of these heaps and uses them more efficiently, effectively doubling the amount of system resources your system can have.

Have you ever had "out of memory" messages when you knew you had plenty of memory left? It wasn't a memory problem, it was simply that you had filled the system resource heaps. That was common in Windows 3.0, but it shouldn't happen as much in Windows 3.1. Many users will never run out of system resources, but it *can* still happen if you load many applications. Each time you start an application you use up some of the resources. If you start Clock, for instance, you may use only 1 or 2%. Start Word for Windows and you will use perhaps 10%. Load a few large programs and you can run low on resources.

What happens then? Things stop working properly. You can't start more applications, for instance, and the Task List dialog box won't open. And you get those irritating "out of memory" messages. At this point the only thing you can do is close applications. However, some applications do not release system resources when you close them. (That's a problem with the application, not Windows.) There is no way to increase the amount of memory that Windows assigns to the system resources.

Controlling Application Swapfiles

Windows uses temporary application swapfiles in Standard mode. (In 386 Enhanced mode it uses the swapfile you specify in the Control Panel's 386 Enhanced dialog box; see Chapter 8 for details.) Each time you start a DOS application Windows creates a file whose name begins with ~WOA (such as ~WOA100B.TMP). This file is generally stored in the directory set in the environment variable TEMP (created in AUTOEXEC.BAT). If there is no TEMP environment variable, it's placed in the root directory of your first hard drive.

You can change the directory by entering the line `swapdisk=` in the [NonWindowsApp] section of the SYSTEM.INI file. You should make sure that the application swapfiles are stored on a disk that has plenty of free space—preferably several megabytes at least (one swapfile may be 512 KB alone). Use the fastest disk drive you have, if possible. And if you are using a RAM drive (explained later in this appendix) and have set the TEMP directory on the RAM drive, you may need to change the swapdisk setting to a real hard drive if you don't have a lot of memory, because Windows will be swapping the swapfiles onto another area of memory—it won't actually free memory. On the other hand, if you have more memory than you need to run your applications, placing the swapfiles on the RAM drive will speed up switching between DOS and Windows applications.

Optimizing Your Hard Disk

Hard disks are never big enough, it seems. The more space you have, the more files you have to fill it. This is especially true of Windows. Where a DOS word processing file may be a few thousand bytes, a Windows file could be a megabyte or more—because it may contain graphics, or special formatting such as various columns, tables, borders, several fonts, and so on.

You shouldn't completely fill your hard disk. You always need space on the disk so Windows can create swapfiles, other temporary files created by some applications when printing or simply working in a document, and to allow you to save new work. It's very frustrating to try to save a document only to be told you have no disk space in which to save it.

There are a few things you can do to maximize your disk space.

- Reduce the size of your swapfile (see Chapter 8). This also reduces the amount of virtual memory available to Windows, which will reduce the number of applications you can open.
- Delete temporary files. Use File Manager's Search command (Chapter 9) to delete old temporary files—only those from *previous* Windows sessions—that were left on your hard drive accidentally. (They should be deleted when you

close Windows, but sometimes they are left when a program crashes.) Look for ~*.*, *.TMP, and WIN386.SWP files. Check the file date and time before deleting so you don't delete files created during the current Windows session.

- Remove unnecessary backup files. Look for *.BAK and *.BKP (Write backup files).
- Remove old programs and document files you don't currently need. Archive them on disk or tape if you may need them again.

Remove Unwanted Windows Files

If there are Windows applications and components you don't use, you can remove them. Perhaps you never use Windows Write or Calculator, or never display any of the desktop wallpapers. Use Windows Setup (see the end of Chapter 1) to selectively remove these files.

Some Windows applications have quite large Help files. You could easily have 5 or 10 MB of help files on your disk, many of which you don't use. Use File Manager's File | Search command to find them, and then delete the ones you don't want. (Help files have the .HLP extension.) Many Windows applications load files you don't need. Check their documentation to see which files may be removed.

Use CHKDSK

When applications—running either in Windows or in DOS—crash, data can get lost on the disk drive. These lost "clusters" of information take up disk space, although you can't see them in a directory listing. DOS has a command called CHKDSK that searches for these lost clusters and converts them to files. You can examine the clusters if you wish, then delete them if you can't use them (they are usually of no use).

You *must* exit Windows before you use this command. At the DOS prompt, change to the disk you want to check (type **c:** and press **Enter**, for instance, to change to drive c:). Then type **chkdsk /f** and press **Enter**. DOS checks your disk and if it finds any lost clusters asks if you want to convert them to files. Type **y**. DOS puts the files in the root directory and names them FILE0001.CHK, FILE0002.CHK, and so on. You can now examine these files in a word processor such as Write (or even Notepad, for small files).

If the file is of no use to you, delete it. You can sometimes recover significant amounts of disk space by deleting all the lost clusters. A file may, on rare occasions, be useful. If a program has just crashed you may be able to restore lost data.

You can also tell DOS you do *not* want to convert the lost clusters to files (by typing **n** when it asks if you want to do so). DOS will fix the clusters and remove the data for you, freeing the disk space automatically.

You can use this command now and again to free wasted disk space, or use it immediately after a program crashes to see if you can recover data.

Unfragmenting Your Hard Disk

Computer files are not always stored in one contiguous space on your hard disk. Files may be spread around the disk, a piece here, a piece there. This lengthens the time it takes to read the file because your disk drive has to do more work. Periodically you should *unfragment* your disk drive (this is sometimes called *optimizing* or *compacting* the drive). A number of utilities are available to do this. Unfortunately neither Windows nor DOS can unfragment a disk.

Before you run a defragmentation program, delete all unnecessary files from your disk, run the DOS CHKDSK command (as just described), and then delete the lost-cluster files. If you are using a DOS-based utility to unfragment your drive, *do not* run it from Windows. Exit Windows first. If you use a *disk-compression* system (to effectively increase the amount of space on a disk drive) such as Stacker, use that system's defragmenter.

Defragmenting a drive will not give you more disk space, but it will speed up disk reads and writes and make Windows and its applications run faster. It may also allow you to create a larger swapfile, giving you more virtual memory.

Using FastDisk

Windows' FastDisk system, also known as 32-bit disk access, can make disk reads and writes much faster—if you have the right hard-disk controller. By default this feature is turned *off*. You can turn it on in Control Panel's 386 Enhanced dialog box, but read the warnings in Chapter 8 before you use it.

Using SMARTDrive

SMARTDrive is a disk *cache*, a program that speeds up disk reads and writes by using memory to *buffer* data. A computer's hard disk is a processing "bottleneck." Your computer can operate many times faster than the fastest hard disk, so when it writes data to the disk or reads from the disk, it has to slow down to do so. A disk cache is like a print spooler, to some degree. Instead of writing directly to, or reading directly from, the disk, the computer uses an area in memory as an intermediate step. When an application wants to write to the disk drive it does so as normal, but the cache processor intercepts the data and places it in memory. The application goes on with other jobs, while the cache processor handles the data, copying it to the disk. This is known as *write behind* caching. (Some disk caches cannot cache while *writing* to disk, only while reading from it. The latest SMARTDrive, however, can cache while both reading and writing.)

If an application wants to *read* from the disk, something similar happens, but with a bit of guess work. The application can read the data as quickly as it comes off the disk, but now the cache has to figure out what the application will want next, and copies that off the disk as well. When the application finally *does* ask for that data it's already available in memory, so the application can read it quickly. For instance, if your application is reading a long series of database records, the cache can figure out which will be needed next. Of course the cache sometimes gets it wrong. This is known as *read ahead* caching. The higher a cache's "hit rate," the more efficient it is.

A disk cache can speed up your system dramatically, so you should use one if at all possible. However, the cache uses memory, so if you don't have much memory you won't be able to use one, or won't be able to create a very large one. Windows automatically loads SMARTDrive. It adds a line like this to the AUTOEXEC.BAT file:

```
C:\SMARTDRV.EXE 2048 512
```

This starts SMARTDrive and tells it to use a 2-MB disk cache (this is the *InitCacheSize*). When running in DOS, it will always use this amount. Windows can reduce the cache size and then dynamically adjust the size according to needs. The last number, 512, indicates the lowest level to which Windows may reduce the cache size. (This is the *WinCacheSize*.) Reducing this value makes more memory available to Windows but reduces the size of the cache at times.

▼ ***Note*** Do not try to use DOS 5.0's commands to "load SMARTDrive high." SMARTDrive automatically loads high.

If you don't specify these figures, Windows uses the defaults according to the amount of extended memory in your system.

Extended memory	***InitCacheSize***	***WinCacheSize***
Up to 1 MB	all the memory	0 (no caching)
Up to 2 MB	1 MB	256 KB
Up to 4 MB	1 MB	512 KB
Up to 6 MB	2 MB	1 MB
Over 6 MB	2 MB	2 MB

There's no ideal, and you may want to try experimenting with these figures. There are some other options you can try.

drive — You can tell SMARTDrive which drives you want to cache. If you don't specify the drives, it will read- and write-cache hard disks, read-cache floppy disks, and ignore CD-ROM and network drives. You will use + and – signs to specify actions. For instance, d– means "don't cache drive D"; d+ means "read- and write-cache drive D"; and d (without either sign) means "only read-cache drive D."

/e:*nnnn* — The amount of the cache SMARTDrive can move at any time. The default is 8192 bytes, but you can also use 1024, 2048, 4096.

/b:*nnn* — The size of the read-ahead buffer. The default is 16384. This is the area in which SMARTDrive stores the information it read from the disk that wasn't actually requested by the application—the data it assumes the application will need next. A large read-ahead buffer can increase the cache's efficiency in some cases. You can make the buffer any multiple of the /e: value.

/c — Tells the cache to write all the cached memory to the hard disk immediately. You can use this option at any time to make the cache write to the disk by simply typing **smartdrv /c** at the DOS prompt and pressing **Enter**. You don't normally need to do so, because SMARTDrive writes to disk as soon as it can. It is possible, in theory, to lose data if you quickly reboot or turn off your computer before it has a chance to write to disk.

/r — Clears the cache and restarts.

/l — Stops SMARTDrive from loading itself into high memory, which it will do automatically in DOS 5.0.

/q — Stops the SMARTDrive status information from appearing on your screen when you use the SMARTDRV command.

/s — Displays information about the current SMARTDrive—the amount of room in the cache, and how many hits and misses the cache has made. This is an indication of its efficiency.

/? — Type **smartdrv /?** at the DOS prompt and press **Enter** to see a list of these options.

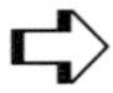 **Tip** The easiest way to experiment with SMARTDrive is to use a controller such as SMARTMON.EXE, which lets you control the cache from a dialog box. This utility is available from Microsoft in the Windows Resource Kit.

You can combine these commands. For instance,

```
smartdrv a+ d- /e:4096 3072 1024 /s
```

This line tells SMARTDrive to read- and write-cache drive A:; to not cache drive D:; to set the element size to 4096, the InitCacheSize to 3072, and the WinCacheSize to 1024; and to display the extra information (about the number of elements, the hits, and the misses, as shown below).

When you use the SMARTDRV command—in AUTOEXEC.BAT or by simply typing at the DOS prompt—SMARTDrive displays information similar to the following:

```
C:\WINDOWS>smartdrv.exe /s
Microsoft SMARTDrive Disk Cache version 4.0
Copyright 1991,1992 Microsoft Corp.

Room for 66 elements of 8,192 bytes each
There have been 53,335 cache hits
    and 6,599 cache misses

Cache size: 540,672 bytes
Cache size while running Windows: 540,672 bytes

            Disk Caching Status

drive   read cache   write cache   buffering
--------------------------------------------
  A:       yes           no            no
  B:       yes           no            no
  C:       yes           yes           no

For help, type "Smartdrv /?".
```

In this example we used the /s switch, which gave us the extra information about elements, hits, and misses. You can also use the /q switch to make sure *none* of this information appears—so it doesn't clutter your screen each time you boot up, for instance.

Using Double Buffering

Some hard-disk controllers support something called *bus mastering*. The controller takes over the bus to transfer the data, and this may cause problems while you are using SMARTDrive because the memory addresses will be mixed up. When running in 386 Enhanced mode the memory addresses for a "virtual" machine won't match the physical addresses. Some bus-mastering controllers use Microsoft's Virtual DMA Services Standard to avoid the problem. Some older ones do not, in which case you must use *double-buffering*.

Double buffering uses a buffer to store and match virtual and physical memory addresses. Windows checks to see if double-buffering is needed when you install it. If it isn't, Windows installs SMARTDrive in the AUTOEXEC.BAT file. If it *is* required, or if Windows isn't sure, Windows adds this line to CONFIG.SYS:

```
device=c:\windows\smartdrv.exe /double_buffer
```

Double buffering on systems that don't require it wastes a small amount of memory and slows performance, so you should remove the line if it's not necessary.

How do you know if it isn't necessary? Type **smartdrv** at the DOS prompt and press **Enter**. You will see a table like this:

```
                Disk Caching Status
drive    read cache    write cache    buffering
---------------------------------------------
  A:         yes            no            no
  B:         yes            no            yes
  C:         yes            yes           -
```

Look in the buffering column. If all the entries say `no`, you don't need buffering. If any entries say `yes` or –, you should use double-buffering.

 ***Note*** Earlier versions of Windows and DOS 5.0 have a SMARTDRV.SYS file that was loaded from the CONFIG.SYS file. Windows 3.1 uses SMARTDrive 4.0 (SMARTDRV.EXE). Use File Manager to search for and delete any copies of SMARTDRV.SYS.

Using a RAM Drive

A *RAM drive* (or *RAM disk*) is a simulated hard disk in your computer's memory. In the same way that you can simulate memory using hard-disk space—by creating swapfiles—you can do the opposite, simulate hard-disk space using memory. That sounds like a paradox, but there are good reasons to do so. RAM is much faster than your hard disk, so you can speed up Windows by running applications from a

RAM drive instead of a hard disk. Also, by placing temporary files on a RAM drive, you automatically remove temporary files left accidentally if your system crashes. You may also want to use a RAM drive if you have a diskless workstation on a network. You will be able to run applications much faster than off the network's drives.

Here's how it works. When you boot your computer, a command in CONFIG.SYS tells the computer that it has another hard-disk drive; the command fools your computer into thinking that part of the computer's memory is disk space. You can then use that memory in exactly the same way you would a hard drive, copying files to it and reading files from it. It appears just like a disk drive; you will see a drive icon in File Manager, for instance, and be able to select the drive from the File Open and File Save dialog boxes, or use the DIR command on it in DOS.

You can use your AUTOEXEC.BAT file to load programs onto the RAM Drive and to set the TEMP directory there. Those programs, and the temporary files being placed there, will operate much more quickly than if they were on a real disk drive. This should, for instance, speed up spooling to the Print Manager, because Print Manager's temporary files are stored in the TEMP directory.

There's an important thing to remember about RAM drives: The information stored in the RAM drive is volatile. If your computer crashes, or if you reboot your computer, you will lose all the data in the RAM drive; you must save any data onto your *real* hard drive before rebooting or turning off your computer. That's not always a problem—you may want to keep data files on the real disk drive and place only executable and temporary files on the RAM drive, for instance. Or you may want to use a batch file to copy the data from the RAM drive back onto the disk drive before you turn off your computer.

Remember also that when you create a RAM drive, you are taking away memory from applications. If you don't have much memory in your computer, you may not be able to set up a RAM drive. You need at least 4 MB, preferably 8 MB or more.

The RAMDrive Command

Enter this line into CONFIG.SYS:

```
device=c:\windows\ramddrive.sys 256 /e
```

This sets up a 256-KB RAM drive in extended memory. Your computer will automatically select a drive letter for you, the next available letter. For instance, if you have drives A:, B:, and C:, the RAM drive will be D:. This line must appear *after* the extended-memory manager (HIMEM.SYS). If you put the RAM drive in expanded memory, using the /a switch, it must appear after the expanded memory manager (EMM386.SYS).

You can modify the command using these options.

RAMDrive Size The size of the disk, in kilobytes. If you don't enter a value, RAMDrive uses 64 KB. For instance, if you enter 1024, DOS creates a 1-MB RAM drive. You can enter from 16 to 4096 (up to 4 MB).

Sector Size The disk-sector size used by the RAM drive. You will probably never need to change this. The default is 512, but you can enter 128 or 245.

Number of Entries The number of files and directories you can place in the RAM drive's root directory. The default is 64, but you can enter from 2 to 1024. You will probably never need to.

/e Tells DOS to put the drive in extended memory.

/a Tells DOS to put the drive in expanded memory. Of course your computer must have expanded memory installed.

If you want to enter a Sector Size, you must enter a RAMDrive Size. If you want to enter the Number of Entries, you must enter both the RAMDrive Size and Sector Size. DOS assumes these three numbers are in order, so the first it sees is the RAMDrive Size, the second the Sector Size, and the third the Number of Entries.

Make sure you use the /e or /a switch, or RAMDrive will use *conventional* memory, which could cause real problems.

As you can see, Microsoft's RAMDrive doesn't let you create a very large RAM drive. If your system has a lot of memory—12 or 16 MB or more—you may want to put more programs into the RAM drive. If so, you will have to use another product. PC-Kwik's RAM drive, for instance, lets you set up 16-MB drives in memory.

Important If you use a disk-compression system such as Stacker, read the system's documentation before attempting to build a RAM file.

Using the RAM Drive

Now that you have created your RAM drive, how do you use it? Add commands to your AUTOEXEC.BAT file. First, change the TEMP directory to the RAM drive. Let's assume the RAM drive is drive D:. Remove the old SET TEMP= line and add these commands:

```
mkdir d:\temp
set temp=d:\temp
```

This creates a directory called TEMP on drive D:, then sets the environment variable called TEMP to that directory. Windows will use the directory for its temporary files. Now, how about placing some application files on the RAM drive? Here's an example of the commands you might use.

```
mkdir d:\deskapp
copy c:\windows\deskapp\book.exe d:\deskapp
copy c:\windows\desktop\white.* d:\deskapp
```

This copies an application called BOOK.EXE (an address book) to a directory on the RAM drive. It also copies the data files (WHITE.ADR and WHITE.DAT) to the RAM drive. There are some other things you will have to change. First, you need to adjust the icons in Program Manager to call the right file when you want to start the application. You may also have to make changes to the WIN.INI file or in the application's own .INI file. For instance, this application has the following lines in WIN.INI:

```
[DeskTop Set]
Apps=c:\windows\deskapp
Data=c:\windows\desktop
```

These lines have to be changed to

```
[DeskTop Set]
Apps=d:\deskapp
Data=d:\deskapp
```

Some applications may also require changes within the application itself to determine the correct path for data files. When you have set the application up correctly, you can start and run it much more quickly. Depending on the speed of your hard disk, an application may open two or three times faster, for instance.

Notice that we have copied *data* files as well as program files. This data is at risk to some degree. In this case it's a phone book, so as long as we don't add or change information, there's no problem. If we do, that information must be copied back to the hard disk before you reboot, restart—or crash. You can use File Manager to do this, or add a batch file to do it when you close Windows. For instance, create a batch file called WINRAM.BAT with these lines.

```
win
copy d:\deskapp\white.* c:\windows\desktop
```

Now, when you type WINRAM and press Enter at the DOS prompt, Windows opens. When you close windows, the data files are automatically copied back to the hard disk. If you use this method, make sure you remember to type **WINRAM** to start, or your data won't be copied when you close Windows. You may even want to name the file WIN.BAT, rename WIN.COM to WINX.COM, and make the first line of the batch file `WINX.COM`. That way you will always run this batch file, and the data will always be copied back to the hard disk.

Another option is to run a batch file from an icon in Program Manager. Then you could update the hard disk periodically if you needed to.

▼ ***Note*** Windows comes with a later version of RAMDRIVE.SYS than DOS 5.0. Use File Manager to search for all copies of RAMDRIVE.SYS on your disk, then delete all but the latest one. Make sure that file is in the directory indicated in the CONFIG.SYS file.

Hardware Upgrades

Windows will run on a 286, but it won't run well. It won't even run well on a 386SX, especially when you are working with graphics and desktop-publishing programs—it will function, perhaps acceptably, but it certainly won't rush to get its work done. Getting the best out of Windows means using the best equipment. This isn't always an option, but if you use Windows every day as a business tool, you should consider using the best equipment you can.

Processor A 286 is too slow for most Windows applications. A 386SX may be passable for some but unusable for others. Consider a 25-MHz 386DX as the minimum for a real Windows workstation. However, you can dramatically improve 386SX performance by adding a video accelerator.

Math Coprocessor Math coprocessors can speed up some programs dramatically, as much as four or five times in some cases. But don't rush out and buy—Windows doesn't use one. Some Windows applications, however—such as Lotus 1-2-3, Microsoft Excel, Arts & Letters, AutoCAD, and Interleaf—are designed to take advantage of a coprocessor. Check your programs' manuals before buying one.

Memory

1 MB does not a Windows machine make. Even 2 MB is the bare minimum, and Microsoft recommends 4 MB; 8 MB or more will let you create a RAM disk and run more programs. Some Windows applications need a great deal of memory. For instance LaserMaster's WinJet 800 (a high-resolution printing system) requires at least 8 MB to run well.

Hard Disk

Many computers are sold with 40- or 60-MB hard drives these days, but Windows applications take up so much room that you can quickly fill such a disk, especially if you work with graphics. Consider 100 MB as a starting point. The more hard-disk space you have available, the larger the swapfile you can create, and the more virtual memory Windows can use.

Monitor

The larger the display the better, especially if you want to use a high resolution. Systems sold with 1024 x 768 or higher resolution and 14-inch monitors are a joke; the text will be too small to read comfortably, so you will probably end up using VGA (640 x 480). Large monitors can be expensive, however. While 19 inches or more is ideal, you may be able to afford only 15 or 16 inches. Compare actual image sizes, not advertised screen sizes; one screen's 15 inches may be larger than another's, especially as many monitors use less of the screen in high-resolution modes. Also look for low dot-pitch size so the text and icons are sharp, non-interlaced, and flicker-free.

Tip It's possible to enlarge text so it is still legible in high resolutions. See the information on IconTitleSize and the [Font] section in Appendix B.

Video Accelerator

Video accelerators help your system manage Windows' graphics—windows, dialog boxes, icons, and so on—more quickly. A fast video accelerator on a slow system can make Windows run faster than a simple VGA card on a fast system. You can improve a system's performance perhaps 10 times or more by installing the right accelerator cards, such as the ATI Graphics Ultra or the Orchid Fahrenheit 1280°. Note, however, that using some accelerator cards in DOS, rather than Windows, can actually slow performance.

A Few More Tips

Here are a few quick ideas to speed up Windows and increase available memory.

- Read Appendix B. It contains many ways to modify the .INI files, some of which may help improve your system's performance.
- Read Chapter 7 for information on multitasking DOS applications.
- Read Chapter 8's section on the 386 Enhanced mode dialog box for more information on multitasking DOS applications.
- Remove unused fonts, using the Control Panel.
- Change your system colors to use only a few, nondithered colors.
- Remove wallpaper and patterns.
- Close all unused applications, including Clock, Notepad, and so on.
- Empty the Clipboard.
- Use the methods in Chapter 11 to speed up printing.
- If you get many "out of memory" messages, increase your swapfile size.

Appendix B

The Windows .INI Files

Windows' .INI files define how Windows and its applications will be configured. Most of the .INI file settings are made from various dialog boxes, in particular the Control Panel. Some, however, can only be changed by directly modifying the .INI file. To save space, when a setting is made from a dialog box we have explained simply where to make the setting (for instance, "Control Panel, Desktop icon, Border Width" means open Control Panel, double-click on the Desktop icon, and use the Border Width option), not what the setting does. If the setting can be made only from the .INI file, we have preceded the name by an asterisk and explained what the setting does.

You may want to scan this appendix—looking at the settings marked by asterisks—just to get an idea of what you can change in the Windows environment.

Tip If you often need to work in an .INI file, set up an icon for it. For instance, set up an icon in Program Manager for WIN.INI. Because .INI files are automatically associated with Notepad, Windows will use the Notepad icon. Of course you can select another if you wish. Double-clicking on the icon will open Notepad, with WIN.INI already loaded. You may also use SYSEDIT, an application that runs four Notepad windows with WIN.INI, SYSTEM.INI, CONFIG.SYS, and AUTOEXEC.BAT. (See Appendix D.)

The settings are shown in each section in alphabetical order. The actual order in which they appear in the .INI files will vary. Also, some of the entries may not appear in your .INI files: Windows uses the default values until you change them, at which time the entries are added to the file. Your files may have entries not mentioned here. Some may be left over from Windows 3.0, settings that used to be valid but no longer are. Others may have been inserted by individual applications. For instance, Paintbrush adds the following section to WIN.INI:

```
[Paintbrush]
width=640
height=480
clear=COLOR
OmitPictureFormat=1
```

This tells Paintbrush how to create the work area when you start the application. Other applications create their own .INI files to store such information.

Important Modifications to systemwide settings in the .INI files do not take effect until you restart Windows. Modifications related to an application that is currently open will take effect when you close and then reopen the application. Remember to make backups of the .INI files before modifying them.

WIN.INI

[Windows]

Beep= Control Panel, Sound icon, Enable System Sounds.

BorderWidth= Control Panel, Desktop icon, Border Width.

CoolSwitch= Control Panel, Desktop icon, Fast "Alt+Tab" Switching.

CursorBlinkRate= Control Panel, Desktop icon, Cursor Blink Rate.

***DefaultQueueSize=** The number of messages an application's message queue can hold. The default is 8, and you shouldn't need to change this option.

Device= Control Panel, Printers icon, Set As Default Printer.

***DeviceNotSelectedTimeout=** The system default value for the Device Not Selected Timeout. This is the number of seconds Windows will wait for a device to turn on before it assumes the device is not going to work. If the timeout is exceeded Windows will not print to the device and may display an error message. The default value is 15 seconds. Individual timeouts can be set for each device in the Connect dialog box (Control Panel, Printers, Connect).

***Documents=** Defines which file extensions indicate a document file. Document files will use the document icon in File Manager. Windows assumes that file extensions included in the [extensions] section of WIN.INI are documents, so they do not have to appear here. Do not include the period, and separate with spaces.

DosPrint= Control Panel, Printers, Connect, Fast Printing Direct to Port.

***DoubleClickHeight=** The number of pixels the pointer can move vertically between mouse clicks in a double-click. If the pointer moves farther, the clicks are regarded as individual clicks. The default is four pixels.

***DoubleClickWidth=** The same as the previous entry, except for horizontal pointer movement.

DoubleClickSpeed= Control Panel, Mouse icon, Double-Click Speed.

KeyboardDelay= Control Panel, Keyboard icon, Delay Before First Repeat.

KeyboardSpeed= Control Panel, Keyboard icon, Repeat Rate.

***Load=** Applications that will load and minimize automatically when you start Windows. Separate each application with a space. Include the path if the file is not in the WINDOWS directory. You can also start minimized applications by placing an icon in the StartUp window and selecting Run Minimized in the icon's Program Item Properties dialog box. This will *not* add the information to the Load= line, however.

***MenuDropAlignment=** 1 aligns the drop-down menus with the right side of the menu title; 0 aligns the menus with the left side (0 is the default).

***MenuShowDelay=** The number of milliseconds that Windows waits before displaying a cascading menu (after you move the highlight onto a menu option with a small triangle). On a 386 the default is 0; on a 286 it is 400. If you *click* on the menu option, Windows displays the cascading menu immediately.

MouseSpeed= Control Panel, Mouse icon, Mouse Tracking Speed.

MouseThreshold1= Control Panel, Mouse icon, Mouse Tracking Speed.

MouseThreshold2= Control Panel, Mouse icon, Mouse Tracking Speed.

***MouseTrails=** The number of pointers shown on-screen if you select Mouse Trails in the Mouse dialog box (Control Panel, Mouse icon).

NetWarn= Control Panel, Network icon.

***Programs=** Defines which file extensions indicate a program file. Program files will use the program icon in File Manager. Windows automatically adds "com exe bat pif." This is not the same as associating a file with an application. That is done with the [Extensions] section.

DosPrint= Control Panel, Printers, Connect, Fast Printing Direct to Port.

***Run=** Applications that will load automatically when you start Windows. Separate each application with a space. Include the path if the file is not in the WINDOWS directory. You can also start applications by placing an icon in the StartUp window. This will *not* add the information to the Run= line, however.

ScreenSaveActive= Control Panel, Desktop icon, Screen Saver Name.

ScreenSaveTimeOut= Control Panel, Desktop icon, Screen Saver Delay.

Spooler= Control Panel, Printers icon, Use Print Manager.

SwapMouseButtons= Control Panel, Mouse icon, Swap Left/Right Buttons.

***TransmissionRetryTimeout=** The system default value for the Transmission Retry Timeout. This is the number of seconds Windows will retry transmission to a printer before it assumes the device is not going to work. If the timeout is exceeded Windows will display a message telling you it cannot print. The default value is 90 seconds for the Windows PostScript driver, 45 seconds for all other printer drivers. Individual timeouts can be set for each device in the Connect dialog box (Control Panel, Printers, Connect).

[desktop]

GridGranularity= Control Panel, Desktop icon, Granularity.

IconSpacing= Control Panel, Desktop icon, Spacing.

***IconTitleFaceName=** The font used for icon titles (the default is MS Sans Serif).

***IconTitleSize=** The size of the font used to display icon titles (the default is 8 points).

IconTitleWrap= Control Panel, Desktop icon, Wrap Title.

***IconVerticalSpacing=** The size of the space between an icon and the one below it, measured in pixels. This is the vertical spacing, while IconSpacing is the horizontal spacing.

Pattern= Control Panel, Desktop icon, Pattern Name.

TileWallpaper= Control Panel, Desktop icon, Tile. You can edit this line to specify a wallpaper that is not in the WINDOWS or SYSTEM subdirectory.

Wallpaper= Control Panel, Desktop icon, Wallpaper File.

[extensions]

This section contains lines that associate document files with applications. You can associate files and applications using the File | Associate command in File Manager. Associations let you start an application and load a file by starting the file itself (see Chapter 9).

When you install Windows, the following lines are automatically added:

```
cal=calendar.exe ^.cal
crd=cardfile.exe ^.crd
trm=terminal.exe ^.trm
```

```
txt=notepad.exe ^.txt
ini=notepad.exe ^.ini
pcx=pbrush.exe ^.pcx
bmp=pbrush.exe ^.bmp
wri=write.exe ^.wri
rec=recorder.exe ^.rec
hlp=winhelp.exe ^.hlp
```

Running a file with the extension on the left of the = sign automatically loads the program on the right of the = sign. The caret (^) is replaced by the name of the file you run, minus the extension, thus loading the file after starting the application. You can add any necessary switches to the program name. If the program is not in the Windows directory, include the pathname. Each extension may appear only once in this list, but each application may appear multiple times.

[intl]

The [Intl] International section controls the dates, times, currency format, and so on, set in the Control Panel's International dialog box. Keywords beginning with i are integers (iCountry, iCurrency, and so on). Keywords beginning with s are strings (s1159, sLanguage, and so on).

[ports]

This section lists your computer's communications ports and files to which you may send printer output (to create print files). You can change the COM-port settings from Control Panel's Ports dialog box. The other settings are edited in WIN.INI. See Chapter 11 for more information about these ports.

[fonts]

This section shows the *screen* fonts loaded when Windows starts. For each TrueType font on your system a .FOT file will be listed in this section, for instance. Here's an example of a font listing.

```
Times New Roman (TrueType)=TIMES.FOT
```

Load new files using the Control Panel's Fonts dialog box. You can edit these settings to modify the size of text in dialog boxes, making it more legible in high resolutions. Windows uses the `MS Sans Serif` line to determine which font is used for dialog box text and icon titles. Extract another font file from the installation disks (see Chapter 1 for information on extracting files), then replace the line with something like this.

```
MS Sans Serif 8,10,12,14,18,24 (VGA res)=SSERIFF.FON
```

This will replace the default VGA file (SSERIFE.FON) with SSERIFF.FON and will make the text larger in VGA, 800 x 600, or 1024 x 768 resolution.

[fontSubstitutes]

This section tells which screen fonts Windows should use if one named in a document is not available. For instance,

```
Helv=MS Sans Serif
Helvetica=Arial
Times=Times New Roman
```

In other words, if Times is used in a document but is not available on your system, Windows uses Times New Roman instead.

[TrueType]

***OutlineThreshold=** The number of pixels per em above which TrueType fonts are rendered as outline fonts instead of bitmap fonts. (An *em* is a typographic term, a measurement of font size.) Bitmaps are faster but use more memory, so decreasing the value can free memory. The default is 256. Do not go over 300.

TTEnable= Control Panel, Fonts, TrueType, Enable TrueType Fonts

***TTIfCollisions=** Determines whether Windows should use the TrueType version of a font if another version with the same name is available on your system. The default is 0, meaning Windows will use TrueType fonts instead of the other type. Set to 1 if you want to use the other type.

TTOnly= Control Panel, Fonts, TrueType, Show Only TrueType Fonts in Application.

[mci extensions]

This section is used by Media Player to determine which media files should be associated with which Media Control Interface drivers. For example,

```
rmi=sequencer
mid=sequencer
wav=waveaudio
```

[network]

drive= File Manager, Disk | Network Connections.

***InRestoreNetConnect=** If set to 1, you will automatically reconnect to the network servers to which you were connected in the last session. You *may* be able to change this from the Control Panel's Network dialog box. Otherwise, editing WIN.INI may work.

port= Control Panel, Printers, Connect, Network. Or Print Manager, Options | Network Connections.

[embedding]

This section contains information about the OLE objects—their descriptions, server applications, and their format. For example,

```
SoundRec=Sound,Sound,SoundRec.exe,picture
Package=Package,Package,packager.exe,picture
PBrush=Paintbrush Picture,Paintbrush Picture,pbrush.exe,picture
Draw=Windows Draw Drawing,Windows Draw
Drawing,C:\WINDOWS\DRAW\DRAW.EXE,picture
```

Do not edit this section. Most changes are done automatically when you load applications. You can also use the *Registration Editor* (REGEDIT.EXE) to change settings.

[Windows Help]

M_WindowPosition= The position and size of the main help window, saved when you closed Help.

H_WindowPosition= The position and size of the History window, saved when you closed Help.

A_WindowPosition= The position and size of the Annotate window, saved when you closed Help.

C_WindowPosition= The position and size of the Copy window, saved when you closed Help.

***IFJumpColor=** Defines the color used for the text that, when clicked on, displays a page of information in another file.

***IfPopupColor=** Defines the color used for the text that, when clicked on, displays a pop-up panel from another file.

***JumpColor=** Defines the color used for the text that, when clicked on, displays another page of information.

***MacroColor=** Defines the color used for text that, when clicked on, runs a help macro.

***PopupColor=** Defines the color used for the text that, when clicked on, displays a pop-up panel.

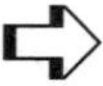

Tip If you want to change any of these colors, open the Control Panel's Colors dialog box. Click on Color Palette, then Define Custom Colors. Define the color you want, then note the red, green, and blue values. For instance,

```
PopupColor=000 000 000
```

provides black text. Use solid colors.

[sounds]

This section holds the sound events assigned in the Control Panel's Sounds dialog box. For instance,

```
SystemQuestion=C:\WINDOWS\TADA.WAV,Question
```

[PrinterPorts]

This section shows the information from the Control Panel's Printers dialog box. For instance,

```
HP LaserJet III=hppcl5a,LPT1:,15,45,LPT2:,15,45
LM WinPrint 800 PS=pscript,WinSpool:,15,45
```

Do not change this directly, because problems may occur if the information doesn't match the information in the [devices] section.

[devices]

This section is for maintaining compatibility with Windows 2.x applications and contains a list of the active printers. These entries are identical to those in the [PrinterPorts] section, but without the timeout values. For instance,

```
HP LaserJet III=hppcl5a,LPT1:,LPT2:
LM WinPrint 800 PS=pscript,WinSpool:
```

[programs]

This section appears only if you move an executable file that has been associated with a data file. If you try to run the data file Windows won't be able to find the application. Instead it displays a dialog box asking where the application is. When you enter the information, Windows saves it in the [Programs] section of the WIN.INI file, so it can find the application the next time it needs it. For example,

```
calendar.exe=C:\windows\dates\calendar.exe
```

Every time you try to start the application by running the data file, Windows looks at the [Extensions] and [Programs] sections of WIN.INI.

[colors]

This section shows the colors used by Windows. For example,

```
Background=255 255 255
AppWorkspace=255 255 255
```

Set these colors from the Control Panel's Colors dialog box.

[Compatibility]

This section tells how to handle certain applications that are not fully Windows 3.1-compatible. For each listed application there is a code that refers to a particular type of handling. For example,

```
TURBOTAX=0x00080000
W4GLR=0x4000
W4GL=0x4000
NETSET2=0x0100
```

[*printername,port*]

If you modify a printers setup using its Setup dialog box (Control Panel, Printers, Setup), Windows adds a section to WIN.INI. For instance,

```
[HP LaserJet III,LPT1]
paper=1
prtcaps=-13440
paperind=0
```

[PostScript,*port*]

If you install a PostScript device and assign soft fonts to it, a section similar to this is added.

```
ATM=placeholder
softfonts=41
softfont1=c:\psfonts\pfm\ae______.pfm
```

```
softfont2=c:\psfonts\pfm\ctr______.pfm
softfont3=c:\psfonts\pfm\cti______.pfm
```

SYSTEM.INI

The SYSTEM.INI file contains important information about the manner in which Windows will run, from Windows drivers to using DOS applications. Much of SYSTEM.INI is rather obscure, containing commands you will almost certainly never use. Many entries are small fixes, added by Microsoft to get around problems with specific applications (mainly DOS applications). Others may be useful, like the DOSPromptExitInstruc=Off command, which removes the instruction box from the DOS Prompt window.

In some cases you will need more information before using some of the more obscure entries. Try using the Microsoft Knowledge Base on CompuServe (see Chapter 14), or Microsoft's technical support.

[boot]

286grabber= Windows Setup, Options|Change System Settings, Display.

386grabber= Windows Setup, Options|Change System Settings, Display.

***CachedFileHandles=** The number of .EXE and .DLL files that may remain open. If you have a problem with running Windows on a network server, try reducing this number from its default of 12. You can enter any number from 2 to 12.

***comm.drv=** The filename of the serial communications driver you are using. Windows enters

```
comm.drv=comm.drv
```

but some applications may modify it. If an application modifies it, you may not be able to access the Advanced features from the Control Panel's Ports dialog box.

display.drv= Windows Setup, Options|Change System Settings, Display.

***drivers=** Filenames or aliases of dynamic link libraries (.DLL) loaded when Windows starts.

fixedfon.fon= The fixed system font used by Windows 2.x applications. Windows Setup, Options|Change System Settings, Display.

fonts.fon= The proportionally spaced system font used by Windows 3.1. Windows Setup, Options|Change System Settings, Display.

keyboard.drv= Windows Setup, Options|Change System Settings, Keyboard.

language.dll= Control Panel, International, Language.

mouse.drv= Windows Setup, Options | Change System Settings, Mouse.

network.drv= Windows Setup, Options | Change System Settings, Network.

oemfonts.fon= The font file for the OEM character set, installed during Setup. Also Windows Setup, Options | Change System Settings, Display.

***shell=** The program that runs as the Windows shell program when you start Windows. By default it is `shell=progman.exe` (Program Manager), but you could also use

```
shell=winfile.exe
```

to open File Manager instead, or even

```
shell=c:\winword\winword
```

to load Word for Windows as the shell (or run any Windows application as the shell). Many third-party shells are available for Windows.

***sound.drv=** The system sound driver you are using.

system.drv= The system hardware driver you are using, set when you run Setup in DOS.

***TaskMan.Exe=** The task-switching application that appears when you press **Ctrl-Esc**. By default TASKMAN.EXE is used (the Task List dialog box). You can add this line to change the application.

[boot.description]

This section shows a list of device descriptions used in Setup. Do not change these; if you do, you won't be able to update drivers with Setup.

[drivers]

This section shows the drivers loaded using the Control Panel's Drivers dialog box. For instance,

```
[drivers]
midimapper=midimap.drv
Timer=timer.drv
Wave=speaker.drv
```

[keyboard]

This section describes the keyboard. All the options are set when you install Windows. Use the Control Panel's International dialog box to change the Language, or use Windows Setup to change the Keyboard System Settings.

[mci]

The Media Control Interface (MCI) section. This lists the drivers installed when you run Setup or added using the Control Panel's Drivers dialog box.

[NonWindowsApp]

This section affects the way in which DOS applications run in Windows. Only a few lines are added by Windows, but you can experiment by adding others.

***CommandEnvSize=** The size of the COMMAND.COM environment; 0 (not modified), or from 160 to 3278. This lets you set a virtual DOS machines' environment size so it is larger than that created by the SHELL=COMMAND.COM command in CONFIG.SYS. You cannot *reduce* the value.

***DisablePositionSave=** If 0 (the default), the window position and font size are saved in DOSAPP.INI when you close the application. If 1, they are not saved, although you can use the Save Settings On Exit in the window's Fonts dialog box to make sure they are saved.

***FontChangeEnable=** If you are using a Windows 3.0 display grabber driver, setting this to 1 may allow you to change fonts in a DOS window.

***GlobalHeapSize=** The size of the buffer used by Standard mode. The default is 0, and probably will never need changing.

***LocalTSRs=** If you load TSRs before you start Windows, each TSR is added to each virtual DOS machine you start. Some TSRs won't work correctly. If you add the TSR's name to this line Windows will make a unique copy of all the code associated with the TSR for each virtual DOS machine, perhaps enabling the TSR to run.

***MouseInDosBox=** Use 0 to turn off mouse support in a DOS window. Or, if you have a Windows 3.0 version of a display grabber file, use 1 to turn the feature on.

***NetAsynchSwitching=** Set this to 1 to allow Windows to switch away from a DOS application, running in Standard mode, after it has made an asynchronous NetBIOS call.

***ScreenLines=** The number of lines displayed in a DOS application (the default is 25). The application itself may be able to override this. You can use this entry to increase the number of lines in the DOS Prompt window, for instance.

***SwapDisk=** The directory in which Windows will place Standard-mode application swapfiles. This overrides the TEMP environment variable in the AUTOEXEC.BAT file for these swapfiles. For example,

```
swapdisk=c:\data\swap
```

[standard]

This section contains information about running in Standard mode. Windows doesn't add anything when you install it. You can enter them to try to improve system performance.

***FasterModeSwitch=** Try setting this to 1 to switch between DOS and Windows applications on a 286 computer. Also set to 1 if you are using a Zenith Z-248 and lose characters while typing, or an Olivetti M-250-E and lose control of the mouse. This has no effect on a 386 or 486. If Windows hangs after you change this, use a DOS editor to remove the line and then restart Windows.

***Int28Filter=** Increasing this value from its default of 10 may improve Windows performance, but it also may interfere with memory-resident software (such as a network shell). The setting indicates the number of INT28h interrupts visible to memory-resident software loaded before Windows. A setting of 10 means Windows filters out all but the tenth interrupt. A setting of 0 filters them all out.

***MouseSyncTime=** Used on an IBM/PS2 mouse interface to determine the length of a mouse data package. The default is 500 milliseconds.

***NetHeapSize=** Try increasing this setting from its default of 8 KB if an application is not running correctly on a network. This is the size of the data transfer buffer. Increasing the buffer size reduces memory available to applications.

***PadCodeSegments=** If your 286 locks up in Standard mode, try setting this to 1. This setting is needed for 80286 C2 stepping, which some 286 systems use.

***Stacks=** Increase this number from its default of 12 if you get a Standard Mode: Stack Overflow message. You can use any value from 8 to 64.

***StackSize=** The size of the interrupt-reflector stacks. Increase the number from its default of 384 KB if you get a Standard Mode: Stack Overflow message.

[386enh]

This section has information about running Windows in 386 Enhanced mode. Entries may refer to the filename of a virtual device driver or, if preceded by an asterisk (*), the name of a virtual device built into the WIN386.EXE file.

32BitDiskAccess= Control Panel, 386 Enhanced, Virtual Memory, Change, Use 32-Bit Disk Access.

***A20EnableCount=** The initial A20 enable count used by the extended-memory manager (HIMEM.SYS).

***AllEMSLocked=** Set this value to On if you are using a disk-cache that uses expanded memory. It overrides the PIF setting for EMS Memory Locked, making sure that the contents of expanded memory are not swapped to disk.

***AllVMsExclusive=** Set this value to On to force all DOS applications to run in exclusive full-screen mode, overriding their PIFs. This may help avoid problems with memory-resident software that is not fully compatible.

***AllXMSLocked=** Set this value to On to lock the contents of all applications into extended memory instead of swapping to disk. It also overrides the PIF XMS Memory Locked settings.

***AltKeyDelay=** Increase this value from its default of 0.005 second if an application has trouble using the Alt key.

***AltPasteDelay=** Increase this value from its default of 0.025 second if an application has trouble using the Alt key.

***AutoRestoreScreen=** This is on by default. It works on VGA screens, with DOS applications that tell Windows they can update their screens. Windows will save the application's display and repaint the screen when you switch back. If you set this to Off, the application must repaint the screen itself. This makes more memory available, but slows down the system. And the application may not be able to repaint the screen automatically.

***BkGndNotifyAtPFault=** If this is On, Windows sends a notification to a DOS application—telling it not to access the display—when it tries to access the display itself. If this is Off, Windows notifies the DOS application when switching. This is set to Off for 8514 displays and TIGA, and On for VGA displays.

CGA40WOA.FON= The filename of the font used for DOS applications with 40-column, 25-line (or fewer) displays. This is set when you run Setup from DOS.

CGA80WOA.FON= The filename of the font used for DOS applications with 80-column, 25-line (or fewer) displays. This is set when you run Setup from DOS.

***CGANoSnow=** Set this to On if you get "snow" on a CGA display.

COM*n*AutoAssign= Control Panel, 386 Enhanced, Device Contention.

COM*n*Base= Control Panel, Ports, Settings, Advanced.

***COMBoostTime=** Try increasing this value from the default of 2 milliseconds if a DOS communications program is losing keyboard characters on the display. This value is the time allowed a virtual machine to process a COM interrupt.

***COM*n*Buffer=** Increase this value from the default of 128 if a communications program is losing data at high baud rates. See also COM*n*Protocol=.

***COMdrv30=** Set this On to improve COM port performance if you are using a Windows 3.0 communications driver.

***COM*n*FIFO=** Set this On if a COM port's 16550 UART should be enabled.

COM*n*Irq= Control Panel, Ports, Settings, Advanced.

***COMIrqSharing=** Set this to On for a MicroChannel or EISA machine on which you want COM ports to share interrupt lines.

***COM*n*Protocol=** Set this to XOFF if a communications program using that port is losing characters in text transfers at high baud rates. Leave blank or remove the line if the application does binary transfers, as it might suspend them. See also COM*n*Buffer=.

Device= The virtual devices being used with Windows 386 Enhanced mode. Also **Display=**, **EBIOS=**, **Keyboard=**, **Network=**, and **Mouse=** are all virtual-device identification lines. Windows Setup assigns these according to your system configuration.

Display= See Device=.

***DMABufferIn1MB=** When On, the Direct Memory Access (DMA) buffer should be in the first 1 MB of memory (above 640 KB), to be compatible with 8-bit bus master cards.

***DOSPromptExitInstruc=** Set this to Off to remove the information box that appears at the top of a DOS Prompt window.

***DualDisplay=** This leaves a memory block unused and available for another display when on. If Off—the default—the memory is available on EGA systems, but not on VGA.

EBIOS= See Device=.

EGA40WOA.FON= The filename of the font used for DOS applications with 40 columns and more than 25 lines. This is set when you run Setup from DOS.

EGA80WOA.FON= The filename of the font used for DOS applications with 80 columns and more than 25 lines. This is set when you run Setup from DOS.

***EISADMA=** Used for EISA machines only. Set to Off to make Windows treat the machine as a non-EISA machine, if you can't run it in 386 Enhanced mode.

You can also use this entry to specify the default transfer size for each DMA channel. For example,

```
EISADMA=0,8
```

means channel 0, 8 bits. The options are 8, 16w (16 words), 16b (16 bits), or 32.

***EMMExclude=** This command tells Windows to exclude an area of memory from use. It also turns off ROM and RAM search code for that block. You can use this to make Windows avoid areas that some adapters use. For instance,

```
EMMExclude=C800-CFFF
```

excludes C800:0000 through CFFF:000F, a block used by some VGA cards. You can have several EMMExclude commands.

***EMMInclude=** This tells Windows to scan a block for memory, regardless of what is there. It takes precedence over EMMExclude.

***EMMPageFrame=** This specifies where Windows should place the 64-KB page frame—it specifies the beginning of the frame. For instance,

```
EMMPageFrame=C400
```

starts the frame at C400:0000.

***EMMSize=** The total extended memory, in KB, available for mapping as expanded memory. By default all the extended memory may be mapped as expanded. This line lets you limit the amount. You can also limit expanded-memory use with the application's PIF.

***FileSysChange=** When Off, File Manager will not receive messages when a non-Windows application creates, renames, deletes, or copies a file. It is On by default in 386 Enhanced mode, Off in Standard mode. It can slow down performance.

***Global=** By default all devices loaded in CONFIG.SYS are global, available to any application. Some virtual devices may specify that a device be local. This entry can override that and make the device global. Make sure the device name is spelled with the same capitalization as in CONFIG.SYS.

***HardDiskDMABuffer=** The amount of memory used for Direct Memory Access buffer. You may need to change this if you are using a DMA hard disk without SMARTDrive, or if double-buffering is not turned on. The default is 0 for AT computers and those using DMA channel 3 and running SMARTDrive, and 64 for Micro Channel computers and computers using DMA channel 3 without SMARTDrive.

***IdleVMWakeUpTime=** This entry forces timer interrupts to "wake up" virtual machines after the specified seconds (1, 2, 4, 8, 16, 32, or 64).

***IgnoreInstalledEMM=** Set this to On if an unrecognized EMM (expanded-memory manager) is controlling physical expanded memory. This should allow Windows to start in 386 Enhanced mode. Make sure before starting that no software is using the expanded memory.

***InDOSPolling=** Set this to On to prevent Windows from running other applications when memory-resident software has the InDOS flag set. This slows down performance slightly.

***INT28Critical=** If you are not using a network, you might try setting this to Off to improve task switching (it's on by default).

***IRQ9Global=** If your system hangs when it reads a floppy-disk drive, set this to On. This entry makes the IRQ9 interrupt global.

***Keyboard=** See Device=.

***KeyBoostTime=** This can improve keyboard response when several applications are running in the background. Increasing the value from the default of 0.001 second increases the amount of processing time Windows assigns to an application when you press a key in that application.

***KeyBufferDelay=** This value is the delay between the keyboard buffer filling and the program entering keyboard inputs. Some programs may need more than the default 0.2 second. You may need this if you lose characters while pasting into a DOS application.

***KeyIdleDelay=** Setting this to 0 can speed up keyboard response in some DOS applications but may have the opposite effect on others. The default is 0.5 second.

***KeyPasteCRSkipCount=** If you lose characters or the screen doesn't update enough while pasting into DOS applications, try increasing this value from the default of 10. Also change KeyPasteSkipCount=.

***KeyPasteDelay=** This value is the length of time between pasting characters into a DOS application. Increase the delay if you lose characters while pasting. The default is 0.003 second.

***KeyPasteSkipCount=** If you lose characters or the screen doesn't update enough while pasting into DOS applications, try increasing this value from the default of 2. Also change KeyPasteCRSkipCount= and KeyPasteDelay=.

***KeyPasteTimeout=** This specifies how long to wait for an application to read keyboard input before Windows changes from fast paste to slow paste. The default is 1 second.

***KybdPasswd=** Used by 8042 keyboard controllers compatible with IBM PS/2 computers. The default of On lets the system use keyboard password security.

***KybdReboot=** If your computer hangs while rebooting, try setting this to Off. If you reboot from windows you will have to press **Ctrl-Alt-Delete** a total of three times to reboot (instead of the normal twice).

***Local=** If a DOS driver doesn't work well, you can add its name to this line to make Windows create a unique version in each virtual DOS machine. The name must match the capitalization used in CONFIG.SYS. Most drivers will not work if added to this line.

***LocalLoadHigh=** With the default of Off, Windows uses all the upper memory area when running with DOS 5.0. If On, Windows doesn't use all the upper memory area, so virtual DOS machines can.

***LocalReboot=** If you want Ctrl-Alt-Delete to reboot your computer rather than display the "This Windows application has stopped responding to the system" message, turn this line On.

***LPT*n*AutoAssign=** These settings may appear if you upgraded from Windows 3.0. They have no effect in 3.1.

***LRU*xxxxxx*=** commands: These values should never need changing.

***MapPhysAddress=** The range of addresses, in MB, that a memory manager preallocates to physical page-table entries and address space. This is only needed if you are using an old memory manager that requires this memory to be set aside.

***MaxBPs=** The maximum number of break points used by a Virtual Memory Manager. You need to change from the default of 200 only if you are using another memory manager.

***MaxCOMPort=** The maximum number of COM ports supported in 386 Enhanced mode. The default is 4.

***MaxDMAPGAdress=** The maximum physical address used for DMA (Direct Memory Address). The default is 0FFFh for non-EISA computers, 0FFFFFh for EISA computers.

MaxPagingFileSize= Control Panel, 386 Enhanced, Virtual Memory, Change, select Type: Temporary, enter **New Size**. By default Windows suggests 50% of the available disk space.

***MaxPhysSize=** The maximum page number the Virtual Memory Manager can manage as a usable page. This may be modified if you are using a device that cannot recognize all of your computer's memory.

***MCADMA=** If you are using an MCA computer but the DMA channels are not implemented, set this line to Off.

***MessageBackColor=** This is the VGA color-attribute number of the color used for screens such as that which appears when you press **Ctrl-Alt-Del**.

***MessageTextColor=** This is the VGA color-attribute number of the color used for the text in screens such as that which appears when you press **Ctrl-Alt-Del**.

***MinTimeSlice=** Control Panel, 386 Enhanced, Minimum Timeslice.

***MinUnlockMem=** This value should never need changing. It is the memory that must remain unlocked when returning to a virtual machine when multiple virtual machines are running. The default is 40 KB.

***MinUserDiskSpace=** Used when creating temporary swapfiles, it tells Windows how much disk space must be left empty. The default is 500 KB.

Mouse= See Device=

***MouseSoftInit=** Set this to Off if the mouse pointer and screen data are distorted in a DOS application. However, if you set it to Off you will not be able to use the mouse in a DOS application started in a window.

***NetAsynchFallback=** With this turned On, Windows will allocate space in a local-memory buffer and prevent a virtual machine from running when it receives a NetBIOS request and there is insufficient global memory to save it. The default is Off.

***NetAsynchTimeout=** Used if NetAsynchFallback is turned On. This value is the time within which Windows must service an asynchronous NetBIOS request. The default is 5.0 seconds.

***NetDMASize=** The DMA buffer size if a network has been installed. The default is 32 on MCA computers, and 0 on non-MCA computers. Windows will use the larger of this value and DMABufferSize=.

***NetHeapSize=** The size of the 386 Enhanced-mode data-transfer buffers used for transferring data on a network. This is in conventional memory, in 4-KB increments. The default is 12.

Network= Windows Setup, Options | Change System Settings, Network.

***NMIReboot=** If On, a reboot occurs when a nonmaskable interrupt is received. The default is Off.

***NoEMMDriver=** Turn this On to stop 386 Enhanced mode from installing the expanded-memory driver.

***NoWaitNetIO=** The default is On, and converts synchronous NetBIOS commands to asynchronous commands.

***OverlappedIO=** This value should never need changing. Turn this On to allow several DOS applications to make read and write requests to a disk before the first request is finished. If InDOSPolling=On the default is Off. If InDOSPolling=Off, the default is On (therefore the default is On).

***PageBuffers=** Used if you turned on 32-bit disk access and have a permanent swapfile, this setting is the number of 4-KB page buffers used to save read and write data. Increasing the value over the default of 4 may improve performance. The value may be from 0 to 32.

***PageOvercommit=** Increasing this value from the default of 4 MB increases the amount of linear address space. This may slow down the system.

***Paging=** Turn this Off to stop Windows from creating temporary swapfiles. You should avoid using this unless you have to stop Windows from using the disk space.

***PagingFile=** The path and filename of the temporary swapfile used in 386 Enhanced mode.

***PerformBackfill=** This line should never need changing.

PermSwapDOSDrive= Control Panel, 386 Enhanced, Virtual Memory, Change, Type: Permanent, Drive.

PermSwapSizeK= Control Panel, 386 Enhanced, Virtual Memory, Change, Type: Permanent, New Size.

***PerVMFiles=** The number of private handles assigned to each virtual DOS machine. This is the same as the FILES= entry in CONFIG.SYS. The default is 10, but if the DOS SHARE command is running the value is ignored. You may have to increase the value if a DOS program will not start.

***PSPIncrement=** The additional memory, in 16-byte increments, reserved for each virtual machine when UniqueDOSPSP=On. The default is 2 (meaning two times 16 bytes), but the value can be from 2 to 64.

***ReflectDosInt2A=** Set this On if running memory-resident programs that need INT 2A.

***ReservedHighArea=** The range of memory Windows will not scan to find unused address space.

***ReservePageFrame=** If set to On (the default), Windows gives preference to EMS page-frame space over conventional memory when allocating DOS transfer buffers. You can turn this Off if you want to run DOS applications that need expanded memory.

***ReserveVideoROM=** Try setting this to On if the text is scrambled in a DOS application.

***ROMScanThreshold=** This entry specifies a parameter used to determine if an area of memory in the adapter area is ROM.

***ScrollFrequency=** The number of lines you can scroll in a DOS application before updating the screen. The default is 2.

***SGrabLPT=** All interrupts sent to the defined port number in a virtual machine are rerouted to the system virtual machine.

***SyncTime=** This is on by default, making Windows synchronize its time with the system clock periodically. See also TrapTimerPorts=.

***SystemROMBreakPoint=** Some memory managers need this to be set to Off.

***SysVMEMSLimit=** The amount of expanded memory that Windows can use in KB. If the value is 0, Windows can't use any of it. If it is –1 it can use all of it. The default is 2048.

***SysVMEMSLocked=** When On this stops Windows swapping DOS applications from expanded memory to the disk, speeding up the DOS applications but slowing down the system as a whole. The default is Off.

***SysVMEMSRequired=** The amount of expanded memory required to start Windows, by default 0 KB.

***SysVMXMSLimit=** The amount of extended memory Windows can assign to a DOS application in KB. A setting of –1 lets an application have as much as it wants. The default is 2048.

***SysVMXMSRequired=** The amount of extended memory required to start Windows in KB. The default is 0.

***TimerCriticalSection=** A positive number ensures that only one virtual machine can receive interrupts at any time. The value is a time in milliseconds, the time within which Windows can feed interrupts to only one machine. Some networks require this entry, but it may slow down system performance. The default is 0.

***TokenRingSearch=** By default Windows searches for a Token Ring Network card. This may interfere with other devices, in which case you can turn this Off.

***TranslateScans=** Turn this On if your keyboard is using nonstandard scan codes.

***TrapTimerPorts=** By default this is On, stopping applications from reading from and writing to the system timer ports. Some applications may run slowly if this is On, in which case you can set it to Off. However, this may slow down Windows' system time. You can turn SyncTime=On to make Windows check the time periodically.

***UniqueDOSPSP=** When On, Windows starts every application at a unique address, making sure that each application in a virtual machine starts in a different place. Different networks require different settings.

***UseableHighArea=** The range of memory that Windows will scan for unused address space. This takes precedence over ReservedHighArea=.

***UseROMFont=** Set this to Off if unusual characters appear on your screen in DOS-application messages. When On (the default), the soft font stored in video ROM is used for messages that appear in DOS applications running full screen, or when switching between applications.

***VGAMonoText=** With this On (the default), Windows ignores the video message space in VGA displays normally used by Monochrome adapters. If Off, Windows can use B000h through B7FF in upper memory if no other device is using them and other applications are not using the VGA adapter's monochrome mode.

***VideoBackgroundMsg=** If this is On (the default) when a background DOS application is suspended or if its display cannot be updated due to low video memory, a message is displayed.

***VideoSuspendDisable=** If this is Off (the default), a DOS application running in the background with a corrupted display will be suspended. If On, the application continues running. (This applies only to VGA.)

***VirtualHDIrq=** When On (the default for AT-compatible machines), this lets Windows 386 Enhanced mode terminate interrupts from the hard-disk controller, bypassing the ROM routine that usually handles the interrupts. Some hard drives may require this turned Off, although that may slow performance.

***WindowKBRequired=** The amount of conventional memory needed to start Windows. The default is 256.

***WindowMemSize=** The amount of conventional memory Windows may use. The default, –1, means it may use all that is available. You can enter a value less than 640 if there isn't enough memory to run Windows in 386 Enhanced mode.

***WindowUpdateTime=** The time, in milliseconds, between updating DOS applications running in a window. The default is 50.

WinExclusive= Control Panel, 386 Enhanced, Exclusive in Foreground.

WinTimeSlice= Two numbers: Control Panel, 386 Enhanced, Windows in Foreground and Windows in Background.

WOAFont= The font used by DOS applications (DOSAPP.FON by default). Enter a filename if you want to use a different one. Also set when you run Setup from DOS and change the CodePage or Display setting.

***XlatBufferSize=** Entering a value higher than the default of 8 KB can improve the performance of some Windows applications that read and write a great deal of information, such as databases. This decreases memory for DOS applications and may interfere with networks using named pipes (such networks may require a value of 4). This entry is in increments of 4 KB. If you enter a value that is not a multiple of 4, Windows rounds it up.

XMSUMBInitCalls= You should not change this. Installing a different extended-memory manager may change it from its default of On.

PROGMAN.INI

The PROGMAN.INI file controls Program Manager. The [Settings] and [Groups] sections contain information about the way you have configured Program Manager—the size and position, the number and kind of groups and program icons, and so on.

There is an option you can add to the [Groups] section.

Startup=, Enter the name of a program group you want to take the place of Program Manager's StartUp group. The applications in the named group will open automatically when you start Windows—the applications in the StartUp group will not.

You can also create a [Restrictions] section that restricts a user from carrying out certain actions. A system administrator might want to use this section. These are the possible entries.

NoRun=1 Disables the File | Run command. If you leave a File Manager icon in a program group, the user can start File Manager and then run any application from there.

NoClose=1 Stops the user from closing Windows, using the Control menu, File | Exit, or Alt-F4.

NoSaveSettings=1 Disables the Options | Save Settings on Exit command, so a user can't change the groups and save the changes. Nor can the user hold Shift and select File | Exit to save settings.

NoFileMenu=1 Removes the File menu. The user can still close Windows by pressing **Alt-F4** or using the Control menu.

EditLevel=1 The user cannot create, delete, or rename groups.

EditLevel=2 Same as Level 1, plus restricts actions carried out on program items—disables File | New, File | Move, File | Copy, and File | Delete.

EditLevel=3 Same as Level 2, plus disables the command line in the Program Item Properties dialog box.

EditLevel=4 Same as Level 3, plus disables all areas in the Program Item Properties dialog box (the user can still view the dialog box).

WINFILE.INI

The WINFILE.INI file contains settings that determine the manner in which File Manager will run when you open it. These settings come from the various menu options and configuration commands that you can use in File Manager.

CONTROL.INI

The CONTROL.INI file contains settings from several of the Control Panel's dialog boxes. For instance, it contains information about the system colors—the scheme currently in use, the available schemes, and the custom colors you have created.

It also contains the desktop patterns, information about special drivers, the screen savers you have configured, the screen-saver password, and so on. Change these settings from the Control Panel.

Appendix C

The Windows Files

Windows has so many files, it's sometimes difficult to know what's what. The following list of file extensions should help you figure it out. This is not a complete listing of all the file extensions you are likely to find in your WINDOWS and SYSTEM directories. Other applications will add their own, so if it isn't in this list it's probably from another program. You could easily find another 10 or 20 different extensions in these directories.

.2GR	286 grabber files, used for transferring data between Windows and DOS applications in Standard mode.
.386	Files that support virtual devices in 386-enhanced mode.
.3GR	386 grabber files, used for transferring data between Windows and DOS applications in 386 Enhanced mode.
.BAK	A backup file. This extension is used by many applications.
.BAT	A DOS batch file.
.BKP	A Write backup file.
.BMP	Bitmap files, used by Paintbrush and Windows wallpaper.
.CAL	Calendar files.
.CFG	A configuration file, such as the configuration file used by MIDI Mapper.
.CHK	Lost cluster files created by the DOS CHKDSK command.
.CLP	Clipboard files, used to save the contents of the Clipboard.
.CNF	WIN.CNF, Windows startup code.
.COM	An executable program file.

.CPL	Control Panel files, used for some Control Panel dialog boxes.
.CRD	Data files used by Cardfile.
.DAT	WINTUTOR.DAT, the Windows tutorial file. REG.DAT, the data file used by the Registration database (for OLE).
.DIB	Device Independent Bitmap, a new database format used by some graphics programs. (It *isn't* device independent!)
.DLL	Dynamic-link library files, used to provide libraries of code, such as information about different languages, standard printer-driver information, program icons, and so on.
.DOC	A common document-file extension, used by applications such as Word for Windows.
.DRV	Driver files, used to operate hardware such as keyboards, printers, graphics boards, and so on.
.EXE	Executable (program) files, such as the files that run Write, Paintbrush, Clock, and so on.
.FON	Font files.
.FOT	TrueType screen font files, associated with .TTF.
.GRP	A Program Manager group file that describes the contents of a program group.
.HLP	Files containing Help information.
.INF	Information files, used in installation and initialization.
.INI	Initialization files, used to set a program's defaults when it starts running.
.IW	Screen saver files.
.LGO	The code that displays the startup logo (in the .RLE file).
.LOD	WINDOWS.LOD, Qualitas 386MAX/BlueMAX.
.LOG	DrWatson report files.
.MID	MIDI (Musical Instrument Digital Interface) files.
.MOD	Grabber files, used for transferring data between Windows and DOS applications.
.MSP	Microsoft Paint format, used by earlier versions of Paintbrush.
.OBJ	IPX.OBJ, a workstation communications driver.
.OLD	A backup of an old file, created automatically by many programs when they modify WIN.INI or AUTOEXEC.BAT, for instance.

.PAL	Color palette files (created by Paintbrush, and used by other graphics programs, also).
.PAR	SPART.PAR, a read-only file used to manage the permanent swapfile. 386SPART.PAR, the permanent swapfile.
.PCX	A bitmap file used by Paintbrush.
.PIF	Program Information Files, used to determine the manner in which DOS applications will operate.
.PS2	Provides support for PS/2 machines.
.REC	Windows Recorder files.
.REG	Registration database template (used by OLE and "drag and drop").
.RLE	The bitmap used by the .LGO file to display the opening logo.
.RLM	TIGAWIN.RLM, TIGA firmware code.
.SCR	Screen-saver files.
.SHH	A system's settings template file, used for creating customized installation setups.
.SRC	.INI file templates.
.SYS	Device and memory drivers, installed from CONFIG.SYS.
.SWP	WIN386.SWP, temporary swapfile.
.TMP	Temporary files, used while carrying out procedures such as printing. ~WOA*.TMP files are Standard-mode application swapfiles.
.TRM	Settings files used by Terminal.
.TSK	MMTASK.TSK, Multimedia background task file.
.TTF	TrueType printer font files, associated with .FOT.
.TXT	ASCII files, used by Windows Notepad.
.VXD	Qualitas product virtual devices.
.WAV	Waveform sound files, used by Sound Recorder and Media Player.
.WPD	PostScript description files, needed by certain printers.
.WR	Windows Write document files.

Appendix D

Troubleshooting Tools

Windows 3.1 includes a couple of important troubleshooting tools: Dr. Watson and Microsoft Diagnostics. It also has an application called System Configuration Editor, which makes working with your WIN.INI, SYSTEM.INI, AUTOEXEC.BAT, and CONFIG.SYS files easier. Windows doesn't automatically create icons for these tools.

Dr. Watson

Windows provides a special "debugging" tool called Dr. Watson. When you load Dr. Watson it sits in the background, waiting for trouble. It keeps a log (called DRWATSON.LOG) that records significant events. When your system locks up or crashes, for instance, Dr. Watson may be able to record important information. You can use this data to debug your own programs or to give to a software publisher's technical support department.

You must create the Dr. Watson icon yourself. Open a new Program Item Properties dialog box and type **DRWATSON.EXE** in the Command Line text box. Now, when you double-click the icon, Dr.Watson opens. All you will see, however, is the icon at the bottom of your screen. (Move the windows out of the way to make sure it's there.)

You might want to put the Dr. Watson icon in the Program Manager StartUp group so it runs automatically each time you open Windows. You could also create an icon to display the Dr. Watson log. Open a new Program Item Properties dialog box, type a description such as "Dr. Watson's Log," and type **NOTEPAD.EXE DRWATSON.LOG** in the Command Line text box. The icon will be the Notepad icon, although you may use the Change Icon procedure

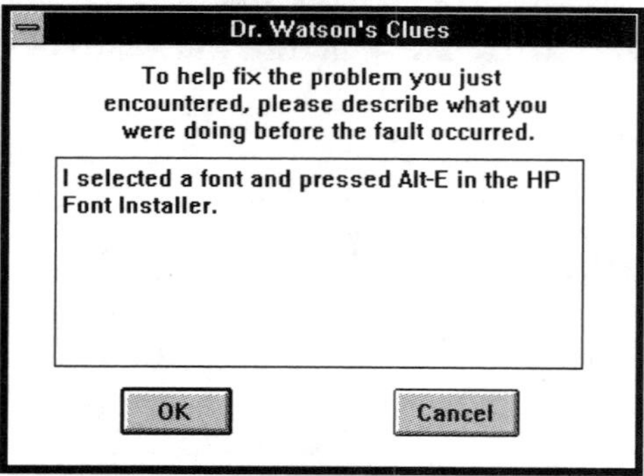

Figure D.1 The Dr. Watson's Clues dialog box

to select the DRWATSON.EXE icon. Now you will be able to display the Dr. Watson log at any time by double-clicking on the icon.

When a problem occurs, Dr. Watson may be able to monitor it (although quite often he cannot). A dialog box like that shown in Figure D.1 appears. Type a description of what happened, and click on **OK**.

The data you enter into the dialog box is added to the DRWATSON.LOG file. Open this file in Notepad to read it. Figure D.2 shows an example. This information probably won't be of use to you unless you are a programmer and want to debug your own program. However, it may be useful to the application's technical support people.

Dr. Watson is being used by many application developers. While often it may not be able to help you fix immediate problems, it's quite likely that it will lead to better, more stable Windows applications in the future.

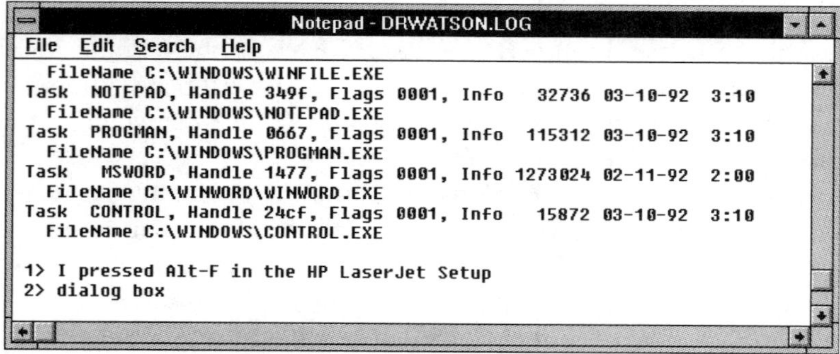

Figure D.2 An example of a Dr. Watson log

Microsoft Diagnostics

Windows 3.1 loads a program called Microsoft Diagnostics (MSD.EXE). You can create an icon for this application if you wish, but it runs better under DOS. To make sure you get an accurate report, you should exit Windows before you use it. In Windows the memory reports may be wrong, along with the IRQ, video, operating system, mouse, disk drives, and COM ports. However, some of its information and procedures will be accurate. You can view information about your computer hardware, network, adapters, LPT ports, TSR Programs, and device drivers. You also can use the printer test, insert commands into SYSTEM.INI, WIN.INI, CONFIG.SYS, and AUTOEXEC.BAT, and search your hard disk for a file and display its contents.

▼ ***Note*** When you start Microsoft Diagnostics in Windows, you may get a Device Conflict, as it checks your communications ports. The way Windows handles the conflict depends on the settings in Control Panel's 386 Enhanced dialog box. If you see a dialog box warning you, select the Microsoft Diagnostics option button and click on **OK**.

Figure D.3 shows the Microsoft Diagnostics screen in a window. To select a report simply click on one of the blocks in the middle of the screen, or press the highlighted letter. To use the menu bar, click on the option or press **Alt** to select the menu bar and then press the highlighted letter to select the menu. Some of the

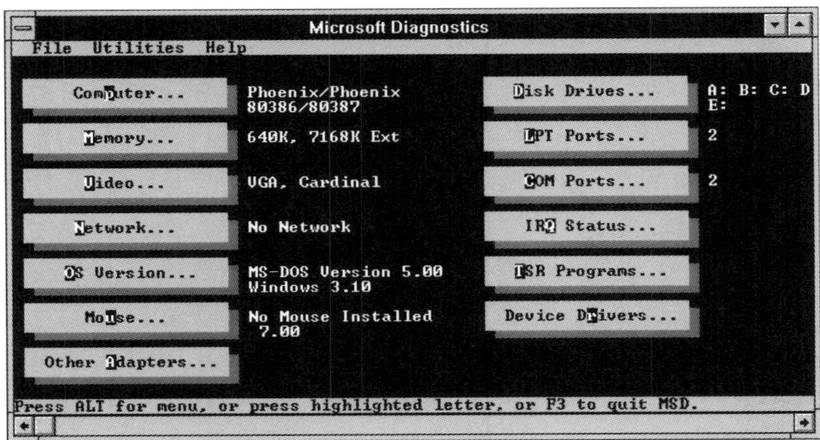

Figure D.3 The Microsoft Diagnostics Window

reports have scroll bars on the right side. You can use the mouse or the Down Arrow key to scroll through these reports.

Here are the reports and features you can use.

Computer	Your computer, BIOS, coprocessor, and so on.
Memory	A visual memory map.
Video	Your video adapter.
Network	Your network.
OS Version	The version of DOS and Windows you are using, and a list of the environment variables you have set.
Mouse	Your mouse, including the IRQ, mouse port, and sensitivity. There's a good chance some of the mouse information will be wrong, even running in DOS.
Other Adapters	Game adapters.
Disk Drives	The sizes and types of your disk drives.
LPT Ports	The status of the LPT ports.
COM Ports	The status of the COM ports.
IRQ Status	The IRQ interrupt settings.
TSR Programs	Shows blocks of memory allocated to programs.
Device Drivers	Device driver information, such as filename, units, header, and attributes.
File I Find File	Searches your disks for a file, and displays the file contents.
File I Print Report	Prints a report; you can select which portions to include.
File I AUTOEXEC.BAT	Displays the AUTOEXEC.BAT file contents. You cannot edit this file or the next three.
File I CONFIG.SYS	Displays the CONFIG.SYS file contents.
File I SYSTEM.INI	Displays the SYSTEM.INI file contents.
File I WIN.INI	Displays the WIN.INI file contents.
File I Exit (F3)	Closes Microsoft Diagnostics.

Utilities | Memory Block Display — Shows a memory map and the allocated memory. Select a program from the list to see where it's located in memory.

Utilities | Memory Browser — Searches ROM for keywords.

Utilities | Insert Command — Lets you insert a command, selected from a list, into SYSTEM.INI, WIN.INI, AUTOEXEC.BAT, or CONFIG.SYS. Select the command, press **Enter**, modify the command parameters, and press **Enter** again to place it in the file.

Utilities | Test Printer — Sends a test document to your printer.

Utilities | Black & White (F5) — Changes the screen to black and white.

System Configuration Editor

SysEdit

The System Configuration Editor is a very useful little tool for working on your important system files. You have to create the icon yourself, using the SYS-EDIT.EXE file. When you double-click on the icon, Windows opens the System Configuration Editor and loads four document windows containing SYS-TEM.INI, WIN.INI, CONFIG.SYS, and AUTOEXEC.BAT (see Figure D.4).

The menu commands are very similar to Notepad's, with a few important differences. You can't open any other files, nor can you Save As. And pressing F3 doesn't open the Find dialog box. You can save the files (however, File | Save saves

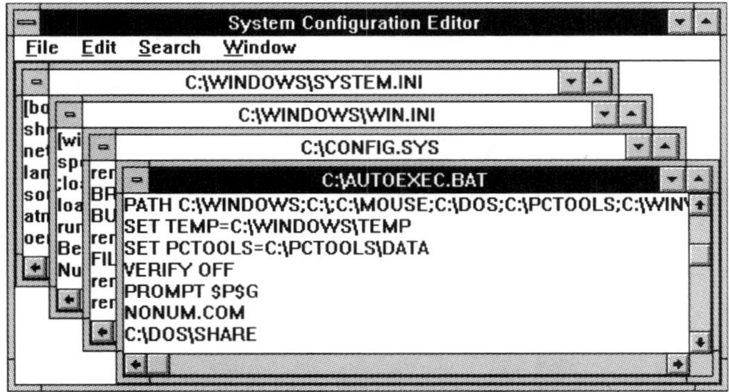

Figure D.4 The System Configuration Editor

only the file in the active document window, not all four). The only way to close a single document window is to use its own Control menu.

The System Configuration Editor has a more limited Edit menu; there's no Time Stamp, and it has a Clear command instead of Delete, although it works just the same. Its Search menu has a Previous command, which searches *backwards*.

The Windows Resource Kit

Microsoft sells a kit that includes a disk of Windows utilities and a book with detailed information about Microsoft Windows. If your job is maintaining Windows workstations, you should buy this kit. The book contains detailed troubleshooting procedures and flow diagrams for everything from finding out why a mouse won't work in a DOS window to figuring out network problems. It includes detailed lists of files, descriptions of .INI file entries, an explanation of how to create automated setup procedures, a hardware compatibility list, and articles about FastDisk, QEMM-386, and Pen Windows.

The resource kit contains these programs.

- **Graphics Viewer** Displays .BMP, .WMF, and .ICO files.
- **Network Assistant** Lets you manage your disk and printer connections and view network information.
- **File Size** A useful extension to File Manager that calculates the total file size of all the files in a directory or directory branch.
- **SMARTDrive Monitor** Lets you control SMARTDrive from a dialog box.
- **System Resource Monitor** Provides a graphical representation of the system resource and total memory use.
- **TopDesk** Lets you create a *virtual desktop*, with each application in a separate *virtual screen*.

Caution Information in the resource kit book that applies to Windows 3.0 is not always identified.

Index